# Fodor's 94
# Mexico

Fodor's Travel Publications, Inc.
New York • Toronto • London • Sydney • Auckland

## Fodor's Mexico

**Editor:** Paula Consolo
**Editorial Assistant:** Amy Hunter
**Contributors:** Ron Butler, Chuck Edgerly, Barbara Franco, Marian Goldberg, Edie Jarolim, Caroline Liou, Wendy Luft, Maribeth Mellin, Eleanor Morris, Denise Nolty, Marcy Pritchard, Frank Shiell
**Researcher:** Mary Ellen Schultz
**Creative Director:** Fabrizio La Rocca
**Cartographer:** David Lindroth
**Illustrator:** Karl Tanner
**Cover Photograph:** Andy Caulfield/Image Bank

**Design:** Vignelli Associates

## Special Sales

# Contents

**Maps and Plans**

# Foreword

We would like to express our gratitude to the Mexican Government Tourist Office and all of the state tourist offices throughout Mexico that helped us in revising this book. We would also like to thank the public relations firm Daniel J. Edelman, Inc., as well as Mexicana airlines and the public relations firm Manning, Selvage, and Lee.

While every care has been taken to ensure the accuracy of the information in this guide, the passage of time will always bring change and, consequently, the publisher cannot accept responsibility for errors that may occur.

All prices and opening times quoted here are based on information supplied to us at press time. Hours and admission fees may change, however, and the prudent traveler will avoid inconvenience by calling ahead.

Fodor's wants to hear about your travel experiences, both pleasant and unpleasant. When a hotel or restaurant fails to live up to its billing, let us know and we will investigate the complaint and revise our entries where the facts warrant it.

Send your letters to the editors of Fodor's Travel Publications, 201 E. 50th Street, New York, NY 10022.

# Highlights'94 and Fodor's Choice

# Highlights '94

The biggest change throughout Mexico this year is that the peso has shed three zeros. What was once 1,000 pesos (P$1,000) is now 1 nuevo peso (NP$1). At press time, both pesos and nuevo pesos were still in circulation, and many public telephones still accepted only the older currency.

**The Yucatán Peninsula**
*Cancún*

The devastation caused by Hurricane Gilbert in 1988 is far in the past. Countless hotels have been made over, and new ones are springing up, although as the authorities become more concerned that Cancún is approaching the saturation point, the growth rate is slowing down. Among the deluxe international properties to open recently is the 370-room **Ritz Carlton.**

The **Cancún Convention Center,** the original venue for the area's cultural events, was razed by Hurricane Gilbert and is being rebuilt. Although it was scheduled to open in 1993, at press time its doors were still closed.

As the hotel inventory plateaus, however, **time-share condominiums** are going up at a feverish pitch—not just in Cancún, but all along the Caribbean coast and on Isla Mujeres as well. In an effort to keep pace with the nearly constant flow of visitors, **charter airlines** have been boosting their service to Cancún and Cozumel from a growing number of gateways.

*Cozumel*

The offshore island of Cozumel is taking steps to curb progress's toll on the environment. Although the new Diamond Resort opened in early 1993, development of several deluxe hotels has been halted; the island museum has embarked on a serious save-the-turtle campaign; and Isla de Pasión—a tiny island off the west coast, previously used for picnic cruises—has been made into a state reserve.

*Isla Mujeres*

An attempt is being made to stop development by having the government declare the entire island a national park. (If that happens, you'll be charged a fee to come ashore here.) Still, there have been some new additions, including the **Condominio Playa Norte Nautibeach,** the **Cristalmar** condo-hotel, and the cozy little **Na-Balam.** The all-inclusive resort **Costa Club** is scheduled to open by 1994, but it probably won't.

Although there is talk of rebuilding the town dock to accommodate cruise ships and of operating an air charter service to Florida, Mérida, Chichén Itzá, and the Guatemalan ruins of Tikal, actual planning has not begun.

*Campeche*

Restoration continues on the ruined Maya city of **Edzná,** the most accessible archaeological site in the state.

*Mérida and the State of Yucatán*  Mérida is becoming increasingly popular with European tourists. Although the city is often used only as a stopover for visits to the archaeological sites, its impressive architecture and numerous cultural events are beginning to draw travelers who stay for a week or more. A new toll road linking Mérida and Cancún is partially completed (Mérida to Valladolid); it reduces driving time by one hour.

**Mexico City**  With the new free trade agreements between the United States and Mexico, the capital city is, more than ever, a destination for business as well as vacation travelers. World-class hotels opening this year include a **Ritz Carlton** and a **Four Seasons,** both on Paseo de la Reforma, and in the city's southern section, the immense **Hilton Pedregal,** which will have three heliports.

**Acapulco**  By 1994 work should be completed on the new highway between Acapulco and Mexico City cutting the driving time to 3½ hours. The city and state governments have built several large parking lots in town to handle the expected increase in tourists arriving by automobile. New air-conditioned buses with reclining seats run every 10 minutes along the Costera Miguel Alemán from the Hyatt to Playa Caleta.

The old El Cano hotel has been beautifully restored and redecorated in nautical colors, but fortunately it still maintains an air of the 1950s. It is now one of the loveliest hotels along the Costera.

In spite of pressure from many hoteliers, the government still won't allow casinos to operate in Acapulco; however, it did approve the opening of Aca Book, an off-track betting parlor, restaurant, and bar that's located on the Costera opposite the Torres Gemelas. A jai alai stadium on the Costera was also in the works at press time.

Almost all new development is concentrated east of the Hyatt Regency—extending almost to the airport, in the area known as Acapulco Diamante. The Westin Camino Real was inaugurated on Puerto Marqués Bay in February 1993, and dozens of condo developments are going up everywhere.

The open-air markets that the government built in an effort to rid the city's streets and beaches from hawkers, are still working, and only rarely will one be bothered by an itinerant vendor who has managed to escape the sharp eye of the law. The municipal beaches, restrooms, and showers are well maintained, but pollution in Acapulco Bay remains a sore point. Swimmers should stick to the hotel pool.

**Baja California and Mazatlán**  The northern third of the Baja California peninsula from Tijuana to Ensenada continues to undergo unprecedented development. Time-share and condominium resorts and hotels and restaurants continue to rise along the oceanfront hills on the coastal corridor. Several major projects including marinas, golf courses, and residences are in the planning stages.

In and around the twin resorts of Cabo San Lucas and San José del Cabo, three new golf-oriented resorts are under construction—at Cabo Real, Cabo del Sol, and Campo de Carlos. Meanwhile, the Jack Nicklaus–designed course at Hotel Palmilla has opened. Work continues on widening the highway between the two towns, where much of the resort development is taking place.

**Telephone Service**   MCI can now be accessed from all phones not restricted to local calls throughout Mexico. Simply dial 95–800–674–7000 to make MCI credit card or collect calls. AT&T can still be reached by dialing **01 or 95–800–462–4240.

**Ground Transportation**   Although unleaded gasoline is easier to find than it was five years ago, if you are not traveling a tourist route you will most likely still have trouble feeding a lead-free motor. Fill up whenever you can.

The first-class train service, the **División del Norte,** has been discontinued. Now the only train service from the border is from Nuevo Laredo or Piedras Negras. Bus-tour enthusiasts will be happy to know that Mexico is now open to motorcoach tours originating in the United States.

# Fodor's Choice

No two people will agree on what makes a perfect vacation, but it's fun and helpful to know what others think. We hope you'll have a chance to experience some of Fodor's Choices yourself while visiting Mexico. We have tried to offer something for everyone and from every price category. For more information about each entry, refer to the appropriate chapters (listed in the margin) within this guidebook.

## After Hours

| | |
|---|---|
| **Acapulco** | Fantasy and Extravaganzza discos |
| **Guadalajara** | Factory, Aranzazu Hotel |
| | Lobby Bar, Fiesta Americana |
| | Plaza Tapatía |
| **Mexico City** | Plaza Garibaldi |
| | Up and down the Zona Rosa |
| **Yucatán** | Carlos 'n' Charlie's, Cancún and Cozumel |
| | Christine and La Boom discos, Cancún |

## Art Festivals

| | |
|---|---|
| **Heartland** | International Cervantes Festival, Guanajuato |
| **Mexico City** | Ballet Folklórico de México |
| | Carnival, Tepoztlán |
| **Oaxaca** | Guelaguetza |

## Buildings and Monuments

| | |
|---|---|
| **Heartland** | Morelia Cathedral |
| | Zacatecas Cathedral |
| | Teatro Juárez, Guanajuato |
| **Mexico City** | Casa de los Azulejos |
| | Castillo de Chapultepec |
| | Palacio de Bellas Artes |
| | Palacio de Iturbide |
| **Oaxaca** | Church of Santo Domingo |

## Day Trips

| | |
|---|---|
| **Acapulco** | Taxco |

| | |
|---|---|
| Chiapas/Tabasco | Lagunas de Montebello |
| Mexico City | Puebla/Cholula |
| | Teotihuacan pyramids |
| | Tepotzotlán |
| Oaxaca | San Bartolo Coyotepec, Teotitlán del Valle |

## Museums

| | |
|---|---|
| Chiapas/Tabasco | CICOM Museum of Anthropology, Villahermosa |
| | Na-Bolom, San Cristóbal de las Casas |
| Heartland | Rafael Coronel Museum, Zacatecas |
| Huasteca | Museum of Contemporary Art, Monterrey |
| Mexico City | Museo Franz Mayer |
| | Museo de Frida Kahlo |
| | Museo Templo Mayor |
| | Museo Nacional de Antropología |

## Off the Beaten Track

| | |
|---|---|
| Chiapas/Tabasco | Yaxchilán |
| Copper Canyon | Batopilas |
| Guadalajara | Tequila |
| Heartland | *Lavandería*, San Miguel de Allende |
| | Paricutín volcano, Uruapan |
| Yucatán | Flamingo preserves during spring nesting season, Río Lagartos National Park |
| | Maya caves at Loltún, Balankanche, and Bolonchén |
| | Boca Paila and Xcalak peninsulas |

## Parks and Gardens

| | |
|---|---|
| Heartland | Jardín la Unión, Guanajuato |
| Huasteca | Gran Plaza, Monterrey |
| Mexico City | Alameda Park |
| | Bosque de Chapultepec |
| | Plaza San Jacinto |

## Shopping

| | |
|---|---|
| Chiapas/Tabasco | Calle Real de Guadalupe, San Cristóbal de Las Casas |
| Guadalajara | Tlaquepaque's shops and boutiques |
| Mexico City | Bazar Sábado |

Fonart stores

La Ciudadela market

Bazar del Centro

**Oaxaca** Daily markets

## Archaeological Sites

**Chiapas/Tabasco** Palenque

**Mexico City** Templo Mayor

Teotihuacan

**Oaxaca** Mitla

Monte Albán

**Huasteca** El Tajín

**Yucatán** Chichén Itzá

Tulum

Uxmal

## Special Moments

**Acapulco** Watching the divers at La Quebrada

A sunset or nightime cruise on Acapulco Bay

**Baja** Whale-watching at Scammon's and San Ignacio lagoons

**Chiapas/Tabasco** Firewalk on Carnival Tuesday, San Juan Chamula

**Heartland** Sunset boat trip to Janitzio, Pátzcuaro

**Yucatán** *Calesa* (horse-drawn carraige) ride through Mérida

Diving near coral formations, Cozumel

Snorkeling in naturla aquarium, Xel-Há

Sunset on Isla Mujeres

## Taste Treats

**Acapulco** *Pescado a la talla* at Beto's Barra Vieja

**Baja** Fresh dorado, wahoo, and lobster

**Guadalajara** Crepes at St. Michel

**Huasteca Country** Shrimp

**Oaxaca** Mole, mescal, fried grasshoppers

**Yucatán** Cochinita píbil

Fresh corn tortillas

Montejo, León Negro, and Carta Clara beers

Tik-In-Chik

## Towns and Villages

| | |
|---|---|
| **Chiapas/Tabasco** | San Cristóbal de las Casas |
| | San Juan Chamula |
| **Heartland** | Guanajuato |
| | Zacatecas |
| | Pátzcuaro |
| **Mexico City** | Coyoacán |

## Views

| | |
|---|---|
| **Acapulco** | Acapulco Bay from the air |
| **Chiapas/Tabasco** | Río Grijalva from CICOM complex, Villahermosa |
| **Heartland** | Zacatecas from the city's aerial tramway |
| **Mexico City** | Popocatépetl and Ixtaccíhuatl volcanoes from the air |

## Hotels

| | |
|---|---|
| **Very Expensive** | Acapulco Princess (Acapulco) |
| | Camino Real, Cancún (Yucatán) |
| | Casa de Sierra Nevada, San Miguel de Allende (Heartland) |
| | Copper Canyon Lodge (Copper Canyon) |
| | Las Brisas (Acapulco) |
| | Marquis Reforma (Mexico City) |
| | Posada del Capitán Lafitte, Mexico's Caribbean Coast (Yucatán) |
| | Mesón de Santa Rosa, Querétaro (Heartland) |
| | Palmilla, San José del Cabo (Baja) |
| | Quinta Real (Guadalajara) |
| | Stouffer Presidente, Cozumel (Yucatán) |
| | Villa Montana, Morelia (Heartland) |
| **Expensive** | Chan Kah, Palenque (Chiapas and Tabasco) |
| | Fiesta Americana (Guadalajara) |
| | Gran Hotel Ancira, Monterrey (Huasteca) |
| | Hotel Posada de Don Vasco, Pátzcuaro (Heartland) |
| **Moderate** | Continental Plaza Playacar, Playa del Carmen (Yucatán) |
| | La Mansión del Bosque, San Miguel de Allende (Heartland) |
| | Na-Bolom, San Cristóbal de las Casas (Chiapas and Tabasco) |
| **Inexpensive** | Frances (Guadalajara) |

Molino de Agua, Puerto Vallarta (Pacific Coast Resorts)

## Restaurants

**Very Expensive** Coyuca 22 (Acapulco)

San Angel Inn (Mexico City)

**Expensive** La Bella Epoca, Mérida (Yucatán)

La Vianda (Guadalajara)

Madeiras (Acapulco)

Restaurante Josecho, Querétaro (Heartland)

**Moderate** El Rey Tacamba, Morelia (Heartland)

Fonda Meson de San José, San Miguel de Allende (Heartland)

La Habichuela, Cancún (Yucatán)

Rincón Maya, Cozumel (Yucatán)

Tasca de Los Santos, Guanajuato

**Inexpensive** Jardines de Chiapa, Chiapa de Corzo (Chiapas and Tabasco)

La Paroquia, Veracruz (Huasteca)

Las Cazuelas (Mexico City)

Normita, San Cristóbal de las Casas (Chiapas and Tabasco)

Restaurante Hotel Posada La Basílica, Pátzcuaro (Heartland)

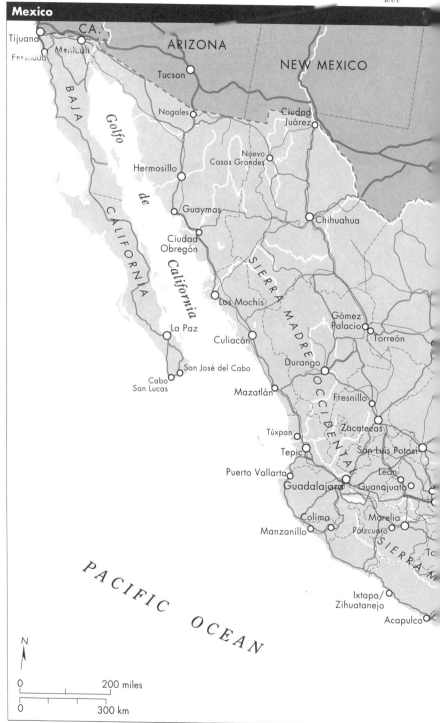

**Mexico**

Tijuana
Ensenada
CA.
Mexicali
BAJA
ARIZONA
NEW MEXICO
Tucson
Nogales
Ciudad
Juárez
Golfo
Nuevo
Casas Grandes
Hermosillo
de
Guaymas
Chihuahua
Ciudad
Obregón
California
SIERRA
Los Mochis
Gómez
Palacio
Torreón
La Paz
Culiacán
MADRE
San José del Cabo
Durango
Cabo
San Lucas
Mazatlán
Fresnillo
Túxpan
Zacatecas
OCCIDENTAL
Tepic
San Luis Potosí
Puerto Vallarta
León
Guadalajara
Guanajuato
Colima
Morelia
Manzanillo
Pátzcuaro
SIERRA M
Te

PACIFIC

OCEAN

Ixtapa/
Zihuatanejo
Acapulco

N

0          200 miles

0          300 km

OKLAHOMA
ARKANSAS
TENN.
MISS.
TEXAS
ALA.
LOUISIANA
Rio Grande
Nuevo
Laredo
Monterrey
Brownsville
Reynosa
Saltillo
Matamoros
Gulf of Mexico
Ciudad Victoria
Ciudad Mante
Tampico
San Miguel
de Allende
Isla
Mujeres
Querétaro
Poza Rica
El Tajín
Mérida
Cancún
Teotihuacán
Chichén Itzá
Tizimín
Mexico City
Veracruz
Uxmal
Cozumel
Toluca
Cobá
Xel-Há
Puebla
Campeche
YUCATAN
Tulum
Cuernavaca
Bahía de Campeche
Chilpancingo
Ciudad del
Carmen
Chetumal
Monte Albán
Coatzacoalcos
Minatitlán
Villahermosa
Caribbean Sea
Oaxaca
Palenque
BELIZE
Tehuantepec
Tuxtla
Gutiérrez
San Cristóbal
de las Casas
Huatulco
Comitán
Golfo de
Tehuantepec
GUATEMALA
Tapachula
HONDURAS
SIERRA MADRE ORIENTAL
SIERRA MADRE DEL SUR

# Mexican States and Capitals

CALIFORNIA
Mexicali ★

ARIZONA

NEW MEXICO

BAJA
CALIFORNIA
NORTE

Golfo

de

California

Hermosillo ★

SONORA

CHIHUAHUA

Chihuahua ★

COAHUILA

BAJA
CALIFORNIA
SUR

La Paz ★

SINALOA

Culiacán ★

DURANGO

Durango ★

ZACATECAS

Zacatecas ★

S
P

Tepic ★
NAYARIT

AGUASCALIENTES
Aguascalientes ★

★

Guanajuato ★
GUANAJUATO

Guadalajara ★
JALISCO

Colima ★
COLIMA

Morelia ★
MICHOACAN

M
T

M

GUERRERO

PACIFIC OCEAN

N

0        200 miles

0        300 km

# Mexico City and Environs

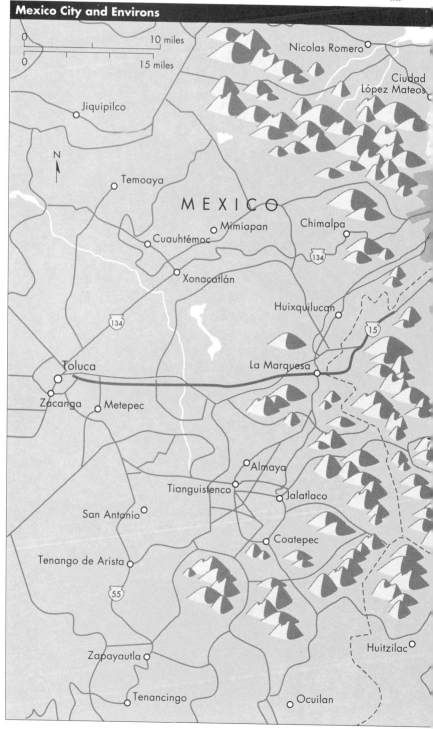

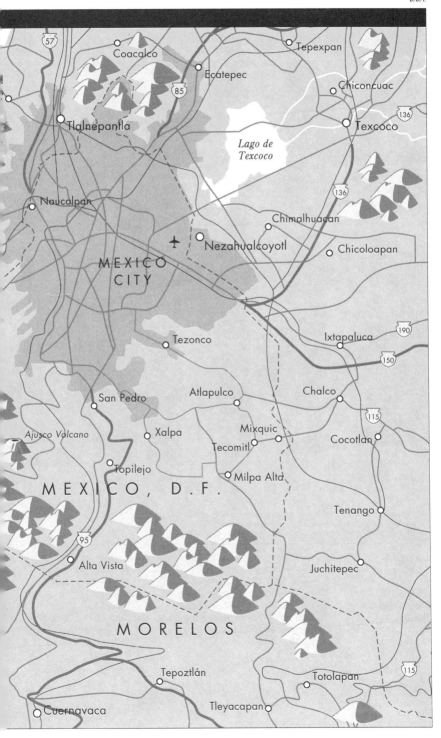

# World Time Zones

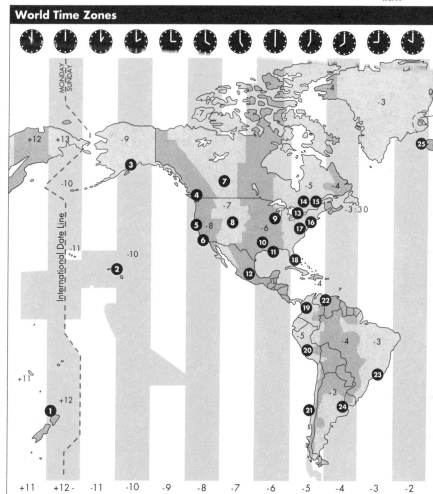

Numbers below vertical bands relate each zone to Greenwich Mean Time (0 hrs.).
Local times frequently differ from these general indications,
as indicated by light-face numbers on map.

| | | | |
|---|---|---|---|
| Algiers, **29** | Berlin, **34** | Delhi, **48** | Istanbul, **40** |
| Anchorage, **3** | Bogotá, **19** | Denver, **8** | Jerusalem, **42** |
| Athens, **41** | Budapest, **37** | Djakarta, **53** | Johannesburg, **44** |
| Auckland, **1** | Buenos Aires, **24** | Dublin, **26** | Lima, **20** |
| Baghdad, **46** | Caracas, **22** | Edmonton, **7** | Lisbon, **28** |
| Bangkok, **50** | Chicago, **9** | Hong Kong, **56** | London (Greenwich), **27** |
| Beijing, **54** | Copenhagen, **33** | Honolulu, **2** | Los Angeles, **6** |
| | Dallas, **10** | | Madrid, **38** |
| | | | Manila, **57** |

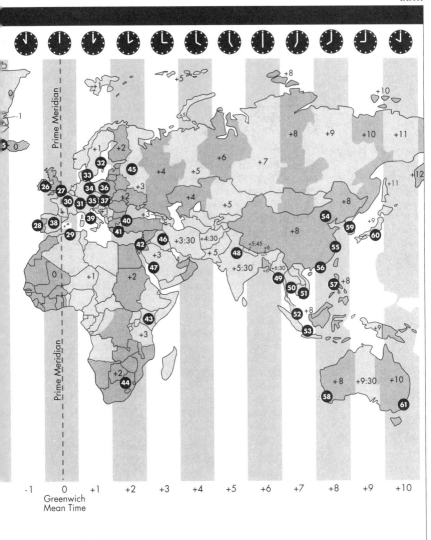

-1    0    +1    +2    +3    +4    +5    +6    +7    +8    +9    +10
Greenwich
Mean Time

# Introduction

*By Erica Meltzer*

*Freelance writer Erica Meltzer lived in Mexico City for three years, working as a writer, translator, meeting planner, and teacher. She is now based in New York and visits Mexico frequently.*

He who has been touched by the dust of Mexico will never again find peace in any land, says an old Mexican proverb. This is not hyperbole. I first went to Mexico when I was 15. I spent several summers there and eventually lived in Mexico City for three years. But I can't stay away.

Gringos have always had complex relationships with this country. Graham Greene wrote a cranky book about his travels in Mexico in the 1930s and finally had to admit that "it was as if Mexico was something I couldn't shake off, like a state of mind." Malcolm Lowry was "afflicted" with Mexico and insisted that he would prefer to die there, yet the Mexicans in his *Under the Volcano* are sinister and manipulative, or hopelessly passive. D.H. Lawrence made "noble savages" of the Indians, and both B. Traven and Katherine Anne Porter wrote compassionately of the downtrodden peasants.

Explaining one's obsession with a place is a monumental and painful task. I remember how strange and glorious it felt as a 15-year-old first-timer to Mexico to see the Maya ruins at Kabah in Yucatán: a gold and amber haze enshrouded the fluted columns and marred friezes, the stillness shattered only by the rustling of iguanas in the tall grasses. And I remember the heat, that throbbing sun, which dampened the mossy, claustrophobic walls in the subterranean vault at Chichén Itzá.

In Mexico City, my friends and I spent all our taco money on booklets at the Museum of Anthropology, then got sick on fresh peanuts in the shell from the marketplace. In Zihuatanejo resident hippies offered as drug-spiked oranges. Everywhere we were followed by young men who knew enough English to tell us what beautiful eyes we had; soon we were able to appreciate the Spanish-language version of those compliments.

When I went to live in the capital in 1979, I resided in four different middle-class neighborhoods not far from the Paseo de la Reforma. It was easy to live there on a limited budget. Eight *tacos al pastor* cost a couple of dollars, and we expatriates were fond of going into the markets to find inexpensive but pretty trinkets for decorating our apartments. There were petty problems to deal with, like having to buy stock in the phone company to get a phone, then waiting as long as six weeks for it to be installed; most people simply "bought" the phone and line from previous tenants so as not to bother with getting their own listing. (These days little has changed, except that it now takes six months to get a phone.)

Sunday mornings we'd go biking in Chapultepec Park, where vendors sold chili-covered white jicamas on sticks, like Popsicles, then have brunch in Polanco. We jogged in the Parque México, in Colonia Condesa, then sat on benches chatting with aging refugees from the Spanish Civil War and World War II. We prided ourselves on knowing the most obscure cantinas downtown and on enduring 12-hour bus rides—sometimes standing room only—to the beaches. It's a mild form of that expatriate malady known as "going native."

Mexico's intellectual and artistic life is fascinating. In the 1920s and 1930s, the country had a literary circle as prestigious and incestuous as Virginia Woolf's Bloomsbury or the Paris of Gertrude Stein. B. Traven palled around with Mexico's most famous cinematogorapher, Gabriel Figueroa, and was godfather to his son. They all knew Diego Rivera, who shared the favors of Tina Modotti with Edward Weston. Rivera and his wife, Frida Kahlo, persuaded President Lázaro Cádenas to give asylum to Leon Trotsky. Trotsky lived in Coyoacán, a colonial village, with Riviera and Kahlo. He had a brief fling with Kahlo before his assassination.

In the 1990s Mexico's tradition of an intellectual elite and of glaring class disparities lives on. Just as during the 300 years of Spanish rule when the "pure-blooded" children of the Spaniards, the Creoles, imposed their sense of superiority on the mixed-blood *mestizos*, so Creoles dominate Mexican cultural and political life today. Many of their parents came to Mexico to escape Franco's Spain, and even their last names give them away: The names are originally Basque, or they boast the aristocratic "de" (as in President Carlos Salinas de Gortari or his immediate predecessor, Miguel de la Madrid Hurtado). This class is collectively personified by the "Thousand Families," and they virtually run the country's media, banking, real estate, industrial, tourism, and public sectors.

The Indians, who account for about 10% of the total population, cannot read of their plight in the nation's print media. Besides the fact that many of the Indians are illiterate and do not understand Spanish, the news media are muzzled. And yet the Indians have not always been passive. There were violent uprisings in the state of Chiapas in 1712 and again in 1869; some 200,000 died in the Yucatán Caste Wars in the 1840s. The Indian community of San Juan Chamula, Chiapas, threw out the local priest in the early 1980s, along with hundreds of their own numbers who had converted to fundamentalist Protestant sects.

Pre-Columbian religious traditions are clung to fiercely. I once visited a *curandero* (shaman) near San Miguel de Allende who broke raw eggs over us to purge the evil spirits. In the church in San Juan Chamula, there are no pews and no altar. The "worship" I witnessed consisted of a man wringing a chicken's neck while his family drank Coca-Cola and burned candles on the floor in front of "Christian" idols. The Day of the Dead ceremonies enacted at candlelit cemeteries in the state of Michoacán, where families place food on the graves of their dead, are rooted in ancient forms of ancestor worship and appeasement of bloodthirsty deities. Mexico's relationship with the Catholic Church has not been a peaceful one: Two periods of violent anticlericalism (in the 1850s and 1920s and '30s) resulted in rioting, the demolition of churches and convents, and the persecution and murder of priests. Yet 93% of the people are baptized Catholics. Religious people are married in two ceremonies: by the state, because civil marriages are the only legally binding ones, and again by the church.

Violence is undeniably a part of Mexican life. Politicians are kidnapped, guerrilla groups hide out in the mountains, labor unions and students demonstrate, sometimes met by police repression. Drunken brawls are common in this country of high alcoholism.

On the other hand—and there *is* always an other hand in Mexico, this country of eros and thanatos, love and death, running madly together—I have had fatherly taxi drivers advise me not to be out on the streets so late and not to trust them by leaving my luggage unattended in the cab. There was the woman in Zihuatanejo who soothed a bad sunburn with a rubdown of crushed tomatoes. One good friend even lent me money, explaining that Mexicans never did that for each other. Students threw parties for me and sent me to their relatives when I traveled in the country. Mexican *pachangas*—celebratory, frequently tipsy, parties—are peerless.

Speaking Spanish is a definite advantage in Mexico. It is the most populous Spanish-speaking country in the world, and it has its own richly expressive vocabulary, a hybrid of Castilian, Indian, and English. I still say *¡híjole!* when something upsets or disgusts me, although I haven't been able to trace its etymology. There are dozens of exclamatory words: *¡Caray! ¡Aguas! ¡Chispas!* Let those roll off your lips and you feel a satisfaction no Anglo-Saxon word can give. Then there are the derogatory adjectives applied with robust enthusiasm to people and situations: *pinche* (damned), *naco* (uncouth) or *mensa* (stupid), and *pendejo* (also stupid, but rather vulgar). Mexicans say *sí, no?* (yes, no?) to mean something like, "it's true, isn't it?" They deride motherhood with *me vale madre* (I couldn't care less) and extol fatherhood with *qué padre* (how wonderful). And there is that ubiquitous little word, so infite in its uses: *ya,* which translates variously as "already," "yet," and—when used alonea s an exclamation—"enough already!" A close friend is a *cuate,* which has a deliciously cozy feel to it that "buddy" cannot possibly duplicate. People's personalities really do change when they speak another language.

Business correspondence seems flowery when compared with North American efficiency, and politeness—not always sincere—is an art. *Mi casa es su casa* (my house is your house) is one of the most-used Mexican expressions of hospitality, but do not take it seriously: I had a long and warm correspondence with one of my Mexican teachers who kept telling me I must come and stay with her, but when I phoned on arrival in Mexico City, she recommended a hotel.

Let a modicum of annoyance or impatience appear in your voice, and you will see how quickly Mexicans take offense. Possibly this tendency arises more often with foreigners than with other Mexicans—proof of an underlying wariness—but I have seen how angry Mexicans can be with one another over a perceived slight or wrong.

*Machismo* has to be addressed. When I lived in Mexico I learned to lower my eyes on the street and camouflage my anatomy. I got so used to the unsolicited male attention that on visits back to the United States, I wondered what was wrong with the men.

Tourism and development are transforming Mexico and its people to the point where the government has admonished the residents of Puerto Vallarta with a wall sign saying, VIVIMOS DEL TURISMO, NO DEL TURISTA (we live off tourism, not off the tourist). And the small colonial towns and fishing villages, such as San Miguel de Allende, Zihuatanejo, and Puerto Escondido, whicha re often described as "charming" and "typical," are now full of Americnas. San Cristóbal de las Casas, however, is not likely to lose its charm for at least 10 years. I imagine that when I go back to Paricutín, the volcano near Uruapan, I will still be able to ride a mule to the lava-covered church spires of the town buried by its last eruption in 1943. I will still enjoy picnics in utter isolation on the banks of Lake Avándaro and buy herbal medicines in the market at Valle de Bravo. Sunny breakfasts at a small hotel in Taxco, overlooking that completely colonial city, will still be possible, as will a night in a dingy has-been hotel of "traditional" or downtown Acapulco. In Mexico City, I can still walk by my apartment building in the Zona Rosa and appreciate its faintly neglected look. For the best buildings in Mexico are *not* the modoern ones; in the capital, at least, the modern ones were the first to fall in the 1985 earthquake. No, it's the slightly dilapidated walk-up flats, furnished 50 years ago with genteel lace, sturdy wooden chairs, and yellowing paintings of the Madonna, that I delight in—down to the last plastic flower and brown clay salsa bowl.

# 1  Essential Information

# Before You Go

## Government Tourist Offices

For a current calendar of events, train schedules and fares, brochures and other general information about travel in Mexico, contact the nearest **Mexican Government Tourism Office.**

**In the U.S.** 405 Park Avenue, Suite 1402, New York, NY 10022, tel. 212/755–7261, fax 212/753–2874; 1911 Pennsylvania Avenue NW, Washington, DC 20006, tel. 202/728–1750, fax 202/728-1758; 128 Aragon Avenue, Coral Gables, FL 33134, tel. 305/443–9160, fax 305/443-1186; 70 E. Lake Street, Suite 1413, Chicago, IL 60601, tel. 312/565–2786, fax 312/606-9012; 2707 N. Loop West, Suite 450, Houston, TX 77008, tel. 713/880–5153, fax 713/880-1833; Center Plaza Building, 45 NE Loop 410, Suite 125, San Antonio, TX 78216, tel. 210/366–3242, fax 210/366-1532; 10100 Santa Monica Boulevard, Suite 224, Los Angeles, CA 90067, tel. 310/203–8191, fax 310/203-8316. If there is no office near you, call 800/262–8900.

The Department of State's **Citizens Emergency Center** issues Consular Information Sheets that cover crime, security, and health risks as well as embassy locations, entry requirements, currency regulations, and other routine matters. (Travel Warnings, which counsel travelers to avoid a country entirely, are issued in extreme cases.) For the latest information on travel in Mexico, stop in at any passport office, consulate, or embassy; call the interactive hotline (tel. 202/647–5225); or, with your PC's modem, tap into the Bureau of Consular Affairs' computer bulletin board (tel. 202/647–9225).

**In Canada** 1 Place Ville Marie, Suite 2409, Montreal, Quebec H3B 3M9, tel. 514/871–1052, fax 514/871-3425; 2 Bloor Street W., Suite 1801, Toronto, Ontario M4W 3E2, tel. 416/925–0704 or 416/925–1876, fax 416/925-6061.

## Tours and Packages

Should you buy your travel arrangements to Mexico packaged or do it yourself? There are advantages either way. Buying packaged arrangements saves you money, particularly if you find a program that includes exactly the features you want. You also get a pretty good idea of what your trip will cost from the outset. Generally, two types of packaged travel arrangements are available: fully escorted tours and independent packages.

Travel agents are your best source of recommendations for both tours and packages. They can sell any of the packages offered by operators listed below, and the cost to you is the same as buying direct. Whatever program you ultimately choose, be sure to find out exactly what is included: taxes, tips, transfers, meals, baggage handling, ground transportation, entertainment, excursions, sports or recreation (and rental equipment if necessary). Ask about the level of hotel used, its location, the size of its rooms, the kind of beds, and its amenities, such as pool, room service, or programs for children, if they're important to you. Find out the operator's cancellation penalties. Nearly everyone charges them, and the only way to avoid them is to buy trip-cancellation insurance (*see* Trip Insurance, *below*). Also ask about the single supplement, a surcharge assessed to solo travelers. Some operators do not make you pay it if you agree to be matched up with a roommate of the same sex, even if one is not found by departure time. Remember that a program that has features you won't use may not be your best bet.

**Fully Escorted Tours** Escorted tours are usually sold in three categories: deluxe, first-class, and tourist or budget class. The most important differences are the price, of course, and the level of accommodations. Some operators specialize in one category, while others offer a range. Most itineraries are jam-packed with sightseeing, so you see a lot in a short amount of time (usually one place per day). To judge just how fast-paced the tour is, review the itinerary carefully. If you are in a different hotel each night, you will be getting up early each day to head out, travel to your next destination, do some sightseeing, have dinner, and go to bed, then you'll start all over again. If you want some free time, make sure it's mentioned in the tour brochure; if you want to be escorted to every meal, confirm that any tour you consider does that. Also, when comparing programs, be sure to find out if the motorcoach is air-conditioned and has a restroom on board.

Look into **American Express Vacations** (300 Pinnacle Way, Norcross, GA, tel. 800/241–1700); **Friendly Holidays** (1983 Marcus Ave., Suite C130, Lake Success, NY 11042, tel. 516/358–1200 or 800/221–9748, fax 516/358–1319), one of the largest wholesalers to Mexico; **GoGo Tours** (69 Spring St., Ramsey, NJ 07446, tel. 201/934–3500 or 800/821–3731), whose programs must be purchased through travel agents; **Mexico Travel Advisors** (1717 N. Highland Ave., Suite 1100, Los Angeles, CA 90028, tel. 213/462–6444 or 800/876–6824, fax 213/461–7559), which has been leading tours to Mexico for over 60 years; **Gadabout Tours** (700 E. Tahquitz Way, Palm Springs, CA 92262, tel. 619/325–5556 or 800/952–5068); and **American Leisure** (9800 Center Pkwy., Suite 800, Houston, TX 77036, tel. 800/777–1980; in TX, 713/988–6098), **Cartran Tours** (1334 Parkview Ave., Suite 210, Manhattan Beach, CA 90266, tel. 800/422–7826), and **Travel Impressions** (465 Smith St., Farmingdale, NY 11735, tel. 516/845–8000 or 800/284–0044), three other leading tour operators to Mexico.

**Independent Packages** Independent packages are offered by airlines, tour operators who may also do escorted programs, and any number of other companies from large, established firms to small, new entrepreneurs. Contact the tour operators above, plus **Asti Tours** (21 E. 40th St., New York, NY 10016, tel. 800/327–4390 or, in NY, 800/535–3711), and look into airline packages from **American Airlines Fly AAway Vacations** (tel. 800/321–2121), **Continental Airlines' Grand Destinations** (tel. 800/634–5555 or 800/284–0303), **Delta Dream Vacations** (tel. 800/872–7786), and **United Airlines' Vacation Planning Center** (tel. 800/328–6877).

**Special-interest Travel** Special-interest programs may be fully escorted or independent. Some require a certain amount of expertise, but most are for the average traveler with an interest and are usually hosted by experts in the subject matter. The price range is wide, but the cost is usually higher—sometimes a lot higher—than for ordinary escorted tours and packages, because of the expert guiding and special activities.

*Adventure* If lying motionless on a beach for a week is your idea of the perfect vacation, don't call **Mountain Travel-Sobek** (6420

**When to Go**

In terms of climate, the dry season—October through May—is the best time to see Mexico. Rain can fall daily during the peak of the rainy season (June–September), when it frequently lasts for hours. Even if it is not raining, much of the country is overcast—a less than perfect condition for a beach vacation.

During the North American winter, December through February, the Mexican resorts—where the vast majority of tourists go—are the most crowded and therefore the most expensive. To avoid the masses, the highest prices, and the worst rains, visit Mexico during October, April, or May. Hotel rates at the beach resorts can be cut by as much as 30% in the shoulder season, 50% in the off-season.

Mexicans travel during traditional holiday periods: Christmas/New Year's, Semana Santa (Holy Week, the week before Easter), and school vacations in the summertime, as well as over extended national holiday weekends, called *puentes* (bridges), and during festivals (*see* Festivals and Seasonal Events, *below*). If you travel then, reserve both lodgings and transportation well in advance.

**Climate**  The variations in Mexico's climate are not surprising considering the size of the country. The coasts and low-lying sections of the interior are often very hot if not actually tropical, with temperatures ranging from 24° to 31°C (75° to 88°F) in winter and well above 32°C (90°F) in summer. A more temperate area ranging from 16° to 21°C (60° to 70°F) is found at altitudes of 1,220–1,830 meters (4,000–6,000 feet). In general, the high central plateau on which Mexico City, Guadalajara, and many of the country's colonial cities are located is springlike year-round.

| *Acapulco* | **Jan.** | 88F | 31C | **May** | 90F | 32C | **Sept.** | 90F | 32C |
|---|---|---|---|---|---|---|---|---|---|
| | | 72 | 22 | | 77 | 25 | | 77 | 25 |
| | **Feb.** | 88F | 31C | **June** | 90F | 32C | **Oct.** | 90F | 32C |
| | | 72 | 22 | | 77 | 25 | | 77 | 25 |
| | **Mar.** | 88F | 31C | **July** | 91F | 33C | **Nov.** | 90F | 32C |
| | | 72 | 22 | | 77 | 25 | | 75 | 24 |
| | **Apr.** | 88F | 31C | **Aug.** | 91F | 33C | **Dec.** | 88F | 31C |
| | | 72 | 22 | | 77 | 25 | | 73 | 23 |

| *Cozumel* | **Jan.** | 82F | 28C | **May** | 89F | 32C | **Sept.** | 89F | 32C |
|---|---|---|---|---|---|---|---|---|---|
| | | 68 | 20 | | 73 | 23 | | 75 | 24 |
| | **Feb.** | 84F | 29C | **June** | 89F | 32C | **Oct.** | 87F | 31C |
| | | 68 | 20 | | 75 | 24 | | 73 | 23 |
| | **Mar.** | 86F | 30C | **July** | 89F | 32C | **Nov.** | 84F | 29C |
| | | 69 | 21 | | 75 | 24 | | 71 | 22 |
| | **Apr.** | 89F | 32C | **Aug.** | 91F | 33C | **Dec.** | 84F | 29C |
| | | 71 | 22 | | 75 | 24 | | 68 | 20 |

| | | | | | | | | |
|---|---|---|---|---|---|---|---|---|
| *Ensenada* | **Jan.** | 64F<br>45 | 18C<br>7 | **May** | 70F<br>54 | 21C<br>12 | **Sept.** | 77F<br>61 | 25C<br>16 |

| | | | | | | | | | |
|---|---|---|---|---|---|---|---|---|---|
| *Ensenada* | **Jan.** | 64F | 18C | **May** | 70F | 21C | **Sept.** | 77F | 25C |
| | | 45 | 7 | | 54 | 12 | | 61 | 16 |
| | **Feb.** | 66F | 19C | **June** | 72F | 22C | **Oct.** | 73F | 23C |
| | | 46 | 8 | | 57 | 14 | | 55 | 13 |
| | **Mar.** | 66F | 19C | **July** | 75F | 24C | **Nov.** | 72F | 22C |
| | | 46 | 8 | | 61 | 16 | | 48 | 9 |
| | **Apr.** | 68F | 20C | **Aug.** | 75F | 24C | **Dec.** | 66F | 19C |
| | | 52 | 11 | | 63 | 17 | | 46 | 8 |
| *Guadalajara* | **Jan.** | 75F | 24C | **May** | 88F | 31C | **Sept.** | 79F | 26C |
| | | 45 | 7 | | 57 | 14 | | 59 | 15 |
| | **Feb.** | 77F | 25C | **June** | 84F | 29C | **Oct.** | 79F | 26C |
| | | 46 | 8 | | 61 | 16 | | 59 | 15 |
| | **Mar.** | 82F | 28C | **July** | 79F | 26C | **Nov.** | 77F | 25C |
| | | 48 | 9 | | 59 | 15 | | 48 | 9 |
| | **Apr.** | 86F | 30C | **Aug.** | 79F | 26C | **Dec.** | 75F | 24C |
| | | 54 | 12 | | 59 | 15 | | 46 | 8 |
| *La Paz* | **Jan.** | 72F | 22C | **May** | 88F | 31C | **Sept.** | 92F | 33C |
| | | 57 | 14 | | 64 | 18 | | 76 | 24 |
| | **Feb.** | 74F | 23C | **June** | 92F | 33C | **Oct.** | 89F | 32C |
| | | 56 | 13 | | 69 | 21 | | 71 | 22 |
| | **Mar.** | 80F | 27C | **July** | 95F | 35C | **Nov.** | 81F | 27C |
| | | 56 | 13 | | 75 | 24 | | 66 | 19 |
| | **Apr.** | 83F | 28C | **Aug.** | 93F | 34C | **Dec.** | 74F | 23C |
| | | 60 | 16 | | 76 | 24 | | 59 | 15 |
| *Mexico City* | **Jan.** | 70F | 21C | **May** | 79F | 26C | **Sept.** | 72F | 22C |
| | | 41 | 5 | | 52 | 11 | | 52 | 11 |
| | **Feb.** | 73F | 23C | **June** | 77F | 25C | **Oct.** | 72F | 22C |
| | | 45 | 7 | | 54 | 12 | | 52 | 11 |
| | **Mar.** | 79F | 26C | **July** | 73F | 23C | **Nov.** | 72F | 22C |
| | | 48 | 9 | | 52 | 11 | | 52 | 11 |
| | **Apr.** | 81F | 27C | **Aug.** | 73F | 23C | **Dec.** | 70F | 21C |
| | | 50 | 10 | | 52 | 11 | | 43 | 6 |
| *Monterrey* | **Jan.** | 68F | 20C | **May** | 88F | 31C | **Sept.** | 88F | 31C |
| | | 48 | 9 | | 68 | 20 | | 70 | 21 |
| | **Feb.** | 73F | 23F | **June** | 91F | 33C | **Oct.** | 81F | 27C |
| | | 52 | 11 | | 72 | 22 | | 63 | 17 |
| | **Mar.** | 79F | 26C | **July** | 91F | 34C | **Nov.** | 75F | 24C |
| | | 55 | 13 | | 72 | 22 | | 55 | 13 |
| | **Apr.** | 86F | 30C | **Aug.** | 93F | 34C | **Dec.** | 70F | 21C |
| | | 64 | 18 | | 72 | 22 | | 50 | 10 |
| *Puerto Vallarta* | **Jan.** | 84F | 29C | **May** | 91F | 33C | **Sept.** | 93F | 34C |
| | | 63 | 17 | | 68 | 20 | | 73 | 23 |
| | **Feb.** | 86F | 30C | **June** | 93F | 34C | **Oct.** | 93F | 34C |
| | | 61 | 16 | | 73 | 23 | | 73 | 23 |
| | **Mar.** | 86F | 30C | **July** | 95F | 35C | **Nov.** | 91F | 33C |
| | | 63 | 17 | | 73 | 23 | | 68 | 20 |
| | **Apr.** | 88F | 31C | **Aug.** | 95F | 35C | **Dec.** | 86F | 30C |
| | | 64 | 18 | | 73 | 23 | | 64 | 18 |

| *San Miguel* | **Jan.** | 79F | 26C | **May** | 91F | 33C | **Sept.** | 82F | 28C |
|---|---|---|---|---|---|---|---|---|---|
| *de Allende* | | 48 | 9 | | 61 | 16 | | 61 | 16 |
| | **Feb.** | 82F | 28C | **June** | 91F | 31C | **Oct.** | 82F | 28C |
| | | 52 | 11 | | 63 | 17 | | 61 | 16 |
| | **Mar.** | 88F | 31C | **July** | 84F | 29C | **Nov.** | 81F | 27C |
| | | 55 | 13 | | 61 | 16 | | 52 | 11 |
| | **Apr.** | 90F | 32C | **Aug.** | 84F | 29C | **Dec.** | 77F | 25C |
| | | 59 | 15 | | 61 | 16 | | 48 | 9 |

*Information*   For current weather conditions for cities in the United States
*Sources*   and abroad, plus the local time and helpful travel tips, call the
**Weather Channel Connection** (tel. 900/WEATHER; 95¢ per
minute) from a touch-tone phone.

## Festivals and Seasonal Events

Mexico has a full calendar of national holidays, saints' days, and
special events; below are some of the most important or unusual
ones. For further information and exact dates, contact the
Mexican Government Tourism Office (*see* Government Tourist
Offices, *above*).

**Jan. 1: New Year's Day** is a major celebration throughout the
country. Agricultural and livestock fairs are held in the provinces; in Oaxaca, women display traditional *tehuana* costumes.
**Jan. 6: Feast of Epiphany** is the day the Three Kings bring gifts
to Mexican children.
**Jan. 17: Feast of San Antonio Abad** honors animals all over Mexico. Household pets and livestock alike are decked out with flowers and ribbons and taken to a nearby church for a blessing.
**Jan.: Feast of the Immaculate Conception** is a religious celebration in which lights and flowers transform Morelia.
**Feb.: Día de la Candelaria,** or Candlemas Day, means fiestas,
parades, bullfights, and lantern-decorated streets. Festivities
include a running of the bulls through the streets of
Tlacotalpan, Veracruz.
**Feb.–Mar.: Carnival** is celebrated throughout Mexico, but most
notably in Mérida and Veracruz, where there are parades with
floats and bands.
**Mar. 21: Benito Juárez's Birthday** is a national holiday that is
most popular in Guelatao, Oaxaca, where Juárez, the beloved
19th-century president of Mexico and champion of the people,
was born.
**Mar.–Apr.: Holy Week** or (Semana Santa) is observed throughout the country with special passion plays during this week
leading up to Easter Sunday.
**Apr.: International Horse Fair** is held in Texcoco, Estado de
México.
**Apr.–May: San Marcos National Fair,** held in Aguascalientes, is
one of the country's best fairs. It features native *matachnes*
(dances performed by grotesque figures), mariachi bands, and
bullfights.
**May 1: Labor Day** is a day for workers to parade through the
streets.
**May 5: Cinco de Mayo** marks the anniversary of the French defeat by Mexican troops in Puebla in 1862.
**May 15: Feast of San Isidro Labrador** is celebrated nationwide
with the blessing of new seeds and animals.
**June 1: Navy Day** is commemorated in all Mexican seaports and
is especially colorful in Acapulco.

**June: Feast of Corpus Christi** is celebrated in different ways. In Mexico City, children are dressed in native costumes and taken to the cathedral on the *Zócalo* (main square) for a blessing. In Papantla, Veracruz, the Dance of the Flying Birdmen, a pre-Hispanic ritual to the sun, is held throughout the day.

**June 24: Saint John the Baptist Day** is a popular national holiday, with many Mexicans observing a tradition of tossing a "blessing" of water on most anyone within reach.

**July 16: Feast of the Virgen del Carmen** is a celebration, with fairs, bullfights, fireworks, sporting competitions, even a major fishing tournament.

**July: Guelaguetza Dance Festival** is a Oaxacan affair that dates to pre-Columbian times.

**Late July: Feast of Santiago** is a national holiday that features *charreadas*, Mexican-style rodeos.

**Aug. 15: Feast of the Assumption of the Blessed Virgin Mary** is celebrated nationwide with religious processions. In Huamantla, Tlaxcala, the festivities include a running of the bulls down flower-strewn streets.

**Aug. 25: San Luis Potosí Patron Saint Fiesta** is the day the town honors its patron, St. Louis, with traditional dance, music, and foods.

**Sept. 15–16: Independence Day** is when all of Mexico celebrates independence with fireworks and parties that outblast New Year's Eve. The biggest celebrations take place in Mexico City.

**Sept. 29: San Miguel Day** honors St. Michael, the patron saint of all towns with San Miguel in their names, with bullfights, folk dances, concerts, and fireworks.

**Oct.: October Festivals** means a month of cultural and sporting events in Guadalajara.

**Oct. 4: Feast of St. Francis of Assisi** is a day for processions dedicated to St. Francis in various parts of the country.

**Oct. 12: Columbus Day** is a national holiday in Mexico.

**Oct.–Nov.: International Cervantes Festival**, in Guanajuato, is a top cultural event that attracts dancers, singers, and actors from a number of different countries.

**Nov. 2: All Soul's Day** or **Day of the Dead** is when Mexicans remember the departed in an oddly merry way, with candy skulls sold on street corners and picnickers spreading blankets in cemeteries.

**Nov. 20: Anniversary of the Mexican Revolution** is a national holiday.

**Nov.–Dec.: National Silver Fair** is an annual Taxco event in which silver is exhibited and sold.

**Dec. 12: Feast Day of the Virgin of Guadalupe** is the day on which Mexico's patron saint is feted with processions and native folk dances, particularly at her shrine in Mexico City.

**Dec. 16–24: Christmas** is the day for processions that lead to Christmas parties and to *piñatas* (decorated, suspended hollow balls) that are broken open to yield gifts. Mexico City is brightly decorated, but don't expect any snow.

## What to Pack

Pack light: Though baggage carts are available now at airports, luggage restrictions on international flights are tight, and you'll want to save space for purchases. Mexico is filled with bargains on clothing, leather goods, arts and crafts, and silver jewelry.

**Clothing** What you bring depends on your destination. For the resorts, bring lightweight sports clothes, bathing suits, and cover-ups for the beach. Bathing suits and immodest clothing are inappropriate for shopping and sightseeing, both in cities and beach resorts. Mexico City is a bit more formal than the resorts and because of its high elevation, cooler. Men will want to bring lightweight suits or slacks and blazers for fancier restaurants; and women should pack tailored dresses. Many restaurants require jacket and tie. Jeans are acceptable for shopping and sightseeing, but shorts are frowned upon for men and women. You'll need a lightweight topcoat for winter and an all-weather coat and umbrella in case of sudden summer rainstorms.

Resorts, such as Cancún and Acapulco, are both casual and elegant; you'll see high-style designer sportswear, tie-dyed T-shirts, cotton slacks and walking shorts, and plenty of colorful sundresses. The sun can be fierce; bring a sun hat (or buy one locally) and sunscreen for the beach and for sightseeing. You'll need a sweater or jacket to cope with hotel and restaurant air-conditioning, which can be glacial. Few restaurants require jacket and tie.

**Miscellaneous** Bring a spare pair of eyeglasses and sunglasses. If you have a health problem that requires a prescription drug, take enough to last the duration of the trip. You can probably find what you need in the pharmacies, but you may need a local doctor's prescription. Bring as much film as you're allowed, because film is expensive in Mexico. Also pack a small flashlight, insect repellent, and a plastic water bottle for carrying your own supply on the road. And don't forget a list of the addresses of offices that supply refunds for lost or stolen traveler's checks.

**Luggage Regulations** Free baggage allowances on an airline depend on the airline, the route, and the class of your ticket. In general, on domestic flights and on international flights between the United States and foreign destinations, you are entitled to check two bags—neither exceeding 62 inches, or 158 centimeters (length + width + height), or weighing more than 70 pounds (32 kilograms). A third piece may be brought aboard as a carryon; its total dimensions are generally limited to less than 45 inches (114 centimeters), so it will fit easily under the seat in front of you or in the overhead compartment. There are variations, so ask in advance. The single rule, a Federal Aviation Administration safety regulation that pertains to carry-on baggage on U.S. airlines, requires only that carryons be properly stowed and allows the airline to limit allowances and tailor them to different aircraft and operational conditions. Charges for excess, oversize, or overweight pieces vary, so inquire before you pack.

On flights between Mexico and another destination outside the U.S., baggage allowances may be determined not by the piece method but by the weight method, which generally allows 88 pounds (40 kilograms) of luggage in first class, 66 pounds (30 kilograms) in business class, and 44 pounds (20 kilograms) in economy. If your flight between two cities abroad *connects* with your transatlantic or transpacific flight, the piece method still applies.

*Safeguarding Your Luggage* Before leaving home, itemize your bags' contents and their worth; this list will help you estimate the extent of your loss if your bags go astray. To minimize that risk, tag them inside and out with your name, address, and phone number. (If you use your home address, cover it so that potential thieves can't see it.) At check-in, make sure that the tag attached by baggage handlers bears the correct three-letter code for your destination. If your bags do not arrive with you, or if you detect damage, do not leave the airport until you've filed a written report with the airline.

*Insurance*   In the event of loss, damage, or theft on domestic flights, airlines limit their liability to $20 per kilogram for checked baggage (roughly about $640 per 70-pound bag) and $400 per passenger for unchecked baggage. On domestic flights, the ceiling is $1,250 per passenger. Excess-valuation insurance can be bought directly from the airline at check-in but leaves your bags vulnerable on the ground. Your own homeowner's policy may fill the gap; or you may want special luggage insurance. Sources include **The Travelers Companies** (1 Tower Sq., Hartford, CT 06183, tel. 203/277–0111 or 800/243–3174) and **Wallach and Company, Inc.** (107 W. Federal St., Box 480, Middleburg, VA 22117, tel. 703/687–3166 or 800/237–6615), underwritten by Lloyds, London.

## Taking Money Abroad

Traveler's checks and all major U.S. credit cards are accepted in most tourist areas of Mexico. The large hotels, restaurants, and department stores accept cards readily. Some of the smaller restaurants and shops, however, will only take cash. Credit cards are generally not accepted in small towns and villages, except in tourist-oriented hotels. When shopping, you can usually get much better prices if you bargain with dollars.

Traveler's Checks   The most widely recognized are **American Express, Barclay's, Thomas Cook,** and those issued by major commercial banks such as **Citibank** and **Bank of America.** American Express also issues *Traveler's Cheques for Two,* which can be signed and used by you or your traveling companion. Although some checks are free, you will usually pay 1% of the checks' face value as a fee.

Be sure to buy a few checks in small denominations to cash toward the end of your trip, when you don't want to be left with more pesos than you can spend. Always record the numbers of checks as you spend them, and keep this list separate from the checks.

Currency   To avoid lines at airport currency-exchange booths, arrive in a
Exchange   foreign country with a small amount of the local currency already in your pocket—a so-called tip pack. **Thomas Cook Currency Services** (630 5th Ave., New York, NY 10111, tel. 212/757–6915) supplies foreign currency by mail.

In Mexico, banks, *casas de cambio* (exchange houses), and bank-operated exchange booths at airports and railroad stations are usually the best places to change money. Rates at banks and airport exchange booths are typically better than at hotels, stores, and privately run exchange firms. You can usually get more pesos for your dollars at Mexican airports or banks than at U.S. airports.

can also write to the **Centers for Disease Control (CDC)** or call their hotline (Center for Preventive Services, Division of Quarantine, Traveler's Health Section, 1600 Clifton Rd., MSE03, Atlanta, GA 30333, tel./fax 404/332–4559). In Mexico you can purchase malaria-preventive Aralen tablets without a prescription. To be effective, the tablets must be taken before entering a malarial region. Dengue fever—a viral disease transmitted by mosquitoes and characterized by high fever, severe headaches, and joint and muscle pain—is becoming more prevalent in parts of Mexico. No specific treatment exists, so take proper precaution: Remain in well-screened areas, wear clothing that covers your arms and legs, and use a mosquito repellent.

Many travelers are eventually hit with an intestinal ailment known facetiously as Montezuma's Revenge or the Aztec Two-Step. Generally, it lasts only a day or two. A good antidiarrheal agent is paregoric, which dulls or eliminates abdominal cramps. You will need a doctor's prescription to get it in Mexico. The National Institute of Health recommends Pepto-Bismol and loperamide (Imodium) for mild cases of diarrhea. Lomotil is no longer recommended because it usually prolongs the infection. If you get sick, rest as much as possible, drink lots of fluids (such as tea without milk), and, in severe cases, rehydrate yourself with a salt-sugar mixture added to water. The best defense against food and waterborne diseases is a smart diet. Stay away from unbottled or unboiled water, ice, raw food, unpasteurized milk, and milk products.

Caution is advised when venturing out in the Mexican sun. Sunbathers lulled by a slightly overcast sky or the sea breezes can be burned badly with as little as 20 minutes' exposure. Use strong sunscreens, and avoid the peak sun hours of noon to 2 PM.

Scuba divers take note: PADI recommends that you not scuba dive and fly within a 24-hour period.

**Finding a Doctor**  The **International Association for Medical Assistance to Travellers** (IAMAT, 417 Center St., Lewiston, NY 14092, tel. 716/754–4883; 40 Regal Rd., Guelph, Ontario N1K 1B5; 57 Voirets, 1212 Grand-Lancy, Geneva, Switzerland) publishes a worldwide directory of English-speaking physicians whose qualifications meet IAMAT standards and who have agreed to treat members for a set fee. Membership is free.

## Insurance

**For U.S. Residents**  Most tour operators, travel agents, and insurance agents sell specialized health-and-accident, flight, trip-cancellation, and luggage insurance as well as comprehensive policies with some or all of these features. But before you make any purchase, review your existing health and homeowner policies to find out whether they cover expenses incurred while travelling.

Companies supplying comprehensive policies include **Access America, Inc.,** underwritten by BCS Insurance Company (Box 11188, Richmond, VA 23230, tel. 800/284–8300); **Carefree Travel Insurance,** underwritten by The Hartford (Box 310, 120 Mineola Blvd., Mineola, NY 11501, tel. 516/294–0220 or 800/323–3149); **Tele-Trip** (Mutual of Omaha Plaza, Box 31762, Omaha, NE 68131, tel. 800/228–9792), a subsidiary of Mutual of Omaha;

**The Travelers Companies** (1 Tower Sq., Hartford, CT 06183, tel. 203/277–0111 or 800/243–3174); **Travel Guard International,** underwritten by Transamerica Occidental Life Companies (1145 Clark St., Stevens Point, WI 54481, tel. 715/345–0505 or 800/782–5151); and **Wallach and Company, Inc.** (107 W. Federal St., Box 480, Middleburg, VA 22117, tel. 703/687–3166 or 800/237–6615), underwritten by Lloyds, London.

## Car Rentals

When considering this option, remember that Mexico is still a developing country. Acquiring a driver's license is more a question of paying someone off than of tested skill, and Mexican men have a tendency to show off on the road—often at the expense of other vehicles and pedestrians. The highway system is very uneven: in some regions, modern, well-paved super highways prevail; in others, particularly the mountains, potholes and dangerous, unrailed curves are the rule.

Major car-rental companies are represented in Mexico, including **Avis** (tel. 800/331–1212, 800/879–2847 in Canada); **Budget** (tel. 800/527–0700); **Dollar** (tel. 800/800–4000); **Hertz** (tel. 800/654–3131, 800/263-0600 in Canada); and **National** (tel. 800/227–7368), known internationally as InterRent and Europcar. Mexico also has its own national and local firms (their rates are frequently less expensive).

**Requirements** Your own U.S., U.K., or Canadian driver's license is acceptable. Mexican rental agencies are more familiar with U.S. and Canadian licenses than with the international driver's licenses issued by the American Automobile Association, which must be obtained before you leave home. You will need to leave a deposit—the most acceptable being a blank, signed credit card voucher. Without a credit card, you may not be able to rent a car.

When you drive in Mexico, it is necessary at all times to carry proof of Mexican auto insurance, which is usually provided by car-rental agencies and included in the cost of the rental. If you don't have proof of insurance and happen to injure someone—whether it's your fault or not—you stand the risk of being jailed.

**Extra Charges** Automatic transmissions and air-conditioning are not universally available; ask for them when you book if you want them, and check the cost before you commit yourself to the rental.

Drop-off charges, for renting a car in one location and dropping it off in another, can be hefty—about 33¢ per kilometer between rental city and drop-off city—and in some places drop-off is not possible at all. **M & M Jeeps** (220 El Cajon Blvd., San Diego, CA, 92104, tel. 619/297–1615, fax 619/297–1617) is the only rental agency in the United States from whom you can rent cars, drive them across the border, and drop them off in Los Cabos without a drop-off charge.

**Cutting Costs** It is always best to book in advance from home. Not only will this give you an American reservation number, but the price will be substantially less. Major international companies have programs that discount their standard rates by 15%–30% if you make the reservation before departure (anywhere from two to 14 days), rent for a minimum number of days (typically three or four), and prepay the rental. Ask about these advance-pur-

varies. U.S. carriers must allow FAA-approved models, but because these seats are strapped into a regular passenger seat, they may require that parents buy a ticket even for an infant under 2 who would otherwise ride free. Foreign carriers may not allow infant seats, may charge the child's rather than the infant's fare for their use, or may require you to hold your baby during takeoff and landing, thus defeating the seat's purpose.

**Publications**
*Newsletter*

*Family Travel Times,* published 10 times a year by Travel With Your Children (TWYCH, 45 W. 18th St., 7th Floor Tower, New York, NY 10011, tel. 212/206–0688; annual subscription $55), covers destinations, types of vacations, and modes of travel; an airline issue comes out every other year (the last one, February/March 1993, is sold to nonsubscribers for $10). On Wednesday, the staff answers subscribers' questions on specific destinations.

*Books*

*Great Vacations with Your Kids,* by Dorothy Jordan and Marjorie Cohen ($13; Penguin USA, 120 Woodbine St., Bergenfield, NJ 07621, tel. 800/253–6476) and *Traveling with Children—And Enjoying It,* by Arlene K. Butler ($11.95 plus $3 shipping per book; Globe Pequot Press, Box 833, Old Saybrook, CT 06475, tel. 800/243–0495 or 800/962–0973 in CT) both help you plan your trip with children, from toddlers to teens. Also from Globe Pequot is *Recommended Family Resorts in the United States, Canada, and the Caribbean,* by Jane Wilford with Janet Tice ($12.95), which describes 100 resorts at length and includes a "Children's World" section describing activities and facilities as part of each entry.

**Tour Operators**

**GrandTravel** (6900 Wisconsin Ave., Suite 706, Chevy Chase, MD 20815, tel. 301/986–0790 or 800/247–7651) offers international and domestic tours for grandparents traveling with their grandchildren. The catalogue, as charmingly written and illustrated as a children's book, positively invites armchair traveling with lap-sitters aboard. **Rascals in Paradise** (650 5th St., Suite 505, San Francisco, CA 94107, tel. 415/978–9800 or 800/872–7225) specializes in programs for families.

## Hints for Travelers with Disabilities

**Organizations**

Several organizations provide travel information for people with disabilities, usually for a membership fee, and some publish newsletters and bulletins. Among them are the **Information Center for Individuals with Disabilities** (Fort Point Pl., 27–43 Wormwood St., Boston, MA 02210, tel. 617/727–5540 or 800/462–5015 in MA between 11 and 4, or leave message; TDD/TTY tel. 617/345–9743); **Mobility International USA** (Box 3551, Eugene, OR 97403, voice and TDD tel. 503/343–1284), the U.S. branch of an international organization based in Britain and present in 30 countries; **Moss Rehab Hospital Travel Information Service** (1200 W. Tabor Rd., Philadelphia, PA 19141, tel. 215/456–9603, TDD tel. 215/456–9602); the **Society for the Advancement of Travel for the Handicapped** (SATH, 347 5th Ave., Suite 610, New York, NY 10016, tel. 212/447–7284, fax 212/725–8253); the **Travel Industry and Disabled Exchange** (TIDE, 5435 Donna Ave., Tarzana, CA 91356, tel. 818/368–5648); and **Travelin' Talk** (Box 3534, Clarksville, TN 37043, tel. 615/552–6670).

**Travel Agencies and Tour Operators**

**Directions Unlimited** (720 N. Bedford Rd., Bedford Hills, NY 10507, tel. 914/241–1700), a travel agency, has expertise in

**The Travelers Companies** (1 Tower Sq., Hartford, CT 06183, tel. 203/277–0111 or 800/243–3174); **Travel Guard International,** underwritten by Transamerica Occidental Life Companies (1145 Clark St., Stevens Point, WI 54481, tel. 715/345–0505 or 800/ 782–5151); and **Wallach and Company, Inc.** (107 W. Federal St., Box 480, Middleburg, VA 22117, tel. 703/687–3166 or 800/237– 6615), underwritten by Lloyds, London.

## Car Rentals

When considering this option, remember that Mexico is still a developing country. Acquiring a driver's license is more a question of paying someone off than of tested skill, and Mexican men have a tendency to show off on the road—often at the expense of other vehicles and pedestrians. The highway system is very uneven: in some regions, modern, well-paved super highways prevail; in others, particularly the mountains, potholes and dangerous, unrailed curves are the rule.

Major car-rental companies are represented in Mexico, including **Avis** (tel. 800/331–1212, 800/879–2847 in Canada); **Budget** (tel. 800/527–0700); **Dollar** (tel. 800/800–4000); **Hertz** (tel. 800/ 654–3131, 800/263-0600 in Canada); and **National** (tel. 800/227– 7368), known internationally as InterRent and Europcar. Mexico also has its own national and local firms (their rates are frequently less expensive).

**Requirements**  Your own U.S., U.K., or Canadian driver's license is acceptable. Mexican rental agencies are more familiar with U.S. and Canadian licenses than with the international driver's licenses issued by the American Automobile Association, which must be obtained before you leave home. You will need to leave a deposit—the most acceptable being a blank, signed credit card voucher. Without a credit card, you may not be able to rent a car.

When you drive in Mexico, it is necessary at all times to carry proof of Mexican auto insurance, which is usually provided by car-rental agencies and included in the cost of the rental. If you don't have proof of insurance and happen to injure someone—whether it's your fault or not—you stand the risk of being jailed.

**Extra Charges**  Automatic transmissions and air-conditioning are not universally available; ask for them when you book if you want them, and check the cost before you commit yourself to the rental.

Drop-off charges, for renting a car in one location and dropping it off in another, can be hefty—about 33¢ per kilometer between rental city and drop-off city—and in some places drop-off is not possible at all. **M & M Jeeps** (220 El Cajon Blvd., San Diego, CA, 92104, tel. 619/297–1615, fax 619/297–1617) is the only rental agency in the United States from whom you can rent cars, drive them across the border, and drop them off in Los Cabos without a drop-off charge.

**Cutting Costs**  It is always best to book in advance from home. Not only will this give you an American reservation number, but the price will be substantially less. Major international companies have programs that discount their standard rates by 15%–30% if you make the reservation before departure (anywhere from two to 14 days), rent for a minimum number of days (typically three or four), and prepay the rental. Ask about these advance-purchase schemes when you call for information. More economical rentals are those that come as part of fly/drive or other packages, even those as bare-bones as the rental plus an airline ticket (*see* Tours and Packages, *above*).

One important thing to keep in mind, however, if you are booking in advance, is that you cannot always count on getting the make and model of your choice upon arrival. The least-expensive rental car—a Volkswagen sedan—may be unavailable, and you might have to settle for a larger, more costly model. Manual transmission cars are more common than automatics.

One last tip: Remember to fill the tank when you turn in the vehicle, to avoid being charged for refueling at what you'll swear is the most expensive pump in town.

**Insurance and Collision Damage Waiver** The standard rental contract includes liability coverage (for damage to public property, injury to pedestrians, etc.) and coverage for the car against fire, theft (not included in certain countries), and collision damage with a deductible—most commonly $2,000–$3,000, occasionally more. In the case of an accident, you are responsible for the deductible amount unless you've purchased the collision damage waiver (CDW), which costs an average $12 a day, although this varies depending on what you've rented, where, and from whom.

Because this adds up quickly, you may be inclined to say "no thanks"—and that's certainly your option, although the rental agent may not tell you so. Planning ahead will help you make the right decision. By all means, find out if your own insurance covers damage to a rental car while traveling (not simply a car to drive when yours is in for repairs). And check whether charging car rentals to any of your credit cards will get you a CDW at no charge. Note before you decline that deductibles are occasionally high enough that totaling a car would make you responsible for its full value.

### Student and Youth Travel

**Hosteling** An **International Youth Hostel Federation** (IYHF) membership card is the key to more than 5,300 hostel locations in 59 countries; the sex-segregated, dormitory-style sleeping quarters, including some for families, go for $7–$20 a night per person. Membership is available in the United States through **American Youth Hostels** (AYH, 733 15th St. NW, Washington, DC 20005, tel. 202/783–6161), the American link in the worldwide chain, and costs $25 for adults 18–54, $10 for those under 18, $15 for those 55 and over, and $35 for families. IYHF membership is available in Canada through the **Canadian Hostelling Association** (CHA, 1600 James Naismith Dr., Suite 608, Gloucester, Ont. K1B 5N4, tel. 613/748–5638) for $26.75, and in the United Kingdom through the **Youth Hostel Association of England and Wales** (Trevelyan House, 8 St. Stephen's Hill, St. Albans, Herts. AL1 2DY, tel. 0727/55215) for £9. For hostel locations in Mexico contact **El Commission National del Deporte, Direccion de Villas Deportivas Jovenes** (Glorieta del Metro Insujentes, Local C-11 Y 12, Col. Juarez, Deleg. Cuauhumoc, CP 06600, Mexico, D. F. tel. 5/525–2926/2974/2699, fax 5/546–7425).

**Discount Cards** For discounts on transportation and on museum and attractions admissions, buy the **International Student Identity Card**

(ISIC) if you're a bona fide student, or the **International Youth Card** (IYC) if you're under 26. In the United States the ISIC and IYC cards cost $15 each and include basic travel accident and sickness coverage. Apply to **CIEE** (*see* address, *above*, tel. 212/661–1414; the application is in *Student Travels*). In Canada the cards are available for $15 each from **Travel Cuts** (*see above*). In the United Kingdom they cost £5 and £4 respectively at student unions and student travel companies, including Council Travel's London office (28A Poland St., London W1V 3DB, tel. 071/437–7767).

**Travel Agencies** The foremost U.S. student travel agency is **Council Travel,** a subsidiary of the nonprofit Council on International Educational Exchange. It specializes in low-cost travel arrangements, is the exclusive U.S. agent for several discount cards, and, with its sister CIEE subsidiary, **Council Charter,** is a source of airfare bargains. The Council Charter brochure and CIEE's twice-yearly *Student Travels* magazine, which details its programs, are available at the Council Travel office at CIEE headquarters (205 E. 42nd Street, New York, NY 10017, tel. 212/ 661–1450) and at 37 branches in college towns nationwide (free in person, $1 by mail). The **Educational Travel Center** (ETC, 438 N. Francis St., Madison, WI 53703, tel. 608/256–5551) also offers low-cost rail passes, domestic and international airline tickets (mostly for flights departing from Chicago), and other budgetwise travel arrangements. Other travel agencies catering to students include **Travel Management International** (TMI, 18 Prescott St., Suite 4, Cambridge, MA 02138, tel. 617/661– 8187) and **Travel Cuts** (187 College St., Toronto, Ont. M5T 1P7, tel. 416/979–2406).

## Traveling with Children

All children, including infants, must have proof of citizenship for travel to Mexico. Children traveling with a single parent must also have a notarized letter from the other parent stating that the child has his or her permission to leave the country. Although children can be listed on parents' tourist cards, it's a good idea to get separate tourist cards for everyone in your family. That way in an emergency one child will be able to leave the country with one parent if necessary.

**Getting There** On international flights, the fare for infants under 2 not occupy-
**Airfares** ing a seat is generally 10% of the accompanying adult's fare; children ages 2–11 usually pay half to two-thirds of the adult fare. On domestic flights, children under 2 not occupying a seat travel free, and older children currently travel on the "lowest applicable" adult fare.

**Baggage** In general, infants paying 10% of the adult fare are allowed one carry-on bag, not to exceed 70 pounds or 45 inches (length + width + height). The adult baggage allowance applies for children paying half or more of the adult fare. Check with the airline for particulars, especially regarding flights between two Mexican destinations, where allowances for infants may be less generous.

**Safety Seats** The FAA recommends the use of safety seats aloft and details approved models in the free leaflet **"Child/Infant Safety Seats Recommended for Use in Aircraft"** (available from the Federal Aviation Administration, APA–200, 800 Independence Ave. SW, Washington, DC 20591, tel. 202/267–3479). Airline policy varies. U.S. carriers must allow FAA-approved models, but because these seats are strapped into a regular passenger seat, they may require that parents buy a ticket even for an infant under 2 who would otherwise ride free. Foreign carriers may not allow infant seats, may charge the child's rather than the infant's fare for their use, or may require you to hold your baby during takeoff and landing, thus defeating the seat's purpose.

**Publications**
*Newsletter* *Family Travel Times,* published 10 times a year by Travel With Your Children (TWYCH, 45 W. 18th St., 7th Floor Tower, New York, NY 10011, tel. 212/206–0688; annual subscription $55), covers destinations, types of vacations, and modes of travel; an airline issue comes out every other year (the last one, February/March 1993, is sold to nonsubscribers for $10). On Wednesday, the staff answers subscribers' questions on specific destinations.

*Books* *Great Vacations with Your Kids,* by Dorothy Jordan and Marjorie Cohen ($13; Penguin USA, 120 Woodbine St., Bergenfield, NJ 07621, tel. 800/253–6476) and *Traveling with Children—And Enjoying It,* by Arlene K. Butler ($11.95 plus $3 shipping per book; Globe Pequot Press, Box 833, Old Saybrook, CT 06475, tel. 800/243–0495 or 800/962–0973 in CT) both help you plan your trip with children, from toddlers to teens. Also from Globe Pequot is *Recommended Family Resorts in the United States, Canada, and the Caribbean,* by Jane Wilford with Janet Tice ($12.95), which describes 100 resorts at length and includes a "Children's World" section describing activities and facilities as part of each entry.

**Tour Operators** **GrandTravel** (6900 Wisconsin Ave., Suite 706, Chevy Chase, MD 20815, tel. 301/986–0790 or 800/247–7651) offers international and domestic tours for grandparents traveling with their grandchildren. The catalogue, as charmingly written and illustrated as a children's book, positively invites armchair traveling with lap-sitters aboard. **Rascals in Paradise** (650 5th St., Suite 505, San Francisco, CA 94107, tel. 415/978–9800 or 800/872–7225) specializes in programs for families.

## Hints for Travelers with Disabilities

**Organizations** Several organizations provide travel information for people with disabilities, usually for a membership fee, and some publish newsletters and bulletins. Among them are the **Information Center for Individuals with Disabilities** (Fort Point Pl., 27–43 Wormwood St., Boston, MA 02210, tel. 617/727–5540 or 800/462–5015 in MA between 11 and 4, or leave message; TDD/TTY tel. 617/345–9743); **Mobility International USA** (Box 3551, Eugene, OR 97403, voice and TDD tel. 503/343–1284), the U.S. branch of an international organization based in Britain and present in 30 countries; **Moss Rehab Hospital Travel Information Service** (1200 W. Tabor Rd., Philadelphia, PA 19141, tel. 215/456–9603, TDD tel. 215/456–9602); the **Society for the Advancement of Travel for the Handicapped** (SATH, 347 5th Ave., Suite 610, New York, NY 10016, tel. 212/447–7284, fax 212/725–8253); the **Travel Industry and Disabled Exchange** (TIDE, 5435 Donna Ave., Tarzana, CA 91356, tel. 818/368–5648); and **Travelin' Talk** (Box 3534, Clarksville, TN 37043, tel. 615/552–6670).

**Travel Agencies and Tour Operators** **Directions Unlimited** (720 N. Bedford Rd., Bedford Hills, NY 10507, tel. 914/241–1700), a travel agency, has expertise in tours and cruises for the disabled. **Evergreen Travel Service** (4114 198th St. SW, Suite 13, Lynnwood, WA 98036, tel. 206/ 776–1184 or 800/435–2288) operates Wings on Wheels Tours for those in wheelchairs, White Cane Tours for the blind, and tours for the deaf, and makes group and independent arrangements for travelers with any disability. **Flying Wheels Travel** (143 W. Bridge St., Box 382, Owatonna, MN 55060, tel. 800/535–6790 or 800/722–9351 in MN), a tour operator and travel agency, arranges international tours, cruises, and independent travel itineraries for people with mobility disabilities. **Nautilus,** at the same address as TIDE (*see above*), packages tours for the disabled internationally.

**Publications**  In addition to the fact sheets, newsletters, and books mentioned above are several free publications available from the Consumer Information Center (Pueblo, CO 81009): "New Horizons for the Air Traveler with a Disability," a U.S. Department of Transportation booklet describing changes resulting from the 1986 Air Carrier Access Act and those still to come from the 1990 Americans with Disabilities Act (include Department 608Y in the address), and the Airport Operators Council's *Access Travel: Airports* (Dept. 5804), which describes facilities and services for the disabled at more than 500 airports worldwide.

Twin Peaks Press (Box 129, Vancouver, WA 98666, tel. 206/ 694–2462 or 800/637–2256) publishes the *Directory of Travel Agencies for the Disabled* ($19.95), listing more than 370 agencies worldwide; *Travel for the Disabled* ($19.95), listing some 500 access guides and accessible places worldwide; the *Directory of Accessible Van Rentals* ($9.95) for campers and RV travelers worldwide; and *Wheelchair Vagabond* ($14.95), a collection of personal travel tips. Add $2 per book for shipping.

## Hints for Older Travelers

**Organizations**  The **American Association of Retired Persons** (AARP, 601 E St. NW, Washington, DC 20049, tel. 202/434–2277) provides independent travelers the Purchase Privilege Program, which offers discounts on hotels, car rentals, and sightseeing, and the AARP Motoring Plan, provided by Amoco, which furnishes domestic trip-routing information and emergency road-service aid for an annual fee of $39.95 per person or couple ($59.95 for a premium version). AARP also arranges group tours, cruises, and apartment living through AARP Travel Experience from American Express (400 Pinnacle Way, Suite 450, Norcross, GA 30071, tel. 800/927–0111); these can be booked through travel agents, except for the cruises, which must be booked directly (tel. 800/745–4567). AARP membership is open to those 50 and over; annual dues are $8 per person or couple.

Two other membership organizations offer discounts on lodgings, car rentals, and other travel products, along with such nontravel perks as magazines and newsletters. The **National Council of Senior Citizens** (1331 F St. NW, Washington, DC 20004, tel. 202/347–8800) is a nonprofit advocacy group with some 5,000 local clubs across the United States; membership costs $12 per person or couple annually. **Mature Outlook** (6001 N. Clark St., Chicago, IL 60660, tel. 800/336–6330), a Sears Roebuck & Co. subsidiary with 800,000 members, charges $9.95 for an annual membership.

Note: When using any senior-citizen identification card for reduced hotel rates, mention it when booking, not when checking out. At restaurants, show your card before you're seated; discounts may be limited to certain menus, days, or hours. If you are renting a car, ask about promotional rates that might improve on your senior-citizen discount.

**Educational Travel**   **Elderhostel** (75 Federal St., 3rd floor, Boston, MA 02110, tel. 617/426–7788) is a nonprofit organization that has offered inexpensive study programs for people 60 and older since 1975. Programs take place at more than 1,800 educational institutions in the United States, Canada, and 45 countries overseas, and courses cover everything from marine science to Greek myths and cowboy poetry. Participants generally attend lectures in the morning and spend the afternoon sightseeing or on field trips; they live in dorms on the host campuses. Unique homestay programs are offered in a few countries. Fees for the two- to three-week international trips—including room, board, tuition, and transportation from the United States—range from $1,800 to $4,500.

**Tour Operators**   **Saga International Holidays** (222 Berkeley St., Boston, MA 02116, tel. 800/343–0273), which specializes in group travel for people over 60, offers a selection of variously priced tours and cruises covering five continents. If you want to take your grandchildren, look into **GrandTravel** (*see* Traveling with Children, *above*).

## Further Reading

The best nonfiction on Mexico blends history, culture, commentary, and travel description. The works below are categorized, but by no means mutually exclusive.

**History**   For decades, the standard texts written by scholars for popular audiences have been *A History of Mexico*, by Henry B. Parkes; *Many Mexicos*, by Lesley Byrd Simpson; and *A Compact History of Mexico*, an anthology published by the Colegio de México. Two journalists recently have made important contributions to the literature on historical and contemporary Mexico: Alan Riding's *Distant Neighbors: A Portrait of the Mexicans*, and Jonathan Kandell's *La Capital: The Biography of Mexico City*. Works focusing on the ancient Mexican Indian cultures include *The Maya* and *Mexico*, by Michael D. Coe; *The Last Lords of Palenque*, by Victor Perera and Robert D. Bruce; and *The Blood of Kings: Dynasty & Ritual in Maya Art*, by Linda Schele and Mary Ellen Miller, a handsome coffee-table book that summarizes ground-breaking work in our understanding of the ancient Maya.

**Culture/ Ethnography**   Excellent ethnographies include Oscar Lewis's classic works on the culture of poverty (*The Children of Sanchez* and *Five Families*); *Juan the Chamula*, by Ricardo Pozas, about a small village in Chiapas; *Mexico South*, by Miguel Covarrubias, which discusses Indian life in the early 20th century; Gertrude Blom's *Baring Witness*, on the Lacandones of Chiapas; and *Maria Sabina: Her Life and Chants*, an autobiography of a shaman in the state of Oaxaca.

**Food**   Two lushly photographed cookbooks capturing the culinary history and culture of Mexico are Patricia Quintana's *The Taste* *of Mexico* (Stewart, Tabori & Chang) and *Mexico the Beautiful Cookbook* (Harper-Collins, 1991).

**Travelogues**   Two of the more straightforward accounts from the early 19th century are the letters of Fanny Calderón de la Barca *(Life in Mexico)* and John Lloyd Stephens's *Incidents of Travel in Central America, Chiapas and Yucatán*. Foreign journalists have described life in Mexico during and after the revolution: John Reed *(Insurgent Mexico);* John Kenneth Turner *(Barbarous Mexico);* Aldous Huxley *(Beyond the Mexique Bay);* and Graham Greene *(The Lawless Roads*, a superbly written narrative about Tabasco and Chiapas, which served as the basis for *The Power and the Glory).* In much the same vein, but more contemporary, are works by Patrick Marnham *(So Far from God),* about Central America and Mexico, and Hugh Fleetwood, whose *A Dangerous Place* is informative despite its cantankerousness. Alice Adams' 1991 *Mexico: Some Travels and Some Travelers There*, which includes an introduction by Jan Morris is now available in paperback; James A. Michener's 1992 novel, *Mexico*, captures the history of the land and the personality of the people. Probably the finest travelogue-cum-guidebook is Kate Simon's *Mexico: Places and Pleasures.*

**Mexican Literature**   Poet/philosopher Octavio Paz is the reigning dean of Mexican intellectuals. His best works are *Labyrinth of Solitude*, a thoughtful, far-reaching dissection of Mexican culture, and the biography of Sor Juana Inés de la Cruz, a 17th-century nun and poet. Latin American literature is increasingly being translated into English. Among the top authors are Carlos Fuentes *(The Death of Artemio Cruz* and *The Old Gringo*), Juan Rulfo *(Pedro Páramo)*, Jorge Ibarguengoitia, and Elena Poniatowska. Recent biographies of the artist couple Frida Kahlo and Diego Rivera (by Hayden Herrera and Bertram D. Wolfe, respectively) provide glimpses into the Mexican intellectual and political life of the '20s and '30s.

**Foreign Literature**   D. H. Lawrence's *The Plumed Serpent* is probably the best-known foreign novel about Mexico, although its noble savage theme is considered slightly offensive today. Lawrence recorded his travels in Oaxaca in *Mornings in Mexico*. A far greater piece of literature is Malcolm Lowry's *Under the Volcano*. The mysterious recluse B. Traven, whose fame rests largely on his *Treasure of the Sierra Madre*, wrote brilliantly and passionately about Mexico in *Rebellion of the Hanged* and *The Bridge in the Jungle*. Also noteworthy is John Steinbeck's novel *The Sea of Cortez.*

# Arriving and Departing

## From the United States by Plane

The number of airlines serving Mexico from the United States is constantly changing as the two nations continue to revise their bilateral agreements. The bankruptcy and later revival of Aeroméxico in 1988 contributed to even more confusion. Since 1986, however, Mexico has been opening the way for more charter flights, an increasingly popular option for inexpensive air service. The country's two major carriers—Aeroméxico and Mexicana—are being supplemented by several smaller airlines serving domestic destinations and a new charter company,

Latur. Significantly lower airfares can frequently be had by flying into Tijuana from southern California and then catching a domestic flight to your final destination.

Flights are either nonstop, direct, or connecting. A **nonstop** flight requires no change of plane and makes no stops. A **direct** flight stops at least once and can involve a change of plane, although the flight number remains the same; if the first leg is late, the second waits. This is not the case with a **connecting** flight, which involves a different plane and a different flight number.

**Airports and Airlines**   Airports with frequent direct (although not always nonstop) service to the United States are Acapulco, Cancún, Cozumel, Guadalajara, Ixtapa, Mazatlán, Mérida, Mexico City, Puerto Vallarta, and San José in Los Cabos.

Airlines specifically serving Mexico from major U.S. cities include **Aero California** (tel.800/237-6225) from Los Angeles; **Aeroméxico** (tel. 800/237–6639) from Houston, Los Angeles, Miami, New York, San Diego, Phoenix and Tucson; **American** (tel. 800/433–7300) from Chicago, Dallas/Fort Worth, Miami, and Raleigh–Durham; **Continental** (tel. 800/525–0280) from Houston and Newark, NJ; **Delta** (tel. 800/241–4141) from Atlanta, Dallas/Fort Worth, Los Angeles, New York, and Orlando (no service to Cancún or Cozumel); **Lufthansa** (tel. 800/645–3880) from Dallas/Fort Worth; **Mexicana** (tel. 800/531–7921) from Chicago, Denver, Los Angeles, Miami, New York, San Antonio, San Francisco, and San Jose; **Northwest** (tel. 800/447–4747) from Tampa, Memphis and Minneapolis to Cancún, Cozumel and Ixtapa; and **United** (tel. 800/538–2929) from Dulles/Washington, Chicago, Orlando, and San Francisco.

**Flying Time**   Mexico City is 4½ hours from New York, 4¼ hours from Chicago, 3½ hours from Los Angeles. Cancún is 4 hours from New York, 3½ hours from Chicago, and 5 hours from Los Angeles. Acapulco is 6 hours from New York, 2 hours from Houston, and 3 hours from Los Angeles.

**Cutting Flight Costs**   The Sunday travel section of most newspapers is a good source of deals. When booking, particularly through an unfamiliar company, call the Better Business Bureau to find out whether any complaints have been registered against the company, pay with a credit card if you can, and consider trip-cancellation and default insurance.

Sometimes it pays to investigate packages that include airfare even if you don't plan to use their hotels, meals, transfers, and other components. Because a packager can book blocks of seats at very reduced costs, an air-hotel package can sometimes cost less than airfare alone.

*Promotional Airfares*   Most scheduled airlines offer three classes of service: first class, business class, and economy or coach. To ride in the first-class or business-class sections, you pay a first-class or business-class fare. To ride in the economy or coach section—the remainder of the plane—you pay a confusing variety of fares. Most expensive is full-fare economy or unrestricted coach, which can be bought one-way or round-trip and can be changed or turned in for a refund.

All the less expensive fares, called promotional or discount fares, are round-trip and involve restrictions. The exact nature of the restrictions depends on the airline, the route, and the season, and on whether travel is domestic or international, but you must usually buy the ticket—commonly called an APEX (advance purchase excursion) when it's for international travel—in advance (7, 14, or 21 days are usual). You must also respect certain minimum- and maximum-stay requirements (for instance, over a Saturday night or at least seven and no more than 30, 45, or 90 days), and you must be willing to pay penalties for changes. Airlines generally allow some changes for a fee. But the cheaper the fare, the more likely the ticket is nonrefundable; it would take a death in the family for the airline to give you any of your money back if you had to cancel. The cheapest fares are also subject to availability; because only a certain percentage of the plane's total seats will be sold at that price, they may go quickly.

*Consolidators* Consolidators or bulk-fare operators—also known as bucket shops—buy blocks of seats on scheduled flights that airlines anticipate they won't be able to sell. They pay wholesale prices, add a markup, and resell the seats to travel agents or directly to the public at prices that still undercut the airline's promotional or discount fares. You pay more than on a charter but ordinarily less than for an APEX ticket, and, even when there is not much of a price difference, the ticket usually comes without the advance-purchase restriction. Moreover, although tickets are marked nonrefundable so you can't turn them in to the airline for a full-fare refund, some consolidators sometimes give you your money back. Carefully read the fine print detailing penalties for changes and cancellations. If you doubt the reliability of a company, call the airline once you've made your booking and confirm that you do, indeed, have a reservation on the flight.

The biggest U.S. consolidator, C.L. Thomson Express, sells only to travel agents. Well-established consolidators selling to the public include **UniTravel** (Box 12485, St. Louis, MO 63132, tel. 314/569–0900 or 800/325–2222); **Council Charter** (205 E. 42nd St., New York, NY 10017, tel. 212/661–0311 or 800/800–8222), a division of the Council on International Educational Exchange and a longtime charter operator now functioning more as a consolidator; and **Travac** (989 6th Ave., New York, NY 10018, tel. 212/563–3303 or 800/872–8800), also a former charterer.

*Charter Flights* Charters usually have the lowest fares and the most restrictions. Departures are limited and seldom on time, and you can lose all or most of your money if you cancel. (Generally, the closer to departure you cancel, the more you lose, although sometimes you will be charged only a small fee if you supply a substitute passenger.) The charterer, on the other hand, may legally cancel the flight for any reason up to 10 days before departure; within 10 days of departure, the flight may be canceled only if it becomes physically impossible to operate it. The charterer may also revise the itinerary or increase the price after you have bought the ticket, but if the new arrangement constitutes a "major change," you have the right to a refund. Before buying a charter ticket, read the fine print for the company's refund policy and details on major changes. Money for charter flights is usually paid into a bank escrow account, the name of which should be on the contract. If you don't pay by credit card, make your check payable to the escrow account (unless you're dealing with a travel agent, in which case, his or her check should be payable to the escrow account). The Department of Transportation's Consumer Affairs Office (I–25, Washington, DC 20590, tel. 202/366–2220) can answer questions on charters and send you its "Plane Talk: Public Charter Flights" information sheet.

Charter operators may offer flights alone or with ground arrangements that constitute a charter package. Well-established charter operators include **Council Charter** (205 E. 42nd St., New York, NY 10017, tel. 212/661–0311 or 800/800–8222), now largely a consolidator, despite its name, and **Travel Charter** (1120 E. Long Lake Rd., Troy, MI 48098, tel. 313/528–3570 or 800/521–5267), with Midwestern departures. **DER Tours** (Box 1606, Des Plaines, IL 60017, tel. 800/782–2424), a charterer and consolidator, sells through travel agents.

**Enjoying the Flight**
Fly at night if you're able to sleep on a plane. Unless you are flying from Europe, jet lag won't be a problem. But still, because the air aloft is dry, drink plenty of beverages while on board. Sleepers usually prefer window seats to curl up against; restless passengers ask to be on the aisle. Bulkhead seats, in the front row of each cabin, have more legroom, but since there's no seat ahead, trays attach awkwardly to the arms of your seat, and you must stow all possessions overhead. Bulkhead seats are usually reserved for the disabled, the elderly, and people traveling with babies.

**Smoking**
Since February 1990, smoking has been banned on all U.S. domestic flights of less than six hours duration; the ban also applies to domestic segments of international flights aboard U.S. and foreign carriers. On U.S. carriers flying to Mexico and other destinations abroad, a seat in a no-smoking section must be provided for every passenger who requests one, and the section must be enlarged to accommodate such passengers if necessary as long as they have complied with the airline's deadline for check-in and seat assignment.

Smoking is permitted aboard all Mexican airlines, which, like all foreign airlines, are exempt from these rules. However, they do provide no-smoking sections, and some nations, including Canada as of July 1, 1993, have gone as far as to ban smoking on all domestic flights; other countries may ban smoking on flights of less than a specified duration.

If smoking bothers you, request a seat far from the smoking section.

## From the United States by Car

There are two absolutely essential things to remember about driving in Mexico. First and foremost is to carry Mexican auto insurance, which can be purchased near border crossings on either the U.S. or Mexican side. If you injure anyone in an accident, you could well be jailed—whether it was your fault or not—unless you have insurance. Guilty until proven innocent is part of the country's *Code Napoleon.*

The second item is that if you enter Mexico with a car, you must leave with it. The fact that you drove in with a car is stamped on your tourist card, which you must give to immigration authorities at departure. If an emergency arises and you must fly home, there are complicated customs procedures to face. The reason is that cars are much cheaper in the United States, and you are not allowed to sell your vehicle in Mexico.

**Insurance** Remember that the domestic insurance on your car is not valid in Mexico. Purchase enough Mexican automobile insurance at the border to cover your estimated trip. It's sold by the day, and if your trip is shorter than your original estimate, a pro-rated refund for the unused time will be issued to you upon application after you exit the country. *Sanborn's Mexican Insurance* (Headquarters, McAllen, TX, tel. 512/686–0711) and *Seguros Atlántico* (All-State reps) have offices in most border cities. Also, try *Instant Mexico Auto Insurance* (tel. 619/428–3583) or *Oscar Padilla Insurance* (619/428-2221), both in San Ysidro, California. All four are experienced and reliable.

## From the United States by Train, Bus, and Ship

**By Train** Rail service from the U.S. border at Nuevo Laredo (across from Texas's Laredo) to Mexico City has become a great deal more pleasant since the 1988 introduction of *El Regiomontano*, which covers the 1,210-kilometer (750-mile) trip in 18 hours. The train stops in Monterrey, Saltillo, and San Luis Potosí; private rooms with bath and one or two berths are available. For service to the U.S. side of the border, call **Amtrak** (tel. 800/872–7245). Information and schedules on Mexican trains are available from **Mexico By Train** (tel. 800/321–1699) in the United States or at local railroad stations in Mexico.

**By Bus** Getting to Mexico by bus is no longer for just the adventurous or budget-conscious. In the past, bus travelers were required to change to Mexican vehicles at the border, and vice versa. Now, however, in an effort to bring more American visitors and their tourist dollars to off-the-beaten-track markets and attractions, the Mexican government has removed this obstacle and a growing number of trans-border bus tours are available.

In addition, gateway cities such as El Paso, Del Rio, Laredo, McAllen, Brownsville, and San Antonio, Texas, and Tijuana are served by several small private bus lines as well as by **Greyhound Lines.** (Check your telephone book for the local number that will connect you with the national switchboard. The Laredo Station number is 210/723–4324.)

**Gray Line Tours** (tel. 512/943–2144 or 800/321–8720) runs four-hour- to seven-day-long bus tours, including shopping tours, across the border. Prices range from $15 for a five-hour excursion to $729 for a nine-day/eight-night Copper Canyon tour.

**Alamo Coaches of San Antonio** (tel. 512/923–8222 or 800/527–3453) offers a reasonably priced three-day trans-border excursion that departs for Monteray every Friday and includes two-night accommodations and a one-day tour.

**By Ship** Many cruise lines include Mexican ports on their ships' itineraries. Most originate from across the Gulf of Mexico, usually Ft. Lauderdale or Miami, and make stops in Key West, Cancún, and Cozumel. Others sail from Los Angeles or San Diego and follow the Pacific coastline. Still others include both coastlines, passing through the Panama Canal. Usually, the best deal on cruise bookings can be found by consulting a cruise-only travel agency. Contact the **National Association of Cruise Only Travel Agencies (NACOA)** (Box 7209, Freeport, NY 11520) for a listing of member firms in a particular state. Enclose a self-addressed stamped envelope.

Among the many cruise lines that ply Mexican waters are **Commodore/Crown Cruise Line** (tel. 800/237–5361), **Holland American Line** (tel. 800/426–0327), **Carnival Cruise Line** (tel. 800/432–5424), **Dolphin** (tel. 800/222–1003), **Epirotiki** (tel. 212/599–1750), **Norwegian Cruise Lines** (tel. 800/327–7030), **Ocean Quest** (tel. 800/338–3483), **Princess Cruises** (tel. 800/421–0522), **Regency** (tel. 800/457–5566), **Royal Caribbean Cruise Line** (tel. 800/327–6700), **Royal Viking Line** (tel. 800/422–8000), and **Society Expeditions** (tel. 800/426–7794).

*Specialty Cruises*   **Oceanic Society Expeditions** (Fort Mason Center, Bldg. E., Suite 230, San Francisco, CA 94123, tel. 415/441-1106 or 800/326-7419) sails for Baja in ships that accommodate 15–25 passengers for whale-watching, encounters with other sea life and snorkeling. Trip costs contribute toward conservation efforts.

**Classical Cruises** (132 E 70th St., New York, NY 10021, tel. 212/794–3200 or 800/252–7745 or 800/252–7746 in Canada, fax 212/517–0077) offers a diverse selection of upscale, special interest cruises on small luxury ships. Participants join sails designed for museums and special interest groups, including arts, culture, and natural history programs with renowned personalities and scholarly lecturers.

# Staying in Mexico

### Tourist Information

The Secretaria de Turismo (SECTUR) operates a 24-hour hot line in Mexico City with multilingual experts providing information on the capital and the entire country. You can also call collect from anywhere in Mexico by adding the prefix 91–5 to the following numbers: 250–0123, 250–0151, or 545–4306.

### Getting Around

**By Plane**   **Mexicana** and **Aeroméxico** provide the bulk of air service within Mexico, and regional airlines have filled in most of the gaps. **Aerocaribe** serves the Yucatán and the Southeast; **Aeromar** serves central Mexico; **Aerocozumel** flies between Cozumel and Cancún; and **Aerovías Oaxaqueñas** flies between Oaxaca and Puerto Escondido and Salina Cruz. Reservations for these carriers can be made in the United States via **Mexicana**. **Aero California** also flies within Mexico, serving Guadalajara, Loreto, Los Mochis, Hermosillo, and Tijuana. Call them directly. **International Airlines** offers connecting service between the large beach resorts and Mexico City. Remember to arrive one hour before your internal flight, as overbooking is common. Collect and recheck your baggage with each plane change to decrease the chances of loss. Be prepared to pay a departure tax on some Mexican domestic flights.

**By Train**   Since 1987 the **Ferrocarriles Nacionales de México** (Mexican National Railways, tel. 5/547–1084) has been putting luxury trains into service around the country, with upgraded dining and club cars, air-conditioning, first-class service, and several with sleeping cars. These services, however, are still available only on certain designated trains. *El Constitucionalista* runs between Mexico City and Querétaro, Irapuato, and San Miguel Allende. *El Jarocho* commutes overnight between the capital and Veracruz, and there are also overnight trains from Mexico City to Guadalajara *(El Tapatío)* and Oaxaca *(El Oaxaqueño)*. Two other trains go as far north as León, Aguascalientes, and Zacatecas. Service to Yucatán, Chiapas, and to Michoacán has not yet been refurbished. The *Expreso del Mar* runs between Nogales (across from Arizona) and Guaymas. There is also an antique narrow-gauge train that runs between Mexico City and Cuernavaca on weekends. Whichever train you take, be prepared for a relatively slow ride and bring a snack. The meals are less than appetizing.

One of the newest and most popular tourist trains coasts alongside the Copper Canyon from Chihuahua to Los Mochis on the Pacific Coast (tel. 14/16–1657). Other railways include the **Chihuahua-Pacific Railway** (tel. 5/54–5325), the **Pacific Railway** (tel. 5/547–2019), and the **Sonora-Baja California Railway** (tel. 5/657–2386).

*Primera especial* (special first-class) tickets on overnight trains entitle passengers to reserved, spacious seats that turn so traveling companions can face each other. *Primera regular* (regular first-class) service is also available on many trains. Second-class tickets are not available from U.S. agents, but first-class seats are not expensive and in terms of comfort, well worth the few extra pesos.

Sleeping accommodations consist of *camarines* (private rooms with bath and one lower berth), *alcobas* (same as *camarines*, but with an upper and a lower berth), and couchettes.

Train tickets must be purchased at least one day in advance, from Mexico City's Buenavista Station, local stations, or local Mexican travel agents, who will, of course, charge you extra. You can also reserve first class tickets and rail-hotel packages in advance (15 to 30 days is recommended) from the United States by calling **Mexico by Train** (tel. 800/321–1699). Another company, **Mexico by Rail,** also sells tickets and rail packages, but be careful: The surface transportation division of the Mexican Government Tourist Board in San Antonio (800/232–4639, fax 210/366–1532) has received numerous complaints regarding their prices and reliability.

**By Bus** Mexican buses run the gamut from comfortable air-conditioned coaches with bathrooms on board (deluxe and first-class) to dilapidated "vintage" buses (second- and third-class) on which pigs and chickens travel and stops are made in the middle of nowhere. While a lower-class bus ride can be interesting if you are not in a hurry and want to see the sights and experience the local culture, these fares are only about 10% less than first-class. Therefore, travelers planning a long-distance haul are well advised to buy the first-class ticket, which, unlike the other classes, can be reserved in advance.

The Mexican bus network is extensive, far more so than the railroads, as buses are the poor man's transportation. Buses go where trains do not, service is more frequent, tickets can be purchased on the spot (except during holidays and on long weekends, when advance purchase is crucial), and first-class buses can be almost as comfortable as trains. Bring something to eat on all overnight bus rides in case you don't like the restaurant where the bus stops, and bring toilet tissue, as rest rooms vary in cleanliness. Smoking is permitted on all Mexican buses.

In large cities, bus stations are a good distance from the center of town. Though there's a trend toward consolidation, some towns have different stations for each bus line. Bus service in Mexico City is well organized, operating out of four terminals. **Central de Autobuses** (Plaza del Angel, Londres 161, tel. 5/533–2047), a travel agency in the capital, will make reservations and send bus tickets to your hotel for a small fee. The best first-class lines include **ADO**, serving Yucatán, Palenque, Villahermosa, and Veracruz from the Eastern Bus Terminal (tel. 5/542–7192) and Matamoros, Pachuca, and Tampico from the Northern Bus Terminal (tel. 5/567–8455); **Cristóbal Colón**, which goes to Chiapas and the Guatemala border from the Eastern Bus Terminal (tel. 5/542–7263); and **Transportes del Norte,** which goes up to the U.S. border from the Northern Bus Terminal (tel. 5/587–5511).

**By Car** For day trips and local sightseeing, engaging a car and driver (who often acts as a guide) for a day can be a hassle-free, more economical way to travel than renting a car and driving yourself. Hotel desks will know which taxi companies to call, and you can negotiate a price with the driver.

*Road and Traffic Conditions* There are several well-kept toll roads in Mexico—primarily of the two-lane variety—covering mostly the last stretches of major highways *(carreteras)* leading to the capital. (*Cuota* means toll road; *libre* means no toll, and such roads are usually not as smooth.) Approaches to most of the other large cities are also in good condition, and the new Northern Border Program (*see* from the United States by Car, in Arriving and Departing, *above*) will be cleaning up some of the ubiquitous potholes. In rural areas, roads are quite poor: Caution is advised, especially during the rainy season, when rock slides are a problem. Driving in Mexico's central highlands may also necessitate adjustments to your carburetor. Generally, driving times are longer than for comparable distances in the United States. *Topes* (road cops, or bumps) are also common; it's best to slow down when approaching a village.

Driving at night is not recommended because of Mexicans' habit of driving without headlights, the difficulty of getting assistance in remote areas, and the risk of banditry. This can occur anywhere, though popular lore has it that such incidents occur primarily in the long, desolate stretches of Baja California and northern Mexico. Common sense goes a long way: If you have a long distance to cover, start early and fill up on gas. Allow extra time for unforeseen occurrences as well as for the trucks that seem to be everywhere. By day, be alert to animals, especially cattle and dogs. (The number of dead dogs lying beside—and in the middle of—Mexican highways is appalling.)

Traffic can be horrendous in the cities, particularly in Mexico City. As you would in metropolitan areas anywhere, avoid rush hour (7–9 AM and 5–7 PM) and lunchtime (1–3 PM). Signage is not always adequate in Mexico, so if you are not sure where you are going, travel with a companion and a good map. Always lock your car, and never leave valuable items in the body of the car (the trunk will suffice for daytime outings).

The Mexican Tourism Ministry publishes a good general road map, available free from its offices. PEMEX, the state-owned oil company, has an excellent, highly detailed road atlas *(Atlas de Carreteras);* Guía Roji puts out current city, regional, and national road maps. PEMEX and Guía Roji publications are available in bookstores; gas stations generally do not carry maps.

*Rules and Safety Regulations* Illegally parked cars are either towed or their license plates removed, which requires a trip to the traffic police headquarters for payment of a fine. When in doubt, park in a lot instead of on the street; your car will probably be safer there, anyway.

If an oncoming vehicle flicks its lights at you in daytime, slow down: it could mean trouble ahead. When approaching a narrow bridge, the first vehicle to flash its lights has right of way. One-way streets are common. One-way traffic is indicated by an arrow; two-way, by a two-pointed arrow. A circle with a diagonal line superimposed on the letter *E* (for *estacionamiento*) means "no parking." Other road signs follow the now-widespread system of international symbols, a copy of which will usually be provided when you rent a car in Mexico.

*Speed Limits* Mileage and speed limits are given in kilometers: 100 kph and 80 kph (62 and 50 mph, respectively) are the most common maximums. A few of the newer toll roads allow 110 kph (68.4 mph). In cities and small towns, observe the posted speed limits, which can be as low as 30 kph (18 mph).

*Fuel Availability and Costs* PEMEX franchises all the gas stations in Mexico. Stations are located at most road junctions, cities, and towns, but do not accept credit cards or dollars. Fuel prices are the same at all stations and about the same as in the United States. Unleaded gas is increasingly easy to find on major tourist routes, but it's still a good idea to fill up whenever you can.

At the gas stations, keep a close eye on the attendants, and if possible, avoid the rest rooms: They're generally filthy.

*National Road Emergency Services* To help motorists on major highways, the Mexican Tourism Ministry operates a fleet of almost 250 pickup trucks, known as the *Angeles Verdes*, or Green Angels. The bilingual drivers provide mechanical help, first aid, radio-telephone communication, basic supplies and small parts, towing, tourist information, and protection. Services are free, and spare parts, fuel, and lubricants are provided at cost. Tips are always appreciated.

The Green Angels patrol fixed sections of the major highways twice daily from 8 AM to 8 PM. If you break down, pull off the road as far as possible, lift the hood of your car, hail a passing vehicle, and ask the driver to notify the patrol. Most bus and truck drivers will be quite helpful. The Green Angels' 24-hour, nationwide hot line is 250–4817.

If you witness an accident, do not stop to help but instead locate the nearest official.

**By Taxi** Taxis in Mexican cities are the best alternative to public transportation, which, though inexpensive, is slow and sometimes patrolled by pickpockets. Always establish the fare beforehand, and always count your change. From the airport, take a government-subsidized cab; the driver will accept the taxi vouchers sold at stands outside the airport, which in theory ensure that your fare is established beforehand. However, in practice you may be overcharged, so prepare yourself by locating the taxi originating and destination zones on a map and make sure your ticket is properly zoned; if you only need a ticket from zone three to zone four, don't pay for a ticket from zone one. Even then, the rates for non-government-subsidized cabs routinely exceed the official taxi rate. In most of the beach resorts, there are inexpensive fixed-route fares, but if you don't ask, or your Spanish isn't great, you may get taken. In the cities, and especially the capital, meters do not always run, and if they do, their rates have usually been updated by a chart posted somewhere in the cab. For distances more than several kilometers, negotiate a rate in advance; many drivers will start by asking how much you want to pay to get a sense of how street-smart you are.

Taxis are available on the street, at taxi stands *(sitios)*, and by phone. Street taxis—usually Volkswagen Beetles—are subsidized cabs and are always the cheapest; large limousines standing in front of hotels will charge far more. Never leave luggage unattended in a taxi.

In addition to private taxis, many cities operate a bargain-price collective taxi service using VW minibuses, both downtown and at the airports. The vehicle itself is called a *combi;* the service, *colectivo* or *pesero.* Peseros run along fixed routes, and you hail them on the street and tell the driver where you are going. The fare—which you pay before you get out—is based on distance traveled. (For information on taxis in Mexico City, *see* Chapter 3.)

## Telephones

The country code for Mexico is 52.

The Mexican telephone system is antiquated. Lines are frequently tied up, the number of digits varies from city to city, obtaining information from the operator is not always possible, and public phones are often out of order. Pay phones in Mexico City have been free since the earthquake of 1985; elsewhere you must carry a good selection of coins.

Local and long-distance calls can also be made from telephone company offices, specially marked shops (usually with a telephone symbol hanging out front), and hotels, although the last place an excessive surcharge on top of the phone tax and value-added tax, which comes to about 58%. For international calls, call collect whenever possible; there is often a charge whether or not the call is completed. Direct dial to the United States is available from most luxury hotels, but if you must go through an operator, expect a long wait to be connected. International operators speak English. Dial 09 to place international calls; 02 for long-distance calls; 04 for local information; 01 for long-distance information.

## Mail

The Mexican postal system is notoriously slow and unreliable; *never* send, or expect to receive, packages, as they may be stolen (for emergencies, use a courier service or the new express-mail service, with insurance). There are post offices *(oficinas de correos)* even in the smallest villages, and numerous branches in the larger cities. Always use airmail for overseas correspondence; it will take anywhere from 10 days to two weeks or more, where surface mail might take three weeks to arrive. Service within Mexico can be equally slow. Postcard rates are NP$1 to the United States and NP$1. 2 to Great Britain. Letters cost NP$1. 5 to the United States and NP$1. 7 to Great Britain.

To receive mail in Mexico, you can have it sent to your hotel or use *poste restante* at the post office. In the latter case, include the words "a/c Lista de Correos" (general delivery) and the zip code. A list of names for whom mail has been received is posted and updated daily by the post office. American Express cardholders or traveler's check holders can have mail sent to them at the local American Express office. For a list of the offices worldwide, request a copy of *Traveler's Companion* from American Express (Box 678, Canal Street Station, New York, NY 10013).

## Addresses

The Mexican method of naming streets is exasperatingly arbitrary. Streets in the centers of many colonial cities (those built by the Spaniards) are laid out in a grid surrounding the zócalo and often change names on different sides of the square; other streets simply acquire a new name after a certain number of blocks. The naming system for numbered streets is identical to the American habit of designating numbered streets as either "north/south" or "east/west" on either side of a central avenue. Streets with proper names, however, can change mysteriously from Avenida Juárez, for example, to Calle Francisco Madero, without any way of knowing where one begins and the other ends. On the other hand, blocks are often labeled numerically, according to distance from a chosen starting point, as in "la Calle de Pachuca," "2a Calle de Pachuca," etc.

Many Mexican addresses have "s/n" for *sin número* (no number) after the street name. This is common in small towns where there are fewer buildings on a block. Similarly, many hotels give their address as "Km 30 a Querétaro," which indicates that the property is on the main highway 30 kilometers from Querétaro.

As in Europe, addresses in Mexico are written with the street name first, followed by the street number. The five-digit zip code *(código postal)* precedes, rather than follows, the name of the city. "Apdo." *(apartado)* means "post office box number."

Veteran travelers to Mexico invariably make one observation about asking directions in the country: Rather than say they do not know, Mexicans tend to offer guidance that may or may not be correct. This is not out of malice, but out of a desire to please. Therefore, patience is a virtue when tracking down an address.

## Tipping

When tipping in Mexico, remember that the minimum wage is the equivalent of $4 a day and that the vast majority of workers in the tourist industry live barely above the poverty line. However, there are Mexicans who think in dollars and know, for example, that in the United States porters are tipped about $1 a bag; many of them expect the peso equivalent from foreigners (NP$3 at press time) but are happy to accept NP$1 from Mexicans. They will complain either verbally or with a facial expression if they feel they deserve more—you and your conscience must decide. Overtipping, however, is equally a problem. Following are some general guidelines, in pesos.

**Porters and bellboys** at airports and at moderate and inexpensive hotels: NP$2 per bag
**Porters** at expensive hotels: NP$4 per bag
**Hotel room service:** NP$1 *(Expensive);* 50 centavos *(Moderate* and *Inexpensive)*
**Maids:** NP$2 per night (all hotels)
**Waiters:** 10%–20% of the bill, depending on service (make sure a 10%–15% service charge has not already been added to the bill, although this practice is not common in Mexico)
**Taxi drivers:** a 10% tip is appreciated by not necessary.
**Gas station attendants:** 50 centavos
**Parking attendants and theater ushers:** 50 centavos

## Opening and Closing Times

**Banks** are open weekdays 9 AM–1:30 PM. In some larger cities, a few banks also open weekdays 4–6 PM, Saturday 10 AM–1:30 PM and 4–6 PM, and Sundays 10 AM–1:30 PM. Banks will give you cash advances in pesos (for a fee) if you have a major credit card. **Stores** are generally open weekdays and Saturdays from 9 or 10 AM to 7 or 8 PM; in resort areas, they may also be open on Sundays. Business hours are 9 AM–7 PM, with a two-hour lunch break (siesta) from about 2 to 4 PM. **Government offices** are usually open 8 AM–3 PM. All government offices, banks, and most private offices are closed on national holidays. **Museums and most archaeological zones** close Mondays, with few exceptions.

## Shopping

Mexico is one of the best countries in the world to purchase *artesanía* (handicrafts), and many items are exempt from duty *(see* Customs and Duties, in Before You Go, *above).* The work is varied, original, colorful, and inexpensive, and it supports millions of families who are carrying on ancient traditions. Though cheap, shoddy merchandise masquerading as "native handicraft" is increasingly common, careful shoppers who take their time can come away with real works of art.

At least three varieties of outlets sell Mexican crafts: indoor and outdoor municipal markets; government-run shops (known as *Fonart*); and tourist boutiques in towns, shopping malls, and hotels. By shopping in the municipal shops or markets you can avoid the VAT, and you'll be able to pay in pesos or dollars. Boutiques usually accept credit cards if not dollars, and although they are overpriced, they are also convenient, and you can bargain. (You may be asked to pay up to 10% more on credit card purchases; savvy shoppers with cash have greater bargaining clout.) The 10% tax (I.V.A.) is charged on most purchases but is often disregarded by eager or desperate vendors.

It is not always true that the closer you are to the source of an article, the better the selection and price are likely to be. Mexico City, Oaxaca, and San Miguel de Allende have some of the best selections of crafts from around the country, and if you know where to go, you will find bargains. Prices are usually higher at beach resorts.

Bargaining is accepted in most touristy parts of Mexico and is most common in the markets. Start by offering no more than half the asking price and then come up very slowly, but do not pay more than 70%. Always shop around. In major shopping areas like San Miguel, shops will wrap and send purchases back to the United States via a package delivery company. In some areas you will be able to have items such as *huaraches* (leather sandals), clothing, and blankets tailor-made. If you are buying anything made of wood, freeze or microwave it to avoid termite infestation. Keep in mind that items made from tortoiseshell and black coral will not be allowed back into the United States.

Mexican craftspeople excel in ceramics, weaving and textiles, silver, gold, and semiprecious stone jewelry, leather, woodwork, and lacquerware; each region has its specialty.

**Ceramics** Blue talavera (Puebla); black (Oaxaca); masks and figurines (Michoacán); also in Jalisco, Taxco, Valle de Bravo, Tlaquepaque, and Chiapas.

**Jewelry** Silver (Taxco, San Miguel, and Oaxaca; be sure purchases are stamped "925," which means 92.5% pure silver); gold filigree (Oaxaca, Guanajuato); semiprecious stones (Puebla, Querétaro).

**Leather** Yucatán, Chiapas, Oaxaca, and Jalisco.

**Metalwork** Copper (Santa Clara del Cobre in Michoacán); tin (San Miguel de Allende).

**Weavings and Textiles** Shawls and blankets (Oaxaca, Jocotopec, near Guadalajara, and Pátzcuaro); *huipiles, guayaberas*, and embroidered clothing (Yucatán and Michoacán); henequen hammocks and baskets (Yucatán); reed mats (Oaxaca, Valle de Bravo); also in the Mezquital region east of Querétaro.

**Woodwork** Masks (Guerrero, Mexico City); *animalitos* (painted wooden animals, Oaxaca); furniture (Guadalajara, Michoacán, San Miguel de Allende, and Cuernavaca); lacquerware (Uruapan, Michoacán, and Olinalá, Guerrero); guitars (Paracho, Michoacán).

## Sports and Outdoor Activities

**Adventure Tours** Trek Mexico (Havre No. 67-305, Col. Juarez, C.P. 6600, Mexico, D.F., tel./fax 52-5-525-5093, 5213, 5113 or 6813) operates volcano climbing, river rafting, spelunking (rafting and exploring underground caves), diving, archaeology, and trekking adventures throughout Mexico. Bilingual guides available upon request.

**Hunting, Fishing, and Bird-watching** The best area for these activities is Baja California and the Sea of Cortés. Deep-sea fishing off the northern Pacific is also renowned. For information on hunting and the hunting calendar, contact the Dirección General de Area de Flora y Fauna Silvestres (Dirección General de Conservación Ecológica de los Recursos Naturales, Río Elba 20, Col. Cuauhtémoc, 06500 México, D.F., tel. 52–5–553–5545). Licenses can be obtained from Mexican consulates in Texas, California, New Mexico, and Arizona, or in Mexico from the Secretaría de Desarrollo Urbano y Ecología. For information on fishing and mandatory permits, contact the Secretaría de Pesca (Alvaro Obregón 269, 06700 México, D.F., tel. 52–5–211–0063).

**Tennis and Golf** Most major resorts have lit tennis courts, and there is an abundance of 18-hole golf courses, many designed by such noteworthies as Percy Clifford, Larry Hughes, and Robert Trent Jones. Contact the Federación Mexicana de Tenis (Durango 225–301, México, D.F., tel. 52–5–514–3759) and the Federación Mexicana de Golf (Cincinati 40, 02710 México, D.F., tel. 52–5–563–9194 or 52–5–563–9195) for information. At private golf and tennis clubs, you must be accompanied by a member to gain admission. Hotels that do not have their own facilities will often secure you access to ones in the vicinity.

**Mountain Climbing, Camping, Hiking** There are mountain climbing centers on the volcanoes outside of Mexico City—Ixtaccíhuatl and Popocatépetl—and on Mt. Orizaba in the state of Veracruz (at 5,750 meters or 18,851 feet, it is one of the highest in the world). Climbing experience is advised, and ropes and crampons are recommended. Avoid climbing during the rainy season. For information and guides, contact the Club de Exploraciones de México (Juan Mateos 146, México, D.F., tel. 52–5–578–5730).

Like mountain climbing, camping is not a particularly popular pastime among the Mexicans. Though many national parks provide free camping facilities, most camping takes place outside them. Camping is best on the Pacific Coast and in Baja, which is endowed with forests of pine, granite formations, and lagoons. An hour out of Mexico City, you can camp and hike at Cumbres de Ajusco, Desierto de los Leones, and La Marquesa. The Chiapas lakelands at Lagunas de Montebello are one of the least explored and most beautiful parts of the country.

**Horseback Riding** Horseback riding is a sport the Mexicans love. The dry ranchlands of northern Mexico have countless stables and dude ranches, particularly in San Miguel de Allende and Querétaro, in the Heartland. Horses can be rented by the hour at all the beaches, and horseback expeditions can be arranged to the Copper Canyon in Chihuahua and the forest near San Cristóbal, Chiapas. A new horse ranch, Taballo del Mar, just opened in Huatulco near Baya Conejos just a short taxi ride from the Huatulco Sheraton (tel. 52–9–581–0055, ext. 784). The Sheraton's travel agency will make arrangements at your request.

**Hot Springs** Mexico is renowned for its *balnearios* (mineral bath springs), which today are surrounded by a cluster of spa resorts and hacienda-type hotels. Most of the spas are concentrated in the center of the country, in the states of Aguascalientes, Guanajuato, México, Morelos, Puebla, and Querétaro.

## Spectator Sports

**Charreada** This Mexican rodeo is a colorful event involving elegant flourishes and maneuvers, handsome costumes, mariachi music, and much fanfare. There are charreadas most Sunday mornings at Mexico City's Rancho del Charro; inquire at the tourist office or a travel agency.

**Soccer** As in Europe, this is Mexico's national sport (known as *futból*). It is played almost year-round at the *Estadio Azteca* in Mexico City as well as in other large cities.

**Other Sports** Jai alai, horse racing, dog racing, cockfights, boxing, and bullfights are practiced all over Mexico. Again, ask at the tourist

1519 Hernán Cortés lands in Mexico, founds Veracruz, determines to conquer. Steel weapons, horses, and smallpox, coupled with a belief that Cortés was the resurrected Topiltzin-Quetzalcóatl, minimize Aztec resistance. Cortés enters Tenochtitlán and captures Moctezuma

## The Colonial Period

1520–1521 Moctezuma is killed; Tenochtitlán falls to Cortés. The last Aztec emperor, Cuauhtemoc, is executed

1528 Juan de Zumarraga arrives as bishop of Mexico City, gains title of "Protector of the Indians"; native conversion to Catholicism begun

1535 First Spanish viceroy arrives in Mexico

1537 Pope Paul III issues a bull declaring that native Mexicans are indeed human and not beasts. First printing press arrives in Mexico City

1546–48 Silver deposits discovered at Zacatecas

1547 Spanish conquest of Aztec Empire—now known as "New Spain"—completed, at enormous cost to native peoples

1553 Royal and Pontifical University of Mexico, first university in the New World, opens

1571 The Spanish Inquisition established in New Spain; it is only abolished in 1820

1609 Northern capital of New Spain established at Santa Fe (New Mexico)

1651 Birth of Sor (Sister) Juana Inés de la Cruz, greatest poet of colonial Mexico (d. 1695)

1718 Franciscan missionaries settle in Texas, which becomes part of New Spain

1765 Charles III of Spain sends José de Galvez to tour New Spain and propose reforms

1769 Franciscan Junipero Serra establishes missions in California, extending Spanish hegemony

1788 Death of Charles III; his reforms improve administration, but also raise social and political expectations among the colonial population, which are not fulfilled

1808 Napoleon invades Spain, leaving a power vacuum in New Spain

## The War of Independence

1810 September 16: Father Miguel Hidalgo y Costilla preaches his *Grito de Dolores*, sparking rebellion

1811 Hidalgo is captured and executed; leadership of the movement passes to Father José Maria Morelos

1813 Morelos calls a congress at Chilpancingo which drafts a Declaration of Independence

1815 Morelos is captured and executed

## The Early National Period

**1821** Vicente Guerrero, a rebel leader, and Agustín de Iturbide, a Spanish colonel converted to the rebel cause rejuvenate the Independence movement. Spain recognizes Mexican independence with the Treaty of Córdoba

**1822** Iturbide is named Emperor of Mexico, which stretches from California through Central America

**1823** After ten months in office, Emperor Agustin is turned out

**1824** A new constitution creates a federal republic, the Estados Unidos Mexicanos; modeled on the U.S. Constitution, the Mexican version retains the privileges of the Catholic Church and gives the president extraordinary "emergency" powers

**1829** President Vicente Guerrero abolishes slavery. A Spanish attempt at reconquest is halted by General Antonio López de Santa Anna, already a hero for his role in the overthrow of Emperor Agustin

**1833** Santa Anna is elected president by a huge majority; he holds the office for 11 of its 36 changes of hands by 1855

**1836** Although voted in as a liberal, Santa Anna abolishes the 1824 constitution. Already dismayed at the abolition of slavery, Texas—whose population is largely American—declares its independence. Santa Anna successfully besieges the Texans at the Alamo. But a month later he is captured by Sam Houston following the Battle of San Jacinto. Texas gains its independence as the Lone Star Republic

**1846** The U.S. decision to annex Texas leads to war

**1848** The treaty of Guadalupe Hidalgo reduces Mexico's territory by half, ceding Texas, New Mexico and California to the U.S.

**1853** Santa Anna agrees to the Gadsden purchase, ceding a further 30,000 square miles to the U.S.

## The Reform and French Intervention

**1855** The Revolution of Ayutla topples Santa Anna and leads to the period of The Reform

**1857** The liberal Constitution of 1857 disestablishes the Catholic Church among other measures

**1858–1861** The civil War of the Reform ends in liberal victory. Benito Juárez is elected president. France, Spain and Britain agree jointly to occupy the customs house at Veracruz to force payment of Mexico's huge foreign debt

**1862** Spain and Britain withdraw their forces; the French, seeking empire, march inland. On May 5, General Porfirio Díaz repulses the French at Puebla

**1863** Strengthened with reinforcements, the French occupy Mexico City. Napoleon III of France appoints Archduke Ferdinand Maximilian of Austria as Emperor of Mexico

**1864** Maximilian and his empress Charlotte, known as Carlota, land at Veracruz

1867 With U.S. assistance, Juárez overthrows Mexico's second empire. Maximilian is executed; Carlota, pleading his case in France, goes mad

1872 Juárez dies in office. The Mexico City-Veracruz railway is completed, symbol of the new progressivist mood

## The Porfiriato

1876 Porfirio Díaz comes to power in the Revolution of Tuxtepec; he holds office nearly continuously until 1911. With his advisors, the *científicos*, he forces modernization and balances the budget for the first time in Mexican history. But the social cost is high

1890 José Schneider, of German ancestry, founds the Cerveceria Cuauhtemoc, brewer of Carta Blanca

1900 Jesús, Enrique, and Ricardo Flores Magón publish the anti-Díaz newspaper *La Regeneración*. Suppressed, the brothers move their campaign to the U.S., first to San Antonio, then to St. Louis

1906 The Flores Magón group publish their Liberal Plan, a proposal for reform. Industrial unrest spreads

## The Second Revolution

1910 On the centennial of the Revolution, Díaz wins yet another rigged election. Revolt breaks out

1911 Rebels under Pascual Orozco and Francisco (Pancho) Villa capture Ciudad Juárez; Díaz resigns. Francisco Madero is elected president; calling for land reform, Emiliano Zapata rejects the new regime. Violence continues

1913 Military coup; Madero is deposed and murdered. In one day Mexico has three presidents, the last being General Victoriano Huerta. Civil war rages

1914 American intervention leads to dictator Huerta's overthrow. Villa and Zapata briefly join forces at the Convention of Aguascalientes, but the Revolution goes on

1916 Villa's border raids lead to an American punitive expedition under Pershing. Villa eludes capture

1917 Under a new constitution, Venuziano Carranza, head of the Constitutionalist Army, is elected president. Zapata continues his rebellion, which is brutally suppressed

1918 CROM, the national labor union, is founded

1919 On order of Carranza, Zapata is assassinated

1920 Carranza is assassinated; Alvaro Obregón is elected president, beginning a period of reform and reconstruction. Schools are built and land is redistributed. In the next two decades, revolutionary culture finds expression in the art of Diego Rivera and José Clemente Orozco, the novels of Martin Luis Guzmán and Gregorio Lopez y Fuentes, and the music of Carlos Chavez

1923 Pancho Villa is assassinated. The U.S. finally recognizes the Obregón regime

1926–1928 Catholics react to government anticlericalism in the Cristero Rebellion

**1934–1940** The presidency of Lázaro Cárdenas leads to the fullest implementation of revolutionary reforms

**1938** Cárdenas nationalizes the oil companies, removing them from foreign control

## Post-revolutionary Mexico

**1951** Mexico's segment of the Pan-American Highway is completed, confirming the industrial growth and prosperity of post-war Mexico. Culture is increasingly Americanized; writers such as Octavio Paz and Carlos Fuentes express disillusionment with the post-revolution world

**1968** The Summer Olympics in Mexico City showcase Mexican prosperity, but massive demonstrations indicate underlying social unrest

**1981–1982** Recession and a drop in oil prices severely damage Mexico's economy. The peso is devalued

**1985** Thousands die in the Mexico City earthquake

**1988** American-educated economist Carlos Salinas de Gortari is elected president; for the first time since 1940, support for the PRI, the national political party, seems to be slipping

# Talking Mexican

*By Kate Simon*

*Bronx native
Kate Simon is the
author of nine
travel books,
including* Mexico:
Places and
Pleasures, *which
remains a classic
after 28 years.*

*"Talking
Mexican" is
excerpted from
her book* Never
Say Ahoritita
Again.

**M**exicans still cherish an art once highly prized among us (think of Emerson, of Melville, of Hawthorne): conversation. They know it takes two to make a good talker—the confident speaker and the eager listener. A Mexican tête-à-tête—except among the dour mountain people, who prefer long, motionless silences—is a graceful act. The talker, carried away by his own mellifluous sounds, often repeats himself. His listener seems to find him fascinating. His eyes glow, he smiles, he melts, he frowns, he is delighted, he is appalled; he is completely immersed in the words and their passion and keeps them going with a gamut of encouragements: *"Claro, pues sí"* ("Of course, obviously"), *"Qué bueno"* ("How nice"), *"Qué lindo"* ("How lovely"), *"¡No me digas!"* ("Don't tell me!"), and, as a sorrowful cadence, *"Ai lástima"* ("What a pity").

Spanish isn't absolutely essential in large centers, although all sorts of doors and amiabilities will open for the traveler who conquers a few Spanish words of greeting and politesse. The Mexican is so delighted with the *"americano"* who tries even a little that he will, with a peculiar delicate empathy, help shape the words you need. A sympathetic Mexican can make you feel that you know Spanish; it's your tongue that is stupid.

Like other languages, but more so, Spanish is heavily embroidered with diminutives. Usually endearments, they also have other uses. They serve as intensifiers of meaning: *Chico* means "small"; *chiquito,* "very small"; and *chiquitito,* "almost invisible." A diminutive also suggests doubt, skepticism. *Hay sol* means that the sun is out, but if you are in an excursion boat under a cloudy sky and the boatman hopefully says there is *solecito,* beg to be taken ashore before the descent of a storm that maddens the lake. An important early lesson in Spanish is the use of *ahora,* meaning "now," which when spoken straight out usually denotes an intention of getting something done reasonably soon. The addition of one diminutive bit—*ahorita*—stretches the distance between promise and deed; *ahoritita* carries us into improbability; *ahorititita* becomes a piece of silliness.

The curious impersonal reflexive *se* conjures up a bewildering world of small satanic forces. One doesn't break a glass. *Se me rompió*—it broke itself, no fault of mine. If you bargain with a market woman, she will not say, "I can't," but *"No se puede"*—"one (little *se*) cannot." A lost object—even my own bag—lost itself, and it wasn't *I* who caused me to be late, but that mischievous bit of fate, *se.*

This deference to unpredictable external powers may bespeak a fatalism whose reverse side is bright casualness. A

Mexican will warmly, charmingly, and with—at the moment—complete sincerity declare his affection, admiration, and profound need to see you again, very soon. Unaccustomed to such quick warmth, you settle into this cozy nest of love, this having been accepted by Mexico. Time passes, nothing happens. You have been forgotten. You feel unlovely, unwelcome, the contemptible "big foot" who ate up vast Texas, responsible for all the world's messes and of course "Yankee imperialism." But it's only *se* that intervened and manipulated your friend's life in some unexpected way that was more attractive, more novel, than the prospect of another encounter with you.

A people who arrange a highly ornamented holiday for their dead and hold in awe the death dance of the bullfight are not inclined to respect precise dates, neat boxes of time. Anything is at any time likely to happen—a flat tire, a nearby fiesta, a change of mood—to be enjoyed *si Dios nos presta el tiempo* ("if God lends us the time"). Another imposing fact about the language is that the word for "to expect" (*esperar*) is identical with that for "to await" and "to hope." You might witness this miracle of linguistic transmutation at a rural train station as your assured expecting melts into vague awaiting and then vaporizes into humble hope—hope that some train that pertains to you will show up, sometime.

**O**ne of the pleasant quirks of the language is the big, baroque, generous phrase that can't mean what it says. Someone gives you his address and adds, *"Esta es su casa"* or *"Aquí tiene su casa"* ("Consider this your home"), or *"Mi casa es su casa"* ("My house is your house")—obviously ridiculous and yet frequently said as proof of boundless, aristocratic generosity (a Don Quixote touch?). Clearly, the only person in Mexican history who took such statements seriously was Cortés, the conquistador who took not only the house and treasures of Moctezuma but the whole of his host's empire. Admire an object and you may be told it is yours. Smile and without making a move say, "Thank you," to which the answer may be, "To serve you" (*"A su servicio"*). "At your command" (*"A sus órdenes"*) often acknowledges a formal introduction. These phrases are not servile or meant to buy favor, but express the courtliness of old Spain.

On the other hand, Spanish can be direct and even harsh. Observe the park signs, which say flatly, "This is yours, take care of it" (*"El parque es suyo, cuídelo"*).

In other areas the touch is delicate, even elegant. One doesn't hit a man with "He is disagreeable," but, instead, one dismisses him as "little amiable." *"Venga por favor tempranito"* takes the pressure off the necessity to be absolutely on time (*temprano*). No one wants to rush you, you must understand, but try to be nice and come on time, mollified and seduced by little *ito*, the most persuasive of Mexican persuasions.

In the wide world of *amor* anything goes; the limits are wide and brilliant, painting the conversational sky with dazzling rainbows. Shelley's "I die! I faint! I fail!" are pale mutterings compared with Mexican strophes of romantic love. A woman must have quite a bit of Spanish to appreciate the flowers of words thrown at her feet. But even a little helps. Not necessarily very young or lovely, she might still have the word *guapa* ("handsome woman") wafted toward her, or if she's fair-haired, like the *Yanquis* from north of the border, she could be called *güerita* ("blondie"). Her lack of response (and there shouldn't be any unless she's ready to face the consequences) might evoke something like "Can't you even say thanks, for God's sake?" ("*¿No puedes decir gracias, por Dios?*"), and this, too, might amuse her if she happens to understand what's going on.

A knowledge of Spanish enables one to discern nuances of class in certain areas of speech. The courtliness of "*hágame el favor*" ("please do me the kindness") moves downward into the middle class with "*por favor*," then becomes the cajoling peasant phrase "*por favorcito.*"

Perhaps most important, it lets one sample the wilder pleasures of Mexican radio, such as its ads for Pepsi-Cola. An old feeble female voice pleads, "Buy me a taco." Old feeble male voice: "Sure, they're delicious." Strong radio voice out of seemingly unrelated space: "Delicious? Pepsi-Cola is more delicious. Drink Pepsi!" This is followed by a female voice shrieking, "I can't stand it anymore. *You* pay the household bills; I can't seem to manage on the money you give me." This time the out-of-the-blue voice says gently, "Calm yourself. Have a Pepsi." Then a siren's voice, quite dulcet, with a tiny rasp of passion: "Darling, please buy me another diamond." Her lover's rich voice: "What? So that you can be even more delicious?" Voice from the blue: "More delicious? Pepsi-Cola is more delicious." Without Spanish and the radio, how could one be grateful for the sponsorship of "*Mox Foctorr de Hawlywoot, naturalmente*"?

# Fiesta

By Octavio Paz

Poet, essayist, and diplomat, Octavio Paz is one of Mexico's most prominent spokesmen. This essay is excerpted from his best-known work, The Labyrinth of Solitude, originally published in 1962.

The solitary Mexican loves fiestas and public gatherings. Any occasion for getting together will serve, any pretext to stop the flow of time and commemorate men and events with festivals and ceremonies. We are a ritual people, and this characteristic enriches both our imaginations and our sensibilities, which are equally sharp and alert. The art of the fiesta has been debased almost everywhere else, but not in Mexico. There are few places in the world where it is possible to take part in a spectacle like our great religious fiestas with their violent primary colors, their bizarre costumes and dances, their fireworks and ceremonies, and their inexhaustible welter of surprises: the fruit, candy, toys, and other objects sold on these days in the plazas and open-air markets.

Our calendar is crowded with fiestas. There are certain days when the whole country, from the most remote villages to the largest cities, prays, shouts, feasts, gets drunk and kills, in honor of the Virgin of Guadalupe or Benito Juárez. Each year on the fifteenth of September, at eleven o'clock at night, we celebrate the fiesta of the *Grito*[1] in all the plazas of the Republic, and the excited crowds actually shout for a whole hour . . . the better, perhaps, to remain silent for the rest of the year. During the days before and after the twelfth of December,[2] time comes to a full stop, and instead of pushing us toward a deceptive tomorrow that is always beyond our reach, offers us a complete and perfect today of dancing and revelry, of communion with the most ancient and secret Mexico. Time is no longer succession, and becomes what it originally was and is: the present, in which past and future are reconciled.

But the fiestas that the Church and State provide for the country as a whole are not enough. The life of every city and village is ruled by a patron saint whose blessing is celebrated with devout regularity. Neighborhoods and trades also have their annual fiestas, their ceremonies and fairs. And each one of us—atheist, Catholic, or merely indifferent—has his own saint's day, which he observes every year. It is impossible to calculate how many fiestas we have and how much time and money we spend on them. I remember asking the mayor of a village near Mitla, several years ago, "What is the income of the village government?" "About 3,000 pesos a year. We are very poor. But the Governor and the Federal Government always help us to meet our expenses." "And how are the 3,000 pesos spent?" "Mostly on

---

[1] *Padre Hidalgo's call-to-arms against Spain, 1810.—Tr.*
[2] *Fiesta of the Virgin of Guadalupe,—Tr.*

fiestas, señor. We are a small village, but we have two patron saints."

This reply is not surprising. Our poverty can be measured
by the frequency and luxuriousness of our holidays.
Wealthy countries have very few: There is neither the time
nor the desire for them, and they are not necessary. The
people have other things to do, and when they amuse themselves they do so in small groups. The modern masses are
agglomerations of solitary individuals. On great occasions
in Paris or New York, when the populace gathers in the
squares or stadiums, the absence of people, in the sense of a
people, is remarkable: There are couples and small groups,
but they never form a living community in which the individual is at once dissolved and redeemed. But how could a
poor Mexican live without the annual fiestas that make up
for his poverty and misery? Fiestas are our only luxury.
They replace, and are perhaps better than, the theater and
vacations, Anglo-Saxon weekends and cocktail parties, the
bourgeois reception, the Mediterranean café.

In all of these ceremonies—national or local, trade or
family—the Mexican opens out. They all give him a
chance to reveal himself and to converse with God, country, friends, or relations. During these days the silent Mexican whistles, shouts, sings, shoots off fireworks,
discharges his pistol into the air. He discharges his soul.
And his shout, like the rockets we love so much, ascends to
the heavens, explodes into green, red, blue, and white
lights, and falls dizzily to earth with a trail of golden
sparks. This is the night when friends who have not ex-
changed more than the prescribed courtesies for months
get drunk together, trade confidences, weep over the same
troubles, discover that they are brothers, and sometimes,
to prove it, kill each other. The night is full of songs and
loud cries. The lover wakes up his sweetheart with an orchestra. There are jokes and conversations from balcony to
balcony, sidewalk to sidewalk. Nobody talks quietly. Hats
fly in the air. Laughter and curses ring like silver pesos.
Guitars are brought out. Now and then, it is true, the hap-
piness ends badly, in quarrels, insults, pistol shots, stab-
bings. But these too are part of the fiesta, for the Mexican
does not seek amusement: He seeks to escape from himself,
to leap over the wall of solitude that confines him during the
rest of the year. All are possessed by violence and frenzy.
Their souls explode like the colors and voices and emotions.
Do they forget themselves and show their true faces? Nobody knows. The important thing is to go out, open a way,
get drunk on noise, people, colors. Mexico is celebrating a
fiesta. And this fiesta, shot through with lightning and delirium, is the brilliant reverse to our silence and apathy, our
reticence and gloom.

According to the interpretation of French sociologists, the
fiesta is an excess, an expense. By means of this squander-

ing the community protects itself against the envy of the gods or of men. Sacrifices and offerings placate or buy off the gods and the patron saints. Wasting money and expending energy affirms the community's wealth in both. This luxury is a proof of health, a show of abundance and power. Or a magic trap. For squandering is an effort to attract abundance by contagion. Money calls to money. When life is thrown away it increases; the orgy, which is sexual expenditure, is also a ceremony of regeneration; waste gives strength. New Year celebrations, in every culture, signify something beyond the mere observance of a date on the calendar. The day is a pause: Time is stopped, is actually annihilated. The rites that celebrate its death are intended to provoke its rebirth, because they mark not only the end of an old year but also the beginning of a new. Everything attracts its opposite. The fiesta's function, then, is more utilitarian than we think: Waste attracts or promotes wealth and is an investment like any other, except that the returns on it cannot be measured or counted. What is sought is potency, life, health. In this sense the fiesta, like the gift and the offering, is one of the most ancient of economic forms.

This interpretation has always seemed to me to be incomplete. The fiesta is by nature sacred, literally or figuratively, and above all it is the advent of the unusual. It is governed by its own special rules that set it apart from other days, and it has a logic, an ethic, and even an economy that are often in conflict with everyday norms. It all occurs in an enchanted world: Time is transformed to a mythical past or a total present; space, the scene of the fiesta, is turned into a gaily decorated world of its own; and the persons taking part cast off all human or social rank and become, for the moment, living images. And everything takes place as if it were not so, as if it were a dream. But whatever happens, our actions have a greater lightness, a different gravity. They take on other meanings and with them we contract new obligations. We throw down our burdens of time and reason.

In certain fiestas the very notion of order disappears. Chaos comes back and license rules. Anything is permitted: the customary hierarchies vanish, along with all social, sex, caste, and trade distinctions. Men disguise themselves as women, gentlemen as slaves, the poor as the rich. The army, the clergy, and the law are ridiculed. Obligatory sacrilege, ritual profanation is committed. Love becomes promiscuity. Sometimes the fiesta becomes a Black Mass. Regulations, habits, and customs are violated. Respectable people put away the dignified expressions and conservative clothes that isolate them, dress up in gaudy colors, hide behind a mask, and escape from themselves.

Therefore the fiesta is not only an excess, a ritual squandering of the goods painfully accumulated during the rest of the year; it is also a revolt, a sudden immersion in the formless, in pure being. By means of the fiesta, society frees itself from the norms it has established. It ridicules its gods, its principles, and its laws: It denies its own self.

The fiesta is a revolution in the most literal sense of the word. In the confusion that it generates, society is dissolved, is drowned, insofar as it is an organism ruled according to certain laws and principles. But it drowns in itself, in its own original chaos or liberty. Everything is united: good and evil, day and night, the sacred and the profane. Everything merges, loses shape and individuality and returns to the primordial mass. The fiesta is a cosmic experiment, an experiment in disorder, reuniting contradictory elements and principles in order to bring about a renascence of life. Ritual death promotes a rebirth; vomiting increases the appetite; the orgy, sterile in itself, renews the fertility of the mother or of the earth. The fiesta is a return to a remote and undifferentiated state, prenatal or presocial. It is a return that is also a beginning, in accordance with the dialectic that is inherent in social processes.

The group emerges purified and strengthened from this plunge into chaos. It has immersed itself in its own origins, in the womb from which it came. To express it in another way, the fiesta denies society as an organic system of differentiated forms and principles, but affirms it as a source of creative energy. It is a true "re-creation," the opposite of the "recreation" characterizing modern vacations, which do not entail any rites or ceremonies whatever and are as individualistic and sterile as the world that invented them.

Society communes with itself during the fiesta. Its members return to original chaos and freedom. Social structures break down and new relationships, unexpected rules, capricious hierarchies are created. In the general disorder everybody forgets himself and enters into otherwise forbidden situations and places. The bounds between audience and actors, officials and servants, are erased. Everybody takes part in the fiesta, everybody is caught up in its whirlwind. Whatever its mood, its character, its meaning, the fiesta is participation, and this trait distinguishes it from all other ceremonies and social phenomena. Lay or religious, orgy or saturnalia, the fiesta is a social act based on the full participation of all its celebrants.

Thanks to the fiesta, the Mexican opens out, participates, communes with his fellows and with the values that give meaning to his religious or political existence. And it is significant that a country as sorrowful as ours should have so many and such joyous fiestas. Their frequency, their brilliance and excitement, the enthusiasm with which we take part, all suggest that without them we would explode. They free us, if only momentarily, from the thwarted impulses, the inflammable desires that we carry within us. But the Mexican fiesta is not merely a return to an original state of formless and normless liberty: The Mexican is not seeking to return, but to escape from himself, to exceed himself. Our fiestas are explosions. Life and death, joy and sorrow, music and mere noise are united, not to re-create or recognize themselves, but to swallow each other up. There is nothing so joyous as a Mexican fiesta, but there is also nothing so sorrowful. Fiesta night is also a night of mourning.

If we hide within ourselves in our daily lives, we discharge ourselves in the whirlwind of the fiesta. It is more than an opening out: We rend ourselves open. Everything—music, love, friendship—ends in tumult and violence. The frenzy of our festivals shows the extent to which our solitude closes us off from communication with the world. We are familiar with delirium, with songs and shouts, with the monologue . . . but not with the dialogue. Our fiestas, like our confidences, our loves, our attempts to reorder our society, are violent breaks with the old or the established. Each time we try to express ourselves we have to break with ourselves. And the fiesta is only one example, perhaps the most typical, of this violent break. It is not difficult to name others, equally revealing: our games, which are always a going to extremes, often mortal; our profligate spending, the reverse of our timid investments and business enterprises; our confessions. The somber Mexican, closed up in himself, suddenly explodes, tears open his breast and reveals himself, though not without a certain complacency, and not without a stopping place in the shameful or terrible mazes of his intimacy. We are not frank, but our sincerity can reach extremes that horrify a European. The explosive, dramatic, sometimes even suicidal manner in which we strip ourselves, surrender ourselves, is evidence that something inhibits and suffocates us. Something impedes us from being. And since we cannot or dare not confront our own selves, we resort to the fiesta. It fires us into the void; it is a drunken rapture that burns itself out, a pistol shot in the air, a skyrocket.

# 3 Mexico City

*By Frank*
*"Pancho" Shiell*

Mexico City is a city of superlatives: It is both the oldest (669 years) and the highest (2,240 meters/7,349 feet) city on the North American continent, and with 22 million inhabitants, it is the most populous city in the world. It is Mexico's cultural, political, and financial core—on the verge of the 21st century but clinging to its deeply entrenched Aztec heritage.

Unfortunately, the single most widely known fact about the capital is that its air is polluted. Many foreigners envision the city as being wrapped in black smog every day; they picture gray skies and streets packed with vehicles. But in reality, although the capital does have a serious pollution problem, it also has some of the clearest, bluest skies anywhere. At 7,349 feet, it often has mild daytime weather perfect for sightseeing and cool evenings comfortable for sleeping. Mornings can be glorious—chilly, and bright with the promise of the warming sun.

In order to comprehend Mexico City, it is necessary to know what it was before the 16th-century arrival of the conquering Spaniards: the refined and flourishing capital of the Aztec civilization. Well over a thousand years after the mysterious demise of the great Toltec city of Teotihuacan—whose gargantuan pyramids just northeast of the city are a must-see—wandering Aztecs in search of their prophesied promised land would build their city upon encountering an eagle, perched on a prickly pear cactus, holding a snake in his beak. In 1325, the official date of the founding of Mexico City (upon which historians disagree), they found it on this very spot. Called Tenochtitlan, even then it was the biggest city in the Western Hemisphere and, according to historians, one of the three largest cities on earth. Tenochtitlan occupied what was then an island in shallow Lake Texcoco, connected to lakeshore satellite towns (now neighborhoods) by a network of *calzadas* (canals and causeways; now freeways). When he first laid eyes on the city, Spanish conquistador Hernán Cortés was dazzled by the glistening metropolis, which reminded him and his men of Venice.

A combination of factors made the conquest possible. The superstitious Aztec emperor Moctezuma II believed the white, bearded Cortés on horseback to be a descendant of the mighty plumed serpent-god Quetzalcoatl, who, according to a tragically ironic prophesy, was suppose to arrive from the east in the year 1519 to rule the land. Moctezuma therefore welcomed the foreigner with gifts of gold and palatial accommodations.

But in return, Cortés initiated the bloody massacre of Tenochtitlan, which lasted almost two years. Joining forces with him was a massive army of anti-Tenochtitlan Indians gathered from other settlements that were fed up with the Aztec Empire's domination and taxation. With the strength of their numbers and the European tactical advantages of brigantines built to cross the lake; imported horses, firearms, and armor; and, inadvertently, smallpox and the common cold, Cortés succeeded in devastating Tenochtitlan. Only two centuries after it was founded, the young Aztec capital lay in ruins, about half of its population dead from battle, starvation, and contagious European diseases to which they had no immunity.

The conquest brought into being a new culture that is more than the combination of its distinct ethnic parts. A philosophical 1964 plaque in the Plaza de las Tres Culturas (Square of the

Three Cultures) north of the downtown section defines it well. The plaque reads: "On the 13th day of August, 1521, defended by the heroic Cuauhtémoc (Moctezuma's successor), Tlatelolco fell under the power of Hernán Cortés. It was neither a triumph nor a defeat. It was the painful birth of the mixed race that is the Mexico of Today."

Cortés began building Mexico City, the capital of what he patriotically named New Spain, the Spanish Empire's colony that would spread north to cover what is now the United States southwest and south to Panama. At the site of the demolished Aztec ceremonial center—now the 10-acre Zócalo—he started building a church (the precursor of the gigantic Metropolitan Cathedral), mansions, and government buildings. He utilized the slave labor—and artistry—of the vanquished native Mexicans. On top of the ruins of their city, and using rubble from it, they were forced to build what became the most European-style city in North America, but unlike the random layout of contemporary medieval European cities, it followed the sophisticated grid pattern of the Aztecs. The Spaniards also drained and filled in Lake Texcoco. They preferred wheels and horses (which they introduced to Mexico) over canals and canoes for transport. Modern urban planners would have objected, because the filled-in lake bed was a soggy support for the immense buildings that have been slowly sinking into it ever since they were built. For much of the construction material they quarried local volcanic porous stone called *tezontle*, which is the color of dried blood and forms the thick walls of many historic downtown buildings.

Cortés had excusable difficulty pronouncing the word *Tenochtitlan*, so he named the city Mexico, after the Mexica (pronounced *meh-SHE-ka*) Indians, the predominant tribe of the Nahuatl-speaking Aztec civilization. (Scholars, long disputing how Tenochtitlan was actually pronounced, have finally agreed on *TEN-och-TEET-lan*, which means the word is no longer written with an accent mark on the last syllable).

During the colonial period, the city grew, and the Franciscans converted the Aztecs to Christianity. In 1571 the Spaniards established the Inquisition in New Spain and burned heretics at its headquarter palace, which still stands in Plaza de Santo Domingo.

More than 200 years later, Mexicans rose up against Spain. The historic downtown street 16 de Septiembre commemorates the "declaration" of the War of Independence. On that date in 1810, Father Miguel Hidalgo rang a church bell and cried out his history-making *grito* (shout) to his countrymen "to recover the lands stolen three centuries ago from our forefathers by the hated Spaniards . . . Viva Mexico!" That "liberty bell," which now hangs above the main entrance to the National Palace, is rung on the eve of every September 16 by the president of the republic.

Travelers flying into or out of Mexico City get an aerial view of the still-remaining portion of Lake Texcoco on the eastern outskirts of the city; at night the vast expanse of city lights abruptly ends at a black void that appears to be an ocean.

In-flight views also provide a panorama of the vast flat 1,482-square-kilometer (572 square-mile) Valley of Mexico, the *Meseta de Anahuac*, completely surrounded by mountains, in-

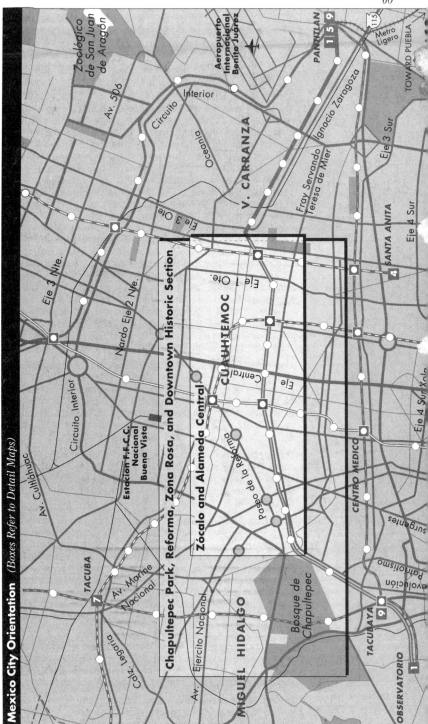

**Mexico City Orientation** *(Boxes Refer to Detail Maps)*

Chapultepec Park, Reforma, Zona Rosa, and Downtown Historic Section

Zócalo and Alameda Central

Zoológico de San Juan de Aragón

Aeropuerto Internacional Benito Juárez

PANTITLAN 1 5 9

Metro Ligero

TOWARD PUEBLA

115

Interior

Av. 506

Circuito Interior

Oceanía

V. CARRANZA

Ignacio Zaragoza

Fray Servando Teresa de Mier

Eje 3 Sur

Eje 4 Sur

SANTA ANITA

Eje 3 Ole

Eje 3 Nte.

Nardo Eje 2 Nte.

Eje 1 Ote.

CUAUHTEMOC

Eje Central

4

Eje 4 Sur Xola

CENTRO MEDICO

Circuito Interior

Av. Cuitláhuac

Estación F.F.C.C. Nacional Buena Vista

Paseo de la Reforma

surgentes

TACUBA 7

Av. Marina Nacional

Av. Ejercito Nacional

Calz. Laguna

MIGUEL HIDALGO

Bosque de Chapultepec

Patriotismo

Revolución

TACUBAYA 9

OBSERVATORIO 1

cluding, on its south side, two extinct and usually snowcapped volcanoes, both well over 17,000 feet high: Popocatepetl and Ixtaccihuatl. The volcanoes are separated by the 2½-mile-high Cortés Pass, from which the arriving conquistador, after a nine-month trek from Veracruz, gazed down for his first astonishing glimpse of Tenochtitlan.

The city lies on a fault similar to the San Andreas in California. In 1957 a major earthquake took a tragic toll, and scars are still visible from the devastating 1985 earthquake (8.1 on the Richter scale); the government reported 7,000 deaths, but according to vox populi the death toll reached 50,000.

Growing nonstop, Mexico City covers about a 1,000-square-kilometer (386 square-mile) area of the valley. The city limits are surrounded on three sides by the state of Mexico and bordered on the south by the state of Morelos. Advertising campaigns and tour packages usually tout Mexico's paradisaical beach resorts and ancient ruins, but cosmopolitan, historic Mexico City is an important destination in itself, more foreign and fascinating than many major capitals on far-away continents. And since so many flights from the United States pass through the capital, visitors should not pass up the opportunity to stop here at least for two days but preferably for five.

# Essential Information

### Arriving and Departing by Plane

**Airports and Airlines**  All roads (and flights) lead to Mexico City. **Mexicana** (tel. 800/531-7921 in the U.S.; 5/325-0990 in Mexico City) has scheduled service from Chicago, Denver, Los Angeles, Miami, New York, San Antonio, San Francisco, and San Jose. It has direct or connecting service at 30 locations throughout the country, and its subsidiary, **Aerocaribe,** serves the Yucatán area. **Aeroméxico** (tel. 800/237-6639 in the U.S.; 5/207-8233 in Mexico City) serves Mexico City daily from Houston, Los Angeles, Miami, New Orleans, New York, Tucson, Phoenix, and San Diego (as well as Tijuana). Aeroméxico offers special low joint fares with certain U.S. airlines for connections from throughout the United States to its Mexico gateway cities. The airline serves some 35 cities within Mexico and has three commuter subsidiaries that offer connections in Mexico City: **Aeromar,** based in Mexico City, flies to cities in central Mexico and on the Gulf [of Mexico] and Pacific coasts. **Aeroponiente** serves cities in the central and Pacific regions from its hub in Guadalajara; **Aerolitoral,** based in Monterrey, serves north-central and Gulf-Coast cities as well as San Antonio, Texas. **Taesa** (tel. 800/328-2372), a fast-growing Mexican airline, has direct flights (but not nonstop) to Mexico City from Chicago and Laredo, Texas. At press time additional U.S. gateways were being planned.

U.S. carriers serving Mexico City include **American, Continental, Delta,** and **United.**

Promotional fares in an almost endless variety are frequently available. Tour and charter packages offer substantial airfare and hotel discounts. If you purchase tickets in Mexico for domestic flights (other than to border cities) you will be charged 10% sales tax (IVA). Also, bear in mind that on some domestic flights, no-shows or those who cancel less than 45 minutes be-

fore their Mexican domestic flight may be charged up to 20% of the ticket price in penalties.

**Between the Airport and Center City**  Customs procedure is unique: At check-in or on the plane, you are handed a very simple declaration form to fill out. Present it with your baggage to the customs inspector, who will ask you to press a button on a post with two lights that looks just like a traffic signal. If the green light flashes, you pass right through; if it's red, your baggage is examined. With this random system, your chance of getting green is, *unofficially*, about 15 to 1 in your favor.

Porters and carts are available in the baggage-retrieval area. Just outside, in the concourse area, there are two banks; at least one is open around the clock. There is also a currency-exchange booth (*casa de cambio*), and Cirrus and Plus automatic teller machines that disburse pesos to Visa and MasterCard holders. (To speed up your arrival even more, bring $50–$75 in pesos with you.) The Mexico City Tourist Office and the Hotel Association both have stands in the arrival areas that can provide information and find visitors a room for the night.

Taxis are available at both the domestic (*nacional*) and international arrival areas. Purchase your ticket at the **Transportación Terrestre** (ground transportation) counters located in the baggage carousel area or just outside at the curb. (Avoid *pirata* taxi drivers offering their services.) Government-controlled fares are based on which *colonia* (neighborhood) you are going to and are usually less than $10 to most hotels. A 10% tip is customary for airport drivers, because they help with baggage. All major car-rental agencies have booths at both arrival areas, but renting a car is not recommended unless you are heading out of town or know Mexico City *very* well.

## Arriving and Departing by Car, Train, and Bus

**By Car**  Proof of vehicle ownership *must* be shown at the Mexican border. Either the title or a letter from a bank giving permission to take the car out of the United States is necessary. Moreover, only the person whose name appears on the Mexican import permit is allowed to drive the vehicle in Mexico. *Always* purchase Mexican car insurance at the border, since uninsured drivers involved in accidents can wind up in jail.

Highways range from toll, four-lane divided superhighways to two-lane highways, and you have the option of taking more scenic paved country roads (watch out for meandering livestock). The maximum speed limit on superhighways is 140 kph (86.9 mph). Obey lower posted speed limits on smaller roads and in populated areas. In remote regions where distance between towns is considerable, it is wise to fill up at every opportunity. Eighty-seven-octane unleaded gasoline, called *Magna Sin*, is now available throughout the republic. During daylight hours highways and major roads are patrolled by the *Angeles Verdes* (Green Angels), whose green trucks are well equipped to provide mechanical assistance to motorists in distress at no charge, courtesy of the Mexican government. It is not advisable to drive at night, especially in mountainous areas.

Throughout Mexico City, a new and *strictly enforced* law, *Un Día Sin Auto* (One Day Without a Car), applies to all private vehicles, including your own. One of several effective measures to reduce smog and traffic congestion, this law prohibits every privately owned vehicle (including out-of-state, foreign, and even rental cars) from being used on one designated weekday. Cars in violation are refused service by parking garages and gas stations, and are inevitably impounded by the police. Expect a hefty fine as well. The weekday is specified by the last number or letter of the license plate. To find out which is your day to be without a car, contact the Mexican Government Tourism Office nearest you, and by all means plan your schedule accordingly.

No matter where you cross the border, you will almost certainly approach Mexico City via Querétaro on Highway 57, a toll expressway that passes through miles of suburbs. Turn off at the Reforma-Centro (*centro* means "downtown") exit and you will be headed for the heart of the capital.

**By Train** Mexico's National Railways have improved dramatically, with modern streamliners such as the *Regiomontano*, which runs daily from Nuevo Laredo, at the Texas border, to Mexico City. It has private cabins with toilet and also "First-Class Special" cars with airplane-style seats. Waiters serve hot meals at the seats or in the dining car, and there is also an observation car with bar. The scenic trip takes 18¼ hours.

**By Bus** Reserved seating is available on first-class Mexican bus lines, which depart throughout the day from major border cities to Mexico City. You can purchase your tickets on the U.S. or Mexican side of the border. If you plan stopovers en route, make sure your ticket is to that stopover city; you can reserve a seat to continue on your journey when you arrive at that point. In Mexico, platform announcements are in Spanish only. From Matamoros, the trip to Mexico City takes about 14 hours; from Laredo, 15 hours; from Ciudad Juárez (El Paso), 24 hours; from Nogales, 40 hours; from Tijuana, 44 hours.

## Getting Around

**By Bus** The Mexico City bus system is used by hundreds of thousands of commuters daily because it's cheap—less than 15¢—and goes everywhere. Buses are packed during rush hours, so, as in all big cities, you should be wary of pickpockets. In Mexican Spanish, the word for bus and truck is the same: *camión*. One of the principal bus routes runs along Paseo de la Reforma, Avenida Juárez, and Calle Madero. This west–east route connects Chapultepec Park with the *Zócalo* (main plaza). Stops are clearly indicated by shelters, signs, and often lines of waiting passengers. A southbound bus also may be taken along Avenida Insurgentes Sur to San Angel and University City, or northbound along Avenida Insurgentes Norte to the Guadalupe Basilica. You can get virtually anywhere in the city by bus; call 5/525-9380 for route information (in Spanish).

Intercity bus tickets can be purchased at **Mexicorama** (tel. 5/525-2050) in the Plaza del Angel arcade in Zona Rosa. The staff speaks English. The arcade has two entrances, one on Londres and the other on Hamburgo, both between Florencia and Amberes.

Buses to other Mexican cities depart from four outlying stations: Central de Autobuses del Norte (going north), Río Cién Metros 4907; Central de Autobuses del Sur (going south),

Taxqueña 1320; Central de Autobuses del Oriente (going east), Zaragoza 200; and Central de Autobuses del Poniente (going west), Río Tacubaya and Sur 122. The metro connects with these terminals, but passengers cannot bring luggage on the metro.

**By Pesero** Originally six-passenger sedans, then vans, and now minibuses with stereo music, *peseros* operate on a number of fixed routes and charge a flat rate (a peso once upon a time, hence the name). Peseros offer a good alternative to buses and taxis. Likely routes for tourists are along the city's major west–east axis (Chapultepec Park/Reforma/Avenida Juárez/Zócalo) and north–south along Insurgentes, between the Guadalupe Basilica and San Angel/University City. Just stand on the curb, check the route sign on the oncoming pesero's windshield, hold out your hand, and it will pick you up. Tell the driver where to stop, or press the button by the door. At press time (January 1993), the fare ranged from less than 20¢ for up to 5 kilometers to about 35¢ for more than 17 kilometers.

**By Subway** Transporting 5 million passengers daily, Mexico City's metro is one of the world's best, busiest, safest, and cheapest transportation systems—the fare is the same as for buses, 40 centavos (less than 15¢). The impeccably clean marble and onyx stations are brightly lit, and modern French-designed trains run quietly on rubber tires. Lines 1, 2, and 3 operate from 5 AM to 12:30 AM on weekdays, 6 AM to 1:30 AM on Saturdays, and 7 AM to 12:30 AM on Sundays and holidays. Lines 4, 5, 6, 7, and 9 operate 6 AM–12:30 AM, 6 AM–1:30 AM, and 7 AM–12:30 AM, respectively. Trains are least crowded between 10 AM and 4 PM. By law, during rush hours, men use separate cars from women and children. There are eight continually expanding lines covering more than 160 kilometers (100 miles): numbers 1 through 7 and the new number 9. A new line that was under construction at press time will bear the number 8. Color-keyed signs are posted all around, and maps and assistance are provided at information desks. At the southern edge of the city, the Taxqueña station connects with the electric train (Metro Ligero) that continues south to Xochimilco. To the southeast, the new Metro Ligero from the Pantitlán station has a projected route all the way to Puebla. The metro is well attended and safe. Some stations, such as Insurgentes, are shopping centers. Even if you don't take a ride, visit the Zócalo station, which has large models of central Mexico City during three historic periods. The Bellas Artes station has replicas of archaeological treasures on exhibit, and inside the Pino Suárez station is a small Aztec pyramid, a surprise discovery during construction.

**By Taxi** The Mexico City variety comes in several colors and sizes. Unmarked *turismo* sedans with hooded meters are usually stationed outside major hotels, however they are uneconomical for short trips. The drivers are almost always English-speaking guides and can be hired for sightseeing on a daily or hourly basis (always negotiate the price in advance). *Sitio* (site) taxis operate out of stands, take radio calls, and are authorized to charge a small premium. Among these, **Servi-Taxis** (tel. 5/516–6020) and **Super-Taxis** (tel. 5/566–0077) offer 24-hour service. Taxis that cruise the streets range from sedans to Volkswagen Beetles—the latter with the front passenger seat removed for more legroom. They are available either when the *libre* (free) light is on or when the windshield sign is displayed. Taxi meters are gradually being converted to the Nuevo Peso system;

# Mexico City Subways

**6 7 El Rosario**

**Politécnico** **5**

Tezozomoc · Azcapotzalco · Ferrería · Vallejo

**Indios Verdes** **3**

Aquiles Serdán

Camarones

Norte 45 · **Instituto del Petróleo**

Lindavista

**Basílica**

Lo Villa

**Martín Carrera** **4 6**

Refinería

Autobuses del Norte

Potrero

Talismán

Panteones · **Tacuba**

**Cuatro Caminos** **2**

Cuitláhuac

Popotla

**La Raza**

Misterios

Bondojito

Colegio Militar

Valle Gómez

**Consulado**

Eduardo Molina

San Juan de Aragón

San Joaquín

Normal

Guerrero

Tlatelolco

Canal del Norte

Oceanía

Polanco

San Cosme

Revolución

**Hidalgo**

Bellas Artes

Morelos

Auditorio

Chapultepec

Sevilla

Insurgentes

Juárez

Allende

Zócalo

San Lázaro

Moctezuma

Terminal Aérea

Constituyentes

Juanacatlán

Cuauhtémoc

**Balderas**

Salto del Agua

I. la Católica

Niños Héroes

Hospital General

Mercad

**Pino Suárez**

San Antonio Abad

**Candelaria**

Fray Servando

Balbuena

Aeropuerto

Hangares

Gómez Farías

**Pantitlán** **1 5 9**

**Tacubaya** **9**

**1**

**Observatorio**

Patriotismo

Chilpancingo

**Centro Médico**

Lázaro Cárdenas

**Chabacano**

Zaragoza

Cd. Deportiva

Mixhuca

Velódromo

Puebla

Metro Ligero

**Jamaica** **4**

**Santa Anita**

TOWARD PUEBLA

San Pedro de los Piños

Etiopía

Viaducto

Xola

San Antonio

Eugenia

Villa de Cortés

Mixcoac

División del Norte

Nativitas

**7**

**Barranca del Muerto**

Zapata

Portales

Coyoacán

Ermita

Viveros

M.A. de Quevedo

General Anaya

Copilco

**2 Tasqueña**

Metro Ligero

**Universidad** **3**

TO XOCHIMILCO (under construction)

N

in taxis with meters that have not been reprogrammed charts are posted on the window with fare equivalents. Meter rates don't necessarily apply at night and on Sundays, so it's best to negotiate the fare before entering the taxi (never "cab"). Taking a taxi in Mexico City is extremely inexpensive and tips are not expected unless you have luggage, when 10% is sufficient.

**By Car** Millions of intrepid drivers brave Mexico City's streets every day and survive, but for out-of-towners the experience can be frazzling. One-way streets are confusing, rush-hour traffic is nightmarish, and parking places can be hard to come by. Police tow trucks haul away illegally parked vehicles, and retrieving them requires fluency in Spanish, detectivelike skills, and the patience of Job (call 5/658–1111 to begin your quest). Visitors can hire a chauffeur for their cars through a hotel concierge or travel service such as American Express. An automobile will come in handy if you plan to explore the nearby communities of Cuernavaca, Taxco, Pachuca, Puebla, and Tehuacán (*see* Excursions, *below*), but don't forget the Day Without a Car program (*see* Arriving and Departing by Car, *above*).

## Important Addresses and Numbers

**Tourist Information** The **Mexico City Tourist Office** (Departamento de Turismo del Distrito Federal) maintains information booths at both the international and domestic arrivals area at the airport, the Buenavista Train Station, Fonart (Av. Juárez 89), and on highways leading into the city. In town, information, brochures, and assistance are available in the lobby of its main office at Amberes 54 at the corner of Londres in the Zona Rosa. For tourist information and advice by phone, dial INFOTUR (tel. 5/525–9380, 5/525–9381, 5/525–9382, or 5/525–9383) from 9 AM to 9 PM daily. Operators are multilingual and have access to an extensive data bank. The **Secretariat of Tourism (SECTUR)** operates a 24-hour multilingual hot line that provides information on both Mexico City and the entire country (tel. 5/250–0123, 5/250–8419, or 5/250–8601). If the lines are busy, keep trying. You can also call collect from anywhere in Mexico by dialing the prefix 91 and any of the above numbers. SECTUR operates a Tourist Information Center at Presidente Masaryk 171 (in Polanco), open Monday–Friday, 8 AM–8 PM.

A new city-government entity, **Agencia del Ministerio Público para Turistas,** has been set up exclusively to assist tourists with legal advice. It has two offices: in the Zona Rosa (Florencia 20, corner of Hamburgo, tel. 5/625–8761) and in the Downtown Historic Center (Argentina corner of San Idelfonso, tel. 5/789–0833). A central phone number for both (tel. 5/625–8618) answers 24 hours a day, 365 days a year.

**Consulates and Embassies** The **U.S. Embassy** (Paseo de la Reforma 305, tel. 5/211–0042) is open weekdays 8:30–5:30 but is closed for American and Mexican holidays. The **Canadian Embassy** (Schiller 529, tel. 5/254–3288) is open weekdays 9–4 and is closed for Canadian and Mexican holidays. The **British Embassy** (Lerma 71, tel. 5/207–2449) is open weekdays 9:30–1 and 4–7 PM.

**Emergencies**
*Police* Dial 06 for police, Red Cross, ambulance, fire, or other emergency situations. If you are not able to reach an English-speaking operator, call the SECTUR hot line (*see* Tourist Information, *above*). For missing persons or cars, call LOCATEL at 5/658–1111.

*Hospital* **American British Cowdray Hospital** (Observatorio and Sur 136, tel. 5/515–8359 or 5/277–5000).

**English-language** **Sanborns**—a mini department-store chain with branches all
**Bookstores** over town, including two along Paseo de la Reforma, one on
Niza in the Zona Rosa, and one downtown on Calle Madero in
the House of Tiles—carries U.S. newspapers and magazines,
paperbacks, and guidebooks. The **American Book Store** at
Calle Madero 25 has an even more extensive selection. *The
News*, a daily English-language newspaper, available at hotels
and on newsstands in the tourist areas, provides a summary of
what is happening in Mexico and the rest of the world with cultural and entertainment listings, daily stock market reports,
and a Sunday travel supplement.

## Telephones

The city code for Mexico City is 5. Thanks to the privatization
of *Telefónos de México* in late 1991, the country's exasperatingly inefficient phone service is gradually being overhauled, but
it will take time to bring the system up to U.S. standards. So
far there is no touch-tone (digital) equipment in Mexico. If you
need touch tone to access U.S. automatic phones or answering
machines, purchase a touch-tone simulator (about $15) at a Ra-
dio Shack or other electronics store and take it with you.

Currently there are various types of public phones that can be
confusing at best. The regular black push-button or dial pay
phones have a coin slot but have been free for local calling ever
since the 1985 earthquake. After about three minutes, a recorded voice may announce *"tiempo transcurrido"* (time's up)
and abruptly disconnect you; just redial. From these and
other types of public phones (*see below*), you can also call long-
distance *por cobrar* (collect) by dialing the operator: 02 for calling within Mexico and 09 for international calls. International
operators speak English.

Information for all of Mexico is 04. For residential listings, as
with the telephone directory, you need to know *both* surnames
of the individual unless the person is a gringo with only one
name. Small businesses are often listed under the owner's
name. Be patient; sometimes it takes the operators awhile to
answer.

New blue- or ivory-colored push-button coin-slot phones with
digital screens often refuse to place calls. When you pick up the
receiver the screen announces *"solo para emergencia"* (only for
emergency calls), and when you try to insert coins, they drop
through to the return slot. This happens because the phone's
coin box is full. On phones that aren't full, the screen instructs
you to insert a minimum amount (at press time phones were
gradually being converted to accept Nuevo Peso coins), but the
phones will swallow large amounts, allowing you to call long-
distance direct. You can't, however, dial the operator. Don't be
disconcerted by the signs on the blue phones giving explicit instructions for inserting a credit card into a vertical slot indicated by an arrow; there is no slot.

The ivory phones have one or two (usually unlabeled) slots—
one at the bottom and, sometimes, one at the top. The top slots
are for Mexican bank cards, but some will accept U.S. Visa or
MasterCard. The bottom slots are for LADATEL *débito* cards,

plastic debit cards that can be purchased at tourist offices and certain newsstands and stores bearing the LADATEL logo. These cards can be purchased in amounts ranging from the equivalent of $2 to about $20. The peso value is printed on the card and designated by the card's magnetic strip. The card can be used repeatedly, for both local and long-distance calls. The digital screen on the phone indicates the descending balance of the card's worth; when the balance is zero, the card is discarded.

You can make long-distance direct-dial (the acronym in Mexico is LADA) calls from LADATEL phones, business or residential phones, and some deluxe hotels. Dial 91 + city area code + number for calls within Mexico; 95 + city area code + number for calls to the United States. LADA codes for Mexican cities and other countries are listed on some phones and in the telephone directory.

You can access AT&T's U.S.A. direct service from most of the new blue-and-ivory push-button public phones in Mexico City by dialing **01 or 95/800–462–4240 (no coins are necessary). This allows you to either charge the call to your AT&T credit card or call collect. For a charge payable by AT&T credit card, the AT&T operator can also connect you to U.S. 800 numbers.

Keep in mind that hotels add a hefty surcharge and tax on all long-distance calls placed through the hotel operator or the Mexico long-distance operator. Also, it is more expensive to call from Mexico to the United States than from the United States to Mexico.

The modernization of the phone system also includes new toll-free 800 phone numbers for calling *within Mexico* (although comparable, they are not linked with U.S. 800 numbers). This service is now being offered by some Mexican hotel chains for reservations and by the airlines Aeroméxico and Mexicana. Separately, some U.S.-based companies such as Radisson Hotels are introducing international 800 numbers for calling toll-free from Mexico to their reservation centers in the United States.

Rotary lines, in which incoming calls automatically bounce to the next available line, are not the norm, as they are in the United States. You may be given several phone numbers for the same place. If one is busy, try another.

With the increasing installation of new phone and fax lines in Mexico City, many phone numbers have been or are in the process of being changed. If you dial a changed number, a recording may intercept with the new number, so it is worthwhile to know the numbers 1 through 9 in Spanish.

## Guided Tours

Mexico City has no dearth of tour operators eager to show you around the capital. You can book tours through the travel desk at most hotels or contact the following reputable tour operators, which can arrange half- and full-day tours or one involving a special interest: **American Express** (Paseo de la Reforma 234, tel. 5/533–0380), **Mexico Travel Advisors (MTA)** (Génova 30, tel. 5/525–7520), and **Línea Gris** (Londres 166, tel. 5/533–1540).

**Orientation** The basic city tour ($15) lasts four hours and takes in the Zócalo, Palacio Nacional, Catedral Metropolitana, and Bosque de Chapultepec. A four-hour pyramid tour costs around $12 and covers the Basílica de Nuestra Señora de Guadalupe and the major ruins at Teotihuacán. The six-hour, light-and-sound version of the pyramid tour is run mid-October through May and costs $16.

**Special-interest** The seven-hour tour ($32) is run on Sunday mornings only and *Cultural* includes a performance of the folkloric dances at the Palacio de Bellas Artes, a gondola ride in the canals of Xochimilco's floating gardens, and a visit to the modern campus of the National University.

*Bullfights* Also on Sundays only are trips to the bullring with a guide who will explain the finer points of this spectacle. This four-hour afternoon tour ($15) can usually be combined with the Ballet Folklórico–Xochimilco trip.

*Nightlife* These are among the most popular tours of Mexico City. The best are scheduled to last five hours and include transfers by private car rather than bus, dinner at an elegant restaurant (frequently Del Lago), a drink and a show at the Plaza Garibaldi, where mariachis play, and a nightcap at Gitanerías, which features Spanish flamenco performances. Nightlife tours begin at $50.

**Walking** Huge as it is, Mexico City is not difficult to negotiate. Both the downtown Centro Histórico and the Zona Rosa are compact and easily walkable. In fact, the best way to see them is on foot.

# Exploring

## Orientation

Most of Mexico City is aligned around two major intersecting thoroughfares: Paseo de la Reforma and Avenida Insurgentes. Administratively, the city is divided into 16 *delegaciones* (districts) and about 400 colonias each with street names fitting a given theme, such as rivers, philosophers, doctors, or revolutionary heroes. The same street can change names as it goes through different colonias, making it a bit more difficult to find an address. Hence most street addresses include the colonia they are in, and, unless you're going to an obvious place, it is very important to tell your taxi driver the name of the colonia.

The principal sights of Mexico City are organized into three tours. You need a full day to cover each thoroughly, though each can be done at breakneck speed in four or five hours. Tour 1, Zócalo and Alameda Park, concentrates on a relatively compact area that can be seen on foot. Its focus is historical, since the Zócalo, its surrounding Centro Histórico, and Alameda Park were the heart of both the Aztec and the Spanish cities. The second tour, taking in Reforma, Zona Rosa, and Chapultepec Park, will necessitate some form of transportation if done in its entirety, but strong walkers can cover most of it on their own. Exploring San Angel and Coyoacán, two suburbs in southern Mexico City, will also require a taxi ride or two. Originally separate colonial towns, both were absorbed by the ever-growing capital, yet they retain their original pueblo charm and tranquillity.

## Highlights for First-time Visitors

Bellas Artes, Tour 1
Castillo de Chapultepec, Tour 2
Museo de Antropología, Tour 2
Museo Frida Kahlo, Tour 3
Palacio Nacional, Tour 1
Plaza Hidalgo, Tour 3
Plaza San Jacinto, Tour 3
Teotihuacan, Excursions
Zona Rosa, Tour 2

## Tour 1: Zócalo and Alameda Central

*Numbers in the margin correspond to points of interest on Zócalo and Alameda Central map.*

The **Zócalo** (formal name: **Plaza de la Constitución**), or main square, of Mexico City was built by the Spaniards on the site of the main temple complex of Tenochtitlan, the capital of the Aztec Empire. Throughout the 16th, 17th, and 18th centuries, the Spaniards and their descendants constructed elaborate churches and convents, elegant mansions, and stately public edifices, many of which have long since been converted to other uses. There is an air of Old Europe to this section of the city, which, in its entirety (the Centro Histórico), is a national monument that has recently undergone a major refurbishing. Imposing buildings are constructed with the ubiquitous blood-red volcanic *tezontle* stone and the quarry stones that the Spaniards recycled from the rubble of the Aztec temples they razed. Throngs of small shops, eateries, cantinas, and street vendors contribute to an inimitably Mexican flavor, even an exuberance.

The downtown area is also consistently filled with people. Travelers should be alert to pickpockets, especially on crowded buses and subways, and avoid dark, deserted streets at night.

The Zócalo is an enormous paved square, the largest in the Western Hemisphere; it and the surrounding structures rose on the Aztec ceremonial center, which once comprised 78 buildings. *Zócalo* means "pedestal" or "base": In the mid-19th century an Independence monument was envisioned for the square, but it was never built. The term stuck, however, and now the word *zócalo* is applied to the main plazas of most Mexican cities. Mexico City's Zócalo (since it's the original, it is always capitalized) is used for government rallies and festive events. It is also the focal point for Independence Day celebrations on the eve of September 16, and is spectacularly festooned during the Christmas–New Year holiday season. Flag-raising and -lowering ceremonies take place here in the early morning and late afternoon.

Around the square are the two most important symbols of
❶ church and state in Mexico. On the north side is the **Catedral Metropolitana** (Metropolitan Cathedral), which, over the centuries, has sunk noticeably into the spongy subsoil. Its lopsidedness is evident when viewed from across the square, but an engineering project to stabilize the structure has been in progress for the past eight years. (Scaffolding was still up at press time.) Construction on the oldest and largest cathedral in Latin America began in 1573 and continued intermittently through-

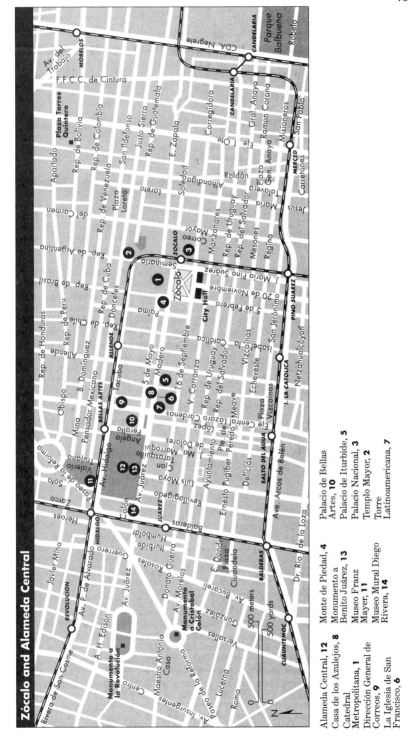

# Zócalo and Alameda Central

Alameda Central, **12**
Casa de los Azulejos, **8**
Catedral Metropolitana, **1**
Dirección General de Correos, **9**
La Iglesia de San Francisco, **6**

Monte de Piedad, **4**
Monumento a Benito Juárez, **13**
Museo Franz Mayer, **11**
Museo Mural Diego Rivera, **14**

Palacio de Bellas Artes, **10**
Palacio de Iturbide, **5**
Palacio Nacional, **3**
Templo Mayor, **2**
Torre Latinoamericana, **7**

out the next three centuries. The result is a medley of Baroque and neoclassical touches. Inside are four identical domes, their airiness made earthbound by rows of supportive columns. There are 5 altars and 14 chapels, mostly in the fussy, Churrigueresque style, an extremely decorative form of Spanish Baroque from the mid-17th century. Like most Mexican churches, the cathedral is all but overshadowed by the innumerable paintings, altarpieces, and statues—in graphic color—of Christ and the saints. *Open daily 8–6.*

Adjacent to the cathedral, the comparatively small 18th-century **Sagrario Church,** also tilted, has an elaborate Churrigueresque facade.

Turn left as you leave the cathedral and walk one block north on Seminario to view the excavated ruins of the **Templo Mayor** (Great Temple of the Aztecs). It was unearthed accidentally in 1978 by electric-company repairmen and has since been turned into a vast and historically significant archaeological site and museum. The temple depicts the myth of the goddess Coyolxauhqui (the moon), who was killed, decapitated, and dismembered by her brother, Huitzilopochtli (the sun), for trying to persuade her 400 other brothers to murder their mother. (Coyolxauhqui's only crime was to become pregnant by touching a feather to her breast.) Captives from rival tribes—as many as 10,000 a year—were sacrificed here to the bloodthirsty Aztec deities, as suggested by the seven rows of leering stone skulls that adorn one side of the structure.

The adjacent **Museo Templo Mayor** contains 3,000 pieces, including ceramic warriors, stone carvings and knives, skulls of sacrificial victims, a rare gold ingot, models and scale reproductions, a room on the destruction of Tenochtitlan by the Spaniards, and the centerpiece, an eight-ton stone disk of the goddess. *Corner of Guatemala and Argentina. Small admission fee. Open Tues.–Sun. 9–5. Call 5/542–1717 to reserve English-language tours.*

Returning to the Zócalo on Seminario, the first building on your left is the vast **Palacio Nacional,** or National Palace, which was initiated by Cortés on the site of Moctezuma's home and remodeled by the viceroys; its current form dates from 1693, although a third floor was added in 1926. Now the seat of government, it has always served as a public-function site. In fact, during colonial times, the first bullfight in New Spain took place in the inner courtyard.

Diego Rivera's sweeping, epic murals on the second floor of the main courtyard have the power to mesmerize. For more than 16 years (1929–45), he and his assistants mounted the scaffolds day and night, perfecting techniques adapted from Renaissance Italian frescoes. The result, nearly 1,200 square feet of vividly painted wall space, is grandiosely entitled *Epic of the Mexican People in Their Struggle for Freedom and Independence.* The larger-than-life paintings represent two millennia of Mexican history, as seen through the artist's vivid imagination. The innocence of pre-Hispanic times is portrayed by idyllic, almost sugary scenes of Tenochtitlan. Only a few vignettes—a lascivious woman baring her leg in the marketplace, a man offering a human arm for sale, and the carnage of warriors—acknowledge other aspects of ancient life. As you walk around the floor, you'll pass images depicting the savage-ry of the conquest and the hypocrisy of the Spanish priests, the noble Independence Movement, and the bloody revolution. Marx appears amid scenes of class struggles, toiling workers, industrialization (which Rivera idealized), the decadence of the bourgeoisie, and nuclear holocaust. The murals are among Rivera's finest works, equal in genius and craftsmanship to works by Da Vinci and Michelangelo. They are also the most accessible and probably the most visited of the artist's paintings. The palace also houses two minor museums—dealing with 19th-century president Benito Juárez and the Mexican Congress—and the liberty bell rung by Padre Hidalgo to proclaim independence in 1810 hangs high on the central facade. It chimes every eve of September 16, while from the balcony below, the president repeats the historic shout for independence known as *el grito. Admission free. Open daily 9–5. Closed holidays.*

As you leave the building turn left and then right onto the south side of the Zócalo, which is occupied by the twin buildings of **Ayuntamiento** (City Hall). The arcade of the western structure is decorated with colonial tiles of the coats of arms of Cortés and other conquistadores. Complete your tour of the square by ❹ heading north, through the arcade, on 5 de Febrero. The **Monte de Piedad** (Mountain of Piety) will be on your left, at the far northwest corner of the Zócalo. It was built in the late 18th century on the site of an Aztec palace to help the poor and currently houses the National Pawn Shop, which sells jewelry, antiques, and other pawned goods. *Open Mon.–Sat. about 10–7.*

**Time Out** At Cinco de Mayo 10 is one of Mexico City's most venerable and atmospheric cantinas, **Bar la Opera** (tel. 5/512–8959). The bar/restaurant has two claims to fame: Pancho Villa supposedly rode his horse into the place and demanded service by shooting a hole in the ceiling (you can still see it); and it was one of the first cantinas to allow women. Stop in for a drink or a snack.

There are two notable sites one block north of Cinco de Mayo on Calle Tacuba: the **Palacio de Minería,** a 19th-century architectural landmark; and the neo-classical **Museo Nacional de Arte** (National Art Museum), which contains a superb collection of pre-Hispanic, religious, and contemporary artwork. *The museum is at Calle Tacuba 8, tel. 5/521–7320. Small admission fee. Open Tues.–Sun. 10–5.*

From Calle Tacuba, walk two blocks south to Calle Madero, one of the city's busiest and most typical streets in terms of its architectural variety. On the south side of Calle Madero, between ❺ Bolívar and Gante, is the **Palacio de Iturbide** (Emperor Iturbide's Palace), which has been converted into a branch of Banamex (Banco Nacional de México). This handsome Baroque structure—note the imposing door and its carved-stone trimmings—was built in 1780 and became the residence of Iturbide in 1822. One of the heroes of the Independence Movement, the misguided Iturbide proclaimed himself emperor of a country that had thrown off the imperial yoke of the Hapsburgs only a year before; his empire, needless to say, was short-lived. Major cultural exhibitions are held in the atrium. *Calle Madero 17. Admission free. Inner atrium open weekdays 9–6, and on weekends during exhibitions.*

**❻ La Iglesia de San Francisco,** built on the site of Mexico's first convent (1524), is located a block west of the palace, on the same side of Calle Madero. Moctezuma's zoo was supposed to have stood on the site in Aztec times. The present 18th-century French Gothic church is one of the newest buildings on the street. The beautiful ceiling paintings are being restored. *Admission free. Open daily.*

**❼** In stark contrast to the church is the **Torre Latinoamericana** (Latin American Tower), once the tallest building in the capital. This 47-story skyscraper was built in 1956, and on clear days the observation deck and restaurant on the top floors afford fine views of the city. *Calle Madero and Eje Central Lázaro Cárdenas. Small admission fee. Observation deck open daily 10 AM–11:30 PM.*

Three other interesting buildings are off Eje Central Lázaro
**❽** Cárdenas, a main thoroughfare. The 17th-century **Casa de los Azulejos** (House of Tiles) is catercorner from the tower, on the north side of Calle Madero at the corner of Callejón de la Condesa. Its well-preserved facade of white, blue, and yellow tiles, iron grillwork balconies, and gray stonework make it among the prettiest Baroque structures in the country. Currently occupied by Sanborns, a chain store/restaurant, it was built as the palace of the Counts of the Valle de Orizaba, an aristocratic family from early Spanish rule. Inside are a Moorish patio, a monumental staircase, and a mural by Orozco. This is a good place to stop for lunch, and the shop (both upstairs and down) has an excellent selection of jewelry and crafts at fair prices. *Calle Madero 4. Open daily 8 AM–10 PM.*

**❾** Continue north on Callejón de la Condesa to the **Dirección General de Correos** (General Post Office) at the corner of Calle Tacuba and Eje Central Lázaro Cárdenas. This neo-Renaissance building (1908) epitomizes the grand imitations of European architecture common in Mexico during the Porfiriato, or dictatorship of Porfirio Díaz (1876–1911). On the upper floor, the **Museo de la Filatelia** exhibits the postal history of Mexico. *Open Mon.–Sat. 8 AM–midnight, Sun. 8–4. Museum open weekdays 9–7. Admission free.*

The most celebrated public building of the Díaz period is the
**❿** **Palacio de Bellas Artes** (Fine Arts Palace), which is diagonally across from the post office, at the corner of Lázaro Cárdenas and Avenida Juárez and across from Alameda Park. It was constructed as an opera house between 1904 and 1934, with time out for the revolution. In addition to being a handsome theatrical venue (the Ballet Folklórico de México performs here, as do other national and international artists), it is renowned both for its architecture—by the Italian architect Adamo Boari, who also designed the post office—and for its paintings by several celebrated Mexican artists, including Rufino Tamayo and Mexico's trio of muralists: Rivera, Orozco, and Siqueiros. In the palace Rivera reconstructed his mural *Man in Control of His Universe,* which was commissioned for and then torn down from Rockefeller Center in New York City, because of its political message (epitomized by the face of Lenin). The marble palace contains a Tiffany stained-glass curtain depicting the two volcanoes outside Mexico City and also houses temporary art exhibits. *Tel. 5/510–1388. Open Tues.–Sun. 10:30–6:30.*

Aficionados of colonial Spanish decorative and applied arts ⑪ should detour at this point to visit the **Museo Franz Mayer,** located one block west of the rear of the Palacio de Bellas Artes, facing the north side of Alameda Park. The museum opened in 1986 in the 16th-century Hospital de San Juan de Dios. Exhibits include wooden chests inlaid with ivory, tortoiseshell, and ebony; tapestries, paintings, and lacquerware; Rococo clocks, glassware, architectural ornamentation; and an unusually large assortment of Talavera ceramics and tiles. Wall plaques explain in detail the history of tiles (*azulejos*), a technique carried from Mesopotamia and Egypt to the Persians, Arabs, and Spaniards, who brought it to Mexico. The museum building is faithfully restored, with pieces of the original frescoes peeking through; classical music plays in the background. *Av. Hidalgo 45, at the Plaza Santa Veracruz, tel. 5/518–2265. Small admission fee except on weekends. Open Tues.–Sun. 10–5. Call ahead for an English-speaking guide.*

⑫ **Alameda Central** (Alameda Park), across Avenida Hidalgo from the Plaza Santa Veracruz, has been one of the capital's oases of greenery and a gracious center for festivities since Aztec times. The Indians held their *tianguis* (market) on the site. In the early days of the Viceroyalty, it was where victims of the Inquisition were burned at the stake. National leaders, from 18th-century viceroys to Emperor Maximilian and President Díaz, clearly envisioned the park as a symbol of civic pride and prosperity: Over the centuries, it has been endowed with fountains, railings, a Moorish kiosk imported from Paris, and ash, willow, and poplar trees. Its most conspicuous man-made ⑬ structure is the white marble semicircular **Monumento a Benito Juárez** (monument to Juárez) on the Avenida Juárez side of the park. It is a fine place for strolling (and resting) and listening to live music on Sundays and holidays.

**Fonart,** the government-owned handicrafts chain, has a store at Avenida Juárez 89, just west of the park (*see* Shopping, be- ⑭ low). At the far western side of the Alameda is **Museo Mural Diego Rivera,** built to display Diego Rivera's controversial mural *Sunday Afternoon Dream in the Alameda Park.* The mural was painted on a wall of the Hotel Del Prado in 1947–48. The controversy was due to Rivera's inscription, "God does not exist," which he later replaced with the bland "Conference of San Juan de Letrán." The mural—one of Rivera's most gentle and poetic—was relocated following the hotel's destruction in the 1985 earthquake. Luckily, the entire wall with the mural was undamaged. It was moved (an engineering feat) in its entirety across the street to the museum built to house it. *Museo Mural Diego Rivera, at Calles Balderas and Colón. Admission free. Open Tues.–Sun. 10–6.*

## Tour 2: Reforma, Reforma, Zona Rosa, and Chapultepec Park

*Numbers in the margin correspond to points of interest on the Chapultepec Park, Reforma, Zona Rosa, and Downtown Historic Section map.*

The Paseo de la Reforma was built by Emperor Maximilian in 1865 to connect the Palacio Nacional with his residence, the Castillo de Chapultepec. It was modeled after the Champs-Elysées in Paris. Reforma is 30 blocks long, so public transportation is recommended if you want to cover all the sights described. Begin at Reforma's northern end, about 2 kilometers (1.2 miles) north of Bellas Artes, in the area known as **Tlatelolco** (Tla-tel-OHL-coh). Before the conquest, Tlatelolco and Tenochtitlan were sister cities, and the domain of Cuauhtémoc, the last Aztec emperor. In modern times its name makes residents shudder, because it was here that several hundred protesting students were massacred by the National Guard in 1968. The 1985 earthquake destroyed an entire housing complex in Tlatelolco, in which hundreds perished.

❶ The center of Tlatelolco is the **Plaza de las Tres Culturas,** so named because Mexico's three cultural eras—pre-Hispanic, colonial, and modern—are represented on the plaza in the form of the small ruins of a pre-Hispanic **ceremonial center** (visible from the roadway); the **Iglesia de Santiago Tlatelolco** (1609) and **Colegio de la Santa Cruz de Tlatelolco** (1535–36); and the ultra-contemporary **Ministry of Foreign Affairs.** The church contains the baptismal font of Juan Diego, the Indian to whom the Virgin of Guadalupe appeared in 1531. The Colegio (college) concentrates on studies of Indian language and culture. *The plaza is bounded on the north by Manuel González, on the west by Av. San Juan de Letrán Norte, and on the east by Paseo de la Reforma, between Glorieta de Peralvillo and Glorieta Cuitláhuac.*

The plaza itself can be seen in passing, but nearby are several other points of interest: the Mercado de Tepito, the Mercado de la Lagunilla, and Plaza Garibaldi. Tepito is a typical market selling tools and used clothing, but it is situated in the midst of some of the worst tenements in the city, at the corner of Aztecas and Héroes de Granaditas. It is not a place for tourists. Six blocks east of Tepito, between República de Chile and
❷ Allende, is the **Mercado de la Lagunilla,** known affectionately as the Thieves' Market. Go on Sundays, when it is busiest, and watch your money: Here, along with the usual flea-market fare, you can find antiques (some of them fake), toys, second-hand books and clothes, semiprecious stones, art, and some handicrafts.

❸ Nearby is **Plaza Garibaldi,** Mexico City's mariachi square (*see* Nightlife, *below*). Pass through here during the day, but return at night, when it resounds with music and festivity until the wee hours, especially on weekends. One warning: Late at night things can get a bit raucous. Choose a cantina, order a tequila; the musicians will be around shortly to serenade you (tipping is essential). On the north side of the square is the Mercado de San Camilito, where typical Mexican food is served. The plaza and its surrounding area have recently been refurbished. *Just east of Av. Lázaro Cárdenas, between República de Honduras and República de Perú.*

From Plaza Garibaldi, return to Paseo de la Reforma and walk west (left). In about 10 minutes you'll reach the junction of Reforma, Avenida Juárez, and Bucareli. Along the stretch of Reforma west of this intersection there are a number of statues erected at the request of Porfirio Díaz to honor illustrious men, including Simón Bolívar, Columbus, Pasteur, and Cuauhtémoc. The most famous of these statues is used by locals
❹ as a geographic point of reference: it is the **Monumento a la Independencia,** a Corinthian column topped by a gold angel (thus the more common "the Angel"). Beneath the pedestal lie

# Chapultepec Park, Reforma, Zona Rosa, and Downtown Historic Section

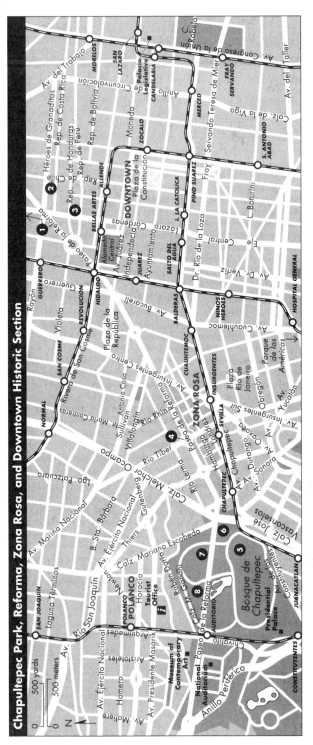

Castillo de
Chapultepec, **5**
Mercado de la
Lagunilla, **2**
Monumento a la
Independencia, **4**
Museo de Arte
Moderno, **6**

Museo Nacional de
Antropología, **8**
Museo Rufino
Tamayo, **7**
Plaza de las Tres
Culturas, **1**
Plaza Garibaldi, **3**

the remains of the principal heroes of the Independence Movement, and an eternal flame burns in their honor.

The Angel marks the midpoint of the western edge of the **Zona Rosa** (Pink Zone), which for years has been the one part of the city in which tourists feel most comfortable because of the plethora of restaurants, cafés, art galleries, hotels, discos, and shops. It is also an affluent residential neighborhood, populated by foreign diplomats and businesspeople (the American Embassy is just across Reforma).

The architecture in the Zona Rosa is appealing. Most buildings, two or three stories high, were originally private homes built in the 1920s for the wealthy. All the streets are wistfully named after European cities; some, such as Genova, are garden-lined pedestrian malls. The appellation Zona Rosa was supposedly applied to lend credence to the neighborhood's aristocratic pretensions.

To enjoy the Zona Rosa, just walk the lengths of Hamburgo and Londres and follow some of the side streets, especially Copenhague—a veritable restaurant row. The large handicrafts market on Londres is officially **Mercado Insurgentes,** though most people call it either **Mercado Zona Rosa** or **Mercado Londres** (*see* Shopping, *below*). Just opposite the market's Londres entrance is **Plaza del Angel,** a small shopping mall where a *minitianguis* (native market) specializes in antiques and curios on Saturdays and Sundays.

**Time Out**    Stop for tea and pastries at one of two tea shops on Hamburgo: **Duca d'Este** on the southeast corner of Florencia (164–B Hamburgo, tel. 5/525–6374) or **Salón de Té Auseba** (159–B Hamburgo, tel. 5/511–3769).

The third area of Reforma covers most of the first of three sections of **Bosque de Chapultepec** (Chapultepec Park). The main entrance to the park lies four blocks southwest of the Zona Rosa. The 1,600-acre park functions as a "green space" for families on weekend outings, cyclists, joggers, and museum goers. It is also one of the oldest parts of Mexico City, having been inhabited by the Mexica (Aztec) tribe as early as the 13th century. The Mexica poet-king Nezahualcoyotl had his palace here and ordered construction of the aqueduct that brought water to Tenochtitlan. Ahuehuete trees (Moctezuma cypress) still stand from that era, when the woods were used as hunting preserves.

The entrance to the park is guarded by the **Monumento a los Niños Héroes** (Monument to the Boy Heroes), consisting of six marble columns adorned with eaglets. In it are buried the six young cadets who wrapped themselves in the Mexican flag and then jumped to their deaths from the ramparts during the U.S. invasion of 1847. (That war may not take up much space in American textbooks, but to the Mexicans it is still a troubling symbol of their neighbor's aggressive dominance: The war cost Mexico almost half of its national territory—the present states of Texas, California, Arizona, New Mexico, and Nevada.)

❺ The **Castillo de Chapultepec,** like the Palacio Nacional, witnessed the turbulence and grandeur of all Mexican history. In its earliest permutations, its home on the Cerro del Chapulín (Grasshopper Hill) was a Mexica palace, where the Indians made one of their last stands against the Spaniards; later it was a Spanish hermitage, gunpowder plant, and military college. Emperor Maximilian used the castle (parts of which date from 1783) as his residence, and his example was followed by various presidents from 1872 to 1940, when Lázaro Cárdenas decreed that it be turned into the **National History Museum.**

Displays on the museum's ground floor cover Mexican history from the conquest to the revolution; the bathroom, bedroom, tea salon, and gardens were used by Maximilian and his wife, Carlotta, during the 19th century. The ground floor also contains works by 20th-century muralists O'Gorman, Orozco, and Siqueiros, whereas the upper floor is devoted to temporary exhibits, Díaz's malachite vases, and religious art. Because it is situated on top of a hill, the Castillo is accessible by car, on foot (10 minutes), or by a free but unreliable shuttle bus and elevator. *Tel. 5/553–6242. Small admission fee. Open Tues.–Sun. 9:30–5.*

Just down the hill from the Castillo is the **Museo Galería de la Lucha del Pueblo Mexicano por su Liberatad,** which goes by the more fanciful **Museo del Caracol** (Museum of the Snail) because of its spiral shape. The museum concentrates on the 400 years from the Viceroyalty to the Constitution of 1917, using dioramas and light-and-sound displays that children can appreciate. *Tel. 5/553–6285. Admission free. Open Tues.–Sun. 9–5.*

**❻** The **Museo de Arte Moderno** (Museum of Modern Art) is just north of the Castillo on the south side of Reforma. Two rooms are devoted to plastic arts from the 1930s to the 1960s; a third focuses on the past 20 years; and a fourth room and annex house temporary exhibits of contemporary Mexican painting, lithography, sculpture, and photography. *Tel. 5/553–6211. Small admission fee. Open Tues.–Sun. 10–6.*

The private collection of painter Rufino Tamayo now has a permanent home in the sleek and austere **Museo Rufino Tamayo.**
**❼** Tamayo's unerring eye for great art is evidenced by paintings and sculptures by such contemporary masters as Picasso, Miró, Warhol, and Henry Moore. *In Chapultepec Park, on the north side of Paseo de la Reforma and west of Gandhi, tel. 5/286–6519. Small admission fee. Open Tues.–Sun. 10–6.*

The greatest museum in the country—and arguably one of the
**❽** finest archaeological museums anywhere—is the **Museo Nacional de Antropología** (National Museum of Anthropology), just west of the Museo Rufino Tamayo. Even its architectural design (by Pedro Ramírez Vázquez) is distinguished. The collection is so extensive—covering some 100,000 square feet—that four hours are barely adequate to see it. However, bilingual guides take you through the highlights in two-hour tours. English guidebooks are available in the bookshop.

Begin in the Orientation Room, which traces the course of Mexican prehistory and the pre-Hispanic cultures of Mesoamerica. There are 12 rooms on the ground floor, including preclassical cultures, Teotihuacan, the Toltecs, Oaxaca, the Maya, and the north and west of Mexico. The so-called Aztec calendar stone and profusely feathered Aztec headdresses, reconstructed Mayan temples, and reproductions of the Mayan paintings from the ruins of Bonampak are just some of the highlights. (The gold diadem from Palenque and other priceless relics, stolen from the museum in the early 1980s, were recovered in June 1989.) Statuary, jewelry, weapons, clay figurines, and pottery evoke the brilliant, quirky, and frequently blood-thirsty civilizations that peopled the subcontinent during Europe's Dark Ages. The nine rooms on the upper floor contain faithful ethnographic displays of current indigenous peoples, using maps, photographs, household objects, folk art, clothing, and religious articles. *Tel. 5/553–6266. Small admission fee. Open Tues.–Sat. 9–6, Sun. and holidays 10–6.*

Other sights in the first section of Chapultepec Park include three small boating lakes; the Casa del Lago, a cultural center and fancy restaurant; a botanical garden; archaeological excavations (visitable by appointment); and the zoo housing Mexico's pandas, gifts from China. **Los Pinos,** the residential palace of the president of Mexico, is located on the park's southern boundary, at Avenida Constituyentes and Parque Lira. It is heavily guarded and cannot be visited. The less crowded second and third sections contain amusement parks (*see* What to See and Do with Children, *below*), the national cemetery, and the **Lienzo Charro** (rodeo).

**Time Out**   After visiting the museums, take a five-minute taxi ride just north of the park to Colonia Polanco, which is quickly upstaging the Zona Rosa as the chic place for shopping and dining. The outdoor tables at **Sanborcito's,** also known as **Restaurante Polanco,** are usually filled by the residents of this well-heeled, tranquil neighborhood. It has a small but moderately priced menu and is especially good for brunch. *Emilio Verde at Julio Castelar, overlooking a lovely park with a statue of Lincoln.*

Reforma wends its leisurely way west into the wealthy neighborhoods of Lomas de Chapultepec, where most of the houses are hidden, fortresslike, behind stone walls.

**Tour 3: San Angel and Coyoacán**

*Numbers in the margin correspond to points of interest on the San Angel and Coyoacán map.*

To explore the southern part of the city—which until 50 years ago was separate suburbs—take a taxi or pesero down Avenida Insurgentes. At 34 kilometers (21 miles), the longest avenue in the city, Insurgentes did not exist as such before the 1920s. It is blaring and unabashedly commercial, epitomizing the functional ugliness of much of Mexico City.

Get off at Avenida La Paz. On the east side of Insurgentes is a bizarre monument to revolutionary leader and onetime president Alvaro Obregón. The gray granite **Monumento al General Alvaro Obregón** marks the spot where the national hero Obregón was gunned down in a restaurant in 1928, and the centerpiece inside is none other than Obregón's hand and forearm—eerily preserved in formaldehyde—which he lost in a 1915 battle.

To make the most out of your visit to the next site, try to come on a Saturday, when the indoor and outdoor handicrafts market known as **Bazar Sábado** (Saturday Bazaar) is operating. Cross Avenida Insurgentes on Avenida La Paz, then take the southern fork off Avenida La Paz (Calle Madero) until you come to the **Plaza San Jacinto.** You are now in San Angel, a little colonial enclave of cobblestone streets, gardens drenched in bougainvillea, stone walls, and pastel houses.

# San Angel and Coyoacán

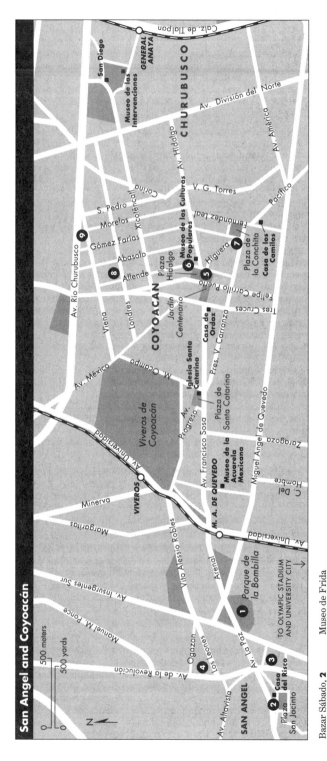

Bazar Sábado, **2**
Casa de la Malinche, **7**
Convento e Iglesia del Carmen, **3**
Monumento al General Alvaro Obregón, **1**
Museo Alvar y Carmen T. de Carrillo Gil, **4**

Museo de Frida Kahlo, **8**
Museo de Leon Trotsky, **9**
Palacio de Cortés, **6**
Parroquia de San Juan Bautista, **5**

Plaza San Jacinto is interesting in its own right. In 1847 about 50 Irish soldiers of St. Patrick's Battalion—who had sided with the Mexican side in the Mexican–American War—had their foreheads branded here with the letter *D* (for deserters) and were then hanged by the Americans. These men had been enticed to swim the Rio Grande and desert the ranks of U.S. General Zachary Taylor by pleas to the historic and religious ties between Spain and Ireland; as settlers in Mexican Texas, they felt their allegiance lay with Mexico, and they were among the bravest fighters in the war. They met their end when the American flag flew over Chapultepec Castle after the death of the *niños héroes* (*see* Tour 2, *above*). A memorial plaque at No. 23 listing their names and expressing Mexico's gratitude for their help in the "unjust North American invasion" now stands in the plaza, where each September a ceremony is conducted in their honor.

One of the prettiest houses facing the plaza—and also open to the public—is the **Casa del Risco**. It dates from the 18th century, and fountains situated in the patio and abutting the eastern wall explode with broken porcelain, tiles, shells, and mosaics. The **Museo de la Casa del Risco** houses a splendid collection of 14th- to 18th-century European and colonial Mexican paintings as well as period furnishings. *Plaza de San Jacinto 5 & 15, tel. 5/548–2329. Small admission fee. Open weekdays 9–3, Sat. 10–3. Closed Sun.*

The Bazar Sábado is off to one side of the plaza and specializes in unique high-quality handicrafts at excellent prices. Outside, vendors sell embroidered clothing, leather goods, wooden masks, beads, *amates* (bark paintings), and trinkets. The better-quality—and higher-priced—goods are found inside, including *animalitos* (painted wooden animals from Oaxaca), glassware, pottery, jewelry, and papier-mâché flowers. There is an indoor restaurant as well. *Open Sat. 10–7.*

After strolling around San Angel, retrace your steps along Calle Madero to Plaza del Carmen, at the corner of Avenida La Paz and Avenida Revolución. The **Convento e Iglesia del Carmen** (Carmelite Convent and Church) were erected by Carmelite friars with the help of an Indian chieftain in 1617; the tile-covered domes and fountains, gardens, and cloisters make these the most interesting examples of colonial religious architecture in this part of the city. The church still operates, but the convent is now the **Museo Regional del Carmen**, with a fine collection of 18th-century religious paintings, icons, mummified corpses, and pre-Hispanic handicrafts. *Av. Revolución 4 at Av. de la Paz. Tel. 5/548–5312. Small admission fee. Open Tues.–Sun. 10–5.*

A large selection of Mexican folk art is on sale at the Fonart branch at Avenida La Paz 17, almost at the corner of Avenida Revolución.

Take Avenida Revolución one block north to the **Museo Alvar y Carmen T. de Carrillo Gil.** This private collection contains murals by Orozco, Rivera, Siqueiros, and other modern artists. *Av. Revolución 1608 at Desierto de los Leones. Tel. 5/548–6467. Open Tues.–Sun. 10–6.*

The next part of the tour is set in Coyoacán, a neighborhood (formerly a village) that extends east of Avenida Insurgentes and about 1 kilometer (less than a mile) from San Angel. Consider taking a taxi to the Plaza de Santa Catarina on Avenida Francisco Sosa, about halfway into the center of Coyoacán, because the tour involves a lot of walking.

Coyoacán means "Place of the Coyotes," and according to local legend, a coyote used to bring chickens to a friar who had saved the coyote from being strangled by a snake. Coyoacán was founded by Toltecs in the 10th century and later settled by the Aztecs, or Mexica. Bernal Díaz Castillo, a Spanish chronicler, wrote that at the time of the conquest there were 6,000 houses. Cortés set up headquarters in Coyoacán during his siege of Tenochtitlan and at one point considered making it his capital. He changed his mind for political reasons, but many of the Spanish buildings left from the two-year period it took to build Mexico City still stand.

Contemporary Coyoacán exudes charm. The neighborhood has had many illustrious residents from Mexico's rich and intellectual elite, including Miguel de la Madrid, president of Mexico from 1982 to 1988; Orozco, the muralist; Gabriel Figueroa, cinematographer for Luis Buñuel and John Huston; the film star Dolores del Río; El Indio Fernández, a film director; and writers Carlos Monsiváis, Elena Poniatowska, and Jorge Ibargüengoitia.

While superficially it resembles San Angel, Coyoacán has a more animated street life. Most of the houses honor the traditions of colonial Mexican architecture, and the neighborhood is very well kept. As you walk east on Avenida Francisco Sosa, a block to your left is the **Viveros de Coyoacán** (Nurseries of Coyoacán), an expansive, tree-filled park. On one side of the Plaza Santa Catarina is the **Iglesia Santa Catarina,** a pretty 16th-century church; in the plaza there is a bust of Mexican historian Francisco Sosa, who lived here and wrote passionately about Coyoacán. Stop in at Avenida Francisco Sosa 202, the **Casa de Jesús Reyes Heroles,** home of the late minister of culture. It is a fine example of 20th-century architecture on the colonial model and is now used as a cultural center. Continuing along Avenida Francisco Sosa, you will pass the 17th-century **Casa de Diego de Ordaz** at the corner of Tres Cruces, a *mudéjar* (Spanish-Arabic) structure adorned with inlaid mortar.

You now stand at the entrance to the **Jardín Centenario,** a large park, surrounded by two important colonial buildings and outdoor cafés. Small fairs and amateur musical performances are frequent occurrences. At the opposite end of the park is the ❺ **Parroquia de San Juan Bautista,** one of the first churches to be built in New Spain. It was completed in 1582, and its door is decorated with a Baroque arch. To the left of the church is the heart of Coyoacán, Plaza Hidalgo, the main square. On the north side of the plaza, across from the church, sprawls the ❻ **Palacio de Cortés,** where Cuauhtémoc was held prisoner. An 18th-century building, it is supposed to have been erected by one of Cortés's descendants from the stones of his original house and is now used as Coyoacán's City Hall.

One of the most powerful symbols of the conquest is located in Coyoacán but, significantly perhaps, is not even marked. This ❼ is the **Casa de la Malinche,** the beautiful, red-stone house of Malinche, Cortés's Indian mistress and interpreter, whom the Spaniards called Doña María and the Indians called Malintzín. Malinche was instrumental in the conquest by enabling Cortés to communicate with the Nahuatl-speaking tribes he met en route to Tenochtitlan. Today she is a much-reviled Mexican symbol of a traitorous xenophile, hence the term *malinchista*, used to describe anything tainted by foreign influences. The legends say that Cortés's wife died in this house, poisoned by the conquistador; they also say he wrote his famous letter to Emperor Charles V in the house. Mysterious noises are said to destroy the peace of the present inhabitants. The house faces a pretty little square called Plaza de la Conchita, in the center of which lies an 18th-century church. *Two blocks east of Plaza Hidalgo on Calle Higuera, at the corner of Vallarta.*

**Time Out**  Return to Plaza Hidalgo for some refreshments before embarking on the next part of the tour. **La Guadalupana,** at the corner of Higuera and Caballocalco, is a popular cantina from the 1920s with snacks (such as shrimp broth and *totopos con frijoles,* a kind of corn tortilla with beans), and one of the few in Mexico City where women can feel comfortable. The quesadillas served in the little restaurants on Higuera have attained citywide fame.

From the plaza, walk five blocks north on Allende to the corner of Londres. Remodeled in early 1992, the bright blue adobe house—the **Museo de Frida Kahlo**—is where the painter Frida Kahlo was born and lived with Diego Rivera from 1929 until their respective deaths in 1954 and 1957. Kahlo has become quite a cult figure in recent years, not only because of her paintings—which consist almost entirely of self-portraits, many of them rather morbid—but because of her bohemian lifestyle and flamboyant individualism. As a child Kahlo was crippled by polio, and several years later she was impaled on a tramway rail; she spent much of her life in casts and excruciating pain. She had countless operations, including the amputation of a leg; was addicted to alcohol and drugs; had affairs with Leon Trotsky and several women; and married Rivera twice and stuck with him, despite his philandering (including an affair with her own sister). Kahlo's astounding vitality and originality are reflected in this house, from the giant papier-mâché skeletons outside and the painted tin retablos on the staircase to the gloriously decorated kitchen, the wheelchair and paintbrushes set up at her easel, and the childlike bric-a-brac in her bedroom. Even if you know nothing about Kahlo, a visit to the museum—also filled with letters, diaries, clothes, and paintings by Kahlo and other great moderns, including Klee and Duchamp—will leave you with a strong, visceral impression of this early feminist. *Londres 127, tel. 5/554–5999. Admission free. Open Tues.–Sun. 10–6.*

Leon Trotsky lived, was murdered, and his ashes were kept a short walk away. Go three blocks east on Londres and then two blocks north on Morelos; his house is on the northwest corner of Viena. From the outside, the **Museo de Leon Trotsky** resembles an anonymous and forbidding fortress, with turrets for armed guards; it is difficult to believe that it is the home and final resting place of one of the most important figures of the Russian Revolution. But that fact only adds to the allure of the house, which is owned by Trotsky's grandson.

Ring the bell to get in. A volunteer will take you through this modest, austere dwelling—anyone taller than five feet must stoop to pass through doorways—to Trotsky's bedroom (with bullet holes in the walls from the first assassination attempt, in which the muralist Siqueiros was implicated), his wife's study, the dining room, and the study where Ramón Mercader finally drove an ice pick into Trotsky's head. (On his desk, cluttered with writing paraphernalia and an article he was revising in Russian, the calendar is open to the fateful day of August 20, 1940.) The volunteers will tell you how Trotsky's teeth left a permanent scar on Mercader's hand; how he clung to life for 26 hours; what his last words were; and how his death was sponsored by the United States. Not all of the volunteers, however, speak English. *Av. Río Churubusco 410, tel. 5/554–0687. Admission free. Open Tues.–Sun. 10–5.*

## What to See and Do with Children

The best place to take children in Mexico is the parks, particularly Chapultepec. It has a **children's zoo** with a miniature railroad for viewing the animals, picnic grounds, and a boating lake. Youngsters can play with the animals, ride ponies, and climb tree houses. *First section of Chapultepec Park. Admission free. Open daily 8–6.*

An amusement park and roller coaster called the **Montaña Rusa** (Russian Mountain; in other words, roller coaster) is located in the third section of the park, along with a man-made lake, restaurant, and *cafetería* (coffee shop).

**Reino Aventura** is a 100-acre theme park on the southern edge of the city, comprising six "villages": Mexican, French, Swiss, Polynesian, American, and Children's World. Shows include performances by trained dolphins. *Carretera Picacho a Ajusco, Km 1.5. Admission: about $12, includes entrance and all rides (discounts for senior citizens and children). Open Tues.–Fri. 10–6, weekends 10–8.*

## Off the Beaten Track

**Colonia Condesa** (full name: Hipódromo de la Condesa) is a residential zone with an oval-shape park, the Parque México, which used to be the Hippodrome, or racetrack, and around which runs Calle Amsterdam on three sides. The colonia was built in 1902–1903 and named for a 17th-century countess (*condesa*). By 1910 the local Jockey Club had opened the Hippodrome, later used for car races and air stunts. During the late 1920s and 1930s, when post-Revolutionary Mexico was returning to stability, a building boom saw the addition of many architecturally similar Art Deco, neo-Hollywood, and neocolonial houses to the neighborhood, giving a pleasant uniformity to the streets.

In the 1940s Condesa was still an elegant residential community, but by the 1950s and 1960s, formerly one-family dwellings were being converted into multifamily apartments. The colonia lost its cachet, and nowadays it is inhabited by many older Jews and Spanish Civil War refugees of more modest means. Because of this European slant, it is not surprising that the neighborhood is one of the few where bagels are sold and where there are several good German restaurants. It's about a 15-minute walk southeast along Sonora from the Monumento a los Niños Héroes, or two blocks west of Avenida Insurgentes on Teotihuacan.

# Shopping

Native crafts and specialties from all regions of Mexico are available in the capital, as are designer threads and modern art. The best, most concentrated shopping area is the **Zona Rosa**, an 18-square-block area bounded by Reforma on the north, Niza on the east, Avenida Chapultepec on the south, and Varsovia on the west. The neighborhood is chock-full of boutiques, jewelry stores, leather-goods shops, antiques stores, and art galleries, as well as dozens of great little restaurants and coffee shops. Day or night, the Zona Rosa is always lively.

**Polanco,** a choice residential neighborhood along the northeast perimeter of Chapultepec Park, is blossoming with fine shops and boutiques, many of which are branches of Zona Rosa or downtown establishments. Many are located in malls like the huge ultramodern **Plaza Polanco** (Jaime Balmes 11).

There are hundreds of equally good shops spread out along the length of Avenida Insurgentes, as well as along Avenida Juárez and in the old downtown area. The major department-store chains are **Liverpool** (at Av. Insurgentes Sur 1310, Mariano Escobedo 425, and in the Plaza Satélite and Perisur shopping centers), **Suburbia** (at Horacio 203, Sonora 180, Av. Insurgentes Sur 1235, and also in Plaza Satélite and Perisur), and **El Palacio de Hierro** (at the corner of Durango and Salamanca), which is noted for fashions by well-known designers at prices now on par with those found in the United States. The posh and pricey shopping mall **Perisur** is out on the southern edge of the city near where the Periférico Expressway meets Avenida Insurgentes. **Plaza Satélite,** an ultramodern mall, is at the city's northern edge on the Anillo Periférico. Department stores are generally open Mondays, Tuesdays, Thursdays, and Fridays from 10 AM to 7 PM, and on Wednesdays and Saturdays from 10 AM to 8 PM.

**Sanborns** is a mini department-store chain with 19 branches in Mexico City alone. Those most convenient for tourists are at Madero 4 (its original store in the House of Tiles, downtown); on the Reforma, one at the Angel monument and another at the Diana Fountain; and in the Zona Rosa, corner of Niza and Hamburgo. They feature a good selection of quality ceramics and handicrafts (they can ship anywhere), and most have restaurants or coffee shops, a pharmacy, and periodical and book departments carrying English-language publications.

Under the auspices of the National Council for Culture and Arts, **Fonart** (National Fund for Fomenting Handicrafts) operates six stores in Mexico City and others around the country. The most convenient locations are at Londres 136, 2nd floor, Zona Rosa, and at Juárez 89, downtown just west of Alameda Park. Prices are fixed, and the diverse, top-quality folk art and handcrafted furnishings from all over Mexico represent the best artisans. Major sales at near wholesale prices are held at the main store-warehouse (Av. Patriotismo 691, Col. Mixcoac) during the second half of March, June, September, and November.

A Saturday "must" for shoppers and browsers is a visit to the **Bazar Sábado** (Saturday Bazaar) at Plaza San Jacinto in the southern San Angel district (*see* Tour 3, *above*). Inside a converted 18th-century mansion, dozens of fine shops sell handicrafts and regional clothing; an art show and handicraft stands are set up in the adjacent square. On Sundays, more than 100 artists exhibit and sell their paintings and sculptures at the **Jardín del Arte** (Garden of Art) in Parque Sullivan, just northeast of the Reforma-Insurgentes intersection. Along the west side of the park, a colorful weekend *mercado* (market) with scores of food stands is also worth a visit.

The following list will get you started. As you explore, you will find hundreds more.

## Zona Rosa

Arcades **La Rosa,** a sparkling new shopping arcade between Amberes and Génova, opened in 1991 and houses 72 prestigious shops and boutiques. It spans the entire depth of the block from Londres to Hamburgo with entrances on both streets. The pink neocolonial **Plaza del Angel** (Londres 161) has a *Centro de Antigüedades* (antiques center) with several fine shops. On Saturday, together with other vendors, they set up a flea market in the arcades and patios. On Sunday bibliophiles gather here to sell, peruse, and buy collectors' books and periodicals.

Clothing **Acapulco Joe's** (3 locations: Amberes 9, also in Polanco at Mazaryk 310 and 318) has great T-shirts, beachwear, and hip unisex sportsclothes. **Rubén Torres** (Amberes 9) has a wide selection of sportswear, from jerseys and jumpsuits to T-shirts and shorts, all nicely designed and well made. **Guess** (Amberes 17) features chic denim sportswear for guys and gals. **Fiorucci** (Londres 138 at Amberes) features famous Italian designer funwear for daytime or evening, activewear, beachwear, T-shirts, and sweaters. Next door at Londres 140, **La Patty's Boutique,** open Sundays, has two floors replete with top Mexican-label casuals for guys and gals.

Designers **Cartier** (Amberes 9, Zona Rosa, and the lobby of the Stouffer Presidente in Polanco) sells genuine designer jewelry and clothes, under the auspices of the French Cartier. However, **Gucci** (Hamburgo 136) has no connection with the European store of the same name; nevertheless, it has a fine sellection of shoes, gloves, and handbags. **Ralph Lauren** (Amberes 21) is the home of Polo sportswear made in Mexico under license and sold at Mexican prices.

Galleries The **Juan Martín Gallery** (Amberes 17) is one of the city's best avant-garde studios. **Galería Círculo** (Hamburgo 112) displays and sells the works of such contemporary artists as Climent and Tamayo, as well as prints by Dalí, Picasso, Miró, and others.

Jewelry The owner of **Los Castillo** (Amberes 41) developed a unique method of melding silver, copper, and brass, and is considered by many to be Taxco's top silversmith. The exclusive **Flato** (Amberes 21) sells original pieces by the internationally known jeweler Paul Flato, who specializes in gold. Taxco silver of exceptional style is sold at **Arte en Plata** (Amberes 24 and Londres 162), with many designs inspired by pre-Hispanic art. **Pelletier** (Amberes 15) sells fine jewelry and watches. **Tane** (Amberes 70, Zona Rosa; Edgar Allan Poe 68, in Polanco; and other locations) is a treasure trove of superb silver works—jewelry, flatware, candelabra, museum-quality reproductions of antique pieces, and bold new designs by young Mexican silversmiths. The **Mexican Opal Company** (Hamburgo 203) is run by Japanese who are very big on opals. They sell set and loose stones as well as a selection of jewelry in silver and gold.

**Leather** For leather goods, you have more than a few choices in Mexico City. **Ginatai** (Niza 46) stocks excellent leather suits, boots, and purses; and **Gaitán** (Copenhague 32, corner of Hamburgo) features an extensive array of leather coats, luggage, golf bags, and saddles. **Aries** (Florencia 14 and Plaza Polanco) is Mexico's finest purveyor of leather goods, with a superb selection of clothes, shoes, and accessories for both men and women. The prices are high. Just down the street, **Antil** (Florencia 22) also specializes in high-quality leather goods.

**Mexican** Browse for fine works of folk art, sculpture, and handicraft, **Handicrafts** from silver to ceramics, in the two-story gallery **Manos Mexicanas** (Amberes 57, near Londres). The **Mercado Insurgentes** (also called **Mercado Zona Rosa**) is an entire block deep, with entrances on both Londres and Liverpool (between Florencia and Amberes). This is a typical neighborhood public market with one big difference: Most of the stalls (222 of them) sell crafts. You can find all kinds of handmade items—including serapes and ponchos, baskets, pottery, silver, and onyx, as well as regional Mexican dresses and costumes.

**Girasol** (Génova 39) has a whimsical selection of hand-loomed fabrics and delightful hand-embroidered gowns and skirts. Handwoven wool rugs, tapestries, and fabrics with original and unusual designs can be found at **Tamacani** (Amberes 38).

**The Unusual** **Arte Popular en Miniatura** (Hamburgo 130) is a tiny shop filled with tiny things, from dollhouse furniture and lead soldiers to miniature Nativity scenes. **Flamma** (Hamburgo 167, at the corner of Florencia) is a town house that sells a beautiful array of handmade candles. **Muller's** (Florencia 52, corner of Londres) has just about everything that can be made from Puebla onyx, from jewelry to dining tables.

## Downtown

The Zócalo and Alameda Park areas have interesting markets for browsing and buying handicrafts and curios; polite bargaining is customary. The biggest is the **Centro Artesanal Buenavista** (Aldama 187, by the Buenavista Central Train Station). **La Lagunilla** market attracts antiques hunters who know how to determine authenticity, and also coin collectors. The best day is Sunday, when flea-market stands are set up outside (on Libertad, just east of Paseo de la Reforma Norte), with everything from collectibles to interesting knickknacks to junk. Within the colonial walls of **La Ciudadela** market (Balderas, about four blocks south of Avenida Juárez) are 344 artisans' stalls selling a variety of good handicrafts from all over the country.

**Museo de Artes Populares** (Museum of Arts and Crafts) could well be a museum but is in fact a large store displaying and selling an array of folk art and handicrafts—pottery, ceramics, glassware, textiles, and more—from practically every region of the country. Housed in an early 18th-century convent (across the street from Alameda Park and the Juárez Monument, at Juárez 44), it is open 7 days a week.

**Bazar del Centro** (downtown, at Isabel la Católica 30, just below Madero) is a restored late-17th-century noble mansion built around a garden courtyard that houses several chic boutiques, top-quality handicraft shops, and prestigious jewelers such as Aplijsa, known for its fine gold, silver, pearls, and gemstones. Other shops sell Taxco silver, Tonalá stoneware, and Mexican tequilas and liqueurs. It is elegant, worth a visit, and also has a congenial bar.

**Portales de los Mercaderes** (Merchants' Arcade) has attracted merchants since 1524. The arcade extends along the entire west side of the Zócalo, between Madero and 16 de Septiembre avenues. Today it is lined with jewelry shops, selling gold (sometimes by the gram) and authentic Taxco silver at prices lower than those in Taxco itself, where the overhead is higher. In the middle of the arcade (Plaza de la Constitución 17) is **Tardán,** an unusual shop specializing in fine quality and fashionable men's hats of every imaginable type and style.

**Celaya** (Cinco de Mayo 13), in the downtown historic section, is a decades-old haven for those with a sweet tooth. It specializes in candied pineapple, papaya, guava, and other exotic fruit, almond-paste, candied walnut rolls, and *cajeta,* a typical Mexican dessert of thick caramelized milk.

**Feders** (2 locations: the factory at Mérida 90 in Colonia Roma and a booth at Bazar Sábado, Plaza San Jacinto 11, San Angel) has great hand-blown glass, Tiffany-style lamps, and artistic wrought iron.

# Sports

**Bullfights**  The main season is the dry season, around November through March, when celebrated *matadores* appear at **Plaza México,** the world's largest bullring, which seats 40,000. Gray Line Tours offers bullfight tour packages (*see* Guided Tours in Essential Information, *above*); or tickets, which range from about $2 to $25, can be purchased at hotel travel desks. Try the bullring ticket booths on Saturdays between 11 AM and 2 PM or Sundays between 11 AM to 3:30 PM for tickets as well. The ring is located next to the Cuidad de Deportes sports complex, and the show goes on at 4 PM. *Calle A. Rodín s/n, Col. Nápoles, tel. 5/ 563–3959.*

**Golf**  The major hotels should be able to arrange guest privileges at private 18-hole courses around Mexico City, except on weekends, when tee times are at a premium. The fashionable **Club Campestre de la Ciudad de México** (Mexico City Country Club) has a golf course, pool, gym, and tennis and fronton courts. Tourists are admitted, but bring your Tourist Card. *Calzada Tlalpan 1978, tel. 5/549–3040.* You can also try the **Club de Golf Country Club** (Constituyentes 561, tel. 5/273–1790 or 5/273– 1803) or the **Club de Golf la Hacienda** (in Tecoluapan, tel. 5/379– 0033). Greens fees are about U.S. $50.

**Horse Racing**  The season at the beautiful **Hipódromo de las Américas** lasts from mid-January through December, when Thoroughbreds run daily except Mondays and Wednesdays. Betting is pari-mutuel. The races are especially enjoyable to watch from the swank Derby or Jockey Club restaurants. Tickets cost about 20 nuevos pesos and can be purchased at hotel travel desks or at the track, which is located in the northwest section of the city near the Querétaro Highway. *Av. Conscripto y Av. Periférico, tel. 5/557–4999.*

**Jai Alai** You can watch and bet on men playing this lightning-fast Basque-style handball game at **Frontón México** (on the northwest corner of the Plaza de la República) daily except Fridays and Sundays, 6 PM–1 AM. Women's matches are played at **Frontón Metropolitano** (Bahía de Todos los Santos 190) daily except Sundays, 4 PM–10 PM. Betting, which goes on while the games are being played, is a fascinating skill in itself; instructions on the betting sheets are in Spanish and English.

**Jogging** There are jogging tracks in Chapultepec Park and at the Villa Olímpica (Olympic Village). Another joggers' favorite is along the pastoral paths of the Coyoacán Nurseries by the Viveros Station of the No. 3 metro line. Early morning runners will probably see young novice bullfighters there going through their training maneuvers. Keep in mind, by the way, that air quality is often poor and this is the highest city in North America—7,349 feet/2,240 meters above sea level—so take it easy until your heart and lungs become accustomed to the altitude.

**Tennis** Tennis buffs should consider staying at one of the hotels (*see* Lodging, *below*) that have courts on site. Other hotels will usually arrange for you to play at semi-private clubs, where court fees are about 55 nuevos pesos per hour. **Club Reyes** (tel. 5/277–2690), three blocks from Bosque Chapultepec, is open daily from 7 AM to 9 PM. Call ahead for reservations. Facilities of the **Club Deportivo Chapultepec** (Chapultepec Sports Club) include a swimming pool, gym, horseback riding, and tennis courts. The Davis Cup matches are played here. *Mariano Escobedo, across from the Hotel Camino Real, tel. 5/589–1200.*

**Water Sports** The best place for swimming is your hotel pool. There are numerous public swimming pools in the city, and the vast **Cuemanco** sports park (Canal de Cuemanco, on the way to Xochimilco) has an immense pool as well as an artificial lake for canoeing. Rowers can ply their sport in the lakes of Chapultepec Park. Rentals are nearby.

# Dining

Mexico City has been a culinary capital ever since the time of Moctezuma. Chronicles tell of the daily banquet extravaganzas prepared for the slender Aztec emperor by his palace chefs. Over 300 different kinds of dishes were served for every meal, comprising vast assortments of meats and fowls seasoned in dozens of ways; limitless fruit, vegetables, and herbs; freshwater fish; and fresh seafood that was rushed to Tenochtitlan from both seacoasts by sprinting relay runners.

Until the 15th century, Europeans had never seen indigenous Mexican eatables such as corn, chilies of all varieties, tomatoes, potatoes, pumpkin, squash, avocado, turkey, cacao (chocolate), and vanilla. In turn, the colonization brought European gastronomic influence and ingredients—wheat, onion, garlic, olives, citrus fruit, cattle, sheep, goats, chickens, pigs (and lard for frying)—and ended up broadening the already complex pre-Hispanic cuisine into one of the most multifaceted and exquisite in the world: traditional Mexican.

Mexico's food, like Mexican art, is just as diverse and abundant as its geography. Distinct regional specialties typify each of the republic's 32 states and even the different provinces within the states. Fresh ingredients are bountiful, recipes are passed

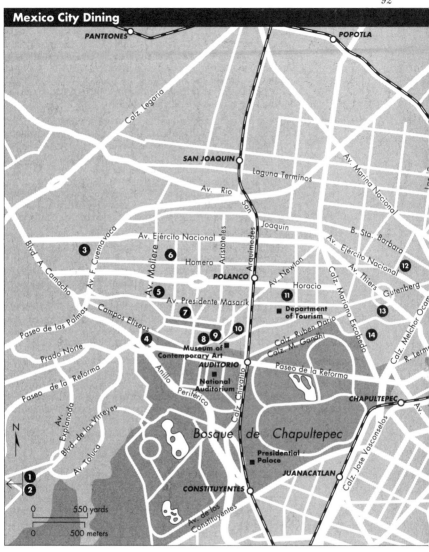

# Mexico City Dining

92

Andersons, **17**

Babieca, **1**

Bellinghausen, **20**

Café de Tacuba, **26**

Champs Elysées, **18**

El Arroyo, **22**

El Buen Comer, **6**

El Parador de
Manolo, **5**

Estoril, **8**

Focolare, **19**

Fonda del
Recuerdo, **12**

Fonda Don Chón, **28**

Fonda El Refugio, **21**

Fouquet's de Paris, **14**

Hacienda de los
Morales, **3**

Isadora, **4**

La Lanterna, **15**

La Petite France, **7**

Las Cazuelas, **27**

Las Mercedes, **13**

Las Palomas, **16**

Les Célébrités, **10**

Lincoln, **24**

Los Irabien, **30**

Maxim's de Paris, **9**

TLATELOLCO

94

s much lov-
es are dis-
ican food
e bewil-

estau-
stab-
on-
d

Magon

NORMAL

Mosqueta

GUERRERO

SAN COSME

Violeta

Rivera de San Cosme

REVOLUCION

Rayón
Rep. de Costa Rica

5 de Mayo

Guerrero

Paseo de la Reforma

Cárdenas

Rep. de Chile

27

BELLAS
ARTES

26

Rep. de
Bolivia

HIDALGO

M. María Contreras

Plaza de la
Republica

Alameda
Central

ALLENDE

Av. Parque Via

Antonio Caso

Sullivan

Av. Juárez

25

Madero

Moneda

Villalongín

Av. Insurgentes Centro

JUAREZ

Independencia

ZOCALO

R. Sena

Río Rhin

24

Eje Central Lázaro Cárdenas

Ayuntamiento

Río Tiber

de la Reforma

19

20

CUAUHTEMOC

Av. Bucareli

BALDERAS

SALTO DEL AGUA

28

Paseo

18

21

Dr. Río de la Loza

I. LA CATOLICA

PINO
SUAREZ

15

17

Londres

Bolívar

SEVILLA

INSURGENTES

Av. Chapultepec

Plaza
Rio de
Janeiro

Av. Dr. Vertiz

L. Boturini

S. Antonio Abad

16

Av. Durango

Av. Oaxaca

Sonora

Obregón

Orizaba

Av. Cuauhtemoc

NIÑOS HÉROES

Dr. Claudio Bernard

SAN ANTONIO
ABAD

Av. Insurgentes Sur

Av. Yucatán

Coahuila

Eje Central Lázaro Cárdenas

HOSPITAL GENERAL

22

23

CENTRO MEDICO

29 30

CHABACANO

down through generations, and preparation requir
ing care and a lot of patience. (Mexican gastronom
mayed by foreigners' glaring misconceptions of Me
no essentially tacos, enchiladas, and burritos; they a
dered by Tex-Mex, and appalled by Taco Bell.)

Today's cosmopolitan Mexico City, with some 15,000 r
rants, is a gastronomic melting pot. Here you can find e
lishments ranging from simple family-style eateries to five-
world-class restaurants. In addition, there are fine internatl
al restaurants specializing in cuisines of practically every f
eign culture. Among them, the most prevalent are Spanish an
haute-cuisine French—France also invaded Mexico and influ
enced its eating traditions.

In the past decade a renaissance of Mexican cooking has
brought about a new wave known as *cocina mexicana moderna*
(modern Mexican cuisine), which is featured in many Mexico
City restaurants. Emphasis is on the back-to-basics, delicate
tastes of traditional regional dishes served in smaller portions
with refined aesthetic presentation. Also significant in this
modern trend is the revival of ancient indigenous cuisine, when
frying and cholesterol phobia were nonexistent, and foods, especially fish, were baked, grilled, or steamed in leaves.

Mexico City mealtime hours are 7–11 AM for breakfast
(*desayuno*), 1–4 PM for lunch (*comida*), and 7 PM–midnight for
dinner (*cena*). At deluxe restaurants, dress is formal (coat and
tie), and reservations are required as noted below. For tourists
on the run there are American-style coffee shops (VIPS,
Denny's, Shirley's, and Sanborns) all over the city; some are
open 24 hours.

The following selection of recommended restaurants is organized by cuisine and price range. Those that are highly recommended (regardless of price range) are indicated by a star ★.

| Category | Cost* |
|---|---|
| Very Expensive | over $35 |
| Expensive | $25–$35 |
| Moderate | $15–$25 |
| Inexpensive | under $15 |

*per person, excluding drinks and service*

### French

After Mexican and international, French restaurants are the
most popular in Mexico City and exist in all price categories.

**Very Expensive** **Fouquet's de Paris.** Don't be put off by the dazzling rug in the
lobby of the Camino Real hotel. Enter the restaurant and you'll
find a haven of peace and tranquillity. The atmosphere tends to
be impersonal, however, and the service formal and sedate. It's
worth reserving a window table for a view of the attractive patio. The dining room, while elegant, won't win any prizes for
interior design. The best pâtés in Mexico and tender, juicy
lamb chops are part of the diverse and stylish menu. Fouquet's
is a pioneer in presenting international cooking festivals, when
visiting chefs raise the standards a notch or two. The desserts

are in a class all their own. Outstanding are the sorbets, such as delicately flavored passion fruit and *guayaba* (guava). The mousses, cakes, and pastries are light and delicious. *Hotel Camino Real, tel. 5/203–2121. Reservations advised. Jacket and tie required. AE, DC, MC, V. No lunch weekends.*

**Expensive** **Champs Elysées.** On the corner of Amberes and Reforma, com-
★ manding an impressive view of the Independence (Angel) monument, is one of the bastions of haute cuisine in Mexico City. Champs Elysées is never far from the top of any list of the best restaurants in the capital. The variety of sauces served with both meat and fish dishes is impressive, with the hollandaise sauce over sea bass or red snapper probably taking top honors. Regulars find either the roast duck (carved at your table) or the pepper steak hard to resist. Vegetables are all steamed to perfect firmness, and of particular note is the fulsome cheese board. *Amberes 1, Zona Rosa, tel. 5/514–0450. Reservations advised. Jacket preferred. AE, DC, MC, V.*

**Moderate** **La Petite France.** Located in the Mediterranean-looking Pasaje de Polanco, this could be on the Côte d'Azur. Tables under a canopy stretch out onto the street, while the yellows and greens of the decor, the many hanging plants, and the white cast-iron furniture suggest dining in a garden. The menu is strong on imagination, with such specialties as fish soup with Pernod and roast lobster with basil. The chicken-liver mousse is a delicate alternative to coarser pâtés such as duck. The stuffed mushrooms and *moules Provençales* (mussels Provençale) are typically Mediterranean dishes that rely on mixed herbs for flavor. Fish dishes loom large, with *truite meunière* (trout, lightly fried and served with lemon), a giant prawn brochette, and deep-fried sea bass claiming most of the attention. The lamb chops are tender, although the mint sauce is an alarming shade of electric green. Beautifully garnished and presented, the dishes catch the eye with a colorful, good selection of steamed vegetables. *Av. Presidente Masaryk 360, Col. Polanco, tel. 5/250–4470 or 5/548–3918. Reservations accepted. Dress: informal. AE, DC, MC, V. No dinner Sun.*

**Inexpensive** **El Buen Comer.** One of the more original Polanco eating spots, El Buen Comer (eating well) consists of not more than 20 tables in the front yard and garage of a private house. It is so popular at lunchtime that reservations are essential. The entrance is discreet and can easily be missed; indeed, the atmosphere inside is more that of a large private lunch party than a restaurant. Oysters are meticulously cleaned and scrubbed before opening and are then left in their own water, not washed under the faucet, as is the usual Mexican habit. They are served with an unusual vinegar and chopped shallot sauce but are so tasty they can be savored with just a squeeze of lime. The four house pâtés are excellent. A favorite main course of the habitués is quiche Lorraine, cooked to order in an individual dish. The quiche royale with shrimp is a must for seafood lovers. The fondues are exquisite. Whole steaks can be served to order with fine herbes, pepper, tartar, or shallots, which are a rare commodity in Mexico. The clientele consists of people from the business community who insist on eating well but don't want a heavy or complicated meal. El Buen Comer makes a great stop after shopping in Polanco. *Edgar Allan Poe 50, Col. Polanco, tel. 5/203–5337 or 5/545–8057. Reservations required at lunch. Dress: casual. No credit cards. Closed Sun.*

## Indian

**Moderate** **Restaurante Tandoor.** There is much cause for rejoicing now that a respectable Indian restaurant has come to town. Owner Niaz Ahmad Siddiqui makes regular tours to the subcontinent to forage for dishes that can successfully be transplanted to Mexico. The venue is a small house in Polanco. The front room can seat about 30 people. The furnishings are makeshift, but no one seems to care; the satisfied customers who line up outside at lunchtime certainly don't. Everything here is homemade in the traditional Indian way. Curries are superlative, and you can choose the desired spiciness. Rave reviews for the chicken and almond curry, which retains its delicate nutty flavor while still having its full spicy impact, and for the mutton *gosht*, a mix of large chunks of mutton cooked with spinach in a mild but complex sauce. All the *vindaloos* (a typical, very hot curry) are mouth searing, and the kitchen even manages a good chicken tandoor. The rice is excellent, made with a selection of sumptuous spices, such as cardamom, caraway, and saffron. Breads such as nan, chapatis, and papadums are also available. *Lope de Vega 341a, Col. Polanco, tel. 5/203–0045. Reservations advised. Dress: informal. AE, DC, MC, V.*

## International

**Very Expensive** **Estoril.** Now in two locations: Rosa Martín runs the establish-
★ ment, occupying an exquisite refurbished 1930s mansion in fashionable Polanco; her daughter Diana manages the original Estoril in an elegant Zona Rosa town house. Both use only the very best ingredients and serve international cuisine with a Mexican flair; their forte, however, is traditional Mexican. The *perejil frito* (fried parsley) is a popular starter. The smoked oyster mousse and cold avocado soup are delicate, while the *caldo de gallina con coñac* (chicken broth with cognac) and *crepas de chicharrón con salsa verde* (fried pork rinds with green sauce) are distinctive. The main dishes offer some unusual taste combinations: giant prawns in Chablis or curry sauces and sea bass in fresh coriander sauce. To finish, try either the delicious *tarte tatin* (an upside-down apple tart with caramel) or the homemade sorbets, especially the refreshing mint flavor. *Zona Rosa: Génova 75, tel. 5/511–3421. Polanco: Alejandro Dumas 24, Col. Polanco, tel. 5/531–4896. Reservations advised. Jacket and tie required. AE, DC, MC, V.*

**Hacienda de los Morales.** This is a Mexican institution and a fine example of a hacienda turned restaurant. The original building dates from the 16th century. The atmosphere is colonial Mexico in the grand style—huge spaces of terra-cotta and luxuriant green, with dark wood beams. One can just glimpse a bygone world in places such as these. The menu combines both international and Mexican cuisines, with some imaginative variations on both. The *sopa de mariscos del Golfo* weighs in as a substantial seafood soup. The walnut soup is served either hot or cold and is a delicate and unusual specialty. Attention to detail is shown in the choice of cured hams—Parma or Serrano—with melon slices. Fish is seemingly unlimited, with a rainbow trout meunière (lightly sautéed in butter, served with lemon juice and parsley), sea bass *marinière* (in a white-wine sauce), and a mixed seafood gratin. The charcoal-broiled grain-fed chicken has a distinct flavor, and the paillard is always of the highest quality. Vegetables are ordered separately, and the sautéed string beans, broccoli, and spinach all arrive lightly cooked with their natural goodness intact. The Hacienda de los Morales is regularly hired for functions, so don't be surprised if there's a lot of activity. *Vázquez de Mella 525, Col. Los Morales, tel. 5/540–3225. Reservations necessary. Jacket advised. AE, DC, MC, V.*

★ **Les Célébrités.** In addition to superb French fare, this elegant restaurant also serves the best in Mexican cuisine. When the Nikko Hotel opened in 1987, chef Joel Roubenchon, one of the creators of nouvelle cuisine in France, came to Mexico to set up this restaurant off the hotel lobby. With him came the ultimate in restaurant technology and a policy of using only the very finest ingredients. He organized an Annual Gastronomy Festival, held in the fall, featuring the creative modern Mexican cuisine of celebrity Mexican chef-author-painter Marta Chapa, whose original work-of-art dishes are now permanently on the menu: medallion of lobster in guayaba sauce; salmon roll stuffed with lemon mousse in grapefruit sauce; and, for dessert, pomegranate sherbet or red and green prickly pear sherbet. *Hotel Nikko, Campos Elíseos 204, Col. Polanco, tel. 5/203–4020. Reservations required. Jacket and tie required for dinner. AE, DC, MC, V. Open Mon.–Fri. 6:30 AM–11 PM. Dinner only Sat. Closed Sun.*

**Maxim's de Paris.** Here you can enjoy the best French food anywhere and, better yet, nouvelle Mexican cuisine prepared by the creative hands of chef Yves Ferrer. His pre-Hispanic *crepas de huitlacoche* (crepes of corn fungus) are a modern delicacy. Inspired by Mexico's great wealth of foodstuffs, Ferrer has conceived original dishes such as fillet of sea bass in jellied sauce of beef bone marrow. Operated under the auspices of the original Maxim's in Paris—the menu has the same design—this spacious but intimate restaurant is located in the Hotel Stouffer Presidente. Decor is Parisian art deco under a stained-glass ceiling; the wine cellar is nonpareil, and the service impeccable. *Hotel Stouffer Presidente, Campos Elíseos 218, Col. Polanco, tel. 5/254–0033. Reservations required. Jacket and tie required. AE, DC, MC, V. Lunch and dinner Mon.–Fri. Dinner only Sat. Closed Sun.*

**Moderate–Expensive**

**Bellinghausen.** This is one of the most pleasant lunch spots in the Zona Rosa. The partially covered hacienda-style courtyard at the back, set off by an ivy-laden wall, is a magnet at lunchtime for executives and tourists alike. A veritable army of waiters, in blue-and-white striped jackets, scurry back and forth serving such tried-and-true favorites as *sopa de hongos* (mushroom soup); a delicious chicken broth served *a la mexicana, with rice, raw onion, avocado, and a coriander garnish; and a filete chemita* (broiled steak with mashed potatoes). The *higaditos de pollo* (chicken livers) with a side order of sautéed spinach is another winner. Sometimes it even has *charalitos* (tiny fish from Lake Patzcuaro), which are a must if available. Other specials include *gusanos de maguey* (worms from the maguey cactus), *cabrito* (baby goat), roast lamb, and Spanish paella. *Londres 95, Zona Rosa, tel. 5/511–9035 or 5/511–1056. Reservations advised. Dress: informal. AE, DC, MC, V. Closed Sun.*

**Inexpensive**

**Andersons.** Mexico is a city of institutions: Andersons is one of its most lighthearted. This is the headquarters of a chain (some branches are called Carlos 'n' Charlies) with outlets in Acapulco, Cancún, and Ixtapa, among other cities. The decor is all card-table green and white. Photographs and paraphernalia of patrons past and present adorn the walls. The menu is international with a dash of Mexican. The place is well known for its multiple varieties of cooked oysters and *ostiones 444* (12 oysters baked with bacon, garlic, and cheese toppings). Other successes include Oriental chicken, which comes in a tangy sweet-and-sour sauce, and the *puntas de filete a la mexicana* (tender and piquant sirloin tips). On the fish side, the *huachinango* (red snapper) in green sauce is an unusual creation. Tables are rather cramped and the service can be fast and furious to the point of being hyper, so don't come if you want a romantic dinner. *Paseo de la Reforma 382, Col. Juárez, tel. 5/525–1006. No reservations. Dress: casual. AE, DC, MC, V.*

### Italian

**Moderate**  **La Lanterna.** The Petterino family has run this two-story restaurant in the same building for 20 years. The downstairs has the rustic feel of a northern Italian trattoria, with the cramped seating adding to the intimacy. Upstairs is more spacious. All the pastas are made on the premises, and the Bolognese sauce, in particular, is a local favorite. The management is especially proud of its *osso buco à la milanaise* (the real bone and not the knuckle, which is often passed off as such). Other dishes worth trying include a raw artichoke salad, *conejo al Salmi* (rabbit in a wine sauce), *filete al burro nero* (steak in black butter), and *saltimbocca à la Romana* (veal and ham in Marsala sauce). *Paseo de la Reforma 458, Col. Cuahtémoc, tel. 5/207–9969. No reservations. Dress: casual but neat. MC, V. Closed Sun.*

### Japanese

**Very Expensive**  **Suntory.** With restaurants in Boston, Singapore, Paris, and São Paulo, the Suntory name has become synonymous with the best in Japanese dining. As you enter, by way of three rocks in a bed of well-raked sand, you are transported into a small-town patio in a dense green garden. In this enchanted world you are not absolved of the difficulty of choice. Is it the teppanyaki room to watch your fresh meat or fish prepared with a variety of vegetables? Or perhaps the shabu-shabu room beckons with wafer-thin sashimi and a copper pot of steaming vegetable broth in which elegant slices of beef are cooked? If you are a raw-fish enthusiast, perhaps the sushi bar? Prices are high, especially for Mexico, but the argument holds that raw materials of the highest quality will always cost, wherever you decide to eat. *Torres Adalid 14, Col. del Valle, tel. 5/536–9432. Reservations advised. Dress: casual but neat. AE, DC, MC, V.*

### Mexican

**Very Expensive**  **Isadora.** Some of Mexico City's most inventive and exciting
★    cooking takes place in this converted private house in Polanco. The three smallish dining rooms have a 1920s feel but are uncharacteristically ascetic—pale walls dabbed with modern-art squiggles. The management sponsors "cooking festivals," and virtually every month the kitchen produces dishes from a different country. The basic menu changes six times a year, and over that same period it will include three Mexican foodfests. What might be called the set menu features coarse duck pâté and excellent seafood pasta, with no holding back on the juicy

prawns, shellfish, and squid. Ice creams, meringues, and chocolate cake for dessert benefit from the addition of the chef's
delicate, pale green mint sauce. *Molière 50, Col. Polanco, tel.
5/520–7901. Reservations necessary. Jacket and tie required.
AE, DC, MC, V. Closed Sun.*

**Los Irabien.** This beautiful dining area filled with leafy plants
and the owner's impressive art collection is a worthwhile stop
for the gourmet and culture hound alike. Chef Enrique
Estrada, who trained at the Waldorf Astoria in New York, is
one of Mexico's finest exponents of nouvelle cuisine à la
Mexicaine. His *ensalada Irabien* triumphs as a mixture of
smoked salmon, abalone, prawn, quail eggs, lettuce, and wa-
tercress; and his *ensalada Valle de Bravo* is no less impressive,
with Serrano ham, apple, quail eggs, mushrooms, Gruyère,
and walnuts. Two outstanding entrées include the nopal cactus
stuffed with fish fillet in garlic and the fillet steak in strawberry sauce *a la pimienta*. Less exotic dishes, such as a juicy prime
rib of beef, are also available, and lavish care in preparation
and presentation is evident in all courses. Los Irabien is one of
the city's breakfast spots par excellence. Where else could one
be tempted by *huevos de codorniz huitzilopochtli* (quail eggs
with tortilla on a bed of *huitlacoche* in a squash-blossom sauce)?
*Av. de la Paz 45, Col. San Angel, tel. 5/660–2382. Reservations
advised. Jacket and tie required. AE, DC, MC, V.*

★ **San Angel Inn.** If architectural style and natural setting were
everything, the San Angel Inn would consistently head the list.
In the south of the city, this magnificent old hacienda and ex-
convent, with its elegant grounds and immaculately tended
gardens, is both a joy to the eye and an inspiration to the palate.
Whether you're enjoying a quiet aperitif on the cool patio or
seated in the exquisitely decorated dining room, the San Angel
Inn will claim the full attention of all your senses. The dark mahogany furniture, crisp white table linens, and beautiful blue-
and-white Talavera place settings all combine to touch just that
right note of restrained opulence. There are many dishes to be
recommended, especially the *crepas de huitlacoche* (corn-fun-
gus crepes) and the *sopa de tortilla* (tortilla soup). The *puntas
de filete* (sirloin tips) are liberally laced with chili, as they
should be, and the huachinango is offered in a variety of ways.
Desserts—from light and crunchy meringues to gâteaux bulg-
ing with cream—can be rich to the point of decadence. *Calle
Palmas 50, Col. San Angel, tel. 5/548–4514 or 5/548–6840. Reservations necessary. Jacket required. AE, DC, MC, V.*

**Expensive** **Lincoln.** Lincoln, with its portrait of the great statesman in the
entrance, is reminiscent of a New England club—leather up-
holstery, discreet dining booths, and plenty of dark wood to
provide a serious, rather disciplined atmosphere. Fish is the
main draw, although the traditional Mexican menu does offer
some meat dishes. The salsa verde, with large chunks of
cheese, onion, and *perejil* (parsley), is an ideal complement to
the appetizers. From there the range and choice are impressive. Soups include such delicacies as *sopa de almejas* (clam
soup), and a thick crab soup. Among the main dishes, the
*huachinango a la veracruzana* is notable. A common dish in
Mexico, it is here distinguished by its extraordinary freshness
and its sauce, which avoids being watery, a common pitfall in
other establishments. The typical *albóndigas en chipotle*
(meatballs in spicy chile sauce) is another favorite. Desserts
are not designed to be stunning; *arroz con leche* (something

like a rice pudding) or *natilla* (liqueur-flavored custard) are an acceptable way to round off a meal. *Revillagigedo 24, Col. Centro, tel. 5/510-1468. Reservations accepted. Dress: casual bul nowl. AE, DC, MC, V.*

**Prendes.** This downtown institution, first opened in 1892, is back in business under new ownership after having been closed down due to earthquake damage. In fact, the building is still tilted. There is an air of history and legend—the president of Mexico dines here, as did his predecessors. Trotsky ate here with Ramón Mercader, who axed him to death two days later. The decor is minimal but is highlighted by the famous Prendes murals, which depict such celebrities as Gary Cooper and Walt Disney dining here. Prendes features some traditional Mexican dishes, but emphasis is now on delicate and decorative nouvelle Mexican cuisine. Oysters, *ceviche* (raw fish marinated in lime juice, tomatoes, onions, and chile) or a cream of maize soup are typical starters. The *filete chemita* (fillet of beef) with some delicious mashed potatoes and the fillet of fish meunière with nuts are two popular main courses. It's a good spot to try when exploring the downtown area. *16 de Septiembre 10, Col. Centro, tel. 5/512-7517. Reservations required. Jacket and tie required. AE, DC, MC, V.*

**Villa Reforma.** Occupying a converted house in the exclusive Lomas de Chapultepec residential area, this secluded restaurant is very popular for lunch on the terrace, candlelight dinner, breakfast at 8—try the *jugo de tuna* (prickly pear juice)— or sumptuous Sunday brunch with music. Previously known for its French provincial fare, Villa Reforma now features innovative nouvelle Mexican cuisine: *sopa "María Candelaria"* (squash blossom soup with corn kernels), *huevos a la poblana* (poached eggs on a tortilla topped with cream cheese and slices of poblano chile), duckling in strawberry sauce, turkey steak in lemon sauce, and huachinango in avocado sauce. Villa Reforma is also famed for its home-baked breads and pastries. *Paseo de la Reforma 2210, Lomas de Chapultepec, tel. 5/596-0123 or 5/596-4355. Reservations advised. Jacket and tie required for dinner. AE, DC, MC, V.*

**Moderate– Expensive**
**El Arroyo.** More than just a restaurant, this dining complex is a famous attraction in itself, complete with its own bullring. Located at the south end of town near the beginning of the highway to Cuernavaca, it was founded over 50 years ago by the Arroyo family and is now run by jovial Jesús ("Chucho") Arroyo. His loyal following includes celebrities, dignitaries and bullfighters, and the place is also enjoyed by families, tourists, and groups (generous menus are available for 15 or more and 100 or more). More than 2,600 people can dine simultaneously in a labyrinth of 11 picturesque dining areas. Typical Mexican specialties—roast baby lamb wrapped in maguey leaves, chicken mole, a dozen types of tacos and much more—are prepared in open kitchens where the copper and ceramic casseroles are big enough to swim in. There's mariachi music galore and the full gamut of Mexican drinks, including pulque. The small bullring is the setting for bullfights with audience participation and not-very-brave bulls, as well as for special banquets and lively fiestas. Breakfast starts at 8 AM and lunch is served until 7 PM. *Insurgentes Sur 4003, Col. Tlalpan, tel. 5/573-4344. Reservations recommended, required for groups. Dress: casual. AE, DC, MC, V. Open daily.*

★ **Fonda El Refugio.** Since it opened in 1954, this fine Zona Rosa restaurant has been internationally known for its exquisite Mexican cuisine that delights even the most delicate palates. A habitual dining place for local devotees, it also offers a delightful introduction to Mexican gastronomy. The first thing you see upon entering this converted two-story town house is a mouthwatering display of homemade cream-pudding desserts. Atmosphere is casual yet classy in the intimate colonial-decor dining rooms. The menu varies daily, with a selection of appetizers, soups, and regional dishes such as chicken mole, assorted *chiles rellenos,* grilled pork chops, and *albóndigas en chile chipotle* (meat balls in chile chipotle sauce). In the fall, the *chiles en nogada* are famous. This traditional dish displays the colors of the Mexican flag—green baked chilies stuffed with ground meat, walnuts, and rice, topped with white cream and red pomegranate seeds. To make selection easy, there is also a set house specialty for each day of the week. Whichever day it is, start with a plate of *botanas* (Mexico's version of hors d'oeuvres) and, in addition to tequila with *sangrita,* try the refreshing *aguas* (fresh-fruit and seed juices) made with *chía* (sage seeds), *jamaica* (hibiscus), or *tamarindo.* After dessert, try *café de olla* (cinnamon-flavored coffee boiled in a clay pot and sweetened with brown sugar). *Liverpool 166, Zona Rosa, tel. 5/528–5823. Reservations recommended. Dress: casual but neat. AE, DC, MC, V. Closed Sun. and holidays.*

**Las Palomas.** In a residential neighborhood not far from the Zona Rosa, this is a congenial meeting place, delightfully decorated with colorful hand-painted tiles, wrought-iron grillwork, flowers, foliage, and art. Socialite-owner-hostess Lila Briones attends loyal customers, who even include some of her rival restaurateurs and chefs, as well as noted journalists, authors, and other cognoscenti in the field of Mexican gastronomy. Lila is faithful to the recipes she inherited from the days of her great-grandmother's country hacienda, such as homemade *tinga* (shreds of beef in a sauce of a blend of chilies of various flavors) and sensational homemade green chicken mole. Her brother Miguelangel barrel-pickles a coveted appetizer of chilies jalapeños with cauliflower, carrots, radishes, onions, and squash. Other specialties include huachinango in homemade avocado sauce, *cochinita pibil* (baby pig Yucatecan style), and *bacalao* (codfish Spanish style, with red and green bell peppers). Among desserts: homemade rice pudding and *natillas* (Spanish-style custards). A folkloric trio and guitarist-balladeer add to the talented milieu. *Cozumel 37, Col. Roma, tel. 5/ 553–7084. Reservations suggested. Dress: casual but neat. AE, MC, V. Open daily for lunch and dinner.*

**Moderate** **Focolare.** Among the prettiest eateries in the Zona Rosa, Focolare's dining area is a covered patio with a fountain in the middle and a high roof attractively decorated with hanging wicker baskets. At the far end, a double blue-tile staircase leads to the second floor and adds to the feeling of spaciousness. This is a great breakfast spot. The buffet caters to the Mexican taste (red-hot chili first thing in the morning), but it also has less violent ways to start the day. Dishes are organized by region; if you are a fan of Oaxaca's chocolate mole sauce, you can enjoy a different one here every day of the week. Yucatecan dishes figure strongly at Focolare. Particularly worthwhile is the cochinita pibil. In fact, if you wanted to do a gastronomic tour of Mexico, Focolare would be a good guide to which places should be given priority. From Puerto Angel, for example, it does a delicious *calamares* dish in a delicate mandarin sauce, supposedly typical of this tiny port on the Oaxacan coast. Another highlight is *cuete de res*, which is a special cut of beef prepared in a sumptuous almond sauce. Service is attentive and one can either eat quickly and be gone or linger over a meal. On Sundays, a healthy brunch is served, accompanied by a live band. *Hamburgo 87, Zona Rosa, tel. 5/511-2679 or 5/511-4236. No reservations. Dress: casual. AE, DC, MC, V.*

**Fonda del Recuerdo.** A solid family restaurant, the *fonda* (inn) has an enviable reputation among tourists and visitors. Every day from 2 to 10, five different groups from Veracruz provide music that creates a festive atmosphere. A traditional Mexican menu features excellent seafood, meat, and *antojitos* (Mexican appetizers). Mixed fish-and-seafood platters for two, four, or eight people, and whole fish or fillets (grilled with garlic or served with tomatoes, onions, and chile) are recommended. Meat from the kitchen's own *parillas* (grills) is always first-rate. The fonda is renowned for its gigantic portions, so you may find there's no room for dessert. If the appetite is willing, however, the *crepas de cajeta al tequila* (crepes of caramelized goat's milk with tequila) are worth trying. The continual party atmosphere and good Mexican cooking from Veracruz make this an excellent dining spot to enjoy with friends. *Bahía de las Palmas 39, Col. Anzures, tel. 5/545-1652. Reservations advised. Dress: informal. AE, DC, MC, V.*

**Fonda Don Chón.** This simple family-style restaurant, deep in downtown, is famed for its pre-Hispanic (indigenously Mexican) dishes. "This highly nutritious cuisine of our ancestors before the discovery of the Americas is also food of the future," says Fortino Rojas, a well-known chef of pre-Hispanic cooking. This restaurant is for the adventurous, although some pre-Hispanic delicacies, such as corn fungus, are featured at some of Mexico's most elegant restaurants. A knowledge of zoology, Spanish, and Nahuatl helps in deciphering the menu, which changes daily. A gamut of products from throughout the republic are prepared fresh every day, and no processed foods are used. *Escamoles de hormiga* (red ant roe), 97% protein, is known as the "caviar of Mexico" for both its deliciousness and its costliness. Another delicacy, also served in small portions, is *gusanos de maguey* (maguey cactus worms) worth $100 a kilo and seen in some tequila bottles, served in tacos or with guacamole. Among exotic entrées are armadillo in sesame mole sauce, iguana soup, and snake (boa or rattle) steak. More traditional specialties include *mixiote de carnero* (barbecued lamb in maguey leaves). The coconut cake dessert is excellent, and live music adds to the atmosphere. *Regina 159, Col. Centro, tel. 5/522-170. No reservations. Dress: casual. AE, MC, V. Open daily 10 AM-7 PM.*

**Las Mercedes.** Styled as a *restaurant de epoca*, Las Mercedes specializes in traditional Mexican food, with some ancient recipes that have stood the test of time. The decor is modern rustic, with furniture from Michoacán and a pleasant terra-cotta and coffee color scheme. Enjoy the variety of fresh-fruit and seed juices (known as *aguas*) and some *sopecitos* (chicken and chorizo on flat tortillas) before beginning your meal in earnest. Both the *sopa de fideos con albondiguitas* (pasta soup with little meatballs) and the *sopa de tortilla* (tortilla soup) make excellent starters. The *lomo de cerdo en salsa de huitlacoche* (pork in a sauce made from the corn-husk fungus) is exceptional. The *plato Mercedes*, a sampling of both the old and the new Mexican cuisines, is highly recommended. Las Mercedes is a good choice for breakfast, when such delicacies as eggs with shrimp, oysters, and asparagus are offered. *Rio Guadalquivir 91, Col. Cuauhtemoc, tel. 5/208–7369. Reservations accepted. Dress: informal. AE, DC, MC, V.*

**Inexpensive** **Café de Tacuba.** This typically Mexican restaurant is an essential breakfast, lunch, dinner, or snack stop for those exploring the city's downtown historic district. Since it opened in 1912, in a section of an old convent, it has charmed locals and visitors with its warm colonial decor and traditional Mexican fare. Colorful hand-painted Talavera tiles from Puebla line the walls. In the rear dining room, huge 18th-century oil paintings depict the historic invention of *mole poblano*, one of Mexico's most original dishes with a sauce of countless ingredients, including a variety of chilies and chocolate. The complex recipe was created by the nuns in the Santa Rosa Convent of Puebla. Of course, mole poblano is on the menu here, as are delicious tamales made fresh every morning—Oaxaca style with black mole and banana leaf or a fluffy Mexico City version. Enjoy pastries galore. *Tacuba 28, Col. Centro, tel. 5/518–4950. No reservations. Dress: casual. MC, V. Open daily.*

★ **Las Cazuelas.** Traditional Mexican cooking at its best is on tap at one of the most famous of the downtown fondas. The open view kitchens are kept immaculately clean, and diners often take a peek at the bubbling *mole* and *pipián* sauces before being seated. (*Mole* is a chocolate-based chile sauce with many other spices; *pipián* is a lightly *picante*, sesame-flavored sauce from the Yucatán, which is often served with poultry.) The large dining area is brightened by hand-painted chairs from Michoacán and by the crisp green-and-white table linen. Ideal Mexican appetizers to share are *entremés ranchero de carnitas* (meat morsels in red sauce) and chicharrón y quesadilla (pork rind and tortillas with melted cheese). All the ingredients, and especially the *chicharrón* (fried pork rinds), are *de primera* (the best quality available). Main courses center around various moles or pipián sauces with pork or chicken. If you like the slightly bitter but spicy, hot taste of the *chile pasilla*, try the *hongos en salsa de pasilla con carne de puerco* (mushrooms with pork). Finish with a *café de olla* (cinammon coffee in a clay mug) and a domestic brandy, then enjoy some fine mariachi singing from a talented and professional group (from 4 to 6 daily). *Rep. de Colombia 69, Col. Centro, tel. 5/522–0689. No reservations. Dress: casual. AE, MC, V.*

## Spanish

**Expensive** **El Parador de Manolo.** A period two-story house was remodeled into this Spanish restaurant in fashionable Polanco. The Bar Porrón on the ground floor serves a variety of Spanish tapas, including an excellent prawn mix in a spicy sauce. In the brasserie-style dining room upstairs, choose from a Spanish menu or from the list of the chef's recommendations. The specially cured Serrano ham is possibly the best in the city, while the *calamares fritos* (fried squid) or the *crepas de flor de calabaza al gratin* (squash-blossom crepes) make other fine starters. Fish dishes are the most appealing for a main course, although the chateaubriand Parador for two (in a black corncob sauce) is truly original. Desserts cater to the Spanish sweet tooth and are less notable. Wines are on display downstairs, as are the fresh fish of the day. *Presidente Masaryk 443, Polanco, tel. 5/545–7723. Reservations accepted. Dress: informal. AE, MC, V.*

**Moderate** **Babieca.** Almost hidden in the growing Lomas shopping complex, the Babieca, despite its rustic decor, could not really be anything other than Spanish (the name is taken from El Cid's horse, and the decor has strong equestrian overtones). This is a wonderful place for tapas, especially if you don't want a heavy meal. There could be nothing more Spanish than the tapas served here: *tortilla de patata* (potato omelet), *abulón* (abalone), *chorizo con chistorra* (dried meats and sausage), *morcilla* (blood sausage), and *gambas al ajillo* (prawns in garlic sauce) are all exquisite. If a full meal beckons, try the *setas a la Provençale* (wild mushrooms in butter, wine, parsley and garlic) to start, then move on to a brochette of giant prawn with a Gruyère gratin. The dessert truffles are superlative, the meringues in chocolate sauce are downright sinful, and the date-and-nut tart is both sticky and irresistible. *Bosques de Duraznos 187, Col. Bosques de las Lomas, tel. 5/596–4601 or 5/596–2625. Reservations advised. Dress: informal. AE, DC, MC, V.*

# Lodging

As might be expected of a megalopolis, Mexico City has 17,000 hotel rooms—enough to accommodate every taste and budget. Though the city is huge and spread out, most hotels are located within the districts listed below, which are not far from one another. Chapultepec Park and the swank Polanco neighborhood are on the west side of the city. Paseo de la Reforma runs from Chapultepec, northeast through "midtown," and intersects with Avenida Juárez at the beginning of the downtown area. Juárez becomes Avenida Madero, which continues east to the downtown historic district and its very core, the Zócalo. The Zona Rosa, replete with boutiques, cafés, restaurants, and night spots, is just south of Reforma in the western midtown area.

The following selection is organized by the major areas of the city and then by price. Highly recommended lodgings are indicated by a star ★.

| Category | Cost* |
|---|---|
| Very Expensive | over $160 |
| Expensive | $90–$160 |
| Moderate | $40–$90 |
| Inexpensive | under $40 |

*All prices are for a standard double room, excluding service charge and sales tax (10%).*

**Airport**

**Expensive** **Fiesta Americana Aeropuerto.** Opened in 1985 and expanded since, this deluxe hotel—with climate control, a satellite color TV, radio, minibar, and purified water in every room—is located over a short footbridge from the airport terminal, making it convenient for those who arrive late and have an early morning flight. For this convenience you pay a price. Day rates (9–6) are available at about half the full rates. *Benito Juárez Airport, 15620, tel. 5/762–0199 or 800/223–2332. 340 rooms and suites. Facilities: purified water, 24-hr room service; restaurant, coffee shop, lobby bar, nightclub, pool, health center with sauna, valet, shops, car rental, garage, facilities for the handicapped. AE, DC, MC, V.*

## Chapultepec Park and Polanco

**Very Expensive**  **Camino Real.** Super luxurious and immense—about the size of
**★**  the Pyramid of the Sun in Teotihuacan—this city within a city hosts heads of state and celebrities as well as business and pleasure travelers. Impressive works of art embellishing the endless corridors and lounges include Rufino Tamayo's mural of *Man Confronting the Universe, Sighs* by painter Pedro Coronel, and an imposing sculpture by Calder. As a result of recent renovation, 100 enlarged rooms with extra-deluxe amenities now make up the fifth-floor Executive Level. Foquet's de Paris restaurant holds French culinary festivals, and the airy Azulejos features Mexican cuisine and special Sunday buffet brunches. The only drawback: It's easy to get lost in the endless corridors of this architectural masterpiece. *Mariano Escobedo 700, 11590, tel. 5/203–2121 or 800/228–3000. 713 rooms and suites. Facilities: gardens, 1 heated pool for general use, 2 pools provided exclusively for suites, 4 tennis courts, health club, 10 bars and restaurants, disco, fully bilingual business center. AE, DC, MC, V.*

**Hotel Nikko México.** One of the city's newest hotels (1987), and part of the Japanese Nikko chain, this property occupies a prime position adjacent to Chapultepec Park and Paseo de la Reforma, and just a five-minute walk to the Anthropology Museum. All rooms and suites feature air-conditioning, a color TV with U.S. Cablevision, refrigerator, radio, and phone with message service. The four Fountain Club executive floors have better rooms and extra facilities. Three top restaurants excel in their gastronomic specialties: Les Celébrités (French), Teppan Grill (Japanese), and El Jardín (Mexican). *Campos Elíseos 204, 11560, tel. 5/203–4800 or 800/NIKKO–US. 771 rooms and suites. Facilities: 24-hr room service, 3 restaurants, bar, 2 pools (1 heated), health club with Nautilus equipment, 3 tennis courts, shopping arcade, travel agency. AE, DC, MC, V.*

**Expensive–**  **Stouffer Presidente México.** Formerly called El Presidente
**Very Expensive**  Chapultepec and still referred to as such, this 42-story business/convention hotel is, like its next-door neighbor, the Nikko, adjacent to Chapultepec Park and the posh Colonia Polanco. The dramatic five-story lobby is a hollow pyramid of balconies, with music presented daily at the lively lobby bar. The rooms are immense, and all have air-conditioning, a color TV, FM radio, and work area. Those on the top two floors afford views of two snowcapped volcanoes. There are a number of smart stores and no fewer than six eateries on the premises, including a branch of Maxim's of Paris. *Campos Elíseos 218, 11560, tel. 5/327–7700, or 800/HOTELS 1. 877 rooms and suites. Facilities: 24-hr room service, 5 restaurants, lobby bar, coffee shop, shopping arcade, baby-sitting service, underground parking garage. AE, DC, MC, V.*

# Mexico City Lodging

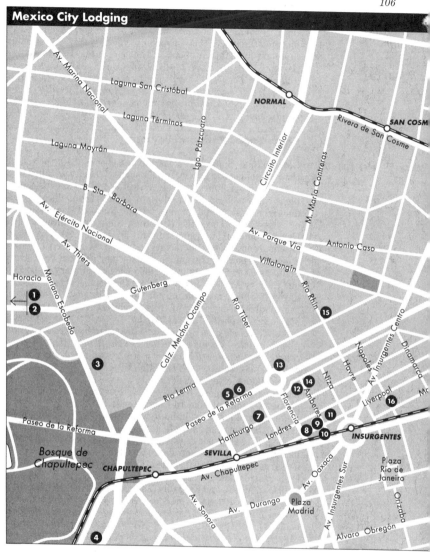

Aristos, **14**
Calinda Geneve, **11**
Camino Real, **3**
Catedral, **21**
Century, **10**
Fiesta Americana
Aeropuerto, **24**

Galería Plaza, **7**
Gran Hotel Howard
Johnson, **23**
Holiday Inn Crowne
Plaza, **18**
Hotel de Cortés, **20**
Hotel Misión
México, **16**

Hotel Nikko
México, **1**
Imperial, **19**
Krystal Rosa, **9**
Majestic Best
Western, **22**
Marco Polo, **12**
María Cristina, **15**

María Isabel Sheraton
Hotel and Towers, **13**
Marquis Reforma, **5**
Park Villa Motel, **4**
Plaza Florencia, **8**
Reforma Clarion, **6**
Sevilla Palace, **17**
Stouffer Presidente
México, **2**

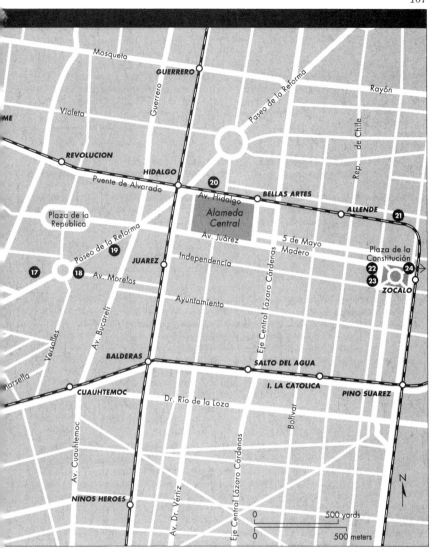

Mosqueta

GUERRERO

Rayón

Paseo de la Reforma

Guerrero

Violeta

Rep. de Chile

ME

REVOLUCION

HIDALGO

Puente de Alvarado

**20**

Av. Hidalgo

BELLAS ARTES

Alameda
Central

ALLENDE

**21**

Plaza de la
Republica

Av. Juárez

5 de Mayo

Madero

Plaza de la
Constitución

Paseo de la Reforma

**19**

Independencia

**22**

**24**

JUAREZ

**17**

**18**

Av. Morelos

**23**

ZOCALO

Eje Central Lázaro Cárdenas

Ayuntamiento

Av. Bucareli

Versalles

BALDERAS

SALTO DEL AGUA

arsella

CUAUHTEMOC

I. LA CATOLICA

PINO SUAREZ

Dr. Río de la Loza

Bolívar

Av. Cuauhtemoc

NINOS HEROES

N

Av. Dr. Vértiz

Eje Central Lázaro Cárdenas

500 yards

0

0

500 meters

**Moderate** **Park Villa Motel.** This two-story colonial hacienda, in a tranquil
★ residential setting, is ideal for travelers with a car. Overlooking its pretty garden is the Restaurant Jardín del Corregidor,
which serves authentic Spanish cuisine. If you are driving,
you'll need to get directions to its secluded site near the southeast side of Bosque de Chapultepec (Chapultepec Park). The
nearest subway stop is Juanacatlán. *Gómez Pedraza 68 (enter
at Constituyentes), 11850, tel. 5/515–5245. 45 rooms. Facilities: restaurant, color TV. No credit cards.*

## Zona Rosa

**Very Expensive** **Galería Plaza.** A Westin Hotel and part of the prestigious
★ Camino Real chain, the Plaza is convenient for shopping and
dining out in the elegant Zona Rosa. It has faultless rooms,
service, and facilities, but once inside it's hard to remember
that you are in Mexico. All rooms have air-conditioning, a
minibar, color satellite TV, and radio. Other advantages include the 24-hour restaurant, a rooftop pool with sun deck, and
a secure underground parking lot. *Hamburgo 195 at Varsovia,
06600, tel. 5/211–0014 or 800/228–3000. 434 rooms and suites.
Facilities: 24-hr room service; shops, concierge, valet parking.
AE, DC, MC, V.*

**Expensive–** **Marco Polo.** Posh and right in the center of the Zona Rosa, this
**Very Expensive** deluxe, small, yet ultramodern all-suite hotel offers the ameni-
★ ties and outstanding personalized service often associated with
a small European property. All rooms feature climate control,
a color cable TV, FM radio, minibar, and kitchenette. Rooms
on the top floor facing north have excellent views of Paseo de la
Reforma, and the U.S. Embassy is close by. In the street-level
Marco Polo Restaurant and Bar you can listen to sophisticated
live jazz at lunch, over cocktails, and at dinner. *Amberes 27,
06600, tel. 5/207–1893. 60 rooms and 4 penthouse suites with
Jacuzzi and terrace. Facilities: valet parking, multilingual
secretarial service. AE, DC, MC, V.*

**Expensive** **Aristos.** This 15-story hotel is on the busy Paseo de la Reforma,
in front of the U.S. Embassy and the Mexican Stock Exchange.
All 360 rooms are well furnished and feature the hues of the
decade: peach and mauve, with brass and wood accents. Each
room also has two phones, a radio, color TV, and an alarm clock.
The business center has a bilingual staff and a message service.
*Paseo de la Reforma 276, 06600, tel. 5/211–0112 or 800/5–
ARISTO. 360 rooms and suites. Facilities: sun deck, sauna,
gymnasium, travel agency, unisex beauty parlor. AE, DC,
MC, V.*
**Century.** This zebra-stripe high rise stands out in the middle of
the Zona Rosa. Rooms have round Roman-style marble baths,
round beds, and semicircular private balconies. Violins add a
romantic touch at the rooftop Regine restaurant, and the
street-level Petit Pois serves a good breakfast and luncheon
buffet. All rooms have a marble bath, color satellite TV, FM radio, minibar, and private balcony. The large penthouse suites
are superb. *Liverpool 152, 06600, tel. 5/584–7111 or 800/221–
6509. 143 rooms. Facilities: 2 restaurants, bar, disco, heated
swimming pool, sauna, massage, car rental, currency exchange, baby-sitting, parking. AE, DC, MC, V.*
**Krystal Rosa.** Part of the Mexican Krystal Hotel chain, this superbly run, recently remodeled high-rise hotel is centrally located and has an excellent view of the city from the pool

terrace. All rooms have a telephone, minibar, and color TV with satellite transmission. *Liverpool 155, 06600, tel. 5/211–0092 or 800/231–9860. 330 rooms. Facilities: restaurant, bar, nightclub, heated pool, business center. AE, DC, MC, V.*

**Plaza Florencia.** This is a modern hotel on a smart shopping street. Rooms are well furnished, cheerfully decorated, and soundproofed against the location's heavy traffic noise; the higher floors have views of the Angel monument. Some large family suites are available. All rooms have air-conditioning, heat, a color TV, and a phone. *Florencia 61, 06600, tel. 5/211–0064. 140 rooms, including 10 suites. Facilities: coffee shop, restaurant, bar, nightclub. AE, DC, MC, V.*

**Moderate** **Calinda Geneve.** A Quality Inn, this friendly, centrally located hotel features a remarkable gallery, the Salón Jardín, containing more plants than a greenhouse and a remarkable stained-glass ceiling. It attracts guests and nonguests alike for cocktails and dining, and a Mexican buffet luncheon is served daily, accompanied by live Mexican music. Colonial-style carved chairs and tables furnish the hotel's pleasant lobby, and the rooms are adequate if a little cramped. All are equipped with air-conditioning, a phone, minibar, and color cable TV. The clientele is almost exclusively non-Mexican. El Jardín restaurant serves wursts and sausage to the accompaniment of American jazz. *Londres 130, 06600, tel. 5/211–0071 or 800/228–5151. 347 rooms. Facilities: travel agency, boutique, grill restaurant, bar with nightly entertainment. AE, DC, MC, V.*

**Inexpensive** **Hotel Misión México.** A part of the Misión chain, this very comfortable hotel is well placed for shopping and sightseeing. All rooms are air-conditioned and have a color TV and telephone. *Nápoles 62, 06600, tel. 5/533–0535. 50 rooms. Facilities: coffee shop, lobby bar. AE, MC, V.*

## Midtown and along the Reforma

**Very Expensive** **María Isabel Sheraton Hotel and Towers.** Don Antenor Patiño, the Bolivian "Tin King," inaugurated this Mexico City classic in 1969 and named it after his granddaughter, socialite Isabel Goldsmith, who owns the Las Alamandas resort on the Pacific coast of Jalisco. The entire hotel was remodeled in 1992, but the glistening brown marble and Art Nouveau details in the lobby and other public areas remain. All guest and public rooms are impeccably maintained, but penthouse suites in the Tower Section are extra spacious and exceptionally luxurious. Rooms are air-conditioned and have minibars and cable TV. Location is prime: next to the Angel, across the Reforma from the Zona Rosa, with Sanborns next door and the U.S. Embassy just across the street. The Sheraton has one informal and two formal restaurants. *Paseo de la Reforma 325, 06500, tel. 5/207–3933 or 800/325–3535. 751 rooms and suites. Facilities: 3 restaurants, bar, outdoor swimming pool, health club with sauna and masseur, business center, shopping arcade, 24-hour room service, concierge, valet parking. AE, DC, MC, V.*

★ **Marquis Reforma.** One of Mexico City's newest and most luxurious, this hotel is within walking distance of the Zona Rosa. It has a striking pink stone and curved glass facade, and its seventh-floor suites have picture-perfect views of Chapultepec Castle. The elegant lobby is furnished in classic European style, with paintings, sculpture, and palatial furniture. Guest-room furniture and decor is Art Deco–inspired. Rooms have minibars and cable TV, and all are air-conditioned. The award-winning La Joya Restaurant specializes in northern Italian cuisine. The casual Café Royal serves both Continental and Mexican dishes. A musical quartet adds atmosphere to the Caviar Bar, a fine setting for tea or cocktails. The fully staffed Corporate Center offers state-of-the-art computer services, and guest-room phones feature a second plug for computers with fax modem. *Paseo de la Reforma 465, 06500, tel. 5/211–3600 or 800/525–4800. 200 rooms, including 84 suites. Facilities: 2 restaurants; bar; gym with Nautilus workout stations, relaxation room, and juice bar; business center; 24-hour room service; concierge; valet parking. AE, DC, MC, V.*

**Reforma Clarion.** Opened in 1988, this all-suite deluxe hotel caters to the business traveler. Facilities include a heliport, limousine service, and free car wash. The exclusive Executive Suites feature either a sauna or a Jacuzzi, and the even more deluxe Clarion Suites have both. All rooms have air-conditioning and a cable TV with movies. The Bellini Restaurant serves international cuisine with Italian accents. The 22-story hotel is located between the Zona Rosa and Chapultepec Park. *Paseo de la Reforma 373, 06500, tel. 5/207–8944 or 800/228–5151. 81 suites. Facilities: restaurant, 24-hr room service, concierge, valet parking. AE, DC, MC, V.*

**Expensive Holiday Inn Crowne Plaza.** Well organized for business travelers and large groups, this establishment has an ample selection of bars, restaurants, and entertainment, including the lively Stelaris rooftop nightclub. There is not much Mexican atmosphere, but even if the sun doesn't shine, you can get a good tan in the solarium. All rooms are equipped with a phone, minibar, and refrigerator. *Paseo de la Reforma 80, 06600, tel. 5/705–1515 or 800–HOLIDAY. 583 rooms. Facilities: restaurant, concierge, bar. AE, DC, MC, V.*

**Imperial.** Opened in 1990, the Hotel Imperial occupies a stately, turn-of-the-century European-style building right on the Reforma alongside the Columbus Monument. Quiet elegance and personal service are keynotes of this Spanish-owned property, which is part of the prestigious HUSA chain. All rooms have a cable TV, automatic-dial phone, air-conditioning, minibar, and an automatic safe. *Reforma 64, 06600, tel. 5/705–4011. 70 rooms, junior and master suites. Facilities: restaurant, café, bar, room service, travel agency, secretarial service. AE, DC, MC, V.*

**Sevilla Palace.** This is a glistening new showplace with five panoramic elevators to its 23 floors and 414 rooms, a covered rooftop pool with Jacuzzi, health club, terraced rooftop lounge with a city view, restaurants, a top-floor supper-club with entertainment, and convention halls with capacities up to 1,000. All rooms have climate control, color satellite TV, and an automatic phone. It's a well-located near the Columbus traffic circle. *Paseo de la Reforma 105, 06030; tel. 5/566–8877. 414 rooms. Facilities: concierge, valet parking. AE, DC, MC, V.*

**Moderate María Cristina.** Full of Old World charm, this Spanish Colonial-
★ style gem is a Mexico City classic. Impeccably maintained since it was built in 1937, the peach-color building surrounds a delightful garden-courtyard that is the setting for its El Retiro bar and Río Nansa restaurant. A 1990 refurbishment has resulted in three new, tastefully decorated apartment–style master suites, complete with Jacuzzis. All rooms have color cable TV, a minibar, and a safe. Located in a quiet residential set-

ting near Sullivan Park, the hotel is just a block from the Paseo de la Reforma and close to the Zona Rosa. *Río Lerma 31, 06500, tel. 5/566–9688. 156 rooms and suites. Facilities: room service, travel agency, boutique, beauty parlor, valet parking. DC, MC, V.*

## Downtown

**Moderate** **Gran Hotel Howard Johnson.** The name was changed, but locals still refer to this establishment by its original (and more appropriate) name: Gran Hotel de la Ciudad de México. Ensconced in what was formerly a 19th-century department store, this older, more traditional hotel has contemporary rooms. Its central location—adjacent to the Zócalo and near the Templo Mayor—makes it the choice of serious sightseers. And its distinctive Belle Epoque lobby is worth a visit in its own right, with a striking stained-glass Tiffany dome, chandeliers, singing canaries in gilded cages, and 19th-century wrought-iron elevators gliding smoothly up and down. All rooms are equipped with a minibar, phone, and satellite color TV. For breakfast (7–11 AM), the fourth-floor Mirador overlooks the Zócalo. The Del Centro restaurant/bar is run by Delmónicos, one of Mexico City's best. At press time, guest rooms at the hotel were being renovated. *16 de Septiembre 82, 06000, tel. 5/510–4040, or 800/654–2000. 125 rooms. Facilities: 2 restaurants, bar, concierge, travel agency, parking. AE, DC, MC, V.*

★ **Hotel de Cortés.** This delightful small hotel is housed in a colonial building (1780) that has been designated a national monument. A major renovation in 1990 has given luster and luxury to the colonial-decor rooms and added two lovely soundproofed suites overlooking Alameda Park. Climate control, a remote control color satellite TV, radio, minibar, and safe are available in each room. The new restaurant also views the park, and a friendly bar opens to the tree-shaded central courtyard and fountain, a lovely setting for tea or cocktails. Every Saturday evening (8–10 PM), a mariachi festival entertains guests and visitors. The Franz Mayer Museum is just a block away, and it's an easy walk to the Zócalo. Loyal guests make reservations through Best Western many months in advance. *Av. Hidalgo 85, 06000, tel. 5/518–2181 or 800/334–7234. 29 rooms and suites. Facilities: restaurant, bar. AE, DC, MC, V.*

**Majestic Best Western.** The atmospheric, colonial-style Hotel Majestic was built in 1937. Its location is perfect for anyone interested in exploring the downtown historic district: it is right on the Zócalo at the corner of Madero. Rooms are comfortable, and the service is efficient and courteous. The seventh-floor dining room and terrace—which feature international and Mexican specialties—have marvelous panoramas of the entire Zócalo. Breakfast is served at 7:30, and the Sunday buffet (1–5 PM) features live Mexican music. It is worth a visit just to see the view, and nonguests are welcome. Colorful hand-painted ceramic tiles and potted plants decorate the public areas. *Madero 73, 06000, tel. 5/521–8600 or 800/528–1234. 85 rooms. Facilities: restaurant, climate control, color TV, minibar. AE, DC, MC, V.*

**Inexpensive** **Catedral.** Located just one block from the Cathedral and Templo Mayor, this older hotel in the heart of the downtown historic district has been completely refurbished inside and out. The once dreary public rooms are now sparkling, with lots of mirrors, chrome, and glass. Rooms are cheerful, and the service is friendly. *Donceles 95, 06000, tel. 5/521-6183. 116 rooms. Facilities: room service, bar, nightclub, coffee shop, travel agency, free parking, laundry. AE, MC, V.*

# The Arts and Nightlife

Mexico City has a rich cultural scene and nightlife, with something for virtually every taste. Good place s to check for current events are the Friday edition of *The News*, a daily English-language newspaper, and *Tiempo Libre*, a weekly listing of activities and events in Spanish. Both are available at newsstands. Free concerts are given Sundays at 1 PM at Chapultepec Castle.

## The Arts

**Dance**  The world-renowned **Ballet Folklórico de México,** directed by Amalia Hernández, offers a stylized presentation of Mexican regional folk dances and is one of the most popular shows in Mexico. The first few acts are great fun, and it's a treat to be in the Palace of Fine Arts, but the music can be repetitious and the "dances" border on corny. Performances are given on Sundays at 9:30 AM and 9 PM and Wednesdays at 6 and 9 PM at the Palace of Fine Arts (Av. Juárez and Eje Central Lázaro Cárdenas, tel. 5/512-3633). Hotels and travel agencies can secure tickets.

Not to be confused with the above is the **Ballet Folklórico Nacional de Mexico,** directed and choreographed by Silvia Lozano. The company performs authentic regional folk dances regularly at the Teatro de la Ciudad, also known as the Mexico City Opera House (Donceles 36, tel. 5/510-2197).

The **National Dance Theater,** a component of the National Auditorium complex in Chapultepec Park, and the **Dance Center** (Campos Elíseos 480, tel. 5/520-2271) frequently sponsor modern dance performances.

**Music**  The primary venue for classical music is the **Palace of Fine Arts** (Av. Juárez and Eje Central Lázaro Cárdenas, tel. 5/512-3633), which has a main auditorium and the smaller Manuel Ponce concert hall. The National Opera has two seasons at the Palace: January–March and August–October. The National Symphony Orchestra stages classic and modern pieces at the palace in the spring and fall.

Another top concert hall is **Ollin Yolitzli** (Periférico Sur 1541, tel. 5/655-3611), which hosts the Mexico City Philharmonic several times a year. The State of Mexico Symphony performs at **Nezahualcóyotl Hall** in University City (tel. 5/655-6511). The **Teatro de la Ciudad** (Donceles 36, tel. 5/510-2197) is also a popular site for a number of musical programs, both classical and popular, year-round. And the **Sala Chopín** (Alvaro Obregón 302, tel. 5/533-1380) presents a number of free musical events throughout the week.

**Theater**  Visitors with a grasp of Spanish will find a wide choice of theatrical entertainment, including recent Broadway hits. Prices are reasonable compared with stage productions of similar caliber in the United States. Though Mexico City has no central theater district, most theaters are a 15- to 30-minute taxi ride from the major hotels. The top theaters include **Hidalgo** (Av.

Hidalgo 23, tel. 5/521–3859), **Julio Prieto** (Nicolás San Juan at Zola, tel. 5/543–3478), **Insurgentes** (Av. Insurgentes Sur 1587, tel. 5/660–2304), and **San Rafael** (Virginia Fábregas 40, tel. 5/592–2142).

## Nightlife

*Night* is the key word to understanding the timing of going out in Mexico City. People generally have cocktails at 7 or 8 PM, take in dinner and a show at 10 or 11, head to the discos at midnight, and then find a spot for a nightcap somewhere around 3 AM. The easiest way for the non-Spanish-speaking visitor to do this is on a nightclub tour (*see* Guided Tours, in Essential Information, *above*). However, those who set off on their own should have no trouble getting around. For starters, Niza and Florencia streets in the Zona Rosa are practically lined with nightclubs, bars, and discos that are especially lively on Friday and Saturday nights. The big hotels offer both bars and places to dance or be entertained, and they are frequented by locals. Outside of the Zona Rosa, Paseo de la Reforma, Avenida Juárez and Insurgentes Sur have the greatest concentration of night spots. Remember that the capital's high altitude makes liquor extremely potent, even jolting. Imported booze is very expensive, so you may want to stick with what the Mexicans order: tequila, rum, and *cerveza* (beer).

**Dinner Theater**  The splashiest shows are found in the big hotels and in Zona Rosa clubs. **El Patio** (Atenas 9, tel. 5/535–3904) is a classic, old-style nightclub with tiny tables, surly waiters, and poor food; go there only if you must see one of the headliners, such as Julio Iglesias or Vicky Carr. **El Gran Caruso** (Londres 25, on the edge of the Zona Rosa, tel. 5/545–1199) is where the waiters sing arias between courses. In the Crowne Hotel Plaza, **Stelaris** (Paseo de la Reforma 80, tel. 5/566–7777) has top entertainers (performing Mon.–Sat. at midnight), good food, and music for dancing. Strolling violinists serenade the patrons of **Regine** (Hotel Century, Londres at Amberes, tel. 5/584–7111). **La Veranda** (María Isabel Sheraton, Paseo de la Reforma 325, tel. 5/211–0001) serves dinner while international-caliber stars perform; afterward the dance floor is open. Mexican headliners perform at **Maquiavelo** (Hotel Krystal Rosa, Zona Rosa, tel. 5/211–0092) Mon.–Sat. at 11 PM and 1 AM.

**Discos**  Dance emporiums in the capital run the gamut from cheek-to-cheek romantic to throbbing strobe lights and ear-splitting music. Most places have a cover charge, but it is rarely more than $10. **Lipstick** (Hotel Aristos, Paseo de la Reforma 274, tel. 5/211–0112) is a longtime favorite where the action begins nightly at around 10. **Cero Cero** (Camino Real, Mariano Escobedo 700, Polanco, tel. 5/545–6560) has live bands as well as tapes and is open every night 9 PM–4 AM. **Le Chic** (Hotel Galería Plaza, Hamburgo at Varsovia, Zona Rosa, tel. 5/211–0014) is small, elegant, with stuffed chairs, and deafening modern sounds. It's open Mon.–Sat. 9 PM–3 AM. The emphasis is on romantic mood music and touch dancing at **Valentino's** (Florencia 36, Zona Rosa, tel. 5/525–2020), which is open Mon.–Sat. 9 PM–4 AM.

**Hotel Bars**  The lobby bars in the **María Isabel Sheraton** (Reforma 325), **Stouffer Presidente México** (Campos Elíseos 218, Polanco), and **Camino Real** (Mariano Escobedo 900, Polanco) are all good bets for a sophisticated crowd and lively music, usually until around midnight.

**After Midnight** **Afro Tramonto** features a raunchy but not overly rowdy show that appeals to gentlemen, though escorted ladies are welcome. *Av. Insurgentes and Sullivan, on the north side of Paseo de la Reforma, tel. 5/546–8807. Cover: $4. Open Mon.–Sat. 10 PM–4 AM.*

**Gitanerías** continues to be an authentic Spanish flamenco nightclub (*tablao*). Now, in addition to a fiery flamenco there is also disco dancing to flamenco and Latin rhythms. Only light supper and drinks are served, and the first show starts at midnight. *Oaxaca 15, Col. Roma, tel. 5/208–2264. Closed Mon.*

The traditional last stop for nocturnal Mexicans is **Plaza Garibaldi,** where exuberant mariachis gather to unwind after evening performances—by performing even more. They play in the square and inside the cantinas and clubs surrounding it; the better ones are **Guadalajara de Noche** (tel. 5/526–5521) and **Tenampa** (tel. 5/526–6176). If the extroverted singer-musicians focus on you, a friendly smile and a tip are expected. *Open daily until 4 AM and even later on Fri. and Sat.*

# Excursions

## Xochimilco, Cuernavaca, and Tepoztlán

This excursion to the south and southwest of Mexico City begins in Xochimilco (*So-chee-MEEL-co*), famous for its floating gardens, where visitors can take rides in gondolalike boats and get a fleeting sense of pre-Hispanic Mexico City. Beyond Xochimilco, in the neighboring state of Morelos, lies Cuernavaca, a weekend retreat for wealthy chilangos and foreigners. The climate in Cuernavaca, just 85 kilometers (53 miles) and an altitude descent of almost 2,500 feet from Mexico City, changes dramatically to lush, semitropical. The city is known for its many Spanish-language schools, the beautiful Borda Gardens, and Diego Rivera murals in the Palacio de Cortés (Palace of Cortés). An overnight stay is recommended. From Cuernavaca we suggest a detour to Tepoztlán, which features a 16th-century Dominican convent.

**Tourist** The **Morelos State Tourist Office** in Cuernavaca is located on the
**Information** south side of the Borda Gardens. *Morelos Sur 802, tel. 73/14–38–60. Open weekdays 9–8, Sat. 9–6, Sun. 9–3.*

**Getting Around** To reach Xochimilco by car, take Periférico Sur to the extension of División del Norte; an alternate route is from Calzada de Tlalpán to Calzada México Xochimilco and then Calzada Guadalupe Ramírez. Xochimilco is 21 kilometers (13 miles) from the Zócalo in Mexico City; the trip should take between 45 minutes and 1 hour, depending on traffic. If Xochimilco is your final destination, you are probably better off taking a taxi. By public transportation, take metro line No. 2 to Taxqueña and then any bus marked Xochimilco.

To continue south by car, return to Periférico Sur, turn left (south) on Viaducto Tlalpán, and watch for signs to Cuernavaca. The *cuota*, or toll road (Rte. 95D), costs about U.S. $5 but is much faster than the *carretera libre*, or free road (Rte. 95).

Route 95D will take you about 1½ hours to cover 85 kilometers (53 miles).

Tepoztlán is 26 kilometers (16 miles) east of Cuernavaca via Route 95D. Buses also run every 20 minutes.

**Exploring Xochimilco** According to legend, the Xochimilcas were the first of the seven Nahuatl tribes to leave Aztlán, the mythical Aztec homeland in the north. Reaching Xochimilco ("the place where flowers are planted") between AD 900 and 1200, they devised a system of *chinampas* (floating gardens) to grow and transport food along the canals of Tenochtitlan. Originally, the gardens were anchored with roots, poles, and mud; as they grew, and the waters receded, they became permanently affixed to the lakebed. Canoes carried the flowers and produce to the capital.

Today Xochimilco is the only place in Mexico where the gardens still exist. Go on a Saturday, when the *tianguis* (market) is most active, or on a Sunday. (Note that Xochimilco is a popular destination for families on Sundays.) On weekdays the place is practically deserted, so it loses much of its charm. Hire a *trajinera* (flower-covered launch); an arch over each launch spells out its name—usually a diminutive for a woman's name—in flowers. As you sail through the canals, you'll pass mariachis and women selling tacos from other launches.

**Exploring Cuernavaca** Downtown Cuernavaca is fairly compact. The most attractive sights are the mansions of the wealthy weekenders set in the hills on the edge of town, but you must be a guest to get in. The four main sites are located near the main square. The **Palacio de Cortés**—Cortés's palace-cum-fortress—now houses the **Museo de Cuauhnáhuac** (Museum of Cuauhnáhuac, the Indian name for Cuernavaca), which focuses on Mexican history before and after the conquest. On permanent exhibit is a collection of some of Diego Rivera's finest murals, which, like those of Mexico City's National Palace, dramatize the history and the horrors of the conquest, colonialism, and the revolution. The beautiful and spacious **Jardín Borda** (Borda Gardens), three blocks west, was designed in the late 18th century by one member of the Borda family (rich miners of French extraction) for one of his relatives; Maximilian and Carlotta visited the gardens frequently, and novelist Malcolm Lowry turned them into a sinister symbol in *Under the Volcano*. Opposite the gardens is the **Catedral de la Asunción,** an architecturally eclectic structure noteworthy for its 17th-century Japanese wall paintings. Diagonally opposite the cathedral is the **Palacio Municipal;** the paintings inside depict life in the city before the Spaniards.

**Exploring Tepoztlán** This tiny village is best known for its pyramid, and for the dances held here during Carnival, when celebrants don bright masks depicting birds, animals, and Christian figures. Anthropologists Robert Redfield and Oscar Lewis both did fieldwork here in the 1950s. The landmark is the multibuttressed Ex-Convent (1559), with fine paneled doors adorned with Indian motifs.

## Cholula, Puebla, and Tlaxcala

The three major destinations on this excursion are located in the state of Puebla. The capital city, also called Puebla, is a good 1½ to 3 hours by car southeast of Mexico City, depending on whether you use the toll highway or the more scenic road.

You can detour along the way to see the volcanoes, Popocate-petl and Ixtaccihuatl, up close. On your return to the capital, consider a stop in Tlaxcala, with its rare church and ex-convent of San Francisco. Cholula, one of the most sacred spots in ancient Mexico, has scores of churches and a pyramid that is considered to be the largest in the world in terms of volume, consisting of several layers built on top of one another over the centuries. The pyramid was an important ceremonial center during pre-Hispanic times; subsequently, the Spaniards built a large church on top of it. Puebla, another well-preserved colonial city only 8 kilometers (5 miles) east of Cholula, was the center of the Spanish tile industry; and the town of Tehuacán, another 115 kilometers (71 miles) southeast, was a thermal spa before Columbus's time. Mexico's best brands of mineral water are bottled there.

**Tourist Information**
The **Puebla Tourist Office** can supply information. *3 Sur 1501, tel. 22/37–50–13. Open daily 10–2 and 4–7.*

**Getting Around**
From Mexico City, head east toward the airport and turn onto Calzada Zaragoza, the last wide boulevard before arriving at the airport; it becomes the Puebla Highway at the toll booth. Route 190D is the toll road straight to Puebla; Route 150 is the free road. To go directly to Cholula, take the exit at San Martín Texmelucan and follow the signs. From Puebla, Cholula is a couple of kilometers west. To stop at the volcanoes, take the free road 33 kilometers (20 miles) to Chalco. From there it is 4 kilometers (2.5 miles) to the Amecameca-Chalco sign, from which you continue 22 kilometers (13.6 miles) on Route 115 to Amecameca. To Tehuacán, follow Route 150 from Puebla for 115 kilometers (71 miles).

**Exploring Cholula**
As you leave Mexico City—if the smog is not too thick—the **volcanoes** will be visible to the south. "Popo" is 5,455 meters (17,887 ft) high. To see it up close you should exit at either of the main highways at Chalco and follow the signs to the Parque Nacional. Popo last erupted in 1802. The legend states that Popocatepetl, an Aztec warrior, had been sent by the emperor—father of his beloved Ixtacchuatl—to bring back the head of a feared enemy in order to win Ixtacchuatl's hand. He returned triumphantly only to find that Ixtacchuatl had killed herself, believing him dead. The grief-stricken Popo laid out her body on a small knoll and lit an eternal torch that he watches over, kneeling. Each of the four peaks composing the volcano is named after different parts of her body—hence its nickname "The Sleeping Lady." (In addition, the silhouette of the volcano resembles the figure of a reclining woman.) Climbing Popo or "Ixta" is for serious mountaineers, but the park, a verdant pine forest, makes a good spot for a picnic.

Most of the 40 colonial churches in Cholula are in poor condition, but 6.4 kilometers (4 miles) south of town, in **San Francisco Acatepec,** is one of the two most stunning and well-preserved churches in the country. Completely covered with Puebla tiles, it has been called the most ornate Poblano Rococo facade in Mexico. Equally unusual is the interior of the church in **Santa María Tonantzintla,** 3.2 kilometers (2 miles) toward Cholula. Its polychrome wood-and-stucco carvings—inset columns, altarpieces, and the main archway—are the epitome of Churrigueresque. Set off by ornate gold-leaf figures of vegetal forms, angels, and saints, the carvings were done by native craftsmen.

Closer to town, the **Great Pyramid** was the centerpiece of a Toltec and then Aztec religious center and consists of seven superimposed structures connected by tunnels and stairways. The Spaniards, as they often did, built a chapel to **Nuestra Señora de los Remedios** (Our Lady of the Remedies) on top of it. Behind the pyramid is a vast temple complex of 43 acres, once dedicated to Quetzalcóatl. *Small admission charge. Open daily 10–5.*

**Exploring Puebla**  Maize was first cultivated in the Tehuacán Valley; later, the region was a crossroads for many ancient Mesoamerican cultures, including the Olmecs and Totonacs. The town of Puebla is notable for its idiosyncratic Baroque structures, which are built of red brick, gray stone, white stucco, and the beautiful Talavera tiles produced from local clay. The Battle of May 5, 1862—resulting in a short-lived victory against French invaders—took place just north of town. The national holiday, Cinco de Mayo, is celebrated yearly on that date in its honor.

While in Puebla, don't miss the **Cathedral.** Onyx, marble, and gold adorn the high altar, designed by Mexico's most illustrious colonial architect, Manuel Tolsá.

The colonial **Convento de Santa Rosa,** now a ceramics museum, contains the intricately tiled kitchen where Puebla's renowned mole sauce was invented by the nuns as a surprise for their demanding gourmet bishop. Puebla is also famous for *camote,* a popular candy made from sweet potatoes and fruit. La Calle de las Dulces (Sweet Street) is lined with shops competing to sell a wide variety of freshly made camote.

**Exploring Tehuacán**  Tehuacán is a good place to stop and relax for a night or two on your way to or from Oaxaca. The principal sight is the **Museo de la Valle de Tehuacán (the Ex-Convento del Carmen),** with exhibits on the development of agriculture. The appeal of "taking the waters" has faded over time, though there are several mineral-water swimming pools at ex-haciendas outside of town.

**Exploring Tlaxcala**  Capital of the tiny state of the same name, Tlaxcala (*Tlas-CA-la*) will interest church lovers. (At Carnival time it also hosts some spectacular dances.) The **monastery complex of San Francisco** (1537–40), which stands atop a hill one block from the handsome main square, was the first permanent Catholic edifice in the New World. The most unusual feature of the church is its wood ceiling beams, carved and gilded after the Moorish fashion. (Moorish, or *mudéjar,* architecture appeared in Mexico only during the very early years after the conquest, when Spain was still close enough in time to the Moorish occupation to be greatly influenced by Arabic architectural styles.) The austere convent, now a museum of history, boasts 18th-century religious paintings and a small collection of pre-Columbian pieces. Near the convent is a beautiful outdoor chapel whose symmetrical rear arches show Moorish and Gothic traces.

The **Palacio de Gobierno** (Government Palace), which occupies the north side of the Zócalo, was built in about 1550. Inside are vivid epic murals of Tlaxcala before the conquest, painted in the 1960s by local artist Desiderio Hernández Xochitiotzin.

About 1 kilometer (less than a mile) west of Tlaxcala is the large, ornate **Sanctuary of Ocotlán.** It dates from the 18th century and was built on the site of a miracle performed by the Virgin. (In 1541, during a severe drought, she answered the

prayers of an Indian by causing water to flow from the ground.)
Noteworthy are the Churrigueresque, white plaster facade,
which conjures up images of a wedding cake; the two Poblano
(red-tile) towers; and, inside, the brilliantly painted and gilded
Camarín chapel.

## Toluca and Valle de Bravo

This excursion to the west of Mexico City encompasses Toluca,
capital of the state of Mexico and renowned for its Friday market but not much else, and Valle de Bravo, a lovely lakeside village popular with vacationing chilangos that because of its
lush, green setting is often called Mexico's Switzerland. We
suggest a brief stop en route at Desierto de los Leones, a
forested national park whose centerpiece is an intriguing Carmelite monastery.

**Tourist Information**  The **Mexico State Tourist Office** in Toluca is located at Edificio
Plaza Toluca. *Av. 5 Lerdo de Tejada Pte. 101, tel. 721/4–10–99.
Open weekdays 9–8, Sat. 9–3.*

**Getting Around**  By car from Mexico City, take Boulevard López Mateos to
Calzada al Desierto de los Leones if you are going to the park.
To go straight to Toluca, follow Paseo de la Reforma all the way
west (it eventually merges with the Carretera a Toluca). Buses
depart Terminal Poniente every 20 minutes. There are two
choices for getting to Valle de Bravo: the winding but scenic
route, which you pick up 3.2 kilometers (2 miles) west of
Zincantepec, or Route 15. The former takes twice as much time
but is worth it if you have the time and enjoy unspoiled mountain scenery.

**Exploring Toluca**  On your way to Toluca, consider a brief stop at the **Desierto de
los Leones**, a 5,000-acre national park 30 kilometers (18.6 miles)
west of Mexico City. Deer and armadillos roam in the pine forest, and there are several walking trails. The focal point is the
ruined 17th-century Carmelite ex-monastery, strangely isolated amid an abundance of greenery. Guides will point out the
incongruous torture chambers. The park played a significant
role during the War of Independence: At a spot called Las Cruces, the troops of Father Hidalgo trounced the Spaniards but
resolved not to go on and attack Mexico City, an error that cost
the insurgents 10 more years of fighting.

The capital of the state of Mexico, Toluca is an industrial town.
Go only on a Friday (market day); but before venturing into the
market, stop at the **Casa de Artesanías** on Paseo Tollocán to get
a feel for the prices. Specialties in the market come from surrounding villages and include serapes, rebozos, coarse wool
sweaters, pottery, and cotton cloth.

**Time Out**  If you fancy a picnic and don't mind a bit of a drive, make a 44-
kilometer (27-mile) detour south of Toluca on Route 130 to
**Nevado de Toluca Park.** At 4,691 meters (15,390 feet), the
Nevado de Toluca, a now-extinct volcano, is Mexico's fourth-
largest mountain; on clear days its crater affords wonderful
views of the valley. Picnickers might also enjoy a stop at **Parque
de los Venados** (Park of the Deer).

**Exploring Valle de Bravo**  Valle de Bravo is colonial, with white stucco houses trimmed
with red balconies, tile roofs, and red-potted succulents clut-
tering the doorways. The town is hilly, many of the streets are

unpaved, and beyond it lies Lake Avándaro, which is surrounded by pines and mountains. Valle was founded in 1530. There are no historical monuments to speak of, but plenty of diversions: boating, waterskiing, and swimming in the lake and its waterfalls, and the more sociable pleasures of the Sunday market, where exceptionally good pottery is the draw. Although Valle is an enclave for artists and the wealthy, it attracts inhabitants who prefer a low profile.

## Basílica de Guadalupe, Teotihuacan, Pachuca, and Tula

Hugging the roads to the north of Mexico City are several of the country's most celebrated pre-Columbian and colonial monuments. The Basílica de Guadalupe, a church dedicated to Mexico's patron saint, and the pyramids of Teotihuacan make an easy day tour, as does the combination of the ex-convent (now a magnificent museum of the viceregal period) at Tepotzotlán and the ruins at Tula. Pachuca, however, is farther north and is more comfortably visited as part of an overnight excursion.

**Tourist Information** The **Hidalgo State Tourist Office** in Pachuca can help you. *Allende 406, tel. 771/3-95-00. Open weekdays and Sat. morning.*

**Getting Around** To reach La Villa de Guadalupe by car, take Avenida Insurgentes Norte to the Pachuca toll road (Rte. 85); the side road for Acolmán is 3 kilometers (1.9 miles) after the toll booth. Buses run every half hour from the Central de Autobuses del Norte to Teotihuacan, and the trip takes about one hour. Pachuca is a good 77 kilometers (48 miles) beyond Teotihuacan and can be reached either by doubling back to Route 85 or along the old road to Pachuca via Epazoyucán.

To get to Tepotzotlán from Mexico City, follow Periférico Norte out to the Carretera a Querétaro. After 41 kilometers (25.4 miles) there is a detour for Tepotzotlán. Tula is about 8 kilometers (5 miles) north of Teotihuacan off Route 57D. Buses to Tula leave Mexico City every 20 minutes; from Pachuca, every 15 minutes.

**Exploring La Villa de Guadalupe** "La Villa"—more formally known as La Villa de Guadalupe, the site of the two Basilicas of the Virgin of Guadalupe—is technically within the northern limits of Mexico City (The No. 3 metro line goes from downtown to the **Basílica** stop). Also, it can easily be visited in combination with the pyramids of Tenochtitlan farther north. From here the Spaniards laid siege to Tenochtitlan in 1521, and in 1867 La Villa served as Porfiro Díaz's headquarters for the ousting of Emperor Maximilian. But the area's symbolic importance derives from the miracle that transpired here on December 12, 1531, when an Indian named Juan Diego received from the Virgin a cloak permanently imprinted with her image so he could prove to the priests that he had indeed had a holy vision. On that date each year, millions of pilgrims arrive, many crawling on their knees for the last few hundred meters, and praying for cures and other divine favors. The **Basílica Vieja** (Old Basilica) dates from 1536, although various additions were made during the intervening centuries; the altar was executed by sculptor Manuel Tolsá. The basilica now houses a museum of ex-votos (votive offerings) and popular religious art, painting, sculpture, and decorative and applied arts from the 15th to the 18th century.

The old church is no longer large enough to accommodate all worshipers. In 1976 the government erected the **Basílica Nueva** (New Basilica), a grotesque and most unchurchlike mass of steel, wood, resinous fibers, and polyethylene designed by Pedro Ramírez Vázquez, who is also the architect of the Museum of Anthropology. It holds 10,000 people; the famous cloak is enshrined in its own altar and can be viewed from a moving sidewalk that passes below it.

**Exploring Teotihuacan** Most tour buses to the ruins stop briefly in **Acolmán** to see the outstanding Gothic church and ex-convent, now a museum. The original Augustinian church (1539) is noteworthy for its vaulted roof and pointed towers; the ornate cloister and Plateresque facade, set off with candelabralike columns, were added a century later by the monks.

Teotihuacan occupies a monumental place in early Mexican history that is easily matched by the physical grandeur and scale of the site itself: The **Pyramid of the Sun** extends over 4,640 square feet and has 248 steps to climb. (Bring comfortable walking shoes, sunscreen or visored hat; women should wear slacks.) Only the pyramids of Cholula and Cheops (Egypt) are larger.

Climbing one pyramid is probably enough for most people; in any event you will have a good view of the smaller **Pyramid of the Moon** at the northern end of the Street of the Dead. Since the entire site encompasses 13 square kilometers (8 square miles), you may actually end up visiting only one or two of the 15 or so complexes. Note the carvings of Quetzalcóatl, the plumed serpent, and Tlaloc, the god of rain, on the Temple of Quetzalcóatl, and the blood-red traces of ancient murals in the Palace of the Jaguar and the Temple of the Plumed Conch Shells.

The artifacts uncovered at Teotihuacan are on display at the Museum of Anthropology in Mexico City. The on-site museum contains only scale models and chronological charts. A light-and-sound show is performed at the site nightly October–May, Tuesday–Sunday at 7 PM.

Seeing the ruins will take two to four hours, depending on how taken you are with the place (or when your tour bus leaves).

**Exploring Pachuca** Capital of the state of Hidalgo, Pachuca was founded by the Spaniards in the early 16th century. The town grew quickly once silver was discovered in the area. It is situated high up in the Sierra Madre and is more appealing for its vaguely colonial ambience than for any individual sight. Among the structures from the viceregal era, see the **Casa de Caja** (1670), built to house the "king's fifth" of all silver mined, which was destined for the Spanish crown. Also downtown is the **Casa Colorada,** the red-stone home of the counts of Regla. The **Museo Nacional de la Fotografía** is housed in the 17th-century Ex-Monastery of San Francisco and specializes in rare photographic archives from the revolution.

**Exploring Tepotzotlán** The **church** and **monastery of San Francisco Javier** at Tepotzotlán rank among the masterpieces of Mexican Churrigueresque architecture. The unmitigated Baroque facade of the church (1682) is the first thing to catch the eye, but inside and out, every square inch has been worked over, like an over-

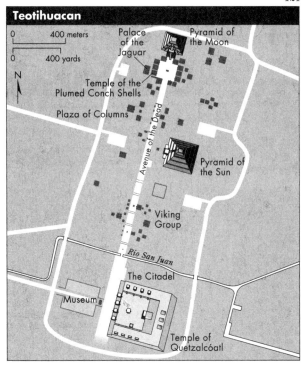

**Teotihuacan**

0 ——— 400 meters

0 ——— 400 yards

N

Palace of the Jaguar

Pyramid of the Moon

Temple of the Plumed Conch Shells

Plaza of Columns

Avenue of the Dead

Pyramid of the Sun

Viking Group

Rio San Juan

The Citadel

Museum

Temple of Quetzalcóatl

dressed Christmas tree. Note especially the gilded, bemirrored Chapel of the Loreto.

**Exploring Tula**   Tula, capital of the Toltecs (its original name was Tollán), was founded in about AD 1000 and abandoned two centuries later. It is the 4.5-meter (15-foot) warrior statues (called *atlantes*), rather than the ruins themselves, that give Tula its fame. These basalt figures tower over Pyramid B, their harsh geometric lines looking vaguely like totem poles. Crocodiles, jaguars, coyotes, and eagles are also depicted in the carvings and represent the various warrior orders of the Toltecs.

# 4  Baja California

# Tijuana

By Maribeth
Mellin

A former senior
editor of San Diego
Magazine,
Maribeth Mellin is
a San Diego–based
freelance writer
and photographer.
She has been
making regular
forays to Mexico
for the past 10
years.

Just 29 kilometers (18 miles) south of San Diego lies Tijuana, Mexico's fourth-largest city. A metropolis, Tijuana can no longer be called a border "town." The official language is Spanish, but many here speak "Spanglish," a mix of Spanish and English. Residents come from throughout Mexico and Central America; visitors come from all over. Tijuana's promoters like to call it "the most visited city in the world," and certainly the border crossing at Tijuana is the busiest in the United States. Tijuana has served as a gigantic recreation center for southern Californians since the turn of the century. Before that it was a ranch, populated by a few hundred Mexicans. In 1911 a group of Americans invaded the area and attempted to set up an independent republic; they were quickly driven out by Mexican soldiers. When Prohibition hit the United States in the 1920s, Tijuana boomed. The Agua Caliente Racetrack and Casino opened in 1929. Americans seeking alcohol, gambling, and more fun than they could find back home flocked across the border, spending freely, which fueled the region's growth. Tijuana became the entry port for what some termed a "sinful, steamy playground," frequented by Hollywood stars and the idle rich. Then Prohibition was repealed, Mexico outlawed gambling, and Tijuana's fortunes dwindled. The Agua Caliente Resort fell into ruin and has never been revived.

The flow of travelers from the north slowed to a trickle for a while, but Tijuana still captivated those in search of the sort of fun that was illegal or just frowned upon at home. The evergrowing numbers of servicemen in San Diego kept Tijuana's sordid reputation alive. Before the toll highway to Ensenada was finished in 1967, travelers going south drove straight through downtown Tijuana, stopping along Avenida Revolución and its side streets for supplies and souvenirs.

The city's population has mushroomed—from 300,000 in 1970 to more than 1.5 million today. The city has spread into canyons and dry riverbeds, over hillsides, and onto ocean cliffs.

City leaders have come to realize that tourism creates jobs and bolsters Tijuana's fragile economy, and have begun to work hard to attract visitors. Avenida Revolución, the main street that was once lined with brothels and bars, has undergone tremendous rehabilitation. Today the avenue is lined with shops and restaurants, all catering to tourists. Park benches and shade trees on brick paths winding away from the traffic encourage visitors to linger and watch the scenery. Many tourists are regulars, with favorite shops and restaurants. San Diegans often travel south of the border just for dinner and become neighbors of sorts, making friends with the locals.

Tijuana's tourist attractions have remained much the same throughout the century. Betting on horses and greyhounds is legal and popular at the Agua Caliente Racetrack. The impressive El Palacio Frontón (Jai Alai Palace), where betting is also allowed, draws crowds of cheering fans to its fast-paced matches.

Some of Spain's and Mexico's greatest bullfighters appear at the oceanfront and downtown bullrings; some of Latin America's most popular musicians and dancers perform at the Cul-

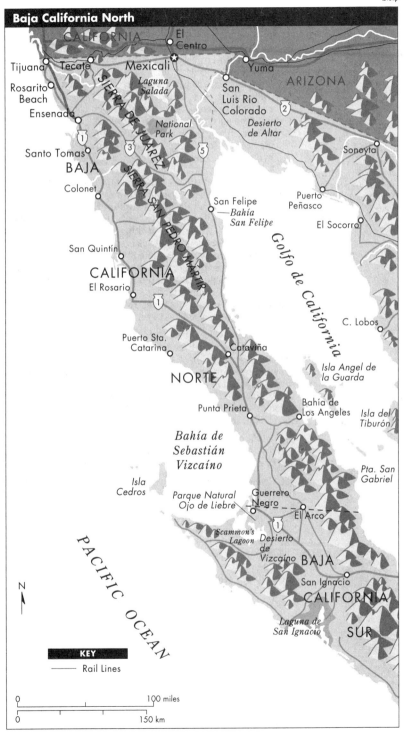

**Baja California North**

CALIFORNIA

El Centro

Tijuana
Tecate
Mexicali
Yuma
ARIZONA

Rosarito Beach

San Luis Rio Colorado

Ensenada

SIERRA DE JUAREZ

Laguna Salada

National Park

Desierto de Altar

Sonoyta

Santo Tomas

BAJA

Colonet

SIERRA SAN PEDRO MARTIR

San Felipe
—Bahía San Felipe

Puerto Peñasco

El Socorro

San Quintín

CALIFORNIA

El Rosario

Puerto Sta. Catarina

Cataviña

NORTE

C. Lobos

Golfo de California

Isla Angel de la Guarda

Punta Prieta

Bahía de Los Angeles

Isla del Tiburón

Bahía de Sebastián Vizcaíno

Pta. San Gabriel

Isla Cedros

Parque Natural Ojo de Liebre

Guerrero Negro

El Arco

Scammon's Lagoon

Desierto de Vizcaíno

BAJA

N

San Ignacio

PACIFIC OCEAN

CALIFORNIA

Laguna de San Ignacio

SUR

**KEY**
— Rail Lines

0 _____ 100 miles
0 _____ 150 km

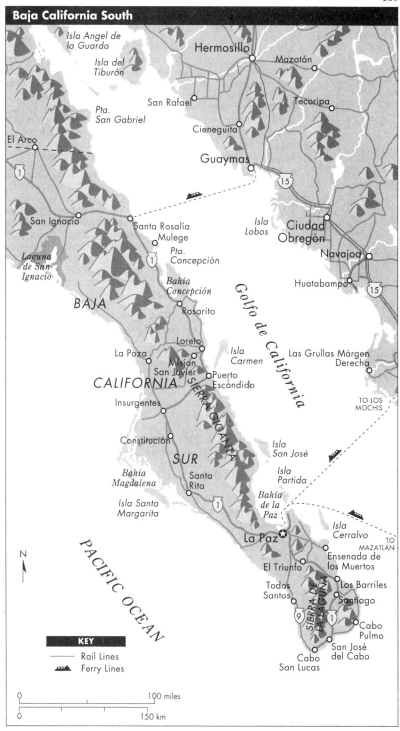

# Baja California South

Isla Angel de la Guarda

Isla del Tiburón

Hermosillo

Mazatán

San Rafael

Pta. San Gabriel

Cieneguita

Tecoripa

El Arco

Guaymas

15

San Ignacio

Santa Rosalía

Mulege

Isla Lobos

Ciudad Obregón

Laguna de San Ignacio

Pta. Concepción

Navajoa

BAJA

Bahía Concepción

Huatabampo

15

Rosarito

Loreto

Isla Carmen

Las Grullas Márgen Derecha

La Poza

Misión San Javier

Puerto Escondido

Golfo de California

TO LOS MOCHIS

CALIFORNIA

SIERRA GIGANTA

Insurgentes

Constitución

Isla San José

SUR

Isla Partida

Bahía Magdalena

Santa Rita

Bahía de la Paz

Isla Santa Margarita

1

Isla Cerralvo

TO MAZATLAN

La Paz

El Triunfo

Ensenada de los Muertos

N

Todos Santos

Los Barriles

PACIFIC OCEAN

SIERRA DE LA LAGUNA

Santiago

9

1

Cabo Pulmo

San José del Cabo

Cabo San Lucas

## KEY

—— Rail Lines

🚂 Ferry Lines

0       100 miles

0       150 km

tural Center; and there are an extraordinary number of places in town that provide good food and drinks.

Shopping is one of Tijuana's other main draws. From the moment you cross the border, people will approach you or call out and insist that you look at their wares. If you drive, workers will run out from auto-body shops to place bids on new paint or upholstery for your car. All along Avenida Revolución and its side streets, shops sell everything from tequila to Tiffany lamps; serious shoppers can spend a full day searching and bargaining for their items of choice. If you intend to buy food in Mexico, get the U.S. customs list of articles that are illegal to bring back so that your purchases won't be confiscated.

The Río Tijuana area, called the Zona Río, is quickly becoming the city's glamorous zone. The area is not far from the border, just past the usually dry riverbed of the Tijuana River along Paseo de los Héroes. This boulevard is one of the city's main thoroughfares, with large statues of historical figures, including one of Abraham Lincoln, in the center of the *glorietas* (traffic circles). The Plaza Río Tijuana, built on Paseo de los Héroes in 1982, was Tijuana's first major shopping center. Pueblo Amigo, a shopping and entertainment complex at the north end of the Zona Río, just 300 meters (328 yards) from the border, has a pedestrian walkway that leads from the border and through the plaza to Boulevard Paseo de los Héroes.

### Arriving and Departing by Plane

**Mexicana** (tel. 800/531–7921), **Aeroméxico** (tel. 800/237–6639), and **Aero California** (tel. 800/237–6225) serve many cities in Mexico, with fares that are often lower than those for flights from the United States. No U.S. carriers fly into Tijuana. The airport is located on the eastern edge of the city, near the Otay Mesa border crossing. The cab fare from the San Ysidro border is about $8 per person; from the Otay Mesa border, about $10. Shuttle services operate Volkswagen vans *(combis)* from the airport to downtown and the borders.

### Arriving and Departing by Car, Trolley, and Bus

**By Car** U.S.–5 and I–805 end at the border crossing in San Ysidro; Highway 905 leads from I–5 and I–805 to the border crossing at Otay Mesa, near the Tijuana airport. Day-trippers often prefer to park their cars on the U.S. side and walk across the border. There are acres of parking lots by the border, charging from $5 to $10 per day. Park at a guarded lot, since break-ins are common. Those driving into Tijuana should purchase Mexican auto insurance, available at many stands along the last exit before the border crossing. On holidays and weekends there can be a wait at the border when traveling into Mexico. The wait to get back into the United States can be as long as two hours, though lines are usually shorter at the Otay Mesa crossing.

Many car-rental companies do not allow their cars to be driven into Mexico. **Avis** (tel. 800/331–1212) permits its cars to go into Baja California as far as the state line at Guerrero Negro. Cars leased from **Courtesy Rentals** (2975 Pacific Hwy., San Diego, 92101, tel. 619/497–4800 or 800/252–9756 in CA) may be taken as far as Ensenada and San Felipe. **M&M Jeeps** (2200 El Cajon Blvd., tel. 619/297–1615) rents two- and four-wheel-drive vehicles with packages covering tours of the entire Baja California Peninsula.

**By Trolley** The **San Diego Trolley** (tel. 619/231–1466) travels from the Santa Fe Depot, at Kettner Boulevard and Broadway, to within 100 feet of the border every 15 minutes during the day (every 30 minutes after 7:30 PM). The 45-minute trip costs $2.

**By Bus** **Greyhound** (tel. 619/239–3266 or 800/528–0447) serves Tijuana from San Diego several times daily. **Mexicoach** (tel. 619/232–5049) has several departures from the Santa Fe Depot to Tijuana. **Baja California Tours** (6986 La Jolla Blvd., #204, La Jolla, CA 92037, tel. 619/454–7166, fax 619/454–2703) has daily bus tours to Tijuana and on to Rosarito, Ensenada, and San Felipe. **Autotransportes de Baja California** (tel. 66/85–8472) links Tijuana with other points in Baja; **Tres Estrellas de Oro** (tel. 66/86–9186) travels into mainland Mexico, and **Autotransportes del Pacífico** (tel. 66/86–9045) has service to the Pacific Coast. The Tijuana Central Bus Station is at Calzada Lázaro Cárdenas and Blvd. Arroyo Alamar (tel. 66/80–9060).

### Getting Around

Although more border stations are being opened, there are still long lines to reenter the United States, so those who plan to spend just a day in Tijuana are advised to park on the U.S. side of the border and walk across. There is a large lot with scores of taxis on the Tijuana side of the border; from there you can reach the airport, the Cultural Center, the Río area, or Avenida Revolución for under $10. The 2-kilometer (1¼-mile) walk to Avenida Revolución is an easy one through Viva Tijuana, an open-air shopping mall completed in 1991. A walkway leads from the border to the Zona Río; follow the signs to Pueblo Amigo on your immediate right after you cross the border.

**By Car** Heavy rains in the winter of 1992–93 destroyed many roads and neighborhoods in Tijuana. Though most of them have been repaired, it's still best to stick to the major thoroughfares. Plenty of signs at the border will lead you to the main highways and to downtown, but once you hit the streets, Tijuana can be very confusing. There are parking lots along Avenida Revolución and at most major attractions; as noted above, it is advisable to leave your car in a guarded lot. If you park on the street, pay attention to the signs. Your license plates will be removed if you park illegally.

The larger U.S. rental agencies have offices at the Tijuana International Airport. Offices in town include **Avis** (Av. Agua Caliente 3310, tel. 66/86–4004); **Budget** (Paseo de los Héroes 77, tel. 66/84–0253); and **National** (Av. Agua Caliente 5000, tel. 66/86–2103).

**By Taxi** Taxis in Tijuana are both plentiful and inexpensive, with fares to all parts of the city running less than $10 per person. Be sure to agree on the price before the car starts moving.

**By Bus** The downtown bus station is at Calle 1a and Avenida Madero (tel. 66/86–9515). Most city buses at the border will take you downtown; the bus to the border from downtown departs from Calle Benito Juárez, also called Calle 2a, between Avenidas Revolución and Constitución. All buses marked "Centro Camionera" go through downtown.

## Important Addresses and Numbers

**Tourist Information** The **Tijuana Chamber of Commerce** is the best source of tourist information. *Av. Revolución and Calle 1, tel. 66/85-8472. Open daily 9-7.*

The **Attorney General for the Protection of Tourists Hot Line** (tel. 66/88-0555) takes calls Monday through Friday to help with tourist complaints and problems.

**Baja Information** (7860 Mission Center Court, Suite 202, San Diego, CA 92108, tel. 619/298-4105; 800/225-2786 in the U.S.; 800/522-1516 in CA) handles reservations for many Baja hotels and arranges a variety of package deals.

There is a **tourism office** (tel. 66/83-1310) directly across the border with maps, newspapers, and English-speaking clerks; it's open daily 9-5. Tourist information booths are located at the foot of Calle 1, just after the pedestrian overpass across the border; at the airport; and at the intersection of Avenida Revolución and Calle 4.

**Emergencies** **Police** (tel. 134); **Red Cross** (tel. 132); **Fire** (tel. 136); **U.S. Consulate** (tel. 66/86-3886).

## Guided Tours

**San Diego Mini-Tours** (837 47th St., San Diego 92113, tel. 619/234-9044) has hourly departures from San Diego hotels to Av. Revolución in Tijuana and back, and connections with a Mexican-operated trolley tour of Tijuana. **Baja California Tours** (6986 La Jolla Blvd., #204, La Jolla, CA 92037, tel. 619/454-7166, fax 619/454-2703) offers specialized Tijuana excursions, including visits to private homes and tours of art galleries and artists' studios.

## Exploring

*Numbers in the margin correspond to points of interest on the Tijuana map.*

**1** At the **San Ysidro Border Crossing,** a pedestrian walkway travels through the Viva Tijuana dining and shopping center and an adjacent lineup of stalls filled with the full spectrum of souvenirs, and then goes up Calle 2 into the center of town.

**2** **Mexitlan** (Av. Ocampo between Calles 2 and 3, tel. 66/38-4101 or 619/531-1112 in San Diego), a fascinating combination of museum and entertainment/shopping center, opened in 1991. Designed by architect Pedro Ramírez Vásquez, Mexitlan has scale models of all the major architectural and cultural landmarks throughout Mexico; restaurants and shops featuring authentic cuisine and folk art; and frequent performances by folkloric dancers and musical groups. High admission fees have hampered Mexitlan's success; the hours have been limited and fees reduced in an effort to attract tourists to this worthwhile exposition. *Admission: adults $5, children under 12 free. Open Wed.–Sun. 10–5 in winter, 10–10 in summer.*

**3** Calle 2 intersects **Avenida Revolución,** now lined with designer-clothing shops and restaurants, all catering to tourists. Shopkeepers call out from their doorways, offering low prices for an odd assortment of garish souvenirs. Many shopping arcades

Avenida Revolución, **3**
Cultural Center, **9**
El Palacio Frontón, **4**
El Toreo de Tijuana, **5**
Hipódromo de Agua
Caliente, **6**
Hotel Fiesta
Americana, **7**
Mexitlan, **2**
Playas Tijuana, **11**
Plaza de Toros
Monumental, **12**
Plaza Río Tijuana, **10**
Río Tijuana, **8**
San Ysidro Border
Crossing, **1**

open onto Avenida Revolución; inside the front doors are mazes of small stands with low-priced pottery and other handicrafts.

**❹ El Palacio Frontón (Jai Alai Palace)** is on Avenida Revolución between Calles 7a and 8a. The Moorish-style palace is a magnificent building and an exciting place for watching and betting on fast-paced jai alai games (*see* Spectator Sports, *below*).

**Time Out**   Among the many restaurants along Avenida Revolución, **La Especial** (Av. Revolución 718, tel. 66/85–6654) is a favorite for Mexican food that hasn't been fancied up for the tourists.

At Calle 11a, Avenida Revolución becomes Boulevard Agua Ca-
**❺** liente and passes by **El Toreo de Tijuana,** where bullfights are held from May to September. A few blocks farther is the
**❻ Hipódromo de Agua Caliente,** or **Agua Caliente Racetrack.** In the Foreign Book area, bettors can wager on races televised via satellite from California. Nearby are the two gleaming, mir-
**❼** rored towers of the **Hotel Fiesta Americana**—Tijuana's glamour spot.

**❽** Between Boulevard Agua Caliente and the border is the **Río Tijuana** area, which runs parallel to the river. With its impressive Cultural Center and shopping complex, this section of town, along Avenida Paseo de los Héroes, is fast becoming Tijuana's Zona Rosa.

**❾** The **Cultural Center** was designed by architects Manuel Rosen and Pedro Ramírez Vásquez, who also created Mexico City's famous Museum of Anthropology. The Cultural Center's exhibits of Mexican history are a perfect introduction for the thousands of visitors whose first taste of Mexico is at the border. The Omnimax Theater, with its curving 180-degree screen, features *El Pueblo del Sol (People of the Sun)* , a cinematic tour of Mexico. Guest artists appear at the Cultural Center regularly. The center's bookstore has an excellent selection on Mexican history, culture, and arts in both Spanish and English. *Paseo de los Héroes and Av. Independencia, tel. 66/84–1111. Admission to the museum: $1.25: museum and Omnimax Theater: $5.50 for English-language shows, $2.30 for Spanish. Open daily 11–8; the English-language version of the film* El Pueblo del Sol *is presented daily at 2 PM.*

**⑩ Plaza Río Tijuana,** the area's largest shopping complex, is across the street from the Cultural Center on Paseo de los Héroes. It is enormous, with good restaurants, department stores, and hundreds of shops. The plaza has become a central square of sorts, where holiday fiestas are held. This stretch of Paseo de los Héroes has been landscaped with shade trees and flowers, and there are long, wide sidewalks leading from the shopping complex to the Cultural Center.

**Time Out**    The restaurant inside the Cultural Center serves fairly good Mexican food throughout the week. It's a good place for just sitting to relax and absorb all you've seen. **Panadería Suzette,** in the Plaza Río shopping center, has an array of Mexican and French pastries; coffee is free with your selection.

**⑪ Playas Tijuana** along the oceanfront is a mix of modest and expensive residential neighborhoods, with a few restaurants and hotels. The long, isolated beaches are visited mostly by locals.
**⑫** The "Bullring by the Sea," **Plaza de Toros Monumental,** is at the northwest corner of the beach area, right by the border. Bullfights are held here on alternate Sunday afternoons from May through September (El Toreo de Tijuana hosts bullfights every second Sunday). Admission to bullfights varies, depending on the fame of the matador and the location of your seat.

### Shopping

The traditional shopping strip is Avenida Revolución, between Calles 1 and 8. The avenue is lined with shops and arcades that display a wide range of crafts and curios. Bargaining is expected on the streets and in the arcades, but not in the finer shops. **Sanborn's** (Av. Revolución and Calle 9) is a nice addition to the strip, with beautiful crafts from throughout Mexico, an excellent bakery, and chocolates from Mexico City. The **Drug Store, Maxim's, Dorian's,**and **Sara's** have good selections of clothing and imported perfumes. **Tolan,** across from the Jai Alai Palace at Avenida Revolución 111, has an impressive variety of high-quality crafts. **Benetton, Guess, Eduardo's** (Av. Revolución 1105), and **Ralph Lauren Polo** (Calle 7) carry sportswear and resortwear. **La Gran Bota** on Avenida Revolución has great cowboy boots; **Espinosa,** with branches on Avenida Revolución and in the Cultural Center, purveys fine silver, brass, and gold jewelry.

The Avenida Revolución shopping area spreads down Calle 1 to the pedestrian walkway leading from the border. The shops in **Plaza Revolución,** at the corner of Calle 1 and Avenida Revolución, stock quality crafts. Begin shopping at the stands along the border-crossing walkway, comparing prices as you travel toward Avenida Revolución. You may find that the best bargains are closer to the border, and can pick up your piñatas and serapes on your way out of town.

**Shopping Centers**  **Plaza Río Tijuana** is described in Exploring Tijuana, *above*, as is **Mexitlán** on Avenida Ocampo, which stocks high-quality folk art from throughout Mexico. **Pueblo Amigo** on Boulevard Paseo de los Héroes is a fanciful pseudopueblo with colonial-style adobe buildings painted in bright blues, greens, and yellows. **Ley,** a gourmet grocery that sells salad by the pint and hard-to-find Mexican delicacies such as fresh mole sauce and pickled carrots and cauliflower, is one of the center's best shops. **Plaza Fiesta,** on Paseo de los Héroes across from Plaza Río Tijuana, has a collection of boutiques, jewelry stores, and stained-glass shops. Next door, the **Plaza de los Zapatos** gathers together more than a dozen stores selling designer shoes imported from throughout the world; in the same complex, **La Herradura de Oro** sells fine hand-tooled saddles.

## Participant Sports

**Golf**  The **Tijuana Country Club** (Blvd. Agua Caliente, east of downtown, tel. 66/81–7855) is open to guests of some hotels. It provides rental clubs, electric and hand carts, and caddies for the 18-hole course.

## Spectator Sports

**Bullfights**  Bullfights, considered artistic spectacles, not sporting events, feature skilled matadors from throughout Mexico and Spain. They are held at **El Toreo de Tijuana** (Av. Agua Caliente just outside downtown) on Sunday at 4 during May through September. In July and August you can also see fights at the **Plaza de Toros Monumental** (Playas Tijuana area, Ensenada Hwy., tel. 66/85–2210) on Sunday at 4.

**Jai Alai**  This ancient Basque sport, in some ways similar to handball but using a large, scooped-out paddle called a *fronton*, is played in the Moorish-style **Palacio Frontón, or Jai Alai Palace.** *Av. Revolución and Calle 8, tel. 66/88–0125. Admission: $3–$5. Closed Thur.*

**Horse and**  At the **Hipódromo de Agua Caliente,**the horses race on Satur-
**Greyhound Races**  day and Sunday at noon, and the dogs race nightly (except Tues.) at 7:45 and afternoons at 2:30 on Monday, Wednesday, and Friday. In the Foreign Book area, gamblers can bet on races taking place in California and shown at Caliente on TV monitors. *Blvd. Agua Caliente at Salinas, tel. 66/81–7811; in San Diego, tel. 619/231–1919.*

**Charreadas**  Amateur cowboy associations compete at one of several rings
**(Mexican Rodeos)**  around town on Sundays. Call 66/83–4105 for information.

## Dining

There is no shortage of good eating in Tijuana, from *taquerías* (taco stands) to gourmet and Continental restaurants; Avenida Revolución resembles one long food court with places for every taste and budget. A few of the best restaurants from the '20s and '30s still attract a steady clientele with their excellent international cuisine and reasonable prices. On an even more moderate scale, there are scores of seafood restaurants and kitchens that serve great Mexican food, unadulterated for foreign tastes. At night the street life often becomes rowdy, with tourists demonstrating the effects of potent Mexican margaritas.

Beef and pork are excellent, both grilled and marinated. Pheasant, quail, rabbit, and duck are popular in the more expensive places. And the seafood is unbeatable. Grilled lobster and shrimp served with beans, rice, and tortillas are fixtures in casual restaurants modeled after those at the popular seaside fishing village of Puerto Nuevo south of Rosarito.

Dress is casual, and reservations are not required unless otherwise noted. Some restaurants add a 15% service charge to the bill. Highly recommended restaurants are indicated by a star ★.

| Category | Cost* |
|---|---|
| Very Expensive | over $20 |
| Expensive | $15–$20 |
| Moderate | $8–$15 |
| Inexpensive | under $8 |

*per person for a three–course meal, excluding drinks and service.*

**Very Expensive** **Alcázar del Río.** Nouvelle cuisine amid mirrors has hit Tijuana with this upscale, see-and-be-seen restaurant. Patrons are the city's success stories—the casually elegant, sophisticated elite. There's a bit of everything considered to be exotic in Tijuana—smoked salmon with capers, Australian lamb, Serrano ham with sweet cantaloupe, cherries jubilee. The halibut with pine nuts is sublimely simple, and the wine list is excellent. *Bd. Paseo de los Héroes 56–5, tel. 66/84–2672. Reservations suggested. Jacket and tie suggested. AE, MC, V.*

**Expensive** ★ **Cilantro's.** This restaurant in the Viva Tijuana center is one of the best places to sample Mexico's regional dishes. *Ceviche* (marinated fish cocktail), *huachinango* (red snapper) with Yucatán herbs, and a rich mole sauce are all expertly prepared. The menu also features burritos and enchiladas for the less adventurous diner. Colorful posters by Mexican artists adorn the dining room, which looks out onto the shopping plaza. An adjoining disco, XS, provides postdining entertainment. *Paseo Tijuana 406, tel. 66/82–8340. AE, MC, V.*

★ **Pedrín's.** One of Tijuana's best seafood restaurants overlooks the Jai Alai Palace from a second-story garden room. Meals include deep-fried fish appetizers, fish chowder, salad, an entrée, and a sweet after-dinner drink of Kahlua and cream. Recommended dishes include *rajas shrimp*, covered with melted cheese and green chilies, and grilled lobster. *Av. Revolución 1115, tel. 66/85–4052. AE, MC, V.*

**Moderate** ★ **La Fonda Roberto's.** Roberto's is by far the best restaurant in Tijuana for traditional cuisine from the many culinary regions of Mexico. Try the *chiles en nogada* (chilies stuffed with raisins and meat and topped with cream and pomegranate seeds), meats with spicy achiote sauce, and many varieties of mole. Portions are small, so order liberally and share samples of many dishes.*Old Ensenada Hwy. (also Calle 16 de Septiembre), near Blvd. Agua Caliente in the Siesta Motel, tel. 66/86–1601. MC, V.*

★ **La Leña.** The sparkling clean white dining room in La Leña faces an open kitchen where chefs grill unusual beef dishes, such as *Gaonera*, a tender fillet of beef stuffed with cheese and guacamole. The owner often visits with his guests, asking their opinion on the menu and offering samples of tripe—only for the strong of stomach. *Bd. Agua Caliente 4560, tel. 66/86–2920; also at Av. Revolución between Calles 4 and 5. AE, MC, V.*

**La Taberna Española.** The mainstay of Plaza Fiesta's multiethnic cafés, this Spanish tapas bar attracts a youthful, sophisticated crowd. The tapa (appetizer) menu is printed in Spanish, but with a bit of imagination you should be able to select a representative sampling, including octopus in its own ink, a plate of spicy sausages, a wedge of Spanish tortilla with potatoes and eggs, and a bowl of fava beans. The interior café is smoky, fragrant, and invariably crowded; sit at the outdoor tables for a better view of the crowd waiting in line. *Plaza Fiesta, Paseo de los Héroes 10001, tel. 66/84–7562. No credit cards.*

**Tía Juana Tilly's.** Popular with both tourists and locals looking for revelry and generous portions of Mexican specialties, this is one of the few places where you can get *cochinita píbil*, a Yucatecan specialty made of roast pig, red onions, and bitter oranges, or the traditionally bitter and savory chicken mole. Part of the same chain is Tilly's Fifth Ave., catercorner to the original on Avenida Revolución. *Av. Revolución at Calle 7, tel. 66/85–6024. AE, DC, MC, V.*

**Inexpensive** **Carnitas Uruapan.** At this large, noisy restaurant, patrons mingle at long wood tables, toasting one another with chilled *cervezas* (beer). The main attraction here is *carnitas* (marinated pork), sold by weight and served with homemade tortillas, salsa, *cilantro* (coriander), guacamole, and onions. *Blvd. Díaz Ordaz 550, tel. 66/81–6181; also at Paseo de los Héroes at Av. Rodriguez, no phone. No credit cards.*

★ **La Especial.** Located at the foot of the stairs leading to an underground shopping arcade, this restaurant attracts diners in search of home-style Mexican cooking at low prices. There's nothing fancy about the seemingly endless basement room—which is never empty. *Av. Revolución 718, tel. 66/85–6654. No credit cards.*

**Señor Frog's.** Heaping plates of barbecued chicken and ribs and buckets of ice-cold bottles of cerveza are the mainstay at this fun and festive formula eatery, one of many in the Carlos Anderson chain. The loud music and laughter make for a raucous atmosphere, and the food is consistently good. *In the Pueblo Amigo Center, Paseo Tijuana, no phone. AE, MC, V.*

## Lodging

Tijuana's hotels are clustered downtown, along Avenida Revolución, near the country club on Boulevard Agua Caliente, and in the Río Tijuana area on Paseo de los Héroes. There are ample accommodations for all price levels, and a number of new hotels are under construction. **Baja Information** can reserve hotel rooms (*see* Important Addresses and Numbers, *above*). **Baja Lodging Services** (4659 Park Blvd., San Diego, CA 92116, tel. 619/491–0682) makes hotel, condo, and private-home reservations throughout Baja. Highly recommended lodgings are indicated by a star ★.

| Category | Cost* |
|---|---|
| Very Expensive | over $90 |
| Expensive | $60–$90 |
| Moderate | $25–$60 |
| Inexpensive | under $25 |

*\*All prices are for a standard double room, excluding service charge and sales tax (10%).*

**Very Expensive** **Fiesta Americana.** The two mirrored towers of the hotel are
**★** Tijuana's most ostentatious landmarks, signs of prosperity and faith in the economic potential of this lucrative border town. The Fiesta Americana often hosts receptions and parties for Tijuana's elite and is considered by many to be the city's most glamorous place for a drink or meal. The rooms on the club floors are particularly extravagant, with separate seating areas, king-size beds, and astounding views of Tijuana's sprawl. *Blvd. Agua Caliente 4558, tel. 66/81–7000 or 800/223–2332. 422 rooms with bath. Facilities: nightclub, restaurant, health club, tennis courts, pool, travel agency. AE, DC, MC, V.*

**Expensive** **Lucerna.** Once one of the most charming hotels in Tijuana, the Lucerna has become run-down, and the rooms are in need of renovation. Still, the lovely gardens, large swimming pool surrounded by palms, touches of tile work, and folk art lend Mexican character to the hotel. The Lucerna's travel agency is particularly helpful with planning trips into Mexico. *Blvd. Paseo de los Héroes and Av. Rodríguez, tel. 66/34–2000 or 800/ LUCERNA. 170 rooms and 9 suites with bath. Facilities: pool, restaurant, coffee shop, nightclub, travel agency. MC, V.*

**Moderate** **Corona Plaza.** Though the exterior of this hotel resembles that of a nondescript office building, the interior is surprisingly pleasant. Rooms, furnished in handsome bleached wood, overlook an atrium lobby and restaurant. For less noise and more air, ask for a second- or third-floor room near the pool. The bullring is within walking distance; other attractions are just a short cab ride away. *Blvd. Agua Caliente 1426, tel. 66/81–8183. Facilities: swimming pool, restaurant. AE, MC, V.*

**La Mesa Inn.** This recently renovated Best Western hotel/motel has a small, shaded pool and rooms you could find anywhere, with tan walls, brown carpet, earthtone decor, and no charm. Stay away from the rooms by the street and pool. *Blvd. Díaz Ordaz 50, tel. 66/81–6522 or 800/528–1234. 125 rooms. Facilities: pool, coffee shop, bar. MC, V.*

**La Villa de Zaragoza.** La Villa is a fairly new, brown stucco motel with a good location—near the Jai Alai Palace and one block from Revolución. It has the nicest rooms downtown in this price range. *Av. Madero 1120, tel. 66/85–1832. 42 rooms. Facilities: restaurant, parking. MC, V.*

**Otay Bugambilias.** There is finally a tourist hotel near the Tijuana airport that's clean and comfortable. The pink, three-story Bugambilias was an instant hit with travelers and those who do business in the Otay Mesa industrial area. The motel-like rooms feature kitchenettes; suites have separate seating areas.

Extras include a small gym, sauna, and swimming pool. *Blvd. Industrial at Carretera Aeropuerto, tel. 66/23–8411 or 800/ 472–1153. 129 rooms. Facilities: restaurant, bar, pool, gym, meeting facilities. MC, V.*

**Inexpensive** **CREA Youth Hostel.** The hostel is set in a quiet, peaceful park and is part of a sports complex. The 20 beds are in same-sex dorms, and there is a cafeteria. *Av. Padre Kino, tel. 66/84–2523 or 66/84–7510. No credit cards.*

## The Arts and Nightlife

Tijuana has toned down its Sin City image; much of the action now takes place at the **Jai Alai Palace** and the racetrack. Several hotels, especially the **Lucerna** and **Fiesta Americana,** feature live entertainment. **Iguanas** (Blvd. Paseo de los Héroes, tel. 66/ 82–4967), at the Pueblo Amigo shopping center, is an 18-and-over club; appearances by New Wave and rock artists draw as many patrons from San Diego as from Tijuana. Cover charge varies with the group.

**La Peña** (Plaza Fiesta, Paseo de los Héroes, tel. 66/84–9410) is currently the hippest music club among the night spots at Plaza Fiesta, with live salsa and rumba bands. The **Hard Rock Cafe** (Av. Revolución 520 between Calles 1 and 2, tel. 66/85–0206) has the same menu and decor as the other offsprings of the London landmark and is immensely popular with locals. For total immersion in the flashy, high-tech disco scene, try **OH! Laser Club** (Paseo de los Héroes 56, tel. 66/84–0267); **Heaven & Hell** (Paseo de los Héroes 10501, tel. 66/84–8484); **The News** (Pueblo Amigo, tel. 66/82–3387); and **Baby Rock** (1482 Diego Rivera, tel. 66/84–0440). Tijuana's discos are elegant and sophisticated, and usually have strict dress codes, with no T-shirts, jeans, or sandals allowed. Stick to high heels and spandex.

# Rosarito Beach

## Introduction

Not long ago, Playas de Rosarito (Rosarito Beach) was a small seaside community with virtually no tourist trade. Part of the municipality of Tijuana, it was an overlooked suburb on the way to the port city of Ensenada. But as the roads improved, and particularly after Baja's Transpeninsular Highway was completed in 1973, Rosarito Beach began to flower. Vacation suites were added along the beach, and time-share and condo units were put up; although as recently as 1980, the Rosarito Beach Hotel was the only major resort in the area.

The '80s brought an amazing building boom to Rosarito. The main street, alternately known as the Old Ensenada Highway and Boulevard Benito Juárez, is now packed with restaurants, bars, and shops. With the completion of a major shopping and convention complex in 1987, Rosarito Beach hit the big time.

Still, it is a relaxing place to visit. Southern Californians have practically made Rosarito (and much of Baja Norte) a weekend suburb. Surfers, swimmers, and sunbathers come here to enjoy the beach, one of the longest in northern Baja: It's an uninterrupted stretch of sand from the power plant at the far north end of town to below the Rosarito Beach Hotel, about 8 kilometers (5 miles) south. Horseback riding, jogging, and strolling are popular along this strand. Whales pass not far from shore on their winter migration; dolphins and sea lions sun on rocks jutting out from the sea. Rosarito has always attracted a varied crowd, and today's group is no exception—an assemblage of prosperous young Californians building villas in vacation developments, retired Americans and Canadians homesteading in trailer parks, and travelers of all ages from all over the world.

Hedonism and health get equal billing in Rosarito. One of the area's major draws is its seafood, especially lobster, shrimp, and abalone. The visiting Americans act as if they've been dry for months—margaritas and beer are the favored thirst-quenchers. People throw off their inhibitions here, at least to the degree permitted by the local constables. A typical Rosarito day might begin with a breakfast of eggs, refried beans, and tortillas, followed by a few hours of horseback riding on the beach. Lying in the sun or strolling through the shops takes care of midday. Siestas are imperative and are usually followed by more shopping, strolling, or sunbathing before dinner, dancing, and sleep.

## Arriving and Departing

Rosarito Beach is 29 kilometers (18 miles) south of Tijuana, on the Pacific coast. There is no airport, but **Tres Estrellas de Oro** (tel. 66/88–9186 in Tijuana) has service between Tijuana and Ensenada, stopping at the bus terminal in Rosarito on Avenida Benito Juárez across from the Rosarito Beach Hotel.

The easiest way to get to Rosarito Beach is to drive. Once you cross the border, follow the signs for Ensenada Cuota, the toll road that runs south along the coast. Take the Rosarito exit, which leads to what is alternately called the Old Ensenada Highway and Boulevard Juárez in Rosarito. The tolls from Tijuana to Rosarito run about $5. Rest rooms are available near the toll booths. Although the alternate free road—Ensenada Libre—has been vastly improved, it is difficult for the first-timer to navigate, but here are directions if you want to try: In Tijuana, drive south on Avenida Revolución to Boulevard Fundadores and bear right. You'll discover that the free road and the toll road merge just north of Rosarito.

Note: The old, free road was forced to close during the torrential rains of early 1993; the damage it incurred has since been repaired. The toll road remained open during the storm but was also damaged by mud slides and flooding. Drive slowly on both roads, and keep an eye out for road work ahead—usually marked by a row of large rocks placed across a lane. These rock barriers can appear out of nowhere and are a major driving hazard.

## Getting Around

Most of Rosarito proper can be explored on foot, which is a good idea on weekends, when Boulevard Juárez has bumper-to-bumper traffic. To reach Puerto Nuevo and points south, continue on Boulevard Juárez (also called Old Ensenada Highway and Ensenada Libre) through town and head south. There is a tremendous amount of construction taking place along this stretch of road, incidentally, with time-share communities and resorts popping up side by side along the oceanfront cliffs. Taxis travel this stretch regularly. Settle the fare before departing. Buses from Tijuana and Ensenada stop across the street from the Rosarito Beach Hotel; if you wish to get off at other beach areas along the way, take a local rather than an express bus.

## Important Addresses and Numbers

**Tourist Information** The tourist information office (Blvd. Juárez, in the Quinta Plaza shopping center, tel. 66/12–0200) has brochures from several hotels and restaurants and copies of the *Baja Times*, a handy tourist-oriented, English-language newspaper. The staff speaks English and is extremely helpful. The Rosarito Convention and Visitors Bureau offers brochures and information packets through its toll-free number in the United States, tel. 800/962–BAJA.

**Emergencies** **Police** (tel. 134); **Fire** (tel. 136); **Red Cross** (tel. 132).

## Exploring

Rosarito Beach has few historic or cultural attractions, beaches and bars being the main draws. Sightseeing consists of strolling along the 5-mile beach or down Boulevard Benito Juárez. Note: Street numbers and addresses are changing along Juárez. To reduce confusion, ask for landmarks when getting directions.

An immense PEMEX gasoline installation and electric plant anchor the northern end of Boulevard Juárez, which then runs along a collection of new shopping arcades, restaurants, and motels. The eight-story **La Quinta del Mar** hotel is the first major landmark, followed by the **Quinta Plaza** shopping center, which has a car wash, pharmacy, bakery, specialty shops, and restaurants, as well as the **tourism office** and the **Centro de Convenciones**, a 1,000-seat convention center. Across the street is the **San Fernando Shopping Center.**

**Rodríguez Park,** on the beach at the end of Calle Rene Ortíz, about midway between La Quinta del Mar and the Rosarito Beach hotels, has barbecue pits, picnic tables, and a nice lawn.

**Time Out** The long glassed-in bar that sits on a little hill between the pool and the beach at the **Rosarito Beach Hotel** (tel. 66/12–1106) is the best place for absorbing the hotel's ambience. You'll have a view of the tiled roof, white adobe balconies, and flowered courtyard around the pool to one side, and the horseback riders, sunbathers, and ocean to the other. The margaritas are a potent reminder that you're in Mexico, and the nachos are fairly good. Have Sunday brunch ($15) in the dining room, overlooking the pool.

## Off the Beaten Track

The most popular side trip from Rosarito Beach, if you go by sheer numbers alone, is **Puerto Nuevo** (Newport) at Kilometer 44 on the old highway. A few years ago the only way you could tell you'd reached this fishing community was by the huge painting of a 7-Up bottle on the side of a building. You'd drive down the rutted dirt road to a row of restaurants where you were served the classic Newport meal: grilled lobster, refried beans, rice, homemade tortillas, butter, salsa, and lime. The meal became a legend, and now at least 30 restaurants have the identical menu. Try one of the family-run places, like Ponderosa (*see* Dining, *below*). Rows of artisans' stands have opened around the restaurants and along the road near Puerto Nuevo, offering pottery, baskets, tacky T-shirts, and a bizarre assortment of souvenirs.

## Shopping

The two major resort hotels have shopping arcades equipped with laundromats, taco stands, and some good crafts stores. The **Calimax** grocery store on Boulevard Juárez is a good place to stock up on necessities.

The shopping arcade near La Quinta del Mar Hotel houses many worthwhile shops. **La Casa del Arte** has wicker and willow furniture, large woven rugs, and hand-carved antique furniture. **Muebles Rangel** sells carpeting and rattan-ware; **Oradia Imports** specializes in French perfumes. **Taxco Curios** offers a good selection of silver jewelry, and the last shop in the arcade, **Interios los Ríos,** has custom-designed furniture and Michoacán pottery. **Santa Fe,** across Juárez from Quinta del Mar, was one of the first shops in town to feature handcrafted rustic furniture. Now several like-minded shops have opened, meeting the demand from the many new vacation-home owners in the area interested in outfitting their places in Mexican style. Equally popular are the handpainted tiles sold at **Artesanias Hacienda** (Blvd. Juárez 97).

**Panaderia La Espiga** is an excellent bakery with several branches along Juárez. At **Casa Torres,** in the Rosarito Beach Hotel arcade, you can purchase high-quality French perfumes for about one-third less than you would pay in the United States.

The highway from Rosarito to Puerto Nuevo is lined with pottery shops and curio stands, where some treasures and bargains are buried amid tawdry souvenirs. Try the back shelves at **Chac Curios, Los Hermanos Curios,** and **Esperanza Curios.**

## Sports and Outdoor Activities

**Fishing** There is a small fishing pier at Kilometer 33 on the Old Ensenada Highway; surf casting is allowed on the beach. There is no place in Rosarito that issues fishing licenses, but tourism officials say licenses are not necessary if you fish from shore. Unfortunately, due to ongoing construction and inadequate sewage facilities, the ocean tends to be polluted, especially in residential areas—it is not a good idea to eat fish caught close to shore.

**Horseback Riding** Horses can be rented at the north and south ends of Juárez and on the beach for $10 per half hour. Check the horses carefully; some are pathetically thin. The number of horses on the beach is now restricted, and the horses are better cared for.

**Surfing** The waves are particularly good at **Popotla,** Kilometer 33, **Calafía,** Kilometer 35.5, and **Costa Baja,** Kilometer 36, on the Old Ensenada Highway.

## Dining

Nearly all of Rosarito's restaurants feature the same items—lobster, shrimp, fresh fish, and steak—at nearly the same prices. A lobster, shrimp, or steak dinner costs about $15. Some restaurants tack a 15% service charge on to your bill. Dress is casual and reservations are not required unless otherwise noted. Highly recommended restaurants are indicated by a star ★.

| Category | Cost* |
|---|---|
| Very Expensive | over $20 |
| Expensive | $15–$20 |
| Moderate | $8–$15 |
| Inexpensive | under $8 |

*per person excluding drinks, and service.*

**Expensive** **Dragon del Mar.** A miniature waterfall greets guests in the marble foyer of this elegant Chinese restaurant, which features a pianist playing relaxing music. Decorated with furniture and paintings imported from China and partitioned with carved wooden panels, the expansive dining room creates an intimate dining experience. The food is well prepared and appealing to the eye as well as the palate. *Blvd. Juárez 283, tel. 661/2–0604. MC, V.*

**La Fachada.** A quiet place by Rosarito standards, La Fachada is preferred by diners seeking a subdued but authentically Mexican atmosphere. The food is good, and a pianist performs soothing ballads in the evening. *Blvd. Juárez 317, tel. 661/2–1785. MC, V.*

★ **La Leña.** The cornerstone restaurant of the Quinta Plaza shopping center, La Leña sits on such a high rise that you can see the ocean from the window tables. La Leña specializes in beef grilled in full view of the diners. The dining room is spacious, with the tables spread far enough apart for privacy. Try any of the beef dishes, especially the tender *carne asada* (grilled strips of beef) with tortillas and guacamole. *Quinta Plaza, tel. 661/2–0826. MC, V.*

**La Misión.** A lovely, quiet restaurant, La Misión has white adobe walls, carved-wood statues in niches, and high beamed ceilings. Gourmet seafood and steak dishes are the specialties. Patio dining is available in an enclosed courtyard. *Blvd. Juárez 182, tel. 661/2–0202. MC, V.*

**Moderate** **Azteca.** The enormous dining room at the Rosarito Beach Hotel has a view of the pool and beach area. Many visitors come here exclusively for the lavish Sunday brunch, where margaritas are the drink of choice. Both Mexican and American dishes are offered, and the size of the portions make up for the erratic quality of the food. *Rosarito Beach Hotel, Blvd. Juárez, tel. 661/2–1106. MC, V.*

**El Nido.** A dark, wood-paneled restaurant with leather booths, this is one of the oldest eateries in Rosarito. It's popular with those who are unimpressed with the newer, fancier establishments. Steaks are grilled over mesquite, and the large central fireplace is a cozy touch. *Blvd. Juárez 67, tel. 661/2-1430. MC, V.*

★ **Mariscos de Rosarito Vince's.** This seafood restaurant and deli is popular with expatriate Americans—they swear that Vince's has the best lobster in town. Mariachis add to the nightly festivities. *Blvd. Juárez 77, tel. 661/2-1253. No credit cards.*

**René's.** One of the oldest restaurants in Rosarito (1924), René's features *chorizo* (Mexican sausage), quail, frogs' legs, and lobster. There's an ocean view from the dining room, a lively bar, and mariachi music. *Blvd. Juárez south of the Rosarito Beach Hotel, tel. 661/2-1020. MC, V.*

**Inexpensive** **La Flor de Michoacán.** Carnitas (marinated pork roasted over
★ an open pit) Michoacán style, served with homemade tortillas, guacamole, and salsa, are the house specialty. The tacos *tortas* (marinated pork kebabs roasted on skewers) and tostadas are great. The surroundings are simple but clean. Takeout is available. *Blvd. Juárez 291, tel. 661/2-1858. No credit cards.*

**Juice'n Juice.** Rosarito's Mexican/health-food restaurant is a no-frills lunch counter with lots of salads, juices, yogurt, and granola. Good cheese enchiladas and other meatless Mexican dishes give vegetarians a chance to sample the local fare. Beef burgers and burritos are also served.*Blvd. Juárez 98, tel. 661/ 2-0338. No credit cards.*

**Los Arcos.** Next to the Rosarito Beach Hotel, this café serves home-style Mexican food and offers open-air dining in summer. *Blvd. Juárez 29, tel. 661/2-0491. No credit cards.*

**Rosarito Village Cafe.** Inexpensive margaritas, mariachis, and takeout Mexican food make this restaurant a popular watering hole; it's also a good place for U.S.-style breakfasts. *Next to Rosarito Beach Hotel. Blvd. Juárez 777, no phone. MC, V.*

**South of** **Calafia.** This eccentric restaurant serves up a terrific ocean
**Rosarito Beach** view with its food. You can dine indoors or sit outside at tables
*Expensive* that perch on terraces down the side of a cliff. Dance floors inside and at the bottom of the cliff are ideal. *Km 35.5 on the Old Ensenada Hwy., tel. 661/2-1581. MC, V.*

★ **La Fonda.** At this popular restaurant, you can sit on an outdoor patio overlooking the beach and sip potent margaritas served with greasy nachos and hot salsa. Fresh lobster, grilled steaks, prime rib, and traditional Mexican dishes are accompanied by a delicious black-bean soup. The bar is usually crowded, and the patrons boisterous. *Km 59 on the Old Ensenada Hwy., no phone. No credit cards.*

*Moderate* **Puerto Nuevo.** Newport is a village of 25 to 30 restaurants that serve the same dishes—grilled lobster or shrimp, Spanish rice, refried beans, and homemade tortillas with melted butter, lime, and hot sauce. Some places have full bars; others serve only wine and beer. **Ortega's,** with at least three branches in Newport and on Rosarito, is the most crowded; **Ponderosa** is smaller and quieter and is run by a gracious family; **Costa Brava** is newer and more elegant, with tablecloths and an ocean view. Lobsters in most places are priced as small, medium, and large—medium is about $15. The seafood served in Newport is no longer caught in local waters, which have become polluted: instead, it's frozen and imported from elsewhere. *Km 44 on the Old Ensenada Hwy., no phones. Most places are open for lunch* *and dinner on a first come, first served basis. Some take credit cards.*

## Lodging

Rosarito's recent building boom has solved the area's legendary room shortage. Several agencies in the United States book reservations at Rosarito hotels and at nearby condo and time-share resorts, which may actually cost less than hotel rooms if you are traveling with a group of four or more. For details, contact **Baja Information** (7860 Mission Center Court, Suite 202, San Diego, CA 92108, tel. 619/298–4105; in the U.S., tel. 800/225–2786; in CA, tel. 800/522–1516), **Baja Lodging Services** (4659 Park Blvd., San Diego, CA 92116, tel. 619/491–0682), or **Baja California Tours** (6986 La Jolla Blvd., #204, La Jolla, CA 92037, tel. 619/454–7166, fax 619/454–2703). Reseservations are a must on holiday weekends. Many hotels require a minimum two-night stay for a confirmed reservation, and inexpensive rooms are hard to find. Highly recommended lodgings are indicated by a star ★.

| Category | Cost* |
| --- | --- |
| Very Expensive | over $90 |
| Expensive | $60–$90 |
| Moderate | $25–$60 |
| Inexpensive | under $25 |

*\*All prices are for standard double room, excluding service charge and sales tax (10%).*

**Expensive** **Rosarito Beach Hotel.** Dating from the Prohibition era, this re-
★ sort is beginning to show its age, but it's still a charmer, with huge ballrooms, tiled public rest rooms, and a glassed-in pool deck overlooking a long beach. Rooms and suites in the low-rise buildings that face the beach are modern, though somewhat sterile; more characterful accommodations in the original building surrounding the swimming pool have been over-hauled. Midweek reduced rates are often available; ocean-view rooms are in the Very Expensive category. A 1930s mansion next door to the hotel has been refurbished as the Casa Playa Spa, a full-service European facility with massage, beauty treatments, exercise equipment, saunas and hot tubs, and a restaurant. *Blvd. Juárez at the south end of town, tel. 661/2–1106 or 800/343–8582; reservations: Box 430145, San Diego, CA 92143-0145. 280 rooms and suites. Facilities: beach, tennis courts, 2 pools, health club, European spa, bar, 2 restaurants, convention center. MC, V.*

**Moderate** **Baja Village.** Completed in 1989, this motel is on Rosarito's main drag, which is very noisy during the day; the advantage is that restaurants, stores, and the beach are all within walking distance. Rooms are carpeted, and some have color TV. *Blvd. Juárez 228 at Via Las Olas, tel. 661/2–0050. U.S. mailing address: Box 309, San Ysidro, CA 92073. 21 rooms, 3 suites. Facilities: parking, restaurant, bar. MC, V.*
**Brisas del Mar.** A modern motel (built in 1992), the Brisas del Mar is especially good for families, since the large pastel rooms comfortably accommodate four persons. A few of the rooms on

the second story have views of the ocean; all have air-conditioning and TV. *Blvd. Juárez at the south end of town, tel. 661/2–2547, 800/MY-PLACE. 66 rooms. Facilities: coffee shop, bar, hot tub. MC, V.*

**Los Pelicanos Hotel.** Completed in 1990, this hotel—one of the few situated directly on the beach—has prices that vary depending on the location of the rooms and the presence or absence of a balcony with an ocean view. The second-story restaurant and bar are popular sunset-watching spots. *Calle Cedros 115, tel. 661/2–0445; U.S. mailing address: Box 3871, San Ysidro, CA 92073. 39 rooms. Facilities: restaurant, bar. MC, V.*

**Inexpensive**    **Cupalas del Mar.** Opened in 1991, this small hotel between Boulevard Juárez and the beach is quieter than most, with sunny, clean rooms and satellite TV. *Calle Guadalupe Victoria 9, tel. 661/2–2490, fax 661/2–2494. 39 rooms. Facilities: pool, parking, hot tub. No credit cards.*

**Motel Quinta Chica.** This motel at the south end of town has little character but comfortable beds. Rooms in the front face the free road and enjoy ocean breezes; those in the back have the constant roar of traffic on the toll road. *Km 26.8 on the Old Ensenada Hwy., tel. 661/2–1300. 90 rooms. Facilities: restaurant and bar across the street. MC, V.*

**South of Rosarito**    **Grand Baja Resort.** A good value for families and groups, this
**Expensive**    resort offers beachfront condo rentals with daily and long-term rates; split the cost of a suite or studio between two couples and you'll be in the Moderate range. All accommodations except the junior suites have kitchenettes. The Grand Baja is a block away from the cluster of Puerto Nuevo lobster restaurants. *Km. 44.5 Old Ensenada Hwy., tel. 661/4–1484; reservations in the U.S.: tel. 800/275–3280. 20 condos. Facilities: pool, tennis courts. MC, V.*

★    **La Fonda.** A longtime favorite with beachgoers, La Fonda has a few well-worn rooms, decorated with carved-wood furniture and folk art, with great views of the ocean. The restaurant and bar are immensely popular; if you plan on getting any sleep, ask for a room as far away from them as possible. *Km 59 on the Old Ensenada Hwy., no phone; reservations in the U.S.: Box 268, San Ysidro, CA 92073. 18 rooms. Facilities: beach, restaurant, bar. No credit cards.*

★    **Las Rocas.** An elegant addition to the strip of older hotels perched on cliffs above the ocean, this hotel is terraced up a hillside, giving all the rooms ocean views. The white building, with blue-and-purple trim, stands out vividly against the surroundings. Some suites have fireplaces, coffeemakers, and microwaves. The pool and whirlpool seem to spill over the cliffs into the ocean. *Km. 37 on the Old Ensenada Hwy., tel. 661/2–2140. 46 rooms, 26 suites. Facilities: pool, whirlpool, restaurant, bar. AE, MC, V.*

**Moderate**    **Plaza del Mar.** This hotel, spa, and oceanfront resort is set beside a public archaeological garden, featuring replicas of Aztecan and Mayan ruins. Accommodations are in long Quonset hut-like buildings clustered around courtyards. *Take the La Misión exit from the toll road and go north 1 mile. Km 58 on the Old Ensenada Hwy., tel. 668/5–9152; reservations in the U.S.: tel. 800/762–6380. 120 rooms. Facilities: pool, hot tub, tennis courts, shuffleboard, restaurant, bar. MC, V.*

**Nightlife**

The many restaurants in Rosarito Beach keep customers entertained with live music, piano bars, or *folklórico* (folk music and
dance) shows; the bar scene is also active. Drinking and driving
laws are stiff—the police will fine you no matter how little
you've had. If you plan to drink, take a cab or assign a designated driver.

There's a lot going on at night at **Rosarito Beach Hotel** (Blvd.
Juárez, tel. 661/2–0144): live music at the ocean-view Beach-
comber Bar and Hugo's; a Mexican Fiesta on Friday nights; and
a live band at the cavernous disco. You can also dance to live music at **Calafia** (Km 35.5 Old Ensenada Hwy., tel. 661/2–1581)—
another spot that has great ocean views–during afternoons
and evenings from Friday through Sunday. **Dragon del Mar**
(Blvd. Juárez 283, tel. 661/2–0604) has a piano bar nightly. You
can kick up your heels to a band at **El Torito** (Blvd. Juárez 318,
no phone) until 2 AM on Friday and Saturday evening. On weekends, **Las Olas** (Blvd. Juárez 298, upstairs) features both live
music and music videos. Rowdy **Rene's** (Blvd. Juárez south of
town, tel. 661/2–1061) has it all: a live dance band, mariachis,
and a wide-screen satellite TV. **Vince's** (Blvd. Juárez 77, tel.
991/2–1253) is another place for getting into the mariachi beat.

# Ensenada

Ensenada is a major port 104 kilometers (65 miles) south of Tijuana on Bahía de Todos Santos. The paved highway (Mexico
Route 1) between the two cities often cuts a path between low
mountains and high oceanside cliffs; exits lead to rural roads,
oceanfront campgrounds, and an ever-increasing number of resort communities. The small fishing communities of San Miguel
and El Sauzal sit off the highway to the north of town, and the
Coronado Islands can be clearly seen off the coast.

Juan Rodríguez Cabrillo first discovered Ensenada, which
means "bay" in Spanish, in 1542. Sebastián Vizcaino named the
region Ensenada-Bahía de Todos Santos (All Saints' Bay) in
1602. Since then the town has drawn a steady stream of "discov-
erers" and developers. First ranchers made their homes on
large spreads along the coast and up into the mountains. Gold
miners followed, turning the area into a boomtown during the
late 1800s. After the mines were depleted, the area settled
back into a pastoral state for a while, but the harbor gradually
grew into a major port for shipping agricultural goods from the
surrounding ranches and farms. Now it is one of Mexico's largest seaports and has a thriving fishing fleet and fish-processing
industry. The smell of fish from the canneries lining the highway can be overpowering at times.

Despite the town's tremendous growth since 1984, Ensenada
remains charming and picturesque. It's a popular weekend destination for southern Californians. There are no beaches in
Ensenada proper, but beaches north and south of town are satisfactory for swimming, sunning, surfing, and camping. During the week Ensenada is just a normal, relatively calm port
city, with a population of about 150,000.

For decades most hotels and bars have catered to groups of
young people intent on drinking and carousing. The beachside

strip between San Miguel and Ensenada has long been a haven
of moderately priced oceanfront motels and trailer parks. But
now there is a concerted effort to attract conventioneers and
business travelers. A group of civic boosters has renovated the
Riviera del Pacifico, the grand old gambling hall turned civic
center that is Ensenada's most stately edifice. The waterfront
area has been razed and rebuilt, with taco stands replaced by
shopping centers, hotels, and the massive Plaza Marina,
opened in late 1992. Several fancy new strip malls have opened
in town, and cruise ships regularly anchor offshore. Developers
have poured close to $15 million into a marina, beachfront
casitas, and a large health club in the Baja Beach and Tennis
Club, built on the ruins of another resort that was started in
the 1960s, when it was falsely rumored that gambling would
again become legal in Baja. The building boom seems to have
created a glut of space, however, and construction will probably slow down for a while.

Ensenada is the last major city for hundreds of miles if you are
traveling south on Mexico Highway 1 or the Transpeninsular
Highway. **San Quintín,** 184 kilometers (115 miles) south of
Ensenada, is an agricultural community said to be the windiest
spot in Baja. Fishing and hunting are the draws here. **Cataviña**
has a gas station and a few small hotels. Farther south are turn-
offs for a dirt road to **San Felipe** and a paved road to **Bahía de los
Angeles.** At the end of Baja Norte, 595 kilometers (372 miles)
from Ensenada, stands a steel monument in the form of an eagle, 42 meters (138 feet) high. It marks the border between the
states of Baja Norte and Baja Sur. The time changes from
Pacific to Mountain as you cross the 28th parallel. **Guerrero
Negro,** Baja Sur's northernmost town, with hotels and gas stations, is 2 kilometers (1¼ miles) south.

## Arriving and Departing by Plane

**Airport and Airlines** Ensenada has only a small airstrip, **Aeropuerto el Cipres** (tel.
667/6–6301), for private planes. Most people who visit
Ensenada drive. Tourist cards are required only if you are traveling south of Ensenada or staying longer than 72 hours.

## Arriving and Departing by Bus, Ship, and Car

**By Bus** Ensenada can be reached by bus from Tijuana, Mexicali, and
Mexico City. **Autotransportes de Baja California** and **Tres
Estrellas de Oro** travel throughout Baja, linking all the major
cities. The bus station is at Avenida Riveroll between Calles 10
and 11, tel. 667/8–6770.

**By Ship** Ensenada is a year-round port for **Carnival Cruise Lines** (tel.
800/232–4666), which sails from Los Angeles twice each week.
**Admiral Cruises** (tel. 800/772–7272) has three- and four-night
cruises from Los Angeles. **Starlite Cruises** (tel. 800/488–7827)
features one-day cruises from San Diego, with gambling on
board ship.

**By Car** Mexico Highway 1, called Ensenada Cuota, is a toll road that
runs along the coast from the Tijuana border to Ensenada. The
toll booths along the road accept U.S. and Mexican currency;
tolls are usually about $2.50. The road is excellent, though it
has some hair-raising curves atop the cliffs and is best driven in
daylight. The free road, called Ensenada Libre, runs parallel

to the toll road off and on, cutting east of the low hills along the coast. Although free, the road doubles your traveling time and is very rough in spots.

## Getting around Ensenada

Most of Ensenada's attractions are situated within five blocks of the waterfront; it is easy to take a long walking tour of the city. A car is necessary to reach La Bufadora, the Chapultepec Hills, and most of the beaches. Buses travel the route from Ensenada through Guerrero Negro at the border between Baja Norte and Baja Sur and continue down to the southernmost tip of Baja.

**By Bus** **Tres Estrellas de Oro** and **Autotransportes de Baja California** cover the entire Baja route and connect in Mexicali with buses to Guadalajara and Mexico City.

**By Taxi** There is a *sitio* (central taxi stand) on Avenida López Mateos by the Bahía Hotel (tel. 667/8–3475). Be sure to set the price before the taxi starts moving. Destinations within the city should cost less than $10.

**By Car** Ensenada is an easy city to navigate in that most of the streets are marked. If you are traveling south, you can bypass downtown Ensenada on the Highway 1 truck route down Calle 10. To reach the hotel and waterfront area, stay with Alternate Highway 1 as it travels along the fishing pier and becomes Boulevard Costero, also known as Lázaro Cárdenas and Carretera Transpeninsular. This road ends at Calle Agustín Sangines, also called Calle Delante, which leads out to Highway 1 traveling south. The parking meters along Ensenada's main streets are patrolled regularly; parking tickets come in the form of either a boot on the car's tires or confiscated license plates. Parking has become horrendous as new shopping centers spring up on former parking lots. The paid parking at the new Plaza Marina at the beginning of Boulevard Costero may be your best option.

**Ensenada Rent-a-Car** (tel. 667/8–1896) has an office on Avenida Alvarado between Lázaro Cárdenas and López Mateos.

## Important Addresses and Numbers

**Tourist Information** The **State Tourist Commission** office (Av. López Mateos 1305, tel. 667/6–2222) is open weekdays 7–7, Saturday 9–1, Sunday 10–1. The **Convention and Visitors Bureau** (tel. 667/8–2411) has a stand with pamphlets and brochures on Boulevard Costero at the waterfront.

**Emergencies** **Police** (Ortíz Rubio and Libertad, tel. 134); **Hospital** (Av. Ruíz and Calle 11, tel. 667/8–2525); **Red Cross** (tel. 132).

**Air Evac International** (tel. 619/425–4400) is an air-ambulance service that travels into Mexico from San Diego to bring injured tourists back to the United States.

**Language Classes** A great way to get to know Ensenada and simultaneously improve your Spanish is to attend weekend or week-long classes at the **International Spanish Institute of Ensenada** (tel. 667/6–0109 or 619/472–0600 in CA).

## Guided Tours

**Baja California Tours** (6986 La Jolla Blvd., #204, La Jolla, CA 92037, tel. 619/454–7166, fax 619/454–2703) offers comfortable, informative bus trips throughout Baja and can arrange special-interest tours. Vans depart daily from San Diego to Ensenada; midweek transportation and hotel packages are a real bargain.

**Las Bodegas de Santo Tomás** (Av. Miramar 666, tel. 667/8–3333), Baja's oldest winery, gives tours and tastings daily at 11 AM, 1 PM, and 3 PM and costs $2. Group tours should be arranged in advance.

**Gordo's Sportfishing** (Sportfishing Pier, tel. 667/8–2190) operates whale-watching trips from December through February. The half-day trip goes to La Bufadora and Isla Todos Santos and costs $25 per person.

## Exploring

*Numbers in the margin correspond to points of interest on the Ensenada map.*

The city of Ensenada, the third largest in Baja, hugs the harbor of **Bahía de Todos Santos.** If you have access to a car, begin your tour of Ensenada by driving north up Calle 2 or east on the Mexico Highway 1 bypass around town into the **Chapultepec Hills** to **El Mirador** (The Lookout). From here you can see the entire Bahía de Todos Santos, from the canneries of San Miguel south to the towns of Punta Banda and La Bufadora.

To tour the waterfront and downtown, you'll be better off on foot. As Highway 1 leads into town from the north, it becomes Boulevard Costero, running past shipyards filled with massive freighters. To the right, between the water and the street, the massive Plaza Marina is completed but far from filled with the expected restaurants and shops. At the northernmost point at the water's edge sits an indoor/outdoor **Fish Market,** where row after row of counters display piles of shrimp as well as tuna, dorado, marlin, snapper, and dozens of other species of fish caught off Baja's coasts. Outside, stands sell grilled or smoked fish, seafood cocktails, and fish tacos. Browsers can pick up some standard souvenirs, eat well for very little money, and take some great photographs. The hot-pink Plaza de Mariscos, which blocks the view of the traditional fish market from the street, is a comfortable place in which to eat. **Boulevard Costero** runs along the waterfront from the market and the **Sportfishing Pier** past new minimalls designed to keep tourists by the waterfront. Many of these half-finished buildings lack tenants thus far, as locals and investors adjust to the rapid changes along the waterfront. At the intersection of Boulevard Costero and Avenida Riveroll is the **Plaza Cívica,** with sculptures of Benito Juárez, Miguel Hidalgo, and Venustiano Carranza. Cruise ships dock offshore from here, and passengers are ferried to the pier, where they can walk to the **Centro Artesenal de Ensenada** shopping center.

**Time Out**  You can't visit the fish market without trying at least one fish taco. Strips of fresh snapper, halibut, or other freshly caught fish are dipped in batter and deep-fried, then wrapped in fresh corn tortillas. Choose your topping—cilantro, salsa, tomatoes,

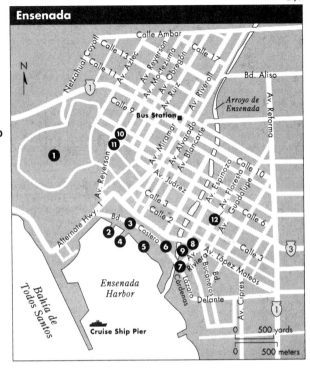

Ensenada

onions, pickled carrots—from an array of dishes set out on the counter.

Boulevard Costero becomes Boulevard Lázaro Cárdenas at
❼ Avenida Riviera, site of the **Riviera del Pacífico.** This rambling
white adobe hacienda-style mansion was built in the 1920s with
money raised on both sides of the border. An enormous gambling palace, hotel, restaurant and bar, the Riviera was a glamorous place frequented by wealthy U.S. citizens and Mexicans,
particularly during Prohibition. When gambling was outlawed
in Mexico and Prohibition ended in the United States, the palace lost its raison d'être. In 1977 the Tourism and Convention
Bureau began refurbishing the palace and its lavish gardens.
During daylight visitors can now tour the elegant ballrooms
and halls, which host occasional art shows and civic events. Riviera del Pácifico is now officially called the Centro Social, Civico
y Cultural de Ensenada (Social, Civic and Cultural Center of
Ensenada), and there are plans to include it in a major con-
vention-center complex along the waterfront. *Blvd. Costero
and Av. Riviera, tel. 667/6–4310. Admission free. Open daily
9–5.*

Ensenada's traditional tourist zone is centered one block east
of the waterfront along **Avenida López Mateos.** High-rise hotels, souvenir shops, restaurants, and bars line the avenue
from its beginning at the foot of the **Chapultepec Hills** for eight
blocks south to the dry channel of the Arroyo de Ensenada.
South of the riverbed, across from a row of inexpensive hotels,
❽ you'll see the **State Tourist Office, Fonart** government crafts

⑨ store, and the **Caliente Foreign Book** (corner of Av. López Mateos and Castillo, tel. 667/6–2133), where horse-racing fans can place their bets on races televised via satellite. Locals shop for furniture, clothing, and other necessities on **Avenida Juárez** ⑩ in Ensenada's downtown area. **Parque Revolución,** near the ⑪ north end of Avenida Juárez at the **Mother's Monument**—a tall, bronze mother holding a child—is the prettiest of the city's parks, with a bandstand, a children's playground, and plenty of comfortable benches in the shade. The city's largest cathedral, ⑫ **Our Lady of Guadalupe,** is at Avenida Floresta and the south end of Juárez.

## Shopping

Most of the tourist shops are located along Avenida López Mateos beside the hotels and restaurants. There are several new two-story shopping arcades with brand-name sportswear stores. Dozens of curio shops line the street, all selling similar selections of pottery, woven blankets and serapes, embroidered dresses, and onyx chess sets.

**Originales Baja** (Av. López Mateos 623) sells large brass and copper birds, wood carvings, and glassware. **Artes de Quijote** (Av. López Mateos 503) has an impressive high-quality selection of carved-wood doors, huge terra-cotta pots, crafts from Oaxaca, and large brass fish and birds. The government-run **Fonart** (Av. López Mateos 1303) is filled with excellent indigenous crafts. **Plaza Hussong's** (Av. Ruiz 337 at Av. López Mateos) is a classy two-story mall completed in early 1992; tenants include a large **Benetton** store and **Lofino's Imports,** displaying European china and crystal. **Avila Imports,** across the street from Hussong's, sells French perfumes, Hummel statues, and crystal. **Librería Banuelos** (Av. Ruíz 370) and **El Spaña** (Av. Ruíz 217) have a good selection of English-language magazines and books. **El Pegaso** (Obregón and Calle Segunda) carries clothing, jewelry, furniture, and crafts from throughout Mexico.

**Centro Artesenal de Ensenada,** a shopping center on the waterfront, caters to cruise-ship visitors. The best shop by far is **Unique Art Center** (no tel.), which carries museum-quality pottery and varied folk art by the indigenous peoples of northern Mexico.

## Sports and Outdoor Activities

Hunting and fishing are popular sports around Ensenada, which calls itself the Yellowtail Capital of the World.

**Sportfishing** Fishing boats leave the **Ensenada Sportfishing Pier** regularly. The best angling is from April through November, with bottom fishing good in the winter. Charter vessels and party boats are available from several outfitters along Avenida López Mateos, Boulevard Costero, and off the sportfishing pier. Trips on group boats cost about $35 per day. Licenses are available at the tourist office or from charter companies.

**Ensenada Clipper Fleet** (pier, tel. 667/8–2185) has charter and group boats.

**Gordo's Sportfishing** (*see* Guided Tours, *above*), one of the oldest sportfishing companies in Ensenada, has a motel on the waterfront, charter boats, group boats, and a smokehouse.

**Golf** **Bajamar** (tel. 667/8–1844) is an excellent 18-hole course 32 kilometers (20 miles) north of Ensenada at the Bajamar condominium and housing resort. The **Baja Country Club** (tel. 667/3–0303) opened in 1991 with 18 holes of golf at a secluded 300-acre course south of Ensenada near Maneadero; it's open to members and guests of the Baja Beach and Tennis Club (Punta Banda, tel. 619/420–8533 in the U.S.).

**Tennis** **Bajamar** and the **Baja Beach and Tennis Club** (*see* Golf, *above*) have courts open to members and guests.

## Beaches

Since the waterfront in Ensenada proper is taken up by fishing boats, the best swimming beaches are south of town. **Estero Beach** is long and clean, with mild waves. Surfers populate the beaches off Highway 1 north and south of Ensenada, particularly at **San Miguel, California, Tres Marías,** and **La Joya** beaches; scuba divers prefer **Punta Banda,** by La Bufadora. Lifeguards are rare; swimmers should be cautious. The tourist office in Ensenada has a map that shows safe diving and surfing beaches.

## Dining

Some restaurants add a service charge of 10% to 15% to your bill in addition to the 15% tax. Dress is casual, and no reservations are necessary unless otherwise indicated. Highly recommended restaurants are indicated by a star ★.

| Category | Cost* |
|---|---|
| Very Expensive | over $20 |
| Expensive | $15–$20 |
| Moderate | $8–$15 |
| Inexpensive | under $8 |

*\*per person for a three-course meal, excluding drinks and service.*

**Expensive** **El Rey Sol.** A family-owned French restaurant over 40 years
★ old, El Rey Sol is in a charming building with stained-glass windows and is decorated with wrought-iron chandeliers and heavy oak tables and chairs. Specialties include French and Mexican presentations of fresh fish, poultry, and vegetables grown at the owner's farm in the Santo Tomás Valley. Appetizers come with the meal; the excellent pastries are baked on the premises. *Av. López Mateos 1000, tel. 667/8–1733. Reservations recommended. Jackets and ties suggested. AE, MC, V.*

**La Casa del Abulón.** The former Kiki's was given a face-lift in 1991, with bouquets of silk flowers, bright pink table linens, and wall murals depicting Neptune and other legends of the sea. But the best additions were a new chef and an ambitious menu featuring abalone prepared in several different ways, along with quail, prime rib, and a superb calamari steak rolled and stuffed with lobster. The menu also lists less expensive

Mexican dishes and burgers. The restaurant has a less-than-perfect ocean view—rock jetties and rusted boats detract from the natural beauty—but in the evening, candlelight and live dance music make it a romantic spot. *Blvd. Costero at Ave. Sangines, tel. 667/6–5785. AE, MC, V.*

**Moderate** **Casamar.** A long-standing, dependable restaurant, Casamar is
★ known for its wide variety of excellent seafood. Large groups, families, and couples fill the main dining room. Lobster and shrimp are prepared in several ways but seem freshest when grilled *con mojo y ajo* (with garlic and butter). The upstairs bar has live jazz on weekend nights. *Blvd. Lázaro Cárdenas 987, tel. 667/4–0417. MC, V.*

**La Hacienda del Viejo.** Also known as El Toro, this large adobe-and-red-tiled restaurant is considered *the* place in town for grilled meats—steak, lamb, and pork—by candlelight. The luncheon menu includes a delectable chicken mole, and the Sunday brunch is a local favorite. *Blvd. Costero 1790, tel. 667/6–0834. MC, V.*

**Taberna Española.** Owner Fernando Ullate has created a warm, comfortable tapas bar and restaurant that has become one of Ensenada's most popular restaurants among locals and visitors alike. The paella alone makes a visit worthwhile; when combined with a pitcher of fruity sangria and a basket of crusty bread, it becomes a memorable feast. Ask about the daily specials. *Blvd. Costero 1982, tel. 667/6–0767. MC, V.*

**Inexpensive** **Cafe Au Lait.** This pretty little French café is a popular lunch spot for fresh sandwiches on pita bread or baguettes, crepes, or baked potatoes smothered with butter and cheese. The pastry counter displays a tempting selection of apple strudel, carrot cake, and a sinful linzer torte, served with cappuccino, espresso, or simple fresh-brewed coffee or teas. *Av. Ruiz 153, tel. 667/4–6647. No credit cards.*

**Plaza Mariscos.** Several fish stands fill this bright pink plaza in front of the fish market. One way to choose your dining spot is by checking out the bowls of condiments arrayed on picnic tables between the stands—if the salsa, onions, cilantro, and pickled vegetables look good, you're bound to like the tacos as well. *Blvd. Costero, no phone. No credit cards.*

## Lodging

Ensenada has become a major resort town, with prices to match. Low-cost places are hard to find, and reservations are a must on holiday weekends, when rates increase as much as 25%. **IMPA/Mexico Information** (7860 Mission Center Ct., Suite 202, San Diego, CA 92108, tel. 619/298–4105, in CA 800/522–1516, elsewhere in U.S. 800/522–1516) handles hotel reservations, tourist information, and group tours, and often has special packages and rates for Baja hotels. Highly recommended lodgings are indicated by a star ★.

| Category | Cost* |
| --- | --- |
| Very Expensive | over $90 |
| Expensive | $60–$90 |

| | |
|---|---|
| Moderate | $25–$60 |
| Inexpensive | under $25 |

*All prices are for a standard double room, excluding service charge and tax (10%).*

**Very Expensive**
★
**Las Rosas.** This elegant pink palace just north of town is by far the most modern hotel in the area; the atrium lobby features marble floors, mint-green-and-pink upholstered couches facing the sea, and a green-glass ceiling that glows at night. All rooms face the ocean and pool; some have fireplaces and Jacuzzis, and even the least expensive accommodations are lovely. The hotel is booked solid most weekends; make reservations far in advance. *Mexico Hwy. 1 north of town, tel. 667/4–4310. 32 rooms and suites. Facilities: pool, hot tub, restaurant, cocktail lounge, jewelry shop, gallery. AE, MC, V.*

**Expensive**
**Corona.** The only hotel on the waterfront, the Corona resembles a little seaside castle, with its white towers and peaks rising above the red-tiled roof. The rooms have bleached-wood furnishings, beige carpeting, tiled baths, and balconies facing the water or downtown. The hotel is almost always full on weekends; reservations are essential.*Blvd. Costero 1442, tel. 667/6–4023; reservations in the U.S.: 482 San Ysidro Blvd., Suite 203, San Ysidro, CA 92173. 93 rooms. Facilities: pool bar, marina, MC, V.*

**Punta Morro.** For seclusion and the sound of crashing surf, you can't beat this all-suites hotel 2 miles north of town beside the university campus. The three-story tan building faces the north end of the bay; the restaurant sits on rock pilings above the waves. Studios and one-, two-, and three-bedroom suites have terraces facing the ocean, kitchenettes, and seating areas; some also feature fireplaces. The large rectangular hot tub is the place for mingling and enjoying the scenery, while the wooden deck that juts out from the cliffs is the spot for those in search of solitude. Stairs lead down to a rocky beach, but the surf is usually too rough for swimming. *Mexico Hwy. 1, 2 mi north of town, tel. 667/8–3507 or 800/726–6426; reservations in the U.S.: Box 434263, San Diego, CA 92143-4263. 30 suites. Facilities: restaurant, bar, pool, hot tub, beach. MC, V.*

**Moderate**
**Villa Fontana.** An architectural oddity in a town full of Spanish tiled roofs, this peak gabled hotel has a New England look. The rooms are decorated in pastels; choose one at the back, away from street noise. There is enclosed parking—a major plus in downtown Ensenada. The hotel has a very reasonably priced sportfishing package that is immensely popular. *Av. López Mateos, tel. 667/8–3434. 60 rooms. Facilities: pool, tour desk. MC, V.*

**Quintas Papagayo.** A bungalow and low-rise seaside establishment opened in 1947, Quintas Papagayo is a place where couples honeymoon and come back each year for their anniversaries. The accommodations are far from spectacular—rustic and homey are better descriptions—but you feel as if you've discovered a special hideaway where everyone remembers your name. Fireplaces, kitchens, patios, and decks are available. *Mexico Hwy. 1 north of town, tel. 667/4–4980 or 667/4–4155; reservations: Box 150, Ensenada, BC 22880, Mexico, or tel. 619/491–0682 in the U.S. 50 rooms. Facilities: pool, restaurant, bar, tennis courts, beach. MC, V.*

★ **San Nicolás.** Hidden behind cement walls painted with Indian murals, this massive resort doesn't look like much from the street. The San Nicolas was built in the early 1970s, but much of it has been refurbished. The suites boast tiled hot tubs; living rooms with deep green carpeting, mauve furnishings, and beveled-glass doors; and mirrored ceilings in the bedrooms. The less extravagant rooms are comfortable and decorated with folk art. A waterfall cascades into the pool and a good restaurant overlooks the gardens. *Av. López Mateos and Av. Guadalupe, tel. 667/6–1901; reservations in the U.S.: Box 4C, San Ysidro, CA 92073, tel. 800/225–2786. 150 rooms and suites. Facilities: 2 pools, hot tub, restaurant, cocktail lounge, disco, convention facilities, shops, cable TV. AE, MC, V.*

**Inexpensive** **Joker Hotel.** A bizarre, brightly colored mishmash of styles makes it hard to miss this hotel, conveniently located for those traveling south of Ensenada. Spacious rooms have private balconies, satellite TV, and phones. *3 mi south of Ensenada on Hwy. 1, tel. 667/6–7201; reservations in the U.S.: 800/678–7244. 20 rooms. Facilities: pool, whirlpool. MC, V.*

### Nightlife

Ensenada is a party town for college students, surfers, and other young tourists. **Hussong's** and **Papa's and Beer** on Avenida Ruíz are rowdy at night. Most of the expensive hotels have bars and discos that are less frenetic.

**La Taberna Espanola** (Blvd. Costero 1982) is a great place to gather for a night-long feast of tapas and sangria and a flamenco show. **Smitty González,** on Avenida Ryerson, attracts devoted disco dancers. **Joy's Discotheque** at Avenidas López Mateos and Balboa is popular with the locals.

# Northeast Baja: Mexicali, Tecate, and San Felipe

**Mexicali,** with a current population estimated at 800,000, shares the Imperial Valley farmland and the border crossing with Calexico, a small California city. The capital of Baja California Norte, Mexicali sees a great deal of government activity and a steady growth of *maquiladoras* (foreign manufacturing plants). Though water is scarce in these largely desert lands, the Mexicali area is blessed with some of the world's richest topsoil, and agriculture is a primary source of income in this section of Mexico. Mexicali is not a tourist destination but rather a place where politicians and bureaucrats meet. A train that reaches points throughout Mexico originates in Mexicali, which is also a point of entry for travelers to the beaches of San Felipe.

The construction of the Imperial Canal in 1902 brought an influx of Chinese immigrants to the region. Their presence is strongly seen in the faces of many inhabitants; Mexicali is a good place to sample Chinese cuisine, and Chinese imports fill the curio shops. After the completion of the Imperial Canal, Mexicali began its prodigious growth, transformed forever from the small mining outpost it had been for years.

At the end of Highway 5, which travels 200 kilometers (125 miles) south of Mexicali along solitary stretches of desert and salt marshes, lies the fishing village of **San Felipe** on the Sea of Cortés. Not until 1948, when the first paved road from the northern capital was completed, did San Felipe become a town of permanent residence. Now it is home to an impressive fishing and shrimping fleet. A hurricane nearly destroyed San Felipe in 1967, but residents rebuilt most of the town, and since then it has grown steadily.

Bahía San Felipe has dramatic changes in its tides. The tides crest at 6 meters (20 feet), and since the beach is so shallow, the waterline can move in and out up to 1 kilometer (about ½ mile). The local fishermen are well aware of the peculiarities of this section of the Sea of Cortés. Many of them visit the shrine of the Cerro de la Virgen (Virgin of Guadalupe), which sits high on a hill at the north end of the bay, before setting sail.

A popular getaway spot for years, San Felipe used to be a place where only hardy travelers in recreational vehicles and campers hid out for weeks on end. Now there are at least a dozen campgrounds on the beaches outside town and a half-dozen hotels in town that fill up quickly during the winter and spring holidays. Dune buggies, motorcycles, and off-road vehicles abound. On weekends San Felipe can be boisterous. The town also draws many sportfishermen, especially in the spring; launches, bait, and supplies are readily available.

**Tecate** is about 144 kilometers (90 miles) west of Mexicali on Highway 2. It is a quiet community, a typical small Mexican town (70,000 population) that happens to be on the border. So incidental is the border to local life that its gates are closed from midnight until 7 AM. Tecate beer, one of the most popular brands in Mexico, is brewed here. Maquiladoras and agriculture are the other main industries. Tecate's primary tourist draw is Rancho la Puerta, a fitness resort that caters to well-heeled southern Californians. A bit farther south, the valleys of Guadalupe and Calafia boast some of Mexico's lushest vineyards. Olives and grain are also grown in profusion here.

### Arriving and Departing by Plane

There are no flights from the United States to the Mexicali International Airport, but flights within Mexico are available on **Mexicana** (tel. 800/531–7921), **Aeroméxico** (tel. 800/237–6639), and regional carriers.

San Felipe has an international airport but no regular commercial flights so far; private and charter planes land there.

### Arriving and Departing by Car, Bus, and Train

**By Car**  Mexicali is located on the border, opposite Calexico, California, approximately 184 kilometers (115 miles) east of San Diego and 88 kilometers (55 miles) west of Yuma, Arizona. Tecate lies on the border between Tijuana and Mexicali on Highway 2. A new toll road opened along this route in 1992. The 134-kilometer (84-mile) journey from Tecate east to Mexicali on La Rumorosa, as the road is known, is as exciting as a roller-coaster ride, with the highway twisting and turning down steep mountain grades and over flat, barren desert. San Felipe lies on the coast, 200 kilometers (125 miles) south of Mexicali via Highway 5. Visitors in this area will not need tourist cards but should purchase Mexican car insurance at agencies near the border.

**By Bus**  Four Mexican bus lines run out of the Mexicali station. **Tres Estrellas de Oro** goes through Tecate on its way to Tijuana; **Transportes del Pacifico** goes to Mexico City and other points on the mainland; **Transportes Norte de Sonora** frequents border towns in Baja and on the mainland; and **Autotransportes de Baja California** goes to San Felipe, Tijuana, and Ensenada. It is possible to purchase reserved seats the day before departure, but only at the bus station (Centro Cívico, Av. Independencia, tel. 65/57–2422).

*Mexicali*  **Central Bus Station** (Centro Cívico, Av. Independencia, tel. 65/57–2422).

*San Felipe*  **Central Bus Station/Autotransportes de Baja California** (Av. Mar de Cortés, tel. 657/7–1039).

*Tecate*  **Central Bus Station** (Av. Benito Juárez and Calle Abelardo Rodríguez, tel. 665/4–1221).

**By Train**  Although there is no train service available through Baja, **El Tren del Pacifico** (Estación de Ferroccarril, Box 3–182, Mexicali, Baja California, Mexico, tel. 65/57–2101) runs from Mexicali to points south in the mainland interior. The station is located at the south end of Calle Ulises Irigoyen, a few blocks north of the intersection of Avenida López Mateos and Avenida Independencia. Trains leave twice daily. The fares are reasonable, and there are several different travel options for which you may make advance reservations.

## Getting Around

**By Car**  The ideal way to see the northeastern part of Baja is to drive your own car or rent one in Mexicali. Most U.S. car-rental agencies do not allow their cars to be taken into Mexico. (*See* Getting Around by Car in the Tijuana section, *above*, for those that do). Be sure to buy Mexican auto insurance before driving into Baja.

Four major rental agencies operate out of the Mexicali airport: **Avis** (tel. 800/331–1212), **Budget** (tel. 800/527–0700), **Hertz** (tel. 800/654–3131), and **National** (tel. 800/227–7368).

**By Taxi**  Taxis are easy to find in Mexicali, Tecate, and San Felipe. Negotiate your fare before you start the trip.

## Important Addresses and Numbers

**Tourist Information**  Information is available at the **Tourist Commission** and **Mexicali Chamber of Commerce** offices (Blvd. López Mateos and Calle Camelias, tel. 65/52–9795). In Tecate, the **State Tourism Office** (1305 Libertad Alley, tel. 665/4–1095) has a full array of pamphlets and an English-speaking clerk; the office keeps rather erratic hours, however. The **San Felipe State Tourism Office** (Av. Mar de Cortés, tel. 657/7–1155) is open weekdays 9–7 and weekends 10–2.

**Emergencies Mexicali**  **Police** (Centro Cívico, tel. 65/2–4443); **Hospital** (Durango and Salina Cruz, tel. 657/5–1666).

*San Felipe*  **Police** (Ortiz Rubio and Libertad, tel. 657/7–1006); **Hospital** (tel. 657/7–1001).

*Tecate*  **Police** (Libertad Alley, tel. 665/4–1176 or 134); **Red Cross** (tel. 132); **Fire** (tel. 136).

## Guided Tours

**Baja California Tours** (6986 La Jolla Blvd., #204, La Jolla, CA 92037, tel. 619/454–7166, fax 619/454–2703) offers comfortable, informative bus trips daily from San Diego to San Felipe; midweek transportation and hotel packages are a real bargain.

## Exploring

Most visitors come to **Mexicali** on business, and the city's sights are few and far between. A tourist-oriented strip of curio shops and sleazy bars is located along Avenida Francisco Madero, one block south of the border. The **Regional Museum,** administered by the Autonomous University of Baja California (UABC), provides a comprehensive introduction to the natural and cultural history of Baja. *Av. Reforma 1998, near Calle L, tel. 65/62–5717. Admission free. Open Tues.–Fri. 9–6, weekends 10–4.*

**Parque Obregón** at Avenida Reforma and Calle Irigoyen and **Parque Constitución** at Avenida México and Zuazua are the only two parks in downtown Mexicali. The **Mexicali Zoo** is in the City Park, **Bosque de la Ciudad,** south of town; the entrance is at the south end of Calle Victoria, between Cárdenas and Avenida Independencia.

If you allocate an hour for exploring **Tecate,** you'll be hard put to fill your time. **Parque Hildalgo,** in the center of town, is a typical Mexican village plaza, with a small gazebo and a few wrought-iron benches. **Parque López Mateos,** on Highway 3 south of town, is the site for dance and band concerts on summer evenings.

**San Felipe** is the quintessential dusty fishing village, with one main street (two if you count the highway into town). The *malecón* (waterfront boardwalk) is little more than a cement sidewalk beside a seawall, with a collection of fishing *pangas* (small boats) clustered at one end. The only landmark in town is the **shrine of the Virgin of Guadalupe,** at the north end of the malecón on a hill overlooking the Sea of Cortés and San Felipe Bay.

## Shopping

**Baldini Importers** in Mexicali (Calle 7 and Av. Reforma) offers a nice selection of imported items. In Tecate, a large artisans' market is located just off the Tecate–Ensenada highway. San Felipe carries the typical array of sombreros, sundresses, and T-shirts, and a large supply of fireworks.

## Sports and Outdoor Activities

*Mexicali*  Golf is played at the **Mexicali Campestre Golf Course** (Km 11.5
*Golf*  on Hwy. 5 south of town, tel. 65/61–7130).

*San Felipe*  The Sea of Cortés offers plentiful sea bass, snapper, corbina,
*Fishing*  halibut, and other game fish. Most hotels can arrange fishing trips; also check at the **Fishing Cooperative** office on Calle Zihuatanejo. Clamming is good here as well.

Long-range fishing trips from San Felipe are available through **Tony Reyes** (tel. 714/538–8010) and **Baja Fishing Tours** (2143 San Diego Ave., San Diego, CA 92110, tel. 800/832–BAJA).

## Dining

Northeast Baja is not known for fine dining, but there are several good Chinese restaurants in Mexicali. Your best bet in San Felipe is seafood, especially fresh shrimp. Dress is casual and reservations are not required. Highly recommended restaurants are indicated by a star ★.

| Category | Cost* |
| --- | --- |
| Expensive | $15–$20 |
| Moderate | $8–$15 |
| Inexpensive | under $8 |

*\*per person for a three-course meal, excluding drinks and service.*

**Mexicali**
*Expensive*
★

**La Misión Dragón.** With its eclectic landscape, this restaurant resembles a combination of a mission house and a Chinese palace. Behind its gates are fountains, a garden, and Asian and Mexican artifacts. The locals hold large dinner celebrations here, and the Chinese food is top-notch. *Av. Lázaro Cárdenas 555, tel. 65/66–4320 or 65/6–4451. MC, V.*

*Moderate*

**Cenaduría Selecta.** This charming restaurant has been serving traditional Mexican food since 1945. Service is formal and efficient, the menus come in wooden folders, and the rows of booths always seem to be filled with locals enjoying themselves. *Av. Arista and Calle C 1510, tel. 65/62–4047. MC, V.*

*Inexpensive*
★

**Casita de Pátzcuaro.** A good place for tacos and burritos, this is a favorite with regulars headed for San Felipe. *Av. López Mateos 648, tel. 65/62–9707. No credit cards.*

**Las Cazuelas.** A nice, clean restaurant, Las Cazuelas serves traditional Mexican dishes and good combination meals. *Av. Benito Juárez 56, tel. 65/64–0649. No credit cards.*

**San Felipe**
*Expensive*

**Alfredo's.** Located in the Las Palmas Hotel, Alfredo's is run by Mexico City restaurateur Alfredo Bellinghieri. The fettuccine Alfredo and lasagna are first-rate, and the tender, tasty *carne asada Siciliano* (grilled beef) is marinated in olive oil and oregano. *Calle Mar Báltico, tel. 657/7–1333. MC, V.*

*Moderate*

**Rubens.** This trailer-park restaurant is a popular hangout for regulars who come to San Felipe year after year. The Coco Loco, a blend of liquors and coconut milk, is reason enough to return, and the shrimp omelet receives high marks. *North of town on Ave. Golfo de California, tel. 65/7–1091. MC, V.*

*Inexpensive*

**Tacos La Gaviota** and **Tacos La Bonita,** both in the downtown area, serve tacos filled with fish, clam, shrimp, or pork at outdoor stands. Straddle a stool at the counter, order one of each, and enjoy a $2 feast. *Av. Mar de Cortés, no phone. No credit cards.*

**Tecate**
*Moderate*

**El Passetto.** The best Italian restaurant in Tecate, El Passetto has superb garlic bread and homemade pasta. The proprietor makes his own wines, which are pretty good. There's live music on weekends. *Callejón Libertad 200, tel. 665/4–1361. MC, V.*

*Inexpensive* **Le Jardine.** The setting is plain and the food simple Mexican fare, but the café tables outside offer a gratifying view of the plaza. *Libertad Alley 274, no phone. No credit cards.*

## Lodging

Hotels are abundant in Mexicali but scarce in San Felipe and Tecate. Accommodations, as a rule, are modest and plain. **IMPA/Mexico Information** (7860 Mission Center Ct., Suite 202, San Diego, CA 92108, tel. 619/298–4105 or 800/522–1516 in CA; 800/522–1516 elsewhere in U.S.) handles hotel reservations for the area. Highly recommended lodgings are indicated by a star ★.

| Category | Cost* |
|---|---|
| Very Expensive | over $90 |
| Expensive | $60–$90 |
| Moderate | $25–$60 |
| Inexpensive | under $25 |

*\*All prices are for a standard double room, excluding service charge and sales tax (10%).*

**Mexicali** **Holiday Inn.** This is the perennial favorite of those doing busi-
*Expensive* ness in the city, with standard rooms and services and no sur-
prises. *Av. Benito Juárez 2220, tel. 65/66–3801; reservations in the U.S.: 800/465–4329. 173 rooms. Facilities: pool, coffee shop, restaurant, bar. AE, MC, V.*

★ **La Lucerna.** The prettiest hotel in Mexicali, La Lucerna has lots of palms and fountains around the pool. *Av. Benito Juárez 2151, tel. 65/66–1000; reservations in the U.S.: Box 2300, Calexico, CA 92231. 200 rooms. Facilities: pool, restaurant, coffee shop, bar. MC, V.*

**San Felipe** **Las Misiones.** A pretty oasis of blue pools and green palms by
*Expensive* the beach, this resort is popular with group tours. Las Misiones is a good choice for travelers who want to get away from it all, but if you want to feel as if you're actually in Mexico, you're better off at a hotel in town. *Av. Misión de Loreto 130, tel. 657/7–1280 or 800/336–5454. 241 rooms. Facilities: restaurant, bar, 3 pools, tennis courts. MC, V.*

*Moderate* **El Cortés.** Probably the most popular hotel in San Felipe, El
★ Cortés has a lively bar, a long, clean beach, and a small pool and hot tub. Some of the rooms have beachfront patios. *Av. Mar de Cortez, tel. 657/7–1055; reservations in the U.S.: Box 1227, Calexico, CA 92231, tel. 706/566–8324. 90 rooms. Facilities: pool, beach, restaurant, bar, boat launch. MC, V.*

**Tecate** **Hacienda Santa Veronica.** Billed as an off-road and dirt-racing
*Expensive* country club, the Hacienda is a pretty countryside resort fea-
turing rooms furnished with Mexican colonial beds, bureaus, and fireplaces. The off-road raceway is set far enough away from the rooms to keep the noise of revving engines from dis-
turbing the guests, and a number of trails for horseback riding traverse the property. *Hwy 2, 2 mi east of Tecate, no phone; reservations in the U.S.: tel. 619/298–4105. 87 rooms. Facili-*

*ties: restaurant, pool, bar, tennis courts, horseback riding, RV park. MC, V.*

**Rancho Tecate.** A family winery has been converted into a peaceful country resort with casitas and a main guest house. A golf course is under construction, with a few holes ready for play. *Hwy 3, 5 mi south of Tecate, tel. 665/4–0011. 37 rooms. Facilities: restaurant, bar, tennis, golf. MC, V.*

## Health Spas

**Tecate**
*Very Expensive*

**Rancho la Puerta.** For those who can afford $1,500 or more a week, Rancho la Puerta is a peaceful, isolated health spa and resort just west of Tecate. Spanish-style buildings with red-tiled roofs and modern glass-and-wood structures are spread throughout the sprawling ranch. Hiking trails lead off into scrub-pine hills surrounding the resort, and a large bright-blue pool is a central gathering spot. Guests stay in luxurious private cottages and usually check in for a week or more, taking advantage of the special diet and exercise regimen to lose weight and shape up. *Hwy. 2, 5 km (3 mi) west of Tecate, tel. 65/4–1005, or 619/744–4222 in CA, 800/443–7565. 80 rooms. Facilities: health club, massage, beauty salon, pool, tennis courts, restaurant. AE, MC, V.*

## The Arts and Nightlife

**Mexicali**

**Teatro del Estado** (tel. 65/64–0757), on Calle López Mateos near the government center, often presents stage hits from Mexico City; dance troupes and musical groups, both classical and modern, are frequently featured as well.

**San Felipe**

The bar at the **El Cortez Hotel** (tel. 657/7–1055) is always crowded. **Hotel Las Misiones** (tel. 657/7–1280) has live music and dancing on weekend nights.

# Guerrero Negro and Scammon's Lagoon

Humans aren't the only travelers who migrate below the border for warmth in the winter months. Every winter thousands of great gray whales swim south from the Bering Sea off Alaska to the tip of the Baja Peninsula. From January to March up to 6,000 stop close to the shore near Scammon's Lagoon—at the 28th parallel, just over the state line between Baja Norte and Baja Sur—to give birth to their calves. Far from diminutive, the newborns weigh about one-half ton and drink nearly 50 gallons of milk each day.

If it weren't for the whales, and the Transpeninsular Highway, which runs near town, few travelers would venture to **Guerrero Negro**, a town of 10,000 located some 720 kilometers (450 miles) south of Tijuana; the name Guerrero Negro, which means Black Warrior, was derived from a whaling ship that ran aground in nearby Scammon's Lagoon in 1858. Near the Vizcaíno desert, on the Pacific Ocean, the area is best known for its salt mines, which provide work for much of the town's population and produce one-third of the world's salt supply. Salt water collects in over 780 square kilometers (300 square miles) of sea-level ponds and evaporates quickly in the desert heat, leaving huge blocks of pure white salt.

Scammon's Lagoon is about 27 kilometers (17 miles) south, down a passable but rough sand road that crosses the salt flats. The lagoon got its name from U.S. explorer Charles Melville Scammon of Maine, who discovered it off the coast of Baja in the mid-1800s. The whales and calves that visited these waters were a much easier and more plentiful prey for the whalers than the great leviathans swimming in the open sea. On his first expedition to the lagoon, Scammon and his crew collected more than 700 barrels of valuable whale oil, and the whale rush was on. Within 10 years, nearly all the whales in the lagoon had been killed, and it took almost a century for the whale population to increase to what it had been before Scammon arrived. It wasn't until the 1940s that the U.S. and Mexican governments took measures to protect the whales and banned the whalers from the lagoon.

Today even whale-watching boats must have permission from the Mexican government to enter Scammon's Lagoon, known in Mexico as Laguna Ojo de Liebre (Hare's Eye Lagoon). The area around the lagoon is now a national park, Parque Natural de Ojo de Liebre (Rabbit's Eye Natural Park). Whale-watching from the shores of the lagoon can be disappointing without binoculars. But it is still an impressive sight to see the huge mammals spouting water high into the air, their 12-foot-wide tails striking the water.

At **Laguna de San Ignacio,** about 100 kilometers (62 miles) south, fishermen will take you out in their boats to get closer to the whales. But for a better view, and an easier stay in this rugged country, travel with an outfitter who will arrange your travel to Guerrero Negro, your accommodations, and your time on the water. The whales will come close to your boat, rising majestically from the water, and sometimes swim close enough to be petted on their crusted backs.

## Arriving and Departing

**By Plane** The closest international airport to Guerrero Negro is in La Paz, 800 kilometers (500 miles) southeast; there is a small airstrip in town.

**By Car and Bus** Guerrero Negro is just south of the Baja Norte/Baja Sur state line, about 720 kilometers (450 miles) from the Tijuana border. **Tres Estrellas de Oro** (tel. 682/2–3063 in La Paz) has buses to Guerrero Negro from La Paz.

## Guided Tours

The best way to see the whales is with a tour company that's familiar with the area. **Baja Expeditions** (2625 Garnet Ave., San Diego, CA 92109, tel. 619/581–3311; 800/843–6967 outside CA), the premier Baja adventure operator in the United States, has whale-watching trips on boats and kayaks. **Baja Discovery** (Box 152527, San Diego, CA 92115, tel. 619/262–0700 or 800/ 829–BAJA) operates a whale-watching camp at Laguna San Ignacio south of Guerrero Negro, with tent camping on an island in the lagoon and boat trips among the whales. **Eco-Tours Malarrimo** (Blvd. Zapata at the entrance to Guerrero Negro, tel. 685/7–0250) conducts guided tours from Guerrero Negro to

Scammon's Lagoon; two hours in a small boat watching the whales runs $30 per person.

## Dining

The best restaurant in town, specializing in seafood, is **Malarrimo**, on Boulevard Zapata near the entrance to town. Though the prices have climbed to the high-moderate range, the food is still worth the cost. Try **Mario's**, on Blvd. Zapata by the El Morro hotel, for seafood and Mexican dishes. The small, pretty **Puerto Viejo** on Boulevard Zapata also offers good standard Mexican dishes and seafood, but prices here are higher.

## Lodging

There are several hotels in Guerrero Negro, none of which is worth visiting as a destination unto itself. Double-occupancy rooms cost from about $25 to $70 per day; rates tend to increase during the peak whale-watching season from January through March. None of the hotels has heat, and winter nights can be downright frigid. Credit cards are not normally accepted, but the hotels do take traveler's checks.

**El Morro.** A small motel operated by the owners of one of the largest hotels in Santa Rosalia, the El Morro is serviceable; the air-conditioned rooms have private baths and hot showers. *Blvd. Zapata, no phone. No credit cards.*
**La Pinta.** A few kilometers outside of town and looking like an oasis of palms in the desert, La Pinta is the largest hotel in town. The clean, functional rooms are dependable, and the setting more attractive than that of other local lodgings, but the rates are very high for the area. Package deals are sometimes available for travelers using the La Pinta hotels throughout the peninsula. *Reservations in the U.S.: tel. 800/336-5454. 26 rooms. Facilities: coffee shop.*
**Malarrimo.** This popular trailer park and restaurant has an eight-room motel, with private baths and TV. It fills up quickly and is one of the best deals in town. *Blvd. Zapata, tel. 685/7-0250.*

# Loreto

On the Sea of Cortés, some 1,200 kilometers (750 miles) south of the U.S. border in California, Loreto's setting is truly spectacular. The gold and green hills of the Sierra Gigante seem to tumble into the cobalt sea. Rain is rare. According to the local promoters, the skies are clear 360 days of the year. There aren't even any bugs—or at least very few—to plague vacationers. The dry, desert climate is not one in which insects thrive.

Loreto was the site of the first California mission. Jesuit priests Eusebio Kino and Juan María Salvatierra settled the area in the 1680s and work began on the mission buildings in 1697. It was from Loreto that Father Junípero Serra, a Franciscan monk from Mallorca, Spain, set out in 1769 to found missions from San Diego to San Francisco—in the land then known as Alta California.

Mexico won its independence from Spain in 1821, and the missions were gradually abandoned. The priests, who were often from Spain, were ordered to return home. Loreto had been the administrative as well as the religious center of the Californias, but with the withering of the mission and the 1829 hurricane that virtually destroyed the settlement, the capital of the Californias was moved to La Paz. A severe earthquake struck the Loreto area in 1877, further destroying the town.

For a century the village languished. The U.S. fishermen who rediscovered the town were a hearty breed who flew down in their own aircraft and went after marlin and sailfish in open launches. Loreto's several small hotels were built to serve this rough-and-ready set; most of the properties were built before 1960, when no highway came down this far and there was no airport worthy of the name.

In 1976, when the coffers were filled with oil revenue, the government tapped the Loreto area for development. Streets were paved in the dusty little village, and telephone service, electricity, potable water, and sewage systems were installed in both the town and the surrounding area. The town even got an international airport. A luxury hotel was built, as was a championship tennis center, where John McEnroe was signed as a touring pro. Then the money dried up, investors could no longer be found, and everything came to a halt. No new hotels have opened since 1980. The Loreto Tennis Tournament, where McEnroe puts in an appearance, moved to Ixtapa.

Today Loreto, with a population of 15,000, is a good place to escape the crowds, relax, and go fishing. The fears of sports enthusiasts that the town would be spoiled have thus far been largely unfounded, though the residential trailer parks are filling up and private homes are clustered in secluded enclaves. Loreto is much the way it was decades ago, except that now it is more accessible.

All that may change if the plans of Fonatur, the government tourism-development agency, go through. Its projects take in some 24 kilometers (15 miles) of coastline. A large marina has gone up at Puerto Escondido, but planned hotels are awaiting construction. Loreto is slated as a bedroom community for the people who will work at the hotels, shops, and restaurants that have yet to be built.

## Arriving and Departing by Plane

**Aero California** (tel.683/3–0500 and 800/237–6225) has daily flights from Los Angeles and La Paz to Loreto's airport, which is 7.2 kilometers (4.5 miles) southwest of town.

## Arriving and Departing by Car, Bus, and Ferry

Loreto is 1,200 kilometers (750 miles) south of the U.S. border via Highway 1. Early starts are recommended to avoid nighttime driving. **Tres Estrellas de Oro** (tel. 662/6–1146 in Tijuana) provides bus services along this route.

The **Sematur ferry** travels from Guaymas on the mainland Pacific coast to Santa Rosalia on the Baja California Peninsula. The ferry departs for the eight-hour trip to the mainland at 8 AM on Wednesday and Sunday, and arrives in Santa Rosalia on Tuesday and Friday at 5 PM. Advance tickets are available at the

Santa Rosalia ferry terminal just south of town on the highway to
Loreto.

## Getting Around

**By Taxi**  Taxis are in good supply, and fares are inexpensive. It is wise to
establish the fare in advance.

**By Rental Car**  The **Thrifty** car-rental agency has a desk in the **Stouffer
Presidente Hotel** (tel. 683/3–0700). Standard sedans and four-
wheel-drive vehicles are available; reserve in advance to be
sure you'll get what you want. There are two gas stations in
Loreto; be sure to fill your tank before heading out on any long
jaunts.

## Important Addresses and Numbers

**The Fonatur Tourist Information Office** (on the east side of the
highway just after the turnoff into Loreto, no phone; closed
Sat. and Sun.) is the only information center in town that's open
at this time. Hotel tour desks may be better sources for basic
facts. **Police,** who may not speak English (tel. 683/3–0035).

## Guided Tours

Picnic cruises to Isla Coronado, excursions into the mountains
to visit the San Javier Mission and view prehistoric rock paintings, and day trips to Mulege can be arranged through hotels.
The local tour operator is **Agencia Loretours** (on the malecón
beside the La Misión hotel, tel. and fax 683/3–5–0088).
**Alfredo's Sportfishing** (on the malecón, Box 39, Loreto BCS
23880, tel. 683/3–0165, fax 683/3–0590) can arrange tours as
well as fishing excursions and is a good source of general information on the area.

## Exploring

One could allocate 15 minutes for a tour of downtown Loreto
and still have time left over. The renovated malecón, built in
1991, has turned the waterfront into a pleasant place for a
stroll: A marina houses the panga fleet and private yachts; the
adjoining beach is a popular gathering spot for locals, especially on Sunday afternoons; and the beach playground has a great
assortment of play equipment for children. The small **zócalo**
(main square) and town center is one block west on Calle
Salvatierra. The only historic sight is **La Misión de Nuestra Señora de Loreto,** the first of the California missions. Founded in
1697 by Jesuit Father Juan María Salvatierra, the church was
the beginning of a chain of missions that eventually stretched as
far as San Francisco and Sonoma in what is now the United
States. The carved stone walls, wood-beam ceilings, gilded altar, and primitive-style portraits of the priests who have
served there are worth seeing. Next door, the **Museum of Anthropology and History,** also called **El Museo de los Misiones**
(open Wed.–Sun 9–4), contains religious relics, tooled leather
saddles used in the 19th century, and displays of Baja's history.
Adjacent to the church is a new shopping complex with boutiques that sell fine silver and crafts.

**Nopoló,** an area being developed for luxury resorts, is about 8
kilometers (5 miles) south of town. The five-star Stouffer

Presidente closed in 1992, but the 9-court tennis complex across the way is still in operation. Between the highway and Nopoló Bay, the first 9 holes of a spectacular 18-hole golf course opened in 1991 after years of construction.

According to Fonatur's plans there will be 5,700 hotel rooms in the Nopoló area, along with about 1,000 private homes and condo units within 10 years. For now, sidewalks and concrete foundation slabs run through fields of weeds and shrubs.

More progress has been made 16 kilometers (10 miles) down the road in **Puerto Escondido,** where the marina contains more than 100 boat slips. Work has begun on a condo complex by the marina, and it is rumored that the long-awaited marina hotel will be built by French investors. Nearby is a recreational vehicle park, **Tripui,** with a good restaurant, a few motel rooms, a snack shop, a bar, stores, showers, a laundry, a pool, and tennis courts. A boat ramp has been completed at the marina; the port captain's offices (tel. 683/3-0656, fax 683/3–0465, open Mon.– Fri. 8–3) are located just south of the ramp. Boaters must pay a fee to launch at the ramp. **Isla Danzante,** 5 kilometers (3 miles) southeast of Puerto Escondido, has good diving and reefs.

Picnic trips to nearby **Coronado Island** , inhabited only by sea lions, may be arranged in Loreto at Nopoló or in Puerto Escondido. Snorkeling and scuba-diving opportunities are excellent.

## Off the Beaten Track

Go north on Highway 1 for 134 kilometers (84 miles) to reach **Mulege,** an old mission settlement and now a charming tropical town set beside a river flowing into the Sea of Cortés. Mulege has become a popular destination for travelers who are interested in exploring the nearby mountains and for kayakers drawn to Bahía Concepción, the largest protected bay in Baja.

Well worth an hour's stroll is **Santa Rosalia,** 64 kilometers (40 miles) north, a dusty mining town with a mix of French, Mexican, and American Old West–style architecture. It's known for its **Iglesia Santa Barbara,** a prefabricated iron church designed by Alexandre-Gustave Eiffel, creator of the Eiffel Tower. Be sure to stop by **El Boleo** (Av. Obregon at Calle 4), the best-known bakery in Baja, where fresh breads bring a lineup of eager customers weekday mornings at 10 AM.

## Shopping

There are few opportunities for shopping in Loreto. Curios and T-shirts are available at shops at the hotels and downtown. **El Alacran,**in the small shopping complex behind the church on Calle Salvatierra, has a remarkable selection of folk art, jewelry, and sportswear. Groceries and ice are available at **El Pescador,** on Calle Salvatierra, the town's only remaining supermarket.

## Sports and Outdoor Activities

Fishing  Fishing put Loreto on the map, especially for the American sports enthusiast. Cabrillo and snapper are caught year-round; yellowtail in the spring; and dorado, marlin, and sailfish in the summer. Visitors who plan to fish should bring tackle with them because the type that is available locally is likely to be primitive and worn. All Loreto-area hotels can arrange fishing, and many own skiffs; the local fishermen congregate with their small boats on the beach at the north end of town. **Alfredo's Sportfishing** (tel. 683/3–0016, fax 683/3–0590) has good guides for anglers.**Sportsman's Tours** (2945 Harding St., Ste. 211, Carlsbad, CA 92008, tel. 619/630–BAJA or 800/234–0618, fax 619/720–0528) organizes fishing trips to Loreto and other spots in Baja.

Golf    The first 9 holes of the 18-hole Loreto Campo de Golf (tel. 683/3–0788), located along Nopoló Bay at the south side of Fonatur's resort development, opened in 1991. Several hotels in Loreto offer golf packages and reduced or free greens fees.

Kayaking    Kayakers who have heard the tales of Baja's gorgeous undeveloped coastline are flocking to the peninsula by the dozens, in groups arranged through outfitters that include **Baja Expeditions** (2625 Garnet Ave., San Diego, CA 92109, tel. 619/581–3311; 800/843–6967 outside CA). Mulege and Bahia Concepción are especially popular for paddling; kayaking tours that include equipment, lessons, and lunch are available from **Baja Tropicales** (Hotel Las Casitas, Box 60, Mulege, BCS Mexico 23900, tel. 685/3–0019, fax 685/3–0340).

Scuba Diving    The coral reefs off Coronado and Carmen islands are an undersea adventure. The scuba specialist is **Fantasia Divers** (tel. 683/3–0700).

Tennis    The **Loreto Tennis Center** (tel. 683/3–0700), 8 kilometers (5 miles) south of Loreto, is open to the public.

Beaches    All Loreto-area hotels are on the water, but the rock-filled beaches that front them are disappointing.

### Dining

There aren't many restaurants in Loreto, but the seafood is excellent no matter where you go. Reservations are not required, and the dress is casual.

| Category | Cost* |
|---|---|
| Very Expensive | over $20 |
| Expensive | $15–$20 |
| Moderate | $8–$15 |
| Inexpensive | under $8 |

*per person for a three-course meal, excluding drinks and service.*

Expensive    **Cesar's.** One block east of the church sits the best restaurant in town, with good seafood and traditional Mexican dishes. Try the giant shrimp stuffed with cheese, wrapped with bacon, and grilled. Bring your own catch of the day and have it prepared however you wish. *Calle Salvatierra at Zapata, tel. 683/3–0203. MC, V.*

Moderate    **The Embarcadero.** This restaurant's open-air deck looking out to the marina and beach is the perfect spot for catching up on the local fishing news. Alfredo's sportfishing is next door, and anglers with their own boats in the marina often stop by for lunch. Fish tacos and grilled-fish dinners are the best choices.*Blvd. Juárez, tel. 683/3–0165. MC, V.*

**Inexpensive** **Café Olé.** The best taquería in town also offers good burgers, ice-cream cones, chocolate shakes, and french fries. *Calle Francisco Madero, tel. 683/3–0496. No credit cards.*

## Lodging

The choices are good, but limited. Highly recommended lodgings are indicated by a star ★.

| Category | Cost* |
|---|---|
| Very Expensive | over $90 |
| Expensive | $60–$90 |
| Moderate | $25–$60 |
| Inexpensive | under $25 |

*\*All prices are for a standard double room, excluding service charge and sales tax (10%).*

**Expensive** **La Pinta.** Part of a chain of Baja California hotels, the La Pinta is a collection of plain brick buildings housing spacious, air-conditioned rooms with satellite TVs. *Blvd. Misión de Loreto, tel. 683/3–0025; reservations in the U.S.: tel. 800/678–7244. 48 rooms. Facilities: pool, 2 tennis courts, restaurant, bar, sportfishing. MC, V.*

**Misión.** This is an old favorite, with one of the most popular swimming pools and second-story bars in town. The rooms and public spaces are in desperate need of renovation, but that doesn't deter the diehard anglers who enjoy being across the street from the marina. *Blvd. Mateos at Calle de la Playa, tel. 683/3–0048, fax 683/3–0648. 54 rooms. Facilities: pool, restaurant, bar, sportfishing. MC, V.*

**Oasis.** This is one of the original fishing camps and a favorite with those who want to spend as much time as possible on the water. Many of the rooms, set amid a tropical oasis of palms, have a view of the water. The hotel has its own fleet of skiffs. *Loreto Beach, tel. 683/3–0112; reservations in the U.S.: tel. 619/491–0682. Facilities: pool, tennis, fishing, boats. MC, V.*

**Moderate** **Plaza Loreto.** Opened in 1992, this was the first new hotel in
★ Loreto in over a decade, and the first right in downtown. Located near the old mission, the two-story hotel has an upstairs bar overlooking the street; 11 rooms have been completed, and another section and pool are under construction. The rooms are by far the best in town, with TVs, coffeemakers, and huge showers. *Paseo Hidalgo, tel. 683/3–0280, fax 683/3–0855. 30 rooms (to be completed in 1993). Facilities: bar, pool. MC, V.*

**Serenidad.** Some 128 kilometers (80 miles) north of Loreto, this hotel is worth the trip. The rooms have fireplaces (nights can be chilly), and the Saturday barbecue is a Baja institution. *Mulege, tel. 685/3–0111; reservations in the U.S.: Box 520, Corona, CA 91720, tel. 714/735–8223. 27 rooms. Facilities: pool, restaurant, airstrip. MC, V.*

**Inexpensive** **Hacienda.** French Canadian Jean-Pierre bought this historic Mulege hacienda in 1992 and is gradually restoring its rooms, including a large ballroom with fireplace. Guests read and lounge in rocking chairs by the pool or at stools along the bar, where snacks and meals are served throughout the day. Special festivities include paella nights, pig roasts, and trips to the nearby cave paintings in the mountains. Even when other hotels in the area are nearly empty, the Hacienda is filled with European travelers attracted by the ambience and incredibly low (by Baja standards) room rates. *Calle Madero, Mulege, tel. and fax 685/3–0021. 18 rooms. Facilities: pool, restaurant, bar, tours. No credit cards.*

## Nightlife

After-dark entertainment is pretty much limited to hotel lobby bars; the fisherfolk drawn to the Loreto area turn in early.

# La Paz

La Paz is one of those cities that make you wish you'd been here 20 years ago. In the slowest of times, in late summer when the heat is oppressive, you can easily see how it must have been when it was a quiet place, living up to its name—"Peace." Today the city has a population of 170,000, with a large contingent of retirees from the United States and Canada. Travelers use La Paz as both a destination in itself and a stopping-off point en route to Los Cabos. Sportfishing is a major lure, though some enjoy La Paz as the most Mexican city on the peninsula, with the feel of a mainland community that has adapted to tourism while retaining its character.

It was commerce that first attracted Hernán Cortés and his soldiers in 1535: The beautiful bay was rich with oysters and pearls. In 1720 the Jesuits arrived to civilize and convert the Indians. Instead, the missionaries inadvertently decimated the local populace by introducing smallpox. Within 30 years, there was no one left to convert.

While the rest of Mexico was being torn apart by revolution, a permanent settlement was established in 1811. La Paz became a refuge for those who wished to escape the mainland wars. In 1829, after then-capital Loreto was leveled by a hurricane, La Paz became the capital of the Californias. Troops from the United States occasionally invaded, but sent word to Washington that the Baja Peninsula was not worth fighting for. In 1853 a different group of invaders arrived from the United States. Led by William Walker, these southerners were intent on making La Paz a slave state but were quickly banished by the Mexicans. Peace reigned for the next century. In 1940, disease wiped out the oyster beds, and with the pearls gone, La Paz no longer attracted prospectors and was left tranquil.

La Paz officially became the capital of Baja California Sur in 1974 and is now the state's largest settlement. It is the site of the power plant for all the state, a fleet of cruise ships, the ferry to Mazatlán, the state bureaucracy, the governor's home, and the state jail. It is the stop-off for fishermen and divers headed for Cerralvo, La Partida, and Espiritu Santo islands, where parrot fish, manta rays, neons, and angels blur the clear waters by the shore, and marlin, dorado, and yellowtail leap out of the deep, dark sea.

La Paz's charm is evident in the early morning. The dull brown hills surrounding the sprawling city turn golden amber; the sea turns aqua blue. The waterfront plaza is empty except for foraging kittens, a half-dozen joggers, and a trickle of workers. In downtown's plaza, Jardín Velazco (Velazco Garden), the pink quartz gazebo shines in the sunlight, and dense trees and blooming hibiscus shade the freshly swept tiled paths. Bells ring in the Catedral de Nuestra Señora de La Paz, and children wearing school uniforms stroll to class arm in arm. At sunset the city grows calm, and Los Pacenos (the peaceful ones), as the residents are called, pause at the waterfront on their way home to watch the sea grow dark again.

### Arriving and Departing by Plane

The La Paz airport, about 16 kilometers (10 miles) north of town, is served by **Aero California** (tel. 682/5–1023 or 800/237–6225), which flies from Los Angeles, Aguascalientes, Culiacán, Guadalajara, Loreto, Los Mochis, Mexico City, and Tijuana to La Paz.

### Arriving and Departing by Car, Bus, and Ferry

**By Car**  La Paz is 1,474 kilometers (921 miles) south of the U.S. border at Tijuana on the Transpeninsular Highway and 211 kilometers (132 miles) north of Los Cabos at the southern tip of the peninsula. The city of La Paz curves along the bay of La Paz and faces the sea in a northwesterly rather than an easterly direction. When you approach the city on Highway 1 from the north, you'll enter from the southwest.

**By Bus**  **Tres Estrellas de Oro** (tel. 682/2–6476) operates buses along the Transpeninsular Highway to the border and Los Cabos.

**By Ferry**  The ferry system connecting Baja to mainland Mexico has been privatized and is constantly undergoing changes in rates and schedules. Currently there are Sematur ferries from La Paz to Mazatlán and La Paz to Topolobampo. Tickets are available at the ferry office at the dock on the road to Pichilingue (tel. 682/5–3833) and at the downtown Sematur office (Av. 5 de Mayo 502, tel. 682/5–8889). Purchase your ticket personally in advance of your trip—and expect confusion. Travelers planning to take cars and motor homes on the ferry to the mainland have experienced considerable difficulty due to ever-changing Mexican customs regulations. At press time drivers were required to make a refundable deposit equal to the value of their car, ensuring that they would return the vehicle to the United States. Check with the Mexican consulate in your area before making plans to take a car to the mainland from Baja.

### Getting Around

**By Rental Car**  A car is not necessary if you plan to stay in town, since taxis are readily available. But if you'd like to explore the more remote beaches, wheels are a must. Rental is about $70 per day for a Volkswagen Beetle, with insurance and unlimited mileage. If you want a sedan or air-conditioning, call ahead to reserve a car. Rental agencies include **Budget** (Paseo Obregón at Hidalgo, tel. 682/2–1097); **Hertz** (tel. 682/2–0919) and **Avis** (tel. 682/2–2651); both at the airport; and **Servitur Autorento** (5 de Febrero at Abasolo, tel. 682/2–1448).

**By Taxi** Taxis are inexpensive, but be sure to set the price with your driver before the cab gets going.

## Important Addresses and Numbers

**Tourist Information** The State Secretary of Tourism (SECTUR) office is located west of downtown on the highway (tel. 682/2–1199, fax 682/2–7722). SECTUR's tourist information center is on the malecón near Calle 16 de Septiembre (tel. 682/2–7975 or 682/2–5939) and is open Monday through Friday, 8–8.

**Emergencies** Police (682/2–6610); Fire (682/2–0054); Red Cross (682/2–1111). Clínica La Paz (Revolución 461, tel. 682/2–0685; 682/2–2800) has English-speaking doctors on staff.

## Guided Tours

Travel agencies in the hotels and along Paseo Obregón offer tours of the city, day-long trips to Los Cabos, sportfishing, and boating excursions.

## Exploring

*Numbers in the margin correspond to points of interest on the La Paz map.*

**The Malecón** The **malecón** is La Paz's sea wall, tourist zone, and main drag ❶ rolled into one. As you enter town from the southwest, Paseo Alvaro Obregón becomes the malecón (waterfront walkway) at a cluster of high-rise condos under construction. A similar project is under way at the west entrance to town, where a golf course and a resort are gradually emerging by the 500-acre ❷ **Fidepaz Marina,** 10 blocks north of the current center of activi-❸ ty. The **State Secretary of Tourism (SECTUR) office** is across from the marina.

**Time Out** If you begin your tour in the evening and can handle frenetic ❹ activity, have your first margarita and some nachos at **La Paz-Lapa.** The portions are gargantuan, and the quality is consistently good. *Paseo Obregón at León, tel. 682/2–6025. Open noon–1 AM. MC, V. Closed Tues.*

❺ La Paz's only true colonial Mexican hotel is **Los Arcos** (Paseo Obregón 498, tel. 682/2–2744). The center courtyard has a fountain surrounded by flowers and is a pleasant place for a short respite, if no one is playing ping-pong nearby.

Shops carrying the predictable assortment of sombreros, onyx chess sets, and painted plaster curios line the next few blocks. Wander through **Artesanías la Antigua California** (Paseo Obregón 220, tel. 682/5–5230) for a sampling of better Mexican crafts—colorful woven baskets from Michoacán and carved masks from Guerero.

❻ **La Perla Hotel** (Paseo Obregón 1570, tel. 682/2–0777) has the best seats on the malecón for watching the steady stream of teens cruising through town in their cars, red and yellow lights twinkling around their license plates and the latest U.S. hits blaring on their radios.

A white arch above the street at the foot of Calle 16 de Septiembre marks the entrance to the center-city area. Across

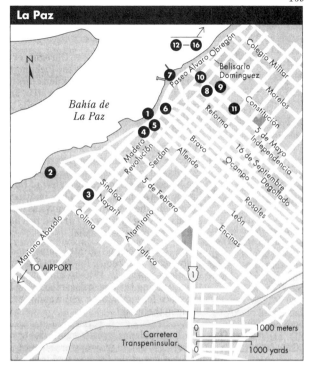

**La Paz**

**7** the street, a two-story white gazebo is the focus of the **Malecón Plaza.** Military bands and mariachis play in the gazebo on weekend nights, when you can barely make it through the crowd of children chasing balloons and the young men eyeing the parade of young women in miniskirts.

**Central La Paz** This downtown district is the busiest in all Baja Sur, with shops crammed together on narrow crowded streets. Browse through **Dorian's,** a large department-store chain at the corner of Avenidas Septiembre and Agosto, for any sundries you might need.

**8** **La Catedral de Nuestra Señora de La Paz** (Our Lady of La Paz Cathedral) is downtown's big attraction. It was built in 1860 near the site of La Paz's first mission, which was established in 1860 by Jesuit Jaime Bravo. It faces the zócalo, which also goes
**9** by the names **Plaza Constitución** and **Jardín Velazco.**

**10** On the opposite end of the plaza is the **Biblioteca de las Californias,** a library specializing in the history of Baja California, with reproductions of the local prehistoric cave paintings, oil paintings of the missions, and the best collection of historical documents on the peninsula. *Madero at Cinco de Mayo, tel. 682/2-2640. Open Mon.–Sat. 8–6.*

One gets an excellent sense of La Paz's culture and heritage at
**11** the **Museum of Anthropology,** constructed in 1983 at the corner of Altamirano and Cinco de Mayo. Exhibits include re-creations of Comondo and Las Palmas Indian villages, photos of cave paintings found in Baja, and copies of Cortés's writings on first sighting La Paz. Many of the exhibit descriptions are writ-

| Category | Cost* |
|---|---|
| Expensive | $15–$20 |
| Moderate | $8–$15 |
| Inexpensive | under $8 |

*per person for a three-course meal, excluding drinks and service.*

**Expensive** **El Bismark.** You've got to wander a bit out of your way to reach
★ El Bismark, where locals go for good, home-style Mexican
food. Specialties include the *cochinita pibil* (marinated pork
chunks) served with homemade tortillas; carne asada served
with beans, guacamole, and tortillas; and enormous grilled lobsters. You'll see families settle down for hours at long wood tables, while waitresses divide their attention between the
patrons and the soap operas on the TV above the bar. *Santos
Degollado and Av. Altamirano, tel. 687/2–4854. MC, V.*
**Restaurant Bermejo.** The most upscale, elegant restaurant in
town has a faithful following of locals and tourists in search of
comfortable booths, candles, and courteous waiters. The menu
is primarily Italian these days. There are a few moderately
priced dishes here, but go all the way and order lobster or filet
Mignon; you won't be disappointed. *Paseo Obregón 498, tel.
682/2–2744. Reservations recommended. AE, MC, V.*

**Moderate** **La Paz-Lapa.** The noise level here is deafening, but this is a fun
place, with a wide-screen TV in the bar and waiters so jolly you
expect them to break into song. The sunset view of the ocean is
terrific, and you're sure to make friends with fellow diners.
The food—your basic beef, chicken, fish, and Mexican selections—is tasty and plentiful. *Paseo Obregón at León, tel. 682/
2–6025. AE, MC, V. Closed Tues.*
**La Terraza.** The newly renovated open-air restaurant at the
Hotel Perla is the best people-watching spot in town, with side-
walk-level tables facing the malecón. The menu includes everything from French toast to pasta—with decent enchiladas,
huevos rancheros, and fresh fish. La Terraza is a good hangout
for morning coffee and afternoon and evening snacks. *Paseo
Obregón under the Hotel Perla, tel. 682/2–0777. MC, V.*
**Samalu.** Owners Santos and Manuel Mompala operate this delightful A-frame palapa in an overgrown garden of palms and
vines. Stick with such house specialties as giant shrimp stuffed
with cheese, wrapped in bacon, and deep-fried, or a thin steak
fillet served with grilled onion and pepper strips, guacamole,
beans, and a cheese enchilada. Be sure to check out the
"Maligator" (half marlin, half alligator) mounted in the bar.
*Rangel between Colima and Jalisco, tel. 682/2–2481. MC, V.*

**Inexpensive** **El Quinto Sol Restaurante Vegetariano.** El Quinto's bright yel-
★ low exterior walls are painted with Indian snake symbols and
smiling suns. The back room is a natural-foods store stocked
with grains, soaps, lotions, oils, and books. The restaurant
serves yogurt with bananas and wheat germ, ceviche tostadas,
and a nonmeat version of *machaca*, a marinated shredded beef
dish. *Belisario Domínguez and Independencia, tel. 682/2–
1692. No credit cards.*
**La Fabula Pizza.** With its turrets and lacy white trim, this
bright yellow two-story building looks like a midwestern Victorian frame home. The pizza parlor inside, crowded and fun,
could be in Ohio. It's got pies with *chorizo* (sausage), beans,

and jalapeños; with smoked oysters and tuna; and with Hawaiian ham and bananas. *Paseo Obregón at 16 de Septiembre, no phone. No credit cards.*

## Lodging

La Paz has hotels clustered along the malecón, with a few of the more expensive places outside town on the road to Pichilingue and the road to the airport. If you're interested in sunbathing and relaxing on the beach, stay outside town. Highly recommended lodgings are indicated by a star ★.

| Category | Cost* |
|---|---|
| Very Expensive | over $90 |
| Expensive | $60–90 |
| Moderate | $25–$60 |
| Inexpensive | under $25 |

*\*All prices are for a standard double room, excluding service charge and sales tax (10%).*

**Expensive** **Club El Moro.** A vacation-ownership resort with suite rentals
★ on a nightly and weekly basis, El Moro boasts a garden of lush palms and a densely landscaped pool area with one of the few hot tubs in town. You can recognize the building by its stark-white turrets and domes; rooms are Mediterranean in style and decor, with arched windows, Mexican tiles, and private balconies. The restaurant is excellent and elegant. *Km. 2 on the road to Pichilingue, tel. and fax 682/2–4084. 17 suites. Facilities: pool, restaurant, bar, tour desk. AE, MC, V.*

**La Concha Beach Resort.** Come to La Concha for its clean, curving beach; modern, well-maintained rooms; and very good restaurant. Some rooms lack TVs, but guests gather around the large-screen TV in an upstairs lounging area, which also has tables for playing cards and games and a small selection of English-language novels. The hotel operates a free shuttle to town twice daily (taxis to town cost $10 each way). *Km 5 on the Pichilingue Rd., tel. 682/2–6544, fax 682/2–6218; reservations in the U.S.: tel. 800/999–2252. 109 rooms. Facilities: pool, 2 tennis courts, restaurant, palapa and lobby bars, gift shop, meeting and banquet rooms. AE, MC, V.*

**Los Arcos.** Many say Los Arcos is the nicest hotel in La Paz, but that depends on the location of your room. Resist the waterfront view and request a room in the central courtyard, where the rush of water in the fountain drowns out the music from the street and the noise from the pool area. All rooms have balconies and TVs. The self-service coffee shop opens early so those headed out on fishing boats can have breakfast and pick up a box lunch. *Paseo Obregón 498 between Rosales and Allende, tel. 682/2–2744; reservations in the U.S.: 4422 Cerritos Ave., Los Alamitos, CA 90720, tel. 213/583–3393 or 800/347–2252. 180 rooms. Facilities: pool, sauna, coffee shop, restaurant, bar, store, sportfishing tours. AE, MC, V.*

★ **La Posada de Englebert.** For 25 years, divers have stayed in La Posada's casitas, which feature wood shutters, haphazardly tiled bathrooms, fireplaces, worn couches in the living rooms, and rocking chairs on the porches. At night, miniature lights twinkle in the palm trees and guitarists stroll among the blue umbrellas on the patio while guests dine on grilled fish and lobster. Saturday-night entertainment alternates between folkloric dancing and a Hawaiian luau. *Av. Reforma and Playa Sur, Box 152, La Paz, BCS 23000, tel. 682/2–4011, fax 682/2–0663. 26 suites, 4 casitas. Facilities: pool, restaurant, palapa bar, private beach. MC, V.*

**Moderate**   **Gardenias.** This large, bright pink motel on the outskirts of town has gardens, a pool and patio, and clean, newly painted rooms. The drawback is its distance from the malecón (about a half-hour walk). *Serdan Nte. 520, tel. 682/2–3088, fax 682/5–0436. 56 rooms. Facilities: pool, restaurant. MC, V.*

**Las Cabañas de Los Arcos.** Next door to, and under the same ownership as, Los Arcos Hotel (*see above*), these small thatched-roof brick cottages are surrounded by trees and flowering hibiscus. Sidewalks lead through the small complex to a pool that is nearly hidden by the trees. The cabanas, which have fireplaces, are a bit run-down but private; for more modern surroundings, stay in the low-rise hotel building by the pool. *Just off Paseo Obregón at the corner of Rosales; reservations in the U.S.: 4422 Cerritos Ave., Los Alamitos, CA 90720, tel. 213/583–3393 or 800/347–2252. 30 rooms. Facilities: pool, access to other facilities at Los Arcos hotel. AE, MC, V.*

**Inexpensive**   **Pension California.** This run-down hacienda, offering clean blue-and-white rooms with baths and a courtyard with picnic tables and a TV, draws backpackers and low-budget travelers. A laid-back, friendly camaraderie prevails. *Av. Degollado 209, tel. 682/2–2896. 25 rooms. Facilities: cooking privileges. No credit cards.*

## The Arts and Nightlife

**El Teatro de la Ciudad** (Av. Navarro 700, tel. 682/5–0004) is La Paz's cultural center. The theater seats 1,500 and is used for stage shows by visiting performers as well as local ensembles.

Nightlife in La Paz centers on the malecón and the **Okey Laser Disco** (Paseo Obregón, tel. 682/2–3133) near La Perla. The mirrored **Disco El Rollo** (tel. 682/2–4000) at the Hotel Palmira plays music videos, recorded salsa, and disco tunes.

# Los Cabos

At the southern tip of the 1,600-kilometer (1,000-mile) Baja California Peninsula, the land ends in a rocky point called **El Arco** (The Arch), a place of stark and mysterious beauty. The waters of the **Sea of Cortés** swirl into the Pacific Ocean's rugged surf as marlin and sailfish leap above the waves. The desert ends in white-sand coves, with cactus standing at their entrances like sentries under the soaring palm trees.

Pirates found the capes at the tip of the peninsula an ideal lookout for spotting Spanish galleons traveling from the Philippines to Spain's empire in central Mexico. Missionaries soon followed, seeking to save the souls of the few thousand local Indians who lived off the sea. The good fathers established the missions of **San José del Cabo** and **Cabo San Lucas** in the mid-1700s, but their colonies did not last long. The missionaries had brought syphilis and smallpox along with their preachings, and by the end of the century the indigenous population had been nearly wiped out.

A different sort of native, the massive gamefish that appeared to be trapped in the swirl of surf where the ocean meets the sea, brought the explorers back. In the 1940s and 1950s the capes became a haven for millionaires, who built lodges on rocky gray cliffs overlooking secluded coves and bays. By the 1960s, lavish resorts had begun to rise in the barren landscape.

Connected by a 20-mile stretch of highway called the Corridor, the two towns that grew around the Spanish missions, Cabo San Lucas and San José del Cabo, were distinct until the late 1970s, when the Mexican government's office of tourism development (Fonatur) targeted the southern tip of Baja as a major resort and dubbed the area Los Cabos.

Fonatur's initial target for development, San José del Cabo is the municipal headquarters for the two towns. A hotel zone was cleared along the long stretch of waterfront on the Sea of Cortés, and a nine-hole golf course and private residential community were constructed south of the town center. But a picturesque downtown, with colored lights in the fountains along the main street, still maintains the languid pace of a Mexican village. Despite the development, San José remains the more peaceful of the two towns and is the one that travelers seeking a quiet escape prefer.

Most of the legendary fishing lodges and exclusive resorts built before the government stepped in were on the Corridor between the two towns. Since the mid-1980s, the area has seen the completion of several private communities and large-scale resorts; two championship-level golf courses and several new hotels are currently under construction along the highway. In 1992 work began on widening the highway along this stretch from two to four lanes, a project that is not likely to be completed until 1994.

Cabo San Lucas, once an unsightly fishing town with dusty streets and smelly canneries, has become the center of tourism activity for the area. It now has an international airport; the sportfishing fleet is headquartered here, and cruise ships anchored off the marina disperse passengers into town. Trendy restaurants and bars line the streets, and massive hotels have risen on every available plot of waterfront turf; a five-story condo/hotel complex along the bay blocks the view from the town's older hotels. Cabo San Lucas has become an in spot for travelers seeking fun, rowdy nightlife, and extensive dining and shopping options.

You need only drive a few miles north of Los Cabos into the desert or along the two coastlines to understand the magnitude of the development that has taken place at the peninsula's tip. Electricity and telephone service end abruptly within 10 miles of Los Cabos: Settlements consist of lone ranches, farms battered by wind and sun, outposts of rugged retirees in rusted motor homes, and isolated hotels operating on their own generators. The true Baja appears in waves of unmitigated heat, clouds of dust, and vistas of desert and sky broken only by thorny cacti and the sight of vultures in flight.

## Arriving and Departing by Plane

The **Los Cabos International Airport** (tel. 684/2–0341) is about 11 kilometers (7 miles) north of San José del Cabo and about 48 kilometers (30 miles) from Cabo San Lucas. **Aero California** (tel. 684/3–0848 or 800/237–6225) flies to Los Cabos from Los Angeles and Phoenix; **Mexicana** (tel. 684/3–0411 or 800/531–7921) from Guadalajara, Mexico City, Mazatlán, Puerto Vallarta, Denver, and Los Angeles; **Alaska Airlines** (tel. 684/2–1015 or 800/426–0333) from Anchorage, Fairbanks, Portland, San Francisco, San Diego, Los Angeles, and Seattle.

Vans shuttle passengers from the airport to the hotels in both towns but don't run from the hotels back to the airport. Many of the hotels have sign-up sheets for guests who wish to share a cab and the $30 or so fare to the airport.

## Arriving and Departing by Car, Bus, and Boat

**By Car**  Mexico Highway 1, also known as the Transpeninsular Highway, runs the entire 1,600 kilometers (1,000 miles) from Tijuana to Cabo San Lucas. The highway is in excellent condition until you reach the road between Cabo San Lucas and San José del Cabo, which is gradually being widened to four lanes.

**By Bus**  **Tres Estrellas de Oro** (tel. 684/2–0200) travels from Tijuana to Los Cabos and between San José and Cabo San Lucas daily. The peninsula-long trip takes about 22 hours.

**By Boat**  Several cruise lines—including **Carnival** (tel. 800/327–9051), **Starlite** (tel. 800/488–7827), **Princess** (tel. 800/421–0522), and **Admiral** (tel. 800/327–0271)—use Cabo San Lucas as a port of call; there is a handicrafts market at the marina designed to accommodate cruise-ship passengers.

## Getting Around

**By Car**  The best way to see the sights is on foot. The downtown areas of San José and Cabo San Lucas are compact, with the plaza, church, shops, and restaurants within a few blocks of one another. If you want to travel frequently between the two towns or to remote beaches and coves, you will need a car.

Most hotels and resorts have car-rental desks; the cost of a Volkswagen Beetle or a Jeep average $60 per day, including tax and insurance, plus 18¢ per kilometer. The following car-rental agencies all have desks at the airport and in one or both towns: **Avis** (tel. 684/2–0680); **Budget** (tel. 684/3–0241); **Dollar** (tel. 684/2–0671); **Hertz** (tel. 684/3–0211); **National** (tel. 684/3–6000); and **Thrifty** (tel. 684/2–1671). **M&M Jeeps** (at the Meliá Cabo Real, tel. 684/3–0754, ext. 1835, or in San Diego, CA, tel. 619/297–1615), which rents two- and four-wheel-drive vehicles, offers a package option. Travelers can rent the vehicles for a one-way trip from San Diego to Los Cabos without a drop-off fee and arrange their own accommodations or they can purchase an all-inclusive self-guided tour package.

**By Taxi**  Cab fares are standardized by the government, but you should confirm the price before you get into the car. The fare between the two towns is about $15.

## Important Addresses and Numbers

**Tourist Information** There is no tourism office in Los Cabos, but there are plenty of makeshift stands where time-share operators seek new clients under the guise of offering information. Unless you have hours to spend listening to sales spiels, you're better off using the tour desk or concierge at your hotel.

**Emergencies** **Police:** Cabo San Lucas (tel. 684/3–0057), San José del Cabo (tel. 684/2–0361); **Hospital:** Cabo San Lucas (tel. 684/3–0102); San José del Cabo (tel. 684/2–0316).

## Guided Tours

With the water as the main attraction, most tours involve getting into a boat and diving or fishing. Nearly everyone takes a ride to El Arco, the natural rock arches at Land's End, and Playa del Amor (Lover's Beach), where the Sea of Cortés blends into the Pacific. Nearly all hotels have frequent boat trips to El Arco; the fare depends on how far your hotel is from the point.

**Chubasco's** (Blvd. Marina 22, Cabo San Lucas, tel. 684/3–0404) offers guided tours on motorcycles and three-wheel off-road motorbikes to remote areas around Los Cabos, including the old lighthouse.

**Pez Gato** (tel. 684/3–0885 or 714/673–4705) has sailing and sunset cruises on a 46-foot catamaran, with live music and free drinks ($40 per person), as well as snorkeling and sailing tours ($25 per person). All trips depart from the marina in Cabo San Lucas; call or stop by the booth at the marina for further information.

## Exploring

You needn't worry about reserving lots of time for sightseeing here—each town can easily be toured in an hour or so. Only a few streets are named, but the towns are small enough for you to find what you're looking for without wandering very far.

**Cabo San Lucas** and **San José del Cabo** are about 32 kilometers (20 miles) apart on Mexico Highway 1. Some hotels in each offer tours to the other town, which is a good way to see the sights; or you can take a taxi between the towns. If you want to check out the lavish fishing resorts or the beaches, you're better off renting a car and stopping off for lunch or a swim along the way.

*Numbers in the margin correspond to points of interest on the Los Cabos Coast, San José del Cabo, and Cabo San Lucas maps.*

**San José del Cabo,** the larger of the two towns, has about 25,000
**❶** inhabitants. The main street is **Boulevard Mijares.** The south end of the boulevard has been designated the tourist zone, with
**❷** the **Los Cabos Club de Golf** as its centerpiece. Fonatur owns
**❸** 4,000 acres along this stretch and has built a **Commercial and Cultural Center** in the middle. A few reasonably priced hotels are situated along this strip, on a beautiful long beach where the surf, unfortunately, is too dangerous for swimming. At the end of the strip, on Paseo San José by the Stouffer Presidente
**❹** hotel, is the **estuary,** a freshwater preserve filled with more than 200 species of birds. A small stand at the road's end rents

boats to paddle through the thick swamp grass of the sanctuary.

**⑤** Take Boulevard Mijares north into town, through a stretch of restaurants and shops. **City Hall** is on your left near Avenida Zaragoza, where Boulevard Mijares ends—a spot marked by a long fountain illuminated at night by colored lights. There is a small, shaded plaza here and, in front of a public library, a mural painted by the children of San José.

**⑥** One block east on Avenida Zaragoza is a large **zócalo** with a white wrought-iron gazebo and green benches set in the shade.
**⑦** The town's **church** looms above the zócalo. Be sure to walk up to the front and see the tile mural of a captured priest being dragged toward a fire by Indians.

Mexicana and Aeroméxico airlines have offices by the zócalo. The bus station, hospital, market, and pharmacies are all located one block south on Avenida Manuel Doblado, and most of the town's souvenir shops and restaurants are clustered in the surrounding streets.

As you drive south on Mexico Highway 1 toward Cabo San
**⑧** Lucas, you'll first pass **Costa Azul,** a good surfing beach, and
**⑨** **Playa Palmilla,** San José's best swimming beach. Above the
**⑩** beach is the **Hotel Palmilla,** a rambling, hacienda-style resort with its own small white adobe chapel. Intensive construction is under way at the Palmilla, including an 18-hole golf course designed by Jack Nicklaus and a resort enclave of more than 1,000 homes and condos. The Cabo Real project a few miles south includes another golf course and the Meliá Cabo Real and Conrad hotels. Still farther south are beaches for swimming and snorkeling, and some spectacular hotels; most worth visit-
**⑪** ing are the **Bahía Chileno** at the **Hotel Cabo San Lucas** and the
**⑫** **Bahía Santa María** at the **Twin Dolphin** hotel. The beaches at both bays have white sand, clear blue water, and schools of fish just offshore.

Highway 1 leads into the center of **Cabo San Lucas,** ending at Kilometer 1 on the Transpeninsular Highway. The main down-
**⑬** town street, Avenida Lázaro Cárdenas, passes a small **zócalo.** Most of the shops, services, and restaurants are located between Avenida Cárdenas and the waterfront.

**Time Out** When the sun's heat has exhausted your energy, stop at the nearest branch of **Helados Bing,** a pink-and-white-striped ice-cream stand that serves delectable cones, shakes, and floats. One is on Boulevard Mijares in San José, and another is located on Highway 1 just north of Cabo San Lucas.

**Boulevard Marina** has been transformed from a dusty main drag into a busy thoroughfare lined with hotels and cafés. Paved walkways now run from here to the hotels and beaches
**⑭** on the east end of town and west to the **Handicrafts Market** at the Cabo San Lucas marina, where new hotels and shopping centers are under construction. The sportfishing fleet is
**⑮** docked in the **Bahía de Cabo San Lucas,** and there are glass-bottom boats available at the water's edge.

**⑯** The most spectacular sight in Cabo San Lucas is **El Arco.** The natural rock arch is visible from the marina and from some of the hotels but is more impressive from the water. A little farther on, and visible from the water, is **El Faro de Cabo Falso**

Los Cabos Coast

Boulevard Mijares, **1**
Church, **7**
City Hall, **5**
Commercial and
Cultural Center, **3**
Estuary, **4**
Los Cabos Club de
Golf, **2**
Zócalo, **6**

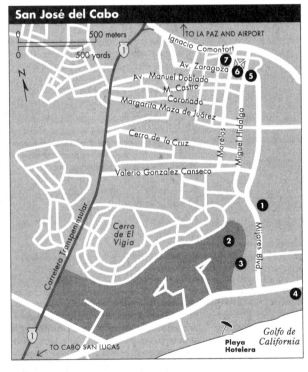

San José del Cabo

Bahía de Cabo
San Lucas, **15**
El Arco, **16**
Handicrafts
Market, **14**
Zócalo, **13**

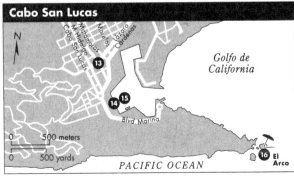

Cabo San Lucas

(Lighthouse of the False Cape). You need a four-wheel-drive vehicle to reach the lighthouse by land. If you don't take at least a short boat ride out to the arches and **Playa de Amor,** the beach underneath, you haven't fully appreciated Cabo.

## Shopping

Shopping may be beating out fishing as the sport of choice in Los Cabos these days. The selection of handicrafts and sportswear in the towns is excellent. In Cabo San Lucas the sportswear shops—**Guess, Ferrioni, Bye-Bye, Cotton Club,** and the like—are clustered at the Plaza Cabo San Lucas on Avenida Madero. Several specialty shops, including **Casa Dupuis,** a gorgeous home-furnishings store, are located in the modernistic Plaza Bonita at the beginning of Boulevard Marina.

Several high-class resortwear boutiques have opened. The best are **Temptations** (Av. Lazaro Cárdenas at Vincente Guerrero, tel. 684/3–1015); **Dos Lunas** (Blvd. Marina, tel. 684/3–1280, and in Plaza Bonita), and **La Bamba** (Guerrero, tel. 684/3–1545). Across Avenida Hidalgo from the zócalo is **La Bugambilia** (tel. 684/3–0625), a gallery with brass and copper animals by Sergio Bustamante and one-of-a-kind belts, purses, and jewelry. **La Paloma,** a few doors down, has beautiful embroidered and appliquéd clothing from Tlaquepaque, an artisans' colony outside Guadalajara.

**Artes Oaxaqueños** on Avenida Hidalgo is a tiny shop stuffed with stunning wood carvings and wool weavings from Oaxaca. **Mama Eli's** (Av. San Lucas, tel. 684/3–1616) has her three display rooms filled with high-quality pottery, jewelry, glasswork, and clothing from throughout Mexico. The gift shop at **Hotel Cabo San Lucas** (Km 14.5 Transpeninsular Hwy.) sells old glass, gorgeous terra-cotta reproductions of Indian statues, and hand-painted beads from China. **Galería El Dorado** (Blvd. Marina, tel. 684/3–0817) sells fanciful bronze sculptures and beautiful watercolor paintings of the beaches of Los Cabos. Wander to the back room which is filled with souvenirs. High-quality folk art from throughout Mexico is also available at **Gattamelata** (tel. 684/3–1166), a rustic stone building on the road to Hotel Hacienda.

At the **Handicrafts Market** in the marina you can pose for a photo with an iguana, plan a ride in a glass-bottomed boat, or browse to your heart's content through stalls packed with blankets, sombreros, and pottery.

Shopping opportunities in **San José del Cabo** occur in the few streets around the zócalo and City Hall. Across Boulevard Mijares from City Hall is **Almacenes Goncanseco,** where you can get film, postcards, groceries, and liquor. **Antigua Los Cabos** on Avenida Hidalgo has handsome carved-wood furniture, woven rugs, and wrought-iron chandeliers. Along Boulevard Mijares, **La Casa Vieja Boutique** (tel. 684/2–0270) carries beautiful hand-knit sweaters, designer dresses, and embroidered *guayaberas* (loose-fitting cotton shirts) for men; **Bye-Bye** has high-quality souvenir T-shirts; **La Mina** displays silver jewelry and leather bags; and **La Bamba** sells colorful hand-painted T-shirts and coveralls. **Galería El Dorado** (tel. 684/2–1987), across from the City Hall on Boulevard Mijares, offers paintings and sculptures from local artists. For fresh produce, flowers, meat, fish, and a sampling of local life in San José, visit the **Mercado Municipal** off Calle Doblado, behind the bus station.

## Sports and Outdoor Activities

**Fishing**  There are more than 800 species of fish in the waters off Los Cabos. Most of the hotels, particularly those along the stretch of highway between the two towns, will arrange fishing charters, which include a captain and mate, tackle, bait, licenses, and drinks. Prices start at $250 per day for a 25-foot cruiser. Some charters provide lunch, and most can arrange to have your catch mounted, frozen, or smoked. Most of the boats leave from the sportfishing docks in the Cabo San Lucas marina. Usually there are a fair number of pangas for rent at about $25 per hour with a five-hour minimum. Dependable companies include **Hotel Palmilla Sportfishing** (Hotel Palmilla in San José del Cabo, tel. 684/2–0583 or 800/637–2226), the **Solmar Fleet** (tel. 684/3–0022 or 800/344–3349), and **Pisces Sportfishing Fleet** (tel. 684/3–0588).

**Diving**  El Arco is a prime diving and snorkeling area, as are several rocky points off the coast. Most hotels offer diving trips and equipment rental. Companies serving divers in Cabo San Lucas include **Amigos del Mar** (near the sportfishing docks at the harbor, tel. 684/3–0022); **Palmilla Divers** (Hotel Palmilla, tel. 684/2–0582); **Cabo Acuadeportes** (at the Hotel Hacienda and Playa Chileno, tel. 684/3–0117); and **Tio Watersports** (at the Melia San Lucas, tel. 684/3–1000).

**Golf**  The nine-hole **Los Cabos Campo de Golf** on Boulevard Mijares in San José, completed in 1988, was the first course and country club in the area. The golf scene has developed considerably since then. In late 1992 the Palmilla opened the first 18 holes of its private 27-hole Jack Nicklaus–designed course. Three other courses are under construction along the Corridor between the two towns: Campo de Carlos, a 750-acre gated community with 36 holes; Cabo del Sol, an 1,800-acre community with three courses, including a public one (slated to open in late 1993); and Cabo Real, with hotels, homes, condos and 27 holes of golf. By 1995 seven courses are expected to be ready for play in Los Cabos.

**Tennis**  The **Los Cabos Campo de Golf** has lighted tennis courts that are open to the public; fees are $6 per hour during the day and $10 per hour at night.

## Beaches

**Cabo San Lucas**  **Playa Médano,** just north of Cabo San Lucas, is the most popular stretch in Los Cabos (and possibly in all Baja) for sunbathing and people-watching. The 3.2-kilometer (2-mile) span of white sand is always crowded, especially on weekends.

**Playa Hacienda,** in the inner harbor by the Hacienda Hotel, has the calmest waters of any beach in town and good snorkeling around the rocky point. **Playa Solmar,** fringing the Solmar Hotel, is a beautiful wide beach at the base of the mountains leading into the Pacific, but it has dangerous surf with a swift undertow. Stick to sunbathing here.

**Playa de Amor** consists of a secluded cove at the very end of the peninsula, with the Sea of Cortés on one side and the Pacific

charbroiled lobster. You'll find the setting so relaxing and charming that you will want to linger well into the night. *Blvd. Mijares 8, tel. 684/2-0499. AE, MC, V. Dinner only.*

*Moderate*
★ **La Paloma.** This restaurant, with an upstairs patio overlooking the Hotel Palmilla's pool and gardens as well as the sea, offers both a sublime setting and unparalleled food. The Continental menu has taken a turn toward lighter, healthier fare. The Sunday brunch is still the most lavish in the area, and worth a few hours of your time, followed by a long siesta. Have at least one meal here. *Hotel Palmilla, Hwy. 1 just north of San José, tel. 684/2-0582. AE, MC, V.*

*Inexpensive* **Café Europa.** Two expatriate Europeans have created a cosmopolitan coffee house in an old home near a small park. Cappuccino, espresso, and coffee brewed by the cup accompany French baguettes, Danish pastries, and smoked salmon with eggs, all served either at a few sidewalk tables or inside by a long wooden bar. Salads washed with purified water and composed of impeccably fresh ingredients make a delightful change from the normal heavy Cabo fare. Light jazz plays in the background of a remarkably urbane scene. *Blvd. Mijares, no phone. MC, V.*
**La Fogata.** The Davida family continues to offer high-quality Mexican dishes, steaks, and seafood in a clean, comfortable dining room, where you will feel like a relative being welcomed home for a good meal. *Calle Zaragoza, tel. 684/2-0480. MC, V.*

## Lodging

The accommodations in Los Cabos are mostly expensive and exclusive. Many of the hotels offer the American Plan (AP) with three meals. A few of the resorts do not accept credit cards and often add a 10%–20% service charge to your bill. Most properties also raise their rates for the December–April high season. Rates here are based on high-season standards. Expect to pay 25% less during the off-season. Highly recommended lodgings are indicated by a star ★.

| Category | Cost* |
|---|---|
| Very Expensive | over $160 |
| Expensive | $90– $160 |
| Moderate | $40–$90 |
| Inexpensive | under $40 |

*All prices are for a standard double room, excluding service charge and sales tax (10%).*

**Cabo San Lucas**
*Very Expensive*
★ **Meliá San Lucas.** From the moment you enter the Meliá and spot El Arco framed by the lobby's arches, you know you're at a hotel where details are important. The blue walls and linens in the rooms complement the views of the aquamarine sea; the outer adobe walls of the terraced hotel buildings glow orange and gold with the changing sunlight. The Meliá has a long beach with calm waters, a spacious hot tub under the palms, and all the equipment you could need for playing on and in the water. *Off Hwy. 1 at Playa Médano, tel. 684/3-4020; reservations in the U.S.: tel. 800/336-3542. 190 rooms and suites. Facilities: beach, 2 pools, hot tub, 3 restaurants, meeting facilities. AE, MC, V.*

*Expensive* **Hacienda.** Set on the tip of a tree-filled point jutting into San Lucas Bay, the Hacienda resembles a Spanish Colonial inn with its white arches and bell towers, stone fountains, and statues of Indian gods set amid scarlet hibiscus and bougainvillea. The white rooms have red-tile floors, tile baths, and folk art hanging on the walls; the bar is a veritable museum of Indian artifacts. *Across from the marina, tel. 684/3–0122; reservations in the U.S.: Box 48872, Los Angeles, CA 90048, tel. 800/733–2226. 112 rooms, suites, and beachfront cabanas. Facilities: beach, pool, restaurant, bar, shops, aquatic center. MC, V.*

★ **Solmar.** From afar, the Solmar looks like a space colony, set against granite cliffs at the tip of Land's End, facing the wild Pacific. In 1992 the rooms were completely redone as suites with tiled baths and separate seating areas, decorated in Mexico/Santa Fe style. A few of the adjacent time-share units with kitchenettes and a private pool area are available on a nightly basis. The surf here is far too dangerous for swimming, but don't miss a stroll along the wide strip of beach. Most visitors hang out around the pool and swim-up bar, joining in with the ever-present musicians. The Solmar's sportfishing fleet is first-rate. *Blvd. Marina, tel. 684/3–0022; reservations in the U.S.: Box 383, Pacific Palisades, CA 90272, tel. 213/459–9861 or 800/344–3349. 66 rooms, 4 suites, 68 condos. Facilities: pool, beach, tennis, aquatic center, restaurant, bar, shops. AE, MC, V.*

*Moderate* **Hotel Marina.** This establishment is conveniently located across from the marina (though the view is now blocked by the massive Plaza Las Glorias hotel/time-share complex). The rooms, with painted blue-and-yellow flowers on the walls, are air-conditioned and the bathrooms have tiled baths. The accommodations facing a courtyard with pools and a whirlpool are quieter than those facing the street. *Blvd. Marina at Calle Guerrero, tel. 684/3–0030. 30 rooms. Facilities: pool, whirlpool, restaurant. MC, V.*

*Inexpensive* **CREA Youth Hostel.** This bare-bones hostel, about 10 blocks from the waterfront, offers very simple dormitory accommodations and private rooms with single beds. There's a courtyard with tables for make-your-own meals, and a TV in the lobby. *Av. de la Juventud, 2 blocks east of Av. Morelos, tel. 684/3–0148. 1 dorm, 11 private rooms. No credit cards.*

**Between the Capes** **Palmilla.** Just outside San José, the Palmilla is a gracious,
*Very Expensive* sprawling hacienda-style resort. Tiled stairways lead up from
★ flower-lined paths to large apartments with hand-carved furniture, French doors opening onto private patios, and tiled baths. Colorful serapes and *molas* (embroidered and appliquéd scenes) hang on the walls. The buildings are spread along a hillside overlooking the beach, with fountains and bougainvillea-draped statues throughout. The service is delightfully personalized, and the Palmilla is a popular honeymoon and hideaway spot. Construction is under way on a large-scale resort development surrounding the hotel. *Hwy. 1 about 8 km (5 mi) from San José, tel. 684/2–1709; reservations in the U.S.: 4343 Von Karman Ave., Newport Beach, CA 92660–2083, tel. 800/637–2226. 62 rooms, 7 suites, 2 villas. Facilities: pool, beach, restaurant, bar, golf course, tennis, water sports, airstrip. AE, MC, V.*

★ **Twin Dolphin.** Sleek and Japanese-modernistic with an austere air, the Twin Dolphin has been a hideaway for the rich and famous since 1977. Guest rooms are in low-lying casitas along a seaside cliff and are furnished in minimalist style. The hotel is worth a visit if only for the reproductions of Baja's cave paintings on the lobby wall. *Km 12, Hwy. 1, tel. 684/3–0496, 213/ 386–3940 in CA, or 800/421–8925 outside CA. 44 rooms, 6 suites. Facilities: pool, beach, restaurant, bar, tennis, water sports. MC, V.*

**Expensive**  **Meliá Cabo Real.** Even if you're staying elsewhere, stop here for a glimpse of the future. This Meliá is incredibly huge and opulent, spread over a hilltop with a meandering crystal-blue pool, fountains, waterfalls, white canopies shading rest areas, and a private beach created by a small jetty jutting from the rocky hillside. Mayan carvings and bas reliefs adorn the walls in the rooms, which all have landscaped terraces. Two other high-end hotels are being completed near the Meliá, along with a large resort development that includes a golf course and an equestrian center. *Km 19.5 Los Cabos Hwy., tel. 684/3–0754; reservations in the U.S.: tel. 800/336–3542. 299 rooms. Facilities: pool, beach, fishing fleet, dive shop, water sports, tennis courts, fitness center, 24-hour room service, 2 restaurants, 24-hour café. AE, MC, V.*

**San José del Cabo**  **Stouffer Presidente Los Cabos.** By far the nicest hotel in San
**Expensive**  José, this property sits at the end of the hotel zone, next to the estuary. It resembles a pueblo set amid beachside cactus gardens. The buildings curve around an enormous blue pool; the rooms have shaded patios, minibars, king-size beds, deep bathtubs, and couches that face the sliding glass doors. *At the end of the hotel zone, tel. 684/2–0038; reservations in the U.S.: tel. 800/472–2427. 250 rooms, including 6 suites. Facilities: beach, pool, tennis courts, satellite TV, 4 restaurants, bar, disco, water sports, horseback riding, fishing charters. MC, V.*

**Moderate**  **Tropicana Inn.** A welcome addition to San José in 1991, this small hotel is a great option for those who aren't desperate to be on a beach. The new stucco buildings frame a pool and palapa bar in a quiet enclave behind San José's main boulevard. The rooms are air-conditioned, have satellite TV, and are maintained to look brand-new. *Blvd. Mijares 30, 684/2–0907. 20 rooms. Facilities: pool, bar, restaurant. MC, V.*

**Inexpensive**  **Hotel San José Inn.** This small hotel, built in 1991, is about a five-minute walk from town and offers simple rooms with concrete floors, showers, and pastel furnishings. The rates are the lowest in town, and the proprietress is very accommodating. *Calle Degollado s/n, tel. 684/2–1428. 15 rooms. Facilities: snack bar. No credit cards.*

**Posada Terranova.** As with many small properties in the area, the Terranova is undergoing changes, with construction continuing on 14 more rooms and a swimming pool. For now, you'll feel as if you're staying in an old hacienda neatly outfitted with private tiled baths in the five colonial-style rooms. Guests return year after year. *Calle Degollado at Zaragoza, tel. 684/2–0534. 5 rooms. Facilities: restaurant, bar. MC, V.*

## Nightlife

The nightlife in Cabo San Lucas took a definite upturn when members of the rock band Van Halen opened **Cabo Wabo** (Calle Guerrero, tel. 684/3–1188). The latest U.S. bands play over an excellent sound system, but the real highlight is the impromptu jam sessions with appearances by Van Halen's many friends in the music business. Music, dancing, and general revelry also reign at **Squid Roe** (Av. Cárdenas), **Giggling Marlin** (Blvd. Marina), **Rio Grill** (Blvd. Marina), and **The One That Got Away** (Calle Guerrero). The best disco in town, **El Oasis** (Av. Cárdenas), now has competition from **Lukas** (Av. Cárdenas at Blvd. Marina) and **Picante** (in Plaza Bonita).

# 5 Pacific Coast Resorts

*By Maribeth Mellin*

*Updated by Wendy Luft*

Across the Gulf of California from the Baja California Peninsula lies Mazatlán, Mexico's largest Pacific port and the closest major Mexican resort to the United States, some 1,200 kilometers (750 miles) south of the Arizona border. This is the beginning of what cruise-ship operators now call the Mexican Riviera, or the Gold Coast. The coastline for the next 1,400 kilometers (900 miles) is Mexico's tropical paradise. The Gulf of California, or the Sea of Cortés, as it is also called, ends just below the Tropic of Cancer, leaving the Pacific coastline open to fresh sea breezes. The Mexican Riviera resorts—Mazatlán, Puerto Vallarta, Manzanillo, Ixtapa, Zihuatanejo, and Acapulco—are therefore less muggy than gulf towns to the north. The water, however, is colder, and waves can get very rough. Deserted palm-fringed bays and tropical jungles border high-rise hotels and luxury resorts, and the emphasis is on enjoying the tropical climate and broad sandy beaches.

The Pacific coast doesn't have the rich cultural heritage of Mexico's inland colonial villages and silver cities, and the history is sketchy at best. This is not an area for touring ruins, museums, and cathedrals, but rather a gathering spot for sun worshipers, sportfishermen, surfers, and swimmers. Sightseeing involves touring the resorts and shopping areas rather than exploring ancient Aztec ruins. Not far from the resort regions are jungle streams and ocean coves that seem remote and undiscovered. The majority of visitors never venture to these isolated sites, preferring instead to immerse themselves in the simultaneously bustling and restful resort lifestyle, where great dining, shopping, and sunbathing are the major draws.

Mazatlán is first and foremost a busy commercial center, thanks to an excellent port and the fertility of the surrounding countryside. More than 600,000 acres of farmland near Mazatlán produce tomatoes, melons, cantaloupes, wheat, and cotton, much of which is shipped to the United States. And nearly all the 150,000 tons of shrimp that are hauled in annually are processed and frozen for the American and Japanese markets.

Sportfishing accounts for Mazatlán's resort status. The port sits at the juncture of the Pacific and the Sea of Cortés, forming what has been called the world's greatest natural fish trap. Mexico's largest sportfishing fleet is based here, and fishermen routinely haul in the biggest catches in size and number on the coast. But fishing is not the only attraction. Hunters are drawn to the quail, duck, and dove that thrive in the hillsides, and surfers find great waves on nearby beaches. Another draw is the relatively low price of accommodations. El Cid, the largest resort on Mexico's Pacific coast, is in the city's Zona Dorada (Golden Zone), as are dozens of high-rise hotels and small *posadas* (inns), all charging about half the going rate of accommodations in Cancún. Between Mazatlán and Puerto Vallarta is Tepic, capital of the state of Nayarit. Tepic is the closest station to the coast for trains from inland Mexico and the U.S. border; travelers headed for Puerto Vallarta or Mazatlán take public buses from here to the coast, some three hours west. For those driving to the coast, Mexico Highway 15 ends here, becoming Mexico Highway 200. The closest coastal town to Tepic is San Blas, some 37 kilometers (23 miles) northwest through the jungle. San Blas is a small seaside village, favored by budget travelers and escapists who eschew the megaresorts.

# North Pacific Coast

ARIZONA

Rio Concepción

Coborca

Nogales

El Desemboque

Magdalena    Cananea    Agua Prieta

Santa Ana

Isla Angel de
la Guarda

El Dátil

Arizpe

Nacozari
de García

Carbo    SONORA

Isla del
Tiburón

Moctezuma

Ures

Hermosillo    Sonora

BAJA
CALIFORNIA
NORTE

Bahía
Kino

San Rafael

Cienaguita

Tecoripa

Yaqui

Guaymas

Santa Rosalía

CHIHUAHUA

Pta.
Concepción

Isla
Lobos

Rosario

Ciudad
Obregón

Mayo

Rosarito

BAJA
CALIFORNIA
SUR

Navojoa

Loreto

Huatabampo

Alamos

Isla
Carmen

Rio Fuerte

Las Grullas
Márgen Derecha

El Fuerte

San Blas

Villa
Constitución

Topolobampo
Harbor

Los Mochis

SINALOA

Isla
San José

Isla
Espíritu
Santo

Guamúchil

N

TO
MAZATLAN

Golfo de California

SIERRA DE LA GIGANTA

Bavispe

Papigochic

| KEY | |
|---|---|
| —— | Rail Lines |
| ---- | Ferry Lines |

0        50 miles
0        75 km

La Paz

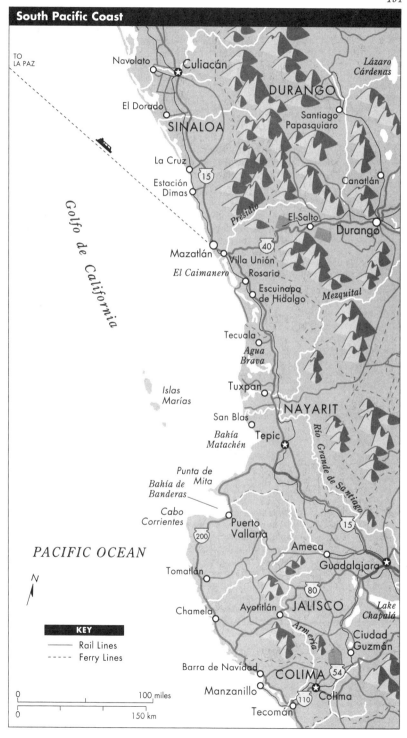

## South Pacific Coast

TO
LA PAZ

Navolato  Culiacán

El Dorado

SINALOA

DURANGO

*Lázaro
Cárdenas*

Santiago
Papasquiaro

La Cruz

Canatlán

Estación
Dimas

15

*Presidio*

El-Salto

Durango

*Golfo de California*

Mazatlán  Villa Unión

40

*El Caimanero*  Rosario

Escuinapa
de Hidalgo

*Mezquital*

Tecuala

*Agua
Brava*

Tuxpan

NAYARIT

San Blas

*Bahía
Matachén*  Tepic

*Islas
Marías*

*Río Grande de Santiago*

Punta de
Mita

*Bahía de
Banderas*

*Cabo
Corrientes*

200

Puerto
Vallarta

15

Ameca

Guadalajara

PACIFIC OCEAN

N

Tomatlán

80

JALISCO

*Lake
Chapalá*

Chamela

Ayotitlán

*Armería*

Ciudad
Guzmán

### KEY

— Rail Lines
--- Ferry Lines

Barra de Navidad

COLIMA

54

Manzanillo  Colima

110

Tecomán

0 _____ 100 miles
0 _____ 150 km

Some 323 kilometers (200 miles) south of Mazatlán is Puerto Vallarta, by far the best-known resort on the upper Pacific coast. The late film director (and sometime resident) John Huston put the town on the map when he filmed Tennessee Williams's *The Night of the Iguana* on the outskirts of the village. One of the movie's stars, Richard Burton, brought Elizabeth Taylor with him—scandalous behavior in 1964, as Burton and Taylor were married but not to each other. Gossip columnists and the Hollywood press flocked to cover the goings-on. In between titterings, stories were filed about the Eden that Huston had discovered—this quaint Mexican fishing village with its cobblestoned lanes and whitewashed, tile-roofed houses. Before long, travel agents were deluged with queries about Puerto Vallarta, a place many had never heard of before.

More than 250,000 people live in Puerto Vallarta today, and upwards of 700,000 tourists arrive each year. The fabled cobblestoned streets are clogged with bumper-to-bumper traffic during the holiday season, and the sounds of construction often drown out the pounding surf. Despite its resort status, parts of Puerto Vallarta are still picturesque. For a sense of the Eden that once was, travel out of town to the lush green mountains where the Rio Tomatlán tumbles over boulders into the sea.

Manzanillo, at the south end of the central Pacific coast, had more of a storybook start than did Puerto Vallarta. Conquistador Hernán Cortés envisioned the area as a gateway to the Orient: From these shores, Spanish galleons would bring in the riches of Cathay to be trekked across the continent to Veracruz, where they would be off-loaded to vessels headed for Spain. But Acapulco, not Manzanillo, became the port of call for the Manila galleons that arrived each year with riches from beyond the seas. Pirates are said to have staked out Manzanillo during the colonial era, and chests of loot are rumored to be buried beneath the sands.

With the coming of the railroads, Manzanillo became a major port of entry, albeit not a pretty one. Forty or 50 years ago, a few seaside hotels opened up on the outskirts of town, which vacationers reached by train. The jet age, however, seemed to doom the port as a sunny vacation spot. Then came Antenor Patiño.

Patiño made millions mining tin in Bolivia. A healthy chunk of that fortune went into building Las Hadas (The Fairies), which, as its name implies, is a sort of fairyland. Inspired by Moorish villages along the Mediterranean, the complex took 10 years to build. The inaugural party in 1974, the "Gala in White," was the social event of the year. Patiño even provided the funds for the government to build a new airport, one that could accommodate his friends' jets. For a while Las Hadas was better known than Manzanillo itself. The film *10* made a star of the resort as well as household names of its stars, Bo Derek and Dudley Moore.

For many visitors, Manzanillo is not so much a city as an airport, the last stop before a holiday begins. Older hotels have been spruced up and condos and all-inclusive resorts built. The Jalisco state line is just a few miles up the coast from the airport. North of the line are the villages of Barra de Navidad, Melaque, Tenacatita, and Costa de Careyes. In these towns and on the isolated beaches between them are self-contained resorts. Colima's tourist industry is working hard to turn the whole coast into a tourist zone. A four-lane toll road now cuts the driving time between Manzanillo and Guadalajara, Mexico's second-largest city, to three hours. On the drawing board are plans to build a $50 million marina complex in downtown Manzanillo, with 230 berths, hotels, restaurants, shops, and a pedestrian walkway along the shore.

The 967-kilometer-long (600-mile-long) coastline on the Gulf of California north of the Mexican Riviera doesn't yet sport a catchy moniker, and the resorts are few and far between. But this corner of northwest Mexico has a character and ambience similar to that of the Baja California Peninsula. The state of Sonora begins at the Arizona border, with the scrubby Sonoran desert extending north into Arizona and New Mexico. Nogales is the main border town, and Americans regularly cross the border in search of bargains and treasures; from Nogales many travelers begin the drive south on Mexico Highway 15 toward the Gulf Coast.

This stretch of the northwest is reminiscent of the old Wild West in the United States. Cowboys ride the range, and ranchero ballads not unlike country-and-western songs emanate from saloons. Irrigated ranchlands feed Mexico's finest beef cattle, and rivers flowing from the Sierra Madre to the east are diverted by giant dams to the once-barren land that now produces cotton, sugarcane, and vegetables. Hermosillo, Sonora's capital, bustles with commerce in the midst of the fertile lands, which turn barren again toward the coast. Kino Bay, 104 kilometers (65 miles) west of Hermosillo, is a quiet beach resort, long favored by travelers in recreational vehicles. Visitors from Arizona seeking more luxurious accommodations have begun building condominiums and private homes along Kino Bay.

The Sierra Madre meets the Sea of Cortés 645 kilometers (400 miles) south of the border at Guaymas, the northwest coast's major resort area. An active city and seaport, Guaymas once drew only the hardy, adventuresome traveler, but hotels and restaurants now abound, along with plans for future developments.

# Mazatlán

Mazatlán is the Aztec word for "place of the deer," and long ago its islands and shores sheltered far more deer than humans. Today it is a city of some 500,000 residents and draws more than 500,000 tourists a year. Sunning, surfing, and sailing have caught on here, and in the winter months visitors from inland Mexico, the United States, and Canada flock to Mazatlán for a break in the sun. From November through April, the temperature range is 21–27°C (70–80°F), and the summer months are not nearly as warm as in the more popular tourist areas farther south. Hotel and restaurant prices are lower than elsewhere on the coast, and the ambience is more that of a fishing town than a tourist haven.

Upscale resorts and ritzy restaurants are not part of Mazatlán's repertoire, though there is a fair dose of luxury at El Cid, Camino Real, and Pueblo Bonito resorts. Work is under way on a 2,000-slip marina to be known as Marina El Sabalo.

The development, which is being undertaken by the El Cid hotel group, calls for a 450-room marina hotel, a yacht club, and nine additional holes added to the hotel's existing 18-hole golf course. The site for the project is the estuary that stretches north from the El Cid golf course to the Camino Real hotel.

Hunting and fishing were the original draw for visitors. At one time, duck, quail, pheasant, and other wildfowl fed in the lagoons; and jaguars, mountain lions, rabbits, and coyotes roamed the surrounding hills. Hunters have to search a little harder and farther for their prey these days, but there's still plenty of wildlife near Mazatlán. The city is the base for Mexico's largest sportfishing fleet; fishermen haul the biggest catches (in size and number) on the coast. The average annual haul is 10,000 sailfish and 5,000 marlin; a record 973-pound marlin and 203-pound sailfish were pulled from these waters.

The Spaniards settled in the Mazatlán region in 1531 and used the indigenous people as a labor force to create the port and village. The center of Mazatlán gradually moved north so that the original site is now 32 kilometers (20 miles) southeast of the harbor.

The port has a history of blockades. In 1847 during the Mexican War, U.S. forces marched down from the border through northeast Mexico and closed the port. In 1864, the French bombarded the city and then controlled it for several years. Mexico's own internal warring factions took over from time to time. And after the Civil War in the United States, a group of southerners tried to turn Mazatlán into a slave city.

Today Mazatlán has the largest shrimping fleet in Mexico. Sinaloa, one of Mexico's richest states, uses Mazatlán's port to ship its agricultural products.

## Arriving and Departing by Plane

**Airport and Airlines** Mazatlán's Rafael Buelna International Airport is serviced by several airlines. **Aeroméxico** (tel. 800/237–6639) has flights from Tucson. **Alaska Airlines** (tel. 800/426–0333) flies in from San Francisco, San Jose, and Los Angeles; **Delta** (tel. 800/241–4141) from Los Angeles; **Aero Litoral** (tel. 800/237–6639) from McAllen, Texas; and **Mexicana** (tel. 800/531–7921) from Denver, Los Angeles, San Francisco, and several Mexican cities.

**Between the Airport and Hotels** The airport is a good 40-minute drive from town. Shuttle services using Volkswagen vans charge about $7 for the trip to the major hotels.

## Arriving and Departing by Car, Train, Bus, and Ship

**By Car** Mazatlán is 1,212 kilometers (751 miles) from the border city of Nogales, Arizona, via Mexico Route 15. An overnight stop is recommended, as driving at night in Mexico can be hazardous.

**By Train** Trains arrive daily from Mexicali, at the California border, and Nogales, at the Arizona border. Others come in from Guadalajara. The train depot is located south of town. Tickets may be purchased at the train station in the neighborhood of Col. Esperanza (tel. 69/84–66–04).

**By Bus** **Transportes Norte de Sonora** has service to Mazatlán from Nogales, Arizona; other companies connect the coast with inland Mexico. The bus terminal is on Av. Insurgentes (tel. 69/81–38–46).

**By Ferry** Ferry service between La Paz and Mazatlán has been privatized and improvements are expected. The ferry departs daily from Mazatlán's Playa Sur terminal at 5 PM and takes about 18 hours to reach La Paz. The fare is $20 for regular passage and nearly $115 for a private cabin for two with bed and bath (tel. 69/81–70–21).

**By Ship** Cruise ships from the **Commodore, Carnival,** and **Princess** lines, among others, include Mazatlán on their winter itineraries.

## Getting Around

Most tourist hotels are located in the Zona Dorada, about 3 kilometers (5 miles) north of downtown, but taxis and buses cruise the strip regularly. A fun way to get around is on the *pulmonías* (open-air jitneys, literally "pneumonias"). The fare, for up to three passengers, starts at about $2 and increases according to the length of the trip. Complaints have been registered, however, about one's susceptibility to fumes from other vehicles.

**By Car** A car is not necessary in town since public transportation is good, but you might want one for a self-guided tour of the area. Rentals usually include free mileage. A Volkswagen Beetle costs about $60 per day with insurance; a sedan with automatic transmission is about $90 per day. The following rental firms have desks at the airport: **Hertz** (Av. Camarón Sábalo 314, tel. 69/83–49–55), and **National** (Av. Camarón Sábalo in the Plaza el Camarón, tel. 69/83–81–11). **Rent Me!,** between the Quijote Inn and the Caravelle hotel, rents antique-type open cars for about $20 an hour (tel. 69/84–64–33).

## Important Addresses and Numbers

**Tourist Information** Information on Mazatlán and city tours is available at the hotels, which do a more thorough job of promoting the area than the tourism office does. The **City Tourism Bureau** is at Paseo Olas Altas 1300, in the Bank of Mexico Building. *Tel. 69/85–12–21. Open Mon.–Sat. 9–1 and 4–7.*

**Consulates** U.S. (Circunvalación 120 Centro, tel. 69/85–22–05); **Canadian** (Hotel Playa Mazatlán, tel. 69/83–73–20).

**Emergencies** The **Public Tourism Ministry** (tel. 69/14–32–22) is an agency of the police department instituted specifically for tourists. **Red Cross** (tel. 69/81–36–90), **24-hour medical clinic** (tel. 69/83–26–00).

## Guided Tours

**Orientation** Tour agencies have offices in most hotels and along the Zona Dorada. Mazatlán's tourist areas are filled with sidewalk stands staffed by persuasive individuals offering free tours of the area along with free drinks and meals. Their true goal is to sell time-shares and condos, and the tour/sales pitch can take up the better part of a day.

The three-hour **City Tour** is a good way to get the lay of the land, particularly downtown, which can be a bit confusing. It includes the Zona Dorada, the cathedral and *zócalo* (main square) downtown, the Mazatlán Arts and Crafts Center, and the waterfront.

**Harbor Cruises** Cruises feature music and dancing and normally last about three hours. Cruises aboard the *Yate Fiesta* (tel. 69/85–22–37) cost about $15 and navigate the bay and the harbor, past the islands and sportfishing fleet. Viajes El Sábalo runs a five-hour tour to **Isla de la Piedra** (Stone Island), with time for lunch and a swim.

The country tour, also called the mountain tour, goes to **Concordia,** known for its furniture makers (a huge wood chair marks the entrance to the small town), then proceeds to **Copala,** a scenic colonial mining town. The jungle tour goes to **San Blas** and the **Rio Tovara** (in the state of Nayarit), where boats travel upriver through mangrove jungle to a small spring-fed pond. The tour companies also offer individual guided tours and sportfishing outings.

## Exploring

*Numbers in the margin correspond to points of interest on the Mazatlán map.*

❶ The **Zona Dorada** (Golden Zone) is the tourist region, and it is from this point that most visitors begin touring the city. Unfortunately, Mazatlán's highlights are spread far and wide, and walking from one section of town to the other can take hours. The best way to travel is via pulmonías, so you can sunbathe and take pictures as you cruise along, although you won't be able to roll up any windows to protect yourself from automobile fumes. If you choose to rent a car and drive, you can tour at your own pace. There are no traffic jams in Mazatlán, except near the market in downtown, where parking can also be a major problem.

❷ The Zona Dorada begins on Avenida Camarón Sábalo at **Punta Camarón** (Shrimp Point), the rocky outcropping on which Valentino's Disco sits, resembling a Moorish palace perched above the sea. Going north, Avenida Camarón Sábalo forms the eastern border of the zone, while Avenida Loaiza runs closer to the beach. In this four-block pocket are most of the hotels, shops, and restaurants, and the majority of nonresidents intent on having a good time sunning, shopping, and partying. Head here to souvenir-shop, hit the discos, and check out the hotel bars.

❸ A stroll through the **Mazatlán Arts and Crafts Center** (Av. Loaiza, tel. 69/13–50–22), at the north end of the zone, will give you a good sampling of the souvenir selection—onyx chess sets, straw sombreros, leather jackets, and Mickey Mouse piñatas. Some of the shops in the center close for siesta from 2 to 4 PM.

**Time Out** **No Name Café,** right in the Arts and Crafts Center, is a good spot for a beer or *agua mineral* (mineral water) and lime. Mexico's version of Baskin-Robbins, **Helados Bing,** has good hot-fudge sundaes and ice cream cones. It's at the corner of Avenida Camarón Sábalo and Avenida Gaviotas. **Panadería Panamá,** also on Camerón Sábalo across from the Las Palmas hotel, is a bakery that has tables where you can sit and enjoy fragrant cinnamon-flavored coffee.

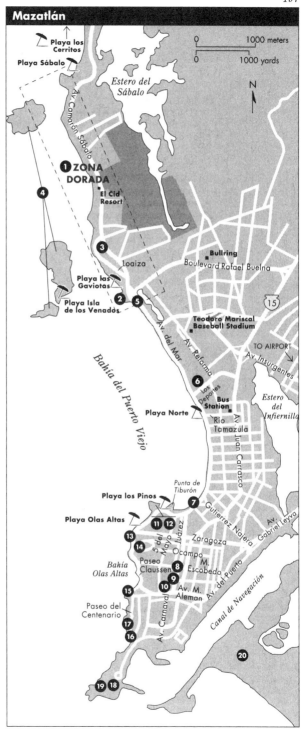

**Mazatlán**

Traveling north, Avenida Loaiza merges into Avenida Sábalo at Avenida Gaviotas, and Avenida Sábalo continues along the coast, past El Cid Resort, one of the largest tourist developments in Mexico. Along the beach side of Avenida Sábalo are some of Mazatlán's largest, most luxurious, and priciest hotels; opposite the beach are many of the better low-cost motels. Along this route there is a good view of Mazatlán's three Pacific
❹ islands—**Isla de los Pájaros** (Bird Island), **Isla de los Venados** (Deer Island), and **Isla de los Chivos** (Goat Island). Just past the Camino Real resort, Avenida Camarón Sábalo becomes Avenida Sábalo Cerritos and crosses over the Estero del Sábalo, a long lagoon popular with bird-watchers. The area north of here will someday be an exclusive touring and resort area; towering condos are already being built.

South of Valentino's, this main road changes names frequently in its 15-mile length. At Punta Camarón it becomes Avenida del
❺ Mar, which leads toward Old Mazatlán. The 10-mile **malecón,** Mazatlán's version of a main highway and beachfront boardwalk, begins here.

❻ **Acuario Mazatlán** (Mazatlán's aquarium) is a few blocks south, down Avenida de los Deportes. The aquarium, with its tanks of sharks, sea horses, eels, lobsters, and multicolored saltwater and freshwater fish, is a must-see. A fanciful bronze fountain and sculpture of two boys feeding a dolphin marks the aquarium's entrance. *Av. de los Deportes 111, tel. 69/81–78–15. Admission: $NP12 adults, $NP6 children. Open daily 9:30–6:30.*

**Time Out** Just before you reach the road to the aquarium, you'll see **Señor Frog** (Av. del Mar, tel. 69/82–19–25), probably the most popular restaurant and bar in all of Mazatlán. There's a souvenir shop at the front that sells T-shirts and assorted paraphernalia bearing the Señor Frog logo. The restaurant is cool, dark, cluttered, and busy. Pace yourself with the margaritas and silver buckets filled with bottles of beer, or you'll never make it to the aquarium.

Avenida del Mar continues south past beaches popular with the locals and travelers staying at the budget hotels across the
❼ street. The **Monumento al Pescador** (Fisherman's Monument) is Avenida del Mar's main landmark, and it is a strange sight. An enormous, voluptuous nude woman reclines on an anchor, her hand extended toward a nude fisherman dragging his nets.

Calle Juárez and Calle Cinco de Mayo intersect with Avenida del Mar and lead to Mazatlán's real downtown, where the streets are filled with buses and locals rushing to and from work and the market. Many travelers never see this part of Mazatlán, but it's worth a visit. Head for the blue-and-gold spires
❽ of the **Mazatlán Catedral,** at Calles Juárez and Ocampo, and you'll be in the heart of the city. The cathedral, built in 1890 and made a basilica in 1935, has a gilded and ornate triple altar, with murals of angels overhead and many small altars along the sides. A sign at the entrance requests that visitors be appropri-
❾ ately attired (no shorts or tank tops inside). The **zócalo,** called **Plaza Revolución,** just across the street, has one of the most fascinating gazebos in Mexico—what looks like a '50s diner inside the lower level and a wrought-iron bandstand on top. The green-and-orange tile on the walls, ancient jukebox, and soda fountain serving shakes, burgers, and hot dogs couldn't make a

more surprising sight. On the streets facing the zócalo are the City Hall, banks, post office, and telegraph office.

⑩ The **Teatro Angela Peralta,** built in 1860 and now beautifully restored, is at Sixto Osuna and Carnaval, about three blocks from the zócalo. It was declared a historic monument in late 1990.

Back along the waterfront, Avenida del Mar becomes Paseo
⑪ Claussen as it heads south, passing by **El Fuerte Carranza,** an old Spanish fort built to defend the city against the French, and
⑫ **Casa del Marino,** a shelter for sailors. Playa los Piños, a popular
⑬ surfing beach, stretches along this road. **High-Divers Park,** where young men climb to a white platform and plunge into the sea, is located nearby. It isn't as exciting as the performance at La Quebrada in Acapulco, but at night when the divers leap carrying flaming torches it's equally spectacular. Some of Mazatlán's best surfing beaches are along this strip.

⑭ The malecón continues past **Cerro de la Nevería** (Icebox Hill). Wealthy landowners in Mazatlán imported ice from San Francisco in the late 1800s and stored it in underground tunnels in
⑮ this hill. The next landmark is the statue of **La Mazatleca,** a bronze nymph rising from a giant wave. Across the street is a small bronze deer, Mazatlán's mascot.

Paseo Claussen leads into Olas Altas, site of Old Mazatlán, the center for tourism in the 1940s. Olas Altas (which means high waves) ends at a small traffic circle. A plaque at the circle bears the state symbol of Sinaloa.

⑯ Above Olas Altas is **Cerro de Vigía** (Lookout Hill), with a lookout point, weather station, and rusty cannon. The view from this windy hill is fantastic, overlooking both sides of Mazatlán, its harbor, and the Pacific. It's a steep climb up and is better
⑰ done by taxi than on foot. The **Centenario Pérgola,** at the top of the hill, was once used by the Spaniards as a place to watch for pirates.

---

**Time Out**   **El Mirador,** on top of Cerro de Vigía, is one of the best seafood restaurants in Mazatlán. If you can't make it for a meal, stop long enough to sample the ceviche (seafood marinated in lime or lemon juice) made with fresh shrimp.

---

At the end of the malecón, the road becomes Paseo Centenario and continues south to the tip of the peninsula. At the tip is
⑱ ⑲ **Cerro del Crestón** (Summit Hill) and **El Faro,** said to be the second-highest lighthouse in the world after Gibraltar, with a range of 36 nautical miles. It takes about 30 minutes to hike up to the lighthouse, but you get a great view of the harbor and sea. This side of the peninsula is devoted to boats, and the road running along the many docks and military installations is called Avenida del Puerto. The sportfishing fleet is anchored at the base of Cerro del Crestón; the next docks north are used by
⑳ cruise ships and merchant vessels. Launches for **Isla de la Piedra** leave from from a small dock by the military base.

---

**Time Out**   Small *palapas* (beach shacks) are sometimes set up along the sportfishing docks; many serve a tasty smoked marlin. The palapas near the launches to Isla de la Piedra sell sugarcane sticks, which look like bamboo and are good for quenching your thirst.

---

## What to See and Do with Children

The **Acuario Mazatlán,** with its tanks of salt- and freshwater
fish, sharks, and films about sea life, is a perfect child-pleaser.
On Sundays in particular, it is packed with families. At the
large playground next door, skateboarders practice their
tricks while the little ones play on the slides and swings. A little zoo sits amid the trees in the botanical garden beside the
aquarium; the most interesting animals are the crocodiles.

## Shopping

In the **Zona Dorada,** particularly along Avenida Camarón
Sábalo and Avenida Rodolfo T. Loaiza, you can buy everything
from piñatas to designer clothing. The best place for browsing
is the **Mazatlán Arts and Crafts Center,** designed as a place to
view artisans at work and buy their wares. Now the center is
filled with shops and boutiques, and the only craft you see is the
fine art of bartering. **No Name Café** restaurant and bar in the
arts center is a good spot in which to have a beer and compare
prices with fellow shoppers. The **Mercado Viejo Mazatlán** and
the **Tequila Tree,** both on Avenida Loaiza, are enormous ware-
house-type stores filled with souvenirs. **Evolución** (tel. 69/13–
08–39), in the Tequila Tree Center, is a new-age bookstore with
a fine collection of English-language books.

For sportswear, visit **Aca Joe, Benetton, Fiorucci, Guess,** and
**Bye-Bye. Sea Shell City** is a must-see; it has two floors packed
with shells from around the world that have been glued,
strung, and molded into every imaginable shape from lamps to
necklaces. Check out the enormous fountain upstairs, covered
with thousands of shells. **Designer's Bazaar,** a two-story shop
near Los Sábalos Hotel, has probably the best selection of high-
quality folk art, leather wallets and belts, hand-embroidered
clothing, and a good sampling of fashionable swimsuits. Leather shops are clustered along the southern end of the Zona
Dorada. Try on soft leather jackets dyed in the latest colors at
the **Leather House** and **Rey Solomon.**

The **Mercado Central,** downtown between Calle Juárez and
Serdán, is a gigantic place filled with produce, meat, fish, and
handicrafts that are sold at the lowest prices in town. It takes
more searching to find good-quality handicrafts, but that's part
of the fun. Browse through the stalls along the street outside
the market for the best crafts.

## Sports and Fitness

Fishing More than a dozen sportfishing fleets operate from the docks
south of the lighthouse. Hotels can arrange charters, or you
can contact the companies directly. Charters include a full day
of fishing, lunch, bait, and tackle. Prices range from $40 per
person on a party boat to $230 to charter an entire boat. Char-
ter companies to contact include **Bill Heimpel's Star Fleet** (tel.
69/82–26–65), **Flota Faro** (tel. 69/81–28–24), **Estrella** (tel. 69/
82–38–78), **El Dorado** (tel. 69/81–62–04), and **De Oro** (tel. 69/
82–31–30).

Golf The spectacular 18-hole course at **El Cid** (tel. 69/13–33–33), designed by Robert Trent Jones, is reserved for members of the
resort, hotel guests, and their guests. There is a nine-hole

course at the **Club Campestre de Mazatlán** (tel. 69/84–74–94), on the outskirts of town on Route 15.

**Hunting** Several species of duck and white-wing doves, mourning doves, and quail abound in the Mazatlán area. The season runs from October through April. **Aviles Brothers** (Box 221, tel. 69/81–37–28) is the most experienced outfitter, arranging licenses and the rental of firearms. The cost of a six-hour hunt is $110 and up, including transportation, retriever, and English-speaking guide.

**Tennis** Many of the hotels have courts, some of which are open to the public. There are a few public courts not connected to the hotels. Call in advance for reservations at **El Cid Resort,** 13 courts (tel. 69/13–33–33); **Racket Club,** 6 courts (tel. 69/12–46–00); and **Club de Tenis Reforma,** 8 courts (tel. 69/13–35–76).

**Water Sports** Jet skis, Hobie Cats, and Windsurfers are available for rent at most hotels, and parasailing is very popular along the Zona Dorada. Scuba diving and snorkeling are catching on, but there are no really great diving spots. The best is around Isla de los Venados. For rentals and trips, contact the following operators: **Caravelle Beach Club** (Av. Camarón Sábalo, tel. 69/13–02–00), **Chico's Beach Club** (Av. Camarón Sábalo 500, tel. 69/14–06–66), **El Cid Resort Aqua Sport Center** (Av. Camarón Sábalo, tel. 69/13–33–33), and **Los Sábalos** (Av. Camarón Sábalo, tel. 69/13–53–37).

## Spectator Sports

**Baseball** The people of Mazatlán loyally support their team, Los Venados, a Pacific League, Triple A team. Games are played at the Teodoro Mariscal Stadium (Av. Deportes) from October through April.

**Bullfights** Spectacles are held most Sunday afternoons between December and Easter. The bullring is located on Boulevard Rafael Buelna and tickets are available through most hotels and from **Valentino's** (tel. 69/84–16–66).

## Beaches

**Playa Los Cerritos** The northernmost beach on the outskirts of town, which runs from Camino Real Resort to Punta Cerritos, is also the cleanest and least populated. The waves can be too rough for swimming, but they're great for surfing.

**Playa Sábalo and Playa las Gaviotas** Mazatlán's two most popular beaches are along the Zona Dorada. There are as many vendors selling blankets, pottery, lace tablecloths, and silver jewelry as there are sunbathers. Boats, Windsurfers, and parasailers line the shores. The beach is protected from heavy surf by the three islands—Venados, Pájaros, and Chivas. You can safely stroll these beaches until midnight and eavesdrop on the social action in the hotels while enjoying a few solitary, romantic moments sans vendors and crowds.

**Playa Norte** This strand begins at Punta Camarón (Valentino's is a landmark) along Avenida del Mar and the malecón and runs to the Fisherman's Monument. The dark brown sand is dirty and rocky at some points, but clean at others, and is popular with those staying at hotels without beach access. Palapas selling cold drinks, tacos, and fresh fish line the beach; be sure to try the fresh coconut milk.

**Playa Olas Altas** Meaning "high waves," this was the first tourist beach in Mazatlán, running south along the malecón from the Fisherman's Monument. Surfers congregate here during the summer months, when the waves are at their highest.

**Playa Isla de los Venados** Boats make frequent departures from the Zona Dorada hotels for this beach on Deer Island. It's only a 10-minute ride, but the difference in ambience is striking; the beach is pretty, uncluttered, and clean, and you can hike around the southern point of the island to small, secluded coves covered with shells.

**Playa Isla de la Piedra** The locals head here on weekends. Entire families, bearing toys, rafts, and picnic lunches, ride over to the island on *pangas* (small, open boats) from the dock near the train tracks. Sixteen kilometers (10 miles) of unspoiled beaches here allow enough room for all visitors to spread out and claim their own space, but this won't be the case for long: Work on another tourist megadevelopment is at a standstill. The project calls for the surrender of 900 acres of the island to a host of hotels, villas, two golf clubs, and tennis and riding clubs. Small shacks and palapas sell drinks and fresh fish, and on Sundays the island looks like a small village, with lots of music and fun.

## Dining

The emphasis in Mazatlán is on casual, bountiful dining, and the prices are reasonable. Shrimp and fresh fish are the highlights; be sure to have a seafood cocktail along the beach. Dress is casual in Mazatlán, although shorts are frowned upon for dinner and most restaurants require footwear at all meals. Chic resortwear is not out of place in establishments like Sr. Peppers, La Concha, and Casa Loma. When you check your bill, be aware that some restaurants, particularly in the hotels, add a service charge of 10% to 15% to your total, as well as 10% tax.

Highly recommended restaurants are indicated by a star ★.

| Category | Cost* |
|---|---|
| Very Expensive | over $35 |
| Expensive | $25–$35 |
| Moderate | $15–$25 |
| Inexpensive | under $15 |

*per person, excluding drinks, service, and sales tax (10%)*

**Very Expensive** **Casa Loma.** An out-of-the-way, elegant restaurant in a converted villa, Casa Loma serves international specialties such as chateaubriand and chicken cordon bleu. Lunch on the patio is less formal. Have a martini made by an expert, and save room for the fine pastries. *Av. Gaviotas 104, tel. 69/13–53–98. Open Oct.–mid-May. MC, V.*

★ **La Concha.** Certainly the prettiest waterside dining spot, La Concha is a large enclosed palapa with three levels of seating at tables spread far apart, a spacious dance floor decked with twinkling lights, and outdoor tables by the sand. Adventurous types might attempt the stingray with black butter or calamari in its ink. The more conservative can try a thick filet Mignon cooked to perfection. A singer croons Las Vegas–style ballads as couples dance. The waiters are proper and refined. La Concha is also open for breakfast. *El Cid Resort, Av. Camarón Sábalo, tel. 69/13–33–33. AE, DC, MC, V.*

**Expensive** **El Marinero.** The best seafood house in Old Mazatlán, this restaurant offers a generous seafood platter, grilled on a hibachi at your table and piled high with frogs' legs, shrimp, oysters covered with melted cheese, and fresh fish. The decor is strictly nautical, with fishing nets, anchors, and seashell-covered lamps. Try the shrimp *machaca*, sautéed in olive oil with tomatoes, chives, and chilies. Machaca is a typical dish, often made with beef and served for breakfast. *Calle Cinco de Mayo 530, tel. 69/81–76–82. AE, D, MC, V.*

**Sr. Peppers.** Elegant yet unpretentious, with ceiling fans, lush foliage, and candlelit tables, Sr. Peppers serves choice steaks and lobsters cooked over a mesquite grill. Enjoy the dance floor and live music. *Av. Camarón Sábalo, across from the Camino Real hotel, tel. 69/14–01–20. AE, MC, V.*

**Moderate** **El Mirador.** A real find on the top of Cerro de Vigía, this unas-
★ suming restaurant has some of the freshest, most flavorful fish around. The ceviche is made with fresh shrimp, chopped and marinated in lime juice with tomatoes, onions, cilantro, and peppers. The salsa and chips are homemade and delicious, and meals include soup, salad, and dessert. Stick with the shrimp and fish, and you'll be delighted. The strong wind atop the lookout tends to whip through the open windows, which can be quite invigorating. *Atop Cerro de Vigía, no phone. MC, V.*

**Señor Frog.** The Carlos Anderson chain's Mazatlán restaurant is as noisy and entertaining as the others. Bandidos carry tequila bottles and shot glasses in their bandoliers, leather belts that held ammunition in the old westerns. Barbecued ribs and chicken, served with corn on the cob, and heaping portions of standard Mexican dishes are the specialty, and the drinking and carousing go on well into the night. The tortilla soup is excellent. *Av. del Mar 225, tel. 69/82–19–25. AE, MC, V.*

**Shrimp Bucket.** In Old Mazatlán under forest-green awnings is the original Carlos 'n Charlie's. The garden patio restaurant is much quieter than its successors—some would call it respectable. Best bets are fried shrimp served in clay buckets and barbecued ribs. Portions are plentiful. Breakfast is also served. It's the place to see where all the Carlos 'n Charlie's action began. *Olas Altas 11, tel. 69/81–63–50. AE, MC, V.*

★ **Tres Islas.** A wonderful palapa on the beach, north of El Quixote hotel, Tres Islas is a favorite with families who spend all Sunday afternoon feasting on fresh fish. Try smoked marlin, oysters *diablo*, octopus, or the seafood platter. The setting is the nicest in town, close to the water with a good view of the three islands. The waiters are friendly and eager to help. *Av. Camarón Sábalo, tel. 69/13–59–32. MC, V.*

**Inexpensive** **Doney.** This big downtown hacienda has been serving great
★ Mexican meals since 1959. The large dining room has old photos of Mazatlán, a high brick ceiling, and embroidered tablecloths, all of which give you the feeling that you're sitting in someone's home. The Doney is named after a restaurant in Rome, though there is nothing Italian about the menu. Try the *chilaquiles* (casserole of tortillas and chile sauce), mole, or fried chicken. The meringue and fruit pies are excellent. *Mariano Escobedo at Calle Cinco de Mayo, tel. 69/81–26–51. AE, MC, V.*

**Jungle Juice.** As you might suspect, the specialties here are unusual fruit-juice concoctions with names like King Kong and Tarzan. But its main attractions are the good food—fish, chicken, and ribs—the satellite TV dish that captures major sports events, and the classic rock and roll that makes this a favorite gathering spot. *Av. de las Garzas and Laguna, tel. 13–33–15. MC, V.*

★ **Karnes en Su Jugo.** A small family-run café on the malecón, with a few outdoor tables and a large indoor restaurant, this establishment specializes in *karnes en su jugo*, literally beef in its juice, a Mexican beef stew, with chopped beef, onions, beans, and bacon—a filling, satisfying meal, especially when eaten with a basket of homemade tortillas. *Av. del Mar, tel. 69/82–13–22. AE, MC, V.*

**Mucho Taco.** This bright blue taco stand in the heart of the Zona Dorada is open 24 hours—a blessing for those who stay out at the discos until the wee hours. The tacos are fresh and tasty, and you can eat at the small sidewalk tables or take your feast back to your room. *Av. Camarón Sábalo, no phone. No credit cards.*

## Lodging

Most of Mazatlán's hotels are in the Zona Dorada, along the beaches. Less expensive places are in Old Mazatlán, the original tourist zone along the malecón—on the south side of downtown. Most hotels raise their rates for the November–April high season; rates are lowest in the summer, during the rainy season. Price categories are based on high-season rates—expect to pay 25% less during the off-season.

Highly recommended lodgings are indicated by a star ★.

| Category | Cost* |
|---|---|
| Very Expensive | over $160 |
| Expensive | $90–$160 |
| Moderate | $40–$90 |
| Inexpensive | under $40 |

*\*All prices are for a standard double room; excluding 10% tax.*

**Expensive** **El Cid.** The largest resort in Mazatlán, and perhaps in Mexico,
★ El Cid has 1,000 rooms spread over 900 acres. A tower contains only suites. A private residential area away from the beach has some impressive homes and villas, most with satellite TV. Soon it will have a private marina. The spacious hotel rooms overlook the pool and beach (one of the longest and cleanest in the area), and the hotel is popular with convention groups as well as lone travelers. The glass-enclosed arcade has nice boutiques, and La Concha is one of the most romantic spots on the beach (*see* Dining, *above*). *Av. Camarón Sábalo, tel. 69/13–33–33; reservations in the U.S., tel. 800/525–1925. 1,000 air-conditioned rooms, suites, and villas. Facilities: 18-hole golf course, 6 pools, 17 tennis courts, 14 restaurants, 2 bars, disco, shops, aquatic center. AE, DC, MC, V.*

**Los Sábalos.** A white high rise in the center of the Zona Dorada, Los Sábalos has a great location, a long clean beach, and lots of action. You feel as though you're a part of things, amid the flight attendants who lay over here, and it's only a short walk to Valentino's, the best disco in town. *Av. Loaiza 100, tel. 69/83–53–33; reservations in the U.S. tel. 800/528–8760. 185 air-conditioned rooms. Facilities: beach, pool, 2 restaurants, 2 bars, tennis courts, health club, shops. AE, DC, MC, V.*

★ **Pueblo Bonito.** By far the most beautiful property in Mazatlán, this all-suite hotel and time-share resort has an enormous lobby with chandeliers, beveled glass doors, and gleaming red-and-white tiled floors. The pink terra-cotta rooms have domed ceilings. An arched doorway leads from the tiled kitchen into the elegant seating area, which is furnished with pale pink and beige couches and glass tables. Pink flamingos stroll on the manicured lawns, golden *koi* (carp) swim in small ponds, and bronzed sunbathers repose on padded white lounge chairs by the crystal-blue pool. This is as elegant as Mazatlán gets. *Av. Camarón Sábalo 2121, tel. 69/14–37–00; reservations in the U.S. tel. 800/262–4500. 250 air-conditioned suites, each with kitchen, dining and living area, and balcony. Facilities: 2 pools, beach, 2 restaurants, tennis courts, bar. AE, DC, MC, V.*

**Westin Camino Real.** Location is the big plus at this property, which is far from the frenzy of the Golden Zone, past a rocky point at the northernmost edge of town. The beach is a bit of a hike from the hotel rooms, through the densely landscaped grounds and down a small hill. The hotel, one of the first in Mazatlán, has undergone drastic renovation; the rooms have shed their '70s earth-tone decor, and a blue, green, and pink color scheme now prevails. If you're more interested in relaxing in peace than in carousing, this is your best bet. *Av. Camarón Sábalo, tel. 69/13–11–11; reservations in the U.S., tel. 800/228–3000. 169 rooms. Facilities: beach, pool, 2 tennis courts, 2 restaurants, bar. AE, DC, MC, V.*

**Moderate** **Holiday Inn.** A consistently good hotel, the Holiday Inn is a long walk from the Zona Dorada, and little traffic runs by. Tour and convention groups fill the 202 rooms and keep the party mood going by the pool and on the beach, where parasailing is a big hit. Children have a small play area with swings and a wading pool, and there is live, upbeat music in the lobby. All of the rooms have been updated in whites and pastels, and there are large sliding glass doors that open to a pretty view of the islands. *Av. Camarón Sábalo 696, tel. 69/13–22–22. 202 air-conditioned rooms. Facilities: pool, beach, restaurant, 2 bars. AE, DC, MC, V.*

★ **Playa Mazatlán.** Palapas are set up on the patios by the rooms in this casual hotel, which is popular with Mexican families and laid-back singles more concerned with comfort than style. The bright, sunny rooms have tiled headboards over the beds and tiled tables by the windows. There's a volleyball net on the beach, and a small taco stand sells good, inexpensive snacks. *Av. Loaiza 202, tel. 69/83–44–44; reservations in the U.S. tel. 800/222–4466. 425 air-conditioned rooms. Facilities: beach, pool, restaurant, bar. AE, DC, MC, V.*

**Inexpensive** **Belmar.** One of the first hotels in Old Mazatlán, built near the turn of the century, the Belmar has seen better days. It must have been charming in its heyday, with its blue-and-white tiled balconies facing a central courtyard. Now the place is a bit shabby. The dark wood arches and doorways haven't seen polish in years, and the furnishings in the rooms are quite rickety, though there are some marvelous antiques among the clutter.

The newer rooms on the waterfront side have shag carpeting and paneled walls. The beach across the street is one of the best for surfing, and downtown and the market are a short walk away. *Olas Altas 166 Sur, tel. 69/85–11–11. 196 rooms. Facilities: beach, pool, parking, coffee shop, bar. MC, V.*

**Bungalows Mar Sol.** This older motel has clean, cluttered rooms furnished in a mishmash of colors and styles. A long garden area fronts the parking lot, and there are lounge chairs, a small fountain, and a palapa-covered ping-pong table, but no pool. The beach is across the street, and though the motel is north of town, buses do stop close by frequently. *Av. Camarón Sábalo 1001, tel. 69/14–01–08. MC, V.*

**Sands.** This is a beachfront hotel with many of the amenities of the larger and more expensive resort hotels, but at a fraction of the price. It is popular with retirees and wanderers who want to stay put for a while. All of the rooms are air-conditioned and have color TVs with some U.S. channels. *Av. del Mar 1910, tel. 69/82–06–00. 86 rooms. Facilities: pool, restaurant, bar. AE, MC, V.*

### Nightlife

**Caracol Tango Palace** at El Cid is Mazatlán's premier night spot. **Valentino's** still draws a glitzy crowd. Its stark white towers rise on Punta Camarón at the beginning of the Zona Dorada. Enjoy easy listening or romantic music here, or opt for rock around the clock on the dance floor.

Also at the Valentino's complex is **Bora Bora** (tel. 69/83–62–12), a casual palapa bar on the beach that stays alive with music and dancing from noon to 4 AM. **Sheik,** a new restaurant extravaganza, is also located here, but it needs a lot of improvement in the food and service departments. Still, don't miss it—stop in during early evening for a drink at least.

**Fandango's,** in the Las Palmas shopping center, is also popular. One of the **Mexican Fiestas,** at the Playa Mazatlan, Holiday Inn, or the Oceano Palace, is also a good entertainment bet; the Fiesta at the Plaza Maya offers a buffet and a two-hour show that includes a performance of the Flying Indians of Papantla. Almost all hotel travel desks can provide you with information on days and times.

# Puerto Vallarta

On the edge of the Sierra Madre range sits one of the most popular vacation spots in Mexico. When Puerto Vallarta first entered the public's consciousness, with John Huston's 1963 movie, *The Night of the Iguana*, it seemed an almost mythical tropical paradise. Indeed, at the time it was a quiet fishing and farming community in an exquisite setting.

Puerto Vallarta's Bahía de Banderas (Bay of Flags) attracted pirates and explorers as early as the 1500s; it was used as a stopover on long sailings, as a place for the crew to relax (or maybe plunder and pillage). Sir Francis Drake apparently stopped here. In the mid-1850s, Don Guadalupe Sánchez Carrillo developed the bay as a port for the silver mines by the Río Cuale. Then it was known as Puerto de Peñas and had about 1,500 inhabitants. It remained a village until 1918, when it was made a municipality by the state of Jalisco and named after Ignacio L. Vallarta, a governor of Jalisco.

In the 1950s, Puerto Vallarta was essentially a pretty hideaway for those in the know—the wealthy and some hardy escapists. After the publicity brought on by *The Night of the Iguana*, tourism began to boom. Puerto Vallarta the fishing village is now PV (as it is called), a city with more than 150,000 residents and an additional 100,000 in the surrounding countryside. Airports, hotels, and highways have supplanted palm groves and fishing shacks. More than 700,000 tourists visit each year, and from November through April cobblestoned streets are clogged with pedestrians and cars. There are now about 10,000 hotel rooms in Puerto Vallarta.

Despite the transformation, every attempt has been made to keep the town's character and image intact. Even the parking lot at the new Gigante supermarket is cobblestoned, and by law any house built in town must be painted white. Visitors still see houses with red-tile roofs on palm-covered hills overlooking glistening blue water. Pack mules clomp down the steep cobblestoned streets. Within 16 kilometers (10 miles) of town are peaceful coves, rivers rushing to the sea, and steep mountain roads that curve and twist through jungles of pines and palms.

In the high season, from December through April, the temperature is in the 70s and 80s, the water temperature in the 60s and low 70s. The off-season brings rain: light afternoon showers in the early summer and major rainstorms in the late summer and fall. You miss out on constant sunshine in the off-season; it's humid and the temperatures are high (in the 80s and 90s), and the mosquitoes can be a nuisance; but you enjoy emptier beaches, warmer water (well into the 70s), and less-crowded streets. You also benefit from a 25% to 30% reduction in room rates and the opportunity to do a little bargaining on rental-car costs.

## Arriving and Departing by Plane

**Airport and Airlines** Puerto Vallarta's **Gustavo Díaz Ordáz International Airport** is 6.4 kilometers (4 miles) north of town, not far from the major resorts. The Mexican airlines have daily flights from Mexico City, Los Cabos, Mazatlán, and Guadalajara, and connecting flights from other Mexican cities. **Mexicana** (tel. 800/531–7921) has service from Chicago, Los Angeles, San Francisco, San Antonio, and Denver; **Aeroméxico** (tel. 800/237–6639) from Los Angeles. Several American carriers also serve Puerto Vallarta, including **Alaska Airlines** (tel. 800/426–0333), **American** (tel. 800/433–7300), **Aero California** (tel. 800/258–3311), **Delta** (tel. 800/221–1212), and **Continental** (tel. 800/525–0280).

**Between the Airport and Hotels** Volkswagen vans provide economical transportation from the airport to hotels, and all the car-rental agencies have desks in the airport.

## Arriving and Departing by Car, Train, Bus, and Ship

**By Car** Puerto Vallarta is about 1,900 kilometers (1,200 miles) from Nogales, Arizona, at the United States–Mexico border, 354 kilometers (220 miles) from Guadalajara, and 167 kilometers (104 miles) from Tepic. Driving to Puerto Vallarta is not difficult, but driving in the city can be horrid. From December to Ap-

Parasailers lift off while sunbathers recline on the sand. Beach toys for rent include everything from rubber inner tubes to Windsurfers. Vendors stroll the beach, hawking lace tablecloths, wood statues, kites, and grilled fish on a stick. Plaza Lázaro Cárdenas is a pretty spot at the north end of the beach. To the south, Playa de los Muertos ends at a rocky point called El Púlpito. PV's tourism promoters have given up trying to change the name of Playa de los Muertos (Beach of the Dead Ones) to Playa del Sol (Beach of the Sun). If you see an address for the latter, head for the former.

**Time Out** Eating grilled fish on a stick at Playa de los Muertos is like having a hot dog on Coney Island: it's what you *do*. Buy it from one of the stands at the south end of the beach, then stroll along and watch the show. For a sit-down break, get a beer and tacos or enchiladas at **El Dorado** at the north end.

**Mismaloya and Boca de Tomatlán** ⓫ A visit to Puerto Vallarta without a side trip to **Playa Mismaloya (Mismaloya Beach)** is nearly unthinkable, since this is where "the movie" was made. The 13-kilometer (8-mile) drive south on Route 200 passes by spectacular houses, some of PV's oldest and quietest resorts, and a slew of condo and time-sharing developments. A pretty cove, somewhat spoiled by La Jolla de Mismaloya, a huge hotel complex built on its shores, Mismaloya is backed by rugged, rocky hills and affords a good view of Los Arcos, a rock formation in the water. Motor launches leave from here for the more secluded beaches of Los Arcos, Las Animas, Quimixto, and Yelapa for about $3.50 per person, per hour.

⓬ **Boca de Tomatlán** is a small village at the mouth of the Tomatlán River. It's a beautiful spot where you can wade in freshwater pools. Just before you reach the dirt road to the beach, there are several large palapa restaurants, including Chee Chee's, which is a massive restaurant, shopping, and swimming-pool complex that spreads down a steep hillside like a small village. Farther along the main road, through Boca, is Chico's Paradise, a large restaurant set amid giant boulders and surrounded by pools and small waterfalls.

### Shopping

Puerto Vallarta can get into a shopper's blood. Chain stores line the main streets, selling designer-label clothing such as **Esprit, Aca Joe,** and **Ralph Lauren** at prices comparable to if not higher than those at home. Prices in the shops are fixed, and American dollars and credit cards are accepted. Bargaining is expected in the markets and by the vendors on the beach, who also freely accept American money. Most stores open at 10, close for siesta at 1 or 2, then reopen from 4 to 8 PM.

**Art** The late Mañuel Lepe is perhaps Puerto Vallarta's most famous artist. His primitive style can be seen in the prints and posters that are still available at several of the galleries and shops around town. Sergio Bustamante, the creator of life-size brass, copper, and papier-mâché animals, has his own gallery, **Sergio Bustamante** (Juárez 275). Other galleries of note include **Galería Uno** (Morelos 561), **Galería Pacífico** (Juárez 519 and Insurgentes 109), **Galería Vallarta** (Júarez 263), and **Galería Brooks/de Gooyer** (Morelos 589).

**Clothing** Most of the brand-name sportswear shops are located along the malecón and down its side streets. Many of these stores also have branches in the shopping centers or along Carretera Aeropuerto. Some of the most popular shops are **Aca Joe** (Díaz Ordáz 588), **Guess** (Morelos and Abasolo), **Ocean Pacific** (Morelos 660), and **Calvin Klein** (Hidalgo and Libertad).

More elegant, dressier clothes, made of soft flowing fabrics in tropical prints, can be found at **Sucesos Boutique** (Libertad and Hidalgo and Olas Altas, in the Los Arcos hotel), which features hand-painted fabrics and fashionable gauze resortwear that is sold in exclusive boutiques throughout Mexico. **El Aguila Descalza** (Corona 179) has designer Josefa's fantastically popular and expensive handwoven cotton caftans, dresses, and skirts embroidered and appliquéd with bright primary-color ribbons. There are also designs by Opus and some beautifully embroidered ethnic clothing. **María de Guadalajara,** in the Puesta del Sol condominiums in Marina Vallarta, carries easy-to-wear clothing for women in gauzy cotton fabrics dyed in luscious colors.

**Folk Art** Few cities in Mexico have a collection of the country's fine folk arts that is as representative as the one in Puerto Vallarta. Masks, pottery, lacquerware, clothing, mirrors, glass dishes, windows and lamps, carved-wood animals and doors, antiques and modern art, hand-dyed woven rugs and embroidered clothing are all available in the markets and from vendors. **Nevaj** (Morelos 223) carries high-quality folk art from Central and South America, including primitive and sublime weavings, bags, shawls, and dresses. **Olinalá** (Lázaro Cárdenas 274, tel. 322/2–4995) is a two-story gallery and shop filled with masks from all over Mexico, as well as lacquered boxes, trays, and bowls from Michoacán. **Arte Mágico Huichol** (Calle Corona 164) features beaded tapestries and weavings from the Huichol Indians of Nayarit. **Majolica** (Calle Corona 191) stocks hand-painted pottery from Puebla. **St. Valentín** (Morelos 574) carries rough-hewn pine and mahogany furniture, handwoven rugs from Oaxaca, and earthenware dishes. **Querubines** (Juárez and Galeana) displays crafts, including ceramics, glassware, and jewelry, from all over Mexico, as well as a wearable collection of intricately embroidered native clothing made from hand-loomed cloth.

**Jewelry** There is a good selection of Mexican silver in Puerto Vallarta, but watch out for fake silver made with alloys. Real silver carries the 925 silver stamp required by the government. It is best to visit a reputable jeweler, such as **Ric Taxco** (Pueblo Viejo shopping center); **Joyería la Azteca** (Juárez 244 and 360) sells silver jewelry from Taxco and its own line of elaborate, heavy silver and gold necklaces and bracelets. **Joyas Finas Suneson** (Morelos 593) specializes in fine silver jewelry and objets d'art by some of Mexico's finest designers.

**Markets** The **Mercado Municipal,** at Avenida Miramar and Libertad, is a typical market plopped down in the busiest part of town. Flowers, piñatas, produce, and plastics are all shoved together in indoor and outdoor stands that cover a full city block. The strip of shops along Río Cuale Island is an outdoor market of sorts, with souvenir stands and exclusive boutiques interspersed with restaurants and cafés. Bargaining at the stalls in the market and on the island is expected.

**Shopping Centers** The highway on the north side of town is lined with small arcades and large shopping centers that are occupied by handicrafts and sportswear shops. The best selections are at **Plaza Malecón,** at the beginning of Díaz Ordáz; **Plaza Marina,** by the airport; the **Gigante Plaza,** by the Fiesta Americana hotel; and **Villa Vallarta,** by the Plaza las Glorias hotel.

## Sports

Swimming, sailing, windsurfing, and parasailing are popular sports at the beachfront hotels. The hotels have stands on the beach offering boat trips and equipment, and you need not be a guest to buy these services.

**Fishing** Sportfishing is good off Puerto Vallarta most of the year, particularly for billfish, roosterfish, dorado, yellowtail, and bonito. The marlin season begins in November. The Fishermen's Association has a shack on the north end of the malecón and offers a variety of options for fishing trips; most hotels can arrange your reservations. Large group boats cost about $60 per person for a day's fishing; the smaller cruisers may be chartered for $150 a day and higher, depending on the size of the boat and the length of the trip. Charters include a skipper, license, bait, and tackle; some also include lunch.

**Golf** **Los Flamingos Country Club** (tel. 322/8–0280) has an 18-hole golf course. Reservations should be made through your hotel a day in advance. The country club is about 12 kilometers (8 miles) north of the airport, and transportation is provided with your reservations. There is a newer, but less shaded, Joe Finger–designed, 18-hole course at the Marina Vallarta complex (tel. 322/1–0171).

**Tennis** Most of the larger hotels have tennis courts. Nonmembers may also play at the **John Newcombe Tennis Club** (tel. 322/4–0123), **Los Tules** (tel. 322/4–4560), and **Los Flamingos Country Club** (tel. 322/8–0280).

**Water Sports** Snorkeling and diving are best at Los Arcos, a natural underwater preserve on the way to Mismaloya. Punta Mita, about 80 kilometers (50 miles) north of Puerto Vallarta, has some good diving spots, as does Quimixto Bay, about 32 kilometers (20 miles) south and accessible only by boat. Experienced divers prefer Las Tres Marietas, a group of three islands off the coast.

Some of the hotels have snorkeling and diving equipment for rent and offer short courses on diving at their pools. For dive trips and rentals, contact the following shops: **Chico's Dive Shop** (Díaz Ordáz 772, tel. 322/2–1895) and **Paradise Divers** (Olas Altas 443, tel. 322/2–4004).

## Beaches

Beaches in Mexico are federal property and are not owned by the hotels; some hotels try to keep their beaches exclusive by roping off an area where the hotel's lounge chairs must be kept.

**Playa Norte** Also known as **Playa de Oro,** this is the northernmost beach, stretching from the marina and cruise-ship terminal to downtown. The beach changes a bit with the character of each hotel it fronts; it is particularly nice by the Fiesta Americana and the Krystal hotels.

**Playa de los Muertos** Dead Men's Beach is the site of a long-ago battle between pirates and Indians. The town's boosters keep trying to change the name to Playa del Sol (Beach of the Sun), but they have not been successful. The budget travelers hang out here, and vendors selling kites, blankets, and jewelry seem as abundant as the sunbathers.

**Playa las Animas and Yelapa** These secluded fishing villages are accessible only by boat. Both villages have small communities of hardy isolationists; of late, Yelapa has attracted more and more foreigners who settle in for good. At Yelapa, take a 20-minute hike from the beach into the jungle to see the waterfalls. Tour groups visit the beaches daily.

## Dining

Puerto Vallarta has so many fine restaurants that it would be impossible to review them all here; hotel restaurants have been listed only if they are exceptional. Dining prices are comparable to those in the United States, and there are few real bargains. Dress is casual in PV, even at the most glamorous spots, though shorts are frowned upon at dinner.

Highly recommended restaurants are indicated by a star ★.

| Category | Cost* |
|---|---|
| Very Expensive | over $35 |
| Expensive | $25–$35 |
| Moderate | $15–$25 |
| Inexpensive | under $15 |

*per person, excluding drinks, service, and sales tax (10%)*

**Very Expensive** **La Perla.** This restaurant and its chef are frequent award winners for their sublime French nouvelle cuisine, service, and ambience. The best dish by far is the sole or salmon topped with pasta, crab, and lime sauce, though the duck with pears and the chateaubriand are also superb. The chef really shows his worth with the pastries, which are renowned throughout PV. There is a separate lounge in the restaurant for after-dinner drinks, coffee, and dessert—by all means try the flaming crepes prepared here. The restaurant is decorated in soft pastels. *Hotel Camino Real, Carretera a Barra de Navidad, tel. 322/3–0123. Reservations advised. AE, DC, MC, V. Dinner only.*

**Expensive** **Chez Elena.** This restaurant is among the town's best. Located
★ up a steep street behind Vallarta's famous crown-topped church, Chez Elena is especially agreeable for an early dinner after enjoying the sunset and a delightful tropical drink on the rooftop El Nido bar. The shrimp dishes are excellent, as is the mixed *satay* (an Indonesian dish consisting of grilled, skewered chicken or meat served with a spicy peanut sauce) and the chicken mole. Top it all off with a perfect brownie and café mulatto. *Matamoros 520, tel. 322/2–0161. Reservations advised. AE, MC, V. Dinner only.*
**El Set.** This restaurant is located at Las Conchas Chinas Hotel, a special spot just south of town. Perched above the cliffs, El Set features rustic wood steps that lead to three dining areas. Try the fajitas or the grilled lobster, but save room for the cara-

mel crepes. Get here in time for the sunset, and stay for the splendid show of city lights. *Hwy. 200 Km 2.5, tel. 322/2–0302. Reservations advised. AE, MC, V.*

★ **Le Bistro.** By far the classiest restaurant along Río Cuale, Le Bistro has a black-and-white tiled bar, gray-and-white striped tablecloths, and handsome waiters. Try the brochette Brubeck, made of grilled giant shrimp and generous hunks of tenderloin. The pecan pie is a must, as is the Russian Quaalude, made with coffee, Frangelico, vodka, and cream. *Río Cuale Island, tel. 322/2–0283. No reservations. AE, MC, V. Closed Sun.*

**Señor Chico's.** On the Alta Vista hill overlooking all of Puerto Vallarta, Señor Chico's is a magnificent spot from sunset into nighttime. The Caesar salad is good, as is any seafood choice, but it's the view that really makes the place. Enjoy live music from 8 to 11 PM. *Púlpito 377, tel. 322/2–3570. Reservations advised. AE, DC, MC, V. Dinner only.*

**Moderate** **Brazz.** A big, airy place decorated with brightly colored piñatas, Brazz is a branch of the Guadalajara chain, known for its generous steaks and chops and good Mexican dishes. The salad bar is the best in town. Mariachi music plays continuously. *Morelos at Galleana, tel. 322/2–0324. Reservations advised. AE, DC, MC, V. Dinner only.*

★ **El Dorado.** A must for at least one lunch, this Playa de los Muertos palapa is popular with American expatriates. The eclectic menu includes spaghetti, burgers, and crepes, but stick with such specialties as dorado-style fish, broiled with a thick layer of melted cheese. *Amapas and Púlpito, tel. 322/2–1511. AE, DC, MC, V.*

★ **Las Palomas.** Breakfast at this malecón café is a daily ritual for many and a place for the reunion of Puerto Vallarta regulars upon their return to town. Have *jugo de lima* (similar to lemonade but made with the region's tart limes). Homesick? Have hot oatmeal with cinnamon and sugar; otherwise, stick with the *huevos con chorizo* (eggs with spicy sausage) and coffee spiced with cinnamon. The people in the mural on one of the walls are all well-known characters in Puerto Vallarta. Stick around town long enough and you'll probably run into a few of them. *Díaz Ordáz at Aldama, tel. 322/2–3675. No reservations. AE, MC, V. ID required for traveler's checks.*

★ **Le Gourmet.** The small Posada Río Cuale hotel has one of the best restaurants in town, offering a great Caesar salad, shrimp à l'orange, and a large choice of flambéed entrées and desserts. The pepper steak, sautéed at your table, is a good choice, and the piano music is a pleasant change from mariachis. *Calle Serdán 284, tel. 322/2–0450. Reservations advised. AE, MC, V. Dinner only.*

**Inexpensive** **Andale.** A Playa de los Muertos hangout and a good spot for an afternoon beer with the locals, this restaurant serves good fettuccine with scallops, great garlic bread, and an unusual chicken *Mestizo* with white wine, pineapple juice, and jalapeño peppers. *Paseo de Velasco 425, tel. 322/2–1054. AE, D, MC, V.*

**The Pancake House.** This has to be the most popular spot in town for breakfast, served from 8 AM until 2 PM. The selection is ample—12 varieties of pancakes, waffles, eggs, French toast—and the coffee is good. *Basilio Badillo 289, no phone. No reservations. No credit cards. Breakfast only.*

★ **La Fuente del Puente.** Located just across from the market, above the riverbank, this outdoor café is popular with budget travelers. The bright pink-and-blue neon along the ceiling is an unusual touch for PV. The prices are low, the food good, and the crowd amiable. *Av. Miramar at the old bridge, tel. 322/2–1141. MC, V.*

**Rito Baci's.** This popular deli and pizza parlor delivers to homes and hotels. The crispy-crusted pizza is excellent, and the sausage spicy and flavorful. Try the sausage sandwich as well. *Calle Ortiz de Domínguez 181, tel. 322/2–6448. MC, V.*

**Tutifruti.** Sample great fresh-squeezed juices at a small stand in the downtown shopping area; choose your desired combination of mango, papaya, melon, and pineapple. Filling *tortas* (sandwiches) cost about $2. *Morelos at Corona, tel. 322/2–1068. No credit cards. Closed Sun.*

## Lodging

Most of PV's deluxe resorts are located to the north; south of downtown and the Río Cuale, in the Playa de los Muertos and Olas Altas areas, the rates are lower. Some of the nicest, older hotels are a few miles south of town. In the winter, budget rooms run $30 to $50, and the large resorts start at $150 per night. Rates go down from April through December by 25%–30%. Reservations are a must at Christmas, New Year's, and Easter.

Highly recommended lodgings in each price category are indicated by a star ★.

| Category | Cost* |
|---|---|
| Very Expensive | over $160 |
| Expensive | $90–$160 |
| Moderate | $40–$90 |
| Inexpensive | under $40 |

**All prices are for a standard double room; excluding 10% tax.*

**Very Expensive**   **Camino Real.** One of PV's first hotels, this Westin hotel sits on a lovely small bay south of town. The rooms have cool marble floors with white furniture and bright pink, yellow, and purple highlights against stark white walls. The hotel has all the five-star touches—from plush robes in the rooms and the feel of an established, comfortable resort to the palapas on the beach and the fragrant white jasmine blooming along the natural waterfall. A newer 11-story tower houses the Royal Beach Club, with 87 rooms and a convention/banquet center. *Carretera a Barra de Navidad, tel. 322/3–0123; reservations in the U.S., tel. 800/228–3000. 337 rooms (80 in new tower). Facilities: beach, 2 pools, children's pool, 2 tennis courts, 5 restaurants and bars, shops. AE, DC, MC, V.*

★  **Fiesta Americana.** A seven-story palapa covers the lobby and a large round bar. The dramatically designed terra-cotta building rises above a deep blue pool that flows under bridges, palm oases, and palapa restaurants set on platforms over the water. The rooms have a modern blue, pink, and lavender color scheme; each has white marble floors, tiled bath with powerful shower, and balcony. The beach bustles with activity—parasailing, windsurfing, boat tours, snorkeling, and, of course, sunbathing. The restaurants are excellent, especially the breakfast buffet by the pool. Of all the full-service resorts, Fiesta Americana has the most tropical and luxurious feel. *Carretera Aeropuerto, tel. 322/4–2010 or 800/FIESTA–1. 291 rooms with bath. Facilities: pool, beach, 4 restaurants, 3 bars, 5 tennis courts, disco, shops, beauty salon, travel agency, Mexican fiestas with fireworks. AE, DC, MC, V.*

★ **Hyatt Coral Grande.** This stunning new hotel south of town is one of the prettiest on the coast, a pale pink palace surrounded by lush landscaping; rushing waterfalls mask the noise from the nearby highway. The lobby is filled with lavish floral arrangements and high-quality folk art and paintings. The rooms are all suites, with pale pink spreads and drapes, glass-top tables and wall-length sliding glass doors, white lounge chairs on the terrace, and white tile floors. The master suites have private whirlpools. *Carretera a Barra de Navidad, tel. 322/3–1234 or 800/233–1234. 120 suites with bath. Facilities: beach, pool, 2 restaurants, 2 bars, tennis court, steam baths, shops, beauty salon, water sports. AE, DC, MC, V.*

**Qualton Club & Spa.** Formerly the Fiesta Americana, the Qualton hotel is a spa, with a fitness center and state-of-the-art machines, a jogging trail running through the hotel grounds, beauty treatments from hydromassage to herbal wraps, nutritional analysis, and computerized exercise and diet regimes. You don't have to be a fitness freak to stay here, though. The rooms in the two wings and main 14-story tower are done in peaceful mauves and blues; deluxe rooms have ocean-view balconies. Meals, drinks, and most sports activities and spa services are included in the room rate, and a "dine-around" program allows guests to sample restaurants in other areas. *Carretera Aeropuerto, tel. 322/4–4446. 219 rooms. Facilities: health spa, 2 pools, hot tub, beach, 3 restaurants, bar. AE, DC, MC, V.*

★ **Villas Quinta Real.** Reminiscent of a Palm Springs estate, this pale pink mansion with white columns is simply but elegantly decorated. Fresh flowers and plants, antiques, and original works of art grace the rooms and corridors of this spacious property. Built in 1990, the Villas Quinta Real includes 50 suites and 25 villas that command views of the golf course of the new Marina Vallarta complex. Though the hotel is not directly on the beach, its amenities are many, and its location between the first and 18th holes of the Marina Vallarta Golf Course makes it ideal for golfers. *Marina Vallarta, Pelicanos 311, 48300, tel. 322/1–0800 or 800/876–5278. 50 suites and 25 1- to 3-bedroom villas. Facilities: golf course, outdoor pool, cable TV, 24-hour room service. AE, MC, V.*

**Expensive** **Continental Plaza Puerto Vallarta.** A heavenly resort for tennis buffs, this Mediterranean-style complex features the John Newcombe Tennis Club, which has 8 courts and offers daily tennis clinics. The resort has a shopping plaza, several restaurants and bars, a large swimming pool, and a nice beach. The Continental Plaza is favored by athletic types. *Carretera Aeropuerto, tel. 322/4–0123, reservations in the U.S., tel. 800/88–CONTI. 429 rooms with bath. Facilities: 8 tennis courts, pool, restaurants, bars, shopping center, beach. AE, DC, MC, V.*

★ **Krystal Vallarta.** A full-service resort that sprawls over acreage equivalent to that of a small town, the Krystal has 460 rooms, including 48 villas, each with a private pool. There are six restaurants, including Tango, which serves Argentine *churrasco* (barbecue), and Kamakura, which serves Japanese food. Not all rooms are by the ocean, but the secluded beach can accommodate all sunseekers. Christine's disco has a knock-'em-dead light show. *Carretera Aeropuerto, tel. 322/4–0202. 412 rooms with bath; 48 villas with bath and pools. Facilities: 2 tennis courts, beach, pools, 6 restaurants, bars, shops, disco, travel agency. AE, DC, MC, V.*

**Marriott Casa Magna.** Located in Marina Vallarta, Puerto Vallarta's newest resort complex, with El Salado beach to the front and the Marina's 18-hole, Joe Finger–designed golf course to the rear, the Marriott Casa Magna is one of Vallarta's newest, largest, and most glamorous hotels. The vast, plant-filled, marble lobbies that open onto the huge pool area are hung with chandeliers. The rooms are decorated with light woods and soft colors. All overlook the bay. And if the water sports, tennis, restaurants, night clubs, and other facilities of the hotel aren't enough, the complex houses a huge shopping center, yacht club, golf course, marina, restaurants, bar, tennis club, and spa. *Marina Vallarta, tel. 322/1–0004 or 800/228–9290. 456 rooms and suites with bath. Facilities: restaurants, pool, beach, tennis, 4 restaurants, bars, disco, tennis. AE, DC, MC, V.*

**Moderate** **Buenaventura.** This hotel's location is ideal, on the edge of
★ downtown, within walking distance (10 blocks or so) of the Río Cuale and, in the opposite direction, of the shops, hotels, and restaurants on the airport highway. From the street it looks rather austere, but just inside the door is an enormous five-story open lobby and bar. The bright, cheerful rooms in yellows and whites have beamed ceilings and pale wood furnishings. *Av. México 1301, tel. 322/2–3737; reservations in the U.S., tel. 800/223–6784. 206 rooms and 4 suites with bath. Facilities: beach, pool, 2 bars, 2 restaurants. AE, DC, MC, V.*

★ **Conchas Chinas.** This hotel is a short distance south of town, but it's one of the most comfortable establishments around, and there is frequent bus service just out the door. The three-story building is set right on the beach, and all 31 rooms and 8 suites face the water. The rooms have dark beams, orange bedspreads, heavy wood furniture, and small kitchenettes. Some rooms have whirlpool bathtubs. There's a small restaurant on the rocky beach, and **El Set,** one of PV's best restaurants, is next door. *Carretera Barra de Navidad Km 2.5, tel. 322/2–0156, reservations in the U.S., tel. 800/424–4441. 31 rooms and 8 suites with kitchenette and bath. Facilities: pool, beach, 2 restaurants. MC, V.*

★ **Las Palmas.** The palapa entrance to Las Palmas is unique—four bamboo bridges suspended from the ceiling and parrots screeching under the palms. The rooms have shared balconies and green and yellow floral spreads and drapes. The accommodations are first-rate for this price category. *Cerrada las Palmas 50, tel. 322/4–0650; reservations in the U.S., tel. 800/995–8584. 153 rooms with bath. Facilities: pool, restaurant, bar, water sports. AE, DC, MC, V.*

**Mar Elena.** These suites on the north side of town are a good bargain for travelers who want a kitchen and living-room setup. The building is rather plain, but the kitchens and bathrooms are beautifully tiled, and the bedrooms have woven rugs on the floors and flowers stenciled on the walls. The pool is on the roof; the beach is a block away. *Carretera Aeropuerto Km 2, tel. 322/4–4425. 30 suites with bath. Facilities: pool. MC, V.*

**Playa Los Arcos.** By far the most popular hotel on the beach by the Río Cuale, Los Arcos has a pretty central courtyard and pool and a friendly air. A glass elevator rises by the pool to the rooms, which have bright orange furnishings and small balconies. *Olas Altas 380, tel. 322/2–0583. 140 rooms with bath. Facilities: beach, pool, restaurant, bar. AE, DC, MC, V.*

Inexpensive **Los Cuatro Vientos.** The most charming small hotel in PV, Cuatro Vientos (meaning Four Winds) is located up a steep hill behind town, tucked among the red-tile-roofed cottages. Its 16 rooms are often booked a year in advance by repeat guests. The simple rooms with arched brick ceilings have colorful flowers stenciled on the walls and folk art knickknacks. The restaurant, **Chez Elena,** is among PV's best, and there's a pleasant rooftop bar open in high season. *Matamoros 520, tel. 322/2–0161. 16 rooms with bath. Facilities: restaurant, bar. AE, MC, V.*

★ **Molino de Agua.** A real find on the Río Cuale, the hotel's bungalows are spread out along the riverbed amid lush trees and flowers. Stone pathways wind under willows, past caged parrots and monkeys, and lead to cottages with wood shutters, yellow tiled bathrooms, and redbrick walls. A bubbling whirlpool sits half-hidden under a willow by the swimming pool. *Vallarta 130, tel. 322/2–1907. 62 rooms with bath. Facilities: beach, whirlpool, restaurant. AE, MC, V.*

★ **Posada de Roger.** One of the least expensive hotels, the Posada de Roger is in many ways the most enjoyable, if you like the company of Europeans and Canadians who are savvy about budget traveling. The showers are hot, the beds soft, and the pool an international meeting spot. You can have your mail held there, and the desk clerks are knowledgeable about other budget hotels and restaurants. *Basilio Badillo 237, tel. 322/2–0836. 56 rooms with bath. Facilities: rooftop pool, restaurant, bar. MC, V.*

★ **Posada Río Cuale.** This small, friendly inn on the south side of Río Cuale has one of the best gourmet restaurants in town (aptly named Le Gourmet) and a nice sense of serenity. The beds are big and cozy, flowers are placed on each nightstand; and with only 21 rooms, it rarely becomes noisy. *Calle Serdán 242, tel. 322/2–0450. 21 rooms with bath. Facilities: pool, restaurant, bar. AE, MC, V.*

## Nightlife

Puerto Vallarta is a party town, where the discos open at 10 PM and stay open until 3 or 4 PM. A minimum $7 cover charge is common in the popular discos, many of which are at the hotels. The Krystal has **Christine's,** which features a spectacular light show set to music from disco to classic rock nightly at 11:30. **Sixties,** at the Marriott, features music for almost all ages, and **Friday López,** at the Fiesta Americana, has karaoke and dancing. Tables start to disappear from the lower level of the **Hard Rock Café** at about 10:30 PM, and by 11 PM the live music starts and there is dancing everywhere. **La Ballena,** at the entrance to the Marina Vallarta complex, has dancing under the stars till dawn. **El Panorama,** at the Hotel La Siesta, is a real nightclub with a floor show and live music. A guitarist plays romantic tunes at **El Nido,** the bar at Los Cuatro Vientos, known for its sunset view. **Iggy's,** at the La Jolla Mismaloya Hotel, is the perfect drinking and dancing spot for those who like to converse without shouting.

Mexican fiestas are popular at the hotels and can be lavish affairs with buffet dinners, folk dances, and fireworks. Reservations may be made with the hotels or travel agencies. Some of the more spectacular shows are at La Iguana Tourist Center, the Krystal, Plaza las Glorias, and the Sheraton. On Thursday nights a Fiesta Brava is held at the Krystal that features a mock bullfight with audience participation. Also on Thursdays, the Meliá hosts a flamenco night with Spanish buffet.

### Excursion from Puerto Vallarta to Manzanillo

The coastline south of Puerto Vallarta is sprinkled with some of the Mexican Riviera's most exclusive and secluded one-of-a-kind resorts. But you'll never see them if you take 200 south—a rugged, twisting road through tropical forest of pines and palms. You've got to venture down some paved and unpaved roads to the coast. Guests usually fly to Puerto Vallarta (two hours north) or Manzanillo (one hour south) and take a taxi or hotel van to the resort. Once there, they stay put for a week or more, leaving only for the requisite shopping spree in PV. Two of the resorts are very expensive—more than $160 a night for a double—but these are all-inclusive, which relieves you of the need to carry cash and calculate tips. Traveling south, the best resorts are in Mismaloya, Tecuán, Careyes, and Tenacatita.

**Lodging** **La Jolla de Mismaloya.** Despite the fact that the overpowering design of this hotel has ruined the view of beautiful Mismaloya Bay, the lucky guests here literally have half of the bay (this is where the movie *The Night of the Iguana* was filmed) to themselves, as well as a fabulous view of Puerto Vallarta's famous arches (rock formations jutting out of the sea). The southern half of the bay is crowded with beachfront restaurants and motor launches that go to even more remote beaches. The hotel's one- and two-bedroom suites have terraces and kitchenettes. Though somewhat out of the way, this is a hotel that consistently gets high marks from its guests. *Off Hwy. 200 at Mismaloya Bay, tel. 322/3–0660; reservations in the U.S., tel. 800/322–2344. 303 suites. Facilities: beach, 3 pools, fitness center, tennis courts, water sports, beach club, bar, disco, restaurant. AE, DC, MC, V. Expensive.*

**Fiesta Americana Los Angeles Locos.** Canadians come here by the charter-jet load, drawn to the amiable surroundings, the all-inclusive drinks and meals, and the chance to relax with friends. Fiesta Americana operates the hotel, which is similar to their other properties in design, with the large, comfortable rooms clustered in a horseshoe-shaped terra-cotta building around the bay. Tours to Puerto Vallarta and Manzanillo are available, and there is a good selection of shops on the property. *Hwy. 200 in Tenacatita, tel. 333/7–0220; reservations in the U.S., 800/FIESTA–1. 205 rooms and suites. Facilities: beach, pool, water and land sports, horseback riding, tours, buffet and restaurant, bar, disco. AE, DC, MC, V. Expensive.*

**Playa Blanca.** This Club Med recently underwent renovation and modernization and has all the services the pioneer all-inclusives are known for—diving, fishing, pool bars, horseback riding, and even a clown school. The food, usually served buffet style, is ample and good, and there are two restaurants where you can be served by waiters. The guests tend to be young and active, and the resort is far from having a feeling of isolation—with 300 rooms, a disco, and a tendency toward rock videos and aerobic classes, the ambience is more celebratory than somnolent. *Off Hwy. 200, next door to Costa Careyes. Reservations in the U.S. 800/CLUB–MED. 300 rooms. Facilities: beach, pool, tennis, horseback riding, water sports, buffet dining halls and 2 restaurants, bar. AE, DC, MC, V. Expensive.*

**El Tecuán.** Small and economical, this beachfront hotel has all the facilities of larger resorts, including its own lagoon, tennis courts, horseback riding, and water sports. *Km. 33.5 Carretera Barra de Navidad–Puerto Vallarta, tel. 333/7–0132. 36 rooms. Facilities: beach, pool, tennis courts, horses, water sports, restaurant/bar. MC, D. Inexpensive.*

# Manzanillo

Tourism is booming in Manzanillo, although compared with other Pacific coast resorts, the town is a sleeper. It has a sprinkling of fine hotels and restaurants, with more being built all the time. Manzanillo is also home to the most opulent resort property on the Mexican coast, Las Hadas.

Nature is undoubtedly Manzanillo's best attraction. Its twin *bahías* (bays), Manzanillo and Santiago, where crystal blue waters lap white-sand shores, have caught outsiders' eyes since Cortés conquered Mexico. In the July–September rainy season, rivers and lagoons swell, forming waterfalls and ponds. White herons and pink flamingos flock to the fertile waters, and white butterflies flutter above the flowers in the chamomile fields (*manzanillo* is Spanish for chamomile).

Santiago Peninsula, which divides Bahía Santiago and Bahía Manzanillo, is the site of Las Hadas (The Fairies) resort. From the water or points above the beach, the resort seems a mirage, a sea of white domes and peaks that radiate in the midday heat. When Bolivian tin magnate Antenor Patiño conceived of this white palace in the early 1960s, Manzanillo was easier to reach by sea than land, a rugged, primitive port that attracted the hardy who didn't mind creating their own tropical paradise. In 1974, when Señor Patiño's retreat was complete, the international social set began to visit Manzanillo, thus putting the city in magazines and on television screens around the world. Even then, Manzanillo remained essentially a port city with only a few tourist attractions.

Manzanillo is still relatively undeveloped. Investors have plenty of land to divvy up for their financially rewarding havens, and existing resorts are spread out. Many shops and hotel desks close for afternoon siesta, and on Sundays most businesses are shut (including restaurants) and everyone heads for the beach.

## Arriving and Departing by Plane

**Airport and Airlines** Manzanillo's **Aeropuerto Internacional Playa de Oro** is 32 kilometers (20 miles) north of town, on the way to Barra de Navidad. **Aeroméxico** (tel. 800/237–6639) and **Mexicana** (tel. 800/531–7921) fly in from several U.S. and Mexican cities. **Mexicana** serves Manzanillo from Guadalajara and Mexico City.

**Between the Airport and Hotels** Volkswagen vans transport passengers from the airport to the major resorts; these shuttle services are less expensive than taxis.

## Arriving and Departing by Car, Train, and Bus

**By Car** The trip south from the Arizona border to Manzanillo is about 2,419 kilometers (1,500 miles); from Guadalajara, it is 332½ kilometers (200 miles); from Puerto Vallarta, 242 kilometers (150 miles). Highway 200 runs along the coast from Tepic, Nayarit, to Manzanillo. Hazardous conditions and unexpected, drastic detours are common.

**By Train** Trains run to Manzanillo from Guadalajara—an adventure for some, but for most it is a tedious trip, lasting a minimum of eight hours and ending at the ship and freight yards outside town.

**By Bus** **Tres Estrellas de Oro** travels to Manzanillo from Nogales, Arizona, at the U.S.–Mexico border, from Mexico City and Guadalajara, and from the coastal towns. Many of the area's resorts are located 1 to 2 kilometers (2 to 3 miles) from the bus stop on the highway.

## Getting Around

**By Car** Cars are almost essential for exploring the area on your own. The highway from Santiago to Manzanillo is commonly called Carretera Santiago–Manzanillo, Manzanillo–Aeropuerto, Salahua–Santiago, or any number of things depending on the closest landmark. It's called the Santiago–Manzanillo Road throughout this chapter to lessen confusion. Route 200 runs north along the coast past Manzanillo and Santiago bays to Barra de Navidad and Melaque; Route 110 goes east to Colima.

Avenida Morelos, the main drag in town, runs from Manzanillo Bay past the port and shipyards to the plaza. If you plan to explore the downtown, park along the waterfront across from the plaza and walk—all the shops and hotels are within a few blocks. **Avis** (tel. 333/3–0190), **Budget** (tel. 333/3–1445), and **National** (tel. 333/3–0611) have offices in the airport, and most big hotels have at least one company represented. **Hertz** has offices at Las Hadas and the Radisson Plaza Sierra hotels. Rates vary depending on where you rent your car, but rentals are generally costly ($60–$100 per day, including insurance). Most offer 200 kilometers (124 miles) free, which should give you enough roaming for one day.

## Important Addresses and Numbers

Street addresses are not often used in Manzanillo; instead, locations are designated by neighborhood—the Las Brisas area, Santiago Peninsula (also known as the Las Hadas Rd.), and so on. Maps with actual street names are rare (or inaccurate).

**Tourist Information** Information on Manzanillo is scanty at best and rarely consistent. The **State Tourism Office** (Blvd. Costero Miguel de la Madrid Km 9.5, tel. 333/3–2277) is supposed to be open weekdays 9–3:30, but call first to be sure. More accurate information is available from tour operators and hotels.

**Emergencies** **Police** (tel. 333/2–1004); **Hospital** (tel. 333/2–0029).

## Guided Tours

The best way to see Manzanillo is with a tour guide. Operators will arrange special-interest or private tours as well as sportfishing trips, sunset cruises, and horseback outings. Most agencies have offices along the highway that encircles Santiago and Manzanillo bays, and most hotels offer at least one agency's services. Agencies include **Bahías Gemelas Agencia de Viajes** (Las Hadas Plaza Albina, tel. 333/3–0204; Manzanillo–Santiago Rd. Km 10, tel. 333/3–1000), **Aeroviajes Manzanillo** (Plaza las Glorias hotel, tel. 333/3–0440; Niños Héroes 96, Km. 1.5 Carr. Manzanillo-Santiago, tel. 333/2–3155), and **Viajes Anfitriones Mexicanos** (Radisson Plaza Sierra Manzanillo, tel. 333/3–1940 or 333/3–2000).

## Exploring

A vacation in Manzanillo is not spent shopping and sightseeing. You stay put, relax on the beach, and maybe take a few hours' break from the sun and sand to survey the local scene casually.

The **Santiago** area is tourist-oriented, with clusters of shops and restaurants by the beach. Plans to build a marina here were announced in late 1992. Public and private developers will invest $50,000,000 to create a downtown marina complex that will have a cruise-ship dock, slips for 240 yachts, a shopping center, and a hotel. The next area to the east, **Salahua,** is a settlement with homes, a baseball field, and restaurants. **Las Brisas** beach is farther south, past the traffic circle and Avenida Morelos, the road to town. Some of the more reasonably priced hotels are located here.

**Downtown** is busy and jam-packed. At the beginning of the harbor, Route 200 jogs around downtown and intersects with Highway 110 to Colima. Avenida Morelos leads past the shipyards and into town. Just before you reach the port, stop at **Laguna de San Pedrito,** where graceful white herons and vivid pink flamingos assemble at sunset. The **zócalo** or **Jardín de Obregón** is right on the main road by the waterfront. It's a small square, quite lively in the evening.

## Shopping

The hotel shops have the best selections of folk art and clothing. Most of the shops are closed from 1 to 4 PM; many are also closed on Sunday. Plaza Santiago has a good Mexican handicrafts store called **Boutique Grivel. Centro Artesanal Las Primaveras,** at Juárez 40 in Santiago, houses a variety of fine folk art. **Galería de Arte** at Plaza Albino (Puerto las Hadas) has paintings and sculptures by contemporary Mexican artists, including Sergio Bustamante and Pal Kepenyes. **Tane,** probably Mexico's most prestigious silver shop for tableware, art objects, and jewelry, is also at Las Hadas.

**Rubén Torres,** set off by itself at Kilometer 13 on the Santiago–Manzanillo Road, has the best sportswear. **Galería Jaramar,** at the Las Hadas arcade, specializes in handwoven fabrics and fine jewelry and creative designs for women. Downtown, the selection of souvenirs and clothing is more typically Mexican. Some of the best spots for crafts and clothing are **El Dorado** and **Maria de Guadalajara.**

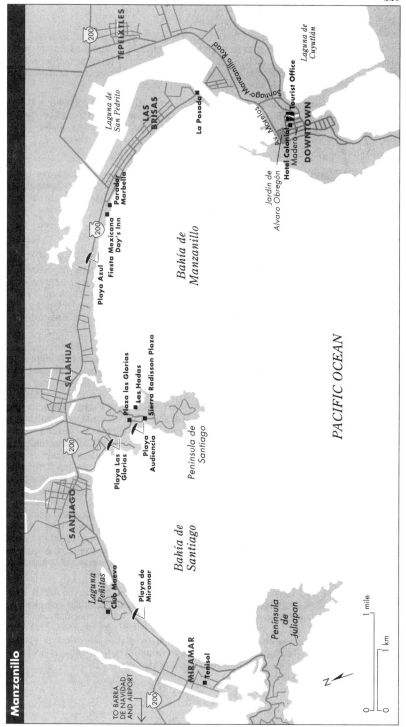

Manzanillo

TEPEIXTLES

Laguna de San Pedrito

LAS BRISAS

La Posada

Santiago-Manzanillo Road

AV. Morelos

Tourist Office

Hotel Colonial

Madero

DOWNTOWN

Laguna de Cuyutlán

Jardín de Alvaro Obregón

Parador Marbella

Fiesta Mexicana
Day's Inn

Playa Azul

Bahía de Manzanillo

SALAHUA

Plaza las Glorias
Las Hadas
Sierra Radisson Plaza

Playa Las Glorias

Playa Audiencia

Península de Santiago

PACIFIC OCEAN

SANTIAGO

Bahía de Santiago

Laguna Peñitas

Club Maeva

Playa de Miramar

MIRAMAR

Tenisol

Península de Juliapan

TO BARRA
DE NAVIDAD
AND AIRPORT

N

0     1 mile
0     1 km

## Sports

Fishing  Manzanillo claims to be the sailfishing capital of the world; the season runs from mid-October through March, with an international sailfish tournament held every November. Blue marlin and dorado are also abundant. Sportfishing charters are available at the major hotels and tour agencies.

Golf  **La Mantarraya** (tel. 333/3–0000), the 18-hole golf course at Las Hadas, designed by Roy Dye, has been rated among the world's 100 best courses by *Golf Digest*. Club Santiago (tel. 333/3–0413) has a nine-hole course designed by Larry Hughes.

Tennis  Most of the resort hotels have tennis courts.

Water Sports  The rocky points off Manzanillo's peninsulas and coves make good spots for snorkeling and scuba diving. Small boats called *pangas* can be rented on some beaches so you can reach the better spots.

## Beaches

In Manzanillo, every day is a beach day, and Sundays are downright festive, with half the town gathered to play onshore. Windsurfing has become quite popular, and jet skis roar about, but there isn't much in the way of parasailing. The sand is a mix of black, white, and brown, with the southernmost beaches the blackest. Most beaches post warning flags if the conditions are dangerous or jellyfish have been sighted.

**Playa Miramar,** at the north end of Santiago Bay, is populated by windsurfers and boogie-boarders. The beach in front of Club Santiago, once the favored hangout for locals, is now accessible only by walking north along the beach from the highway or by passing the guards at the club gates. The main stretch of beach is across the highway from Club Maeva. **Playa Audiencia,** in a cove along the north side of Santiago Peninsula, is a small beach between two rock outcroppings—it's a good spot for snorkeling. (The local Indians supposedly granted Cortés an audience on the beach—thus the name.) The Radisson Plaza Sierra Manzanillo hotel is located in the middle of the beach, making public access limited. **Playa Azul,** also called Playa Santiago, is a long strand that runs from Santiago along Manzanillo Bay to Playa Las Brisas. The surf runs rough along the north end; swimming is better toward Las Brisas. South of town is **Playa Cuyutlán,** a black-sand beach on the open sea. Legend has it that the great *ola verde* (green wave) rises some 30 feet each spring during the full moon. In reality, the surf is high in spring but not quite as big as the original ola verde, which took the tiny town of Cuyutlán by surprise in 1959.

**Barra de Navidad** and **San Patricio Melaque,** to the north, have popular beaches that are good for surfing in the fall months. Palapa restaurants along the beach serve fresh fish. In Barra there are panga trips to a small island just offshore, where unbroken seashells are abundant. When the tide is low, it is possible to walk along the beach from Barra to Melaque, a distance of about 6 kilometers (almost 4 miles).

## Dining

Manzanillo has some good restaurants, several with scenic views of the jungle and water that compensate for their lack of culinary excitement. As more shops appear along the Santiago–Manzanillo Road, so do restaurants that are geared toward tourists. Dress is usually casual but not sloppy (no bathing suits or bare feet), even in the more expensive restaurants, although in L'Récif and Legazpi women and men usually wear chic resortwear. Reservations are almost never necessary, but we have indicated those places that do accept them. Be aware that some restaurants, particularly in the hotels, add a 10%–15% service charge to your tab, as well as 10% tax.

Highly recommended restaurants are indicated by a star ★.

| Category | Cost* |
|---|---|
| Very Expensive | over $35 |
| Expensive | $25–$35 |
| Moderate | $15–$25 |
| Inexpensive | under $15 |

*per person, excluding drinks, service, and sales tax (10%)*

**Very Expensive**
★ **Legazpi.** Manzanillo's only gourmet restaurant is at Las Hadas, and it is beautiful. The service is white-gloved perfection, but friendly rather than pretentious, and the food is decidedly elegant. The emphasis is on caviar and smoked salmon, consommés and bisques, seafood and steaks with French sauces, and wonderful pastries. *Las Hadas, tel. 333/3–0000. Reservations accepted. Jacket and tie suggested. AE, DC, MC, V. Dinner only. Closed Wed. and Fri.*

**Expensive** **El Vaquero.** The setting is reminiscent of a cowboys' saloon, and the emphasis is on beef, marinated and seasoned as *carne asada* or grilled as good old American steaks. Some steaks are served and priced by weight to satisfy the healthiest appetite. *Crucero Las Brisas, tel. 333/3–1654. Reservations not required. Dress: casual. MC, V.*

★ **L'Récif.** Situated in a fantastic cliff-top setting far from town, L'Récif has a breathtaking view and a swimming pool—you can go for lunch, spend the afternoon sunning and swimming, then stay for dinner. The restaurant's owner is French, and the menu includes pâté with Armagnac, quail with muscat, and mango mousse. The Sunday brunch (served only in winter) is a must. *Off the Santiago–Manzanillo Rd., north of Santiago, at the sign for Vida del Mar, tel. 333/3–0624. Reservations accepted. Dress: casual. AE, MC, V.*

**Moderate**
★ **La Bamba.** This patio and indoor restaurant along the highway is considered by locals to be the best place for Mexican food, congenial company, and soft music. *Plaza La Bamba, Km 11 Blvd. Costero Miguel de la Madrid, tel. 333/4–0794. Reservations accepted. Dress: casual. AE, MC, V. Dinner only.*

**Manolo's.** The lobster and shrimp are reasonably priced, and the Mexican dishes are tasty at this longtime favorite for great seafood dinners and steaks. *Santiago–Manzanillo Rd., tel. 333/3–2140. Reservations accepted. Dress: casual. AE, MC, V. Dinner only. Closed Sun.*

*Las Hadas beach, access to the Las Hadas golf course, tennis courts. AE, MC, V.*

**Inexpensive** **Hotel Colonial.** This was once the grandest hotel in Manzanillo. Although the Colonial has gone downhill since its heyday, it's still the best place to stay in downtown, a block away from the noise of the plaza. *Av. México 100, tel. 333/2–1080. 38 rooms with bath. Only some of the units have air-conditioning. Facilities: restaurant, bar. MC, V.*

**Parador Marbella.** This hotel is one of the few reasonably priced places on the beach. The best rooms are on the ocean; each has a tiny balcony under the palms. The furnishings are plain and mismatched—pink sheets contrast with brown and rust bedspreads and red and yellow plastic flowers on the nightstand. *Santiago–Manzanillo Rd., Km 9.5, tel. 333/3–1103. 60 rooms with bath. Facilities: pool, restaurant, bar. MC, V.*

## Nightlife

During the high season, there is nightlife at two discos on the Santiago–Manzanillo Road—**Mirage** (tel. 333/3–2333) and **Enjoy** (tel. 333/3–2839)—and at **Cartouche** (tel. 333/3–0000) at Las Hadas. The **Legazpi** (tel. 333/3–000) piano bar at Las Hadas is also a good spot for a nightcap. At **Bugatti's** (tel. 333/3–2929) there's a piano bar and dancing that goes on until the wee hours. **VOG** (tel. 333/3–1875) is a new disco that may be worth a visit.

# Sonora

*Updated by Edie Jarolim*

Sonora, Mexico's second-largest, second-richest state, is a vacationland with its own band of devoted followers, many from Arizona, just across the border, who use the coast of Sonora as their beach playground.

Mexico Highway 15 begins at the border town of Nogales, running inland through Hermosillo, the capital of Sonora, until it reaches the Gulf of California (also called the Sea of Cortés), at Guaymas, 418 kilometers (261 miles) to the south. The Sonoran Desert dominates the landscape along this route as it does in southern Arizona. In northern Sonora long stretches of flat scrub are punctuated by towering saguaros and organ-pipe cacti. The scenery begins to get more dramatic as you head south: Brown hills and then mountains rise against the vast sky as you approach the coastal resort of Guaymas.

In 1540 Francisco Vázquez de Coronado, governor of the provinces to the south, was the first Spaniard to walk the plains of Sonora. More than a century later, Fray Eusebio Francisco Kino led a missionary expedition to Sonora and founded several towns in the state. For the next three centuries no one paid much attention to Sonora, and it was not part of the Mexican territory that ended up under the American flag after the War of 1847. International squabbles over Sonora bloomed and faded away as the border became a haven for Arizona outlaws. During the last quarter of the 19th century, Porfirio Díaz, dictator of Mexico for 30-odd years, moved to secure the state by settling it. For Don Porfirio, however, developing the region was a mistake—the men who overthrew him in the revolution came from Sonora. In fact, Mexico was ruled by the Sonora dynasty for almost a quarter of a century. The Mexican Revolution brought prosperity to Sonora, and the state continues to thrive. Its inhabitants have adopted modern farming techniques that allow them to grow not only enough wheat for Mexico but also enough for export.

Route 2 leads into Sonora from Baja California, hugging the U.S. border. There are many crossing points, but most people entering from the United States do so at Nogales (adjacent to the U.S. town of Nogales, Arizona), which is also a point of entry for winter fruit and vegetables exported to the United States. A bustling town, Nogales can become fairly rowdy on weekend evenings, when under age Tucsonians head here to drink, but it has some good restaurants, and visitors can find fine-quality crafts and furnishings in addition to the usual border schlock.

Below Nogales is Magdalena, where the grave of Father Kino was discovered in 1966. His remains are in a mausoleum outside Mission San Francisco Xavier, one of the 22 missions he founded. A million-dollar monument to the memory of this pioneer priest also stands here. To the northeast of Magdalena is Cananea, a mining center made famous for its jail by a Mexican song. Today Sonora leads the nation in copper mining, its huge, open pits spewing out about 80% of Mexico's production.

Hermosillo (population about 600,000) is the capital of the state, a status it has held on and off since 1831. It is the seat of the state university and benefits from the cultural activities of that institution. Although the city's name, to those who know a bit of Spanish, sounds as if it means "little beauty," it actually honors José María González Hermosillo, one of the leaders in Mexico's War of Independence. Settled in 1742 by Captain Agustín de Vildosola and a contingent of 50 soldiers, Hermosillo was originally called Pitic, the Pima name for "the place where two rivers meet." A business center for the state of Sonora, Hermosillo is largely modern, but some lovely plazas and parks hark back to a more graceful postcolonial past.

Some 104 kilometers (65 miles) west of Hermosillo lies Kino Bay on the shore of the Sea of Cortés. The coast highway is excellent, and the beaches are magnificent. For many years, Kino Bay was undiscovered except by the RV owners and others who sought the unspoiled and beautiful, but a great change has recently taken place. The area is a convenient distance south of Phoenix and Tucson and thus a good location for a series of fine condos that have been constructed for American owners.

Guaymas (population 225,000), about 135 kilometers (83 miles) south of Hermosillo (and Kino Bay), is an active port where visitors come to do some serious fishing. The port was founded in 1771 and christened San Fernando de Guaymas. A nearby Jesuit mission was named San José de Guaymas. The city's off-the-beaten-path tranquillity may soon come under the heading of "what used to be." Government and private concerns have selected this area for intense economic development. Guaymas is slated to become an international "megaport," designed to compete with the Port of Los Angeles for Pacific Rim shipping traffic. In addition, currently inadequate tourist facilities are being expanded with a view toward turning Guaymas into a major resort with several deluxe hotels. Already there is a Club Med, a new Howard Johnson's resort, and the San Carlos Country Club, which has an 18-hole golf course, a dozen tennis courts, and two swimming pools. (Hotels can arrange for temporary memberships so guests can use country-club facilities.) It is hoped that plans will also include the provision of some means of adequate public transportation.

South of Guaymas, Route 15 continues toward Mazatlán by way of Ciudad Obregón and Navojoa, both of which are modern agricultural and industrial centers. Alamos, the most authentic colonial-style town in Sonora and a Mexican national monument, is 53 kilometers (32 miles) east of Navojoa. Coronado camped here in 1540, and a Jesuit mission was established in 1630, but the town really boomed when silver was discovered in the area during the 1680s. Wealth from the mines financed Spanish expeditions to the north—as far as Los Angeles and San Francisco during the 1770s and 1780s—and the town became the capital of the state of Occidente, which combined the provinces of Sinaloa and Sonora, from 1827 to 1832. A government mint was established here in 1864. The mines closed by the end of the 19th century and the town went into decline, but today Alamos, with many houses beautifully restored by Americans who have settled here, serves as a showcase of its glorious past.

## Important Addresses and Numbers

**Hermosillo** There is a **tourist information office** at the Palacio Administrativo (Calles Tehauntapec and Comonfort, tel. 62/14–63–04 or 800/4–SONORA from the U.S.).

*Emergencies* **Police** (tel. 62/16–15–64), **Red Cross** (tel. 62/14–07–69), **Hospital** (tel. 62/12–18–70).

*U.S. Consulate* The consulate is on Calle Monterrey, in back of the Hotel Calinda (tel. 62/17–26–13 and 17–23–75 [emergencies]).

**Guaymas** **Tourist Information** is at Avenida Serdán 441, between Calles 12 and 13, 2nd floor (tel. 622/2–5667 or 622/4–2932).

*Emergencies* **Police** (tel. 622/2–0030), **Red Cross** (tel. 622/2–0879), **Hospital** (tel. 622/2–0122).

**Alamos** The **tourist information office,** located on the main plaza (Calle Juárez 6, tel. 642/8–04–50), is open Monday–Friday 9–2 and 4–6, Saturday 9–2.

## Arriving and Departing By Plane

**Airport and Airlines** **Aeroméxico** (tel. 800/237–6639) has daily flights to Hermosillo from Tucson ($70 one-way) and Los Angeles ($123 one-way); service daily to Guaymas from Tucson ($92); and flights on Tuesday, Thursday, and Sunday from Phoenix ($149 one-way). The airline also offers direct flights to Hermosillo from many cities in Mexico—including Mexico City, Chihuahua, Ciudad Obregón, Guadalajara, and Tijuana—and from La Paz and Mexico City to Guaymas; connections to other U.S. cities can be made from these points.

## Arriving and Departing by Car, Train, and Bus

**By Car** Many visitors to Sonora travel by car from Tucson via I–19 and Mexico 15. The highways are paved and quite good but are best driven during the day. Highway 15 is now a divided four-lane highway, making the ride much quicker and easier than it used to be. This convenience, however, doesn't come cheap: Tolls on the road through the state, already high, were raised even more in early 1993 to pay for the highway improvement. Drivers heading down to Alamos can now expect to pay approximately $30 in fees.

**By Train** The train arrives in Hermosillo and Guaymas daily from Nogales and Mexicali.

**By Bus** **Elite** (tel. 62/13–06–10 in Hermosillo) runs a deluxe air-conditioned coach daily from Nogales to Hermosillo (around $10). Frequent buses travel to Hermosillo and Guaymas from Nogales, Tijuana, and Mexicali via **Tres Estrellas de Oro** and **Transportes de Sonora.** There's no point in calling these companies; just show up at the bus station to purchase your ticket.

## Getting Around

By far the easiest way to get around is by automobile, either yours or a rented one. Guaymas and its beaches are particularly spread out, and the only convenient means of transportation is a car. Most hotels have car-rental agencies. Buses between towns are frequent and inexpensive; the train runs daily but is unreliable and scheduled at inconvenient hours. There is ferry service from Guaymas to Santa Rosalia on the Baja coast, leaving at 10 AM. The crossing takes about seven hours and returns on the same day at 11 PM. At this time, management of the ferry is changing, and schedules are erratic. Check with the Guaymas tourism office (*see* Important Addresses and Numbers, *above*) for the latest information and schedule. Cars can be shipped on the ferry; reserve at least three days in advance.

**By Rental Car** Car-rental agencies include **Hertz** (Blvds. Rodriguez and *Hermosillo* Tamaulipas, tel. 62/14–85–00 and 62/12–07–35) and, across the street, **Budget** (tel. 62/14–30–33).

*Guaymas* Here the agencies to contact are **Budget** (tel. 622/2–1450) and **Hertz** (tel. 622/2–1000), both on the main highway.

## Exploring Sonora

**Hermosillo** Although Hermosillo is usually just considered a jumping-off point for Kino Bay or Guaymas, it has a number of attractions in its own right, as well as the best accommodations and restaurants in the area. The city's main boulevard is lined with monuments to Sonora's famous sons: Adolfo de la Huerta, Alvaro Obregón, Plutarco Elías Calles, and Abelardo Rodríguez (after whom the boulevard is named), all presidents of the state after the revolution. At the center of town, the **Plaza Zaragoza** boasts the impressive Catedrál de San Agustín (1878), recently regilded at great expense. Across from the cathedral is the Palacío de Gobierno del L'Estado, its graceful courtyard surrounded by somewhat disjunctive modern murals depicting Sonoran history, and between the two buildings sits an ornate Victorian gazebo. On the south edge of town, the **Plaza de los Tres Pueblos** marks the original settlement.

Two museums are worth a visit: overlooking the city, on the Cerro la Campana (Hill of Bells), the **Museo de Sonora,** a former penitentiary, now hosting a variety of regional history displays; and the **Museo de la Universidad de Sonora** (on Blvds.

**Adventures** (c/o Hotel Armida, Carraterra Internacional Salida Norte, tel. 622/4–3035).

## Beaches

All the main beaches of the state have paved access roads. There are hotels and restaurants at San Carlos and in Guaymas, in Puerto Peñasco, and at Kino Bay. Miles and miles of secluded beaches run along the Sea of Cortés, but access is difficult and there are no facilities.

## Dining

| Category | Cost* |
| --- | --- |
| Very Expensive | over $20 |
| Expensive | $15–$20 |
| Moderate | $8–$15 |
| Inexpensive | under $8 |

*per person excluding drinks, service, and sales tax (10%)*

**Alamos**   **Las Palmeras.** This modest restaurant, with high beamed ceilings and wood furniture, serves up tasty Mexican fare, including especially good green-corn tortillas. Located off the southeast corner of the plaza, this is a fun spot to people-watch from one of the outdoor tables. Las Palmeras opens at 7 AM for breakfast. *Calle Lázaro Cárdenas 9, tel. 642/8–0065. No reservations. Dress: casual. MC, V. Inexpensive–Moderate.*

**Polo's.** *Carne asada* (grilled strips of beef), pork chops, and other meat dishes are the most popular offerings at this restaurant, but the chicken enchiladas are also well prepared. Set in a former residence that's more than 225 years old, Polo's is not fancy, but its brightly colored tablecloths help to create a cheerful atmosphere. *Av. Zaragoza 4, tel. 642/8–0001 or 642/8–0003. No reservations. Dress: casual. MC, V. Moderate.*

**Guaymas/**   **Del Mar.** On the main street of town, this place does surf and
**San Carlos**   turf Guaymas style. A series of small dining rooms with beamed ceilings and tiled floors are separated by bricked arches, from which hang fishing nets and assorted flotsam and jetsam. The fish Santo Domingo (broiled local bass with mushrooms, green peppers, and melted cheese) is popular, as is the mixed seafood grill. *Av. Serdán 17, tel. 622/2–4650. Reservations accepted. Dress: casual. AE, MC, V. Expensive.*

**El Paradise.** This small restaurant in town features seafood. Fresh fish is prepared in several ways but is best simply grilled with oil and garlic. *Abelardo Rodríguez 20, Guaymas, tel. 622/2–1181. No reservations. Dress: casual. No credit cards. Moderate.*

**Rosa's Cantina.** Picnic tables fill two large dining rooms where diners feast on ample breakfasts of eggs with *chorizo* (sausage) or *huevos rancheros* (Mexican-style eggs). The tortilla soup is great for lunch or dinner. *Carretera San Carlos at Satélite 296, tel. 622/6–0307. No reservations. Dress: casual. MC, V. Inexpensive.*

**Hermosillo**   **La Siesta.** A family-run inn, La Siesta is known for its fine cuts of Sonoran beef. *Blvd. Kino Norte and 1° de Mayo, tel. 62/14–39–89. No reservations. Dress: casual. MC, V. Expensive.*

**Xochimilco.** This is a friendly place popular with locals and regulars visiting from across the border, serving typical Sonoran dishes. *Av. Obregón 5, tel. 62/13–34–89. No reservations. Dress: casual. AE, MC, V. Expensive.*

**El Chalet de la Guitarra.** A small, intimate restaurant specializing in pastas and other Italian dishes. *Blvd. Kino at Villareal, tel. 62/14–91–41. Reservations accepted. Dress: casual. MC, V. Moderate.*

**Hotel Bugambilia Restaurant.** A small dining room with beamed ceilings and red-checked tablecloths, this cheerful place serves excellent tortilla soup and Mexican-style veal cutlets. *Blvd. Kino 712, tel. 62/14–50–50. Dress: casual. No reservations. AE, MC, V. Moderate.*

**Kino Bay** **El Pargo Rojo.** As befits a restaurant near the sea, this plain but friendly dining room has a nautical motif. Entrées include an excellent *sopa de marisco* (seafood soup) and fresh flounder stuffed with clams, scallops, and shrimp. There's live music on weekend nights. *Av. Mar de Cortez 1426, tel. 624/2–0205. Dress: casual. Reservations accepted. AE, MC, V. Expensive.*

## Lodging

| Category | Cost* |
|---|---|
| Very Expensive | over $90 |
| Expensive | $60–$90 |
| Moderate | $25–$60 |
| Inexpensive | under $25 |

*\*All costs are for a standard double room; excluding 10% tax.*

**Alamos** **Casa de los Tesoros.** This hotel, the House of Treasures, is a picturesque and romantic converted 18th-century convent. The rooms are former nuns' cells and have fireplaces, tiled baths, antique furnishings, and high-quality handicrafts on the walls. The hotel was recently purchased by a group of investors from southern California who plan to redecorate and upgrade the food—an important improvement, because room rates from October through April include meals. *Av. Obregón 10, Box 12, 85760, tel. 642/8–0010, fax 642/8–0400. 14 rooms. Facilities: pool, shops, gardens, restaurant, bar, parking. MC, V. Expensive–Very Expensive.*

★ **Casa Encantada.** Set on the main square, this lovely bed-and-breakfast owned by a California couple is the converted 250-year-old mansion of one of Alamos's former Spanish mine owners. Rooms retain a colonial character, with high, beamed ceilings, fireplaces, and carved-wood furnishings, but all have tiled private baths and good lighting. The copious breakfast, served on a plant-filled patio overlooking a small pool, might include frittatas, fresh fruit, and home-baked breads. *Calle Juárez 20, 85760, tel. 642/8–0482 or 800/422–5485, fax 714/752–2331. 10 rooms. Facilities: pool, gardens, bicycles, meeting room. MC, V. Expensive.*

**Guaymas/San Carlos Bay** **Club Med Sonora Bay.** Although San Carlos is expanding rapidly in its direction, this Club Med is still secluded from the main tourist area, its verdant 42-acre complex spread behind a large gate fronted by saguaro cactus. Accommodations are characteristically charming but plain, and the range of available ac-

tivities is as great as one would expect from the chain. All
meals, drinks, tips—and many sports, such as sailing and
scuba diving—are included. It's worth paying extra for the
dawn horseback ride to the foothills of the nearby Sierra Madre. *Playa de los Algodones, San Carlos 85400, tel. 622/6-
0176, 800/CLUB-MED for U.S. reservations; fax 622/6-0070.
375 rooms. Facilities: beach, pool, 2 saunas, 31 tennis courts,
sailboats, Windsurfers, golf course, horseback riding, restaurant, bar. AE, MC, V. Very Expensive.*

**Howard Johnson's.** Forget the familiar orange roofs: This huge
structure, rising from San Carlos Bay en route to Club Med, is
thoroughly, strikingly pink. Opened in February 1992, this is
the most luxurious hotel in Sonora, with an impressive marble-
floor atrium lobby that opens out onto a large pool and beach.
Rooms are done in an attractive contemporary style, with
pastel-patterned bedspreads and drapes, rattan-style wood
furnishings, faux-burnished copper lamps, and beige carpeting. All have safes and minibars, and rooms on the first two
floors have balconies. *Mar Barmejo, 4, Los Algodones, Box
441, San Carlos 85506, tel. 622/6-0777 or 800/654-2000 for
U.S. reservations, fax 622/6-0778. 148 rooms, 25 suites. Facilities: 2 restaurants, snack bar, 2 bars, 2 pools, Jacuzzi, exercise room, video game room, 2 tennis courts, volleyball, water
sports and fishing center, horseback riding, car rental, travel
agency, beauty salon, shops. AE, MC, V. Very Expensive.*

**Hotel Armida.** Close to downtown Guaymas and its restaurants
and shops, this sand-colored, Mediterranean-style hotel features a large, well-kept pool; a good coffee shop where locals
gather for power breakfasts; and an excellent steak house, El
Oeste. Rooms in the hotel's old section are dark, with ill-
matched furnishings. The larger, brighter accommodations in
the newest section, done in light wood, are worth the higher
rates; many have balconies overlooking the pool. *Carretera Internacional, Box 296, Guaymas 85420, tel. 622/2-5220 or 800/
732-0780 for U.S. reservations, fax 622/2-0448. 80 rooms, 45
suites. Facilities: 2 restaurants, coffee shop, bar, pool, disco,
laundry service, room service, car rental, hunting and fishing
tours, free airport transfers. AE, MC, V. Moderate–Expensive.*

**Playas de Cortés.** This fine, older hotel, built in the colonial
style, is set amid lush gardens that lead down to the sea. The
rooms are furnished with hand-carved antiques and many have
fireplaces; unfortunately, accommodations are not as well-
maintained as they might be. *Bahía Bocochibampo, tel. 622/1-
1224 or 622/1-1048, fax 622/1-0135. 120 rooms. Facilities: restaurant, bar, pool, shop, private beach, parking, gardens, tennis, water sports. AE, DC, MC, V. Moderate–Expensive.*

**Fiesta San Carlos.** This small, well-maintained hotel on the bay
has mismatched furnishings but a comfortable feeling. Accommodations with kitchens are available. Breakfast is included in
the room rate. *San Carlos Bay, tel. 622/6-0229. 33 rooms. Facilities: restaurant, bar, pool, parking. MC, V. Moderate.*

★ **Las Playitas.** The best deal in town, this combination trailer
park/motel on Guaymas Bay has plain but characterful
rooms—with tinwork mirrors and beamed ceilings, opening
out onto a cobblestoned, bougainvillea-lined path—for $22 a
night ($15 if you stay for at least a week). Even if you don't sleep
here, come out for the lively, eclectically decorated restaurant
and bar. The food is good and inexpensive, but if you'd rather
eat what you caught that day, you can get it cooked up with

trimmings added for a small price. *Carreterra al Varadero Nacional, tel. 622/2-2727 and 622/2-2753. 29 bungalows with shower, 93 RV spaces. Facilities: pool, pier, restaurant, bar, live weekend entertainment. MC, V. Inexpensive.*

**Hermosillo** **Holiday Inn.** This full-service property is the largest in town and popular among business travelers. The decor is predictable, but some rooms have excellent views, and the beds are large and firm. *369 Blvd. Kino, tel. 62/15-11-12 or 62/15-18-20, 800/HOLIDAY for U.S. reservations; fax 62/15-14-90. 222 rooms. Facilities: restaurant, cafeteria, lobby bar, pool, Jacuzzi, disco, shops, video bar, tennis, travel agency, beauty parlor. AE, MC, V. Expensive.*

**Valle Grande Pitic.** Two-thirds of the attractive rooms in this contemporary Spanish-style hotel look out on extensive, well-kept gardens and a good-size pool. The staff, geared toward accommodating the many Mexican business travelers who stay here, don't all speak English. *Blvd. Kino and Ramon Corral, tel. 62/14-45-70. 144 rooms with shower. Facilities: nightclub, bar, restaurant, pool, direct-dial long distance, beauty parlor, travel agent, gift shop. AE, MC, V. Expensive.*

**Kino.** Probably the best of the downtown hotels, the Kino has nonetheless seen better days. There's a nice garden in the back, but public areas look worn. Rooms are clean if not exciting, and all have TVs and phones. *Piño Suárez 151 Sur, tel. 62/13-31-31, fax 62/12-38-52. 114 rooms. Facilities: restaurant, pool, sauna, garden, parking. AE, MC, V. Moderate.*

**Kino Bay** **Posada del Mar.** The most pleasant property in Kino Bay, the Posada is decorated mission style, with folk art on the brick walls in the rooms and pretty gardens by the pool. *Mar de Cortéz and Creta, Box 132, tel. 62/42-01-55; in Hermosillo, tel. 62/18-12-05. 48 rooms. Facilities: beach, restaurant, bar, pool, gardens, parking. MC, V. Moderate.*

**Posada Santa Gemma.** A good place for families, this hotel consists of two-story bungalows with fireplaces, full kitchens, and upstairs balconies overlooking the sea. *Blvd. Mar de Cortéz, tel. 62/42-00-26. 14 bungalows, each with 2 bedrooms and kitchen. Facilities: beach, grocery store. MC, V. Moderate.*

## Nightlife

**Guaymas/ San Carlos** Nightlife in Guaymas can be found at the following locales: **Xanadu,** a disco located at Malecón Malpica; **Bar El Yate,** a sports bar at the Marina San Carlos; **Casanova Discoteque,** at the Armida Hotel (Carreterra Internacional Salida Norte); **Charles Baby,** for the younger set, at Avenidas Serden and Malecón; **Las Playitas** bar (*see* Lodging, *above*) on weekends; and **Pappas Tappas,** on the main highway of San Carlos.

**Hermosillo** Hermosillo is home to several lively night spots: **Bar Ali Baba** at the Plaza Pitic, Boulevards Kino and Roman Yocupicio; **Disco Sonovision** at the Hotel San Alberto; and **Blocky'O Disco,** Rodríguez at Aguascalientes.

# 6 The Copper Canyon: From Los Mochis to Chihuahua City

By Edie Jarolim

Edie Jarolim is a freelance writer currently living in Tucson, Arizona.

The magnificent series of gorges known collectively as the Copper Canyon (in Spanish, *Barranca del Cobre*) is the real hidden treasure of the Sierra Madre. Inaccessible to the casual visitor until 30 years ago and still largely uncharted, the canyons may now be explored by taking one of the most breathtaking rides in North America: The *Chihuahua al Pacifico* railroad whistles down 661 kilometers (410 miles) of track, crossing 86 tunnels and 35 bridges through rugged country as rich in history and culture as in physical beauty.

The barrancas of the Sierra Tarahumara, as this portion of the Sierra Madre Occidental is known, are on the western edge of the Pacific "Ring of Fire." Formed by seismic and volcanic activity, which at the same time hurled a good quantity of the earth's buried mineral wealth to the surface, the canyons were carved throughout the millennia by the Urique, Septentrion, Batopilas, and Chinapas rivers and further defined by wind erosion. Totaling more than 1,452 kilometers (900 miles) in length and capable of enveloping four of the Arizona Grand Canyons, the gorges are nearly a mile deep and wide in places; the average height of the peaks is 8,000 feet, and some rise to more than 12,000 feet. Four of the major barrancas—Copper, Urique, Sinforosa, and Batopilas—descend deeper than the Grand Canyon, Urique by nearly 1,500 feet.

The idea of building a rail line to cross this region was first conceived in 1872 by Albert C. Owen, an idealistic American socialist. Owen met with some success initially. More than 1,500 people came from the states to join him in Topolobampo, his utopian colony on the Mexican west coast, and in 1881 he obtained a concession from Mexican president General Manuel Gonzáles to build the railroad. Construction on the flat stretches near Los Mochis and Chihuahua presented no difficulties, but eventually the huge Sierra Madre mountains got in the way of Owen's dream, along with the scourge of typhoid and disillusionment within the community.

After Owen abandoned the project in 1893, it was taken up in 1900 by American railroad magnate and spiritualist Edward Arthur Stilwell. One of Stilwell's contractors in western Chihuahua was Pancho Villa, who ended up tearing up his own work during the Mexican Revolution in order to impede the movement of government troops. By 1910, when the Mexican Revolution started, the Mexican government had taken charge of building the railroad line, but progress was very slow until 1940, when surveying of the difficult Sierra Madre stretch finally began in earnest. Some 90 years and more than $100 million after it started, the Ferrocarril Chihuahua al Pacifico was dedicated on November 23, 1961.

The rail line no longer starts at Topolobambo but at nearby Los Mochis. Chihuahua City, at the other end of the line, was established in 1709. Today Chihuahua, the capital of the state of that name and a prosperous economic center, derives its wealth from mining—the Spanish discovered silver in the region as early as 1649—as well as from ranching, agriculture, and lumber.

The Tarahumara Indians, who once occupied the entire state of Chihuahua, were not unaffected by the foreign activity in the area: They were forced to serve in the mines by the Spanish and on the railroad by the Mexicans and the Americans. The threat

the Sierra Madre foothills, is more scenic than the railroad route via the plains area. Driving is a good option if you have an all-terrain vehicle, because there are many worthwhile, if difficult, excursions into the canyons from Creel. A new road from Chihuahua to Bahuichivo via Divisadero has recently been finished, but an all-terrain vehicle is still advised. A route to Urique Canyon is also planned.

**By Train**
*Los Mochis*
The Ferrocarril Pacífico, which travels from Nogales to Guadalajara, stops at the San Blas (Sufragio) station between Los Mochis and El Fuerte. Arriving at about 2 AM, it is not a viable option for most. But if you don't mind spending the night at a no-frills train station, you can pick up the *Chihuahua al Pacífico* train here the next morning at about 6:45.

*Chihuahua*
The daily train that runs between Ciudad Juárez and Mexico City stops in Chihuahua at 10 PM and takes about 4½ hours. Fares vary; the best seats, *primera especial* or *servicio estrella*, cost about the same as the bus (*see* By Bus, *below*).

*Copper Canyon*
A new luxury touring train makes a round-trip run from Nogales through the Copper Canyon area. **Sierra Madre Express of Tucson** (Box 26381, Tucson, AZ 85726, tel. 602/747–0346 or 800/666–0346) offers eight-day, seven-night trips from Tucson approximately six times a year. Two other tour operators, **Tauck Tours** (Box 5027, Westport, CT 06881, tel. 800/468–2825) and **RFD Travel** (5201 Johnson Dr., Mission, KS 66205, tel. 800/365–5389), charter the train and its personnel for similar excursions the rest of the time. Traveling on the same track as the *Chihuahua al Pacífico*, the train stops in Cerocahui, Posada Barrancas, and Creel. Prices run from about $2,200 to $2,650 per person, based on double occupancy.

**By Bus**
*Los Mochis*
The **Tres Estrellas de Oro, Transportes del Pacífico,** and **Transport Norte de Sonora** bus lines all leave every hour from Nogales to Los Mochis; with luck, the trip should take about 12 hours. The cost is approximately $27.

*Chihuahua*
The **Transportes de Norte, Chihuahuenses,** and **Omnibus de México** lines run clean, air-conditioned buses from Ciudad Juárez to Chihuahua; these leave approximately every 15 minutes from 7 AM to 8 PM. The cost of the trip, which takes about five hours, is approximately $10. Buses shuttle between El Paso and Ciudad Juárez every two hours; the price is $3.

**By Boat**
The **Baja Express** (tel. 682/563–11 or 682/563–13 in La Paz) has catamaran service every day except Wednesday from La Paz to Topolobampo; it takes about four hours, and costs vary from $37 to $47. A slower ferry runs every day except Saturday; the trip takes about eight hours and costs about $11.

## Getting Around

**By Car**
*Los Mochis*
Car companies in town include **Budget** (Leyva and Angel Flores, behind the Santa Anita Hotel, tel. 681/5–83–00, fax 681/5–84–00); **National** (Leyva 127 Nte., tel. 681/2–65–52); and **Aga** (Leyva and Callejón Municipal, tel. 681/2–53–60).

*Chihuahua*
**Avis** (Av. Universidad 1703, tel. 14/14–19–99), **Hertz** (Av. Revolución 514, tel. 14/16–64–73), and **Budget** (Av. Independencia 1205, tel. 14/16–09–09) all have offices at the airport also.

**By Taxi**
*Los Mochis* Taxis are easy to find but not very cheap for long distances. You're better off renting a car to Topolobampo. It costs about $17 to get to the airport from downtown Los Mochis.

*Chihuahua* Easy to find, taxis can be engaged at your hotel or hailed on the street. Since fares are negotiable, always agree on a price before entering the cab. You'll usually pay less if you speak Spanish.

**By Train**
*Copper Canyon* The Ferrocarril Chihuahua al Pacífico line runs two trains daily in each direction from Chihuahua and Los Mochis. The one designed for tourists, with plush seats and a bar and dining car, is called *El Tren Estrella*. Eastbound, this train departs from Los Mochis at 6 AM and arrives in Chihuahua 12 hours later; westbound, it departs from Chihuahua at 7 AM and arrives in Los Mochis around 7 PM (most of the time, but problems with the weather may cause long or short delays). Tickets can be purchased through almost any hotel in Los Mochis or Chihuahua or directly at the train station. The price is about $29 each way, but there's a 15% charge for any stopovers en route. These should be arranged at the time of ticket purchase. Reservations (tel. 14/12–22–84 or 14/15–77–56 in Chihuahua, tel. 681/5–7775 in Los Mochis) should be made at least a week in advance during the busy months of July and August and around Christmas and Easter.

The second-class train leaves an hour later from each terminus but makes many stops and is scheduled to arrive 3½ hours later in both directions than the first-class train. Though it is less comfortable, this train is a good way to meet the locals. Don't rely on served snacks—bring your own food. No reservations are needed; prices are approximately $8.50 each way.

It's possible to ship your car on the train, but it's not worth the expense or the bother. If you're driving down to Los Mochis, you're better off leaving your car there and taking the train round-trip. If you're coming via Chihuahua, however, you should consider driving to Creel and doing a round-trip from there (*see* Arriving and Departing by Car, *above*).

# Exploring the Copper Canyon

Imagine visiting the Grand Canyon in the days before it was tamed by tourist facilities, and you'll have some sense of what a trip through the Copper Canyon will be like—for better and for worse. That is, with the opportunity to encounter a relatively untouched natural site come some of the attendant discomforts of the rustic experience. But if you are careful in your choice of time to visit and are properly prepared, the trip's myriad rewards should far outstrip any temporary inconveniences.

You'll see some beautiful scenery if you just ride the railroad, including a panoramic look at Copper Canyon during a 15-minute stop at Divisadero, but you'll only experience a fraction of what the canyons have to offer if you don't get off the train. If possible, plan on a night in Cerocahui (Bahuichivo stop), one at Posado Barrancas or Divisadero (the train stations are 10 minutes apart), and one or two at Creel.

About 60% of the people who visit the Copper Canyon come via Los Mochis, which is the easiest route if you're traveling from California or Arizona. It's also by far the most desirable route if you come in winter, because some of the best scenery is to be seen at the western end of the ride and you're likely to miss it if you approach Los Mochis in the evening. Your choice of route matters less in the extended daylight hours of summer.

Unless you are planning to head down deep into the barrancas, winter—December through February—is not the best time to come; many of the hotels in the region are inadequately prepared for the cold, and the minor rainy season in January renders some of the roads for side excursions impassable. The warm months are May through September; the rainy season, June through September, brings precipitation for a short period every day, but this shouldn't interfere with your enjoyment in any way. It's temperate in the highlands during the summer; if you're planning to hike down into the canyons, however, remember that the deeper you go, the hotter it will get. The best months to visit are October and November, when the weather is still warm and rains have brought out all the colors in the Sierra Tarahumara.

Many people visit during Christmas and Easter, specifically to see the Tarahumara celebrations of those holidays. Closely related to the Pima Indians of southern Arizona, the Tarahumara are renowned for their running ability. (*Tarahumara* is a Spanish corruption of *Raramuri*, which means "running people" in their language; it is said that in earlier times they survived as hunters by chasing deer to the point of collapse.) Around Christmas, Easter, and other religious feast days, the Tarahumara compete in races that can last up to three days. The men run in small groups, kicking a wooden ball for a distance of 161 kilometers (100 miles) or more. On these and other feast days, tribal elders consume peyote or *tesguino*, a sacred fermented corn liquor.

*Numbers in the margin correspond to points of interest on the Copper Canyon map.*

❶ The first stop on the western end of the rail line, **Los Mochis** (population about 300,000) is an agricultural boomtown; its location near the harbor at Topolobampo and the railroad makes it the export center of the state of Sinaloa, which produces many of Mexico's basic crops. Visitors can tour Benjamin Johnston's sugar refinery, the Ingenio Azucarero, around which the town grew. Near Johnston's estate you can still see the American colony, the group of brick bungalows that housed his associates, as well as a workers' hostel and the country club. Not far away, on Calles Obregón and Mina, the Museo Regional de Los Mochis has rotating exhibits of paintings and crafts by local artists, and the public library next door displays pictures of the early days of the city.

Cottonwood trees and bougainvillea line the highway from Los Mochis to **Topolobampo;** on both sides of the road are fields planted with crops ranging from sugarcane to marigolds and mangos (36 varieties are produced here). Once the site of Albert Owen's utopian colony and the center of the railroad building activity in the area, Topolobampo is now considered a suburb of Los Mochis, 15 minutes away. A huge tuna-packing factory sits at the entrance to the bay, and local fisherman—

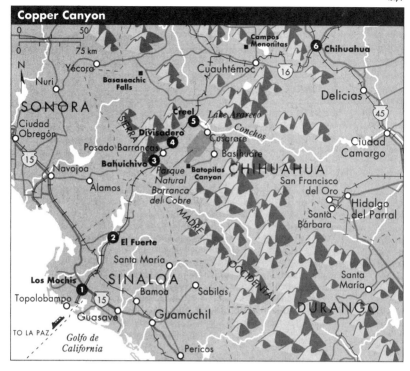

Copper Canyon

90% of the population—ply the harbor in small shrimp boats; they compete for their catch with the many dolphins that cavort in the bay. Isla El Farallón, just off the coast, is a breeding ground for the sea lions that gave the town its name: In the language of the Mayo Indians who once dominated the area, Topolobampo means "watering place of the sea lions."

Eighty kilometers (50 miles) east of Los Mochis, **El Fuerte** is a small colonial town, named after the 17th-century fort built by the Spaniards to protect against attacks by the local Mayo, Sinaloa, Zuaque, and Tehueco Indians. Originally called San Juan de Carapoa, it was founded in 1564 by Spanish conquistador Don Francisco de Ibarra and a small group of soldiers. Located on the central El Camino Real route, El Fuerte was at one time the frontier outpost from which the Spanish set out to explore and settle New Mexico and California. For three centuries, it was also a major trading post for gold and silver miners from the nearby Sierras and the most important commercial and farming center of the area; it was chosen as Sinaloa's capital in 1824 and remained so for several years. Some intact colonial mansions remain in what is now a rather sleepy town of 25,000; one of the best is the Hotel Posada Hidalgo (*see* Lodging, *below*). Most of El Fuerte's historic houses are set off the cobblestone streets leading from the central plaza; a number of them have been converted into government offices.

If you want to catch an extra hour and a half of sleep, spend the night at El Fuerte and board the train at 7:30 AM. As the train ascends almost 1,800 meters (5,906 feet) into the mountains from here to Bahuichivo, it passes through 54 tunnels and over 24 bridges, including the longest and highest ones of the rail system. The scenery shifts from Sinaloan thorn forest, with cactus and scrublike vegetation, to the pools, cascades, and tropical trees of the Río Septentrion canyon, to the oak and pine forest that begins to take over past Temoris, where a plaque marks the dedication of the railroad by President López Mateos in 1961.

**❸** From the train station at **Bahuichivo,** two hotels have buses that make the 45-minute ride up the bumpy, unpaved road to the quiet mountain village of **Cerocahui.** This is a good place to get a sense of how people live in the canyon area. Next door to the Hotel Misión is a Jesuit mission, established around 1690 by Juan María de Salvatierra, who proselytized widely in the region; it is said that because the Tarahumara were the most difficult Indians to convert, he considered this mission his favorite among the many he founded. Nearby, the church operates a boarding school for Tarahumara children. Visitors can hike or ride horses to two nearby waterfalls and to a silver mine (closed since 1988), but the prime reason to come to Cerocahui is its accessibility to Urique Canyon. It's a kidney-crunching ride to the Cerro del Gallego lookout point, where amid mountains spread against the horizon, you can make out the Urique River and the town of Urique, a slim thread and a dot on the distant canyon bottom. On the way up you'll pass a Tarahumara cave where Indian women sell baskets; nearby, a shrine to the Virgin is strikingly set against a spring in the mountainside surrounded by tropical foliage. From Cerro del Gallego the road continues down the canyon into the old mining town of Urique, which has a few basic hotels and restaurants. A public bus makes the trip from Cerocahui a few times a week, but many visitors opt for the round-trip, full-day tours offered by the local hotels (*see* Lodging, *below*).

For the most comfort in the most spectacular setting on the route, get off at the Posada Barrancas or the Divisadero stop.
**❹** There's little to do in **Divisadero,** a postage stamp of a place on the Continental Divide, but it's impossible to remain unastounded by the vistas of the Copper Canyon, said to have derived its name from the facts that copper used to be mined in the area and that the canyon turns copper-colored at sunset. You can also glimpse a bit of the distant Urique and Tararechua canyons from here. A popular excursion that takes about four hours round-trip whether you're traveling on two feet or on horseback, is a visit to Bacajipare, a Tarahumara village.

**❺** Nestled in pine-covered mountains, **Creel** is a rugged mining and logging town that grew up around the railroad station. The largest settlement in the area, it's a gathering place for Tarahumara Indians seeking supplies and markets for their crafts. It's easy to imagine American frontier towns at the turn of the century looking like Creel—without, of course, the backpacking contingent that makes this town its base. A cluster of small hotels here offer tours to the many points of interest in the area. It's 12 miles from Creel to Cusarare, an Indian village that hosts a 300-year-old mission built by the Jesuits for the Tarahumara. En route, you'll pass limpid-blue Lake Arareco and the Valley of the Mushrooms, with its strange volcanic-rock formations. An impressive waterfall can be reached by an easy 2 ½-mile hike from Cusarare through a lovely piñon forest. If the unpaved roads are passable, consider taking the longer trips to the Recohuata Hot Springs, a fairly strenuous hike down from the rim of the Tararecua Canyon, and to El Tejaban, a spectacular overlook at the Copper Canyon. It's a five-hour drive along rough roads to Basaseachic Falls, and you'll have to stay overnight if you want to visit Batopilas (*see* Off the Beaten Track, *below*), but several worthwhile day trips en route to the latter include Basihuare, where huge vertical outcroppings of rock are crossed with wide horizontal bands of color; the Urique Canyon overlook, affording a perspective of that barranca that differs from the one at Cerocahui; and La Bufa, site of a former Spanish silver mine.

After the peaceful Copper Canyon, the sprawling city of ❻ **Chihuahua,** with nearly 1 million inhabitants, may come as a bit of a jolt. Two of the most famous figures in Mexico's revolutionary wars are closely tied to the city. Father Miguel Hidalgo, the father of Mexican independence, and his coconspirators were executed by the Spanish here in 1811. And Chihuahua was home to General Pancho Villa, whose revolutionary army, the División del Norte (Army of the North), was decisive in overthrowing dictator Porfirio Díaz in 1910 and securing victory in the ensuing civil war. In addition, Benito Juárez, known as the Abraham Lincoln of Mexico, made Chihuahua his base in 1865 during the French invasion of the country.

Whatever you do, don't miss a visit to the Museo Histórico de la Revolución en el Estado de Chihuahua, better known as **Pancho Villa's House.** Villa lived in this home, completed in 1909, with his second wife, Luz Corral (he had three wives, none of whom he divorced). She stayed here until her death on June 6, 1981, willing the residence to the government, which restored it as a national museum. The 50 small rooms that used to board Villa's bodyguards have been converted into exhibition rooms displaying artifacts of Chihuahua's cultural and revolutionary history. Parked outside the museum's courtyard is the bullet-ridden 1919 Dodge in which Villa was assassinated in 1923 at the age of 45. *Calle Décima 3014, tel. 14/16–29–58. Admission: less than $1. Open daily 10–1 and 3–7.*

Another must see is the **Catedral** on the central Plaza de la Constitución. Construction on this beautiful Baroque structure was started by the Jesuits in 1726, but not completed until 1825 because of Indian uprisings in the area. The exterior is made of the pinkish limestone quarried in this region; inside, the opulent church has altars made of Carrera marble, a 24-karat solid gold ceiling, a beautiful cedar-and-brass carved depiction of St. Peter and St. Paul, and a huge German-made organ. In the back of the cathedral, the Museum of Sacred Art displays the work of seven local artists of the 18th-century Mexican Baroque tradition, as well as commemorations of the 1990 visit of Pope John Paul II. *Admission: 50¢. Open weekdays 10–2 and 4–6.*

At the nearby Plaza Hidalgo, the **Palacio del Gobierno** (State Capitol) was built by the Jesuits as a convent in 1882. Converted into government offices in 1891, it was destroyed by a fire in the early 1940s and rebuilt in 1947. Murals around the patio by artist Pino Mora depict famous episodes from the history of the state of Chihuahua; a plaque commemorates the spot where Father Hidalgo was shot on the morning of July 30, 1811. *Open daily 8–6.*

hours round-trip, including a half-hour hike at the end, where the trail is too narrow for the horses. From Divisadero, the trip to Bacajipare, a Tarahumara village in the Copper Canyon, affords stunning vistas; it's an exciting four-hour ride round-trip, but it's not for the faint of heart.

# Dining and Lodging

## Dining

Along the Copper Canyon trail you'll encounter rustic areas where there are few eateries besides those connected with lodges, as well as sophisticated culinary centers like Chihuahua.

In Los Mochis and Topolobampo your best bet is seafood. Restaurants tend to be inexpensive. At the hotels in Cerocahui and Divisadero/Posada Barrancas, food is included in the price of the room. Don't even think about dieting here: You'll get three freshly cooked, hearty meals a day, served family style, often with meat courses and dessert at both lunch and dinner. There are a few more dining options in Creel, where, in addition to the hotel dining rooms, there are a number of inns along the town's main street, Avenida López Mateos; **La Cabana** and **Lupita** both offer good, inexpensive Mexican fare.

You'll have the most choice in Chihuahua. The state is a large producer of beef, so upscale steakhouses and places serving *carne asada* (charbroiled strips of marinated beef) abound, but a variety of Mexican specialties and seafood flown in from the coast is also available. Many of Chihuahua's well-appointed international restaurants are located in the Zona Dorada, on Calle Juárez starting from its intersection with Calle Colón.

Highly recommended restaurants are indicated by a star ★.

| Category | Cost* |
|---|---|
| Very Expensive | over $20 |
| Expensive | $15–$20 |
| Moderate | $8–$15 |
| Inexpensive | under $8 |

*\*per person, excluding drinks, service, and sales tax (10%)*

## Lodging

Accommodations in this area tend to fall into two categories: comfortable but characterless in the large cities and charming but to varying degrees rustic in the small ones. In Cerocahui, Divisadero/Posada Barrancas, and Creel, all the hotels send buses or cars to meet the train; if you don't have a reservation, you'll have to make a quick decision and then hop on a vehicle sent out by the hotel of your choice. During the summer and around Christmas and Easter, it's important to book in advance. Where indicated, rates for hotels include meals.

Highly recommended lodgings are indicated by a star ★.

| Category | Cost* |
|---|---|
| Very Expensive | over $90 |
| Expensive | $60–$90 |
| Moderate | $25–$60 |
| Inexpensive | under $25 |

*All prices are for a standard double room, excluding 10% tax.*

**Batopilas**
*Dining and Lodging*

**Riverside Lodge.** A restored late-19th-century hacienda, this new (1992) lodging is quirkily charming. Each of the high-ceilinged rooms is individually decorated—one with a prayer niche, for example, another with vintage Elizabeth Taylor posters—but all have spacious private baths and huge, soft feather duvets. Only partially wired for electricity, the accommodations have an odd mix of kerosene reading lamps and electrical outlets for hair dryers. The home-cooked meals are excellent, and guests are free to raid the refrigerator and liquor cabinet (just sign the book; you'll be billed later). The lodge must be booked as part of a package with the Copper Canyon Lodge in Cusarare (*see below*), which has the same owner; minimum three-day stay. *Batopilas; contact Copper Canyon Lodges, 1100 Owendale Dr., Ste. G, Troy, MI 48083, tel. 313/ 689–2444 or 800/77–MEXICO, fax 313/689–9119 for reservations. 15 rooms. Facilities: patio, library, afternoon tea, guided hikes and walking tours. MC, V. Very Expensive (meals included).*

**Cerocahui**
*Dining and Lodging*

**Hotel Misión.** Part of the Balderrama chain—the Copper Canyon's equivalent of the Grand Canyon's Fred Harvey hotel empire—this is the only tourist accommodation in town. The main house, which looks like a combination ski lodge and hacienda, contains the hotel's office, small shops, dining room, bar, and lounge. In winter, guests huddle for warmth around two large fireplaces, the prime sources of heat and light: Cerocahui isn't wired for electricity, and the hotel uses its generator for only a few hours at night, generally from 7 to 9:30 PM. The plain but characterful rooms, with beamed ceilings and Spanish Colonial-style furnishings, are a pyromaniac's dream: They're equipped with fuel and matches for guests to light the wood-burning stove and a kerosene lamp for light. *Cerocahui (train stop: Bahuichivo; mailing address: Santa Anita Hotel, Box 159, Los Mochis, Sinaloa), tel. 681/5–7046, ext. 432, fax 681/2–0046. 30 rooms with bath. Facilities: gift shop, restaurant, bar, vineyard (which produces red and white wine sold at the hotel). AE, MC, V. Very Expensive (meals included).*

**Paraiso del Oso Lodge.** Opened in 1990, this lodge offers plain rooms with simple wooden furniture handmade by locals. Guests must stoke the stove for heat at night, since there is no electricity here. A huge window-filled lobby affords excellent views of the cliffs above the lodge, and a gift shop carries local crafts as well as wares from other parts of Mexico. *3 miles outside of Cerocahui; contact Columbus Travel, Rte. 12, Box 382B, New Braunfels, TX, 78132, tel. 512/885–2000 or 800/843–1060 for reservations. 16 rooms with bath. Facilities: Dining room, gift shop, tours. MC, V in U.S.; cash or personal checks only on premises. Very Expensive (meals included).*

**Chihuahua**
*Dining*

**El Galeón.** Nautical almost to the point of inducing seasickness, this upscale seafood restaurant serves steak and chicken as well as fish. Yachty details include a bell tower, rigging, and a pirates' deck; in the downstairs bar, which has live music on Tuesday through Saturday nights, fish swim behind simulated portholes. You can get everything here from seabass, conch, and eel (a specialty) to lobster; the *camarones a la plancha*, grilled jumbo shrimp served with rice pilaf and steamed vegetables, is a good choice. *Av. Juárez 3312 B, tel. 14/15–20–50. Reservations accepted. Jacket advised. AE, DC, MC, V. Expensive.*

★ **Club de Los Parados.** Thirty-seven years of Chihuahua's history have passed through the doors of this landmark restaurant, set in an adobe-style house that would seem more at home in New Mexico. It was started by Tony Vega, a wealthy cattle rancher who died two years ago, as a place for him to come with his fellow ranchers. The story goes that when they went out drinking, the one who sat (or fell) down first had to pick up the tab; Los Parados means "the standing ones." Excellently grilled steaks and chicken as well as tasty Mexican specialties are served in a large room, decorated in muted southwestern colors, with a wood-burning kiva fireplace; the *carne asada* (charbroiled strips of marinated beef) with guacamole is particularly good. A private dining room is lined with photographs of Tony Vega and all the important people in town, including native Chihuahuan Anthony Quinn. *Av. Juárez 3616, tel. 14/15–95–85. Reservations accepted. Dress: casual but neat. AE, V. Moderate.*

**La Calesa.** A large, dimly lit room with wood paneling and red tablecloths and curtains, this looks like the classic steakhouse it is. The onion soup and chile with *aserdo* (a local cheese) make good appetizers. The filet Mignon and ribeye steaks from the area are particularly recommended as entrées; try the former cooked in garlic with shrimp and mushrooms. The clubby bar has a good selection of wines and liquors. *Av. Juárez 3300, tel. 14/12–85–55 and 14/16–12–22. Reservations recommended for large groups. Dress: casual. AE, MC, V. Moderate.*

**El Taquito.** Three blocks south of the Palacio del Gobierno, this modest restaurant specializes in tacos and other typical Mexican dishes, although the dining room, with vines and black-and-white etchings of local scenes on the wall, looks somewhat Mediterranean. The chiles relleños, enchiladas suizas, and chicken burritos with mole sauce are all good choices; you can get a bottle of sangria to accompany your meal for about $6. *Venustiano Carranza 1818, tel. 14/12–71–81. No reservations. Dress: informal. No credit cards. Inexpensive.*

**La Parilla.** A good place to take a break from downtown sightseeing, this fast-food eatery across the street from the Hotel San Francisco will delight dedicated carnivores. After the waiter hands you an order form/menu on which you mark your choice, he'll come over with a tray bearing the cuts of meat being offered that day. A strolling guitarist makes the rounds of this plain, white-walled room with plastic tables and chairs and an open grill in the back. The *menu turístico* includes steak with mashed potatoes, soup, and salad for about $6.50; you'll get your own grill if you order the house special, *parillados*, a sirloin platter served with guacamole and chile sauces as well as potatoes. *Victoria 420, tel. 14/50–58–56. No reservations. Dress: informal. No credit cards. Inexpensive.*

*Lodging*   **Villa Suites.** This property, opened in 1988, combines comfort,
★           style, and convenience: Ten minutes from the downtown sights

but set off in a quiet area, it is the first all-suite hotel in Chihuahua. Each of the rooms, tastefully decorated in contemporary style with a green or blue and beige color scheme, has a kitchenette with stove, dishwasher, and coffeemaker, as well as a VCR and an exercycle. A complimentary Continental breakfast buffet is served at the Clubhouse, which also houses the hotel's indoor pool, Jacuzzi, and exercise equipment. Eager to accommodate the many American business travelers who stay here, the English-speaking staff is friendly and helpful. *Escudero 702, tel. 14/14–33–50. 72 suites with private bath. Facilities: restaurant, indoor and outdoor pool, spa, health club, ping-pong, basketball, free videos, cable TV, room service, laundry. AE, DC, MC, V. Very Expensive.*

**Posada Tierra Blanca.** Across the street from the Palacio del Sol but considerably less expensive, this modern motel-style property is convenient to the downtown sights. Rooms, decorated in red and black with pseudo-antique furnishings, are large and well heated in winter; all have TVs. The striking *Stages of Man* mural in the lobby was painted by Pina Mora, the same artist who decorated the courtyard of the Palacio del Gobierno (*see* Exploring, *above*). *Niños Heroes 100, tel. 14/15–00–00. 103 rooms with bath. Facilities: restaurant, pool, piano bar. AE, MC, V. Moderate.*

**Victoria.** This lovely hotel, built in 1940, used to be *the* place to stay in town. It's seen better days—rooms, decorated in pinks and blues, are a bit small and carpets are somewhat worn—but the public areas, with blue-and-white tiles, carved-wood archways, and wrought-iron electric candelabras, have lost none of their charm. The best rooms look out over the pretty garden surrounding a large swimming pool. *Av. Juárez and Colón, tel. 14/10–05–47. 131 rooms with bath. Facilities: TVs in room, restaurant, bar, pool, car-rental company, travel agency. AE, D, DC, MC, V. Moderate.*

**Creel**
***Dining and Lodging***
★

**Copper Canyon Lodge.** About 15 miles from the train station, near Cusarare Falls and overlooking a piñon forest, this rustic hotel couldn't have a nicer setting. The pine-walled rooms, with their light-wood, Spanish-style furnishings and tiled modern baths, are very attractive, and the lodge where hearty meals are served family style is cozy and appealing. The only catch is that there's no electricity. The kerosene lamps are fine for light year-round. You'll just have to get used to bounding out of bed on cold winter mornings to light the wood-burning stove. *Apdo. Postal #9, Creel 33200, Chih., tel. 145/60179; contact Copper Canyon Lodges, 1100 Owendale Dr., Ste. G, Troy, MI 48083, tel. 313/689–2444 or 800/77–MEXICO, fax 313/689–9119 for reservations. 23 rooms. Facilities: restaurant, bar, gift shop. Very Expensive (meals included).*

***Dining***

**The Steak House.** The restaurant of the Hotel Cascada, this is a fun place to have dinner; taped music and a good bar draw both locals and tourists in the evening. As the name suggests, steak is the focus of the menu, but there are tasty seafood dishes, all reasonably priced, as well. *Av. López Mateos 49, tel. 145/6–01–51. No reservations. Dress: casual. MC, V. Moderate.*

**Tio Molcas.** Reopened in 1992 after being remodeled, this brightly lit, cheerful restaurant has light-wood furniture, pink woven place mats, and local native art on the walls. Along with the standard Mexican fare on the menu, you'll find such unusual dishes as *bistec Raramuri*—steak served barbecued with tomatoes and cheese Tarahumara style. There's also a large selection of seafood entrées. Open for breakfast. *Av. López Mateos. No phone. No reservations. Dress: casual. No credit cards. Inexpensive.*

**Lodging**   **Parador de la Montaña Motel/The Little Resort.** Built 19 years ago, the Parador is considered the fanciest hotel in town, but it's showing its age. The furniture is dark—as is the lighting—and unappealing, and the rooms smell like Lysol; Recently remodeled rooms still have the same cheerless decorating scheme, but the hotel is used by many tour operators and is frequently booked up, so its bar and restaurant are often lively in the evening. *Av. López Mateos 44, tel. 145/6–00–75, fax 145/6–00–85. Reservations: Allende 114, Chihuahua, Ch. tel. 14/10–45–80, fax 14/15–34–68. 50 rooms with shower. Facilities: restaurant, bar, gift shop, TV and phone in room. AE, MC, V. Moderate.*

★ **Margarita's.** If a small boy at the train station offers to take you to Margarita's, go with him. Otherwise you might miss one of the best deals in town: There's no sign on the door, and even if you follow directions (right off the main town plaza, between the two churches perpendicular to each other), you're likely to think you're walking into a private kitchen when you open the door. At this gathering spot for backpackers, you can get anything from a bunk bed in the dorm ($5) to a double room with two beds (around $8 per person); all prices include a tasty home-cooked breakfast and dinner. The rooms, with wrought-iron lamps, light-wood furnishings, and clean, modern baths, are as pleasant as anything you'll find for twice or three times the price. Owner Margarita just opened up a new, more upscale place with a proper restaurant near the Parador de la Montaña Motel; room rates there are still a bargain at $27 for a double, including dinner. *Av. López Mateos y Parroquia 11, tel. 145/6–00–45. 21 rooms, most with private bath. Facilities: restaurant. No credit cards. Inexpensive.*

**Divisadero/Posada Barrancas**
**Dining and Lodging**
**Hotel Cabanas Divisadero-Barrancas.** The two other hotels in the area have nearby lodges for viewing the Copper Canyon, but this is the only property that overlooks it directly; the dining room and rooms Room Nos. 1 through 10 in the old section and 35 through 52 in the new section all enjoy panoramic views. The old rooms, with dark furnishings, have decks, while the new ones, somewhat farther from the dining room but lighter in decor, have balconies. Food and service get mixed reviews from the international visitors who sign the guest log, but you're not likely to notice what you're eating when you look out of the dining-room window. *Reservations: Calle 71, #1216, Box 661, Chihuahua, Chih., tel. 14/10–33–30 and 14/15–11–99, fax 14/15–65–75. 52 rooms with shower. Facilities: gift shop, restaurant, bar. AE, MC, V. Very Expensive (meals included).*

**Hotel Mansion Tarahumara.** It's a bit disconcerting to come across a red-turreted, medieval-style castle out here in barranca country, but somehow this whimsical property works. The newest (1988) hotel in the area and the least expensive, it is also the nicest. All the rooms (15 of them in individual cabins) have light-pine furniture beautifully designed in Spanish contemporary style. The newest units have pine-log walls; the older rooms feature gray cobblestone walls that match the castle's exterior. The large dining room with its high-vaulted ceiling is hard to keep warm in winter but has wonderful views of the Sierra Madre. *Apdo. Postal No. 1666–C, Chihuahua, Ch., tel. 14/15–47–21 and 14/10–24–93, fax 14/16–54–44. 46 rooms with* *bath and fireplace. Facilities: restaurant, stables, bar, disco, gift shop. AE, MC, V. Very Expensive (meals included).*

**Hotel Posada Barrancas.** A good base from which to explore the Barranca del Cobre, this member of the Balderrama chain has just added a new annex. These 39 new rooms, done in light wood, are your best bet; the older accommodations have undistinguished dark, contemporary-style furnishings, pseudo-stucco walls, and linoleum-tile floors. From the vertical beams in the main lodge/dining room hang strings of butterfly cocoons used in Tarahumara ceremonial dances, sometimes performed at the hotel in the evening. Rates include four meals (two lunches) instead of the usual three. *Posada Barrancas; reservations: Hotel Santa Anita, Box 159, Los Mochis, Sin., tel. 681/2–00–46. 78 rooms with fireplace and bath. Facilities: restaurant, bar, exercise room, gift shop. AE, DC, MC, V. Very Expensive (meals included).*

**El Fuerte**
*Dining and Lodging*
★

**Hotel Posada Hidalgo.** You'll be transported back to a more gracious era at this lovely restored hacienda, with its lush tropical gardens and cobblestone paths. Designated an Historic Landmark in 1913, it was built in 1895 by Rafael Almada, a rancher and the richest man in nearby Alamos; he had furniture shipped from as far as San Francisco for his lavish home, where he entertained the local elite. It's difficult to choose between the larger rooms with balconies, set off of a lobby filled with period artifacts, and the ones that open out onto the gardens; all are decorated with rough-hewn handcrafted furniture in Spanish Colonial style. *Langostino* (crayfish) is a specialty of the hotel dining room. *Hidalgo 101, tel. 681/3–0242; reservations: Hotel Santa Anita, Box 159, Los Mochis, Sin., tel. 681/57046, fax 681/2–00–46. 40 rooms with bath. Facilities: dining room/bar, gardens, pool, disco. AE, DC, MC, V. Moderate.*

**Los Mochis**
*Dining*

**El Farallón.** With its nautical decor and murals, the dining room of this simple restaurant sets the tone for the excellent fish served here. *Obregón 495, corner Angel Flores, tel. 681/2–14–28. No reservations. Dress: informal. MC, V. Inexpensive.*

*Lodging*

**Hotel Santa Anita.** The central reservations link of the Balderrama chain, this downtown hotel is also an informal information center for what's happening along the *Chihuahua al Pacífico* route, as well as the place to book tours. Built in 1959, the property has been renovated continually; rooms are large and tastefully furnished in muted pastels, with comfortable modern furniture. All have cable TV, and many have hair dryers, unusual for this part of the country. *Leyva and Hidalgo, Apdo. 159, Los Mochis, Sin., tel. 681/5–70–46, fax 681/2–00–46. 133 rooms with bath. Facilities: restaurant, bar, travel agency, gift shop. AE, DC, MC, V. Expensive.*

**El Dorado.** On the main street of town and, as a result, noisy as well as convenient to restaurants and shops, this modest motel/hotel is both a clean establishment and a good value. Rooms are light-filled and have TVs; a small pool is set among palm trees in the back. *525 N. Leyva, corner Valdez, tel. 681/5–11–11, fax 681/9–16–81, 93 rooms with bath. Facilities: coffee shop, bar, pool, travel agency. AE, MC, V. Moderate.*

**Posada Barrancas** (*See* **Divisadero,** *above.*)

**Topolobampo**
*Dining*

**Yacht Hotel.** Open to cool breezes from Topolobampo Bay, this hotel restaurant is a pleasant place for enjoying well-prepared Mexican dishes as well as the fresh seafood caught in the small fishing boats that sail by. *Yacht Hotel, on the waterfront, tel. 681/2-38-62. No reservations. Dress: informal. MC, V. Inexpensive.*

# Nightlife

Sitting around and chatting with fellow guests in your lodge is about the extent of nighttime activity in the heart of Sierra Madre country, though occasionally one of the hotels in Divisadero/Posada Barrancas will have performances in the evening by Tarahumara dancers. In Creel, head to **The Steak House, Tio Molcas,** or the **Parador de La Montaña Motel** (*see* Dining and Lodging, *above*) for an after-dinner drink. Things are a bit more lively in Los Mochis, where locals kick up their heels at **Fantasy** (Hotel Plaza Inn, Leyva and Cardenas, tel. 681/5-80-20) and **Morocco** (Leyva and Rendon, tel. 681/2-13-88), two downtown discos, but Chihuahua has the most nightlife options in the area. **La Reggae** (Blvd. Ortiz Mena and Bosque de la Reina, tel. 14/15-47-55) draws a crowd with dancing feet for its rock'n'roll bands. At **Chihuahua Charlie** (Av. Juárez 3329, tel. 14/17-70-65), DJs spin discs nightly; come early for dinner—the food is as good as the music. The popular **La Puerta de Alcalá** (Revolución 1608, tel. 14/15-83-93) disco sometimes has live music. The bar at the **Hotel San Francisco** (Calle Victoria 409, tel. 14/16-77-70) features a good lounge singer.

# 7 The Heartland of Mexico

By Laura Anne
Broadwell

A New York–based
freelance writer,
Laura Anne
Broadwell lived in
Michoacán for six
months, where she
apprenticed with a
Tarascan Indian
weaver and taught
English to
Mexican students.
She currently
writes for a
variety of business
and travel
magazines.

Updated by
Eleanor S. Morris

Mexico's heartland, so named for its central location, has neither the beaches of the west coast nor the ruins of Yucatán. Rather, this fertile farmland along with the surrounding mountains is known for its leading role in Mexican history, particularly during the War of Independence, and for its especially well-preserved examples of colonial architecture. The Bajío *(ba-HEE-o)*, as it is also called, corresponds roughly to the states of Guanajuato and parts of Querétaro and Michoacán. In the hills surrounding the cities of Guanajuato, Zacatecas, Querétaro, and San Miguel de Allende, the Spaniards found silver in the 1500s, leading them to colonize the area heavily.

Three centuries later, wealthy Creoles (Mexicans of Spanish descent) in Querétaro and San Miguel took the first audacious steps toward independence from Spain. When their clandestine efforts were discovered, two of the early insurgents, Ignacio Allende and Father Miguel Hidalgo, began in earnest the 12-year War of Independence. One of the bloodiest skirmishes was fought in the Alhóndiga de Granaditas, a mammoth grain-storage facility in Guanajuato that is now a state museum.

When Allende and Hidalgo were executed in 1811, another native son, José María Morelos, picked up the independence banner. This mestizo priest turned soldier, with his army of 9,000, came close to gaining control of the land before he was killed in 1815. Thirteen years later, the city of Valladolid was renamed Morelia in his honor.

Many travelers barrel past the Bajío to points north or west of Mexico City. But there are many reasons others make it their destination. Some stop for a few days to browse in the shops of San Miguel or Guanajuato for bargains in silver and other local crafts. Others venture to the state of Michoacán, renowned for its folklore and folk crafts, especially ceramics and lacquerware.

For those who stay longer, the rewards are ample, as each of these colonial cities has a wealth of architectural styles. La Parroquia, the Gothic-style parish church of San Miguel de Allende, designed by an Indian mason, puts a Gallic touch on an otherwise very Mexican skyline; Guanajuato boasts a 17th-century Baroque centerpiece, the Basílica Colegiata de Nuestra Señora; Zacatecas, a national monument city, has the best example in Mexico of a Mexican Baroque cathedral; in Morelia, the 200-foot Baroque towers of the central cathedral are among the tallest in Mexico; and in Pátzcuaro and Querétaro, the ornate 16th-century colonial mansions surrounding the city squares have been converted into hotels and government offices.

Driving through the Bajío, especially scenic Michoacán, is recommended. Within hours the landscape can change from lakeside pine forests to lush subtropical terrain. Day-trippers from Pátzcuaro can explore the crater of an extinct volcano in San Juan Parangaricútiro or the ruins of an ancient Tarascan Indian capital, Tzintzuntzán. Harried city dwellers often head to the state of Querétaro for the weekend, where they unwind in the thermal springs of San Juan del Río and Tequisquiapan. Though the restorative powers of these springs have never been proved scientifically, the waters are said to ease arthritis pain, cure insomnia, and improve digestion.

# Heartland

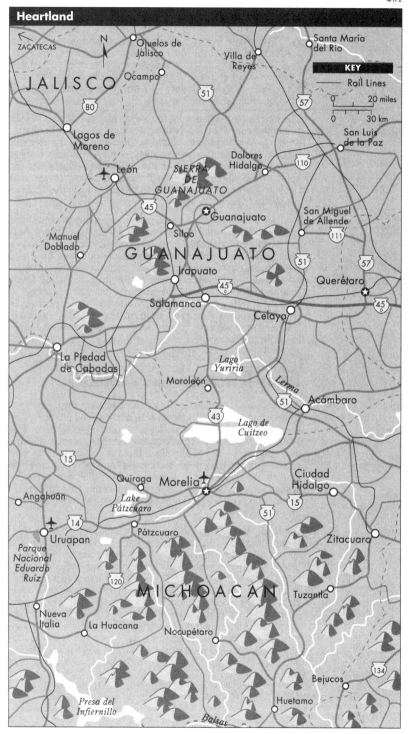

ZACATECAS

**JALISCO**

Otuelos de Jalisco

Santa María del Río

Villa de Reyes

Ocampo

80

Lagos de Moreno

San Luis de la Paz

Dolores Hidalgo

51

León

*SIERRA DE GUANAJUATO*

110

45

Guanajuato

San Miguel de Allende

Silao

111

Manuel Doblado

**GUANAJUATO**

51

Irapuato

57

45

Querétaro

Salamanca

45

Celaya

*Lago Yuriria*

La Piedad de Cabadas

Moroleón

*Lerna*

51

Acámbaro

43

*Lago de Cuitzeo*

15

Quiroga

Morelia

Ciudad Hidalgo

Angahuán

14

*Lake Pátzcuaro*

51

15

Pátzcuaro

Uruapan

Zitacuaro

*Parque Nacional Eduardo Ruíz*

120

**MICHOACAN**

Tuzantla

Nueva Italia

La Huacana

Nocupétaro

134

Bejucos

*Presa del Infiernillo*

Huetamo

*Balsas*

Long after the War of Independence ended in 1821, the cities of the Bajío continued to play a prominent role in Mexico's history. Three major events took place in Querétaro alone: In 1848 the Mexican-American War ended with the signing of the Treaty of Guadalupe Hidalgo; in 1867 Austrian Maximilian of Hapsburg, crowned emperor of Mexico by Napoleon III of France, was executed in the hills north of town; 50 years later the Mexican Constitution was signed here.

The heartland today honors the events and people that helped to shape modern Mexico. In ornate cathedrals or bucolic plazas, down narrow alleyways or high atop hillsides, the traveler will discover monuments—and remnants—of a heroic past. During numerous fiestas, the visitor can savor the region's historic spirit. On a night filled with fireworks, off-key music, and tireless celebrants, it's hard not to be caught up in the vital expression of national pride.

Tourism is welcomed in the heartland, especially in these hard economic times, and tourists are treated naturally by residents, who go about their lives in an ordinary fashion. Families visit parks for Sunday picnics, youngsters tussle in school courtyards, old men chat in shaded plazas, and Tarascan women in traditional garb sell their wares in crowded *mercados* (markets). Though a tour operator or vendor may attempt to persuade foreign passersby to part with their money, rarely is the overture less than good-natured. Unlike areas where attractions have been specifically designed for tourism, the Bajío relies on its historic ties and the architectural integrity of its cities to appeal to the traveler.

# San Miguel de Allende

San Miguel de Allende first began luring foreigners in the late 1930s when Stirling Dickinson, an American, and prominent locals founded an art school in this mountainous settlement. The school, now called the Instituto Allende, has grown in stature over the years—as has the city's reputation as a writers' and artists' colony. Walk down any cobblestoned street and you're likely to see residents of various national origins. Some come to study at the Instituto Allende or the Academia Hispano-Americana, some to escape the harsh northern winters, and still others to retire.

Cultural offerings in this town of about 110,000 reflect its large American community. There are literary readings, art shows, a lending library, and aerobics classes. Nevertheless, San Miguel retains its Mexican characteristics and warrants further exploration. The town was declared a national monument in 1926. Wandering down streets lined with 18th-century mansions, you'll also discover fountains, monuments, and churches, all reminders of the city's illustrious —and sometimes notorious—past. The onetime headquarters of the Spanish Inquisition in New Spain, for example, is located at the corner of Calles Hernández Macías and Pila Seca; the former Inquisition jail stands across the way.

## Arriving and Departing

**By Plane**  **Continental** (tel. 800/525–0280), **Mexicana** (tel. 800/531–7921), and **Aeromexico** (tel. 800/237–6639) now offer international service from Chicago, Houston, and Los Angeles to nearby **Leon International Airport,** which is one hour from San Miguel. Taxis from the airport to downtown cost about $25.

**By Car**  Driving time from Mexico City to San Miguel takes roughly four hours via Route 57 (to Querétaro) and Route 111 (Querétaro to San Miguel). The newly completed freeway saves a half hour in travel time by bypassing Querétero. Cars can be rented at various outlets in Mexico City; in San Miguel, **Renta de Autos Gama** (Calle de Hidalgo 3, tel. 465/2–08–15), has a limited selection of standard-shift compacts available.

**By Train**  First-class train service between Mexico City and San Miguel is available daily via the **Mexican National Railways** (tel. 5/547–5819 or 5/547–3190). The *Constitucionalista* departs Mexico City at 9 AM and arrives in San Miguel at 2 PM; the reverse trip leaves San Miguel at 2 PM and arrives in Mexico City at 7 PM. The round-trip fare costs $55; tickets are best purchased one day in advance. The price includes either a full breakfast or dinner. The San Miguel train station (tel. 465/2–00–07) is located on La Calzada de Estación (Station Highway).

Train service is also available from Nuevo Laredo, Mexico, near the U.S.-Mexican border at Laredo, Texas. The train leaves Nuevo Laredo at 7 PM and arrives at San Miguel at 2 PM. The return trip leaves San Miguel at 2 PM and arrives in Nuevo Laredo at 9 AM. The round-trip fare costs $110.

Train schedules are subject to change without notice. In the United States, call Mexico By Rail, tel. 800/228–3225.

**By Bus**  Direct bus service is available daily between the Central del Norte (North Bus Station) in Mexico City and the new Central de Autobuses in San Miguel. Several major lines—including **Flecha Amarilla, Herradura de Plata, Primera Plus,** and **Tres Estrellas de Oro**—offer frequent service; travel time is about four hours. Inexpensive, second-class bus service is also available from San Miguel to other area cities.

## Getting Around

San Miguel de Allende is best negotiated on foot, keeping in mind two pieces of advice. The city is 1,870 meters (more than a mile) above sea level, so visitors not accustomed to high altitudes may tire quickly during their first few days there. Streets are paved with rugged cobblestone, and some of them do not have sidewalks. Sturdy footwear, such as athletic or other rubber-soled shoes, is therefore highly recommended.

**By Taxi**  Taxis can easily be hailed on the street or found at taxi stands such as **Sitio Allende** in the main plaza (tel. 465/2–05–50), **Sitio San Francisco** on Calle Juárez (tel. 465/2–02–90 or 465/2–01–92), or **Sitio San Felipe** on Calle Mesones (tel. 465/2–04–40). Flat rates to the bus terminal, train station, and other parts of the city apply.

## Important Addresses and Numbers

**Tourist Information**   The **Delegación de Turismo** is located in the center of town on the southeast corner of Plaza Principal (also called El Jardín) to the left of La Parroquia (parish church). Climb the steps of the outdoor restaurant La Terraza and turn right; the tourist office is next to the pizza stand. Most of the brochures here are in Spanish, but an English-speaking staff member can help with basic information. You can also pick up a good map of the city that locates major hotels, restaurants, and historic attractions. *Plaza Principal s/n, tel. 465/2–17–47. Open weekdays 10–2:45 and 5–7, Sat. 10–1, Sun. 10–noon.*

**U.S. Consulate**   The U.S. Consular agent is Colonel Phil Maher. *Calle Hernández Macías 72, tel. 465/2–23–57 during office hours; tel. 465/2–00–68 or 465/2–09–80 for emergencies. Open Mon. and Wed. 9–1 and 4–7; Tues. and Thurs. 4–7.*

**Emergencies**   **Police** (tel. 465/2–00–22). **Ambulance–Red Cross** (tel. 465/2–16–16).

*Hospital*   The staff at **Union Médica** (Calle de San Francisco 50, tel. 465/2–22–33 and 465/2–17–61) can refer you to an English-speaking doctor.

*Pharmacies*   San Miguel has many pharmacies, but American residents recommend **Botica Agundis,** where English speakers are often on hand. *Calle de Canal 26, tel. 465/2–11–98. Open daily 10 AM–midnight.*

**Money Exchange**   Banks will change dollars or traveler's checks at certain hours of the day, usually in the morning. Lines, however, are often long and move slowly. A better bet is the **Casa de Cambio.** *Calle del Correo 15, tel. 465/2–17–06. Open weekdays 9–2 and 4–6, Sat. 9–12.*

**English-language Bookstores**   **El Colibrí,** *Sollana 30, tel. 2–07–51. Open Mon.–Sat. 10–2 and 4–7.*
**Lagundi,** *Calle de Canal 21, tel. 2–08–30. Open Mon.–Sat. 10–2 and 4–7, Sun. 11–3.*

**Travel Agencies**   Major agencies are **Viajes Vértiz** (American Express representative at Calle de Hidalgo 1A, tel. 465/2–18–56 and 465/2–04–09; fax 465/2–16–95); **Viajes San Miguel** (Hotel Real de Minas, tel. 465/2–25–37); and the **Travel Institute of San Miguel** (Calle Cuna de Allende 11, tel. 465/2–00–78).

**Business Services**   **La Conexion** (Aldama 1, tel./fax 465/218–87 or 465/2–23–12) offers 24-hour answering and fax service, a Mexico address for receiving mail, lock boxes, a Macintosh computer center, and other services.

### Guided Tours

The **Travel Institute of San Miguel** (tel. 465/2–00–78) offers two walking tours of the city conducted in English. At press time, each cost $10 per person. Its orientation tour takes in the central plaza, churches, mansions, museums, and public buildings, and also provides practical advice on the town's pharmacies, newsstands, library, and post office. The tour of historic San Miguel takes travelers by minibus to El Mirador (the lookout). Visitors then walk down a winding cobblestoned street to El Chorro natural springs, through Juárez Park, past the bullring, to La Parroquia, and finally to the Allende Museum. They also offer guided tours of other sections of the Bajio.

## Exploring

*Numbers in the margin correspond to points of interest on the San Miguel de Allende map.*

Most of San Miguel's historic sights are clustered in the downtown area and can be seen in a couple of hours. Begin at the **❶** main plaza, commonly called **El Jardín** (the garden). Seated on one of its gray wrought-iron benches, you'll quickly get a feel for the town: Old men with canes exchange tales, youngsters in school uniform bustle by, fruit vendors hawk their wares, and bells from the nearby La Parroquia pierce the thin mountain air at each quarter hour.

**❷** Leaving El Jardín, cross Calle del Correo to reach **La Parroquia** on the south side of the plaza. This imposing pink Gothic-style parish church, made of local *cantera* sandstone, was designed in the late 19th century by self-trained Indian mason Ceferino Gutiérrez, who sketched his designs in the sand with a stick. Gutiérrez was purportedly inspired by postcards of European Gothic cathedrals. Since the postcards gave no hint of what the back of those cathedrals looked like, the posterior of La Parroquia was done in quintessential Mexican style.

La Parroquia still functions as a house of worship, though its interior has been changed over the years. Gilded wood altars, for example, were replaced with neoclassical stone altars. The original bell, cast in 1732, still calls parishioners to mass several times daily.

**❸** Three blocks from La Parroquia, the **Iglesia de San Francisco,** on Calle Juárez, has one of the finest Churrigueresque facades in the state of Guanajuato. (José Churriguera, a 17th-century Spanish architect, was noted for his extravagantly decorative Baroque style.) Built in the late 18th century, the church was financed by donations from wealthy patrons and by revenue from bullfights. Topping the elaborately carved exterior is the image of Saint Francis of Assisi; below are sculptures of Saint John and Our Lady of Sorrows, as well as a crucifix.

Continue a few steps north on Calle Juárez until you reach Calle Mesones and the colorful **Mercado Ignacio Ramírez.** During the week the market occupies the small plaza directly in front of the Oratorio de San Felipe Neri and spills over onto the surrounding streets (for about six blocks). This market is particularly active on Sundays, when country folk come to town with pigs, chickens, and other livestock and succulent produce. During the week, rows of fresh fruits and vegetables are supplemented by racks of cheaply made clothing, inexpensive American toys, and blaring Mexican-made tapes and records. The dome of the **❹** **Oratorio de San Felipe Neri** is visible just beyond the market. This church, located across the market plaza on Calle de los Insurgentes, was built by local Indians in 1712. The pink stone of the eastern facade (with its figure of Our Lady of Solitude) is a remnant of the original chapel; its newer southern front was built in an ornate Baroque style. In 1734 the wealthy Count of Canal paid for an addition to the Oratorio. His **Templo de Santa Casa de Loreto** (dedicated to the Virgin of Loreto) is just be-

Heading downhill, walk briefly through a neighborhood of whitewashed houses before reaching the north entrance to ⑩ **Parque Benito Juárez,** a favorite of joggers, sweethearts, and children. The five-acre park—the largest in San Miguel—is a shaded labyrinth of evergreens, palm trees, and gardens. Take a few minutes to stroll around, or find a bench and observe the activity around you.

Return to the north rim of the park, where Calle Aldama turns into Calle Diezmo Viejo. Continue until the imposing terra-cotta-colored La Huerta Santa Elena is in front of you. From ⑪ here turn left and walk one block uphill to reach the **Lavandería,** one of San Miguel's most endearing places. At this outdoor public laundry—a collection of cement tubs set above Juárez Park—local women gather daily to wash clothes and gossip as their predecessors have done for centuries. Though some women claim to have more efficient washing facilities at home, the lure of the spring-fed troughs—not to mention the chance to gossip—brings them daily to this shaded courtyard.

Calle de Recreo, the road above the Lavandería, heads north back toward the plaza. At times narrow and dusty, it leads uphill past quiet pastel-colored residences and lovely views of the surrounding mountains. To return to town, follow Recreo north for several blocks until you reach Calle del Correo. Make a left, and in three blocks you'll be back at the main plaza.

⑫ For energetic exploration, consider a climb to **El Mirador** (the lookout). One block before town, turn right off Recreo onto Calle Hospicio. Follow Hospicio for three blocks until you reach Calle Pedro Vargas, a narrow, busy two-way street. Make a right and head uphill. Soon you'll notice a statue of Ignacio Allende on your left; a panorama of the city, mountains, and reservoir will be below on your right. The vista is most commanding at sunset, and chances are you won't be alone, as El Mirador is popular with both locals and tourists.

The walk back to town is an approximately 15-minute downhill trek. (Calle Pedro Vargas hits Calle del Correo, which takes you back to the plaza.) Taxis are usually available and the trip back should cost no more than $1.

---

**Off the Beaten Track**

Roughly 50 kilometers (30 miles) north of San Miguel via Route 51 is the town of **Dolores Hidalgo,** which played an important role in the fight for independence. It was here, before dawn on September 16, 1810, that Father Miguel Hidalgo—the local priest—gave an impassioned sermon to his clergy that ended with the cry, "Mexicanos, Viva México!" At 11 PM on September 15, politicians throughout the land repeat the "grito," signaling the start of Independence Day celebrations. On September 16 (and only on this day), the bell in Hidalgo's parish church is rung.

**Casa Hidalgo,** the house where the patriot lived, is now a museum. It contains copies of important letters Hidalgo sent or received and other independence memorabilia. *Calle Morelos 1, tel. 468/20–1–71. Open Tues.–Sat. 10–6, Sun. 10–5. Admission: about $3.*

The town is also known for its output of hand-painted ceramics, most prominently tiles and tableware. Dolores Hidalgo can be reached easily by bus from San Miguel de Allende. Buses depart frequently from the Central de Autobuses; travel time is about one hour.

## Shopping

For centuries San Miguel's artisans have been creating a wide variety of crafts ranging from straw products to metalwork. Though some boutiques in town (including a branch of Benetton) may be a bit pricey, there are good buys on silver, brass, tin, woven cotton goods, and folk art.

**Jewelry** Established in 1963, **Joyería David** has an extensive selection of gold, silver, copper, and brass jewelry, all made on the premises. A number of pieces contain Mexican opals, amethysts, topaz, malachite, and turquoise. *Calle Zacateros 53, tel. 465/2–00–56. Open Mon.–Sat. 9–8. AE, V.*

Other recommended jewelers include:

**Beckmann Joyería,** *Calle Hernández Macías 115, tel. 465/2–16–13. Open Mon.–Sat. 9–2 and 4–7. AE, V.*
**Platería Cerro Blanco,** *Calle de Canal 17, tel. 465/2–05–02. Open Mon.–Sat. 11–2 and 5–8. AE, MC, V.*
**Platería y Joyería Julio,** *Calle del Correo 8, tel. 465/2–02–48. Open Mon.–Sat. 9–2 and 4–8, Sun. 9–2. AE, MC, V.*

**Clothing** **El Pegaso** sells hand-embroidered blouses and dresses from Mexico and Guatemala as well as leather goods, hand-painted masks, jewelry and men's and children's clothing. The second floor contains rare folk art. A small café is located in the middle of the store. *Corregidora 6, tel. 465/2–13–51. Open Mon.–Sat. 10–2 and 4–7:30. AE, MC, V.*

For chic designer clothing, try **Casa Canal,** *Calle de Canal 3, tel. 465/2–04–79, fax 465/2–10–86. Open weekdays 9–2, 4–7; Sat. 10–2, 4–8. AE, V.* **De Selva,** *Calle de Selva, Umarán 1. Open daily 10–7. No credit cards.* **Sidell,** *Jesus, 21, tel. 465/2–04–86. Open Mon.–Sat. 10–1:30 and 4:30–6:30. MC, V.* A **Benetton** outlet is located in the Plaza Colonial, a minimall with an upscale restaurant, a coffee shop, an English-Spanish bookstore, and designer shops. *Calle de Canal 21, tel. 465/2–08–30. Open Mon. and Tues. 10:30–8, Wed. and Thurs. 10:30–2 and 4–8. Fri. 10:30–8, Sat. 10:30–5:30. AE, MC, V.*

**Brass and Tinware** Several stores in town sell locally crafted metal objects, such as plates and trays, chests, mirrors, and decorative animals and birds. The best selections can be found at: **La Carreta de Arte,** *Calle Zacateros 26-A, tel. 465/2–17–32, open Mon.–Sat. 9–2 and 4–8, Sun. 9–2, MC, V;* and **Casa Cohen,** *Reloj 12, tel. 465/2–14–34, open Mon.–Sat. 9–2 and 4–6. MC, V.*

**Folk Art** For hand-painted masks, ceremonial art objects, and other regional handicrafts, try **Cactus,** *Calle Zacateros 39. Open Mon.–Sat. 10–3 and 5–8, Sun. 11–4. AE, MC, V.* **La Calaca,** *Mesones 93. Open Mon.–Wed., Fri. and Sat. 11–2 and 4–7, Sun. 11–2. No credit cards.* **Artes de México,** *Aurora 47 at the Dolores Hidalgo exit, tel. 465/2–07–64, open Mon.–Sat. 9–7:30, AE, DC, MC, V;* **Arte Reve Tonatiu/Meztli,** *Calle de Umarán 24, tel. 465/2–08–69, open Mon.–Sat. 10–2 and 5–8, Sun. 10–4, MC, V;* and **Casa Maxwell,** *Calle de Canal 14, tel. 465/2–02–47, open weekdays 9–2 and 4–7, Sat. 10–2 and 4–8, AE, MC, V.*

## Sports

**Participant Sports**  Travelers who enjoy the sporting life will find good facilities for swimming, tennis, horseback riding, and golf at deluxe and first-class hotels situated near the Instituto Allende or on the outskirts of town. (The San Miguel tourist office can provide a list of these properties.) The **Hotel Hacienda Taboada** (Km 8 on the Dolores Hidalgo Hwy., tel. 465/2–08–50) has simmering thermal pools that are open to the public for a nominal fee. The **Club de Golf Malanquin** (Km 3 on the Celaya Hwy., tel. 465/2–05–16) features a heated pool, steam baths, tennis courts, and nine holes of golf, all of which are open to the public.

**Spectator Sports**  Visitors who want to witness the pageantry of a traditional Mexican bullfight can do so at the **Plaza de Toros Oriente** (situated off Calle de Recreo) several times a year. The most important contest takes place during the last week of September when St. Michael the Archangel, the town's patron saint, is commemorated. Posters announcing fights are set up in El Jardín in the center of town and at the Fonda La Mesa del Matador restaurant at Calle Hernández Macías 76.

## Dining

For its size, San Miguel has a surprising number of international restaurants (about 170 at last count). The recent influx of Americans has given rise to new Tex-Mex and health-food establishments; a European influence has contributed to nearly authentic French, Italian, and Spanish cuisines. Regional Mexican food is available in a variety of price ranges. Much of this fare is made from pork, chicken, or ground beef and often broiled, fried, or covered with a bread-crumb batter. Dishes are prepared with onions or garlic and served with a red or green chile sauce.

Highly recommended restaurants are indicated by a star ★.

| Category | Cost* |
| --- | --- |
| Very Expensive | over $20 |
| Expensive | $15–$20 |
| Moderate | $8–$15 |
| Inexpensive | under $8 |

*\*per person, excluding drinks and service*

**Very Expensive**  **La Vendimia.** Fast becoming one of San Miguel's most excellent restaurants, La Vendimia offers cuisine described by chef Jack Jesse as Continental with a touch of southern California. In a setting designed and furnished by a local Mexican artist, the British cordon bleu Jesse serves such dishes as the house salad of scallops and almonds in a warm soya dressing, sea bass in shrimp sauce and delicious gazpacho, oysters pancetta, fillet of beef Toreado as well as English high tea and fish-and-chips. The happy hour on the patio from 6 to 8 PM Monday–Saturday features flamenco and other lively guitar music. *Hidalgo 12, tel. 465/2–26–45. Reservations suggested. Dress: casual. AE, MC, V.*

**Expensive** **La Antigua Restaurant y Tapa Bar.** The name of this restaurant is something of a joke, as it only opened in 1990. A cheerful room with fewer than a dozen tables (each with a baby-blue tablecloth and a vase of orange carnations) and a polished wood bar that can seat up to 15 people, La Antigua puts its clientele in the mood for a large variety of tapas with its European café furniture and Spanish bolero music. Among its specialties are *queso antiguo*, baked cheese with chilies; *chisterra*, a sliced and fried Spanish-style sausage; *camarones con tocineta*, jumbo shrimp fried with bacon; and *pulpo antiguo*, squid sautéed in garlic and herbs. All dishes are served with bread or tortillas. *Calle Canal 9, tel. 465/2–25–86. Reservations accepted. Dress: casual. AE, MC, V. Closed Tues.*

**La Princesa.** More upscale restaurants have opened in San Miguel recently, but La Princesa is still *the* place to go for intimate dining. The romantic ambience is enhanced by cloth-covered tables, dark wood paneling, lazily turning ceiling fans, a large wine selection, and musicians who entertain from 8 PM to 3 AM. The Executive Menu, served daily 1–8 PM, includes soup, one of eight entrées (ranging from fillet of red snapper to Mexican-style stuffed peppers), dessert, coffee or tea, and a complimentary margarita. After 8 PM the menu features steak dishes, including chateaubriand for two, and the prices climb. *Calle de Recreo 5, tel. 465/2–14–03. Reservations not accepted. Dress: informal. AE, MC, V.*

**Moderate** **Fonda Meson de San José.** On a tree-shaded cobblestone patio
★ inside a complex of small shops, this well-established restaurant offers German as well as Mexican cuisines. Owner-chef Angela Merkel is enthusiastic about her roulade, potato pancakes, and German chocolate cake and once a month invites other local chefs to display their talents. The German buffet, originally offered for Oktoberfest, is in great demand. *Mesones 38, no phone. Reservations not accepted. Dress: casual. No credit cards. Open daily 1–10 PM.*

**Mamá Mía.** It might seem odd to order Italian food in Mexico, but Mamá Mía has a satisfying assortment of pastas and pizzas, as well as a decent *fettuccine bolognese* and *spaghetti parmesana*. House specials include *fettuccine Alex* (flat egg noodles with white wine, ham, cream, and mushrooms) and *fettuccine à la Mexicana* (with ground sausage, peppers, onions, and tomatoes). Folk musicians entertain on the lush outdoor patio come dusk. *Calle de Umarán 8, tel. 465/2–20–63. Reservations not accepted. Dress: informal. MC, V.*

**Inexpensive** **Quinta Loreto.** Although it is a little off the beaten track, this restaurant—located in a motel with the same name—opens off a large garden. Diners have the option of sitting either in the large, plain dining room or on the terrace overlooking the garden. The generous portions and the daily *comida corrida* (fixed-menu lunch) make this an excellent choice for low-priced dining. *Calle Loreto 15, tel. 465/2–00–42. Reservations not accepted. Dress: informal. No credit cards.*

## Lodging

San Miguel has a wide selection of hotels ranging from cozy bed-and-breakfasts to elegant all-suite properties. Rooms fill up quickly during summer and winter seasons, when northern tourists migrate here in droves. Make reservations several months in advance if you plan to visit at these times.

Highly recommended accommodations are indicated by a star
★.

| Category | Cost* |
|---|---|
| Very Expensive | over $90 |
| Expensive | $60–$90 |
| Moderate | $25–$60 |
| Inexpensive | under $25 |

*All prices are for a standard double room, excluding 10% tax.*

**Expensive–** **Casa de Sierra Nevada.** Once the home of the archbishop of Gua-
**Very Expensive** najuato and the marquise of Sierra Nevada, this elegant coun-
**★** try-style inn (built in 1850) hosted George Bush in 1981 and
continues to attract ambassadors, diplomats, heads of state,
film stars, and bullfighters. Its complex of four colonial buildings, on either side of a cobblestoned street a few blocks from
La Parroquia, contains 18 individually decorated suites and
five standard rooms. Lace curtains, handwoven rugs, chandeliers, and prints by artist Diego Rivera adorn some rooms; fireplaces, cozy private terraces, and skylights enhance others.
From the terrace of room No. 1, there's an excellent view of La
Parroquia. *Calle Hospicio 35, 37700, tel. 465/2–04–15 and 465/
2–18–95, or 800/223–9868; 800/372–1323 or 212/696–1323 from
N.Y.; fax 465/2–23–37. 18 rooms with bath. Facilities: formal
restaurant; multilingual receptionist; facials, massage, and
acupuncture (by appointment only); medical evacuation; pool
under construction. No credit cards.*

**Expensive** **Villa Jacaranda.** An all-suite hotel located near the Parque
Benito Juárez, the Villa Jacaranda boasts a full range of amenities. Rooms, though unimaginatively decorated, have space
heaters and cable TVs (with channels from the United States).
The hotel's Cine/Bar shows American movies Tuesday–Saturday at 7:30 PM and live sports events on a giant screen. The price
of admission—roughly $3—includes a drink. *Calle Aldama 53,
37700, tel. 465/2–10–15 or 465/2–08–11, fax 465/2–08–83. 15
suites with bath. Facilities: restaurant, pool, Jacuzzi, cable
TV. AE, MC, V.*

**Moderate** **La Mansión del Bosque.** Located on a quiet side street across
**★** from the Parque Benito Juárez, this renovated hacienda
opened as a guest house and restaurant in 1968. Its American
owners, George and Ruth Hyba, cater to long-term guests in
the winter and more transient visitors in the off-season. The
hotel, which operates on a Modified American Plan that includes breakfast and dinner, has guest rooms with such homey
touches as handwoven cotton spreads, locally made throw rugs
and artifacts, and bookshelves. Many rooms feature working
fireplaces as well as private, plant-filled terraces. The lounge
off the foyer has books and magazines, a telephone for long-distance calls, and a house cat that watches over the premises.
*Calle Aldama 65, 37700, tel. 465/2–02–77. 23 rooms with bath.
Facilities: restaurant, bar. No credit cards.*
**Posada de las Monjas.** This 19th-century structure has been
operating as a hotel for the past 50 years. It caters to long-term
students (from the Instituto Allende or Academia Hispano-
Americana) but welcomes guests of shorter duration. Rooms
are furnished in a colonial style, with some furniture in the old

wing looking worn enough to be authentically colonial. The rooftop public terrace has tables and lounge chairs and offers commanding views of mountains and city. Some rooms have fireplaces, and there's a communal television in the lobby. *Calle de Canal 37, 37700, tel. 465/2-01-71. 65 rooms with bath; 37 are located in a new wing. Facilities: restaurant, bar, solarium, laundry service. AE, DC, MC, V.*

★ **Posada de San Francisco.** This colonial-style property, located on the main plaza downtown, resembles an old Spanish monastery—a crucifix hangs in the lobby beneath a stone archway, and some rooms have crosses over the beds. Rooms on the plaza will appeal to people-watchers, but on weekends and during the busy season these quarters can be rather noisy. For a quieter setting, request a room on the second or third floor (some overlook nearby mountains and churches) or one inside, facing the bougainvillea-draped courtyard. *Plaza Principal 2, 37700, tel. 465/2-14-66, 465/2-00-72, or 465/2-24-25. (All three numbers also serve as fax lines). 71 rooms, suites, and junior suites with bath. Facilities: patio restaurant, bar, lounge. AE, MC, V.*

**Villa Mirasol.** Carmen Avery has taken over local art dealer Josh Klingerman's Casa de LuJo. Each of the lodging's seven rooms is decorated with original prints, oil paintings, pastels, and small sculptures. All have either a private or shared terrace; the ones facing Calle Pila Seca have beautiful vistas of the surrounding hills. Located on a quiet and secluded street no more than a 10-minute walk from the principal plaza, Villa Mirasol includes in its price a rich breakfast, such as *chilaquiles* (baked tortillas with cheese and chicken) or Mexican-style scrambled eggs with chilies, tomatoes, and onions, as well as coffee and pastries in the afternoon. A private house until 1983, most of the hotel's rooms are flooded with sunlight during the day. Its cozy and intimate atmosphere affords visitors a welcome distinction from the larger, less personal hotels in the area. It also offers its guests use of the Club de Golf free of charge. Given its size, reservations are recommended. *Pila Seca 35, 37700, tel. 465/2-15-64. 7 rooms with bath. Facilities: cable TV. MC, V.*

## The Arts and Nightlife

San Miguel, long known as an artists' colony, continues to nurture that tradition today. Galleries, museums, and art shops line the streets near El Jardín, and two government-run salons—at **Bellas Artes** (Calle Hernández Macías 75) and the **Instituto Allende** (Ancha de San Antonio 20)—showcase the work of a variety of Mexican artists. For a sampling of regional talent, visit the **Galería San Miguel** (Plaza Principal 14, tel. 465/2-04-54), **Galería Atenea** (Calle Cuna de Allende 15, tel. 465/2-07-85), and the **Kligerman Gallery** (Calle de Umarán 6, tel. 465/2-09-51). If a rather large painting or photograph strikes your fancy, don't despair: Some gallery owners will ship your newfound treasure back to the States for you.

Nightlife in San Miguel is also plentiful. On most evenings you can readily satisfy a whim for a literary reading, an American movie, a theatrical production, or a turn on a disco dance floor. The most up-to-date listings of events can be found in the English paper *Atención San Miguel*, published every Friday. The bulletin board at the public library (Calle de los Insurgentes 25) is also a good source of current events.

**La Taberna de los Reyes** (Hidalgo 3, no phone) features dance music from 9 until 2 Thursday through Sunday, with dinner/theater on Wednesday at 9:30. Other places that feature live music include: **Pancho and Lefty's** (Calle Mesones 99, tel. 465/2–19–58), rock, jazz, and blues bands, depending on the night; **La Fragua** (Calle Cuna de Allende 3, tel. 465/2–11–44), traditional Mexican bands; **Mamá Mía** (Calle de Umarán 8, tel. 465/2–20–63), Peruvian folk music and classical guitar; **El Jardín** (San Francisco 4, tel. 465/2–17–06), piano bar; **Laberintos Disco** (Calle Ancha de San Antonio 7, tel. 465/ 2–03–62); and **El Ring Disco Club** (Calle de Hidalgo 25, tel. 465/2–19–98).

# Guanajuato

Once Mexico's most prominent silver-mining city, Guanajuato is a colonial gem, tucked into the mountains at 6,700 feet. This provincial state capital is distinguished by twisting cobble-stoned alleyways, pastel-walled houses, 15 shaded plazas, and a vast subterranean roadway (where a rushing river once flowed). In the center of town is Alhóndiga de Granaditas—an 18th-century grain-storage facility that was the site of the first battle in Mexico's War of Independence from Spain.

The city comes alive in mid-October with the International Cervantes Festival, a two-week-long celebration of the arts. Day-to-day affairs, however, continue as usual. Students still rush to class with books tucked under their arms, women eye fresh produce at the Mercado Hidalgo, and old men utter greetings from behind whitewashed doorways. On weekend nights, *estudiantinas* (student minstrels dressed as medieval troubadours) serenade the public in the city squares.

At first Guanajuato's underground roadways and poorly marked streets may seem daunting. Armed with a good map and a sense of adventure, however, you can enjoy exploring the city's hidden passages. If you do get lost, just remember that the top of the Alhóndiga (which can be seen from many spots in town) points north, and the spires of the Basílica Colegiata Nuestra Señora de Guanajuato, at the Plaza de la Paz, point south.

## Arriving and Departing

**By Plane**   **Aeroméxico** (tel. 800/237–6639) offers service from Mexico City to Léon **International Airport,** 34 miles north of Guanajuato. The one-hour taxi ride from the airport to town costs about $25.

**By Car**   Guanajuato is 432 kilometers (268 miles) northwest of Mexico City via Route 57 (to Querétaro) and Route 45 (through Celaya and Irapuato), approximately a five-hour drive.

**By Train**   **Mexican National Railways'** first-class *Constitucionalista* leaves Mexico City daily at 7 AM and arrives in Guanajuato at 2 PM; the return trip leaves Guanajuato at 2:30 PM and arrives in Mexico City at 9:30 PM. The round-trip fare costs $60, including a boxed meal. Tickets should be purchased one day in advance.

Train schedules are subject to change without notice. In the United States, call Mexico By Rail, tel. 800/228–3225.

**By Bus** Direct bus service is available between the Central del Norte (North Bus Station) in Mexico City and Guanajuato's Central Camionera. Several lines—including **Flecha Amarilla** and **Estrella Blanca**—offer hourly service; travel time is about five hours. Frequent inexpensive bus service is available from Guanajuato to other Bajío cities.

## Getting Around

Don't bother with a car in Guanajuato. Many of the attractions are within strolling distance of one another and located between Avenida Juárez and Calle Positos, the city's two major north–south arteries. The twisting subterranean roadway—El Subterráneo—also has a primarily north–south orientation.

**By Taxi** Nonmetered taxis can be hailed on the street or found at *sitios* (taxi stands) near the Jardín la Unión, Plaza de la Paz, and Mercado Hidalgo. Traffic moves north on Avenida Juárez and Calle Positos and south along the underground road system.

## Important Addresses and Numbers

**Tourist** The **Guanajuato tourist office** is at Plaza de la Paz 14, at the
**Information** back of a courtyard (tel. 473/2–15–74, 473/2–00–86, or 473/2–19–84, fax 473/2–41–52; open weekdays 8:30–7:30, weekends 10–2). There is also a tourist information kiosk at the Central Camionera bus station. Maps and brochures (mostly in Spanish) are available at both locations.

**Emergencies** **Police** (tel. 473/2–02–66). **Ambulance-Red Cross** (tel. 473/2–04–87). Since few people in Guanajuato have a good command of English, in an emergency it's best to contact your hotel manager or the tourist office.

*Hospital* **Hospital General** (tel. 473/2–08–59 or 473/2–08–50).

**Travel Agencies** **Viajes Georama,** the American Express representative, is at Plaza de la Paz 34 (tel. 473/2–59–09, 473/2–19–54, or 473/2–51–01, fax 473/2–35–97). **Wagon-Lits Viajes** has an office in the lobby of Hotel Real de Minas (Calle Nejayote 17, tel. 473/2–18–36 or 473/2–23–11). **Viajes Mandel,** is at Plaza de la Paz 62 (tel. 473/2–60–37 or 473/2–71–95, fax 473/2–60–89).

## Guided Tours

**Transporte Exclusivo de Turismo** (Av. Juárez and Calle 5 de Mayo, tel. 473/2–59–68) is a kiosk that offers several tours of Guanajuato and its environs. A 3½-hour tour, with an English-speaking guide, of the Museum of Mummies, the church and mines of Valenciana, the monument to Pípila, the Panoramic Highway, subterranean streets, and residential neighborhoods costs $18 per person. A five-hour evening tour of the Pípila monument and one or two nightclubs, including one drink, is about $20 per person. Estudiantinas perform during the weekend tours.

## Exploring

*Numbers in the margin correspond to points of interest on the Guanajuato map.*

Many of Guanajuato's major attractions are located within an oblong downtown loop. After picking up a detailed city map at the tourist office (corner of Av. Juárez and Calle 5 de Mayo), find the market by walking south on Avenida Juárez 1½ blocks ❶ until you reach **Mercado Hidalgo** on your right. The 1910 cast-iron-and-glass structure is reminiscent of English Victorian stations and markets. Though the balcony stalls try to lure tourists with tacky T-shirts and cheap plastic toys, the lower level is replete with authentic local wares, including fresh produce, peanuts, honey-drenched nut candies, and colorful basketry. Vendors line the sidewalks in front of the market, hawking flowers and local crafts.

As you leave the market, continue south on Avenida Juárez until the road splits near the Jardín Reforma. (Av. Juárez, crowded and heavy with exhaust fumes, veers to the right; keep to the left and cut down Calle Reforma, a short alleyway lined with shops.) Bear right at the end of Calle Reforma and you'll come to two pleasant courtyards: Plaza San Roque, which hosts outdoor performances during the fall Cervantes Festival, and, just beneath it, Plaza San Fernando, a shady square where many bookfairs are held.

This short detour will return you to Avenida Juárez, where the ❷ road climbs slightly toward **Plaza de la Paz**. Built from 1895 to 1898, this square is surrounded by some of the city's finest colonial buildings. Chief among them is the 18th-century residence of the count of Rul and Valenciana, owner of the country's richest silver mine of the time. The two-story structure, located at the corner of Avenida Juárez and Callejón del Estudiante, was designed by famed Mexican architect Eduardo Tresguerras.

❸ Toward the back of the plaza is the imposing **Basílica Colegiata de Nuestra Señora de Guanajuato,** a 17th-century Baroque church painted a striking yellow. Inside is the oldest Christian statue in Mexico: the highly venerated jewel-laden 8th-century wood statue of the Virgin, which, as one story goes, was a gift in 1557 from Philip II of Spain. On the Friday preceding Good Friday, miners—accompanied by floats and mariachi bands—parade to the basilica to pay homage to the Lady of Guanajuato.

As you pass the plaza, bear to the right and continue south ❹ along Avenida Juárez. Within a few blocks on your left is **Jardín la Unión,** a tree-lined plaza that is Guanajuato's central square. On Thursdays and Sundays musical performances take place in the bandshell. At other times, impromptu groups of musicians break into song along the plaza's shaded tile walkways.

**Time Out**   For alfresco dining, try the terrace at the **Hotel Museo Posada Santa Fe.** The menu includes pricey specialties, such as broiled trout and chicken with mole sauce, but a cappuccino and slice of cake will cost about $2. *Plaza Principal at Jardín la Unión 12, tel. 473/2–00–84. Open 7 AM–11 PM. AE, DC, MC, V.*

Another outdoor café, **El Agora,** located down an alley off the plaza's southeast corner, has cheaper offerings. A four-course lunch, including soup, rice, an entrée, and dessert, costs less than $3. *El Agora del Baratillo, tel. 473/2–33–00. Open 8 AM–10 PM. No credit cards.*

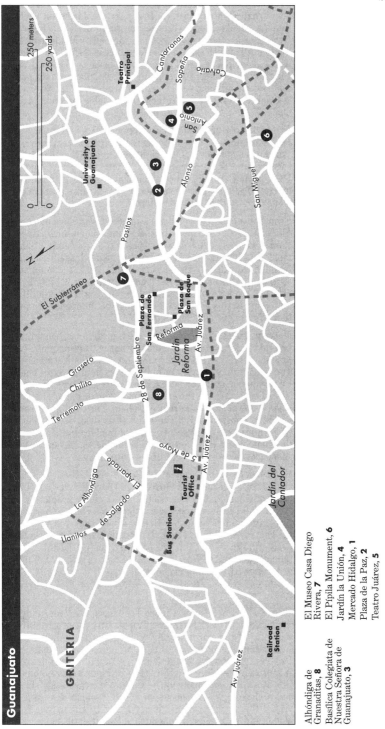

Alhóndiga de
Granaditas, **8**
Basílica Colegiata de
Nuestra Señora de
Guanajuato, **3**

El Museo Casa Diego
Rivera, **7**
El Pípila Monument, **6**
Jardín la Unión, **4**
Mercado Hidalgo, **1**
Plaza de la Paz, **2**
Teatro Juárez, **5**

❺ The ornate **Teatro Juárez** is just past the Jardín on Calle de Sopeña. Adorned with bronze lion sculptures and figures of Greek muses, the theater was inaugurated by Mexican dictator Porfirio Díaz in 1903 with a performance of *Aida*. It now serves as the principal venue of the annual Cervantes Festival, when the city resounds with symphony recitals, plays, dance performances, movies, and *callejoneadas* (student street serenades). A brief tour of the plush interior is available for a nominal fee. *Open Tues.–Sun. 9:15–1:45 and 5–7:45.*

❻ From Teatro Juárez you can walk or take a taxi or bus to **El Pípila Monument**. If you choose to walk (it's a steep climb that takes nearly an hour), bear right on Calle de Sopeña just past the theater. A sign marked *Al Pípila* will direct you onto Callejón de Calvario, which eventually leads to the hillside memorial. If you prefer to save energy, you can hire a taxi or catch a bus marked Pípila from the Jardín.

From the monument you'll see a splendid panorama of the city. You can also pay tribute to the young miner, nicknamed El Pípila, who was one of the martyrs of the independence movement. El Pípila crept into the Alhóndiga de Granaditas (where Spanish Royalists were hiding) and, with a stone shield strapped to his back, set the front door ablaze. El Pípila died, but the Spanish troops were captured by Father Miguel Hidalgo's army in this early battle, giving the independence forces their first major military victory.

Heading back to town, pick up Calle Cantarranas, a main street behind the Jardín la Unión. You'll pass the **University of Guanajuato** (tel. 473/2–41–50) on your right. This institution was begun as a Jesuit seminary in 1732 (the original Baroque church, La Compañia, still stands next door) and became a state university in 1945. Among the school's most famous alumni is Diego Rivera, one of Mexico's great muralists. The current university building, constructed in the 1950s, was designed to blend in with the town's architecture, but its modern interior betrays the colonial facade. If you do wander inside, check out the bulletin boards for notices of cultural events in town.

Head briefly uphill past middle-class residences. This road, ❼ Calle Positos, leads to **El Museo Casa Diego Rivera**—the birthplace of Guanajuato's illustrious son. On view are family portraits, the bed in which Rivera slept as a child, other family furniture, and 97 works by Rivera, among them his studies for the controversial mural that was commissioned for Rockefeller Center in New York City. The painting, completed in 1933, contained a portrait of Russian revolutionary Vladimir Lenin and was removed immediately after it was first displayed. *Calle Positos 47. Open Tues.–Sat. 10–1:30 and 4–6:30, Sun. 10–2:30.*

Calle Positos weaves past more residences and eventually becomes Calle 28 de Septiembre. The massive stone structure on ❽ the left with horizontal slit windows is the **Alhóndiga de Granaditas**, one of the city's most prominent attractions. This 18th-century grain-storage facility was a fortress during the War of Independence and the site of El Pípila's courageous act. It is now a state museum with exhibits on local history, crafts, and archaeology. The hooks on which Spanish Royalists displayed the decapitated heads of Father Hidalgo, Ignacio Allende, and two other independence leaders still hang on the exterior. *Calle 28 de Septiembre #6, tel. 473/2–11–12. Admission: about $3, Sun. free. Open Tues.–Sat. 10–2 and 4–6, Sun. 10–4. Group tours for up to 30 people are available during museum hours.*

A little more than a mile north from the Alhóndiga is the **Iglesia de San Cayetano,** known all over Guanajuato as **La Valenciana.** Constructed over 20 years in the latter part of the 18th century, it is one of the most well-known colonial churches in all of Mexico. The pink stone facade is brilliantly, baroquely ornate. Inside are three altars, each hand-carved in wood and covered in gilt, in separate styles: Plateresque, Chiaroscuro, and Baroque. There are also fine examples of religious painting from the viceregal period. La Valenciana is included in the guided tour of the city; there are also frequent buses from the center.

Return to Calle 5 de Mayo, one block north of the Alhóndiga. If you make a left, you'll be back at Avenida Juárez, where you began your journey. From here you can take a taxi to the **Museo de la Momias,** at the north end of town. At the museum, mummified human corpses—once buried in the nearby municipal cemetery—are on display. Until the law was amended in 1958, if a gravesite had not yet been paid for, the corpse was removed after five years to make room for new arrivals. Because of the mineral properties of the local soil, these cadavers (the oldest is about 100 years old) were in astonishingly good condition upon exhumation. The most gruesome are exhibited in glass cases. *Panteon Municipal. tel. 473/2–06–39. Admission: about 75 cents. Open Tues.–Sun. 9–6.*

## Dining

Guanajuato's better restaurants are located in hotels near the Jardín la Unión and on the highway to Dolores Hidalgo. For simpler fare, private establishments around town offer a good variety of Mexican and international dishes.

Highly recommended restaurants are indicated by a star ★.

| Category | Cost* |
| --- | --- |
| Very Expensive | over $20 |
| Expensive | $15–$20 |
| Moderate | $8–$15 |
| Inexpensive | under $8 |

*per person, excluding drinks and service*

**Very Expensive**
★
**El Comedor Real.** Continental cuisine served in a medieval environment defines El Comedor Real. The bright, whitewashed, and brick-domed restaurant in the Hotel Castillo Santa Cecilia serves such specialties as *filete pimiente* (steak au poivre); breaded trout with tartar sauce, and fish soup with vegetables. Troubadours perform every Friday and Saturday at 10:30 PM at La Cava, the bar next door. *Carretera a la Valenciana s/n, tel. 473/2–04–85. Reservations advised on weekends. Jacket suggested. AE, DC, MC, V.*

**Moderate**
**El Retiro.** This traditional Mexican restaurant up the street from the Teatro Juárez lives up to its name, the Retreat. Though it is often crowded for the main midday meal, at other

times you can relax with a steaming cappuccino and listen to classical music. A full comida corrida runs about $5; for more substantial fare, try the mole poblano with chicken, broiled steak with mushroom sauce, or a Spanish omelet. *Calle de Sopeña 12, tel. 473/2–06–22. Reservations not accepted. Dress: informal. MC, V.*

**Restaurant Valadez.** Dark wood-paneled walls give way to large windows overlooking the Teatro Juárez at this downtown restaurant. House dishes include *filete à la Tampiqueña* (beefsteak served with guacamole, cheese enchiladas, and beans), hamburger Valadez (topped with cheese and bacon), and crepes with tequila and blackberries. The bar serves Campari, Dubonnet, and tequila drinks for less than $2. *Jardín la Unión 3, tel. 473/2–11–57. Reservations not accepted. Dress: informal. AE, DC, MC, V.*

★ **Tasca de Los Santos.** This cozy restaurant, located across the street from the Basílica, specializes in Spanish and international cuisines. Recommended dishes include the *sopa de mariscos* (shellfish soup with shrimp, clams, and crabs), *pollo al vino blanco* (chicken in white-wine sauce with tomatoes, onions, olives, raisins, almonds, and parsley), and *filete parrilla* (grilled beef with baked potatoes and spinach). *Heuvos Reina* is a delicious light dish consisting of eggs and mushrooms baked in a cheese and wine sauce. Dine indoors or outside under white umbrellas on the Plaza, with a view of the fountain. A variety of music, ranging from French to Russian, enhances the cosmopolitan mood. *Plaza de la Paz 28, tel. 473/2–23–20. Reservations not accepted. Dress: informal. MC, V.*

**Inexpensive** **Cafeteria Nueva.** Cheap and plentiful food attracts the university crowd to this spartan eatery. A midday meal, consisting of soup, Mexican rice, a chicken or beef dish, dessert and coffee, costs about $2. The service can be slow, but vibrant music and a lively crowd will keep you entertained. While you wait, note the posters of Mexican art on the walls. *Jardín la Unión at Allende 3, tel. 473/2–40–40. Reservations not accepted. Dress: informal. No credit cards.*

## Lodging

Guanajuato's less expensive hotels are located near the bus station, along Avenida Juárez and Calle de la Alhóndiga. Moderately priced and upscale properties are near the Jardín la Unión and on the outskirts of town. It's best to secure reservations at least six months in advance if you plan to attend the Cervantes Festival, which usually runs from mid- to late October.

Highly recommended lodgings are indicated by a star ★.

| Category | Cost* |
|---|---|
| Expensive | $60–$90 |
| Moderate | $25–$60 |
| Inexpensive | under $25 |

*\*All prices are for a standard double room, excluding 10% tax.*

**Expensive** **Hotel Museo Posada Santa Fe.** This colonial-style property, located at the Jardín la Unión, has been in operation since 1862. Large historic paintings by local artist Don Manuel Leal hang in the wood-paneled lobby; a sweeping carpeted stairway leads to second-floor quarters. Each room, decorated in warm, autumnal colors, has a wood minibar, black-and-white TV, and telephone. Rooms facing the plaza can be noisy; quieter rooms face narrow alleyways. *Plaza Principal at Jardín la Unión 12, 36000, tel. 473/2–00–84 or 2–02–07, fax 473/2–46–53. 47 rooms with bath. Facilities: restaurant, bar, rooftop terrace with Jacuzzi, satellite TV. AE, DC, MC, V.*

★ **Parador San Javier.** This immaculately restored hacienda was converted into a hotel in 1971. In fact, a safe from the Hacienda San Javier and old wood trunks still decorate the large, plant-laden lobby. The rooms are clean and have modern appointments: lace curtains, crisp coverlets, and blue-and-white-tiled baths. The 16 rooms reached via a stone archway have some rugged colonial details. A word of caution: Large convention groups sometimes use the facility. *Plaza Aldama 92, 36000, tel. 473/2–06–26. 115 rooms with bath. Facilities: 2 restaurants, bar, café, disco, outdoor swimming pool, gardens, bullring. AE, DC, MC, V.*

**Inexpensive** **Hotel Socavón.** One of Guanajuato's newer hotels, this modest five-story property was built in 1981. Open-air walkways, with views of surrounding mountains, lead to guest quarters. Each room has a wood-beamed ceiling, is simply furnished with a bed and a desk, and has a modern bath. Fourth-floor corner rooms offer some good views; second-floor rooms are near the hotel restaurant. *Calle de la Alhóndiga 41A, 36000, tel. 473/2–48–85 or 473/2–66–66. 37 rooms with bath. Facilities: restaurant. AE, MC, V.*

## The Arts and Nightlife

Guanajuato, on most nights a somnolent provincial capital, awakens each fall for the **International Cervantes Festival.** During two weeks in October world-renowned actors, musicians, and dance troupes (which have included the Bolshoi Ballet) perform nightly at the Teatro Juárez and at other venues in town. The **Plaza San Roque,** a small square near the Jardín Reforma, hosts a series of *Entremeses Cervantinos*—swashbuckling one-act farces by classical Spanish writers. Grandstand seats require advance tickets, but crowds often gather by the edge of the plaza for free. If you plan to be in Guanajuato for the festival, contact the Cervantes ticket office in Mexico City (Emerson 304, Colonia Polanco, tel. 905/250–0095) at least six months in advance for top-billed events.

At other times of the year, nightlife in Guanajuato is mostly relegated to dramatic, dance, and musical performances at the **Teatro Juárez** (Calle de Sopeña, tel. 473/2–01–83) and the **Teatro Principal** (Calle Hidalgo, tel. 473/2–15–23), which has begun showing American movies several times a week. Some hotels, including the Parador San Javier and the Castillo Santa Cecilia, provide evening musical entertainment. There are also several nightclubs located in or near the downtown area, including **Discoteque El Pequeño Juan** (Panorámica Al Pípila at Callejón de Guadalupe, tel. 473/2–23–08), whose panoramic view of the city at night is stunning, and the small but lively **Discoteque La Fragua** (Calle Tepetapa 45, tel. 473/2–27–15).

## Excursion to León

León, 56 kilometers (35 miles) northwest of Guanajuato, is best known as the shoemaking capital of Mexico. It is also an important center for industry and commerce. With more than 1 million people, it is the state's most populous urban area.

If you know footwear and have the time (and patience) to browse through the downtown shops, you may find some good buys in León. First try the Plaza de Zapatos, a mall with 70 stores located on Boulevard Adolfo López Mateos roughly one block from the bus station. From here take a taxi west (about a 10-minute ride) to the Zona Peatonal, a pedestrian zone with several shoe stores. On Calle Praxedis Guerrero there are various artisans' stands selling leather goods.

Flecha Amarilla buses leave Guanajuato's Central Camionera every 15 minutes for León; the ride takes about 45 minutes and costs less than $1. Pick up a map of León at the tourist office in Guanajuato.

# Zacatecas

In colonial days Zacatecas was the largest silver-producing city in the world, and sent great treasures of the precious metal to the king of Spain. Still a large silver-mining center, with factories producing silver jewelry and trade schools training apprentices in the fine art of handmade silver craft, Zacatecas is a relatively undiscovered jewel for tourists. Although it is a state capital with a population of some 300,000, it has the feel of a much smaller place; the town is kept spotlessly clean by Zacatecan pride, under a mandate by the governor of the state of Zacatecas. This destination is also famous for its historical role as the scene of one of Pancho Villa's most spectacular battles and for its 18th-century colonial architecture.

One of the town's unique charms is the *tambora*, a musical walk up and down the streets and alleyways led by a *tamborazo*, a typical local band that shatters the evening quiet with merriment. Also known as a *callejóneada* (*callejón* means "alley"), the tambora is a popular free-for-all, in which everyone along the way either joins in the procession or leans from balconies and doorways to cheer the group on. During the December *feria* (festival), the tamborazos play night and day as they serenade the Virgin of Zacatecas.

## Arriving and Departing

**By Plane**  **Mexicana** (tel. 800/531–7921) has service to Zacatecas from Mexico City. In Zacatecas the Mexicana Airlines office is located on Hidalgo (tel. 492/2–7429, 492/2–7470, or 492/2–3248). The airport is 18 miles north of town; Aerotransports (tel. 492/25–946) provides transportation. A taxi ride to town will cost about $25.

**By Car**  Zacatecas is 603 kilometers (375 miles) northwest of Mexico City via Route 57 (to Querétero and San Luis Potosi) and Route 49, approximately a 7½–8-hour drive.

**By Bus**  **Omnibus de México** operates several first- and second-class buses daily from Mexico City to Zacatecas.

## Getting Around

You can reach most of the town-center attractions by foot, although you will need to rent a car or hire a taxi if you want a tour of a mine or take a ride on the Teleferico (cable car) to the top of Cerro de la Bufa with its monuments, chapel, and museum. Be sure to wear sturdy footwear. The city has an excellent and inexpensive bus system.

## Important Addresses and Numbers

**Tourist Information**
The **Zacatecas tourist office** (Dirección de Turismo; Ave. Hidalgo 601, tel. 492/2–66–83; open weekdays 8–3 and 6–8) is located near the town cathedral. A small adjoining information booth remains open seven days a week. The state **Delegación de Turismo** is at Boulevard Lopez Mateos 923–A (tel. 492/2–67–50 or 492/2–67–51).

**Emergencies**
**Police** (tel. 492/2–66–83). **Red Cross** (tel. 492/2–30–05). **Emergency Service,** dial 06 (locally). Since English is not generally spoken in Zacatecas, it's best to contact your hotel manager or the tourist office in case of an emergency.

*Hospital*
Tel. 492/3–30–00.

**Travel Agencies**
**Viajes Mazzoco** (Enlace 313, tel. 492/2–08–59). **Turismo Marxal** (Hidalgo 413, tel. 492/2–36–93).

## Guided Tours

**Cantera Tours,** (Mercado Gonzalez Ortega Loc. A–21, tel. 492/2–90–65) offers a five-hour tour that covers Zacatecas and neighboring regions. Cost: approximately $12 per person. The company's Callejoneada Zacatecas tour includes the tambora, as well as wine and mescal. Cost: approximately $15 per person.

## Exploring

The elaborately carved 18th-century Mexican Baroque **cathedral** on Avenida Hidalgo is considered one of the best examples of this style in the country. Each of the three facades tells a different legend, while a fourth tale has it that an anticlerical governor of the state took the cathedral's silver cross and baptismal font to mint Zacatecas's first silver coins.

Adjoining the cathedral is the **Plaza de Armas** and the Governor's Palace, an 18th-century mansion containing flower-filled courtyards and, on the main staircase, a powerful mural depicting the history of Zacatecas.

Across the street stand two more of the town's beautiful 18th-century colonial buildings, both declared national monuments. They are built from native pink stone and have lacey ironwork balconies. One of them now houses the **Paraiso Radisson Hotel,** and the other is presently a municipal building called the **Palacio de la Mala Noche** (Palace of the Bad Night). Legend has it that this was the home of a silver-mine owner who was so often called upon to help the needy that he built a hidden door from which he could enter and leave the palace undisturbed. One night a terrible storm was raging, yet a worker had the temerity to pound on the front door. He finally gained entrance with his good news: silver had been found in a mine considered exhausted. Up the hill along the side of the palace, you will find the so-called hidden door.

In the Plaza Santo Domingo north of the cathedral, the **Pedro Coronel Museum** was originally a Jesuit monastery and then used as a jail in the 18th century. The museum is one of a kind in Mexico and Latin America, housing the work of Zacatecan artist and sculptor Pedro Coronel and his extensive collection of the works of Picasso, Dali, Miró, Braque, and Chagall among others, as well as an abundance of art from Africa, China, Japan, India, Greece, and Egypt. *Admission: Weekdays about 50¢; Sun. free. Open Fri.-Wed. 10-2 and 4-7, Sun. 10-2 and 4-5.*

The fine 17th-century Templo De Santo Domingo is adjacent to the museum. It has a Baroque facade and inside are some old paintings of religious subjects in gold leaf.

**Time Out** The **Cafe Y Neveria Acropolis** (Ave. Hidalgo at Plazuela Candelario Huizar, tel. 492/2-12-84), alongside the cathedral, is an ice-cream parlor in the daytime and a coffeehouse at night. Come here for Turkish coffee (under $1), ice cream, and other desserts. Breakfast is served from 8:30 to 12:30.

Heading south on Avenida Hidalgo you will come to **Teatro Calderon,** opened in 1891. It was restored to its former glory in 1987 and is one of the city's many fine examples of colonial architecture.

Not to be confused with the Pedro Coronel Museum is the **Rafael Coronel Museum** (the men were brothers), located in the Exconvento de San Francisco, out of the town center toward Lómas del Calvario. Its 18th-century facade of mellowed pink tones conceals a rambling structure of open-arched corridors, all leading through garden patios to rooms that contain an amazing collection of some 3,700 masks. Saints and devils, wise men and fools, animals and humans, make up this startling assortment of handmade *máscaras* (masks) used in regional festivals all over Mexico. There is also an outstanding display of puppets. *Northeast of downtown, off Vergel Nuevo, between Chaveño and Garcia Salinas. Admission: About 50¢. Open Tues.-Sun. 10-5.*

At Cerro del Grillo (Cricket Hill) on the northeast side of the city you can catch the **Teleferico,** the only cable car in the world that crosses an entire city (it runs from 12:30 PM to 7:30 PM daily). True, it crosses at the narrowest point, but it presents a magnificent panoramic view of the city and its many Baroque church domes and spires. At the cost of a little more than a dollar, the ride takes you up to Cerro de la Bufa. The price is the same whether you ride both ways or walk one, and going up is quite a climb.

**Cerro de la Bufa,** the trademark of the city, is the site of Pancho Villa's definitive battle against dictator Victoriano Huerta in June 1914. The spacious **Plaza de la Revolución,** paved with the three shades of pink Zacatecan stone, is crowned with three huge equestrian statues of Villa and two other heroes, Felipe Angeles and Panfilo Natera. Also on the site are the Museo de la Toma de Zacatecas (open Tues.-Sun. 10-5; admission free), which has nine rooms filled with historic objects such as guns, newspapers, furniture, and clothing from the days of Pancho Villa; and a chapel dedicated to the patron of the city, **The Sanctuary of the Virgin of Patrocinio.** The very tip-top of the hill has an observatory, a meteorological facility. You'll need to get special permission from the Zacatecas tourist office to visit the observatory. The Eden Mine (El Mina Eden), which functioned from 1586 until the 20th century, is now a tourist attraction. From the entrance on Antonio Dovali off Avenida Torreon beyond the Alameda Garcia de la Cadena, an open mine train runs down into the underground tunnels; there is a small gift shop at the entrance. The tour (there is a nominal fee) is in Spanish, but you'll have no trouble imagining what the life of the miners was like. Be sure to wear sturdy shoes, and remember that mines are pretty dark. This one is no exception; through much of the tour, your only light may be the guide's flashlight. Farther down the train track there is another stop at, of all places, a discotheque! (*See* Nightlife, *below.*) *The mine is open daily noon–7:30 PM.*

Finally, since this is a silver town, you won't want to miss a visit to the **Centro Platero Zacatecas** (tel. 492/2–10–27), a school and factory for fine handmade silver jewelry and other items. In the 18th-century mansion of one Don Ignacio de Bernardez, you can watch student silversmiths master this fine tradition. Jewelry and other silver products are for sale on the premises (Ex-Hacienda de Bernardez, Colonia Bernardez, tel. 492/3–10–07) or in the factory's shop located downtown in **Centro Commercial El Mercado,** a group of boutiques in what was once a covered market, located on Calle Hidalgo next to the cathedral.

## Dining

Several of Zacatecas's better restaurants are located in hotels; another is right in El Mercado, the boutique area on Calle Hidalgo near the cathedral. Other popular restaurants can be found on Avenida Juárez, which intersects Hidalgo. To the north Juárez changes its name to Avenida Torreon along the Alameda Garcia de la Cadena, a pleasant public garden walk.

Highly recommended restaurants are indicated by a star ★.

| Category | Cost* |
|---|---|
| Very Expensive | over $20 |
| Expensive | $15–$20 |
| Moderate | $8–$15 |
| Inexpensive | under $8 |

*per person, excluding drinks and service*

**Very Expensive** **Quinta Real.** In the Quinta Real hotel, this elaborate, formal restaurant with white tablecloths and flowers on the tables serves fine Continental cuisine, with such specialties as medallion of beef in a tangy port sauce and desserts flambéed at the table. There is also a bar. *434 Ave. Rayon and Gonzales Ortega, tel. 492/2–84–40. Reservations suggested. Dress: informal but not casual. AE, MC, V.*

**Expensive** **Candiles.** This popular downtown meeting place is situated in the Paraiso Radisson hotel, a great place to observe the local business crowd as well as the interesting assortment of hotel guests. Candiles has cream and vermilion walls, arches, and soft lighting. Black lacquer slatted chairs contrast with white tablecloths and crystal. The impressive menu includes both Continental and regional dishes. Try the veal marsala or the *filete pimienta* (steak with peppercorns). *Paraiso Radisson Hotel, Av. Hidalgo 703, tel. 492/2-61-83. Dress: casual. No reservations. AE, DC, MC, V.*

**La Cuija.** Zacatecas specialties such as an appetizer basket filled with four sweet varieties of cactus flower, peeled and juicy, are the rule here. Also try the *pollo adobada* (chicken in a rich chili sauce) or *carne a la Mexicana* (beef grilled with tomatoes, onion, and salsa). The decor approximates a wine cellar, and in addition to fine food, the restaurant serves wine from the owner's Cachola Vineyards (*see* Excursions, *below*). *Centro Commercial El Mercado, tel. 492/2-82-75 or 492/2-63-95. Reservations suggested. Dress: informal. AE, MC, V.*

**Inexpensive** **Rancho Viejo.** This informal ranch-style restaurant serves tasty dishes with a Zacatecan flavor, including *huchepos* (tamales with sour cream) and enchiladas covered with vegetables and a rich red chili sauce. *Carretera Panamericana 101, tel. 492/2-67-47. Reservations accepted. Dress: informal. No credit cards.*

## Lodging

Many of Zacatecas's best lodgings are in the city's treasured historic buildings, which have been preserved in all their 18th- and 19th-century beauty. Others are situated in the surrounding mountains and have wonderful views of the picturesque city as well as the silver-mined hills.

Highly recommended lodgings are indicated by a star ★.

| Category | Cost* |
|---|---|
| Very Expensive | over $90 |
| Expensive | $60–$90 |
| Moderate | $25–$60 |
| Inexpensive | under $25 |

*All prices are for a standard double room, excluding 10% tax.*

**Very Expensive** **Quinta Real.** This hotel must be one of the most unusual in the country—or any country. It has been built around the country's oldest bullring and the second bullring ever built in the Western Hemisphere. Although spirited bullfight music plays softly in the background, matadors no longer face the bulls here. Instead, the terrazo-paved ring provides a unique view for the 49 guest rooms, each with a balcony overlooking the *plaza de toro*. Large and bright, the rooms are decorated in pastel fabrics that compliment the traditional furniture. The bar occupies some of the former bull pens, and an outdoor restaurant (*see* Dining, *above*) with bright-yellow umbrellaed tables occupies two levels of the spectator area. *434 Ave. Rayon and Gonzales Ortega, tel. 492/2-84-40. Facilities: restaurant, café, bar. AE, DC, MC, V.*

**Expensive** **Paraiso Radisson.** Facing the Plaza des Armas and the cathedral in the heart of Zacatecas, the Paraiso Radisson is situated in one of the city's beautiful old colonial buildings and has been declared a national monument. The pink-stone facade dates from the 18th century, and the additional construction matches perfectly. Rooms are decorated in cream, blue, and fuschia and furnished with copies of Spanish antiques as well as modern pieces. Those facing the plaza are susceptible to late-night and early morning tamborazo music during festivals; on the other hand, from your small balcony you'll get a great view of the goings-on. The rooms facing the interior courtyard are quieter. *Ave. Hidalgo 703, Colonia Centro, tel. 492/2–61–83. Reservations in Mexico City, tel. 5/533–11–95 or 800/90-0-90; in the U.S., tel. 800/333-3333. 116 rooms with bath. Facilities: restaurant, bar with live music, convention room, satellite TV, indoor parking. AE, DC, MC, V.*

**Moderate–Expensive** **Hotel Gallery.** This Best Western is located only three blocks from the historic town center. From the bay windows of its front rooms you can see over the rooftops of the whitewashed dome of Templo San José, one of Zacatecas's Baroque churches. The hotel is one of the most modern in Zacatecas. Rooms have a cool color scheme of blue, green, and white; furnishings include Mexican chests painted white and lacy white ironwork headboards. Bathrooms are marble. The staff is extremely friendly and helpful. *Blvd. Lopez Mateos y Callejón del Barro, tel. 492/2–33–11; in Mexico City, 5/525–90–81, 5/525–90–82, or 5/525–90–83. 134 rooms with bath, including 3 junior suites and a Suite Presidencial, all with satellite TV and individual climate control. Facilities: restaurant and coffee shop, bar, nightclub, meeting rooms, indoor swimming pool, sauna, 2 squash courts, indoor parking. AE, DC, MC, V.*

**Moderate** **Motel del Bosque.** *Bosque* means "forest" or "woods" in Spanish, and this clean and quiet motel near the green belt offers a superb view of Zacatecas. Close to the Teleferico station at Cerro del Grillo high above the city, yet not terribly far from the center, the motel has clean, carpeted bungalows spread along the hillside in rows and divided by cobblestone parking areas. *Paseo Diaz Ordaz, tel. 492/2–07–45, 492/2–07–46, or 492/2–07–47. 70 rooms with bath. Facilities: restaurant, TV, parking. MC.*

## Nightlife

If only for its uniqueness, a must-visit is El Malacate (tel. 492/2–30–02) the discotheque in the Mina El Eden, a stop on the Eden Mine train and more than 1,000 feet underground. It's best to make reservations at this popular place, which is both crowded and noisy. At the opposite end of the height spectrum is El Elefante Blanco (Mina La Gallega 15, tel. 492/2–71–04), another discotheque but this time one with a panoramic view of the city. There's live music in the lobby bar of the Paraiso Radisson, and the Hotel Gallery has a nightclub with live entertainment (*see* Lodging, *above*).

## Excursions to Zona Archaeologica La Quemada and Cachola Vins

**Zona Archaeologica La Quemada,** about 50 kilometers (30 miles) southwest of Zacatecas, is an archaeological site, once an ancient city that was already a ruin before the advent of the Spaniards in the 16th century. Seven different Indian cultures built one community atop the other, and the present site rises high above the plain. The spot is totally undeveloped as a tourist attraction, making the climb quite rugged, but once you reach the top, the whole area spreads out below you. The edifices, what remains of them, appear to be constructed of thin slabs of stone wedged into place. The principal aesthetic draw is a group of rose-colored ruins containing 11 large round columns built entirely of the same small slabs of rock seen in the rest of the ruins. *Nominal admission and free on Sunday. Open Tues.–Sun. 10–5.*

Another Zacatecas side trip is a jaunt to the award-winning vineyard **Cachola Vins,** in Valle de las Arsinas. In the valley the cold winters, mild springtimes, and temperate summers have produced a silver medal for the vineyard's 1986 Cachola French Columbard at the VINEXPO 1991 in France. Tours of the vineyard are best arranged beforehand, especially if you would like a tasting. *Cachola Vins, Cruce de Carretera Panamericana, Km. 634, Las Arsinas, Guadalupe, Zacatecas, tel. 492/2–72–56.*

# Querétaro

A state capital and industrial center of nearly 800,000 people, Querétaro, like other Bajío cities, has played a significant role in Mexican history. In 1810, in the home of Josefa Ortiz de Dominguez, a heroine of the independence movement, known as La Corregidora, the first plans for independence were hatched. In 1848 the Mexican-American War was concluded in this city with the signing of the Treaty of Guadalupe Hidalgo. Emperor Maximilian made his last stand here in 1867 and was executed by firing squad in the Cerro de las Campañas (Hill of the Church Bells) north of town. A small memorial chapel, built by the Austrian government, marks the spot. A gigantic statue of Benito Juárez crowns a park on the crest of the hill just above it. In 1917 the Mexican Constitution, which still governs the land, was signed in this city.

Throughout Querétaro there are markers, museums, churches, and monuments that commemorate the city's heroes and historic moments. A prevailing sense of civic pride is evident in the impeccably renovated mansions, the flower-draped cobblestoned pedestrian walkways, and the hospitable plazas, which are softly lit at night. The people are among the most congenial in central Mexico and are quick to share their favorite sites and tales with travelers.

Querétaro is also renowned for opals—red, green, honey, and fire stones, as opposed to the blue Australian kind. However, visitors should beware of street vendors, who may sell opals so full of water that they crumble shortly after purchase; depend upon reputable dealers (*see* Shopping, *below*).

Though Querétaro's boundaries extend for some distance, the historic district is in the heart of town. A day or two can easily be spent here, visiting museums, admiring the architecture, and learning the local history.

## Arriving and Departing

**By Car** Querétaro is 220 kilometers (136 miles) northwest of Mexico City, a three-hour drive via Route 57. Cars can be rented at various outlets in Mexico City; in Querétaro try **Budget** (Av. Constituyentes Oriente 73, tel. 463/2–43–45), **Auto Rent** (Av. Constituyentes Oriente 24, tel. 463/4–20–39), or **National** (Calle 13 de Septiembre #34, tel. 463/6–35–44).

**By Train** First-class train service between Mexico City and Querétaro is available daily on **Mexican National Railways** (tel. 905/547–5819 or 905/547–3190 in Mexico City; 463/2–17–03 in Querétaro). The *Constitucionalista* departs from Mexico City at 7 AM and arrives in Querétaro at 10 AM; the return trip leaves Querétaro at 7 PM and arrives in Mexico City at 9:30 PM. Tickets should be purchased one day in advance; the round-trip fare of $40 includes a full breakfast or dinner. Train schedules are subject to change without notice. In the United States, call Mexico By Rail, tel. 800/228–3225.

**By Bus** Direct bus service is available daily between the Central del Norte (North Bus Station) in Mexico City and Querétaro's Central de Autobuses. Major lines—including **Flecha Amarilla, Omnibus de México, Tres Estrellas de Oro,** and **Transportes del Norte**—offer frequent service; travel time is about three hours. Frequent inexpensive bus service is available from Querétaro to other heartland cities.

## Getting Around

Many of Querétaro's historic sites are within walking distance of one another in the downtown district and can be reached by a series of walkways that are closed to automobile traffic most of the day. If you want to venture farther afield, you will find that buses and taxis run frequently along the main streets and are inexpensive.

## Important Addresses and Numbers

**Tourist Information** The **Dirección de Turismo del Estado** is located near the Plaza de la Independencia. City maps and brochures of the state of Querétaro are available, and the bilingual staff is extremely helpful. *Calle 5 de Mayo #61, tel. 463/12–91–00, 463/14–01–79 or 463/14–04–28. Open weekdays 9–3 and 6–8, weekends 10–1.*

An additional tourist information office is located at Av. Constituyentes Oriente 15 (tel. 463/14–32–73, fax 463/9–14–63).

**Emergencies** **Police** (tel. 463/16–19–37). **Ambulance-Red Cross** (tel. 463/12–17–06 or 463/12–83–01). **Protectur** (tel. 463/14–04–28) offers legal assistance with robberies, fraud, and detention/arrest.

*Hospital* **Sanatorio Alcocer Pozo** (Calle Reforma 23, tel. 463/12–01–49 or 463/12–17–87).

**Money Exchange** **Casa de Cambio de Querétaro** (Av. Madero 6–101, tel. 464/14–42–55 or 464/14–39–03) is open Monday–Thursday 9–3, Fri., 9–1:30.

**Travel Agencies** **Wagons-Lits Viajes** (Centro Comercial Plaza Niza at Zaragoza y Tolsa 3, tel. 463/14–30–20).

**Business Services** **La Conexción** (Juárez 153 N, tel./fax 463/12–34–25) offers 24-hour answering and fax service, a Mexican address for receiving mail, lock boxes, a Macintosh computer center, and more.

## Guided Tours

On request, the tourist office conducts a free 90-minute English-language walking tour of the city's historic landmarks. To arrange a city tour, call the office (*see* Important Addresses and Numbers, *above*) one day in advance.

## Exploring

*Numbers in the margin correspond to points of interest on the Querétaro map.*

The city's most noteworthy sites are near the tourist office. Pick up a map, make a right, and walk directly to the **Plaza Independencia** or **Plaza de Armas**. Bordered by carefully restored colonial mansions, this immaculate square is especially lovely at night, when the central fountain is lit. Built in 1824, the fountain is dedicated to the Marquis de la Villa del Villar, who constructed Querétaro's elegant aqueduct and provided the city with drinking water. The old stone aqueduct with its 74 towering arches still stands at the east end of town, though it no longer brings water into the city.

The **Palacio Municipal**, also known as the Palacio de la Corregidora, is on the plaza's northwest corner. Today it houses municipal government offices, but in 1810 it was the home of Querétaro's mayor-magistrate (El Corregidor) and his wife, Josefa Ortiz de Domínguez (La Corregidora). On many evenings conspirators—including Ignacio Allende and Father Miguel Hidalgo—came here under the guise of participating in La Corregidora's literary salon. When the mayor-magistrate learned that they were actually plotting the course for independence, he imprisoned his wife in her room. La Corregidora managed to whisper a warning to a coconspirator, who notified Allende and Hidalgo. A few days later, on September 16, Father Hidalgo tolled the bell of his church to signal the beginning of the fight for freedom. A replica of the bell can be seen atop the Palacio Municipal.

Continue around the square counterclockwise. At Plaza Independencia 4 is the Palacio de Justicia, and beside it, **Casa de la Cultura** (the sign out front reads "*Bazar Ideas y Artesanias*"). The Baroque palace, also known as **Casa de Ecala**, has its original facade. As the story goes, its 18th-century owner adorned his home so ornately to better his neighbor. When the neighbor complained, City Hall stepped in and halted construction.

Just past the Casa de la Cultura is Avenida Libertad Oriente, one of the city's bougainvillea-draped pedestrian walkways. Turn west here and walk two blocks to reach Calle Corregidora, named after the heroine. Bear right again, and in the middle of a long block you'll find the entrance to the **Museo Regional de Querétaro**. This bright yellow 17th-century Franciscan monastery displays the works of colonial and European artists in addition to historic memorabilia, including early copies of the Mexican Constitution and the table on which the Treaty of Guadalupe Hidalgo was signed. *Calle Corregidora 12, tel. 463/*

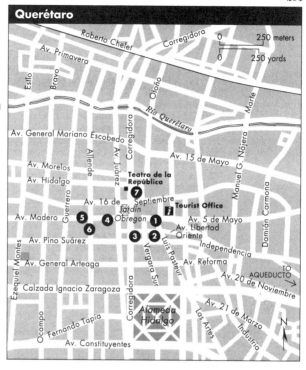

**Querétaro**

*2–20–36 or 463/2–20–31. Admission, about $3. Open Mon., Wed.–Sat. 10–6; Tues. 10–3:30.*

Cross the street to Avenida Madero, another "pedway," this one lined with shops. (Cars have use of the street between 2 and 4 PM daily.) The **Jardín Obregón,** the city's main square, will be on your right. You'll also pass a number of lapidary shops selling opals (not blue like Australian opals but beautiful nonetheless) and other locally mined gems. If you're in the market for loose stones or opal jewelry, do some comparison shopping, as you're apt to find better prices here than in the United States.

One block past Avenida Juárez on the corner of Allende Sur, you'll see the former **Casa de la Marquesa** on your left at No. 41. The structure currently houses Querétaro's Center of Cultural Services, but it was once the ostentatious home of the Marquesa de la Villa del Villar, who apparently had a penchant for things Arabic. Notice the studios on the second floor, one of which is covered with Middle Eastern tiles.

Cross Allende to reach the neoclassical **Fountain of Neptune** next to the Church of Santa Clara at the corner of Calle Allende. It was built in 1797 by Eduardo Tresguerras, the renowned Mexican architect and a native of the Bajío. The fountain originally stood in the orchard of the Monastery of San Antonio, but when the monks faced serious economic problems, they sold part of their land and along with it the fountain.

From the fountain, make a left on Calle Allende and walk nearly one block to a fine example of Baroque architecture, the **State Museum of Art,** housed in an 18th-century Augustinian monastery that contains a collection of European and Mexican paintings from the 17th through the 20th centuries. *Calle Allende 14, no phone. Admission: about 35¢. Open Tues.–Sun. 11–7.*

Retrace your steps back to Calle Corregidora. Make a left and walk one block to Calle 16 de Septiembre. Across the street is

❼ the **Jardín de la Corregidora**, prominently marked by a statue of the heroine. Behind this monument stands the **Arbol de la Amistad** (Tree of Friendship). Planted in 1977 in a mixture of soils from around the world, the tree symbolizes Querétaro's hospitality to all travelers.

**Time Out**  At the Jardín de la Corregidora you may want to find a bench and sit for a while. This is the calmest square in town, with many choices for outdoor eating (*see* Dining, *below*).

## Shopping

**El Rubio,** just off Querétaro's Plaza Principal, is a reputable dealer for opals and other gems. The owner, Señora Villalon, provides information on the mining, care, and value of opals. *Av. Madero #3 Pte, tel. 463/12–09–84. Open Mon.–Sat. 10–2. Closed Sun.*

## Dining

Many of Querétaro's dining spots are located near the main plaza (Jardín Obregón), along Calle Corregidora, near the Teatro de la República, and particularly in the Jardín de la Corregidora. There are more upscale restaurants in hotels on the Plaza Independencia or off Route 57, north of the city. In early evenings women set up stoves in a square near the Plaza Independencia and tempt passersby with cheap and hearty fare, but for health reasons, food cooked on the street should be avoided throughout Mexico.

Highly recommended restaurants are indicated by a star ★.

| Category | Cost* |
|---|---|
| Very Expensive | over $20 |
| Expensive | $15–$20 |
| Moderate | $8–$15 |
| Inexpensive | under $8 |

*\*per person, excluding drinks and service*

**Expensive**  **Fonda del Refugio.** Situated in the Jardín de la Corregidora, this restaurant offers intimate indoor and outdoor dining. Inside, fresh flowers adorn white-clothed tables; outside, comfortable leather chairs face the surrounding gardens. Seafood and beef fillets are a specialty; order the fillet of beef cooked in red wine, lemon, mustard, and peppers, or the scallops prepared in marsala. Cocktails are served on the terrace at night. *Jardín de la Corregidora 26, tel. 463/12–07–55. Reservations not accepted. Dress: informal. AE, DC, MC, V.*

★  **Restaurante Josecho.** Bullfight aficionados and other sports fans frequent this highway road stop as much for the lively atmosphere as for the food. Wood-paneled walls are hung with hunting trophies, including geese, elk, bears, and leopards; waiters celebrate patrons' birthdays by banging on pewter plates and blasting a red siren. Though the place can be raucous, it does quiet down at night, when a classical guitarist performs. House specialties include *filete Josecho* (steak with cheese and mushrooms), *filete Chemita* (steak sautéed in butter and onions), and shrimp crepes smothered in a cheese and tomato sauce. *Dalia 1, next to the Plaza de Toros Santa María, tel. 463/14-02-29. Reservations not accepted. Dress: informal. AE, DC, MC, V.*

**Moderate** **El Cortijo de Don Juan.** At lunchtime businessmen and families favor this garden location, making it the busiest spot in the shaded Jardín. Vendors, too, stroll by with a variety of wares, from homemade cheeses to large, inflatable crayons; and children sing songs for a small donation. Free snacks are served with drinks in the afternoon, or you can order from a menu that includes *pollo adobado* (chicken in a rich chile sauce), *jamón serrano* (a proscuitto-type ham), and *paella Valenciana* (rice casserole with chicken, sausage, and seafood), served on Saturdays only. The inside rooms are filled with photos of famous matadors; a bull's head is mounted prominently on the wall. *Jardín de la Corregidora 14, tel. 463/12-97-08. Reservations not accepted. Dress: informal. AE, DC, MC, V.*

**Inexpensive** **Comedor Vegetariano Natura.** This natural-foods kitchen, one of a chain of four in Querétaro, will be of interest to the vegetarian traveler. (A second one, not far away, is located at Juárez 47, off Plaza Obregón.) Traditional vegetarian fare, such as soy burgers with cheese, is on the menu, as are Mexican-influenced dishes, such as guayaba- or papaya-flavored yogurt, enchiladas stuffed with soy and cheese, or a vegetarian alternative to *huevos rancheros* (Mexican-style eggs). Vitamins, protein powders, and natural soaps are also in stock. *Vergara Sur 7, tel. 463/14-10-88. Reservations not accepted. Dress: informal. No credit cards. Closed Sunday.*
**La Mariposa.** Celebrating more than 50 years in business, La Mariposa is easily recognized by a wrought-iron butterfly (mariposa) over the entrance. This is the place for light Mexican lunches—enchiladas, tacos, tamales, and *tortas* (sandwiches). *Angela Peralta 7, tel. 463/12-11-66 or 463/12-48-49. Reservations not accepted. Dress: casual. No credit cards.*

## Lodging

Several new properties in various price ranges have opened in Querétaro in the past 10 years. Lower-priced hotels are located near the main plaza and thus tend to be noisy; newer high rises are near the bus station but are quiet inside; and deluxe properties, including a Holiday Inn, are on the outskirts of town.

Highly recommended lodgings are indicated by a star ★.

| Category | Cost* |
| --- | --- |
| Very Expensive | over $90 |
| Expensive | $60–$90 |

sal suffrage, racial equality, and the demise of the hacienda system.

The city today still pays tribute to Morelos: His former home has been turned into a museum, and his birthplace is now a library. Morelia's colonial heritage is preserved by its status as a national monument. The city is also forward-thinking. It's the site of a politically liberal university that often holds rallies supporting social and political causes. Look closely along Avenida Madero and you'll see political fliers posted on buildings.

Morelia has the dubious distinction of being the candy capital of Mexico. So strong, in fact, is the sweet-eating tradition that the city houses a *Mercado de Dulcería*, or sweets market. If you want to sample some local confections (made from candied fruit or evaporated milk), walk over to Calle Gómez Farías, three blocks west and a half block north of the main plaza.

Morelia is also the home of writers, artists, philosophers, and poets, as well as American retirees. To explore Morelia and its surrounding hillside neighborhoods thoroughly would take some time. However, if you stroll through the historic plazas and frequent the cafés (as many locals do), you will begin to feel the city's vitality.

## Arriving and Departing

**By Plane** There are daily flights between Francisco Mujica International Airport, 24 kilometers (15 miles) north of Morelia, and Mexico City's International Airport on **Aeromar Airlines** (tel. 800/237–6639; 451/3–05–55 in Morelia; 5/627–0207 in Mexico City). Flights are subject to cancellation, and flight times change often and must be confirmed one day in advance. The 25-minute taxi ride from the airport to Morelia costs about $15.

**By Car** Recent construction on Federal Highway 126 has cut travel time from Mexico City to Morelia (302 kilometers/187 miles). The drive now lasts about 3 hours and 45 minutes. Take the highway through Toluca, Atlacamulco, Contepec and Maravatio. Cars can be rented at various locations in Mexico City. In Morelia, **Budget** has an office at the Misión Hotel (tel. 451/5–00–23) but will pick up clients at the airport.

**By Train** There is daily train service between Mexico City and Morelia on **Mexican National Railways** (tel. 451/2–29–18). The *Purepecha* leaves Mexico City at 10 PM, arriving in Morelia at 6:30 AM; the return train leaves Morelia at 11 PM and arrives in Mexico City at 9:30 AM. The round-trip fare costs $60. There are no sleeping cars, but seats recline. Train schedules are subject to change without notice. In the United States, call Mexico By Rail, tel. 800/228–3225.

**By Bus** Direct bus service is available daily between the Terminal Poniente (West Terminal) in Mexico City and Morelia's Central de Autobuses. Several bus lines offer frequent service; the most direct trip, which takes five hours, is on Herradura de Plata (via Corta). Frequent inexpensive bus service is also available from Morelia to other points in Michoacán and throughout the heartland.

## Getting Around

As in many of the heartland cities, Morelia's principal sights are near the center of town and you can reach them on foot. Street names in Morelia change frequently, especially on either side of Avenida Madero, the city's main east–west artery. Taxis in Morelia can be hailed on the street or found near the main plaza. Buses run the length of Avenida Madero.

## Important Addresses and Numbers

**Tourist Information**  The **Secretaría Estatal de Turismo** in the Palacio Clavijero provides city maps and brochures of the state of Michoacán. Only a few of the brochures are in English, however. *Calle Nigromante 79, tel. 451/3–26–54. Open daily 9–2 and 4–8.*

Federal tourism offices are located at Santos Delgollado 340, (tel. 451/2–01–23 or 451/2–05–22).

**Emergencies**  Police (tel. 451/2–22–22). **Ambulance-Red Cross** (Cruz Rojo; tel. 451/4–51–51 or 4–50–25). **Consumer Protection Office** (tel. 451/2–40–49).

*Hospital*  **Municipal Hospital** (tel. 451/2–22–16).

**Money Exchange**  **Casa Cambio Valladolid** (Portal Matamoros 86, tel. 451/2–85–86) is open Monday–Saturday, 9–2 and 4–6.

**Travel Agencies**  **Viajes Lopsa** is the American Express representative. (Service Las Américas, Local 27, Artilleros del 47, tel. 451/4–19–50 or 4–77–16). **Servicios Establecidos Para el Turismo** is located at Portal Hidalgo 229 (tel. 451/2–36–64).

## Guided Tours

The following operators conduct tours of Morelia: **Autoturismo Morelia** (Calle Colima 486, tel. 451/4–08–26), **Michoacán Tour Guides and Conductors Association** (Calle Nigromante 79, tel. 451/3–26–54), **Tours Lindo Michoacán** (Calle Colima 486, tel. 451/4–99–43), **Transportación Turística Valladolid** (Av. Lázaro Cárdenas 1966, 2nd floor, tel. 451/4–73–84).

## Exploring

*Numbers in the margin correspond to points of interest on the Morelia map.*

**❶** Many of Morelia's points of interest are located within a few blocks of the main square, the **Plaza de Armas** or **Plaza de los Mártires**. Several rebel priests were brutally murdered on this site during the War of Independence, and the plaza is named after them. Today, however, the square belies its violent past: Sweethearts stroll along the tree-lined walks, vendors sell mounds of peanuts, placards boast of cultural events, and lively, recorded music blasts from a silver-domed bandshell.

**❷** Slightly east of the plaza lies Morelia's famed **Catedral**, a majestic structure built between 1640 and 1744. It is known throughout Mexico for its 200-foot Baroque towers, among the tallest in the land, and for its 4,600-pipe organ, one of the finest in the world. The organ is on the balcony at the back of the cathedral. An international organ festival is held here each May.

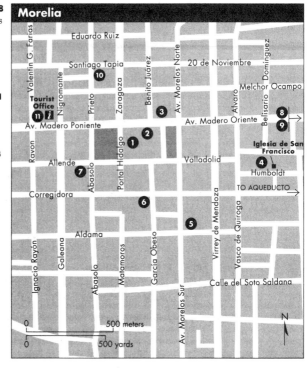

As you leave the cathedral, cross Avenida Madero and walk to
❸ the **Palacio de Gobierno**. This former Tridentine Seminary,
built in 1770, has had such notable graduates as independence
hero José María Morelos, social reformer Melchor Ocampo, and
the first emperor of Mexico, Agustín de Iturbide. Striking murals decorate the stairway and second floor. Painted by local
artist Alfredo Zalce in the early 1960s, they depict dramatic,
often bloody scenes from Mexico's history. From the second
floor you can catch a glimpse of the cathedral's spires across the
way. *Av. Madero 63, tel. 451/2–78–72. Open daily 7 AM–11 PM.*

From the palace, walk four blocks east along Avenida Madero
(past a number of banks) until you reach Calle de Belisario
Domínguez. Make a right and walk one block to the Church of
San Francisco. To the rear of the church, in the former convent
❹ of San Francisco, is the entrance to the **Casa de las Artesanías
del Estado de Michoacán**. This two-story marketplace is a vir-
tual cornucopia of crafts from around the state. In the 16th century, Vasco de Quiroga, the bishop of Michoacán, helped the
Tarascan Indians develop artistic specialties so they could be
self-supporting. The rooms display the work the Tarascans still
produce: copper goods from Santa Clara del Cobre, lacquerware from Uruapan, straw items and pottery from Pátzcuaro,
guitars from Paracho, macabre ceramic figures from Ocumi-
cho. Upstairs in the **Museo Michoacana de las Artesanías,** which
is open daily 9–8, some of these items are showcased behind
glass while artists demonstrate how they are made. Though the
market offers an excellent selection of goods, prices are often

better in the indigenous villages. If you plan to explore these outlying towns, you may want to do your shopping there.

❺ Next, visit the **Casa Museo de Morelos**, a home acquired in 1801 by the independence leader Morelos. Generations of the Morelos family lived here until 1934. Walk two blocks south on Calle Vasco de Quiroga, a street lined with vendors, until you reach Calle del Soto Saldana. Walk west another two blocks to Avenida Morelos Sur. The museum, now owned by the Mexican government, is the corner building on your right. The two floors contain family portraits (including one of Morelos's mother, who, he said, "gave him constant spirit and strength"), a copy of Morelos's birth certificate, various artifacts from the independence movement (such as a camp bed used by Ignacio Allende), and the blindfold Morelos wore for his execution. A guide conducts an excellent free tour (in Spanish only). *Av. Morelos Sur 323. Small admission fee. Open daily 9–6:30.*

From the museum, walk one block north to Calle Corregidora, then one block west to Calle García Obeso. On this corner
❻ stands **Casa Natal**, Morelos's birthplace, now a library and national monument housing mostly history and literature books (as well as two murals by Alfredo Zalce). Be sure to visit the courtyard in back. It's a tranquil square, adjacent to the Church of San Agustín, with rosebushes, evergreens, and wild poinsettias; a marker and an eternal flame honor the fallen hero. *Calle Corregidora 113. Admission free. Open weekdays 9:30–2 and 4–8, Sat. 9:30–3:30 and 4:30–7, Sun. 9:30–3.*

Walk west on Calle Corregidora until you reach Calle Abasolo; head north one block to Calle Allende, where you'll find the
❼ **Museo Michoacana.** An 18th-century former palace, the museum traces the history of Mexico from its pre-Hispanic days through the Cardenista period, which ended in 1940. President Lázaro Cárdenas, a native of Michoacán, was one of Mexico's most popular leaders because of his nationalization of the oil industry and his support of other populist reforms. The ground floor contains an art gallery, plus archaeological exhibits from Michoacán and other parts of Mexico. Upstairs is an assortment of colonial objects, including furniture, weapons, and religious paintings. *Calle Allende 305, tel. 451/2–04–07. Admission: about $3. Open Tues.–Sat. 9–7, Sun. 9–2.*

From the museum take Calle Abasolo one block north to return to Avenida Madero. The plaza will be one block to the east.

**Time Out** When you've finished your tour, walk across the street to the *portales*. A number of popular sidewalk cafés are set among these colonial stone arcades. For a sandwich or a fruit cocktail, or a good selection of juices, coffees, and teas, try **Café Catedral.** No one will mind if you linger over a book or newspaper for the better part of an hour. *Portal Hidalgo 213, tel. 451/2–32–89. Open 8 AM–10 PM. No credit cards.*

After refueling at the portales, continue east on Avenida Madero to the **Bosque Cuauhtémoc**, Morelia's largest park. This
❽ walk should take about 15 minutes, providing you aren't sidetracked en route by temptations such as Helados Bing (Av. Madero 422), an ice-cream shop offering more than 20 flavors.

Avenida Madero forks as you near the park. Keep to the right, passing the **Fountain of the Tarascans** on a square to your left.

Just past the square, Morelia's mile-long **aqueduct** begins. This structure, which consists of 250 arches, was built in 1785 and was once the city's main source of drinking water. It's particularly beautiful at night when its arches — some rising to 30 feet—are lit.

Two blocks farther (Madero is now called Avenida Acueducto) is the entrance to Bosque Cuauhtémoc. If you happen by during the week, you may encounter university students studying (or lounging) beneath the palms and evergreens; on weekends, especially Sundays, the park is filled with families on outings.

**❾** Continue past the park entrance for two blocks to the **Museo de Arte Contemporáneo** on your right, where the works of contemporary Mexican and international artists are on view. *Av. Acueducto 18. Small admission fee. Open Tues.–Sun. 10–2 and 4–8.*

On the corner of Guillermo Prieto and Santiago Tapia, directly across from a small plaza with statues of Don Quiroga de Vasco **❿** and Miguel de Cervantes, is the **Museo del Estado,** a history museum in a stately mansion once the home of Augustín de Iturbide, Mexico's only native-born emperor. *Guillermo Prieto 176. Admission free. Open daily 9–2 and 4–8 in summer; 9–2 and 4–7 in winter.*

**⓫** For those who have a sweet tooth, the **Mercado de Dulces** (candy market) is just behind the tourist office at the corner of Av. Madero Poniente and Valentín Gómez Farías. All sorts of local sweets are for sale, such as *ate*, a candied fruit. The market is open daily 9–9.

### Dining

Some of Michoacán's tastiest dishes—Lake Pátzcuaro white fish, tomato-based Tarascan soup, such corn products as *huchepos* and *corundas*, and game (rabbit, quail, and kid)—are featured at Morelia restaurants. Traditional chicken and beef fare are also available, as well as international dishes. As a rule, more upscale restaurants are located in hotels near the plaza and on the outskirts of town.

Highly recommended restaurants are indicated by a star ★.

| Category | Cost* |
|---|---|
| Moderate | $8–$15 |
| Inexpensive | under $8 |

*per person, excluding drinks and service*

**Moderate**
**★** **Boca del Rio.** Large picture windows opening onto a busy intersection provide lots of light for this cheerful restaurant, which claims to have fresh fish and seafood trucked in daily from Sinaloa and Veracruz. Located between the bus station and the Mercado de Dulces, it provides light snacks, such as *cocktel de camarones* (shrimp cocktail) or *sopa de mariscos* (a rich broth filled with clams, mussels, shrimp and crab), and heartier fare, such as *pescadillos* (tostados stuffed with lightly cooked, marinated fish and served with a salad) or *jaiba rellena* (crabs stuffed with mushrooms and cheese and liberally seasoned with garlic). *Valentín Gómez Farías 185, tel. 451/2–99–74. Reservations accepted. Dress: informal. AE, DC, MC, V.*

★ **El Rey Tacamba.** Friendly, attentive service and brightly colored decorations mark this three-year-old restaurant, located on the north side of the Plaza de Armas. Among its specialties are *mixiote de carnero*, a piquant (although not spicy) mutton dish, first stewed and then steamed in banana leaves; *pollo moreliano*, chicken roasted in a rich, red chile sauce and served with enchiladas covered in vegetables; and *carne tampiqueña*, a grilled flank steak accompanied by guacamole, refried beans, and tostadas. *Portal Galeana 157, tel. 451/2-20-44. Reservations accepted. Dress: informal. MC, V.*

**El Paraíso.** To jump-start your day, have a cup of the strong, rich cappuccino at El Paraíso. Breakfasts—the recommended meal at this downtown eatery—run the gamut from eggs and pancakes to fresh fruit, granola, and exotic juices (watermelon, mango, pineapple, and guayaba). The specialty is *jamón Paraíso*, fried eggs, ham, and grated cheese. The plain surroundings—Formica tables and yellow-tiled walls—don't deter locals. *Portal Galeana 103, tel. 451/2-03-74. Reservations not accepted. Dress: informal. MC, V.*

★ **Los Comensales.** This garden restaurant, a downtown favorite among the bullfight crowd, is set in an old colonial house north of the main plaza. Tables are spaced casually around a plant-filled courtyard where caged birds sing briskly. Regional dishes include *pollo de plaza* (chicken with enchiladas, carrots, potatoes, and cheese) and *huchepos* (tamales and sour cream). For breakfast, try *calabaza con leche* (baked squash with brown sugar and milk). *Calle Zaragoza 148, tel. 451/2-93-71. Reservations not accepted. Dress: informal. No credit cards.*

**Inexpensive** **Café del Bosque.** During the week, university students frequent this 1960s-style restaurant. It's tacky—floral carpet and bright green booths—but the food is good and fairly cheap. Most students can afford sandwiches or burgers; if you feel like spending a bit more, order *pollo moreliano* (chicken with enchiladas, vegetables, and french fries) or *carne à la Mexicana* (grilled beef cooked with onions, tomatoes, lemon juice, and salsa). There's a small but pleasant terrace for outdoor dining. *Plaza Rebullones, Local C-7, tel. 451/3-28-13. Reservations not accepted. Dress: informal. AE, MC, V.*

## Lodging

Morelia offers a number of pleasant colonial-style properties both in the downtown and outlying areas. Generally, the cheapest hotels are located near the bus station, moderately priced selections are clustered around the plaza (or on nearby side streets), and deluxe resort properties are in or near the Santa María hills.

Highly recommended lodgings are indicated by a star ★.

| Category | Cost* |
|---|---|
| Very Expensive | over $90 |
| Expensive | $60–$90 |
| Moderate | $25–$60 |
| Inexpensive | under $25 |

*All prices are for a standard double room, excluding 10% tax.*

## Getting Around

Many of Pátzcuaro's principal sites are located near the Plaza Vasco de Quiroga and Plaza Bocanegra in the center of town. Taxis and buses to the lake can also be found at these main squares. If you want to visit surrounding villages, taxi drivers will drive you for a reasonable rate. Be sure to agree on a fee before setting out.

## Important Addresses and Numbers

**Tourist Information**  The **Delegación de Turismo** distributes city maps and brochures (in Spanish). *Portal Hidalgo 9, off the Plaza Vasco de Quiroga, tel. 454/2–09–67. Open weekdays 9–2 and 4–7, Sat. 9–7, Sun. 9–4.*

A tourist office is also located at **La Casa de Los Once** (Patios, Loc. 11, tel. 454/2–10–18).

**Emergencies**  **Police** (tel. 454/2–05–65). **Ambulance** (tel. 454/2–18–89).

*Clinic*  **Centro Médico Quirúrgico** (Portal Hidalgo 76, tel. 454/2–19–98); **Hospital Civil** (tel. 454/2–02–85).

*Pharmacy*  **Farmacia La Paz** (at the corner of La Paz and Bocanegra in the Plaza Bocanegra tel. 454/2–08–10).

**Money Exchange**  **Banca Promex** (Portal Regules 9, tel. 454/2–24–66), **Banamex** (Portal Allende 54, tel. 454/2–10–00, 454/2–15–13, 454/2–15–14 or 454/2–15–16), **Bancomer** (Zaragoza 23, tel. 454/2–03–34 or 454/2–09–52). Many Pátzcuaro restaurants and hotels do not accept traveler's checks, though some will take major credit cards.

## Exploring

*Numbers in the margin correspond to points of interest on the Pátzcuaro map.*

Most of Pátzcuaro's sites can be visited in a few hours, but the town deserves to be explored at a leisurely pace. Begin at the
❶ **Plaza Vasco de Quiroga,** the larger of two downtown squares. A tranquil courtyard surrounded by ash trees and 16th-century mansions (since converted into hotels and shops), the plaza commemorates the bishop who restored dignity to the Tarascan people. During the Spanish conquest, Nuño de Guzmán, a lieutenant in Hernán Cortés's army, committed atrocities on the local population in his efforts to conquer western Mexico. He was eventually arrested by the Spanish authorities, and in 1537 Quiroga was appointed bishop of Michoacán. Attempting to regain the trust of the indigenous people, he established a number of model villages in the area and promoted the development of commerce among the Tarascans. Quiroga died in 1565, and his remains were consecrated in the basilica.

❷ From the plaza, cross over to the **tourist office** at Portal Hidalgo 9, where you can collect maps and brochures on the region. (As you face the front of Quiroga's statue, Portal Hidalgo is the street to your right.) As you leave the office, turn right again and continue around the plaza until you reach Calle Dr. José María Coss on the east side.

Turn right on this street, and in less than a block you'll see a
❸ long cobblestoned walkway leading to **La Casa de los 11 Patios,**

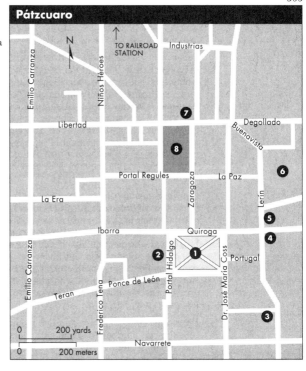

an 18th-century convent with a number of high-quality shops featuring Tarascan handiwork. As you meander through the gardens and courtyards, you'll encounter weavers producing large bolts of cloth, artists trimming black lacquerware with gold, and seamstresses embroidering blouses. Children may approach you and ask if you'd like to hear the history of the Casa. In return they expect a small donation. If you plan to shop in Pátzcuaro, this is a good place to start. You can view the selection of regional goods and begin to compare prices.

As you leave the shops, continue up a stone walkway to Calle Lerín. Though only one block east of the plaza, its aging stone walls and whitewashed houses with sloping tile roofs have an ancient feel about them. Another block down (past Calle Portugal) is the **Templo de la Compañia**, Michoacán's first cathedral. It was begun in 1540 by order of Vasco de Quiroga and completed in 1546. When the state capital was moved to Morelia some 20 years later, the church was taken over by the Jesuits. Today it remains much as it was in the 16th century. Moss has grown over the crumbling stone steps outside; the dank interior is planked with thick wood floors and lined with bare wood benches. Though not architecturally striking, a visit inside the cathedral will transport you four centuries into the past.

Continue down Calle Lerín another half block to the **Museo de Artes Populares** on your right. The Colegio de San Nicolás Obispo in the 16th century, this museum today displays colonial and contemporary crafts, such as ceramics, masks, lacquerware, colonial paintings, and ex-votos in its many rooms. Behind this building is a *troje* (traditional Tarascan wood house) braced atop a stone platform. *Admission: about $3. Open Tues.-Sat. 9-7, Sun. 9-3.*

Directly down Calle Lerín and across a cobblestoned courtyard **❻** is **La Basílica de Nuestra Señora de la Salud.** Out front Tarascan women sell hot tortillas, herbal mixtures for teas, and religious objects. From this point you can glimpse Lake Pátzcuaro in the distance. The church was begun in 1554 by Vasco de Quiroga but was never completed. Throughout the centuries others— undaunted by earthquakes and fires—took up the cause and constructed a church in honor of the Virgin of Health. Near the main altar is a statue made of cornstalk paste and orchid "juice." Several masses are still held here daily; the earliest begins shortly after dawn.

Continue downhill from the basilica for about two blocks to **❼** reach the **Biblioteca Pública Gertrudis Bocanegra.** In the back of this library is a vast mural depicting in great detail the history of the region and of the Tarascan people. It was completed by Juan O'Gorman in 1942. If you look closely at the bottom, you may be able to make out images of Vasco de Quiroga, portrayed as friend and protector of the Indians, and Gertrudis Bocanegra, a local heroine who was shot in 1814 for refusing to divulge the revolutionaries' secrets to the Spaniards. *Open weekdays 9-7, Sat. 9-1.*

From the library, continue again to your right for a half block to the large outdoor **mercado** sprawled along Calle Libertad and its side streets. At times the road is so crowded with people and their wares—fruit, vegetables, beans, rice, herbs, and sponges—that it is difficult to walk. On Friday, market day, the street is particularly packed. If you press on for about a block, you'll see an indoor market to your left, filled with more produce, large hanging slabs of meat, vendors selling hot food, and a variety of cheap trinkets.

When you've completed your market stroll, retrace your steps down Calle Libertad. Across the street from the library, stop **❽** in at the **Plaza Bocanegra.** This square, marked by a statue of the local heroine, is just one block north of Plaza Vasco de Quiroga, your starting point. While Bocanegra is the smaller of the two squares, it is the center of Pátzcuaro's commercial life. Bootblacks, pushcart vendors, and bus and taxi stands to Lake Pátzcuaro are all found in this plaza.

**Time Out**    Before heading to the lake, sit in the shady square for a moment and enjoy a rich Michoacán ice-cream or fruit bar. Then grab a taxi or the San Bartolo/Lago bus to the *embarcadero* (wharf).

A 10-minute ride will take you to the tranquil shores of Lake Pátzcuaro. There are a few lakeside restaurants here that serve fresh white fish and other local catches. Amble along the dock or peek into the waterfront crafts shops. If you have time, a boat trip to **Janitzio** (the largest of Lake Pátzcuaro's five islands) is highly recommended.

Wooden launches, with room for 25 people, depart for Janitzio daily from 8 AM to 5 PM. Purchase round-trip tickets at a dockside office (where prices are controlled by the tourist department). The ride to Janitzio takes about 30 minutes and is particularly beautiful in late afternoon, when the sun is low in the sky. Once you're out on the lake, fishermen with butterfly nets may approach your boat. The nets are no longer used for fishing, but for a small donation these locals will let you take their picture.

On most days (November 2 being the exception), Janitzio is a quiet island inhabited by Tarascan Indians. It is crowned by a huge statue of independence hero José María Morelos, which is accessible by cobblestoned stairway. Though the road twists past many souvenir stands as it ascends, don't be discouraged. The view from the summit—of the lake, the town, and the surrounding hills—is well worth the climb. Inside the statue are some remarkable murals that spiral up from the base to the tip of the monument.

**Nightlife**  The Dance of Los Viejitos (Old Men), a widely known Mexican native dance, is performed on Saturday evenings at the Hotel Posada de Don Vasco (tel. 454/2–02–27). A buffet dinner with entertainment costs approximately $13.

## Off the Beaten Track

The remains of **Tzintzuntzán,** the ancient capital of the Tarascan Indian kingdom, lie 17 kilometers (10.5 miles) northeast of Pátzcuaro. When the Spanish came to colonize the region in the 16th century, some 40,000 Tarascans lived and worshiped in this lakeshore village, which they called "place of the hummingbirds." The ruins of their pyramid-shape temples, or *yacatas,* still stand today and are open to the public for a small admission charge. Visitors can also find vestiges of a 16th-century Franciscan monastery where Spanish friars attempted to convert the Indians to Christianity. Though Tzintzuntzán lost some prominence when Bishop Vasco de Quiroga moved the seat of his diocese to Pátzcuaro in 1540, the village is still well known for its handicrafts. The Tarascan Indians turn out a variety of products in straw and ceramics that are sold in numerous shops along the main street of town. To reach Tzintzuntzán, take the bus marked Quiroga from Pátzcuaro's Central Camionera; travel time is about 30 minutes.

## Dining

Most restaurants in Pátzcuaro specialize in seafood. In addition to whitefish (which is featured on most menus), look for *trucha* (trout) and *charales* and *boquerones* (two small, locally caught fish served as appetizers). Tarascan specialties, such as a tomato-based soup, are also common. As a rule restaurants are located around the two plazas and in hotels. Since the large meal is served at midday, many dining establishments are shuttered by 9 PM.

Highly recommended restaurants are indicated by a star ★.

| Category | Cost* |
|---|---|
| Moderate | $8–$15 |
| Inexpensive | under $8 |

*per person, excluding drinks and service*

**Moderate** **La Casona.** This unpretentious restaurant on Plaza Vasco de Quiroga, with whitewashed walls and white ceiling *vigas* (beams), is brightened by orange tablecloths. The house specialties include *caldo de pesca* (fish soup), and *pescado blanca* (whitefish), among other local dishes. *Plaza Vasco de Quiroga 65, tel. 454/2–11–79. Reservations not accepted. Dress: casual. MC, V.*

**Inexpensive** **El Patio.** Though this newly renovated restaurant features
★ mouth-watering whitefish platters, it's possible to duck in at midday for just a strong cappuccino or glass of local wine. (There are several varieties of wine; waiters can help you choose among them.) For a late-afternoon snack, a plate of quesadillas with a side order of guacamole is highly recommended. For full-blown meals, try the whitefish served with salsa, vegetables, and french fries. *Plaza Vasco de Quiroga 19, tel. 454/2–04–84. Dress: informal. DC, MC, V.*

**Restaurante Gran Hotel.** Though this one-room restaurant is connected to the Gran Hotel, it is independently owned and attracts a mix of locals and tourists to its midday meal. The furnishings are simple: tables covered with amber-colored cloths and set beneath wood chandeliers. The food is good and wholesome. Specialties include lightly breaded whitefish and chicken with mole sauce. Tarascan soup (with a tomato base, cheese, cream, and tortillas) is also worth trying. *Portal Regules 6, tel. 454/2–04–98. Reservations not accepted. Dress: informal. No credit cards.*

★ **Restaurante Hotel Posada La Basílica.** From a corner table in this glass-enclosed restaurant, patrons have views of the mountains, the lake, and tile-roofed homes. Open for breakfast and lunch (8 AM–4 PM), this dining spot offers such regional specialties as broiled trout with garlic, fried charales, and *sopa de corunda* (tamales with cheese and cream). Mexican-style eggs and a fresh-fruit platter are recommended morning fare. *Calle Arciga 6, tel. 454/2–11–08. Reservations not accepted. Dress: informal. No credit cards.*

**Restaurante Los Escudos.** This colonial-style restaurant, located on the Plaza Vasco de Quiroga, is frequented by foreigners who stay in the adjoining hotel. The varied menu ranges from club sandwiches to multicourse midday meals. Two particularly tempting treats are the Tarascan soup and *pollo especial Los Escudos* (chicken sautéed in tomato sauce and vegetables). Checked tablecloths and yellow chimney lamps create a cozy atmosphere. *Portal Hidalgo 74, tel. 454/2–01–38 or 454/2–12–90. Reservations not accepted. Dress: informal. MC, V.*

## Lodging

Though Pátzcuaro has no deluxe properties, there is an ample number of clean, moderately priced hotels. Most are located on or within a few blocks of the Plaza Vasco de Quiroga. Several more expensive properties are situated on Avenida Lázaro Cárdenas, the road to Lake Pátzcuaro. If you're planning to be in town on or near November 2, the Mexican Day of the Dead, make hotel reservations at least six months in advance.

Highly recommended lodgings are indicated by a star ★.

| Category | Cost* |
|---|---|
| Expensive | $60–$90 |
| Moderate | $25–$60 |
| Inexpensive | under $25 |

*All prices are for a standard double room, excluding 10% tax.*

**Expensive** **Hotel Posada de Don Vasco.** Located several minutes out of
★ town on the road to Lake Pátzcuaro, this sprawling resort hotel
offers a wide range of indoor and outdoor amenities. Its 30 new
rooms are thickly carpeted and have either balconies or patios;
the older quarters, decorated in a colonial style, are smaller
and open onto a courtyard. The manicured grounds are relatively quiet despite the occasional rumbling of a passing bus or
truck. *Av. Las Americas 450, 61500, tel. 454/2-02-27 or 454/
2-27-04, fax 454/2-02-62. 103 rooms with bath, including 4
suites. Facilities: restaurant, pool, tennis and badminton
courts, bowling alley, billiard tables. AE, DC, MC, V.*

**Moderate** **Hotel Posada La Basílica.** This colonial-style inn, housed in a
17th-century building, faces the Basilica of the Virgin of
Health. On some mornings strains from a postdawn mass filter
softly into the hotel; in the evenings, when there's a fair across
the way, louder, more resonant music is audible. Though noisy,
the property deserves a positive mention for its comfortable,
individually decorated rooms. Thick wood shutters cover floor-
to-ceiling windows, walls are trimmed in hand-painted colonial
designs, and the rugs are handwoven. Some rooms have fireplaces, but check with management before attempting to use
them, as not all of them are functional. *Calle Arciga 6, 61600,
tel. 454/2-11-08 or 454/2-11-81; reservations 454/2-06-59. 11
rooms with bath. Facilities: restaurant, fireplaces (in lobby
and 7 rooms). No credit cards.*

**Los Escudos.** The 16th-century home of the Count de la Lama
and the Marquis de Villahermosa de Alfaro on the Plaza Vasco
de Quiroga is today a cozy hotel. Its courtyards brim with potted plants, and some guest rooms contain small murals of
Tarascan Indian scenes. Ten rooms situated in back and
shielded from street noise open onto an outdoor patio. Twenty-
five rooms have color TVs; five rooms offer fireplaces. *Portal
Hidalgo 73, 61600, tel. 454/2-01-38 or 454/2-12-90, fax 454/2-
27-56. 30 rooms with bath. Facilities: restaurant. MC, V.*

★ **Mansión Iturbe.** This hotel, housed in a 17th-century mansion,
still retains much of its colonial charm. Plant-filled courtyards
are ringed by stone archways. Rooms have large wood-and-
glass doors; their interiors are partially carpeted and decorated with red-and-black checked spreads and drapes. The
tranquil second-floor courtyard has a good view of the neighborhood. *Portal Morelos 59, 61600, tel. 454/2-03-68. 12 rooms
with bath. Facilities: restaurant, tobacco/souvenir shop. MC,
V.*

**Mesón del Gallo.** Located on a fairly quiet side street near the
Casa de los 11 Patios, this two-story property offers modern
rooms in a garden setting. In the rooms, beds have wood-and-
tile headboards and magenta spreads and drapes. Suites, complete with minibars, are furnished in more subdued hues. The
pool is encircled by bougainvillea, fruit trees, and a rock garden. When the second-floor banquet room is rented out for afternoon parties, the decibel level rises. *Calle Dr. José María*

*Coss 20, 61600, tel. 454/2-14-74, fax 454/2-15-11. 25 rooms with bath, including 5 suites. Facilities: restaurant, bar, pool. AE, MC, V.*

## Excursion to Uruapan

The subtropical town of **Uruapan,** located about 64 kilometers (40 miles) west of Pátzcuaro, is distinctly different from its lakeside neighbor. At an elevation of 5,300 feet, it is a populous, commercial center with a warm climate and lush vegetation. The town's name is derived from the Tarascan word *urupan,* meaning "where the flowers bloom."

Uruapan can be reached from Pátzcuaro by either car or bus. Route 14 is the most direct route between the two cities. There is also frequent bus service on the Flecha Amarilla and other major lines; travel time is about 70 minutes.

You can see several points of interest within a few hours. The first, **La Huatapera,** is located off Uruapan's Plaza Principal. This 16th-century hospital has been converted into the **Museo Regional de Arte Popular.** It houses a collection of crafts from the state of Michoacán, including an excellent display of lacquerware made in Uruapan. *Tel. 452/2-21-38. Open Tues.-Sun. 9:30-1:30 and 3:30-6.*

The **Mercado de Antojitos,** an immense, sprawling market, begins directly in back of the museum and extends quite a distance north along Calle Constitución. Along the road are Tarascan Indians selling large mounds of produce, fresh fish, beans, homemade cheese, and a variety of cheap manufactured goods. If you travel south along Calle Constitución, you'll come to a courtyard where vendors have set up cooking stoves and sell hot food to passersby.

Another recommended eatery is the **Parrilla Tarasca,** a two-level restaurant specializing in grilled meats. For a delicious treat, try the *carne asada;* it's served with grilled scallions, avocado, and *frijoles charros,* a popular Mexican side order of beans in broth. The varieties of salsa are also outstanding. *Calle Alvaro Obregón 4, no phone. Open daily 8-11. MC, V.*

Head over to the **Parque Nacional Eduardo Ruiz,** located about a half mile from the Plaza Principal off Calle Independencia. Stroll through the verdant acreage to the source of the River Cupatitzio and abundant fountains, waterfalls, and springs.

Eleven kilometers (7 miles) south along the river is the magnificent waterfall at **Tzaráracua.** At this point the Cupatitzio plunges 150 feet off a sheer rock cliff into a riverbed below; a rainbow seems to hang perpetually over the site. Buses marked Tzaráracua leave sporadically from the Plaza Principal in Uruapan. You can also take a taxi or drive there via Avenida Lázaro Cárdenas.

Farther afield, about 32 kilometers (20 miles) north of Uruapan, lies the extinct **Paricutín volcano.** Its initial burst of lava and ashes wiped out the nearby village of San Juan Parangaricutiro in 1943. Today travelers can visit this buried site by hiring gentle mountain ponies and a Tarascan guide in the town of Angahuan. To reach Angahuan, take the Los Reyes bus from Uruapan's Central Camionera or go by car via the Uruapan-Carapan highway.

# 8 Guadalajara

*Updated by*
*Chuck Edgerly*

Traditions are preserved and customs perpetuated in Guadalajara; it's a place where the siesta is an institution and the fiesta an art form. The city is the birthplace of *el jarabe tapatío* (the Mexican hat dance), *charreadas* (rodeos), mariachis, and tequila.

Mexico's second-largest city, Guadalajara is engaged in a struggle to retain its provincial ambience and colonial charm as its population approaches 6 million. Emigrés from Mexico City after the devastating 1985 earthquake and staggering numbers of the rural poor seeking employment have created a population explosion that strains the capacity of public services and the city's often outdated infrastructure. Visitors to the city can enjoy the tree-lined boulevards, parks, plazas, and stately Churrigueresque architecture, but recent years have indeed brought traffic jams and occasional heavy pollution, coming from the industrial zone outside of the city, to the downtown area.

Guadalajara has always been one of the most socially traditional and politically conservative cities in Mexico. It has also been the seat of Christian fundamentalism and was one of the strategic areas of the *Cristeros*, a movement of Catholic fanatics in western Mexico in the 1920s. *Tapatíos*, as the city's residents are called, even seem to take a certain amount of pride in their straight and narrow outlook. The International Gay and Lesbian Association (ILGA) wanted to hold its 1991 annual conference here, but such a public outcry ensued—protests ranging from mass marches to death-threatening graffiti to indignant newspaper editorials—that the municipal and state government refused permission. At the last minute, the convention found a friend in Acapulco.

Still, Tapatíos are historically accustomed to challenge and change. (The name comes from *tlapatíotl*, or three units or purses of cacao or tortillas used as currency by the Indians of Jalisco.) Within 10 years of its founding in 1532, the location of the city changed three times. In 1542, the City Council again deliberated on a new site for the fledgling municipality. After days of discussion and indecision, an intrepid woman, Doña Beatriz de Hernández, rose to address the assembly: "If you cannot make up your minds, I will. The only place suitable to build the capital is in the center of the Atemajac Valley, where the city can expand."

The governor immediately accepted the proposal, which placed Guadalajara on a mile-high plain of the Sierra Madre, bounded on three sides by rugged cliffs and on the fourth by the spectacular Barranca de Oblatos (Oblatos Canyon). A near-perfect semitropical climate and proximity to the Pacific Ocean (240 kilometers/150 miles) ensure warm, sunny days with just a hint of humidity and cool, clear nights.

Geographically isolated from the rest of the republic during the nearly 300 years of Spanish rule, the city cultivated and maintained a political and cultural autonomy. By the end of the 16th century, tons of silver were flowing into Guadalajara from area mines, creating the first millionaires of what was then known as New Galicia. Under orders from Spain, much of the wealth was lavished on magnificent churches, residences, and monuments. Many of these reminders of the golden era still stand in a series of contiguous plazas in downtown Guadalajara. The imposing 16th-century cathedral is the symbol of the city and an ideal starting point for a leisurely day or two of exploration.

The city also has numerous modern attractions and activities, including a new zoo, a planetarium, and the immense Parque Agua Azul, which has carnival rides, a minitrain, swimming pool, and Sunday concerts. There are exhibitions of contemporary art at the Instituto Cultural Cabañas and in private galleries throughout the city, and tours of Museo Orozco, the former home and studio of Guadalajara's most famous muralist, José Clemente Orozco.

Guadalajara is also a great place for shopping. The Mercado Libertad, Latin America's largest enclosed market, and El Baratillo, the world's largest flea market, offer a seemingly endless variety of merchandise and the opportunity to bargain with vendors. The Plaza del Sol, Latin America's biggest shopping mall, and Calle Esteban Alatorre, encompassing eight city blocks with more than 60 shoe stores, sell products you could buy at home, but usually with much lower price tags.

The suburbs of San Pedro Tlaquepaque (*Tla-kay-PAH-kay*) and Tonalá produce some of Mexico's finest and most popular traditional crafts and folk art, including intricate blown-glass miniatures, jewelry, silver and copperware, leather and hand-carved wood furniture, and handwoven clothing. In Tlaquepaque, located on the southeastern fringe of Guadalajara, more than 300 shops line pedestrian malls and plazas. This charming town, which gained international acclaim for its production of ceramics, is also the birthplace of mariachi music.

Tonalá *(Toe-na-LA)* is 8 kilometers (5 miles) east of and centuries removed from its commercial neighbor. One of Mexico's oldest pueblos, Tonalá is a quiet village with dusty, cobblestoned streets and adobe houses. Only in the past few years have craftsmen—primarily ceramicists—welcomed tourists into their homes and workshops.

Perhaps it is the Mexican arts and culture, perhaps the favorable exchange rate, perhaps the springlike climate; whatever the reason, more than 25,000 U.S. and Canadian citizens have retired in the Guadalajara area. The majority reside along the shores of Lake Chapala, Mexico's largest inland body of water. In the towns of Chapala (45 kilometers, or 28 miles, south of Guadalajara) and nearby Ajijic *(Ah-he-HEEK)*, residents enjoy most of the amenities and services they were accustomed to north of the border.

Finally, it is worth noting the tragedy that befell Guadalajara in April 1992. More than 200 citizens died in a succession of sewer explosions that went off mid-morning on the 23rd. As a tourist, you will not directly encounter the effects—they were restricted to a working-class neighborhood of the city where virtually no visitor attractions exist—but residents of the city suffered greatly. At press time, the areas affected were still under reconstruction.

# Essential Information

## Arriving and Departing by Plane

**Airport and Airlines** Libertador Miguel Hidalgo International Airport (tel. 3/689–0249) is 16.6 kilometers (11 miles) south of Guadalajara. Unfortunately, Guadalajara's only commercial airport is frequently unable to meet the demands of the increased air service to the city. A new international terminal is planned in the next decade.

Aeroméxico (tel. 800/237–6639) and **Mexicana** (tel. 800/531–7921) have nonstop service from many major U.S. cities. Through Dallas, **American Airlines** (tel. 800/433–7300) provides service to Guadalajara from all cities in its system. **Continental Airlines** (tel. 800/525–0280) provides the same service through Houston. Nonstop flight times are: from Chicago, 4 hours; Dallas, 2 hours; Los Angeles, 2 hours and 40 minutes; and New York, 4 hours and 50 minutes.

**Between the Airport and Downtown** **Autotransportes Aeropuerto** (tel. 3/689–00–32) is a *combi* (VW minibus) service to city hotels and other destinations in the Guadalajara area. Fares, based on distance from the airport, are between $8 and $14 per person.

*By Van*

*By Taxi* Taxis charge between $12 and $18 to city hotels. You can bargain with drivers, but make sure you both agree on the fare before you enter the cab.

*By Limousine* **Royal Limousines** (Miguel de Cervantes 382, Sector Juárez, tel. 3/642–5605) has chauffeur-driven stretch limousines to downtown Guadalajara for $55.

*By Car* The Chapala Highway 23, a well-paved four-lane thoroughfare, stretches north from the airport to the city. The 30-minute trip can be delayed by slow-moving caravans of trucks and weekend recreational traffic. To reach downtown hotels, just past El Tapatío Resort, turn left from the highway onto Calzada Gonzales Gallo and then right onto Av. 16 de Septiembre at Parque Agua Azul; to hotels on Avenida López Mateos Sur, just past El Tapatío Resort, turn left from the highway onto Calzada de las Torres, which turns into Calzada Lázaro Cárdenas.

Most international and domestic car-rental agencies have booths at the airport in both the domestic and the new international terminals.

## Arriving and Departing by Train and Bus

*By Train* To celebrate the 100th anniversary of railroad passenger service in 1988, the Mexican government spent millions to improve service and facilities. The upgrading of Mexico's rail system makes it a comfortable and economical option for traveling to Guadalajara. The scenic trip from the border cities—including Ciudad Juárez, Nogales, and Tijuana—takes 34 hours and features new cars and hot meal service. Information about the Mexican National Railways, including schedules and fares, can be obtained from any Mexican Government Tourism Office. The Estación de Ferrocarril (train station, tel. 3/650–0570) is located at the south end of Avenida 16 de Septiembre, near Parque Agua Azul.

10

8

okkK

**By Bus** First-class, air-conditioned buses with rest rooms provide daily service to Guadalajara from most major cities on the border. **Greyhound** (tel. 800/237–8211) has lists of the telephone numbers of bus terminals in border cities served by Mexican bus lines. English-speaking representatives of the Mexican carriers will give you schedule and fare information. The **Nueva Central Camionera** (New Central Bus Station tel. 3/657–5180 or 3/657–7225) is located 9.6 kilometers (6 miles) southeast of downtown Guadalajara on the highway to Zapotlanejo.

## Important Addresses and Numbers

**Tourist Information State Tourist Offices** The main office is well stocked with timely information on area hotels, restaurants, and attractions, and has a helpful, bilingual staff. *Calle Morelos 102, in the Plaza Tapatía, tel. 3/658–0049. Open weekdays 9–9, weekends 9–1.*

Branch offices are located in **Tlaquepaque** (Guillermo Prieto 80, near the main entrance to El Templo Parroquial de San Pedro, the parish church, tel. 3/635–1503), and **Zapopan** (20 de Noviembre No. 103, in the Municipal Palace, tel. 3/633–0571). *All offices are open weekdays 9–8:30, Sat. 9–1.*

*Municipal Tourism Office* The **Guadalajara Tourist Office** has a very limited amount of printed information. *Av. Vallarta and Los Arcos (the Arches), tel. 3/616–3333. Open weekdays 9–3, Sat. 9–1.*

The **Guadalajara Visitors and Convention Bureau** sometimes has a selection of maps and brochures. *Chamber of Commerce building, Av. Vallarta Poniente 4095, tel. 3/647–9331. Open weekdays 9–5.*

*Associations and Organizations* The U.S. and Canadian communities are eager to provide information and recommendations and answer any questions about the Guadalajara area.

**American Society of Jalisco.** The Personal Services Committee chairman is Judy Furton (tel. 3/621–2348). *San Francisco 3332, in Chapalita, tel. 3/621–2395. Open weekdays 9:30–4:30.*

**New Yorkers.** This group, which meets the first Sunday of each month at 5 PM at members' homes, is made up of people who have lived, worked, or gone to school in New York. Contact Gail Benedict (tel. 3/615–2091).

**Unitarian Fellowship.** This club meets every Sunday at noon at the American Society of Jalisco (*see* address, *above*); contact chairperson Gail Benedict (tel. 3/615–2091).

**Publications** *Retiring in Guadalajara* (Retiring in Guadalajara Publications, Apdo. 5-409, Guadalajara, Jalisco, Mexico, tel. 3/621–2348 or 3/647–9924), by Fran and Judy Furton, is a detailed, up-to-date newsletter for prospective American and Canadian retirees. It discloses tons of information on living costs, housing and work opportunities, medical services, English-speaking organizations, and the sundry advantages of retirement in Guadalajara. Mr. and Mrs. Furton offer one free issue in response to written requests.

*MRTA: Mexico Retirement and Travel Assistance* (Box 2190–23, Henderson, NV 89009) provides information on Mexican life and tips on sightseeing and recommends restaurants. It is published quarterly and is available free at tourist information offices and hotels in the area.

*The Colony Reporter* (Duque de Rivas 254, Guadalajara, Jalisco, Mexico, tel. 3/615–2177), a weekly newspaper in its 30th year of publication, is the best of a mixed lot of English-language periodicals. Its stories and community and cultural listings provide a great deal of information otherwise unavailable. It is sold for $1 at newsstands and hotels.

**Consulates** **United States** (Progreso 175, near the intersection of Av. Chapultepec and Av. La Paz, tel. 3/625–2700; after-hours emergency tel. 3/630–3131).

**Canada:** Offices are in the Fiesta Americana Guadalajara (Aurelio Aceves 225, tel. 3/625–3434).

**Emergencies** **City police** (tel. 3/617–6060); **state police** (tel. 3/622–3886); **highway patrol** (tel. 06); **fire department** (tel. 3/619–5241 and 3/623–0833); **Cruz Roja** (Red Cross) (tel. 3/613–1550), and **Cruz Verde** (Green Cross) (tel. 3/643–7190).

*Hospitals* **Hospital del Carmen** (Tarascos 3435, near the Plaza México, tel. 3/647–1048), **Hospital México-Americano** (Colomos 2110, tel. 3/641–3141), and **Hospital Santa María Chapalita** (Niño Obrero 1666, in the Chapalita neighborhood, tel. 3/621–4050).

*Doctors* The U.S. Consulate (*see* Consulates, *above*) maintains a list of English-speaking doctors. All major hotels have the names of doctors who are on 24-hour call.

**English-language** **Sandi Bookstore** features a variety of newspapers, magazines, **Bookstores** and books. *Tepeyac 718 in the Chapalita neighborhood, tel. 3/621–0863. Open weekdays 9:30–2:30 and 3:30–7, Sat. 9–2.*

**Late-night** **Farmacias Guadalajara** has several branches that are open 24 **Pharmacies** hours. *Avenida Las Americas 2, tel. 3/615–8516; Av. Javier Mina 221, tel. 3/617–8555.*

**Travel Agencies** Many of the city's 150 travel agencies are in the two hotel zones, El Centro (downtown) and on Avenida López Mateos Sur (on the southwest side of the city). There is an American Express office at Avenida Vallarta 2440, near Los Arcos (tel. 3/616–1928).

**Telephones** At press time, the pay phones found on street corners, many of *Local Calls* them around the Plaza Tapatía, still accepted only the old 100-peso coins. All major hotels have telephones in the lobbies from which guests can make local calls at no charge.

### Opening and Closing Times

**Banks** are open weekdays 9–1:30. A few branch offices located in shopping centers are now open on Saturday 9–1.

**Museums** are open Tuesday–Sunday 9–4 generally, but hours may vary.

**Stores** in downtown Guadalajara and in shopping malls are open weekdays 10–8, Saturday 10–6; Sunday hours vary.

### Getting Around

Guadalajara's major attractions are best seen on foot. For points of interest outside the city center, Guadalajara has an inexpensive, well-organized public transportation system.

**By Bus** This is without a doubt the most economical and efficient but least comfortable means of traversing the city. Buses run every few minutes between 6 AM and 10:30 PM from the center of the city to all local attractions, including Tlaquepaque and Zapopan. The 20¢ fare makes buses the preferred mode of transportation for Guadalajara natives, so expect to stand during daylight hours.

**By Tram** The *tren ligero* (light train) runs along Avenida Federalismo from the Periférico (city beltway) Sur to Periférico Norte, near the Benito Juárez Auditorium. The system, which is clean, safe, and efficient, has 16 trains running at five-minute intervals between 19 stations and costs about 25¢. A second line, running east–west along Av. Juarez, is under construction.

**By Taxi** Taxis are readily available and reasonably economical. Tell the driver where you are going and agree on a fare *before* you enter the cab. Fare schedules, listing prices to downtown and all major attractions, are posted in the lobby of all hotels. *Sitios* (cab stands) are located near all hotels and attractions.

## Guided Tours

**City Tours** **Copenhagen Tours** (tel. 3/621–1008 or 3/629–7964) has several city tours, with admission to attractions included in the price. Transport can be by van or car. The branch office is located at Boulevard de las Cordilleras 152; phone for hotel pickup.

**Panoramex** (Calzada Federalismo Sur 948, tel. 3/610–5109 and 3/610–5005), Guadalajara's largest tour company, provides city tours and day-long excursions to Tequila, Lake Chapala, and Tlaquepaque for about $30, including lunch. Air-conditioned buses with bilingual guides depart from Los Arcos and Parque San Francisco each morning.

**Royal Limousines** (Miguel de Cervantes 382, Sector Juárez, tel. 3/642–5605) offers a variety of city and area tour packages in a stretch limousine with bilingual guide; domestic liquor is included in all tours. Limousines can also be rented for $40 per hour for self-guided tours. Phone for reservations between 9 and 2 and between 4 and 7 daily.

**Personal Guides** The federal government maintains a list of licensed bilingual guides. These guides charge $12 per hour for orientation or special-interest tours in their own automobiles. Included in the list are Carlos Garcia (tel. 3/632–4509), Ramiro Romo (tel. 3/642–4646), and Roberto Arellano Deyran (tel. 3/657–8376). Most hotels have a list of guides available on short notice.

**Calandrias** You can hire a horse-drawn carriage in front of the Museo Regional, the Mercado Libertad, or Parque San Francisco. The charge is about $10 for a half-hour tour and about $17 for a full hour, for up to four passengers. Few drivers speak English, so stop by the Federal Tourist Office (*see* Important Addresses and Numbers, *above*) first and ask for brochures that describe the attractions in downtown Guadalajara.

# Exploring the Guadalajara Area

Beginning around 1960, 20th-century architecture started to threaten the historical integrity of this provincial state capital. In the early 1980s, city fathers declared a 30-square-block area in the heart of the city a cultural sanctuary. The 16th-century buildings here are connected by a series of large Spanish-style plazas where today's inhabitants enjoy life: young children chase gaily colored balloons, young lovers cuddle on tree-shaded park benches, and grandparents stroll hand in hand past vendors and marble fountains. At nearby Mariachi Plaza the nostalgic songs and music of costumed troubadors can be heard. The downtown walking tour (Tour 1) visits the churches, monuments, and museums of colonial Guadalajara.

The second tour focuses on the traditional arts and crafts of Tlaquepaque and Tonalá, two towns that are a 20-minute drive from downtown Guadalajara. The third tour covers the lakeside towns of Chapala and Ajijic, 45 kilometers (28 miles) south of Guadalajara. This scenic area is a weekend retreat for wealthy Tapatíos and a retirement haven for *norte-americanos*.

## Highlights for First-time Visitors

Catedrál
Instituto Cultural Cabañas
Museo Regional de la Cerámica
Regional Museum of Guadalajara
Restaurant with No Name
Teatro Degollado
Nueva Posada, Ajijic
Tonalá market (Thursday and Sunday)

## Colonial Guadalajara

*Numbers in the margin correspond to p oints of interest on the Guadalajara map.*

**❶** The focal point of downtown is the **catedrál,** consecrated in 1618. It is an intriguing mélange of architectural styles, the result of design and structural modifications during the 60 years of construction. Its emblematic twin towers replaced the original much shorter ones, which were toppled in the devastating earthquake of 1818. The interior contains fine examples of 16th-through 18th-century Spanish art and decor. Ten of the silver and gilt altars were gifts of King Fernando VII (in appreciation of Guadalajara's financial support of Spain during the Napoleonic Wars); the 11th, of sculpted white marble, was carved in Italy in 1863. The altar and statue dedicated to Our Lady of the Rose are exquisite. The statue, carved from a single piece of balsa wood, was a gift from King Charles V in the 16th century. The image and remains of Saint Innocence, brought here from the catacombs of Rome, are on the left side of the main altar. On the walls of the cathedral hang some of the world's most beautiful *retablos* (altarpieces); above the sacristy is the priceless 17th-century painting of Bartolomé Esteban Murillo, *The Assumption of the Virgin*. The sign near the front door requests

319

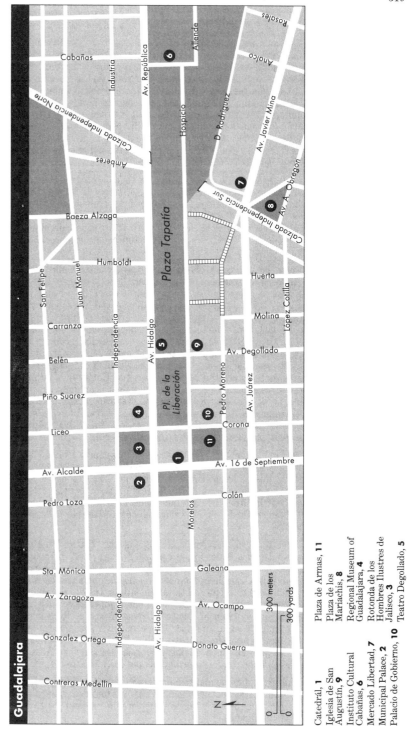

Catedrál, **1**
Iglesia de San
Augustín, **9**
Instituto Cultural
Cabañas, **6**
Mercado Libertad, **7**
Municipal Palace, **2**
Palacio de Gobierno, **10**

Plaza de Armas, **11**
Plaza de los
Mariachis, **8**
Regional Museum of
Guadalajara, **4**
Rotonda de los
Hombres Ilustres de
Jalisco, **3**
Teatro Degollado, **5**

that visitors be appropriately attired. *Av. Alcalde between Av. Hidalgo and Calle Morelos. Open daily 7 AM–9 PM.*

The main entrance to the cathedral overlooks the **Plaza de la Ciudad de Guadalajara,** a spacious square that is ideal for serious people-watching, since Tapatíos use it as a shortcut. Walk across Avenida Hidalgo from the north side of the plaza (to your left as you face the cathedral) to the **Municipal Palace** (City Hall). Though this building has a colonial facade, it was not built until 1952. You may wish to stop in to see the mural by Gabriel Flores—a prominent and prolific Tapatío—on the center stairwell (you may *have* to visit the palace to pay a 50¢ fine to retrieve your front license plate—traffic police remove them from illegally parked cars).

Directly across Avenida Alcalde, on the north side of the cathedral, is the **Rotonda de los Hombres Ilustres de Jalisco** (Monument to the Illustrious Men of Jalisco). A tree-shaded rotunda encircled by 17 Doric columns, it is actually a mausoleum containing the remains of 11 of Jalisco's favorite sons. Surrounding the monument are brass sculptures representing those who are buried inside.

From the east side of the monument, walk across Calle Liceo to the **Regional Museum of Guadalajara** (also known as the State Museum). Constructed at the end of the 17th century, this stately Baroque and colonial building served as a seminary until 1918. Since then, it has housed the art, archaeology, and history museum. The first-floor galleries, which surround a courtyard of Roman arches and tropical gardens, contain artifacts and memorabilia that trace the history of western Mexico from prehistoric times through the Spanish conquest. In the main gallery are the royal carriages of Emperor Maximilian and President Juárez. On the second floor is an impressive collection of works by European and Mexican artists, including Bartolomé Esteban Murillo and Diego Rivera. *Av. Hidalgo between Calle Liceo and Pino Suárez, tel. 3/614–9957. Admission: about $4.50; Sun. free. Open Tues.–Sun. 9–3:45.*

Occupying the next block to the left on Avenida Hidalgo is the **Palacio de Legisladores** (Legislative Palace). Over the past 300 years this building has been a customs house, tobacco warehouse, and *posada* (inn). On the next block, across Calle Belén, is the **Palacio de Justicia** (Hall of Justice), the state courthouse. This colonial building was originally part of the city's first convent.

Directly across Avenida Hidalgo is the **Teatro Degollado,** Guadalajara's famous opera house. Inaugurated in 1866, the magnificent structure was modeled after Milan's La Scala. Above the Corinthian columns gracing the entranceway is a relief depicting Apollo and the seven Muses. Inside, red and gold balconies ascend to a multitiered dome adorned with Gerardo Suárez's depiction of Dante's *Divine Comedy.* Reopened in September 1988 after a year-long renovation, the theater is the permanent home for the Guadalajara Philharmonic and the Ballet Folklórico. Open during performances (*see* The Arts and Nightlife, *below,* for information) and daily 10 AM–2 PM.

Walk around to the rear to **Founders Square.** According to tradition, this is the spot on which the city was founded; the sculpted frieze of the theater's rear wall depicts the ceremony with 60 of the founding fathers.

You are now at the head of the **Plaza Tapatía,** a five-block-long pedestrian mall that ends at the **Instituto Cultural Cabañas.** The plaza is lined with stores and galleries and filled with trees, fountains, and whimsical sculptures.

**Time Out**  An outlet of the city's most popular ice-cream franchise, **Helados Bing** is located two blocks east of the Teatro Degollado on the north side of the plaza, just east of the Children's Fountain. For natives, a stop at Helados Bing is a custom (if not an obsession); for tourists, it is a welcome respite from an afternoon of sightseeing. Choose from 30 flavors of pasteurized ice cream and find a shaded bench where you can take in the activity.

**⑥** On the east end of the plaza is the **Instituto Cultural Cabañas,** the city's cultural center. Bishop Juan Cruz Ruíz Cabañas founded an orphanage in this building in 1801, and it was home for 400 orphans and indigent children until the 1970s. The rooms, which surround 23 flower-filled patios, contain permanent and revolving art exhibits. The central dome of the main chapel displays a series of murals painted by José Clemente Orozco in 1938–39. *The Man of Fire,* which depicts a man enveloped in flames who is ascending toward infinity and yet not consumed by the fire, represents the spirit of mankind. It is generally considered to be his finest work. There is a permanent exhibit of Orozco's paintings, cartoons, and drawings in Room 189. Ask the attendant at the front desk for an English-speaking guide. *Calle Cabañas 8 at the Plaza Tapatía, tel. 3/ 617–4322. Admission: about $2. Open weekdays 10–6, weekends 9–3.*

As you leave the Instituto, walk back west through the Plaza Tapatía to the **Quetzalcóatl Fountain** at the center of the plaza; **⑦** turn left and walk down the stairs to get to the **Mercado Libertad** (Liberty Market). Inside this modern three-story building is Latin America's largest enclosed market. Within a three-square-block area you can browse over 1,000 privately owned stalls selling everything that is grown, manufactured, or handmade in Mexico.

Turn left as you leave the market and cross Avenida Javier Mina (we recommend that you use the pedestrian overpass to avoid the constant flow of traffic) to **Iglesia de San Juan de Díos** (San Juan de Díos Church). In front of the church, you will see a line of colorful calandrias, each behind a patient, motionless **⑧** horse. Next to the church is the **Plaza de los Mariachis,** a picturesque little plaza where mariachi groups perform. While the action and ambience are best during the evening, you might enjoy a break from sightseeing in one of the cafés. A mariachi serenade is $5 a song.

From the intersection in front of the church, turn right on Calzada Independencia; walk two blocks and then go back up the stairs to Plaza Tapatía. Turn left as you enter the mall and continue west for four blocks (giving you the opportunity to see the stores on this side of the plaza) to the oldest church in the **⑨** city, **Iglesia de San Augustín** (St. Augustine Church), at Avenida Degollado and Calle Morelos. Though this venerable building has been remodeled many times since its consecration in 1574, the sacristy has been preserved in its original form. The building to the left of the church, originally a cloister of the

Augustinian monks, is now the School of Music of the University of Guadalajara. This is a good place to hear street musicians.

As you leave the church, turn left and continue down Calle Morelos to Avenida Corona, turn left again and walk a half block to ⑩ the main entrance of the **Palacio de Gobierno** (Governor's Palace). A Churrigueresque and neoclassical structure built in 1643, it is the residence of the governor of the state of Jalisco and the site of Orozco's most imaginative and passionate murals. As you enter the palace, on the stairwell to your right is a dramatic mural depicting Father Hidalgo and the Mexican people's struggle for freedom. Its inspiration was Father Hidalgo's 1810 proclamation abolishing slavery in Mexico. *Open weekdays 9–6.*

⑪ As you leave the palace, cross Avenida Corona to the **Plaza de Armas.** Trees and benches in this lovely square surround an ornately sculpted kiosk, a gift from France in 1910.

## Tlaquepaque and Tonalá

Tlaquepaque is known throughout the country as an arts-and-crafts center. The distinctive hand-painted pottery, sold in stores throughout the town, was first fashioned here by Tonaltecan Indians in the mid-16th century. The small village remained virtually isolated until June 13, 1821, when the Mexican Treaty of Independence was signed here. Soon after, the wealthy residents of Guadalajara, who had used the village as a weekend retreat, began to build palatial mansions in which to spend the summers. Many of these magnificent buildings have been restored, and today they house shops and restaurants.

During this period, according to one legend, a growing French colony living in the area was (inadvertently) responsible for naming one of Mexico's most renowned musical institutions. French aristocrats hired groups of street singers and musicians to entertain at weddings. The French word *mariage* was soon transformed into *mariachi.*

In 1870 the art of glass-blowing was introduced from Europe. As people started coming to purchase the pottery and intricate glass creations, more artisans—weavers, jewelers, and woodcarvers—arrived and built workshops. A new tradition was born.

In 1973 downtown Tlaquepaque underwent a major renovation, the highlight of which was the creation of a wide pedestrian mall. Twentieth-century commercialism had arrived. You can spend the day browsing in the shops and boutiques and stop at lunch to listen to the lively songs of the mariachis.

The village of Tonalá, 10 minutes by car from Tlaquepaque, is one of the oldest pueblos in Mexico. It was both the pre-Hispanic capital of the Indians of the Atemajac Valley and the capital of New Spain. Captain Juan de Oñate moved the city of Guadalajara here in 1532. Within three years, however, unfriendly Indians and a lack of water had forced the Spaniards to abandon the location.

Over the past 400 years, the village has existed in contented seclusion. The simple adobe houses and dusty streets belie the artistic refinement of Tonalá's residents. It is in this small pueblo that most of the ceramics and pottery sold in Tlaquepaque (and in many other parts of the world) are made. Behind the tall gray walls, families create the lovely ceramics, cobalt blue-glassware, and playful animals with the same material and techniques their ancestors used centuries ago. On Thursdays and Sundays, this merchandise is sold at bargain prices at one of the best *tianquis* (markets) in all of Mexico.

*Numbers in the margin correspond to points of interest on the Tlaquepaque map.*

The 20-minute ride from downtown Guadalajara to **Tlaquepaque** will cost about $7 in a cab. Take Avenida Revolución southeast from the city; at the Plaza de la Bandera (at the intersection of Calzada del Ejército), jog to your right onto Boulevard Tlaquepaque and into the town. When you reach the *glorieta* (traffic circle), follow the circle around to Avenida Niños Héroes. The first intersection is Calzada Independencia (the pedestrian mall), where you'll begin your tour on foot.

❶ Turn left and walk one block to the **Museo Regional de la Cerámica** (Regional Museum of Ceramics). Exhibits in the museum, housed in a colonial mansion, trace the evolution of ceramics in the Atemajac Valley during the past century. There is also an exhibit of Indian folk art from the area and prize-winning entries from the national ceramics competition. *Calle Independencia 237, tel. 3/635–5404. Admission free. Open Tues.–Sat. 10–4, Sun. 10–1.*

❷ Walk across the street to the **Sergio Bustamante Gallery,** whose work is found in galleries throughout the world. You can purchase one of Bustamante's whimsical sculptures for considerably less here. Silver- and gold-plated jewelry and bronze sculptures are on display in this modern gallery; the flamingos under the waterfall in the rear are real. *Calle Independencia 236, tel. 3/639–5519. Open Mon.–Sat. 10–7.*

❸ Next door is Tlaquepaque's oldest blown-glass factory, **Artmex la Rosa de Cristal.** The store contains a large variety of hand-blown glass objects and figures; the intricate miniatures are surprisingly inexpensive. Plan to arrive before lunch so you can go into the factory (open weekdays 10–2, Sat. 10–12) and watch the craftsmen shove long tubes into a white-hot fire, retrieve a bubbling glob, and in a few minutes create one of the pieces you saw in front. *Calle Independencia 232, tel. 3/639–7180. Open Mon.–Sat. 10–6, Sun. 10–2.*

❹ On the next block east is **Bazar Hecht,** a 12-room hacienda filled with hand-carved furniture, antiques, and designer fashions. The Hecht family is known throughout Mexico for its high-quality, ornately sculpted tables and chairs. Part of the fun is wandering through this beautiful building, wondering what it would have been like to grow up in the colonial ambience of 19th-century Tlaquepaque. *Calle Independencia 158, tel. 3/ 635–22–41, fax 3/657–0316. Open Mon.–Sat. 10–2:30 and 3:30–6:30.*

Turn left as you leave Bazar Hecht and left again at the next corner (Prisciliano Sánchez); walk one block along Calle Morelos, which, with Calle Guillermo Prieto, forms an L-shaped arcade. In the center of the arcade is the **Templo Parroquial de San Pedro** (Parish Church of St. Peter). Franciscan friars founded the church during the Spanish conquest, naming it in honor of San Pedro de Analco. According to custom, the town was named after the principal church, and in 1915 the name was

Artmex la Rosa de Cristal, **3**

Bazar Hecht, **4**

El Parián, **7**

Ken Edwards Gallery, **6**

Museo Regional de la Cerámica, **1**

Sergio Bustamante Gallery, **2**

Templo Parroquial de San Pedro, **5**

Tonalá, **8**

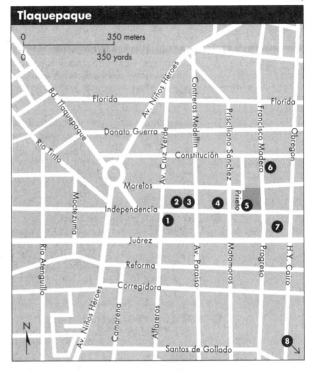

officially changed to San Pedro Tlaquepaque. The altars of Our Lady of Guadalupe and Saint Joseph are intricately carved in silver and gilt; the chapel of the Daughters of Mary has a most effectual oil painting of *La Purísima. Open daily 7 AM–9 PM.*

**Time Out**    Turn right as you leave the church and walk through the arcade; when you reach Constitución, make another right. At the next intersection, with Madero, turn right yet again and walk a half block to the **Restaurant with No Name,** considered by food critics and patrons to be one of Mexico's best culinary establishments. There are tables both indoors and on the patio of this 17th-century colonial mansion. High adobe walls surround the hacienda and the extensive gardens, which are filled with orchids and exotic birds. The restaurant serves Spanish nouvelle cuisine, a combination of pre-Hispanic and modern recipes. Daily entertainment includes *suave* jazz and traditional Mexican music. *Francisco Madero 80, tel. 3/635–4520 or 3/635–9677. Reservations for large parties. Dress: casual. AE, DC, MC, V.*

**6**    The next door to the left is the **Ken Edwards Gallery.** In 1959 Mr. Edwards developed a technique to transform the fragile Tonalá pottery into a lustrous, hardened, glazed stoneware. The store is filled with brightly colored, hand-painted plates, cups, and vases. Prices are much less than you would pay outside Mexico; ask to see the seconds, some real bargains. *Madero 70, tel. 3/635–5456 or 3/635–2426. Open Mon.–Sat. 10–6:30, in summer and winter high seasons, Sun. 12–5.*

# American Express offers Travelers Cheques built for two.

American Express® Cheques *for Two*. The first Travelers Cheques that allow either of you to use them because both of you have signed them. And only one of you needs to be present to purchase them.

Cheques *for Two* are accepted anywhere regular American Express Travelers Cheques are, which is just about everywhere. So stop by your bank, AAA* or any American Express Travel Service Office and ask for Cheques *for Two*.

AMERICAN EXPRESS **Travelers Cheques**

# SUDDENLY, MEXICO AND THE STATES ARE A WHOLE LOT CLOSER.

Introducing AT&T *USADirect*® Service from Mexico. Just dial the access number below

and get home in seconds. Making your international calls simple is all part of **The i Plan**℠ from AT&T.

## CALL THE U.S. FROM MEXICO WITH EASE. DIAL 95-800-462-4240.*

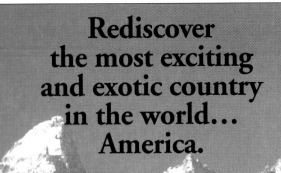

**❼** One block south of the gallery is **El Parián**, a square block of outdoor cafés frequented by mariachis anxious to perform. El Parián (named after the Chinese section of Manila, with which the conquistadors traded) is the heart of Tlaquepaque. The atmosphere is festive, if not boisterous, on weekends. The shops in the arcades around El Parián should be used only to compare prices; do your shopping in the galleries and boutiques on Calzada Independencia or another main street.

**Tonalá** The village of **Tonalá** is a 10-minute ride (about $7 for a cab)
**❽** from Tlaquepaque. Take Avenida Revolución south to Carretera Tonalá and make a left on the Carretera into Tonalá. Follow Avenida Tonalá (the same street you were on) to the main square in the center of the village. Follow Avenida Juárez one block away from the plaza to reach **La Iglesia Parroquial** (the parish church) built in 1533. Inside is a sculpture of Pope Pius IX.

From the northwest corner of the plaza, at Calles Hidalgo and Zapata, walk west (left) one block on Calle Zapata to Avenida Morelos, then right a half block to the **workshop of Jorge Wilmot** (Av. Morelos 76–88, no phone). This factory produces intricately designed, hand-painted stoneware ceramic plates, cups, and figurines that are sold throughout the world. Unfortunately, the opening hours of this shop, like many others in the village, vary greatly, although the artist lists his hours as weekdays 10–6 and Saturday 10–5.

Turn right as you leave the workshop, and right again at the next intersection, to the **Museo Nacional de la Cerámica** (National Ceramics Museum). On exhibit are the ceramics and pottery of several Mexican states dating from pre-Columbian times to the present. There is also a workshop and a small store. *Constitución 110, tel. 3/683–0494. Admission free. Open Tues.–Fri. 10–5, weekends 10–3.*

Turn left and continue a half block on Avenida Morelos to the **workshop of Ken Edwards**. Meet the man who revolutionized the centuries-old technique of firing ceramics. Either Edwards or his wife is usually on hand to show visitors their facilities. *Av. Morelos 184, tel. 3/683–0313. Open weekdays 10–6.*

The Thursday and Sunday markets have expanded to all-day affairs that cover dozens of blocks. Under low-slung tarps you will find blue glassware, ceramics, leather goods, and odd icons and figurines at incredibly low prices.

## Lake Chapala and Ajijic

This tour visits the lakeside communities of Chapala and Ajijic. Unfortunately, Lake Chapala—Mexico's largest inland body of water—is polluted, and water levels have been so low in the past few years that some Mexican ecologists predict there will be no lake at all in a few years' time. It does, however, provide a setting for spectacular sunsets, afford enough humidity to keep the abundant bougainvillea blooming, and ensure that there are no drastic temperature fluctuations.

The town of Chapala is 45 kilometers (28 miles) south of Guadalajara, on the northwest shore of the lake. With its proximity to the large city and its comfortable climate, it is surprising that tourists did not frequent the area until the late 19th century. Then-President Porfirio Díaz heard that aristocrats had discovered the ideal place for weekend getaways. The president began spending holidays here in 1904. Soon summer homes were built, and in 1910 the Chapala Yacht Club opened. Word of the town, with its lavish lawn parties and magnificent estates, spread quickly to the United States and Europe.

Nowadays this town of 35,000 attracts a less influential but equally fun-loving assortment of visitors. On weekends the streets are filled with Mexican families. During the week American and Canadian retirees stroll along the lakeside promenade, play golf, and relax on the verandas of downtown restaurants.

Five miles west of Chapala, along the Carretera Chapala-Jocotepec is the village of Ajijic, featuring several blocks of art galleries and crafts shops. Despite this commercial influence, its small-town ambience is still defined by its narrow cobblestoned streets, whitewashed buildings, and gentle pace.

**Lake Chapala** *Numbers in the margins correspond to points of interest on the Lake Chapala Area map.*

From downtown Guadalajara take Calzada del Federalismo south to Calzada Lázaro Cárdenas (the Sports Stadium is on the corner); turn left on Calzada Cárdenas and continue south. Follow the signs as Calzada Cárdenas converges with the newly expanded and resurfaced Highway 23 to Mexico City; the trip takes 50 minutes. There is also frequent bus service to Chapala from Guadalajara's old bus station on the corner of Calles Analco and Cinco de Febrero. From the Chapala bus station there are buses every hour to Ajijic.

After passing the turnoff to Ajijic, the highway becomes Avenida Madero as you enter Chapala. Follow Avenida Madero down to the **San Francisco Church,** two blocks north of the lake and easy to spot with its blue neon crosses on its twin steeples. Park your car. The church was built in 1528 and reconstructed in 1580. In 1538 Franciscan Friar Miguel de Bolonio founded the town and began to convert the Taltica Indians to Christianity. Their chief was named Chapalah, from which the name Chapala originated.

Walk across the street to the **Hotel Nido** (Av. Madero 201, tel. 376/5–2116), the oldest hotel on the lake. It was built in the beginning of the century to accommodate President Porfirio Díaz and his entourage during their frequent visits. In the 1940s Mexican film star Maria Felix spent the first of her numerous honeymoons at the Nido, and the dark high-ceilinged lobby still feels like the scene of a melodrama waiting to happen. There are pictures of turn-of-the-century Chapala on the walls and a picturesque patio and garden in the rear. (The hotel has 30 rooms with bath, a restaurant and bar, and an outdoor swimming pool. There are no phones or TVs in the rooms.)

Turn right as you leave the hotel and walk two blocks to the lake. On the corner of Av. Madero and Paseo Ramón Corona is the **Cazadores Restaurant,** once the summer home of the Braniff (Airlines) family, an ideal place to enjoy a cool liquid refreshment and watch the action along the *malecón* (lakeside promenade). Walking left down the Paseo Ramón Corona as you leave the restaurant, you will pass a number of open-air cafés featuring *pescado blanco* (white fish). Because of the pollution of the lake, we do not recommend that you partake of this

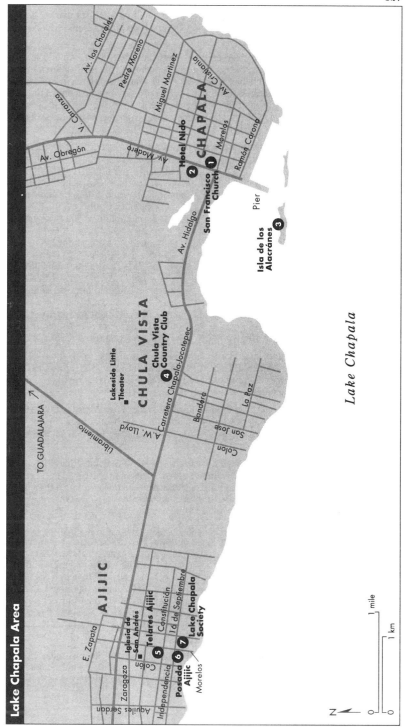

Lake Chapala Area

Lake Chapala

regional delicacy. There is a small **handicrafts market** at the end of the Paseo Ramón Corona (two blocks from Avenida Madero).

Walk back to Avenida Madero and then to the end of the pier, where *marineros* (sailors) rent boats that will take you for a tour of the lake or its islands. The most popular trip is to **Isla de los Alacránes** (Scorpion Island) to enjoy a meal in one of the tiny restaurants there. The price for a round-trip cruise is between $20 and $35 (for the launch, with a capacity of six adults). There are also plans for a ferry to run to the island hourly.

Return to your car and take a right at the traffic light (the only one in town) onto Avenida Hidalgo. You will be heading west to the village of Ajijic. Three kilometers (2 miles) from Chapala is the community of **Chula Vista,** the most American colony in Mexico. On the hillside north of the road, there are dozens of condos. Among them is the **Chula Vista Country Club,** a favorite of the local *norteamericano* community. The "billygoat" golf course here affords the golfer great vistas of the lake as well as a workout, since the rugged terrain cannot be negotiated by golf cart. *Paseo de Golf No. 1, tel. 3/765–2281.* Just west of the Chapala suburb, above the PAL Trailer Park (and next to the Oak High School) is the new 120-seat **Lakeside Little Theater** (tel. 376/5–2368), which stages English-language musicals and plays throughout the year. There is a small cafeteria in the trailer park. The **Lake Chapala Department of Tourism** is 1.6 kilometers (1 mile) west of the trailer park. *Auditorio Ribera de Chapala, tel. 376/5–31–36. Open weekdays 9–3, Sat. 9–1.*

Ajijic   As you enter Ajijic, turn left onto Avenida Colón and continue two blocks until you reach the plaza and the **Iglesia de San Andrés** (Church of St. Andrew). Weekly events and festivities take place on this lovely plaza.

Park your car at the plaza and walk down Morelos toward the lake; along the way you can stop in at the many stores and boutiques that sell everything from designer fashions to traditional arts and crafts.

Walk in and watch weavers work on traditional hand looms at **Telares Ajijic.** Indian women weave cotton, wool, and acrylic into fabrics used for both native costumes and designer fashions. *16 de Septiembre No. 1, tel. 376/5–24–02. Open 9–2 and 4–7.*

Where Calle Morelos meets the lake, you'll find the **Posada Ajijic,** a hacienda-style building that is the social, commercial, and political convocation center for Ajijic residents. Many people come to the restaurant and bar, under sculpted wood archways, for the daily happy hour and stay to watch the spectacular sunsets. For the past few years, members of the Huichole Indian tribe have set up shop in a corner of the lush gardens, where they weave their colorful serapes. *Frente al Lago, esquina Morelos, Ajijic, Jalisco, 45920, tel. 376/5–44–22 and 376/5–33–95.*

Backtrack to 16 de Septiembre to find the headquarters of **Lake Chapala Society,** a nonprofit organization that can answer your questions about the area. *16 de Septiembre No. 16A, no phone. Open weekdays 10–1.*

**Time Out** Stop in for some authentic Mexican atmosphere and cooking at the popular **El Mesón de Ajijic.** Enter through a flower-filled courtyard to dine either inside or on the patio. The white stucco walls, red-tile ceiling, and an antique fireplace will put you in the mood for some serious Mexican food. The *pollo al vino blanco* (chicken sautéed in a rich white-wine sauce) is a favorite of the locals. Don't miss the desserts: crepes suzette, bananas Foster, and strawberries Romanoff. *Av. Hidalgo 17, tel. 376/ 5–36–11. Reservations recommended on weekends. Dress: casual. AE, MC, V.*

**Lodging** After a few days of fuming in Guadalajara's traffic, you may find the clean air and tranquillity of the lake area an agreeable change. Hotel Nido (*see above*), in Chapala, is a good choice, as is Nueva Posada, *below.*

*Ajijic* **Nueva Posada.** Although only recently opened by the former owner of the Posada Ajijic, the Nueva Posada is already a favorite of honeymooners and other vacationers. Its colonial architecture, with hand-painted motifs on pastel stucco walls, suggests coolness and relaxation. The landscaping draws you to the lakeside, framed in bougainvillea. Rooms are spacious, airy, and well lit, with colonial furniture and original watercolors. The hotel also provides fine entertainment each night, typically an American jazz trio or tropical music. To top it off, chef Lorraine Rousseau's eclectic menu is quickly becoming popular with expatriates. *Donato Guerra No. 9 Apdo. 30 C.P. 45920, tel. 3/765–3395, fax 3/765–4495. 12 rooms with bath. Facilities: restaurant, nightclub, bar, bottled water. MC, V.*

## Museums in Guadalajara

Many of Guadalajara's museums are free, and the rest charge a nominal fee.

**Las Calas Cultural Center** (Tepeyac 1156, in Chapalita, tel. 3/ 647–0383 or 3/642–0779) holds monthly exhibitions of contemporary and postcolonial art. It also has a vegetarian café in an enclosed patio and evening concerts on Wednesday, Friday, Saturday, and Sunday nights. *Gallery open Tues.–Sun. 8 AM– 11 PM.*

**Museo de la Ciudad de Guadalajara** opened in 1992 to commemorate 450 years since the founding of the city. The building was once a hacienda; now it houses collections of artwork, artifacts, and reproductions of documents that provide extensive information about the city's development. *Av. Independencia 684, between Barcenas and Medellin, tel. 3/658–2531. Admission: $1. Open Tues.–Sat. 10–5, Sun. 10–3.*

**Museo de Arqueología de Occidente de México** (Archaeological Museum of Western Mexico) houses artifacts from the states of Colima, Jalisco, and Nayarit. *Calzada Independencia and Calzada del Campesino, in front of Parque Agua Azul. Admission: 35¢. Open daily 10–2 and 4–7.*

**El Museo Orozco.** The artist's workshop was converted into a museum after his death in 1949. It contains a large collection of his paintings and frescoes. *Aurelio Aceves 27, just west of Los Arcos, tel. 3/625–3365. Admission: 35¢. Open Tues.–Sat. 10–4, Sun. 10–2.*

## What to See and Do with Children

**Parque Agua Azul** is Guadalajara's largest and most popular park. Amid acres of trees and flowers are carnival rides, tropical birds in cages, a geodesic dome filled with butterflies, and a swimming pool. *Calzada Independencia Sur and Calzada Gonzales Gallo. Admission: 35¢. Open 6 AM–8 PM.*

**Planetario Severo Díaz Galindo** (The Planetarium). A modern facility with astronomy shows and aeronautical displays, the planetarium also features exhibits that allow children to test the forces and laws of nature. *Av. Ricardo Flores Magón 599, tel. 3/637–2959. Admission: about 75¢. Open Tues.–Sun. 10–7.*

**Zoológico Guadalajara** (Guadalajara Zoo). Located in the Barranca Huentitán (Huentitán Canyon), the zoo has 1,800 animals representing 250 species. For 50¢ a train provides guided tours. The adjacent *Selva Mágica* (Magic Jungle) amusement park has carnival rides and attractions. *Paseo del Zoológico 600 next to the Planetarium, tel. 3/638–4306. Admission: about $1. Open Tues.–Sun. 10–6.*

## Off the Beaten Track

Many of the activities at the **Rancho Río Caliente** health resort and vegetarian, alcohol-free spa are literally in hot water—therapeutic hot mineral water. You can steam away your mental tensions and body toxins in front of the 20-foot-high wall of volcanic rock and then dip into one of the mineral-water-filled swimming pools. The resort offers sparse but comfortable accommodations, facials and massages, T'ai Chi instruction, hiking, horseback riding, and classes in yoga and body awareness. *Apdo. 1187, Guadalajara, Jalisco, tel. 3/615–7800. The spa is 30 km (19 mi) from Minerva Fountain on Hwy. 15.*

**Barranca de Oblatos** (Oblatos Canyon). Ten kilometers (6 miles) northeast of downtown Guadalajara via Calzada Independencia is a spectacular 2,000-foot-deep gorge. The view from the top of the canyon is impressive.

**Basilica of the Virgin of Zapopan** (Calzada Avila and Av. Las Américas, 6 mi northeast of downtown). The church, with an ornate Plateresque facade and Mudejar tiled dome, was consecrated in 1730. It is known throughout Mexico as the home of La Zapopanita, Our Lady of Zapopan. The 10-inch-high statue is venerated as the source of many miracles in and around Guadalajara. Every year on October 12, more than 1 million people crowd the streets leading to Zapopan as the Virgin is returned to the basilica after a five-month absence during which she visits every church in the city.

Centuries ago the Tiquilas, a small Nahuatl-speaking tribe, established a settlement 56 kilometers (35 miles) northwest of Guadalajara in **Tequila** in the picturesque Jaliscan countryside. The Tiquilas discovered that the heart of the maguey cactus exuded *mezcal* (a kind of honey). When fermented, it produced a highly appreciated drink, which they called tequila. Today you can tour the famous Sauza Distillery or one of the other modern distilleries in town. Follow the signs, and plan to arrive between 10 AM and 1 PM.

The modern administration building of the **Universidad de Guadalajara** houses the first murals painted by Orozco after he returned to Guadalajara at age 53. In addition to these two power-ful works—located behind the stage and in the dome of the au-ditorium—there are beautiful murals by Amado de la Cueva and David Alfaro Siqueiros. *Av. Juárez at Tolsa, 2 mi west of downtown, tel. 3/625–8888. Open 8–9.*

Behind the university building is the **Templo Expiatorio** (Tolsa and Av. Francisco Madero). Though this church is nearly a cen-tury old, construction is still under way, albeit at a leisurely pace. The church is modeled after the Cathedral of Orvieto in Italy, and it is an outstanding example of unadulterated Gothic architecture.

## Sports

Golf
Golf clubs that admit foreign travelers include **Atlas Golf Club** (Carretera Guadalajara-Chapala, in front of Montenegro Park, tel. 3/689–0085), the **San Isidro Golf Club** (highway to Zacate-cas, Km 14.5, tel. 3/633–2814 or 3/633–2728), and the **Chula Vista Country Club** (tel. 376/5–22–81). If you have credentials from a U.S. golf club, you can play at the **Guadalajara Country Club** on weekdays (tel. 3/641–4045 or 3/641–4002).

Tennis
Try **Tennis Del Sol** (Av. Tizoc 17, tel. 3/622–3831), **Tennis Patria** (Plaza Patria, tel. 3/633–3811), or the **Holiday Inn** (tel. 3/634–1034), which allows nonguests to use its courts for a fee.

Fitness Clubs
The **Hyatt, Fiesta Americana,** and **Holiday Inn** fitness clubs are open to nonmembers. At **Gold's Gym** (Chimalhuacán 3574, off Av. López Mateos Sur, tel. 3/647–8594) guest passes are avail-able for about $7 per day.

Bullfights
*Corridas* begin at 4:30 PM every Sunday in October and every other Sunday from November through April at **Plaza Nuevo Pro-greso.** You can buy tickets for either the *sol* (sunny) or *sombra* (shady) side of the bullring. Since the action does not begin un-til just before sunset, opt for the cheaper seats on the sunny side. *Calzada Independencia across from the Estadio Jalisco, tel. 3/625–1974. Admission: $6–$22.*

Charreadas
The Mexican rodeo takes place at **Lienzo Charros de Jalisco** ev-ery Sunday at noon. The *charros* (cowboys) compete in 10 events; mariachis perform during breaks in the action. *Campo Charro Jalisco, Dr. R. Michel, 577, next to Agua Azul Park, tel. 3/619–3232. Admission: about $3.*

Soccer
**Estadio Jalisco.** Professional soccer matches are on Saturday at 8:45 PM and sometimes on Sunday at 2 PM. *The north end of Calzada Independencia, near the bullring, tel. 3/637–0563. Admission: 75¢–$7.*

# Shopping

Shoppers in Guadalajara can choose from a broad variety of high-quality merchandise at low prices. Of course, you will also find low-quality products at high prices; *caveat emptor.* Store hours are traditionally 10–2 and 4–7 on weekdays, Saturdays 9–2. Many large stores, however, are open daily and don't close for siesta.

## Malls

In Guadalajara, as in all major cities, shopping malls are springing up everywhere; the city now has 24 of them.

**Plaza del Sol.** The city's largest mall has 500,000 square feet of commercial space, enough room for 300 businesses and services and parking for 500 cars. *Av. López Mateos and Mariano Otero (across from the Hyatt Hotel), tel. 3/621–5950. Open weekdays 10–8, weekends 10–6.*

**Plaza México.** There are 100 commercial establishments in the city's second most popular shopping mall. *Av. México 3300, at the corner of Calle Yaquis, on the city's west side, tel. 3/647–0098. Open weekdays 10–8, weekends 10–6.*

**Plaza Galería del Calzado.** The 60 stores in this new mall all sell shoes. Guadalajara is one of Mexico's leading shoe centers, and high-quality footwear and accessories are sold here, many at cheaper prices than in the States. *Av. México and Calle Yaquis, next to the Plaza México, tel. 3/647–6422. Open weekdays 10–7, weekends 10–4.*

## Traditional Arts and Crafts

**Tlaquepaque and Tonalá** Artisans in these two towns produce some of the finest handiwork in Mexico. Tlaquepaque's 300 stores and galleries, and Tonalá's workshops and factories are replete with ceramics, pottery, jewelry, leather, blown glass, brass, and copper creations. *Located on the southeastern fringe of Guadalajara. Most stores are open weekdays 10–2 and 4–7, Sat. 10–6.*

## Markets

In **Mercado Libertad,** Latin America's largest enclosed market, more than 1,000 vendors sell everything from clothing to crafts to live animals and gold watches. *Calzada Independencia and Av. Javier Mina. Open weekdays 9–2 and 4–8, weekends 9–6.*

**El Baratillo** is the world's largest flea market. Thirty city blocks are lined with stalls, tents, and blankets piled high with new, used, and antique merchandise. *On Calle Juan Zavala, east of Mercado Libertad. Open Sun. 6–2.*

**Tianquis,** the twice-weekly market in Tonalá, has glassware, leather goods, ceramics, and rustic crafts at bargain prices. *Located south and west of the village center between the bus terminal and the cathedral. Open Thurs. and Sun., sun up to sundown.*

# Dining

The quality and variety of Guadalajara's restaurants have improved to accommodate the tastes and budgets of the international business community. While native restaurateurs and chefs continue to present traditional and classic Mexican dishes, a new breed of immigrant *cuisinier* has introduced such ethnic delicacies as French Creole *chicken sauté Louisiane,* classic Japanese *shabu shabu,* and Spanish *paella.* Many restaurants close early, so if you are accustomed to dining after 9 PM, it's advisable to call first to check if the establishment remains open.

Highly recommended restaurants are indicated by a star ★.

| Category | Cost* |
|---|---|
| Very Expensive | over $35 |
| Expensive | $25–$35 |
| Moderate | $15–$25 |
| Inexpensive | under $15 |

*per person excluding drinks, service, and sales tax (10%)*

**Very Expensive**
★ **Place de la Concorde.** Booths throughout the elegant multilevel restaurant overlook Minerva Fountain and surround the baby-grand piano, where a pianist provides a musical backdrop for outstanding French cuisine. Specialties include appetizers such as *vol-au-vent* (escargot and mushrooms sautéed in oil and garlic) and tureen of rabbit in rich port sauce; entrées such as tenderloin steak encircled by giant shrimp and medallions of beef in an imaginative sweet grape sauce; and desserts flambéed tableside. *Hotel Fiesta Americana, tel. 3/625–3434, ext. 3077. Reservations advised on weekends. Dress: formal. AE, DC, MC, V. Closed Sun.*

**Expensive** **Cazuelas Grill.** Pedro Olivares personally oversees the operation of this family-operated restaurant and entertainment lounge. Cazuelas Grill serves traditional cuisine both inside and on an open-air patio with red-tiled floor and bamboo ceiling. Two mariachi shows are presented each day (3:30 and 6:30), featuring the songs and music of Guadalajara's best groups; live contemporary Mexican rock music for dancing follows at 10 PM. *Pollo parrilla* (mesquite-grilled chicken) and *borrego al pastor* (barbecued goat) are two specialties. The tangy barbecued ribs are popular with visitors from north of the border. *Av. López Mateos Sur 3755, 2 blocks south of the Holiday Inn, tel. 3/631–5780. Reservations advised for dinner. Dress: casual. AE, MC, V. Closed Christmas Eve.*

★ **La Vianda.** Classical Mexican elegance pervades this intimate bilevel room overlooking a neat, lush garden; cobalt-blue water glasses provide a charming accent to the white-on-white decor. Chef Salvador Rodriguez masterfully combines traditional native recipes with New Orleans Creole. The extensive dinner menu changes monthly. Some of the chef's specialties are crabmeat crepes in a rich hollandaise sauce, a spicy shrimp Creole in a tangy tomato sauce, and mignonettes of veal Normandy. *Av. Chapalita 120, tel. 3/621–7823. Reservations advised. Dress: casual but neat. AE, DC, MC, V.*

**Moderate**
★ **Copenhagen.** The decorative tilework of Tonalá artisan Jorge Wilmot covers the walls of this restaurant, which bills itself as the Paella Place. Since 1952 the Copenhagen has featured the famous dish of Valencia, Spain. The secret of a great paella lies in the texture of the rice. The grain in both presentations, *Copenhagen* (in white wine) and *à la marinera* (with seafood), is loose and dry but still tender. The menu also features beef and seafood entrées. Copenhagen is also the unofficial headquarters for Guadalajara's jazz aficionados; it showcases some of the city's best jazz musicians, who entertain each evening at 8 PM. *López Cotilla and Marcos Castellanos, tel. 3/625–2803. Reservations advised on weekends. Dress: casual. AE, DC, MC, V. Closed May 1 and Dec. 25.*

**Guadalajara Grill.** Fun and revelry share top billing with the food at this Carlos 'n Charlie's affiliate. The large, trilevel room is decorated with Mexican knickknacks and antique street lamps; turn-of-the-century photographs of Guadalajara are displayed in the foyer and on the back wall. The tender barbecued baby ribs are by far the favorite of both natives and tourists. Shrimp lovers will be happy to find the crustaceans grilled, baked, boiled, or served in a casserole. Enthusiastic waiters promote the convivial atmosphere and urge patrons to join in the fun. There is live entertainment every evening. *Av. López Mateos 3771, tel. 3/631–5622. Reservations recommended. Dress: casual. AE, MC, V. Closed on national holidays.*

**La Copa de Leche.** This downtown, family-owned and -operated restaurant is an institution in Guadalajara. You can choose from three distinct dining areas: El Portal, a sidewalk café; El Balcon, an open-air terrace overlooking Avenida Juárez; and the main dining room with traditional Mexican decor, a 40-foot ceiling, and an antique fireplace. Specialties include *pescado California* (California white fish sautéed in a sauce of avocados and oranges and then bathed in butter), *camarones copa de leche* (giant shrimp smothered with bacon and cheese), and *pierna de cerdo* (pork shank baked in a tangy port wine sauce); for dessert try one of the flambés. *Av. Júarez 414–B, tel. 3/614–7976. Reservations advised on weekends. Dress: casual. AE, MC, V. Closed on national holidays.*

**La Rinconada.** This enclosed patio of a restored colonial mansion houses hanging plants, stone pillars, hand-carved doors with frosted glass windows, and a piano and bass duo plucking out American standards. La Rinconada exudes an old-plantation graciousness in a centrally located position on Calle Morelos between the Teatro Degollado and the Instituto Cultural Cabañas. Specialties of the house include shrimp scampi (jumbo shrimp cooked in white wine and garlic sauce), prime rib, and the *Plato Mexicano Arrachera*, a flank steak served with guacamole, enchiladas, and beans and rice. Schedule your private parties in the rooms in the back. *Calle Morelos 86, tel. 3/613–9914. Reservations accepted. Dress: casual but neat. AE, DC, MC, V.*

**Moravia.** Both Tapatios and tourists come to enjoy the elegant ambience and superb Continental cuisine. A full-length stained-glass window in the rear of the main room overlooks manicured gardens. Appetizers include select oysters Rockefeller (eight choice oysters on the half-shell lightly breaded and covered with a rich mornay sauce) and piñon crème with spinach soup, a Moravian specialty. Entrées include fish fillet Florentina (tender white-fish fillets in a tangy white-wine sauce served on a bed of spinach) and *filete pimienta*, steak in a green peppercorn and cream sauce. *López Mateos Nte. 1143 on the corner of Colomos, tel. 3/641–8487. Reservations recommended on weekends. Dress: casual. AE, MC, V. Closed on Sun. and national holidays.*

**Inexpensive**
★

**Dainzu.** Pablo Garcia Ojeda introduced the cuisine of Mexico's southern state of Oaxaca to the city in 1986. The restaurant takes its name from the centuries-old Mixtec ruin just outside of Oaxaca City. The twelve-table room has white plaster walls and a red-tiled ceiling, with regional posters and ornamentation on the walls. Generous portions are brought to you on hefty white ceramic plates. Featured among the Oaxacan specialties are tender beef, pork, and chicken dishes prepared in a tangy green or black mole sauce (the thick dark sauce of chocolate, chilies, onions, and more than a dozen other spices and herbs), and *pollo almendro* (chicken smothered in onions). Traditional Mexican specialties include a combination plate of tacos, enchiladas, and tamales. Complete the Oaxacan experience with a mug of *chocolate caliente* (hot chocolate) and sweet *pan de Oaxaca*. Tell your cabdriver to take Calle Mariano Otero to the *Chocolate Ibarra* (chocolate factory), and then turn east to Avenida Diamante (between the Plaza del Sol and the Plaza Arboledas). *Av. Diamante 2598, tel. 3/647-5086. No reservations. Dress: casual. No credit cards. Closed Mon.*

**La Chata.** Dark-toned beams and brick archways are offset by Day-Glo plaid tablecloths in this popular Jaliscan restaurant. Chef Martina's special soups include *caldo Halpeña*, a thick stew of chicken, avocado, rice, and cheese. Specials include such spicy roasted meat dishes as *carne tampiqueña*, served with rice, beans, and enchiladas. A good complement to this is a cool, sweet *horchata*, a drink made from rice and brown sugar simmered in milk then chilled. There is another La Chata downtown, with the same authentic feel and the same gaudy/distinctive tablecloths. *Av. Lopez Mateo Sur, across from the Holiday Inn, tel. 3/632-4532. No reservations. Dress: casual. V, MC. Closed on national holidays.*

**La Trattoria.** Michelli Primucci's Italian eatery has swiftly become the favorite of the city's American and Canadian communities. Under the vigilant eye of Michelli's brother-in-law Alberto, this unpretentious, squeaky-clean restaurant churns out superb Italian dishes that are reasonably priced. The *combination la trattoria* is lasagna, fettuccine, and spaghetti in a zingy house sauce. In addition to pasta plates, the restaurant offers a limited selection of beef and seafood entrées. All meals come with a trip to the salad bar. The popularity of La Trattoria is increasing to include a large contingent of young natives—especially for Saturday-night dates. *Av. Niños Héroes 3051, tel. 3/622-1817. No reservations. Dress: casual. AE, MC, V. Closed Christmas.*

**Saint Michel.** This is a unique addition to Guadalajara's growing register of restaurants. You would expect to find the front dining room, with its stone walls and arches, in a French castle; the room to the rear has a contemporary Mexican flair, with beige walls, beamed ceilings, and a pleasant view of the patio and gardens. Saint Michel serves more than 50 varieties of crepes, half of which are desserts. Crepe specialties include *Azteca* (with chicken and cheese), beef Stroganoff (with thin slices of beef and mushrooms in a red-wine sauce), *Scissy* (with strawberries, cheese, and cream), and *Gran Amirante* (with shrimp in a thick white-wine sauce). Meals include a trip to the salad bar. *Av. Vallarta 1700, tel. 3/630-1820. Reservations advised. Dress: casual. AE, DC, MC, V. Closed on national holidays.*

# Lodging

Until 20 years ago, most of Guadalajara's hotels were in the downtown area. As commercial interest in the city grew and businesses began springing up throughout the metropolitan area, hotels were constructed on Avenida López Mateos, a 10-mile strip extending from Minerva Fountain to the Plaza del Sol shopping center. Expo-Guadalajara (Latin America's largest convention center) opened in 1987, and the city's hotels immediately began major remodeling projects to accommodate the convention business.

Guadalajara today offers a fine variety of hotels in all price ranges. Hotels in this city follow the tradition initiated by the hotels in resort areas of raising prices every year on December 15. An excellent time to visit Guadalajara is from the beginning of October (during the *Fiestas de Octubre)* until mid-December.

Call ahead if you're apprehensive about noise levels outside your hotel room. Many hotels are located on busy intersections, and you'd be well advised to consult the reservation clerk on the matter of a room away from the hubbub.

The rates given are based on the year-round or peak-season price; off-peak (summer) rates may be slightly lower. Highly recommended lodgings are indicated by a star ★.

| Category | Cost* |
| --- | --- |
| Very Expensive | over $160 |
| Expensive | $90–$160 |
| Moderate | $40–$90 |
| Inexpensive | under $40 |

*\*All prices are for a standard double room; excluding 10% tax.*

**Very Expensive**    **Holiday Inn.** Those who come to Guadalajara for its eternally springlike climate will enjoy the Holiday Inn. There are expansive, well-tended gardens; jacaranda, tulip, and rubber trees providing shade; and a large pool and sunbathing area to take full advantage of the outdoors. Indoors, everything is just as well tended, and the staff is efficient and bilingual. The rooms, renovated in 1992, feature marble baths, upholstered furniture, carpeting, and lots of natural light. Choose a room in the tower for a view of the mountains or one surrounding the courtyard, making a stroll through the parklike greenery readily accessible. *Av. Lopez Mateos Sur 2500, 45050, tel. 3/634–1034, fax 3/648–1564. 300 rooms, including 7 suites. Facilities: 2 restaurants, cafeteria, 2 bars; disco; outdoor pool and jacuzzi; tennis courts, putting green, health club, children's playground; car rentals; VCRs in all rooms and free movies. AE, DC, MC, V.*

★   **Quinta Real.** Stone and brick walls, colonial arches, and objets d'art highlight the classical Mexican architecture in all public areas of this luxury hotel, located in a quiet residential neighborhood on the city's west side. Suites are plush and intimate, with select neocolonial furnishings, including glass-topped writing tables with carved-stone pedestals, fireplaces with marble mantelpieces, and original art. Bathrooms are tiled, with marble sinks and bronze fixtures (some suites have sunken tubs with Jacuzzis). Deluxe rooms, located in the newly completed tower, are more lavish, though removed from the gardens below. *Av. México 2727, 44680, tel. 3/615–0000, fax 3/ 630–1797. 53 suites and 23 deluxe rooms. Facilities: restaurant, piano bar/lounge, small pool with Jacuzzi, boutique, lim-*

*ousine transfer to airport, English-language TV channels, purified water system. AE, DC, MC, V.*

**Expensive** **Camino Real.** A 15-minute cab ride from downtown will bring you to this sprawling resort located 3.2 kilometers (2 miles) west of Minerva Fountain. By day, you can relax in the shade of rubber and jacaranda trees; by night, you can enjoy the turn-of-the-century Aquellos Tiempos restaurant or live entertainment in La Diligencia lounge. The rooms are in two-story wings surrounding manicured lawns and tropical gardens. They are large and have placid pastel color schemes, matching bedspreads and curtains, and modern furniture. Those in the rear wing face busy, noisy Avenida Vallarta. *Av. Vallarta 5005, 45050, tel. 3/647–8000 or 800/228–3000, fax 3/647–6781. 205 rooms. Facilities: 2 restaurants, bar with live music, executive lounge, coffee shop, 5 pools, tennis court, putting green, children's playground, English-language TV channels, purified water system, baby-sitting service. AE, DC, MC, V.*

**Carlton.** The only first-class property in downtown Guadalajara, this modern 20-story tower hotel was totally remodeled in 1988. The oversize rooms with light beige walls and ceilings have matching dark-blue curtains and bedspreads. Public areas are well maintained but sparsely decorated; the rear gardens and fountain are surrounded by ivy-draped walls. Though the hotel is convenient for tourists, it caters to the business traveler. The upper floors offer a spectacular view of the city and a retreat from the horrendous street noise. Service, though friendly, has been less than efficient of late. *Av. Niños Héroes 105, at the corner of Av. 16 de Septiembre, 44100, tel. 3/614–7272, fax 3/613–5539. 222 rooms including 5 suites. Facilities: restaurant, 2 bars, discotheque, outdoor heated pool, health club, video disco club. AE, MC, V.*

★ **Fiesta Americana.** The dramatic glass facade of this luxury high rise faces the Minerva Circle. The location, warm contemporary Mexican ambience, and excellent service make this hotel a popular choice for both business travelers and tourists. Four glass-enclosed elevators ascend above the 11-story atrium lobby and adjoining Lobby Bar (one of Guadalajara's most popular night spots). The ample rooms have a pastel color scheme, modern furnishings (including molded seating and desk areas), and panoramic city views. The hotel presents a German Cafe Night (Thursday), an Italian Fiesta (Friday), and an International Buffet (every day in the Chula Vista cafeteria). The best rooms are on the upper floors, well away from the revelers down in the Lobby Bar. *Aurelio Aceves 225, 45050, tel. 3/625–3434 or 800/223–2332, fax 3/630–3725. 394 rooms, including 39 suites. Facilities: restaurants, including the gourmet Place de la Concorde; cafeteria; 3 bars; shopping center; outdoor heated pool; 2 lighted tennis courts, complete health club (with health-food bar); English-language TV channels; purified water system. AE, DC, MC, V.*

**Hyatt Regency.** This imposing pyramidal structure dominates the hotel strip. Opened in 1983, the Hyatt is popular with vacation charter groups and business travelers seeking the comfortable uniformity the hotel chain affords. Street-level escalators lift you past cascading waterfalls to the plush 12-story atrium lobby; two glass-enclosed elevators whisk you up to your floor. Spacious rooms, redecorated in 1990, feature hypoallergenic carpets and queen- or king-size orthopedic mattresses. The hotel's indoor Polaris Ice Skating Rink (the only such facility in the city) is open to nonguests. The Hyatt succeeds in integrating varied restaurant, club, and common areas and providing all with consistently good service by an attentive staff. For the best city view, request a room on an upper floor facing the bustling Plaza del Sol shopping center. *Av. López Mateos Sur and Moctezuma, 45050, tel. 3/622–7778 or 800/ 228–9000, fax 3/622–9877. 346 rooms with bath, including 29 suites. Facilities: 2 restaurants; 2 bars; pool; VIP club and business center with a bilingual staff; large, upscale shopping arcade; complete health club; English-language TV channels; purified water system. AE, DC, MC, V.*

**Moderate** **Calinda Roma.** Located on a busy downtown street, this hotel caters to business travelers and senior citizens, with discounts offered to the latter. It has a spacious lobby with cushioned chairs and a fireplace. The Roma's finest feature, however, is its rooftop, with gardens, a swimming pool, and a panoramic view of old Guadalajara that is worth checking out even if you're not staying here. The rooms are unspectacular and need renovation, with tired-looking corridors and furniture that appears more often lined up than arranged. *Av. Juárez 170, 44100, tel. 3/614–8650, fax 3/614–2629. 172 rooms with bath, including 3 suites. Facilities: restaurants, bar, bottled water. AE, DC, MC, V.*

**De Mendoza.** Mature travelers and tour groups from the United States and Canada often choose this downtown hotel because of its convenient location (on a quiet side street just one block from the Teatro Degollado) and charming postcolonial architecture and ambience. Beamed ceilings, hand-sculpted wood furniture and doors, and wrought-iron railings decorate public areas and rooms. The staff is bilingual and will be glad to direct you on a tour of historical sights that are right outside the door. *Venustiano Carranza 16, 44100, tel. 3/613–4646, fax 3/613– 7310. 110 rooms with bath, including 17 suites. Facilities: restaurant, pool, bottled water. AE, DC, MC, V.*

**Fénix.** This mid-rise downtown hotel caters to business travelers and national tourists. The lobby is active and busy and the staff efficient. The location, just off a principal downtown intersection, makes this hotel an ideal choice for the short-term visitor. The comfortable standard-size rooms, remodeled in 1988, have simple appointments and furnishings. The Co-Co Bar is one of Guadalajara's livelier venues, and guests are allowed free admission. *Av. Corona 160, 44100, tel. 3/614–5714, fax 3/ 613–4005. 255 rooms with bath, including 25 suites. Facilities: restaurant, bar, disco, nightclub, shops, English-language TV channels, bottled water. AE, DC, MC, V.*

**Plaza Del Sol.** Location and price make families and young adults head for this hotel's two towers rising over the south end of the Plaza del Sol shopping center. The intimate Solaris Restaurant and the Bar Sol provide enjoyable and romantic evenings. Public areas and rooms feature glossy white walls trimmed in aquamarine or mauve. The accommodations have modern furniture and wall-to-wall carpeting. Rooms in the newer tower are a bit larger and have a view of the shopping center below. *Av. López Mateos and Calle Mariano Otero, 45050, tel. 3/647–8790, fax 3/622–9865. 355 rooms with bath, including 14 suites. Facilities: restaurant, cafeteria, bar, nightclub, outdoor swimming pool, solarium, English-language TV channels, bottled water, AE, DC, MC, V.*

**Posada Guadalajara.** Rooms in this colonial-style hotel's four contiguous six-story towers open onto airy, wrought-iron railed hallways overlooking the small patio and circular pool. The unassuming accommodations are clean and comfortable, with traditional appointments. In addition to a loyal cadre of international patrons, the Posada welcomes visiting sports teams. Depending on your disposition (and the age and inclinations of your fellow guests), you will find the evenings here to be either festive or raucous. The hotel is just south of Calzada Lázaro Cárdenas (arterial access to downtown). *Av. López Mateos Sur 1280, 45050, tel. 3/621–2022. 180 rooms with bath, including 18 kitchenette suites. Facilities: restaurant, rooftop bar, outdoor heated pool, English-language TV channels, bottled water. AE, DC, MC, V.*

**Inexpensive**  **Diana.** Mexican and European tourists favor this six-story hotel, located two blocks from Minerva Fountain. The white stucco lobby adjoins a small lounge and busy restaurant. Standard-size rooms have white-on-white walls and ceilings with brightly patterned curtains and bedspreads; all have desks and window air conditioners. The best rooms are on the upper floors in the rear, away from the activity and traffic on Yáñez; suites have private saunas. *Circunvalacion Agustín Yáñez 2760, 44100, tel. 3/615–5510. 200 rooms with bath, including 4 suites. Facilities: restaurant, cafeteria, bar, outdoor heated pool, English-language TV channels, bottled water. AE, DC, MC, V.*

★ **Frances.** The brothers Oliveros carefully renovated Guadalajara's oldest hotel (1610), preserving and restoring its original architecture and charm. During reopening ceremonies in 1981, the four-story downtown hotel was designated a national monument. The venerable Frances has a three-story enclosed atrium lobby with stone columns and colonial arches surrounding a polished marble fountain and cut crystal-and-gilt chandelier. Even if you're not a guest, you may enjoy a ride in the antique cage elevator that holds three adults. Though room sizes vary, all share a colonial ambience, with rose-colored stucco walls, polished wood floors, and high-beamed ceilings. For the best city views, ask for a room facing Calle Maestranza. The Frances is ideal for travelers willing to exchange the amenities of a modern hotel for the hospitality of Guadalajara's grande dame. *Calle Maestranza 35, 45050, tel. 3/613–1190. 60 rooms with bath. Facilities: 2 restaurants, bar with live music, TV with English-language channels, bottled water. AE, DC, MC, V.*

# The Arts and Nightlife

Guadalajara has a reputation as a cultural and performing arts center. During the past 20 years, the active U.S. and Canadian communities have developed a schedule of English-language cultural events. You can attend a performance, an exhibition, or a recital almost any day of the year.

## The Arts

**Symphony**  **Filarmónico Jalisco** (tel. 3/614–4773 or 3/613–1115), conducted by Maestro Guadalupe Flores, performs Sundays and Fridays at the Teatro Degollado.

Music **Teatro Degollado** (Degollado and Belén, tel. 3/614–4773 or 3/
614–1614), a magnificent theater built in 1886 and totally remodeled in 1988, presents nationally and internationally famous artists for performances throughout the year. The new
velvet seats are comfortable, the acoustics are excellent, and
the central air-conditioning is a treat.

**Concha Acústica,** the outdoor theater in Parque Agua Azul,
presents festivals of music and dance every Sunday at 5 PM.

**Instituto Cultural Cabañas** (Calle Cabañas and Hospicio, tel. 3/
617–3097 or 3/618–6003), built in 1810, has 23 flowered patios
and permanent and revolving art exhibits. Theater, dance, and
musical performances take place on an open-air stage within
the institute. The Instituto also has a movie theater.

**Las Calas Cultural Center** (Av. Tepeyac 1156, tel. 3/647–0383 or
3/647–0279) is open as a café, art gallery, and gift shop by day
and for a variety of performances each night. It emphasizes
traditional dance, theater, and music, but also presents jazz,
new age, and 60s shows.

**Plaza De Armas.** Every Sunday and Thursday evening, the
**State Band of Jalisco** performs at 6:30 PM. On Tuesday evening,
the **Municipal Band of Guadalajara** performs at 6:30 PM.

Ballet **Ballet Folklórico of the University of Guadalajara** performs traditional Mexican folkloric dances and music in the Teatro
Degollado every Sunday at 10 AM.

## Nightlife

Guadalajara is not known for its nightlife. The nightclubs in
major hotels provide good local entertainment and, occasionally, internationally known recording artists. The best hotel
clubs are the **Lobby Bar,** in the Hotel Fiesta Americana; **Memo-
ries,** in the El Tapatío; **La Diligencia,** in the Camino Real; and
**La Fiesta,** in the Holiday Inn.

Discos You can dance all night at **Oz** (Av. Mariano Otero and Av. López
Mateos) and **Osiris** (Calzada Lázaro Cárdenas 3898). Hotel
discos include **Da Vinci,** in the Holiday Inn, and **The Factory,** in
the Hotel Aranzazú.

Peña As in the coffeehouses of the 1960s, patrons sit around a small
stage at **Peña Cuicacalli** (Av. Niños Héroes 1988, tel. 3/625–
4690) and listen to jazz, blues, and folk, or Latin American music Wednesday through Saturday nights.

# 9  Acapulco

By Anya Schiffrin

Now based in Turkey, Anya Schiffrin is a well-traveled freelance writer whose credits include the Village Voice and such British publications as City Limits, Time Out, and New Society.

Updated by Wendy Luft

For sun lovers, beach bums, and other hedonists, Acapulco is the ideal holiday resort. Don't expect high culture, historic monuments, or haute cuisine. Anyone who ventures to this Pacific resort 260 miles south of Mexico City does so to relax. Translate that as swimming, shopping, and nightlife. Everything takes place against a staggeringly beautiful natural backdrop. Acapulco Bay is one of the world's best natural harbors, and it is the city's centerpiece. By day the water looks clean and temptingly deep blue; at night it flashes and sparkles with the city lights.

The weather is Acapulco's major draw—warm waters, almost constant sunshine, and year-round temperatures in the 80s. It comes as no surprise, then, that most people plan their day around laying their towel on some part of Acapulco's many miles of beach. Both tame and wild water sports are available—everything from waterskiing to snorkeling, diving, and the thrill of parasailing. Less strenuous possibilities are motorboat rides and fishing trips. Championship golf courses, tennis courts, and the food/crafts markets also occasionally lure some visitors away from the beach, but not out of the sun.

Apart from these options, most people rouse themselves from their hammocks, deck chairs, or towels only when it is feeding time. Eating is one of Acapulco's great pleasures. You will find that in most dishes the ingredients are very fresh. Seafood is caught locally, and restaurateurs go to the *mercado* (market) daily to select the produce, meats, and fish for that night's meals. There are many good no-frills, down-home Mexican restaurants. Prices are reasonable and the food in these family-run places is prepared with care—spiced soups filled with red snapper (and red snapper heads), baskets filled with hot corn tortillas instead of bread. Eating at one of these spots gives you a glimpse into the real Mexico: office workers breaking for lunch, groups of men socializing over a cup of coffee.

At night Acapulco is transformed as the city rouses itself from the day's torpor and prepares for the long hours ahead. Even though Acapulco's heyday is past, its nightlife is legendary. This is true despite the fact that many of the city's discos look as if they were designed in the early '70s by an architect who bought mirrors and strobe lights wholesale. Perpetually crowded, the discos are grouped in twos and threes, so most people go to several places in one night. Last year's disco hits and huge fruity cocktails are trademarks of the Acapulco disco experience.

A relaxed, holiday atmosphere pervades Acapulco; shorts and T-shirts are the standard dress. The Mexicans you meet are friendly, and many travelers return to Acapulco every year to catch up on friendships begun on a previous vacation. The only drawback to this laid-back air is that everything takes much longer than you might expect. But there is no point in getting annoyed—just sit back and relax while you wait.

Acapulco was originally an important port for the Spanish, who used it to trade with countries in the Far East. The Spanish built Fuerte de San Diego (Fort San Diego) to protect the city from pirates, and today the fort houses a historical museum with exhibits about Acapulco's past. The name of the late Teddy Stauffer, an entrepreneurial Swiss, is practically synonymous with that of modern Acapulco. He hired the first cliff divers at La Quebrada in Old Acapulco and founded the Boom Boom Room, the town's first dance hall, and Tequila A Go-Go, its first discotheque. The Hotel Mirador at La Quebrada and the area stretching from Caleta to Hornos beaches, near today's Old Acapulco, were the center of activity in the 1950s, when Acapulco was a town of 20,000 with an economy based largely on fishing.

Former President Miguel Alemán Valdés bought up miles of the coast just before the road and the airport were built. The Avenida Costera Miguel Alemán bears his name today. Since the late 1940s, Acapulco has expanded eastward so that today it is one of Mexico's largest cities, with a population of approximately 2 million. Currently under development are a 3,000-acre expanse known as Acapulco Diamante and the areas known as Punta Diamante and Playa Diamante.

# Essential Information

## Arriving and Departing by Plane

**Airport and Airlines** From the United States: **American** (tel. 800/433–7300) has nonstop flights from Dallas; connections from Chicago and New York through Dallas. **Continental** (tel. 800/525–0280) has nonstop service from Houston. **Delta's** (tel. 800/241–4141) nonstop service is from Los Angeles. **Mexicana** (tel. 800/531–7921) has nonstop service from Chicago and connecting service from New York, Miami, Los Angeles, San Antonio, San Francisco, and San Jose, California, all via Mexico City. **Aeromexico's** (tel. 800/237–6639) flight from New York to Acapulco stops in Mexico City. Other major carriers fly into Mexico City, where you can make a connection to Acapulco.

From Canada: **Sunquest** (tel. 800/776–3000) has charter service from Toronto on a biweekly basis using La Tur airlines; **Delta** has flights from most major Canadian cities via Los Angeles to Acapulco; **Canadian Holidays** (tel. 800/387–7663) has nonstop charter flights from Toronto to Acapulco.

From the United Kingdom: There are no direct flights to Acapulco, though the following airlines have service via Mexico City or major U.S. or European cities: **Air France** (tel. 081/759–2311); **Iberia** (tel. 071/437–5622); and **KLM** (tel. 081/568–9144).

From New York via Dallas, flying time is 4½ hours; from Chicago, 4¼ hours; from Los Angeles, 3½ hours.

**Between the Airport and City Center** Private taxis are not permitted to carry passengers from the airport to town, so most people rely on **Transportes Terrestres,** a special airport taxi service. The bus system looks confusing, but there are dozens of helpful English-speaking staff to help you figure out which bus to take.

Look for the name of your hotel and the number of its zone on the overhead sign on the walkway in front of the terminal. Go to the desk for your zone and buy a ticket for an airport taxi that goes to your zone. The ride from the airport to the hotel zone on the trip costs about $8. The drivers are usually helpful and will often take you to hotels that aren't on their list. Tips are optional. The journey into town takes 20 to 30 minutes.

## Arriving and Departing by Car, Ship, Train, and Bus

**By Car** A car can be handy in these parts, but we don't recommend that you drive from either the United States or Canada. Except for major highways, the roads are not well maintained and distances from the border are great. If you prefer to see the sights by car, we suggest renting a car once you're there. Whether you drive from the United States or Canada or rent a car in Acapulco, bear in mind that Mexico is a developing country and things are much different than in North America or Western Europe. Unleaded gasoline is now available at the green-and-white Pemex stations along major tourist routes, but sometimes you'll find the supply has been depleted. It's a good idea to fill up your tank whenever possible, especially before starting out on long stretches of road. Spare parts are another worry. Parts for a Ford or Chevy are plentiful, but getting a new transmission for a Toyota or Mercedes is not easy.

The trip to Acapulco from Mexico City takes about six hours, but many people opt for going via Taxco. A new, privately built and run, 4-lane toll road connecting Mexico City with Acapulco is almost finished and most certainly will be completed by publication date. Although expensive (it will cost about $60 in tolls one way) it will cut driving time between the two cities from 6 hours to 3½ hours.

**By Ship** Many cruises include Acapulco as part of their itinerary. Most originate from Los Angeles. Cruise operators include **Carnival Cruise Lines** (tel. 800/327–9501); **Clipper Cruise Line** (tel. 800/325–0010); **Cunard Line** (tel. 800/221–4770); **Holland America Lines** (tel. 800/426–0327); **Krystal Cruises** (tel. 310/785–9300); **Princess Cruises** (tel. 800/421–0522); **Royal Caribbean Cruise Line** (tel. 800/327–6700); **Royal Cruise Line** (tel. 800/227–4534); **Royal Viking Line** (tel. 800/422–8000); and **Seaborn Cruise Line** (tel. 415/391–7444). Bookings are generally handled through a travel agent.

For details on freighter travel to or from Mexico, consult **Pearl's Travel Tips** (9903 Oaks La., Seminole, FL 34642, tel. 813/393–2919, fax 813/392–2580).

**By Train and Bus** There is no train service to Acapulco from anywhere in the United States or Canada. Buses to Acapulco can be boarded on the U.S. side of the border, but the trip is not recommended; even the most experienced travelers find the journey exhausting and uncomfortable. Bus service from Mexico City to Acapulco, however, is excellent. First-class buses are comfortable and in good condition, and the trip takes 5 hours. They leave every hour on the half-hour from the Tasqueña station. A first-class ticket costs about $18. There is also deluxe service, called *Servicio Diamante*, with airplanelike reclining seats, refreshments, rest rooms, air-conditioning, movies, and hostess service. The deluxe buses leave four times a day, also from the Tasqueño station, and cost about $40.

## Getting Around Acapulco

Getting around in Acapulco is quite simple. You can walk to many places and the bus costs only 20¢. Taxis cost less than they do in the United States, so most tourists quickly become avid taxi takers.

**By Bus** The buses tourists use the most are those that go from Puerto Marqués to Caleta and stop at the fairly conspicuous metal bus stops along the way. If you want to go from the zócalo to The Strip, catch the bus that says *"La Base"* (the naval base near the Exelaris Hyatt Regency). This bus detours through Old Acapulco and returns to the Costera just east of the Ritz Hotel. If you want to follow the Costera for the entire route, take the bus marked "Hornos." Buses to Pie de la Cuesta or Puerto Marqués say so on the front. The Puerto Marqués bus runs about every half hour and is always crowded. If you are headed anywhere along the Costera Miguel Alemán, it's best to go by the Aca Tur bus. For 60¢ you can ride in deluxe, air-conditioned buses that travel up and down the main drag from the Hyatt to the Caleta hotels every 10 minutes.

**By Taxi** How much you pay depends on what type of taxi you get. The most expensive are hotel taxis. A price list that all drivers adhere to is posted in hotel lobbies. Fares in town are usually about $1.50 to $5; to go from downtown to the Princess Hotel or Caleta beach is about $10 to $15. Hotel taxis are by far the plushest and are kept in the best condition.

Cabs that cruise with their roof light off occasionally carry a price list but usually charge by zone. You need to reach an agreement with these drivers, but the fare should be less than it would be at a hotel. There is a minimum charge of $1.50. Some taxis that cruise have hotel or restaurant names stenciled on the side but are not affiliated with an establishment. Before you go anywhere by cab, find out what the price should be and agree with the driver on a price. You can usually persuade one to overcharge you by only 50¢ to $1. Alternatively, you can hand him the correct fare when you arrive, but that could lead to a nasty scene in which the disappointed driver argues with you for more money.

The cheapest taxis are the little Volkswagens. Officially there is a $1.50 minimum charge, but many cab drivers don't stick to it. A normal—i.e., Mexican-priced—fare is $1 to go from the zócalo to American Express, but lots of luck getting a taxi driver to accept that from a tourist. Rates are about 50% higher at night and though tipping is not expected, Mexicans usually leave small change.

You can also hire a taxi by the hour or the day. Prices vary from about $15 an hour for a hotel taxi to $10 an hour for a street taxi. Never let a taxi driver decide where you should eat or shop, since many get kickbacks from some of the smaller stores and restaurants.

**By Motorscooter** Little Honda motorscooters can be rented from a stand outside CiCi, the children's water park on the Costera. They are also available at the Plaza Hotel. Cost: $15 to $20 for up to four hours, depending on the size, or $30 to $40 per day.

**By Horse and Carriage** Buggy rides up and down The Strip are available on weekends. Bargain before you get in—they cost about $20 a half hour.

## Important Addresses and Numbers

**Tourist Information** The **State of Guerrero Department of Tourism (SEFOTUR)** will help you find your way around and answer questions. The office is in the Centro Internacional, tel. 74/84–70–50. It is open Monday through Saturday from 9 to 3 and 6 to 9. Much more helpful is the **Secretaía de Turismo,** across from the Aurrerá, Costera Miguel Alemán 187, which is open weekdays 8–8, Saturday and Sunday 10–6. The staff speaks English, has brochures and maps on other parts of Mexico, and can help you find a hotel room. Tel. 74/85–12–49 or 74/85–13–04.

**Consulates** The consular representative for the United States is Lambert Jean Urbaneck. His office is in the Club del Sol Hotel on the Costera, tel. 74/85–72–07. The Canadian representative is Diane McLean de Huerta, and her office is on the mezzanine level of the Club del Sol Hotel, tel. 74/85–66–21.

**Emergencies** **Police,** tel. 74/85–08–62.

The **Red Cross** can be reached at tel. 74/84–41–22 or 74/84–41–23. Two reliable hospitals are **Hospital Privado Magallanes,** Wilfrido Massiue 2, tel. 74/85–65–44, and **Hospital Centro Médico,** J. Arevalo 99, tel. 74/82–46–92.

**Doctors and** Your hotel and the Secretaría de Turismo can locate an En-
**Dentists** glish-speaking doctor. But English-speaking doctors don't come cheap—house calls are about $50. The Secretaría de Turismo has a list of dentists and suggests Dr. Guadalupe Carmona, Costera Miguel Alemán 220–101, tel. 74/85–71–76, or Dr. Arturo Carmona, Costera Miguel Alemán 220, Suite 110, tel. 74/85–72–86.

**English-language** English-language books and periodicals can be found at
**Bookstores** Sanborns, a reputable American-style department-store chain, and at the newsstands in some of the larger hotels. Most reading material costs more than you would pay at home. Many small newsstands and the Super-Super carry the *Mexico City News*, an English-language daily newspaper with a Sunday-edition travel section that occasionally carries articles about Acapulco. Every day several pages are devoted to foreign news drawn from the wire services, with reprints of articles from the *Washington Post, New York Times*, and *Los Angeles Times*. These newspapers, as well as *USA Today*, are available at most hotels and at Sanborns. *Time* and *Newsweek* magazines are also available.

**Travel Agencies** **American Express,** at Costera Miguel Alemán 709, tel. 74/84–60–60, and **Viajes Wagon-Lits,** at Scenic Highway 5255 (Las Brisas Hotel), tel. 74/82–28–64.

## Guided Tours

**Orientation Tours** There are organized tours everywhere in Acapulco, from the red-light district to the lagoon. Tours to Mexican fiestas in the evenings or the markets in the daytime are easy to arrange. Tour operators have offices around town and desks in many of the large hotels. If your hotel can't arrange a tour, contact **Consejeros de Viajes** at the Torre de Acapulco, Costera Miguel Alemán 1252, tel. 74/84–74–00, or **Acuario,** Costera Miguel Alemán, opposite the Plaza Hotel, tel. 74/85–61–00.

**Special-interest** The Acapulco Princess runs a Mexican cooking school featur-
**Tours** ing the techniques of executive chef George Olah, who teaches dishes from the Aztec time to nouvelle Mexican. The school is limited to 20 participants per session, and there are two 5-day/4-night sessions a year. Contact the Acapulco Princess hotel, tel. 800/223–1818.

# Exploring Acapulco

Acapulco is a city that is easily understood, easily explored. During the day the focus for most visitors is the beach and the myriad activities that happen on and off it—sunbathing, swimming, waterskiing, parasailing, snorkeling, deep-sea fishing, and so on. At night the attention shifts to the restaurants and discos. The Costera Miguel Alemán, the wide boulevard that hugs Acapulco Bay from the Scenic Highway to Caleta Beach (a little less than 5 miles), is central to both day and night diversions. All the major beaches, big hotels—minus the more exclusive East Bay properties, such as Las Brisas, Pierre Marqués, and the Princess—and the shopping malls are off the Costera. Hence most of the shopping, dining, and clubbing takes place within a few blocks of the Costera, and many an address is listed only as "Costera Miguel Alemán." Because street addresses are not often used and streets have no logical pattern, directions are usually given from a major landmark, such as CiCi or the zócalo.

Old Acapulco, the colonial part of town, is where the Mexicans go to run their errands: mail letters at the post office, buy supplies at the Mercado Municipal, and have clothes made/repaired at the tailor. Here is where you'll find the zócalo, the church, and Fort San Diego. Just up the hill from Old Acapulco is La Quebrada, where, four times a day, the cliff divers plunge into the surf 130 feet below.

The peninsula just south of Old Acapulco contains remnants of the first version of Acapulco. This primarily residential area has been prey to dilapidation and abandonment of late, and the efforts made to revitalize it—such as reopening the Caleta Hotel and opening the aquarium on Caleta Beach and the zoo on Roqueta Island—haven't met with much success. The Plaza de Toros, where bullfights are held sporadically, is in the center of the peninsula.

If you arrived by plane, you've had a royal introduction to Acapulco Bay. Driving from the airport, via the Scenic Highway, the first thing you see on your left is the golf course for the Acapulco Princess. Just over the hill is your first glimpse of the entire bay, and it is truly gorgeous, day or night.

*Numbers in the margin correspond to points of interest on the Acapulco map.*

❶ **La Base,** the Mexican naval base next to Plaza Icacos, anchors the eastern terminus of the Costera. There are no tours.

❷ The **Centro Cultural Guerrerense** is on the beach side of the Costera, just past the Hyatt Regency. It has a small archaeological museum and the Zochipala art gallery with changing exhibits. *Admission free. Open weekdays 9–1 and 5–8.*

❸ CiCi (short for Centro Internacional para Convivencia Infantil), on the Costera, is a water-oriented theme park for children. There are dolphin and seal shows, a freshwater pool with wave-making apparatus, water slide, miniaquarium, and other attractions. *Admission: $7 adults, $5 children. Open daily 10–6.*

About a half mile past CiCi, on the right side of the Costera, is
❹ **Centro Internacional** (the Convention Center), not really of in-

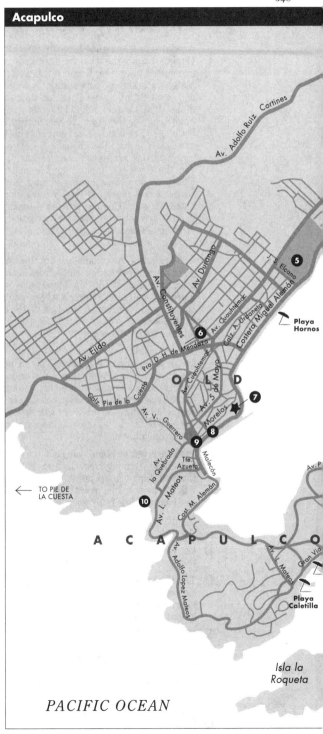

Centro
Internacional, **4**
Centro Cultural
Guerrerense, **2**
CiCi, **3**
El Fuerte de
San Diego, **7**
La Base, **1**
La Quebrada, **10**
Mercado Municipal, **6**
Papagayo Park, **5**
Waterfront, **8**
Zócalo, **9**

Av. Rancho Acapulco

Paseo del Farallón

Golf Course

Cabo Solitario

Av. Almirante

Av. Almirante Cristobal Colón

Magallanes

Horacio Nelson

Av. Cuauhtemoc

Av. W. Massieu

Diana Glorieta

Costera Miguel Alemán

Costera Miguel Alemán

Costera Miguel Alemán

**Playa Condesa**

**Playa Icacos**

**4**

**3**

**2**

**1**

**Playa Hornitos**

Punta Guitarrón

*Bahía de Acapulco*

Escénica

Carretera

**E A S T**

**B A Y**

TO AIRPORT →

o del Rey

ropical

**Playa Caleta**

Punta Bruja

*Bahía de Puerto Marqués*

**Playa Roqueta**

TO PUNTA DIAMANTE →
AND BARRA VIEJA

N

0 — 880 yards

0 — 800 meters

terest unless you are attending a conference there. There is a **Mexican Fiesta** on Tuesday, Thursday, and Saturday nights from 7 to 10:30 ($45 pays for the show, dinner, and open bar; entrance to the show alone is $16).

**❺** Continue along the Costera, through the heart of The Strip, until you reach **Papagayo Park,** one of the top municipal parks in the country for location, beauty, and variety. Named for the hotel that formerly occupied the grounds, Papagayo sits on 52 acres of prime real estate on the Costera, just after the underpass at the end of The Strip. Though the park is designed for children, there is plenty for all ages to enjoy. Youngsters enjoy the life-size model of a Spanish galleon like the ones that once sailed into Acapulco when it was Mexico's capital of trade with the Orient. There is an aviary, a roller-skating rink, a racetrack with mite-size racecars, a replica of the space shuttle *Columbia*, bumper boats in a lagoon, and other rides. The aviary is Papagayo's best feature: Hundreds of species of birds flitter overhead as you amble down shaded paths. *Admission free, though rides cost $1–$3.50. Open daily 10–6.*

**❻** The sprawling **Mercado Municipal,** a few blocks from the Costera, is Acapulco at its most authentic. It is also the city's answer to the suburban shopping mall. Locals come to purchase their everyday needs, from fresh vegetables and candles to plastic buckets and love potions. Go between 10 AM and 1 PM and ask to be dropped off near the *flores* (flower stand) closest to the souvenir and crafts section. If you've driven to the mercado, locals may volunteer to watch your car; be sure to lock your trunk and tip about 35¢.

The stalls within the mercado are densely packed together but luckily are awning-covered, so things stay quite cool despite the lack of air-conditioning. From the flower stall, as you face the ceramic stand, turn right and head into the market. There are hundreds of souvenirs to choose from: woven blankets, puppets, colorful wooden toys and plates, leather goods, baskets, hammocks, and handmade wooden furniture including child-size chairs. You can also find some kitschy gems: Acapulco ashtrays and boxes covered with tiny shells or enormous framed pictures of the Virgin of Guadalupe. Bargaining hard is the rule: Start at half the asking price. The exception is silver. Under no circumstance should you pay more than one-fourth the asking price for hallmarked jewelry. A bracelet will be offered for $50, but the price should drop to less than $20 within five minutes. The silver vendors speak English.

The mercado is patronized primarily by Mexicans and, like many markets, is divided into departments. One area sells locally made brushes and wooden spoons. In another, artisans put finishing touches on baskets and wooden furniture. There are dozens of exotic blossoms—many arranged in FTD-like centerpieces—in the flower market. Prices are a fraction of what you'd pay at home. The beans, spices, and vegetable section has a number of unfamiliar tropical products. There is even a stand offering medicinal herbs from China along with good luck charms. Allow at least an hour and a half to take it all in.

**❼** Built in the 18th century to protect the city from pirates, **El Fuerte de San Diego** is on the hill overlooking the harbor next to the army barracks in Old Acapulco. (The original fort, destroyed in an earthquake, was built in 1616.) The fort now houses the **Museo Historico de Acapulco,** under the auspices of Mexico City's prestigious Museum of Anthropology. The exhibits portray the city from prehistoric times through Mexico's independence from Spain in 1821. Especially noteworthy are the displays touching on the Christian missionaries sent from Mexico to the Far East and the cultural interchange that resulted. Exhibits are mounted in separate air-conditioned rooms of the old fort. *Tel. 74/82–38–28. Admission: $4. Open Tues.–Sun. 10:30–4:30.*

**❽** Acapulco is still a lively commercial port and fishing center. If you stroll along the **waterfront,** you'll see all these activities at the commercial docks. The cruise ships dock here, and at night Mexican parents bring their children to play on the small tree-lined promenade. Farther west, by the zócalo, are the docks for the sightseeing yachts and smaller fishing boats. It's a good spot to join the Mexicans in people-watching.

**❾** The **zócalo** is the center of Old Acapulco, a shaded plaza in front of **Nuestra Señora de la Soledad,** the town's modern but unusual—stark-white exterior with bulb-shaped blue and yellow spires—church. If there is any place in Acapulco that can be called picturesque or authentic, the zócalo is it. Overgrown with dense trees, it is the hub of downtown, a spot for socializing. All day it's filled with vendors, shoeshine men, and people lining up to use the pay phones. After siesta, they drift here to meet and greet. On Sunday evenings there's music in the bandstand. There are several cafés and news agents selling the English-language *Mexico City News,* so tourists lodging in the area linger here, too. The Sanborns just off the zócalo is where locals stop to read the newspaper over a leisurely breakfast before starting off to work. In the afternoon and evening it's a popular spot for drinks and meals. Retired Canadians and American tourists also hang out here, leafing through English-language newspapers and magazines (no one seems to mind—it's a Sanborns tradition) or lingering for hours over a cup of coffee. Around the zócalo are several souvenir shops, and on the side streets you can get hefty, fruity milk shakes for about 50¢. The flea market, inexpensive tailor shops, and Woolworth's (*see* Shopping, *below*) are nearby.

**Time Out** The café at 455 de Mayo, below the German restaurant, serves *churros* every afternoon beginning at 4. This Spanish treat of fried dough dusted with sugar and dipped in hot chocolate is popular at *merienda,* which means "snack."

**❿** A 10-minute walk up the hill from the zócalo brings you to **La Quebrada.** This is home to the famous Mirador Hotel and a large silver shop, Taxco El Viejo (*see* Shopping, *below*). In the 1940s this was the center of action for tourists, and it retains an atmosphere reminiscent of its glory days. Most visitors eventually make the trip here because this is where the famous cliff divers jump from a height of 130 feet every evening at 7:30, 8:30, 9:30, and 10:30. The dives are thrilling, so be sure to arrive early. Before they dive, the brave divers say a prayer at a small shrine near the jumping-off point. Sometimes they dive in pairs; often they carry torches.

**What to See and Do with Children**

CiCi and **Papagayo Park** (*see above*). Children might also like to see the aquarium on Caleta beach, where there are also swimming pools, a toboggan, scuba diving, and (for rent) jet skis, inner tubes, bananas (inflatable rubber tubes pulled along the beach by motorboats), and kayaks—not to mention clean rest rooms. From here you can take the launch to Roqueta Island for a visit to the small zoo, or a glass-bottomed boat to La Quebrada and Puerto Marqués. *Aquarium admission: $7 adults, $5 children. Ferry service to Roqueta Island, including zoo admission: $4. Glass-bottomed boat: $7.*
**Palao's.** This restaurant on Roqueta Island has a sandy cove for swimming, a pony, and a cage of monkeys that entertain the youngsters. Children enjoy the motorboat ride out to the island. Other good restaurants for children are **Beto's Mimi's Chili Saloon,** and **Carlos 'n Charlies** (*see* Dining, *below*).

# Shopping

There is quite a lot of shopping to do in Acapulco, and the abundance of air-conditioned shopping malls and boutiques makes picking up gifts and souvenirs all the more pleasurable. Except for the markets, most places close for siesta. The typical hours of business are 10–1 and then 4–7, though these hours vary slightly. Most shops close on Sunday.

Though the fall of the peso has given most travelers to Acapulco a shopping edge, those who master the art of bargaining and understand how the Mexican sales tax (IVA) works will have their purchasing power increased even more (*see* Shopping *in* Staying in Mexico, Chapter 1).

### Gift Ideas

Mexicans produce quantities of inexpensive collectibles and souvenirs such as colorful serapes, ceramics, glassware, silver, straw hats, leather, shell sculptures, wooden toys, carved walking canes, and, in season, Christmas ornaments. Most of these trinkets can be found everywhere. In fact, you may tire of the stalls that fill the flea markets, all selling seemingly identical selections of archaeological artifact replicas, bamboo wind chimes, painted wooden birds (about $3.50 to $10 each), 50¢ shell earrings, shell sculptures, sets of wooden dishes, wall hangings, rugs, embroidered jackets, shirts, and dresses. Prices in these flea markets are often quite low, so it makes sense to buy outside the shops or to visit the shops first, note the prices, and then venture to the markets to try to beat the store prices. Many of these flea markets were set up by the government in a successful effort to get hawkers off the streets and beaches. Bargaining is essential in these situations. There is always some unscrupulous vendor who tries to sell unsuspecting tourists a $5 bracelet that he bought from a wholesaler for only 50¢ that morning. It's best to buy articles described as being made from semiprecious stones or silver in reputable establishments. If you don't, you may find that the beautiful jade or lapis lazuli that was such a bargain was really cleverly painted paste, or that the silver was simply a facsimile called *alpaca*. Real sterling should always be stamped with the "sterling" or .925 hallmark. The large AFA (Artesanías Finas de Acapulco) crafts shop, though, has fixed prices and will ship, so this is the place to purchase onyx lamp stands and other larger items (*see* Food and Flea Markets, *below*). Clothes are another reasonably priced gift item. There are a couple of fashionable boutiques that sell designer clothes, but the majority of shops stock cotton sportswear and casual resort clothes. Made-to-order clothes are well made and especially reasonable. Otherwise be careful, since quality is not high and many goods self-destruct a few months after you get back home.

## Shopping Districts

The biggest shopping strip surrounds the Fiesta Americana Condesa Hotel and is where you can find Gucci, Acapulco Joe, Ocho Rios, Rubén Torres, Fiorucci, and others. Downtown (Old) Acapulco doesn't have many name shops, but this is where you'll find the inexpensive tailors patronized by the Mexicans, lots of little souvenir shops, and the flea market with crafts made for tourists. The tailors are all on Calle Benito Juárez, just west of the zócalo. Also downtown are Woolworth's and Sanborns.

## Food and Flea Markets

The **Mercado Municipal** is described in Exploring, *above*.

**El Mercado de Artesanías** is a 20-minute walk from the zócalo. Turn left as you leave Woolworth's and head straight until you reach the Multibanco Comermex. Turn right for one block and then turn left. When you reach the Banamex, the market is on your right. There are also "flea market" signs posted. The market itself is shamelessly inauthentic; everything here is made strictly for foreign consumption, so go just for the amusement. It is a conglomeration of every souvenir in town: fake tribal masks, the ever-present onyx chessboards, the $25 hand-embroidered dresses, imitation silver, hammocks, ceramics, even skin cream made from turtles. (Don't buy it because turtles are endangered and you won't get it through U.S. Customs.) *Open daily 9–9.* If you don't want to make the trip downtown, try **Noa Noa** on the Costera at Calle Hurtado de Mendoza. It's a cleaner, more commercial version of the Mercado Municipal and has T-shirts and jewelry, as well as the dozens of souvenirs available in the other markets.

**Artesanías Finas de Acapulco (AFA)** is one block north of the Costera behind the Baby O disco. All the souvenirs you have seen in town and lots more are available in 13,000 square feet of air-conditioned shopping space. AFA also carries household items, complete sets of dishes, suitcases, leather goods, and conservative clothing, as well as fashionable shorts and T-shirts. The staff is helpful. AFA ships to the United States and accepts major credit cards.

The **Crafts Shop**, in the same building as Taxco El Viejo in La Quebrada before you reach the Mirador Hotel, not only has all the usual crafts but also the best selection of glassware in Acapulco.

Two blocks west of the zócalo is **Calle José M. Iglesia,** home to a row of little souvenir shops that have a smaller selection than the big markets but many more T-shirts and more shell sculptures, shell ashtrays, and shell key chains than you ever imagined possible.

## Art

**Contemporary Art Gallery,** at the Hyatt Regency, carries the work of contemporary Mexican artists, including Leonardo Nierman, as well as handicrafts that almost border on art. *Open Mon.–Sat. 10–8.*

**Galería Rudic,** across from the Continental Plaza, is one of the best galleries in town, with a good collection of top contemporary Mexican artists, including Armando Amaya, Leonardo Nierman, Norma Goldberg, Trinidad Osorio, José Clemente Orozco, and José David Alfaro Siqueiros. *Open weekdays 10–2 and 5–8.*

**Galería Victor** is the most noteworthy shop in the El Patio shopping center across from the Hyatt Continental. On display is the work of the late Victor Salmones. *Open 10–2 and 4–8. Closed Sun.*

The sculptor **Pal Kepenyes** continues to receive good press. His jewelry is available in the Hyatt Regency arcade. It's also on display in his house at Guitarrón 140. Good luck with his perennially busy phone number, tel. 74/84–37–38.

**Sergio Bustamante's** whimsical painted papier-mâché and giant ceramic sculptures can be seen at the Princess Hotel shopping arcade and at his own gallery (Costera Miguel Alemán 711-B, next to American Express). **El Dorado Gallery,** next door, carries works by his former partner, Mario Gonzáles.

## Boutiques

The mall section (*see below*) lists clothing shops, but there are a few places, mainly near the Fiesta Americana Condesa Hotel, that are noteworthy. **Mad Max** has tasteful cotton separates in bold colors for children and shirts sporting the shop's logo (all about $20). **Ocho Ríos** has a line of smashing women's bathing suits for equally smashing bodies. **Acapulco Joe, Rubén Torres, Polo Ralph Lauren, Benetton,** and **OP** are scattered around the Costera, too. At No. 143 are three interconnected shops: Explora, Poco Loco, and Maria de Guadalajara. **Explora** and **Poco Loco** stock shirts imprinted with beer and alcohol logos, with casual separates and bathing suits as well. The **Maria de Guadalajara** line of comfortable casual clothes for women is made from crinkly cotton in subdued and pastel colors. There are also a few high-fashion boutiques that will make clothes to order, and many can alter clothes to suit you, so it is always worth asking.

**Nautica,** in the Galería Plaza, is a boutique stocked with stylish casual clothing for men.

In Plaza Bahía, **Marithé and François Girbaud** carry a selection of very stylish casuals, designed in France and made in Mexico for men and women.

**Marietta** is located on the Costera at the Torre de Acapulco. It has a large collection that ranges from simple daywear to extravagantly sexy party dresses. This is a standby for expatriates in Acapulco. Though the clothes may seem expensive (cotton dresses from $70 to $150), they are quite a bit cheaper than they would be in the United States. The store also has a good selection of men's shirts.

**Pit,** located in the Princess arcade, is another bonanza. It carries a smashing line of beach cover-ups and hand-painted straw hats, as well as bathing suits and light dresses.

**Custom-made Clothes** The most famous of the made-to-order boutiques is **Samy's** at Calle Hidalgo 7, two blocks west of the zócalo, a crammed little shop next to a florist. It boasts a clientele of international celebrities and many of the important local families. Samy, the charming owner, takes all customers to heart and treats them like old, much-loved friends. He makes clothes for men and women, all in light cottons. The patterns are unusual and heavily influenced by Mexican designs, with embroidery and gauze playing a supporting role in the Samy look. The outfits are appropriate for trendy over-30s. Anything that doesn't fit can be altered, and Samy will even work with fabric that you bring in. Prices start at about $30. There is also a ready-to-wear line.

**Esteban's,** the most glamorous shop in Acapulco, is on the Costera near the Club de Golf. Like Samy, Esteban will make clothes to order and adapt anything you see in the shop. The similarity ends there, however. Esteban's clothes are far more formal and fashionable. His opulent evening dresses range from $200 to $1,000, though daytime dresses average $120. If you scour the racks, you can find something for $100. Esteban has a back room filled with designer clothes.

## Jewelry

**Aha,** on the Costera next to the Crazy Lobster, has the most unusual costume jewelry in Acapulco. Designed by owner Cecilia Rodriguez, this is really campy, colorful stuff that is bound to attract attention. Prices range from $12 to $300.

**Emi Fors** (Galería Plaza and the Continental Plaza) are tony jewelry shops owned by Mrs. Fors, a former Los Angelino. The stores stock gold, silver, and some semiprecious stones.

**Arles,** at the Galería Acapulco Plaza, carries the beautiful Oro de Monte Alban collection of gold replicas of Oaxacan artifacts, as well as watches, handicrafts, and handpainted tin soldiers.

## Silver

Many people come to Mexico to buy silver. Taxco, three hours away, is one of the silver capitals of the world. Prices in Acapulco are lower than those in the United States but not dirt-cheap by any means. Bangles start at $8 and go up to $20; bracelets range from $20 to $60. Just look for the .925 sterling silver hallmark, or buy the more inexpensive silver plate that is dipped in several coats *(baños)* of silver. **Miguel Pineda** and **Los Castillo** are two of the more famous design names. Designs range from traditional bulky necklaces (often made with turquoise) to streamlined bangles and chunky earrings. Not much flatware can be found, although Emi Fors and Taxco El Viejo do carry some.

**Taxco El Viejo** (La Quebrada 830), in a large colonial building in Old Acapulco, has the largest silver selection in Acapulco. Pieces seen all over town crop up here, as do more unusual designs. Also for sale are flatware and a large range of ornamental belt buckles. If you buy several pieces, you can request a discount. Beware of heavy-handed sales techniques such as offering to send a taxi to pick you up at your hotel, a tactic meant to make you feel obligated to buy something.

**La Joya** (Acapulco Plaza) stocks a good collection of inexpensive silver jewelry in modern designs and an extensive array of low-priced bangles (in the $6 range). Joya sells wholesale and will give a 30% discount on every item. *Open weekdays 9–6, Sat. 9–5.*

**Dudu** (Acapulco Princess shopping center) has the finest selection of silver jewelry and decorative pieces in town. There are signed pieces by Los Castillo (including brightly colored high-temperature ceramic dinnerware inlaid with silver) and enameled pieces by Miguel Pineda.

## Malls

Malls are all the rage in Acapulco, and new ones are constantly being built. These range from the lavish air-conditioned shopping arcade at the Princess to rather gloomy collections of shops that sell cheap jewelry and embroidered dresses. Malls are listed below from east to west.

The **Princess's** cool arcade is one of Acapulco's classiest, most comfortable malls. Serious shopping takes place here. Best bets are quality jewelry, clothes, leather, accessories, and artwork. Even if you are staying on The Strip, it is worth the cab ride out here just to see the shops.

La Casita, which carries Mexican-inspired clothes for women, is the only shop left in **Plaza Icacos,** at the bottom of the hill, across from the Hyatt Regency. Across from the Fiesta Americana Condesa Hotel is the **Plaza Condesa,** which offers a cold-drink stand, an Italian restaurant, a weight-training center, and a greater concentration of silver shops than you'll find anywhere else in Acapulco. Next door to Plaza Condesa is a high-tech, two-story building with a gym, OP for trendy sportswear, Rubén Torres, Acapulco Joe, and two branches of Mad Max. The multilevel **Marbella Mall,** at the Diana Glorieta, has Peletier Paris jewelers and Bing's Ice Cream, as well as several restaurants and a Century 21 office. **Aca Mall,** which is on the other side of the Diana Glorieta, is all white and marble. Here you'll find Polo Ralph Lauren, Esprit, Ferrioni, Aca Joe, Express, and Marti (which carries a huge variety of sports equipment). **El Patio,** across from the Hyatt Continental, has two recommendable art galleries, Gucci, and a fairly generic collection of clothing and silver shops.

**Plaza Bahía,** next to the Acapulco Plaza, is a huge, completely enclosed and air-conditioned mall where you could easily spend an entire day. Here you'll find Docker's; Nautica; Benetton; Aspasia, which carries a line of locally designed glitzy evening dresses and chunky diamanté jewelry; Bally; Armando's Girasol, with its distinctive line of women's clothing; restaurants and snack bars; Marti; a video-games arcade; and silver and handicraft shops. The list goes on and on.

**Galería Plaza** is a new two-story structure of lusciously air-conditioned shops built around a courtyard. Except for the silver, you could find many similar items at home. But this is a good

place for picking up cotton sportswear or a pretty dress to wear
to a disco. For fancier duds, try Arles upstairs. Guess! is one
block west as you leave the plaza. Across from the Galería Plaza
is the **Flamboyant Mall,** similar in style to El Patio.

### Department Stores

**Sanborns** is the most un-Mexican of the big shops. It sells English-language newspapers, magazines, and books, as well as a
line of high-priced souvenirs, but its Mexican glassware and ceramics cannot be found anywhere else in town. This is a useful
place to come for postcards, cosmetics, and medicines. Sanborns's restaurants are recommended for glorified coffee-shop
food. *The branch adjacent to the Condesa, Costera Miguel Alemán 209, is open until 1 AM; the downtown branch, Costera
Miguel Alemán 1206, closes at 10:30 PM.*

Two branches of **Aurrerá** and **Gigante,** all on the Costera, and
the **Super Super** downtown sell everything from light bulbs and
newspapers to bottles of tequila and postcards. If you are missing anything at all, you should be able to pick it up at either of
these stores or at the **Comercial Mexicana,** a store a little closer
to The Strip. *Open until 9 PM.*

**Woolworth's,** at the corner of Escudero and Matamoros streets
in Old Acapulco, is much like the five-and-dime stores found all
over the United States but with a Mexican feel. You can purchase American brands of shampoo for less than they cost at
home, as well as paper goods, cheap clothes, handmade children's toys, and the ubiquitous Acapulco shell ashtrays. There
are also several mini-Woolworths along the Costera. *Open until
9 PM.*

# Sports and Fitness

### Participant Sports and Fitness

Acapulco has lots for sports lovers to enjoy. Most hotels have
pools, and there are several tennis courts on The Strip. The
weight-training craze is beginning to catch on, and gyms are
opening. You'll find one at Plaza Condesa across from the Fiesta Americana Condesa Hotel.

Fishing  Sailfish, marlin, shark, and mahimahi are the usual catches.
Head down to the docks near the zócalo and see just how many
people offer to take you out for $30 a day. It is safer to stick with
one of the reliable companies whose boats and equipment are in
good condition.

Fishing trips can be arranged through your hotel, downtown at
the Pesca Deportiva near the *muelle* (dock) across from the
zócalo, or through travel agents. Boats accommodating 4 to 10
people cost $150–$500 a day, $40 to $60 by the chair. Excursions usually leave about 7 AM and return at 1 or 2 PM. You are
required to get a license ($7) from the Secretaría de Pesca above
the central post office downtown, but most fishing outfits take
care of this. Don't show up during siesta, between 2 and 4 in the
afternoon. For deep-sea fishing, **Arnold Brothers** (Costera
Miguel Alemán 205, tel. 74/82–18–77) has well-maintained
boats for five passengers (four lines). Small boats for freshwater fishing can be rented at **Cadena's** and **Tres Marías** at Coyuca

lagoon. **Divers de México** (*see* Scuba Diving, *below*) rents chairs on fishing boats for about $35 per person.

**Fitness and Swimming**  Acapulco weather is like August in the warmest parts of the United States. This means that you should cut back on your workouts and maintain proper hydration by drinking plenty of water.

**Acapulco Princess Hotel** (Carretera Escénica, Km 17, tel. 74/8 4–31–00) offers the best fitness facilities, with five pools, 11 tennis courts, and a gym with stationary bikes, Universal machines, and free weights. Because the Princess is about 9 miles from the city center, you can even swim in the ocean here, avoiding the pollution of Acapulco Bay. Beware: The waves are rough and the undertow is strong.

**Villa Vera Spa and Fitness Center** (Lomas del Mar 35, tel. 74/ 84–03–33) has a new spa and fitness center and is equipped with exercise machines (including step machines), free weights, and benches. Masseuses and cosmetologists give facials and massages inside or by the pool, as you wish. Both the beauty center and the gym are open to nonguests.

**Westin Las Brisas** (Carretera Escénica 5255, tel. 74/84–15–80) is where you should stay if you like to swim but don't like company or competition. Individual casitas come with private, or semiprivate, pools; the beach club has two saltwater pools, a Home Fitness System, and workout machines.

Most of the major hotels in town along the Costera Miguel Alemán also have pools.

**Golf**  There are two 18-hole championship golf courses shared by the Princess and Pierre Marqués hotels. Reservations should be made in advance (tel. 74/84–31–00). Greens fees are $65 for guests and $85 for nonguests. There is also a public golf course at the Club de Golf (tel. 74/84–07–81) on The Strip across from the Acapulco Malibú hotel. Greens fees are $30 for nine holes.

**Jogging**  The only real venue for running in the downtown area is along the sidewalk next to the seafront Costera Miguel Alemán. Early morning is the best time, since traffic is heavy along this thoroughfare during most of the day and the exhaust fumes can make running unpleasant. The sidewalk measures close to 5 miles. The beach is another option, but like beaches everywhere, the going is tough, with soft sand and sloping contours. Away from the city center, the best area for running is out at the Acapulco Princess Hotel, on the airport road. A 2-kilometer (1.2 mi) loop is laid out along a lightly traveled road, and in the early morning you can also run along the asphalt trails on the golf course.

**Scuba Diving**  **Divers de México** (tel. 74/82–13–98), owned by a helpful and efficient American woman, provides English-speaking captains and comfortable American-built yachts. A four- to five-hour scuba-diving excursion, including equipment, lessons in a pool for beginners, and drinks, costs about $45 per person. If you are a certified diver, the excursion is $35; if you bring your own equipment, it is $30.

**Arnold Brothers** (*see* Fishing, *above*) also runs daily scuba-diving excursions and snorkeling trips. The scuba trips cost $30 and last for 2½ hours.

**Tennis** Court fees range from about $3 to $20 an hour during the day and are $3–$5 more in the evening. Nonhotel guests pay about $5 more per hour. Lessons, with English-speaking instructors, are about $25 an hour; ball boys get a $2 tip.

**Acapulco Plaza,** 3 hard-surface courts, 2 lighted for evening play (tel. 74/84–90–50). **Acapulco Princess,** 2 indoor courts, 9 outdoor (tel. 74/84–31–00). **Club de Tennis and Golf,** across from Hotel Malibu, Costera Miguel Alemán (tel. 74/84–07–81). **Hyatt Regency,** 5 lighted courts (tel. 74/84–12–25). **Pierre Marqués,** 5 courts (tel. 74/84–20–00). **Tiffany's Racquet Club,** Avenue Villa Vera 120, 5 courts (tel. 74/84–79–49). **Villa Vera Hotel,** 3 outdoor lighted clay courts (tel. 74/84–02–24).

**Water Sports** Waterskiing, broncos (one-person motorboats), and parasailing can all be arranged on the beach. Parasailing is an Acapulco highlight and looks terrifying until you actually try it. Most people who do it love the view and go back again and again. An eight-minute trip costs $15 (tel. 74/82–20–56). Waterskiing is about $20 an hour; broncos cost $30 for a half hour. Windsurfing can be arranged at Caleta and most of the beaches along the Costera but is especially good at Puerto Marqués. At Coyuca Lagoon, you can try your hand (or feet) at barefoot waterskiing. The main surfing beach is Revolcadero.

## Spectator Sports

**Bullfights** The season runs from Christmas to Easter, and *corridas* are held—sporadically—on Sundays at 5:30. Tickets are available through your hotel or at the Plaza de Toros ticket window (open Mon.–Sat. 10–2 and Sun. 10:30–3; tel. 74/82–11–81). Tickets cost from $20 to $25, and a $25 seat in the first four rows—in the shade (*sombra*)—is worth the extra cost. Also check the local paper and signs around town to find out if any noteworthy matadors can be seen in action.

## Beaches

The lure of sun and sand in Acapulco is legendary. Every sport is available and you can shop from roving souvenir vendors, eat in a beach restaurant, dance, and sleep in a *hamaca* (hammock) without leaving the water's edge. If you want to avoid the crowds, there are also plenty of quiet and even isolated beaches within reach. However, some of these, such as Revolcadero and Pie de la Cuesta, have very strong undertows and surfs, so swimming is not advised. Despite an enticing appearance and claims that officials are cleaning up the bay, it remains polluted. If this bothers you, we suggest that you follow the lead of the Mexican cognoscenti and take the waters at your hotel pool.

Beaches in Mexico are public, even those that seem to belong to a big hotel. The list below moves from east to west.

**Barra Vieja** About 16 miles east of Acapulco, between Laguna de Tres Palos and the Pacific, this magnificent beach is even more inviting than Pie de la Cuesta because you're not bothered by itinerant peddlers and beggars.

**Revolcadero** A wide, sprawling beach next to the Pierre Marqués and Princess hotels, its water is shallow and its waves are fairly rough. People come here to surf and ride horses.

**Puerto Marqués**  Tucked below the airport highway, this strand is popular with Mexican tourists, so it tends to get crowded on weekends.

**Icacos**  Stretching from the naval base to El Presidente, this beach is less populated than others on The Strip. The morning waves are especially calm.

**Condesa**  Facing the middle of Acapulco Bay, this stretch of sand has more than its share of tourists, especially singles. The beachside restaurants are convenient for bites between parasailing flights.

**Hornos and Hornitos**  Running from the Paraiso Radisson to Las Hamacas hotels, these beaches are packed shoulder to shoulder with Mexican tourists. These tourists know a good thing: Graceful palms shade the sand, and there are scads of casual eateries within walking distance.

**Caleta and Caletilla**  On the peninsula in Old Acapulco, these two beaches once rivaled La Quebrada as the main tourist area in Acapulco's heyday. Now they attract families. Motorboats to Roqueta leave from here.

**Roqueta Island**  A ferry costs about $4 round-trip, including entrance to the zoo; the trip takes 10 minutes each way. Acapulqueños consider Roqueta Island their day-trip spot.

**Pie de la Cuesta**  You'll need a car or cab to reach this relatively unpopulated spot, about 15 minutes west of town. A few rustic restaurants border the wide beach and straw palapas provide shade.

# Dining

Dining in Acapulco is more than just eating out—it is the most popular leisure activity in town. Every night the restaurants fill up, and every night the adventurous diner can sample a different cuisine: Italian, German, Japanese, American, Tex-Mex, and, of course, plain old Mex. The variety of styles matches the range of cuisines: from greasy spoons that serve regional specialties to rooftop gourmet restaurants with gorgeous views of Acapulco Bay. Most restaurants fall somewhere in the middle, and on The Strip there are dozens of palapa (palm frond)–roofed beachside restaurants, as well as wildly decorated rib and hamburger joints popular with visitors under 30.

One plus for Acapulco dining is that the food is garden fresh. Each morning the Mercado Municipal is abuzz with restaurant managers and locals buying up the vegetables that will appear on plates that evening. Although some top-quality beef is now being produced in the states of Sonora and Chihuahua, many of the more expensive restaurants claim that they import their beef from the States. Whether or not they're telling the truth, the beef is excellent in most places. Establishments that cater to tourists purify their drinking water and use it to cook vegetables. In smaller restaurants, ask for bottled water with or without bubbles (*con* or *sin gas*).

The top restaurants in Acapulco can be fun for a splurge and provide very good value. Even at the best places in town, dinner rarely exceeds $45 per person, and the atmosphere and views are fantastic. Ties and jackets are out of place, but so are shorts or jeans. Unless stated otherwise, all restaurants are open daily from 6:30 or 7 PM until the last diner leaves.

Highly recommended restaurants are indicated by a star ★.

| Category | Cost* |
|---|---|
| Very Expensive | over $35 |
| Expensive | $25–$35 |
| Moderate | $15–$25 |
| Inexpensive | under $15 |

*per person excluding drinks, service, and sales tax (10%)*

## Very Expensive

**Continental** **Bella Vista.** This al fresco restaurant in the exclusive Las Brisas area has fantastic sunset views of Acapulco. Its recently expanded menu offers a wide variety of dishes that range from Asian appetizers to Italian and seafood entrées. Try the delicious (and spicy!) Thai shrimp, sauteed in sesame oil, ginger, Thai chili, and hoisin sauce, or the red snapper Etouffee, cooked in Chardonnay, tomato, herbs, basil and oyster sauce. *Carratera Escéncia 5255, tel. 74/84–15–80, ext. 500. Reservations required. AE, DC, MC, V.*
**Maximilian's.** An exception to the rule that says hotels don't serve top-quality food, Maximilian's is a haven for American expatriates who like to dress up and come for a treat. It is one of few beachside restaurants that have air-conditioning. Lobster bisque, duck, and seafood cooked with classic ingredients are the specialties, and steak is available, too. *Acapulco Plaza, tel. 74/85–80–50. Reservations advised. AE, DC, MC, V.*

**French** **Le Gourmet.** Although its food is wildly inconsistent, this restaurant is thought by many to be one of Acapulco's premier establishments. Many people staying down on the Costera brave the 15-minute taxi ride to partake of a tranquil meal in a plush setting. The French menu has all the classics: vichyssoise, steak au poivre sautéed in cognac, and such Acapulco favorites as lobster and red snapper fillets. The atmosphere is luxurious and genteel, with roomy, comfortable chairs, silent waiters, and air-conditioning. *Acapulco Princess Hotel, tel. 74/84–31–00. Reservations advised. AE, DC, MC, V.*

**Gourmet** **Coyuca 22.** This is possibly the most expensive restaurant in
**★** Acapulco; it is certainly one of the most beautiful. Diners eat on terraces that overlook the bay from the west, on a hilltop in Old Acapulco. The understated decor consists of Doric pillars, sculptures, and large onyx flower stands near the entrance. Diners gaze down on an enormous illuminated obelisk and a small pool. The effect is that of eating in a partially restored Greek ruin sans dust. The tiny menu centers on seafood, with lobster the house specialty. Prime rib is also available. *Avenida Coyuca 22 (a 10-minute taxi ride from the zócalo), tel. 74/82–34–68 or 74/83–50–30. Reservations required. AE, DC, MC, V. Closed Apr. 30–Nov. 1.*

**Japanese** **Suntory.** At this traditional Japanese restaurant you can dine either in a blessedly air-conditioned interior room or in the delightful Oriental-style garden. It's one of the few Japanese restaurants in Acapulco and also one of the only deluxe restaurants that is open for lunch. Specialties are the sushi and the teppan-yaki, prepared at your table by skilled chefs.

# Acapulco Dining and Lodging

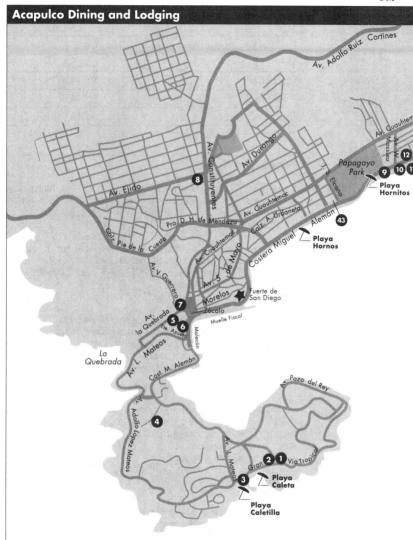

**Dining**

Acapulco Fat Farm, **6**
Bella Vista, **39**
Beto's, **21**
Blackbeard's, **20**
Carlos 'n Charlies, **23**
Casimiro's, **17**
Coyuca 22, **4**
D'Joint, **27**
El Cabrito, **30**
Embarcadero, **31**
Hard Rock Café, **29**

Hard Times, **26**
Le Gourmet, **41**
Los Rancheros, **35**
Madeiras, **38**
Maximilian's, **15**
Mimi's Chili
Saloon, **19**
Miramar, **36**
100% Natural, **13**
Paradise, **18**
Sirocco, **43**
Suntory, **32**

Tlaquepaque, **8**
Zapata, Villa y
Compañiá, **34**
Zorrito's, **11**

**Lodging**

Acapulco Plaza, **15**
Acapulco Princess, **41**
Autotel Ritz, **12**
Belmar, **2**
Boca Chica, **3**
Camino Real Acapulco
Diamante, **42**
Copacabana, **33**
Fiesta American

3

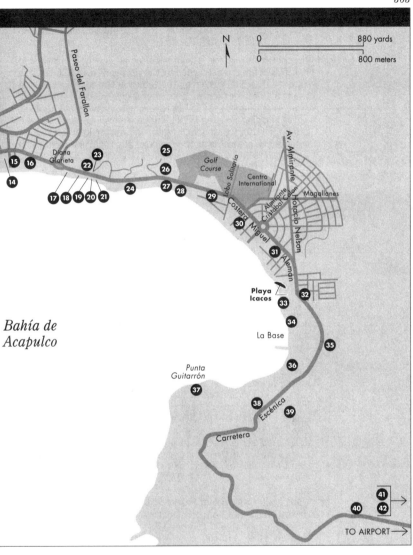

363

Condesa Acapulco, **24**    Pierre Marqués, **40**

Gran Motel
Acapulco, **16**
Hotel Acapulco
Tortuga, **22**
Hotel Misión, **5**
Hyatt Regency
Acapulco, **34**
Las Brisas, **39**
Maralisa Hotel and
Beach Club, **14**
Paraíso Radisson, **9**

Plaza las Glorias El
Mirador, **7**
Ritz, **10**
Royal El Cano, **28**
Sheraton
Acapulco, **37**
Suites Alba, **1**
Villa Vera, **25**

*Suntory, Costera Miguel Alemán 36, across from the La Palapa hotel, tel. 74/84–80–88. Reservations advised for dinner only. AE, DC, MC, V.*

**Seafood** **Blackbeard's.** A dark, glorified coffee shop with a pirate-ship motif, Blackbeard's—owned by the proprietors of Mimi's Chili Saloon—has maps covering the tables in the cozy booths, and the walls are adorned with wooden figureheads. Every movie star, from Bing Crosby to Liz Taylor, who ever set foot here has his or her photo posted in the lounge. A luscious salad bar and jumbo portions of shrimp, steak, and lobster keep customers satisfied. A new disco on the premises starts throbbing at 10:30 PM. *Costera Miguel Alemán, tel. 74/84–25–49. Reservations advised. AE, DC, MC, V.*

## Expensive

**American** **Carlos 'n Charlies.** This is without a doubt the most popular res-
★ taurant in town; a line forms well before the 6:30 PM opening. Part of the Anderson group (with restaurants in the United States and Spain as well as Mexico), Carlos 'n Charlies cultivates an atmosphere of controlled craziness. Prankster waiters, a joke-ster menu, and eclectic decor—everything from antique bullfight photos to a tool chest of painted gadgets hanging from the ceiling—add to the chaos. The crowd is mostly young and relaxed, which is what you need to be to put up with the rush-hour traffic noise that filters up to the covered balcony where people dine. The menu straddles the border, with ribs, stuffed shrimp, and oysters among the best offerings. *Costera Miguel Alemán 999, tel. 74/84–12–85 or 84–00–39. No reservations. AE, DC, MC, V.*

**Embarcadero.** A nautical motif pervades Embarcadero, which is well loved by both Acapulco regulars and resident Americans. It is designed to look like a wharf with the bar as the loading office. Wooden bridges lead past a fountain to the thatched eating area, piled high with wooden packing crates and maps. The food is American with a Polynesian touch. You can have deep-fried shrimp with garlic sauce, tempura, chicken, or steak. The "salad barge" is enormous. *Costera Miguel Alemán, south-east of CiCi Park, tel. 74/84–87–87. Open 6 PM–midnight. No reservations. AE, DC, MC, V. Closed Mon. out of season.*

★ **Hard Rock Café.** A bar, restaurant, and dance hall filled with rock memorabilia, this is one of the most popular spots in Acapulco, and with good reason. The southern-style food—fried chicken, ribs, chili con carne—is very well prepared and the portions are more than ample. The taped rock music begins at noon, and a live group starts playing at 11 PM. There's always a line at the small boutique on the premises where you can buy sports clothes and accessories bearing the Hard Rock label. *Costera Miguel Alemán 37, tel. 74/84–66–80. Reservations advised. AE, MC, V.*

**Continental** **Madeiras.** It vies with its neighbor, Miramar, for most chichi
★ place in Acapulco, and there are fierce arguments as to which has the best food. Madeiras is very difficult to get into; many people make reservations by letter before their arrival. At the very least, call the minute you get to Acapulco. Children under 8 are not welcome, however. All the tables at Madeiras have a view of glittering Acapulco by night. The furniture is certainly unusual: The bar/reception area has art nouveau–style carved chairs, plump sofas, and startling coffee tables made of glass

resting on large wooden animals. All the dishes and silverware were created by silversmiths in the nearby town of Taxco. Dinner is served from a four-course, prix fixe menu and costs about $25 without wine. Entrées include the delicious Spanish dish of red snapper in sea salt, tasty chilled soups, stuffed red snapper, and a choice of steaks and other seafood, as well as the *crepas de huitlacoche* (huitlacoche, or cuitlacoche, is a corn fungus that was a delicacy to the Aztecs). Desserts are competently prepared but have no special flair. There are two seatings, at 6:30 and 9. Unfortunately, diners coming at the later time may find selections limited. *Scenic Highway just past La Vista shopping center, tel. 74/84–73–16. Reservations required. AE, DC, MC, V.*

**Mexican**  **Zapata, Villa y Compañiá.** This is a Mexican version of the Hard Rock Café, where the music and food (excellent) are strictly Mexican and the memorabilia is Mexican Revolution, with guns, hats, and photographs of Pancho Villa. The definite highlight of an evening here is a visit from a sombrero-wearing baby burro, so be sure to bring your camera. *Hyatt Regency, Costera Miguel Alemán 1, tel. 74/84–28–88. No reservations. AE, DC, MC, V.*

**French**  **Miramar.** Light wooden furniture and a fountain provide the
★  decoration for this understated place, but the real glamour comes from the view of the bay and the flickering lights of Acapulco. Traditional dishes, such as pâté and lobster thermidor, are served alongside classics with a new twist: ceviche with a hint of coconut and red snapper papillote. Shrimp mousse and duck are both specialties. Miramar is not as intimate as its neighbor, Madeiras, and many large groups from the Princess book long tables, so the noise level is rather high. *Scenic Highway at La Vista shopping center, tel. 74/84–78–74. Reservations advised. AE, DC, MC, V. Closed Sept.–Oct.*

## Moderate

**American**  **D'Joint.** Locals as well as tourists love D'Joint—a claustrophobic restaurant with a funky, publike atmosphere and a popular sports bar—so, in season, prepare for a wait. In addition to the usual steaks, salads, and nachos, prime rib is the house specialty. The four types of roast beef sandwiches are another hit. After your meal, try "sexy coffee"—cappuccino with liqueur. *Costera Miguel Alemán 79, next door to the Hotel Acapulco Malibú, tel. 74/84–19–13. No reservations. AE, DC, MC, V. Closed 1 week in summer.*

**Mexican**  **Los Rancheros.** With a view of the water in the posh East Bay, here's Mexican food at about half what you'd pay at Madeiras or Miramar. The decor is colorful, folksy Mexican with paper streamers, checked tablecloths, and lopsided mannequins in local dress. Specials include *carne tampiqueña* (fillet of beef broiled with lemon juice), chicken enchiladas, and *queso fundido* (melted cheese served as a side dish with chips). Live music daily noon to midnight. *Scenic Highway just before Extasis disco (on the left as you head toward the airport), tel. 74/84–19–08. MC, V.*

**Mixed Menu**  **Hard Times.** With an unusually large menu for Acapulco, Hard
★  Times features the usual Tex-Mex dishes as well as plenty of barbecue, fresh fish, and the largest salad bar in town. The dining area is an attractive open terrace, with a partial view of the

bay. Although it is right in the center of The Strip, Hard Times is a tranquil haven—decorated with palms and incandescent lights—in which to enjoy generous portions of American food and, sometimes, jazz. Arrive early; there is often a wait in high season. *Costera Miguel Alemán, across from the Calinda Quality Hotel (look for the red neon lights), tel. 74/84–00–64. Reservations advised during high season. AE, DC, MC, V. Closed Sun. during summer.*

**Seafood** **Paradise.** This is the leading beach-party restaurant. T-shirted waiters drop leis over your head as you arrive and hand roses to the ladies. The menu (primarily seafood) has the same number of dishes as drinks, a pretty good indicator of what this place is like. Paradise has one of the biggest dance floors in Acapulco and live music day and night. Chaos reigns at lunchtime (from 2 to 5), and the mood picks up again from 8:30 to 10:30. Expect a young crowd. *Costera Miguel Alemán 107, next to Mimi's Chili Saloon, tel. 74/84–59–88. No reservations. AE, DC, MC, V.*

**Sirocco.** This beachside eatery is numero uno for those who crave Spanish food in Acapulco. The tiled floors and heavy wooden furniture give it a Mediterranean feel. Specialties include *pulpo en su tinta* (octopus in its own ink) and 10 varieties of fresh fish. Order paella when you arrive at the beach—it takes a half hour to prepare. *Costera Miguel Alemán, across from Aurrerá, tel. 74/85–23–86 and 74/85–94–90. Reservations not required. AE, MC, V. Open 2–10 PM.*

---

### Inexpensive

**Health Food** **100% Natural.** Six family-operated restaurants specialize in ★ light, healthful food—yogurt shakes, fruit salads, and sandwiches made with whole-wheat bread. The service is quick and the food is a refreshing alternative to tacos, particularly on a hot day. Look for the green signs with white lettering. *Costera Miguel Alemán 204, near the Acapulco Plaza, tel. 74/85–39–82. Another branch is at the Casa de la Cultura, tel. 74/81–08–44. No credit cards.*

★ **Zorrito's.** The old Zorrito's, a rather dingy but popular café, is no longer, but a new, very clean restaurant of the same name is now attracting tourists. The menu features a host of steak and beef dishes, and the special, *filete tampiqueña*, comes with tacos, enchiladas, guacamole, and frijoles. *Costera Miguel Alemán and Anton de Alaminos, next to Banamex, tel. 74/85–37–35. No reservations. AE, MC, V. Open 9 AM–6 AM.*

**Mexican** **Casimiro's.** The specialty at this beachfront restaurant is seafood, but it is also a good source for some generic yet well-prepared Mexican dishes. *Costera Miguel Alemán, behind the Continental Plaza, tel. 74/84–30–08. No reservations. AE, MC, V.*

**El Cabrito.** This is another local favorite for true Mexican cuisine and ambience. The name of the restaurant—"the goat"—is also its specialty. In addition, you can choose among mole; forged cheese; jerky with egg, fish, and seafood; and other Mexican dishes. *Costera Miguel Alemán, between Mariscos Pipo and Ninas, tel. 74/84–77–11. No reservations. MC, V.*

★ **Mimi's Chili Saloon.** Right next door to Paradise is this two-level wooden restaurant decorated with everything from Marilyn Monroe posters to cages of tropical birds and a collection of ridiculous signs. It's frequented by those under (and frequently over) 30 who gorge on Tex-Mex, onion rings, and excellent burgers and wash them down with peach and mango daiquiris. Or the waiters will bring you anything on the menu next door at Blackbeard's. Be prepared for a wait in the evenings. *Costera Miguel Alemán, tel. 74/84–25–49, at Blackbeard's. No reservations. AE, MC, V. Closed Mon. and Labor Day (May 1).*

★ **Tlaquepaque.** As hard to find as it is to pronounce, this is one of the best restaurants in Acapulco. It's well worth the 15-minute cab ride into the northwestern residential section of Acapulco (tell your driver it is around the corner from where the Oficina de Tránsito used to be). Owner/chef José Arreola was a chef at the Pierre Marqués for 15 years and he takes his job very seriously. Don't insult him by asking if the water is purified or if the vegetables are safe. The menu is 100% Mexican, excellent and authentic. If your party numbers four or more, Señor Arreola likes nothing better than to select a family-style meal, which can include quail liver tostadas, deep-fried tortillas, and *chiles rellenos.* The alfresco dining area sits on a stone terrace bordered by pink flowering bushes and an abandoned well. The outside tables have a perfect view of the kitchen filled with locally made pots. Thursday is *pozole* day, when a thick soup of hominy and pork is served. *Calle Uno, Lote 7, Colonia Vista Alegre, tel. 74/85–70–55. Reservations advised Thurs. only (pozole day). Closed Mon. Cash only.*

**Mixed Menu** **Acapulco Fat Farm.** High-school and college students at the Acapulco Children's Home run this cozy place in the center of town. The specialties include ice cream made with all natural ingredients, U.S.-style cakes and pies, sandwiches, hamburgers, and good Mexican food as well. The background music is classical, which is unusual for Acapulco, and there's an exhibition of paintings and masks as well as a book exchange. *Juárez 10, tel. 74/83–53–39. No reservations. No credit cards.*

**Seafood** **Beto's.** By day you can eat right on the beach and enjoy live mu-
★ sic; by night this palapa-roofed restaurant is transformed into a dim and romantic dining area lighted by candles and paper lanterns. Whole red snapper, lobster, and ceviche are recommended. There is a second branch next door and a third—where the specialty is *pescado a la talla* (fish spread with chili and other spices and then grilled over hot coals)—at Barra Vieja beach. *Beto's, Costera Miguel Alemán, tel. 74/84–04–73. Beto's Safari, Costera Miguel Alemán, next to Beto's, tel. 74/84–47–62. Beto's Barra Vieja, Barra Vieja beach, no phone. Reservations unnecessary. AE, MC, V.*

# Lodging

Accommodations in Acapulco run the gamut from sprawling, big-name complexes with nonstop amenities to small, family-run inns where hot water is a luxury. Wherever you stay, however, prices will be reasonable compared with those in the United States, and service is generally good, since Acapulqueños have been catering to tourists for 40 years. Accommodations above $90 (double) are air-conditioned (but you can find air-conditioned hotels for less) and include a minibar, TV, and a view of the bay. There is usually a range of in-house restaurants and bars, as well as a pool. Exceptions exist, such as Las Brisas, which, in the name of peace and quiet, has banned TVs from all rooms. So if such extras are important to you, be sure to ask ahead. If you can't afford air-conditioning, don't panic. Even the cheapest hotels have cooling ceiling fans.

Because Acapulco is a relatively new resort, it lacks the con verted monasteries and old mansions found in Mexico City. But the Costera is chockablock with new luxury high rises and local franchises of such major U.S. hotel chains as Hyatt and Shera-ton. Since these hotels tend to be characterless, your choice will depend on location and what facilities are available. Villa Vera, Acapulco Plaza, Las Brisas, and both Hyatts have tennis courts as well as swimming pools. The Princess and Pierre Marqués share two 18-hole golf courses, and the Malibú is across from the Club de Tennis and Golf. All major hotels can make water-sports arrangements.

In Acapulco geography is price, so where you stay determines what you pay. The most exclusive area is the Acapulco Diamante, home to some of the most expensive hotels in Mexi-co. Travelers come here for a relaxing, self-contained holiday; the Acapulco Diamante hotels are so lush and well equipped that most guests don't budge from the minute they arrive. The minuses: Revolcadero Beach is too rough for swimming (though great for surfing), and the East Bay is a 15-minute (expensive) taxi ride from the heart of Acapulco. There is also very little to do in this area except dine at three of Acapulco's better restau-rants (Madeiras, Casa Nova, and Miramar) and dance at the glamorous Extravaganzza and Fantasy discos.

Highly recommended hotels are indicated by a star ★.

| Category | Cost* |
|---|---|
| Very Expensive | over $160 |
| Expensive | $90–$160 |
| Moderate | $40–$90 |
| Inexpensive | under $40 |

*All prices are for a standard double room, excluding 10% sales (called IVA) tax.*

### Acapulco Diamante

Very Expensive **Acapulco Princess.** This is the first hotel you'll see as you leave
★ the airport. Three pyramid-shaped buildings, the Princess has the largest capacity of any hotel in Acapulco. The hotel's fact sheet makes fascinating reading: 50 chocolate cakes are con-sumed daily and 2,500 staff meals are served. The Princess is one of those megahotels that is always holding at least three conventions, with an ever-present horde in the lobby checking in and greeting their fellow dentists or club members. But more rooms equals more facilities. The Princess has seven res-taurants, seven bars, a disco, tennis, golf, and great shopping in a cool arcade. The pool near the reception desk is sensation-al—fantastic tropical ponds with little waterfalls and a slatted bridge leading into a swimming/sunning area. It forms a jungle backdrop to the lobby, which is always fresh and cool from the ocean breezes. Rooms are light and airy, with cane furniture and crisp yellow-and-green rugs and curtains. Guests can also use the facilities of the hotel's smaller sibling, the Pierre Marqués; a free shuttle bus provides transport. Accommoda-

tions include breakfast and dinner (mandatory in high season). *Box 1351 Playa Revolcadero, tel. 74/69–10–00 or 800/223–1818. 1,019 balconied rooms, with bath. Facilities: two 18-hole golf courses, 11 tennis courts (2 indoor), 5 freshwater pools, 1 saltwater pool, 7 restaurants, 7 bars, disco, banquet rooms. AE, DC, MC, V.*

**Camino Real Acapulco Diamante.** Acapulco's newest hotel was not yet open at press time. It's set on a secluded beach surrounded by tropical gardens and has "modern Mexican" decor. *Playa Pichilingue, tel. 74/81–22–80 or 800/228–3000. 153 rooms with ocean view, 2 terraced pools, tennis courts, fitness center, shopping arcade, restaurants, bars. AE, DC, MC, V.*

★ **Las Brisas.** Set high on a hillside and across the bay from most of the other main hotels, Westin's Las Brisas hotel remains distinct in Acapulco for the secluded haven it provides its guests. This self-contained luxury complex covers 110 acres and has accommodations that range from one-bedroom units to deluxe private casitas, complete with private pools that are small yet swimmable. All have beautiful bay views. Most of the facilities are open only to guests, though outsiders with a reservation may dine at the El Mexicano restaurant any day except Wednesday and Saturday, and La Concha Beach Club is open to nonguests on Wednesday for shrimp and fillet night. Everything at Las Brisas is splashed with pink, from the bedspreads and staff uniforms to the stripe up the middle of the road. Attention to detail is Las Brisas's claim to fame: minibars are stocked with cigarettes, liquor, and snacks, and fresh hibiscus blossoms are set afloat in the pools each day. Hotel registration takes place in a comfortable lounge to avoid lines, and guests are served tropical mixed drinks to sip. There are almost three employees per guest during the winter season. Transportation is by white-and-pink Jeep. You can rent one for $75 a day, plus tax, gas, and insurance; or, if you don't mind a wait, the staff will do the driving. And transport is necessary—it is a good 15-minute walk to the beach restaurant, and all the facilities are far from the rooms. There is an art gallery and a few other stores. On Thursday there is a jungle picnic, and Friday night is Mexican Fiesta. Tipping is not allowed, but a service charge of $22 a day is added to the bill. The rate includes Continental breakfast. *Carretera Escénica 5255, tel. 74/84–15–80 or 800/228–3000, fax 74/84–22–69. 300 rooms with bath. Facilities: beach club, fitness machines, 2 saltwater pools, 1 freshwater pool, Jacuzzi and sauna, 5 lighted tennis courts, water sports, 4 restaurants, 2 bars, 2 conference rooms. AE, DC, MC, V.*

★ **Pierre Marqués.** This hotel is doubly blessed: It is closer to the beach than any of the other East Bay hotels, and guests have access to all the Princess's facilities without the crowds. In addition, it has three pools and five tennis courts illuminated for nighttime play. Rooms are furnished identically to those at the Princess, but duplex villas and bungalows with private patios are available. Many people stay here to relax, then hit the Princess's restaurants and discos at night—the shuttle bus runs about every 10 minutes. Accommodations include mandatory breakfast and dinner in high season. *Box 1351, Playa Revolcadero, tel. 74/84–20–00 or 800/223–1818. 344 rooms with bath. Facilities: two 18-hole golf courses, 5 lighted tennis courts, 3 pools, valet service, bar, 2 restaurants, shops. Open only during the winter season. AE, DC, MC, V.*

**Expensive** **Sheraton Acapulco.** Perfect for those who want to enjoy the sun and the sand but don't have to be in the center of everything, this Sheraton is isolated from all the hubbub of the Costera and is rather small in comparison with the chain's other properties in Mexico. The rooms and suites are distributed among 17 villas that are set on a hillside on secluded Guitarrón beach 6 miles (10 km) east of Acapulco proper. Rooms for the handicapped and nonsmokers are available, and all units have private balconies and a sweeping view of the entire bay. *Costera Guitarrón 110, tel. 74/81–22–22 or 800/325–3535. 198 rooms and 15 suites with bath. Facilities: 2 pools, 3 restaurants, 3 bars, water sports. AE, DC, MC, V.*

## The Strip

"Costera" is what locals call the Costera Miguel Alemán, the wide shoreline highway that leads from the bottom of the Scenic Highway, around the bay, then past Old Acapulco. The Paraíso Radisson Acapulco Hotel anchors the end of The Strip. This area is where you'll find discos, American-style restaurants, airline offices, and the majority of the large hotels. It is also home base for Americans—lounging on the beaches, shopping in the boutiques, and generally getting into the vacation spirit. Acapulco's best beaches are here, too. The waves are gentle and water sports are plentiful. Hotels on the Costera take full advantage of their location. All have freshwater pools and sun decks, and most have restaurants/bars overlooking the beach, if not on the sand itself. Hotels across the street are almost always cheaper than those on the beach. And because there are no private beaches in Acapulco, all you have to do to reach the water is cross the road.

**Very Expensive** **Hyatt Regency Acapulco.** Another megahotel that you never have to leave, this property is popular with business travelers and conventioneers. (Ex-President López Portillo used to stay in—what else?—the Presidential Suite.) All the rooms were recently redecorated in soft pastels. Five tennis courts, five restaurants (including a beachside seafood place and a Mexican dining room), five bars, and a lavish shopping area provide the action. The Hyatt is a little out of the way, a plus for those who seek quiet. Rooms on the west side of the hotel are preferable for those who want to avoid the noise of the maneuvers at the neighboring naval base. *Costera Miguel Alemán 1, tel. 74/84–28–88 or 800/223–1234. 690 rooms with bath. Facilities: 5 tennis courts, pool, sauna and massage, shops, 4 restaurants, 5 bars, 6 conference rooms, parking. AE, DC, MC, V.*

★ **Villa Vera.** A five-minute drive north of the Costera leads to one of Acapulco's most exclusive hotels. Guests are primarily affluent American business travelers, actors, and politicians. This luxury estate, officially the Villa Vera Hotel and Racquet Club, is unequaled in the variety of its accommodations. Some of the villas, which were once private homes, have their own pools. Casa Lisa, the swankiest, costs $1,500 a day. Standard rooms, in fashionable pastels and white, are not especially large. No matter. No one spends much time in the rooms. The main pool, with its swim-up bar, is the hotel's hub. During the day, guests lounge, lunch, snack, and swim here (a diet menu is available for calorie-conscious guests). By night they dine at the terraced restaurant, with its stunning view of the bay. There's a new exercise facility, and three championship tennis courts host the annual competition for the Miguel Alemán and Teddy Stauffer cups. For guests who don't have their own cars, transportation is provided by hotel Jeep. Book well in advance; guests have been known to make reservations for the following year as they leave. *Box 560, Lomas del Mar 35, tel. 74/84–03–33 or 800/223–6510. 80 rooms with bath. Facilities: pool with swim-up bar, 3 lighted tennis courts, sauna and massage, water sports, beauty salon, restaurant, banquet room. AE, DC, MC, V.*

**Expensive** **Acapulco Plaza.** This Holiday Inn resort is the largest and one of the newest hotels on the Costera. Like the Princess, the Plaza has more facilities than many Mexican towns: 12 bars and restaurants, four tennis courts, Jacuzzis, steam baths, and two pools. The Plaza Bahía next to the hotel is the largest shopping mall in town. The lobby bar is most extraordinary—a wooden hut, suspended by a cable from the roof, reached by a gangplank from the second floor of the lobby. About 35 people can fit inside the bar, which overlooks a garden full of flamingos and other exotic birds. Guest rooms tell the same old story: pastels and blond wood replacing passé dark greens and browns. People rave about the rooms and facilities, but we have heard several reports of inferior service and unfriendly treatment at the front desk. *Costera Miguel Alemán 123, tel. 74/85–80–50 or 800/HOLIDAY. 1,008 rooms with bath. Booked solid Dec. 20–Jan. 3. Facilities: health club, sauna, freshwater pools, 4 lighted tennis courts, water sports, 5 restaurants, 7 bars, conference rooms. AE, DC, MC, V.*

**Copacabana.** Here's a good buy if you yearn for a modern hotel in the center of things. The staff is efficient and helpful, the ambience relaxed and festive. The lobby and pool (with a swim-up bar) are always crowded with people enjoying themselves. The psychedelic pseudo-Mexican lemon-and-lime hues pervade the halls and bedrooms. *Tabichines 2, tel. 74/84–32–60 or 800/221–6509. 422 rooms, showers only. Facilities: pool, 2 restaurants, 2 bars, shops, conference rooms. AE, DC, MC, V.*

★ **Fiesta Americana Condesa Acapulco.** Right in the thick of the main shopping/restaurant district, the Condesa, as everyone calls it, is ever popular with tour operators. The rooms are furnished with wall-to-wall pastel plushness. This is the best hotel on the Costera. *Costera Miguel Alemán 1220, tel. 74/84–28–28 or 800/FIESTA–1. 500 rooms with bath. Facilities: 2 pools, water sports, 4 restaurants, bar, conference rooms. AE, DC, MC, V.*

**Royal El Cano.** One of Acapulco's traditional favorites has been completely remodeled, while still (thankfully) maintaining its '50s flavor. The interior decorators get an A+: The rooms are snappily done in white and navy blue, with white tiled floors and beautiful modern bathrooms. The only exception is the lobby, which is excruciatingly blue. There's a delightful outdoor restaurant, a more elegant indoor one, and a pool that seems to float above the bay with whirlpools built into the corners. *Costera Miguel Alemán 75, tel. 74/84–19–50. 340 rooms with bath. Facilities: 2 restaurants, bar, freshwater pool, banquet rooms. AE, DC, MC, V.*

**Moderate** **Autotel Ritz.** A good buy for its fairly central location, this hotel attracts bargain hunters and senior citizens. The uncarpeted rooms are simply decorated, but the furniture is chipped and smudged with paint. Facilities include a restaurant, a decent-size pool with a bar, and room service until 9 PM. Rooms not on the Costera are reasonably quiet. A useful note for nonguests: The long-distance surcharge is half what it is at many other hotels. *Avenue Wilfrido Massieu, Box 886, tel. 74/85–80–23 or 800/448–8355. 100 rooms with bath. Facilities: pool, restaurant, bar. AE, DC, MC, V.*

**Gran Motel Acapulco.** This is a find for its reasonable price and central location. Bare walls and floors and blond-wood furniture give the newly decorated rooms a monastic appeal. The small pool has a bar, but there is no restaurant. Ask to stay in the old section, where the rooms are larger and quieter and have a partial beach view. *Costera Miguel Alemán 127, tel. 74/85–59–92. 88 rooms with bath. Facilities: pool, 3 lighted tennis courts, bar, parking. MC, V.*

**Hotel Acapulco Tortuga.** A helpful staff and prime location make the "Turtle Hotel" an appealing choice. It is also one of the few nonbeach hotels to have a garden (handkerchief-size) a beach club (in Puerto Maqués), and a pool where most of the guests hang out. At night the activity shifts to the lobby bar, with the crowd often spilling out onto the street. The downside of this merriment is the noise factor. The best bet is a room facing west on an upper floor. All rooms have blue-green pile rugs and small tables. Breakfast is served in the lobby café; lunch and dinner can be taken in the more formal restaurant. *Costera Miguel Alemán 132, tel. 74/84–88–89 or 800/832–7491. 252 rooms with bath. Facilities: pool, swim-up bar, lobby bar, 2 restaurants, coffee shop, conference rooms. AE, DC, MC, V.*

★ **Maralisa Hotel and Beach Club.** Formerly the Villa Vera's sister hotel, this hotel, located on the beach side of the Costera, is now a part of the Howard Johnson chain. The sun deck surrounding two small pools—palm trees and ceramic tiles—is unusual and picturesque. The rooms are light, decorated in whites and pastels. This is a small, friendly place; all rooms have TVs and balconies, and the price is right. *Box 721, Calle Alemania, tel. 74/85–66–77 or 800/654–4656. 90 rooms with bath. Facilities: 2 pools, private beach club, water sports, restaurant, bar. AE, DC, MC, V.*

★ **Paraíso Radisson.** The last of the big Strip hotels is a favorite of tour groups, so the lobby is forever busy. The rooms look brighter and roomier since the management replaced the heavy Spanish-style furniture with light woods and pastels. Guests lounge by the pool or at the beachside restaurant by day. The rooftop La Fragata restaurant provides a sensational view of the bay at night. The pool area is rather small and the beach can get crowded, but the restaurants are exceptionally good and the staff couldn't be nicer. Book early—in high season the hotel is often filled with tour groups. *Costera Miguel Alemán 163, tel. 74/85–55–96 or 800/228–9822. 422 rooms with bath. Facilities: pool, sauna, 2 restaurants, coffee shop, bar, water sports, shops, 5 conference rooms. AE, DC, MC, V.*

★ **Ritz.** From its brightly painted exterior, it's clear that the Ritz is serious about vacations. The lobby is also seriously colorful. Parties are a hotel specialty; outdoor fiestas are held weekly, and Friday is Italian night in the Los Carrizos restaurant. The pink-and-rattan rooms add to the 1950s beach-party flavor. *Box 259, Costera Miguel Alemán and Magallanes, tel. 74/85–75–44 or 800/527–5919. 252 rooms with bath. Facilities: pool, wading pool, sauna, water sports, beach clubs, 3 restaurants, 3 bars (including a beach bar), conference rooms. AE, DC, MC, V.*

## Old Acapulco

Moving off The Strip and west along the Costera leads you to downtown Acapulco, where the fishing and tour boats depart and the locals go about their business. The central post office, Woolworth's, and the Mercado Municipal are here, along with countless restaurants where a complete meal can cost as little as $5. The beaches here are popular with Mexican vacationers, and the dozens of little hotels attract Canadian and European bargain hunters.

**Expensive** **Boca Chica.** This small hotel is in a secluded area on a small pen-
★ insula, and its terraced rooms overlook the bay and Roqueta Island. It's a low-key place that's a favorite of Mexico City residents in the know. There's a private beach club with a natural saltwater pool for guests and a seafood, sushi, and oyster bar. Accommodations include mandatory breakfast and dinner in high season. *Caletilla Beach, tel. 74/83–66–01 or 800/346–3942. 40 rooms. Facilities: 2 pools. AE, DC, MC, V.*

**Moderate** **Belmar.** With its white exterior and green awnings, this stately resort hotel—typical of the 1950s—looks like a ship landlocked in the middle of a huge garden. It's situated on a hill a few blocks from Caleta beach and is a favorite with budget travelers. The rooms are spacious, simple, clean, and comfortable, with large terraces. The walls are white, but almost everything else is some shade of green. This is one of the few Acapulco hotels with a rooftop restaurant; it has a great view of the bay. *Av. de los Cumbres and Gran Vía Tropical, tel. 74/82–15–26. 70 rooms with bath (50 with air-conditioning, 20 with fans). Facilities: pool, wading pool, miniature golf, restaurant, bar. AE, MC, V.*

**Plaza las Glorias El Mirador.** The old El Mirador has been taken over by the Plaza las Glorias chain, which is part of the Sidek conglomerate responsible for marina and golf developments all over Mexico. Very Mexican in style—white with red tiles—the Plaza las Glorias is set high on a hill with a spectacular view of Acapulco and of the cliff divers performing at La Quebrada. *Quebrada 74, tel. 74/83–11–55. 143 rooms with bath. Facilities: 3 pools, 2 restaurants (including La Perla restaurant/nightclub). AE, DC, MC, V.*

**Inexpensive** **Hotel Misión.** Two minutes from the zócalo, this attractive budget hotel is the only colonial hotel in Acapulco. The English-speaking family that runs the Misión lives in a traditional house built in the 19th century. A newer structure housing the guest rooms was added in the 1950s. It surrounds a greenery-rich courtyard with an outdoor dining area. The rooms are small and by no means fancy, with bare cement floors and painted brick walls. But every room has a shower, and sometimes there is even hot water. The Misión appears in several European guidebooks, so expect a Continental clientele. The best rooms are on the second and third floors; the top-floor room is large but hot in the daytime. *Calle Felipe Valle 12, tel. 74/82–36–43. 27 rooms, showers only. No credit cards.*

**Suites Alba.** Situated on a quiet hillside in "Acapulco Tradicional," the Alba is a resort-style hotel that offers bargain prices. All rooms and bungalows are air-conditioned and have a kitchenette, private bath, and terrace. There is no extra charge for up to two children under 12 sharing a room with relatives, which makes it especially popular with families. Caleta and Caletilla beaches are within walking distance, but the hotel provides free shuttle service to Caleta during the winter season. *Grand Via Tropical 35, tel. 74/83–00–73. 250 rooms, 3 pools, tennis court, beach club, 3 restaurants, bar, minisupermarket. MC, V.*

# The Arts and Nightlife

Acapulco has always been famous for its nightlife, and justifiably so. For many visitors the discos and restaurants are just as important as the sun and the sand. The minute the sun slips over the horizon, The Strip comes alive with people milling around window-shopping, deciding where to dine, and generally biding their time till the disco hour. Obviously you aren't going to find great culture here; theater efforts are few and far between and there is no classical music. But disco-hopping is high art in Acapulco. And for those who care to watch, there are live shows and folk-dance performances. The tour companies listed in the Exploring section can organize evening jaunts to most of the dance and music places listed below.

## Entertainment

The **Acapulco International Center** (also known as the convention center) has two shows nightly featuring mariachi bands, singers, and the "Flying Indians" from Papantla. The show with dinner and drinks costs about $42; entrance to the show alone is $16. Performances begin at 7:30 and 10. For $30, there's a Mexican fiesta at the **Marbella Shopping Center** on Monday, Wednesday, and Friday nights during the winter season, and on Wednesday and Friday, off-season, at 8 PM. On Friday, at El Mexicano restaurant in **Las Brisas** hotel, the fiesta starts off with a *tianguis* (marketplace) of handicrafts and ends with a spectacular display of fireworks.

The famous **cliff divers** at La Quebrada (*see* Exploring Acapulco, *above*) perform every night. **Divers de México** organizes sunset champagne cruises that provide a fantastic view of the spectacle from the water. For reservations, call 74/82–13–98, or stop by the office downtown near the *Fiesta* and *Bonanza* yachts. The *Fiesta, Bonanza* (tel. 74/83–18–03 for both), and *Aca Tiki* (tel. 74/84–61–40) all run nightly cruises of the bay that include dinner, drinks, and a show. All boats leave from downtown near the zócalo. Many hotels and shops sell tickets, as do the ticket sellers on the waterfront. At the Colonial, on the Costera, there's a professional **ski show** Tuesday through Sunday at 9 PM (tel. 74/83–91–07).

In spite of the lobbying efforts of many of Acapulco's hoteliers, the local government has not allowed casinos to open in Acapulco. Instead, there is **Aca Book,** a race and sports betting parlor. Shown live are direct transmissions of greyhound and horse races and other major international sports events, such as boxing, baseball, football, and basketball. To set the tone, there's a New York–style deli and bar. Aca Book is located at Costera Miguel Alemán 112, across from the Torres Gemelas condominiums (tel. 74/84–40–00) and is open daily from 10:30 AM to 1:30 AM.

Don't forget the nightly entertainment at most hotels. The big resorts have live music to accompany the early evening happy hour, and some feature big-name bands from the United States for less than you would pay at home. Many hotels sponsor theme parties—Italian Night, Beach Party Night, and similar festivities.

## Dance

**Nina's** is a dance hall specializing in salsa music. *On The Strip near CiCi, tel. 74/84-24-00.*

**Antillanos** has replaced the old Cats, which is, sadly, no more. Now it's all palm "trees" and lanterns, the crowd is mostly local, and the music is strictly salsa and tropical. The live groups start playing at 10:30, and at midnight there's a drag show. The $15 cover charge includes local-brand drinks. *Juan de la Cosa 32, tel. 74/82-72-35. Open Tues.-Sun.*

## Discos

The legendary Acapulco discos are open 365 days a year from about 10:30 PM until they empty out, often not until 4 or 5 AM. Reservations are advisable for a big group, and late afternoon or after 9 PM are the best times to call. New Year's Eve requires advance planning.

Except for Tiffany, Fantasy, and Extravaganzza, all the discos are on The Strip and, except for Le Dome, are in three different clusters. They are listed here roughly from east to west:

**Tiffany,** the posh disco at the Princess Hotel, is a bit more sedate than other places in town. It's great for people who enjoy conversation as well as dancing because the sound system directs the music toward the dance floor. *Princess Hotel, tel. 74/84-33-95.*

**Extravaganzza.** Acapulco's most splendiferous disco was inaugurated in late 1989. Word has it that it cost more than $3 million to build—absolutely everything was imported—and it has the ultimate in light and sound. It accommodates 700 at a central bar and in comfortable booths, and a glass wall provides an unbelievably breathtaking view of Acapulco Bay. No food is served, but Los Rancheros is just a few steps away. The music (which is for all ages) starts at 10:30. *On the Scenic Highway to Las Brisas, tel. 74/84-71-64.*

**Fantasy** is without a doubt one of the most exclusive of all the discos in Acapulco. If there are any celebrities in town, they'll be here, rubbing elbows with or bumping into local fashion designers and artists—since Fantasy is quite snug, to put it nicely. As we've said already, this is one of the only discos where people really dress up, the men in well-cut pants and shirts and the women in racy outfits and cocktail dresses. The crowd is 25–50 and mainly in couples. Singles gravitate toward the two bars in the back. A line sometimes forms, so people come here earlier than they do at other places. By midnight the dance floor is so packed that people dance on the wide windowsills that look out over the bay. At 2 AM there is a fireworks display. The capacity is 300, so although seating is cramped, all seats have a view of the floor. "Siberia" consists of an upstairs balcony. Around the floor are long plastic tubes filled with illuminated bubbles, and there is a good light show. In spite of everyone's proximity to the sound system, it is just possible to have a conversation—although not about anything complicated. A glassed-in elevator provides an interesting overview of the scene and leads upstairs to a little shop that stocks T-shirts and lingerie. *On the Scenic Highway, next to Las Brisas, tel. 74/84–67–27.*

**Magic** is all black inside and has a fabulous light show each night after midnight. This is a good-size place with tables on tiers looking down at the floor. This is one of the few discos where on weekdays you can find a fair number of Mexicans. Any day of the week, this is a good bet to catch up on the Top 10 from Mexico City, as well as the American dance hits. The atmosphere is friendly and laid-back. *Across the Costera from Baby O, tel. 74/84–88–15.*

**Baby O** and Le Dome (*see below*) are both old favorites. Even midweek, Baby O is packed. The dance floor is a New York City subway at rush hour, the bar is Grand Central Terminal. Coming here is not a comfortable experience, nor is it quiet or peaceful; it is total chaos. Baby O bucks the trend of most discos in Acapulco. Instead of the usual mirrors and glitz, Baby O resembles a cave in a tropical jungle, with simple plants and walls made of a strange, stonelike substance. The crowd is 18–30 and mostly tourists, although many Mexicans come here, too. In fact, this is one of Acapulco's legendary pickup spots, so feel free to ask someone to dance. When the pandemonium gets to you, retreat to the little hamburger restaurant. Watch your step at all times, however, to avoid falling on the tables and waiters. The architect clearly thought he was designing for acrobats. *Costera Miguel Alemán 22, tel. 74/84–74–74.*

**Hard Rock Café,** filled with rock memorabilia, is part bar, part restaurant, part dance hall, and part boutique (*see* Dining, above). *Costera Miguel Alemán 37, next to CiCi, tel. 74/84–66–80.*

**Le Dome,** an Acapulco standby, is still one of the hot spots. Even before the music starts at 11:30, there is already a small crowd at the door, and in spite of the capacity of 800, this club is always full. Le Dome doesn't look very different from other clubs on The Strip—it has the usual black wall and mirror mix, although it does have a larger video screen than most. Le Dome is the only club in Acapulco, if not in the world, where you can play basketball, yes, basketball, every Wednesday. Winners get a bottle of tequila. *Costera Miguel Alemán 402, next door to Fiorucci, tel. 74/84–11–90.*

**Discobeach** is Acapulco's only alfresco disco and its most informal one. The under-30 crowd sometimes even turns up in shorts. The waiters are young and friendly, and every night they dress to a different theme. One night they're all in togas carrying bunches of grapes, the next they're in pajamas. Other nights feature a Hawaiian luau or a mock bullfight. Every Wednesday, ladies' night, all the women receive flowers. The coco loco is the house special. *On The Strip, 1 minute east of Eve's, tel. 74/84–70–64.*

**News** is billed as a "disco and concert hall." Disco it is—and it's enormous, with seating for 1,200 people in love seats and booths, but "concert hall" is just a figure of speech. There are different theme parties and competitions nightly—bikini contests on Tuesday and Carnival Night (with lambada and limbo contests and a Brazilian-style show) on Thursday. Winners walk off with a bottle of champagne or dinner for two; occasionally the prize has been a trip to Hawaii. From 10:30 (opening time) to 11:30, the music is slow and romantic; then the disco music and the light show begin, and they go on till dawn. *Costera Miguel Alemán, across from the Hyatt Regency, tel. 74/84–59–02.*

**La Ballena Marea & Waves** is the latest disco to hit the Costera. The decor of this open-air disco is psychedelic; the atmosphere frenetic. Revelers have little sympathy for the guests whose rooms are right next door at the Continental Plaza. When the young crowd tires of dancing, they can watch videos, fill up on hot dogs, hamburgers, nachos and the like, or play a game of volleyball. On Sundays there are dance contests. *Costera Miguel Alemán, next to the Continental Plaza, tel. 74/81–03–62.*

**Planet** is very sophisticated. The seats are comfortable armchairs and sofas with a good view for people-watching. The managers wear suits, and the disco is an art gallery—the walls are covered with tasteful renditions of the beach and other typical Mexican scenes. In addition to the usual videos and disco music, there is a show every night during the winter season (Friday and Saturday night during the rest of the year), complete with mariachis. This club is less crowded than most. There is always room to dance. The crowd is mostly Mexican. *Calle Vicente Yañez Pinzón 12, just behind Delirio, tel. 74/84–82–95.*

# Excursions from Acapulco

### Taxco, the Silver City

It's a picture-postcard look—Mexico in its Sunday best: white stucco buildings nuzzling cobblestoned streets, red-tiled roofs and geranium-filled window boxes bright in the sun. Taxco (pronounced *TAHSS-co*), a colonial treasure that the Mexican government declared a national monument in 1928, tumbles onto the hills of the Sierra Madre in the state of Guerrero. Its silver mines have drawn people here for centuries. Now its charm, mild temperatures, sunshine, and flowers make Taxco a popular tourist destination.

Hernán Cortés discovered Taxco's mines in 1522. The silver rush lasted until the next century, when excitement tapered off. Then in the 1700s a Frenchman, who Mexicanized his name to José de la Borda, discovered a rich lode that revitalized the town's silver industry and made him exceedingly wealthy. After Borda, however, Taxco's importance faded, until the 1930s and the arrival of William G. Spratling, a writer/architect from New Orleans. Enchanted by Taxco and convinced of its potential as a silver center, Spratling set up an apprentice shop, where his artistic talent and his fascination with pre-Columbian design combined to produce silver jewelry and other artifacts that soon earned Taxco its worldwide reputation as the Silver City. Spratling's inspiration lives on in his students and their descendants, many of whom are the city's current silversmiths.

**Getting There** There are several ways to travel to Taxco from Acapulco, and all involve ground transport.

*By Car* It takes about 2½ hours to make the drive from Acapulco to Taxco, using the newly open toll road from Mexico City. It is also common practice to hire a chauffeured car or a taxi. Check with your hotel for references and prices.

*By Bus* First-class **Estrella de Oro** buses leave Acapulco several times a day from the Terminal Central de Autobuses de Primera Clase (Av. Cuauhtemoc 1490, tel. 74/85–87–05). The cost for the approximately four-hour ride is about $11 one-way. The Taxco terminal is at Avenida John F. Kennedy 126 (tel. 762/2–06–48). First-class **Flecha Roja** buses depart Acapulco several times a day from the Terminal de Autobuses (Ejido 47, tel. 74/83–12–51). The one-way ticket is about $10. The Taxco terminal for this line is at Avenida John F. Kennedy 104 (tel. 762/2–01–31).

**Getting Around** Unless you're used to byways, alleys, and tiny streets, maneuvering anything bigger than your two feet through Taxco will be difficult. Fortunately, almost everything of interest is within walking distance of the zócalo. Minibuses travel along preset routes and charge only a few cents, and Volkswagen bugs provide inexpensive (average $2) taxi transportation. Remember that Taxco's altitude is 5,800 feet. Wear sensible shoes for negotiating the hilly streets, and if you have come from sea level, take it easy on your first day.

**Exploring** *Numbers in the margin correspond to points of interest on the Taxco Exploring map.*

❶ Begin at the **zócalo,** properly called **Plaza Borda,** heading first into the **Church of San Sebastián and Santa Prisca,** which domi-
❷ nates the main square. Usually just called **Santa Prisca,** it was built by French silver magnate José de la Borda in thanks to the Almighty for his having literally stumbled upon a rich silver vein. The style of the church—sort of Spanish Baroque meets Rococo—is known as Churrigueresque, and its pink exterior is a stunning surprise.

Just a block from the zócalo, behind Santa Prisca, is the
❸ **Spratling Museum,** formerly the home of William G. Spratling (*see* Introduction, *above*). This wonderful little museum explains the working of colonial mines and displays Spratling's collection of pre-Columbian artifacts. *Porfirio Delgado and El Arco. Small entrance fee. Open Tues.–Sat. 10–5.*

❹ **Casa Humboldt,** a few blocks away, was named for the German adventurer Alexander von Humboldt, who stayed here in 1803. The Moorish-style 18th-century house has a finely detailed facade. It now houses a museum of colonial art. *Calle Juan Ruiz Alarcón 6. No entrance fee. Open Fri.–Sat.*

❺ Down the hill from Santa Prisca is the **Municipal Market,** which is worth a visit, especially early on Saturday or Sunday morning.

**Time Out** Around the plaza are several *neverías* where you can treat yourself to an ice cream in a delicious fruit flavor, such as coconut.

**Off the Beaten Track** About 15 minutes northeast of Taxco are the Caves of Cacahuamilpa (Grutas de Cacahuamilpa). The largest caverns in Mexico, these 15 large chambers comprise 12 kilometers (8 miles) of geological formation. Only some caves are illuminated. A guide can be hired at the entrance to the caves.

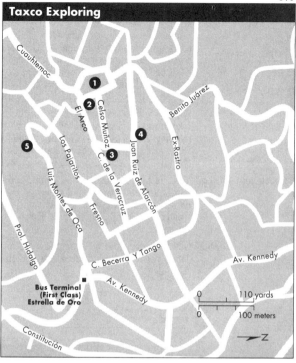

**Shopping**

*Silver* Most of the people who visit Taxco come with silver in mind. Three types are available: sterling, which is always stamped .925 (925 parts in 1,000) and is the most expensive; plated silver; and the inexpensive *alpaca*, which is also known as German silver or nickel silver. Sterling pieces are usually priced by weight according to world silver prices, and of course fine workmanship will add to the cost. Work is also done with semiprecious stones; you'll find garnets, topazes, amethysts, and opals. If you plan to buy, check prices before leaving home. When comparison shopping in the more than 200 silver shops in Taxco, you will see that many carry almost identical merchandise, although a few are noted for their creativity. Among them:

**Galería de Arte Andrés** (Av. John F. Kennedy 28) has unique designs created by the personable Andrés Mejía.
**Pineda's Taxco** (Plaza Borda) has fine designs and fine workmanship.
**Los Castillo** (Plazuela Bernal 10) is the most famous and decidedly one of the most exciting silver shops; it's known for innovative design and for combining silver with ceramics and such other metals as copper and brass. The artisans are disciples of Spratling.
**The Spratling Workshop** (south of town on Highway 95) turns out designs using the original Spratling molds.
**Joyería Elena Ballesteros** (Celso Muñoz 4) is a very elegant shop with work of outstanding design.

*Local Wares* Lacquered gourds and boxes from the town of Olinala, masks, bowls, straw baskets, bark paintings, and many other handcrafted items native to the state of Guerrero are available from strolling vendors and are displayed on the cobblestones at "sidewalk boutiques." **Arnoldo's** (Palma 1) has an interesting collection of ceremonial masks. **Gracias a Dios** (Bernal 3) has women's clothing, with brightly colored ribbons and appliqués, designed by Tachi Castillo, as well as a less original selection of crafts. **La Calleja** (Calle Arco 5, 2nd floor) has a wide and well-chosen selection of native arts and handicrafts.

Sunday is market day, which means that artisans from surrounding villages descend on the town, as do visitors from Mexico City. It can get crowded, but if you find a seat on a bench in Plaza Borda, you're set to watch the show and peruse the merchandise that will inevitably be brought to you.

**Sports and Fitness** You can play golf or tennis, swim, and ride horses at various hotels around Taxco. Call to see if the facilities are open to nonguests. Bullfights are occasionally held in the small town of Acmixtla, 6 km (3.75 mi) from Taxco. Ask at your hotel about the schedule.

**Dining** Gastronomes can find everything from tagliatelle to iguana in Taxco restaurants, and meals are much less expensive than in Acapulco.

| Category | Cost* |
|---|---|
| Very Expensive | over $20 |
| Expensive | $15–$20 |
| Moderate | $8–$15 |
| Inexpensive | under $8 |

*per person excluding drinks, service, and sales tax (10%)*

★ **La Ventana de Taxco.** Mario Cavagna traveled from Como, Italy, to Taxco with many of his favorite recipes intact. That food, coupled with Mexican specialties and a fantastic view, makes this the town's finest restaurant. *Hacienda del Solar Hotel, Hwy. 95, south of town, tel. 762/2–05–87. Reservations required on weekends. Dress: casual. MC, V. Very Expensive.*

**Pagaduría del Rey.** In the Posada Don Carlos, south of town via Avenida John F. Kennedy, this restaurant has a long-standing reputation for Continental fare served in comfortable surroundings. *Calle H. Colegio Militar 8 (Colonia Cerro de la Bermeja), tel. 762/2–34–67. Reservations not necessary. Dress: casual. Open daily breakfast–dinner. MC, V. Very Expensive.*

**Toni's.** Prime rib and lobster are the specialties. There's also a great view and a romantic setting. *Monte Taxco Hotel, tel. 762/2–13–00. Reservations required. Dress: casual. AE, DC, MC, V. Very Expensive.*

**Cielito Lindo.** This charming restaurant features a Mexican-international menu. Give the Mexican specialties a try—for example, *pollo en pipian verde,* a chicken simmered in a mild, pumpkinseed-based sauce. *Plaza Borda, tel. 762/2–06–03. Open daily, breakfast–dinner. No reservations. Dress: casual. MC, V. Expensive.*

★ **La Taberna.** This is another successful venture of the proprietors of Bora Bora, Taxco's popular pizza place. The menu is varied, with the likes of pastas, beef Stroganoff, and crepes to choose from. *Benito Juárez 8, tel. 762/2-52-26. Reservations suggested. Dress: casual. MC, V. Expensive.*

★ **Bora Bora.** Exceptionally good pizza is what's on the menu here. *Callejón de las Delicias 4, behind Paco's Bar, tel. 762/2-17-21. No reservations. Dress: casual. MC, V. Moderate.*

**Piccolo Mondo.** More casual than its neighbor, Toni's, this place serves pizza baked in a wood-burning brick oven and meats and chicken charcoal-broiled at your table. *Monte Taxco Hotel, tel. 762/2-13-00. Reservations advised. Dress: casual. AE, DC, MC, V. Closed Mon.-Thurs. Moderate.*

**Señor Costilla.** That's right. This translates as **Mr.** Ribs, and the whimsical name says it all. The Taxco outpost of the zany Anderson chain serves ribs and chops in a restaurant with great balcony seating. *Plaza Borda, tel. 762/2-32-15. Reservations advised. Dress: casual. MC, V. Moderate.*

**La Hacienda.** In the Hotel Agua Escondida, this charming restaurant serves Mexican and international specialties. The best buy: the daily prix fixe meal called a *comida corrida. Guillermo Spratling 4, tel. 762/2-06-63. Open daily, breakfast-dinner. No reservations. Dress: casual. MC, V. Inexpensive.*

**Los Arcos.** This local favorite serves international cuisine in a delightful patio setting. *At the Hotel los Arcos, tel. 762/2-18-36. Reservations advised. Dress: casual. AE, MC, V. Inexpensive.*

**Lodging** Whether your stay in Taxco is a one-night stopover or a few days' respite from the madness of Acapulco, there are several categories of hotel to choose from within Taxco's two types: the small inns nestled on the hills skirting the zócalo and the larger, more modern hotels on the outskirts of town.

| Category | Cost* |
|---|---|
| Very Expensive | over $90 |
| Expensive | $60–$90 |
| Moderate | $25–$60 |
| Inexpensive | under $25 |

**All prices are for standard double room, exluding 10% sales (called IVA) tax.*

★ **Hacienda del Solar.** This intimate and elegant small resort (off Hwy. 95 south of town) has well-appointed rooms. Its restaurant is the top-notch La Ventana de Taxco (*see above*). *Box 96, 40200, tel. 762/2-03-23. 22 rooms with bath. Facilities: 1 tennis court, pool, restaurant. MC, V. Very Expensive.*

**Monte Taxco.** A colonial style predominates at this hotel, which has a knockout view and two restaurants, a disco, and nightly entertainment. *Box 84, Lomas de Taxco, 40200, tel. 762/2-13-00. 188 rooms, suites, and villas with bath. Facilities: 3 tennis courts, 9-hole golf course, horseback riding, 3 restaurants, disco. AE, DC, MC, V. Very Expensive.*

★ **Posada de la Misión.** Laid out like a village, this hotel is close to town and has dining-room murals by the noted Mexican artist Juan O'Gorman. *Box 88, Cerro de la Misíon 84, 40230, tel. 762/2-00-63. 150 rooms with bath. Facilities: pool, tennis court. AE, DC, MC, V. Very Expensive.*

**Agua Escondida.** A favorite with some regular visitors to

Taxco, this small hotel has simple rooms decorated with Mexican-style furnishings. *Guillermo Spratling 4, 40200, tel. 762/2–07–26. 50 rooms with bath. Facilities: pool, La Hacienda restaurant. MC, V. Moderate.*

**De la Borda.** Long a Taxco favorite, but getting very run-down now, the hotel's rooms overlook town from its hillside perch. There's a restaurant with occasional entertainment, and many bus tours en route from Mexico City to Acapulco stay here overnight. *Box 6, Cerro del Pedregal 2, 40200, tel. 762/2–00–25. 95 rooms with bath. Facilities: pool, restaurant. MC, V. Moderate.*

**Loma Linda.** This is a basic motel on the highway just east of town. *Av. John F. Kennedy 52, 40200, tel. 762/2–02–06. 55 units. Facilities: pool, restaurant, bar. AE, MC, V. Moderate.*

**Posada de los Castillo.** This inn in town is straightforward, clean, and good for the price. *Juan Ruiz de Alarcón 7, 40200, tel. 762/2–13–96. 15 rooms. Facilities: restaurant, bar. DC, MC, V. Moderate.*

**Rancho Taxco-Victoria.** This in-town hotel, in two buildings connected by a bridge over the road, is under the same management as the De la Borda and suffers from the same neglect. It has its rooms done in classic Mexican decor. There's also the requisite splendid view. *Box 83, Carlos J. Nibbi 5, 40200, tel. 762/2–02–10. 64 rooms with bath. Facilities: 2 pools, restaurant, bar. AE, MC, V. Moderate.*

**Santa Prisca.** The patio with fountains is a plus at this colonial-style hotel. *Cena Obscuras 1, 40200, tel. 762/2–00–80. 40 rooms. Facilities: restaurant, bar. AE, MC, V. Moderate.*

**Los Arcos.** An in-town inn, Los Arcos has a fine restaurant (*see Dining, above*). *Calle Juan Ruiz de Alarcón, 40200, tel. 762/2–18–36. 25 rooms with bath. Facilities: heated pool, restaurant. MC, V. Inexpensive.*

**The Arts and Nightlife**

**The Arts**

Taxco has no abundance of cultural events, but it's noted for its festivals, which are an integral part of the town's character. These fiestas provide an opportunity to honor almost every saint in heaven with music, dancing, marvelous fireworks, and lots of fun. The people of Taxco demonstrate their pyrotechnical skills with set pieces—wondrous "castles" made of bamboo. (Note: Expect high occupancy at local hotels and inns during fiestas.)

**January 18,** the feast of Santa Prisca and San Sebastián, the town's patron saints, is celebrated with music and fireworks.

**Holy Week,** from Palm Sunday to Easter Sunday, brings processions and events that blend Christian and Indian traditions, the dramas involving hundreds of participants, images of Christ, and, for one particular procession, black-hooded penitents. Most events are centered on Plaza Borda and the Santa Prisca Church.

**September 29,** Saint Michael's Day (Dia de San Miguel), is celebrated with regional dances and pilgrimages to the Chapel of Saint Michael the Archangel.

In **early November,** on the Monday following the Day of the Dead celebrations on November 1 and 2, is the day the entire town takes off to a nearby hill for the Fiesta de los Jumiles. The *jumil* is a crawling insect that is said to taste strongly of iodine and is considered a great delicacy. Purists eat them alive, but others prefer them stewed, fried, or combined with chili in a hot sauce.

In **late November or early December,** the National Silver Fair (Feria Nacional de la Plata) draws hundreds of artisans from around the world for a variety of displays, concerts, exhibitions, and contests held around the city.

*Nightlife*  Travelers should satisfy their appetite for fun after dark in Acapulco. Although Taxco has one or two discos, a couple of piano bars, and some entertainment, the range is limited.

Still, you might enjoy spending an evening perched on a chair on a balcony or in one of the cafés surrounding the Plaza Borda. Two traditional favorites are the **Bar Paco** and **Bertha's,** where a tequila, lime, and club-soda concoction called a Bertha is the house specialty.

Or immerse yourself in the thick of things, especially on Sunday evening, by settling in on a wrought-iron bench on the zócalo to watch children, lovers, and fellow people-watchers.

Most of Taxco's nighttime activity is at the Monte Taxco hotel, either at the **Windows** discotheque or at **Tony Reyes's,** where the price of the show includes a performance of the Papantla fliers, dancing, drinks, and transportation. On Saturday nights there's a buffet, a terrific fireworks display (Taxco is Mexico's fireworks capital), and a show put on by the hotel's employees.

Some of the best restaurants, including La Ventana de Taxco, have music.

## Ixtapa and Zihuatanejo

In Ixtapa/Zihuatanejo, 3½ hours by car (250 kilometers/150 miles) up the coast from Acapulco, you can enjoy two distinct lifestyles for the price of one—double value for your money.

Ixtapa/Zihuatanejo is a complete change of pace from hectic Acapulco. The water is comfortably warm for swimming, and the waves are gentle. The temperature averages 78° year-round. During the mid-December–Easter high season, the weather is sunny and dry, and in the June–October rainy season the short, heavy showers usually fall at night.

Ixtapa (pronounced *eeks-TAH-pa*), where most Americans stay—probably because they can't pronounce Zihuatanejo (*see-wha-tah-NAH-ho*)—is big, modern, and scarcely 17 years old. Exclusively a vacation resort, it was invented and planned, as was Cancún, by Fonatur, Mexico's National Fund for Tourism Development. Large world-class hotels cluster in the Hotel Zone around Palmar Bay, where conditions are ideal for swimming and water sports, and just across the street are a couple of football fields' worth of shopping malls. The hotels are well spaced; there's always plenty of room on the beach, which is lighted for strolling at night; and the pace is leisurely.

Zihuatanejo, which means "land of women" in Purepecha, the language of the Tarascan Indians, lies 7 kilometers (3 miles) to the southeast. According to legend, Caltzontzin, a Tarascan king, chose this bay as his royal retreat and enclosed it with a long protective breakwater, which is known today as Las Gatas. Zihuatanejo is an old fishing village that has managed to retain its charm; but it's also the area's municipal center and its *malecón* (waterfront) and brick streets are lined with hotels, restaurants, and boutiques.

**Getting There**
*By Plane* You can fly direct to Ixtapa on **Mexicana Airlines** from San Francisco and Los Angeles via Guadalajara, and from Chicago via Mexico City. **Delta** flies to Ixtapa nonstop from Los Angeles. Both **Mexicana** and **Aeromexico** have daily nonstop service from Mexico City and most other major cities in Mexico, but there is no direct air service from Acapulco. **Taesa Airlines** offers daily nonstop service between Mexico City and Ixtapa.

*By Car* The trip from Acapulco is a 3½-hour drive over a good road that passes through small towns and coconut groves and has some quite spectacular ocean views for the last third of the way. At three inspection stops, soldiers checking for drugs and arms generally only look into the car and wave you on.

*By Bus* **Estrella de Oro** and **Flecha Roja** offer deluxe service (which means that the air-conditioning and toilets are likely to be functioning) between Acapulco and Zihuatanejo. The trip takes about five hours and costs $6. You must reserve and pick up your ticket one day in advance and get to the terminal at least a half hour before departure. Estrella de Oro buses leave from the Terminal Central de Autobuses de Primera Clase (Av. Cuauhtémoc 1490, tel. 74/85–87–05). The Flecha Roja buses leave from the Terminal de Autobuses (Ejido 47, tel. 74/83–12–51).

**Escorted Tours** Most Acapulco-based travel agencies can set up one-day tours to Ixtapa/Zihuatanejo for about $50–$150, including guide, transportation (car, minibus, or bus), and lunch. If your hotel travel desk can't make these arrangements for you, contact **Turismo Caleta** (Calle Andrea Dória 2, tel. 74/84–61–72), **Fantasy Tours** (Costera Miguel Alemán 50, tel. 74/84–25–28), or **Excursiones Acapulco** (Costera Miguel Alemán 40, Suite 204, tel. 74/84–65–54).

**Getting Around** Unless you plan to travel great distances or visit remote beaches, taxis and buses are by far the best way to get around. Rental cars cost about $100 per day; Jeeps about $75.

*By Taxi* Taxis are plentiful, and fares are reasonable. The average fare from the Ixtapa Hotel Zone to Zihuatanejo, Playa La Ropa, or Playa Quieta is about $5. There's no problem getting cabs, and there are taxi stands in front of most hotels.

*By Bus* The buses that operate between the hotels and from the Hotel Zone to downtown Zihuatanejo run approximately every 20 minutes and charge about 20¢.

*By Motor Scooter* Scooters can be rented at **Hola Renta Motos** (next door to the Mac's Prime Rib restaurant in the Los Patios shopping center; no phone) for $10–$15 an hour.

*By Pedicab* Pedicabs (*caracachas*) decorated with balloons can be rented in the shopping mall across the street from the Dorado Pacifico hotel for $10 per hour. Bikes cost $2 per hour. The rental tent is open daily 9–8.

*By Car* Rental-car offices in Zihuatanejo: **Dollar** at the Dorado Pacífico hotel (tel. 753/3–20–25) and at the Hotel Krystal (tel. 753/3–03–33, ext. 1110), and **Hertz** (Calle Nicolás Bravo 9, tel. 753/4–30–50 or 753/4–22–55). In Ixtapa: **Avis's** only office is in the airport (tel. 753/4–22–48), and the other companies have branches

there. Jeeps can be rented at the airport from **Dollar** (tel. 753/
4–23–14).

**Exploring** No matter where you go in Ixtapa/Zihuatanejo, you get the
fresh-air, great-outdoors feeling of a place in the making, with
plenty of room to spare.

Zihuatanejo is a tropical charmer. The seaside promenade
overlooks the town dock and cruise-ship pier; tiny bars and restaurants invite you to linger longer. From town the road soars
up a hill that has a handful of restaurants and hotels perched on
breezy spots overlooking the bay. Another sprinkling of hotels
surround pancake-flat **Madera Beach. La Ropa,** farther along,
is Zihuatanejo's most popular beach and the location of one of
Mexico's best small hotels, Villa del Sol. **Las Gatas** beach, beyond, lined with dive shops and tiny restaurants, is also popular
but is accessible only by water.

At the opposite end of the area, about five minutes beyond the
Ixtapa Hotel Zone, is pretty **Playa Quieta,** a small beach used
by Club Med. From here you can take a boat ride to **Isla Ixtapa,**
about $1, and spend a wonderful day in the sun far from other
people. Once the boat lands, take the path to the other side of
the island for better sunning and swimming.

For another perspective, take a 6½-hour cruise for $45 on
**Brisas del Mar's** 12-passenger trimaran *Tri-Star* (tel. 753/4–
27–48) or on the *Las Brisas,* operated by **Sailboats of the Sun**
(tel. 753/4–20–91). Both set sail from the Puerto Mío marina in
Zihuatanejo and include open bar (domestic drinks), live music,
dancing, and a fresh-fish lunch at Ixtapa Island. Both the *Tri-
Star* and *Las Brisas* have two-hour sunset cruises of
Zihuatanejo Bay. On Thursday, and Saturday nights, the *Tri-
Star* operates "The Night Flight"; $40 includes live music,
snacks, open bar, and dancing.

**Shopping** At last count there were seven shopping malls in Ixtapa. La
Puerta, the first one built, is now flanked by terra-cotta-colored Ixpamar, colonial-style Los Patios, and bright white Las
Fuentes. The ubiquitous **Aca Joe** and **Polo Ralph Lauren** are in
Las Fuentes, as is **Africán,** which carries 100%-cotton safari-
style clothing for men and women. **Scruples** is in La Puerta;
**Chiquita Banana,** a good source of decorative items for your
house, and **La Fuente,** which sells clothes with native-inspired
designs, are in Los Patios. **El Huazteco,** which sells some of the
best folk art in the state, is in Ixpamar. Don't let the modern
facades and sparkling decor fool you: Most prices are within everyone's range. There is sometimes free live entertainment on
the patio at Ixpamar.

Downtown Zihuatanejo has a municipal minimarket and a host
of tiny stores. You must go inside to discover bargains in souvenirs and decorations, T-shirts, and embroidered dresses. On
Calle Vicente Guerrero is one of the best handicrafts shops in
all of Mexico—**Coco Cabaña,** which is owned by the same people who run Coconuts restaurant. **Los Almendros,** at Calles
Guerrero and Alvarez, has an especially good selection of
handpainted ceramics from Oaxaca, and at **La Zapoteca,** on the
waterfront, you'll find hand-loomed woolen rugs, wall hangings, and hammocks. On Calle Juan N. Alvarez, Indians sell
baskets and other handmade wares that they bring from the
surrounding areas.

**Sports and Fitness** Although several hotels have tennis courts and there are two beautiful championship golf courses in Ixtapa, most of the outdoor activities in Ixtapa/Zihuatanejo center on the water. At the **water-sports center** in front of Villa del Sol on La Ropa you can arrange for waterskiing, snorkeling, diving, and windsurfing.

*Deep-sea Fishing* Boats with captain and crew can be hired at the **Cooperativa de Lanchas de Recreo and Pesca Deportiva** (Av. Ruíz Cortines 40 at the Zihuatanejo pier; tel. 753/4–20–56) or through **Turismo Caleta** (La Puerta shopping center in Ixtapa, tel. 753/3–04–44). The cost is $80 to $100 for a boat with two lines and up to $250 for a boat with four to six lines.

*Golf and Tennis* The **Ixtapa Golf Club** (tel. 753/3–11–63) is open to the public. The greens fee is $35; tennis costs $8 an hour in the daytime, $10 at night. Caddies cost $10 a round and carts go for $26. A second 18-hole golf course is located at **Marina Ixtapa.**

*Horseback Riding* You can rent horses at La Manzanilla Ranch, near Playa La Ropa, and at Playa Linda. **Turismo Caleta** (La Puerta shopping center, tel. 753/3–04–44) picks tourists up at their hotel and transports them to either of these locations.

*Parasailing* You can try this scary-looking sport on the beach in the Ixtapa Hotel Zone. A 10-minute ride will cost about $15.

*Sailing* Hobie Cats and larger sailboats are available for rent at La Ropa Beach for $20–$60 per hour.

*Scuba Diving* **Carlos** operates day and night diving excursions on Las Gatas, and **Oliverio,** who is now over 70, runs diving excursions on Ixtapa Island. Both have kiosks on the beach. A one-tank dive with either costs about $25 to $30. The **Zihuatanejo Scuba Center,** at Calle Cuauhtémoc 3 (tel. 753/4–21–47), is operated by marine biologist Juan Barnard Avila. The staff, which includes some expatriate Americans, is enthusiastic and knowledgeable. The single-tank dive costs $45 ($40 if you have your own gear); the double-tank dive costs $70 ($60 without equipment) and includes two separate dives and lunch.

*Windsurfing* This popular activity can be arranged at Las Gatas and La Ropa beaches for about $20 per hour—$30 per hour with lessons.

**Dining** Meals are generally less expensive in downtown Zihuatanejo than in Ixtapa or in the restaurants up in the hills, and even the most expensive ones will cost considerably less than you'd pay in Acapulco. The restaurants will fall at the lower end of our price categories, verging on the category below, and casual dress is acceptable everywhere. A delicious, inexpensive snack is a *licuado*, a milk shake made with fresh fruit. It's both filling and nutritious and usually costs about $1.

| Category | Cost* |
| --- | --- |
| Very Expensive | over $35 |
| Expensive | $25–$35 |
| Moderate | $15–$25 |
| Inexpensive | under $15 |

*per person excluding drinks, service, and sales tax (10%)*

*Ixtapa* **Bogart's.** This restaurant is romantic and elegant, with Moorish/Arabic decor and an international menu. The *Crepas Persas* filled with cheese are topped with sour cream and caviar. Or try *Suprema Casablanca*: chicken breasts stuffed with lobster then breaded and fried. *Hotel Krystal, Playa Palmar, tel. 753/ 3–03–33. Reservations required. No shorts or T-shirts. AE, DC, MC, V. Expensive.*

**El Faro.** El Faro sits atop a hill next to the funicular that goes up to the Club Pacifica complex. It has an extensive menu that includes *camarones en salsa de albahaca* (shrimp in a basil sauce), piano music, and a spectacular view. *Playa Vista Hermosa, tel. 753/3–10–27. Reservations advised. Dress: casual. AE, MC, V. Expensive.*

**El Sombrero.** This popular place serves Mexican food, seafood, and international dishes. The potpouri Mexicana, with chicken in mole sauce, an enchilada, and a spicy sausage, is a good introduction to real Mexican cookery. *Los Patios Shopping Center, tel. 753/3–04–39. Reservations advised. Dress: casual. MC, V. Closed Sun. Expensive.*

★ **Las Esferas.** This place in the Westin Ixtapa is a complex of two restaurants and a bar. **Portofino** specializes in Italian cuisine and is decorated with multicolored pastas and scenes of Italy. In **El Mexicano** the specialties are obviously Mexican, as is the decor—bright pink tablecloths, Puebla jugs, a huge tree of life, antique wood carvings, and blown glass. *Playa Vista Hermosa, tel. 753/3–21–21, ext. 3444. Reservations necessary at Portofino, advised at El Mexicano. No shorts or T-shirts. AE, DC, MC, V. Expensive.*

**Villa de la Selva.** Just past the Westin Ixtapa, this restaurant has tables set up on multilevel terraces under the stars. Excellent international dishes, grilled steaks, and seafood are served in a romantic setting, and special lighting after dark illuminates the sea and the rocks below. *Paseo de la Roca, tel. 753/3–03–62. Open daily 6–midnight. Reservations advised. Dress: casual. AE, MC, V. Expensive.*

**Carlos 'n Charlies.** Hidden away at the end of the beach, this outpost of the famous Anderson's chain serves pork, seafood, and chicken in a Polynesian setting almost on the sand. It has a minizoo, too. *Next to Posada Real Hotel, tel. 753/3–00–35. No reservations. Dress: casual. AE, DC, MC, V. Moderate.*

**Da Baffone.** The atmosphere is easy and informal at this well-run Italian restaurant with two dining areas; you can choose the air-conditioned dining room or the open-air porch. Try the spaghetti *siubeco*, prepared with cream, peppers, shrimp, and wine. *La Puerta Shopping Mall, tel. 753/3–11–22. Reservations advised. Dress: casual. AE, MC, V. Moderate.*

**Café Onyx.** Mexican and international dishes are served under an awning at this alfresco eatery. *Across from the Holiday Inn, in the Galerías shopping mall. No phone. No reservations. Dress: casual. MC, V. Inexpensive.*

★ **Nueva Zelanda.** This is a fast-moving cafeteria with good food that you order by numbers. Chicken enchiladas with green sauce, *sincronizadas* (flour tortillas filled with ham and cheese), and the licuados are all tasty. Families with young children gather here, and there is usually a line on weekends. Dinner for two can cost less than $8. *Behind the bandstand, no phone. No reservations. No credit cards. Inexpensive.*

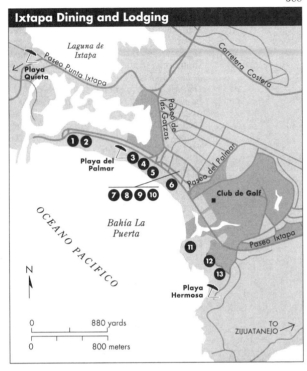

**Dining**
Bogart's, **3**
Café Onyx, **8**
Carlos 'n Charlies, **1**
Da Baffone, **7**
El Faro, **11**
El Sombrero, **9**
Las Esferas, **12**
Nueva Zelanda, **10**
Villa de la Selva, **13**

**Lodging**
Dorado Pacífico, **5**
Krystal Ixtapa, **4**
Posada Real, **2**
Stouffer Presidente, **6**
Westin Ixtapa, **12**

**Ixtapa Dining and Lodging**

Laguna de Ixtapa
Paseo Punta Ixtapa
Playa Quieta
Carretera Costera
Paseo de las Garzas
Playa del Palmar
Paseo del Palmar
Club de Golf
Bahía La Puerta
OCEANO PACIFICO
N
Paseo Ixtapa
Playa Hermosa
0      880 yards
0      800 meters
TO ZIJUATANEJO

*Zihuatanejo*   Restaurants in Zihuatanejo are usually small and friendly. Talking to people can be part of the fun. If you want to find out what the town is about, go to the bar before dinner.

**Coconuts.** Excellent seafood and salads are served in elegant surroundings. *Calle Agustín Ramírez 1, tel. 753/4-25-18. Reservations required. Dress: casual. AE, MC, V. Closed Sept.–Oct. Expensive.*

★ **Villa del Sol.** This restaurant, in the hotel that bears the same name, has earned a worldwide reputation for excellent quality and service. The international menu is prepared by Swiss, German, and Mexican chefs. *Hotel Villa del Sol, Playa La Ropa, tel. 753/4-22-39. Dinner reservations advised. Dress: casual. No credit cards. Expensive.*

**Casa Elvira.** Joaquin Vasquez, the owner, claims that this is the oldest restaurant in town—it's been around since 1956. It's quaint and clean, decorated with talavera tiles from Puebla and handicrafts from Pátzcuaro, and the prices are reasonable. There's a fairly large selection of fish and seafood, including an excellent *parrillada de mariscos* (seafood grill), as well as such traditional Mexican dishes as poblano peppers stuffed with cheese and *puntas de filete albañil* (a kind of goulash). *Paseo del Pescador 16, tel. 753/4-20-61. MC, V. Moderate.*

**Garrabos.** A delightful restaurant that specializes in seafood and Mexican cuisine. Try the seafood brochettes. *Calle Juan N. Alvarez 52, near the church and museum, tel. 753/4-29-77. Reservations advised. Dress: casual. MC, V. Moderate.*

★ **Pepper's Garden.** This Mexican restaurant has beautifully carved doors that lead onto the patio dining area and many pic-

Be sure to cut out these instructions and store in your wallet. Your hot connection to Mexico will always be at your fingertips!

# Now dial a hot number from Mexico to the U.S.

95-800-674-7000

## MCI introduces new MCI CALL USA® Service from Mexico. It's convenient, inexpensive, and you don't even have to be an MCI customer.

Now you can call the United States from all over Mexico*, conveniently and inexpensively, with the ease, value and reliability of MCI®, one of the world's largest telecommunications companies.

Just dial 95-800-674-7000 to place your call from most telephones in Mexico. Then you can have it charged to your MCI account, your local telephone card, (Pacific Bell, New York Telephone or Southwestern Bell, for example) or just call collect. It's that simple.

You'll save up to 9% over AT&T**. So remember, before you fly south of the border, be sure you have a trusted amigo: the MCI Card®.

It's the hottest thing to happen in Mexico since the chili pepper!

**To receive your own MCI Calling Card, or for more information, simply call MCI Customer Service in the U.S. at 1-800-444-3333. It's that easy!**

\* Except from public telephones that will only allow local calling.
\*\*Savings based on an 8 minute MCI CALL USA call from Tijuana versus, AT&T USADirect service rates effective 5/93.

# 95-800-674-7000

### Just dial this number to call the U.S. from Mexico. It's that simple!

See next page for other <u>HOT</u> MCI worldwide locations.

# Here are your hot numbers for the rest of the world...

| COUNTRY | MCI TOLL-FREE ACCESS/OPERATOR NUMBERS | COUNTRY | MCI TOLL-FREE ACCESS/OPERATOR NUMBERS |
|---|---|---|---|
| Argentina | 001-800-333-1111 | Hong Kong(WR) | 800-1121 |
| Australia | 0014-881-100 | Italy~ | 172-1022 |
| Austria~(WR) | 022-903-012 | Japan~ | 0039-121 (KDD)^ |
| Bahamas(WR) | 1-800-624-1000 | | 0066-55-121 (IDC)^ |
| Bolivia~ | 0-800-2222 | Mexico% | 95-800-674-7000 |
| Brazil | 000-8012 | Nicaragua(WR)< | 166 |
| Cayman Islands | 1-800-624-1000 | Panama | 108 |
| Chile(WR) | 00* - 0316 |   Military Bases: | 2810-108 |
| Colombia(WR) | 980-16-0001 | Peru## | 001-190 |
| Costa Rica~ | 162 | Puerto Rico(WR)@ | 1-800-950-1022 |
| Dominican Rep. | 1-800-751-6624 | Singapore | 8000-112-112 |
| Ecuador | 170 | Taiwan~(WR) | 0080-13-4567 |
| El Salvador~ | 195 | Trinidad & Tobago | Special Phones Only |
| France~(WR) | 19*- 00 -19 | United King.(WR) | 0800-89-0222 |
| Germany++(WR) | 0130-0012 | Uruguay | 000-412 |
| Haiti(WR) | 001-800-444-1234 | U.S. Vir. Isl. (WR) @ | 1-800-950-1022 |
| Honduras | 001-800-674-7000 | Venezuela+~ | 800-1114-0 |

A $2.00 surcharge, plus a per minute rate applies to each MCI CALL USA call.
Third party billed/collect call surcharge is $5.50.

+   Limited Availability.
++   Service available on a limited basis in eastern Germany.
\*   Wait for second dial tone.
%   Service from public telephones may be limited.
##   When dialing outside of Lima, the access number is 190.
<   When dialing outside of Managua, dial 02 first.
^   KDD & IDC are international communications carriers in Japan.
~   Public telephones may require deposit of coin or telephone card for dial tone.
@   At tone, dial 0+area code+number. At second tone, dial your 14 digit card number.
(WR) MCI WORLD REACH® country. Country-to-country calling available. May not be available
to/from all international locations. Certain restrictions apply.

## How To Use MCI CALL USA®:

1. Dial the toll-free MCI Access Number for the country you are in.
2. You will automatically be connected to an MCI Operator in the U.S., who will request the number you wish to reach and the method of payment for the call. MCI Card, U.S. local telephone card, and collect calls are accepted.
3. Your call is then completed.

Be sure to cut out these instructions and store in your wallet. Your hot connections to the world will always be at your fingertips!

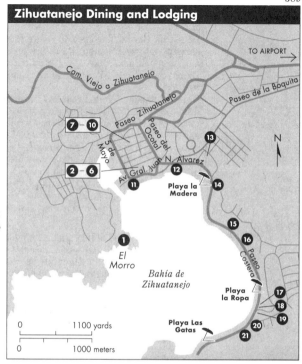

Zihuatanejo Dining and Lodging

turesque colonial touches. *Calle Ignacio Altamirano 46, tel. 753/4–37–67. Reservations suggested. Dress: casual. MC, V. Moderate.*

★ **Tabaga.** *Pescado Yugoslavia* (fillet of fish prepared with cheese, potatoes, and vegetables) is just one of the tasty seafood dishes served in this quaint, newly renovated place across from the Aeromexico office. *Calle Juan Alvarez and Cinco de Mayo, tel. 753/4–26–37. No reservations. Dress: casual. MC, V. Moderate.*

**Zi Wok.** Stir-fried seafood with a Mexican accent is served at this hilltop restaurant with a panoramic view of the bay. The specialty of the house is fresh tuna with broccoli, accented with green chilies. *Carretera Escénica a Playa la Ropa, tel. 753/4–45–10. Reservations advised. Dress: casual. Dinner only. MC, V. Moderate.*

**La Bocana.** This restaurant is a favorite with locals as well as visitors. The service is good and the seafood is a treat. You can eat three meals a day here. Musicians sometimes stroll through. *Calle Juan N. Alvarez 13, tel. 753/4–35–45. Dress: casual. MC, V. Inexpensive.*

**La Gaviota.** A mini-beach club where you can spend an afternoon swimming and sunning after having a seafood lunch. Lots of locals like this one, and the bar is pleasant. Ask the taxi driver to come back for you around 4 PM. *On Playa La Ropa, tel. 753/4–38–16. No reservations. Dress: casual. MC, V. Inexpensive.*

**La Perla.** At Doña Raquel's popular seaside restaurant and video sports bar, the hands-down favorite is *Filete La Perla*, a fish fillet baked in aluminum foil with cheese, garlic, onion, and tomato. *Playa La Ropa, tel. 753/4-27-00. Dress: casual. Open daily 9:30 AM-10 PM. MC, V. Inexpensive.*

**La Sirena Gorda.** The specialty here is seafood tacos (try the shrimp-and-bacon combo), meals are served in rustic yet pleasant surroundings. *Paseo del Pescador 20-A, tel. 753/4-26-87. Dress: casual. MC, V. Open Thurs.-Tues. 7 AM-10 PM. Inexpensive.*

★ **Nueva Zelanda.** From breakfast through dinner everybody drops in to this little coffee-shop-style eatery, which serves *tortas* (Mexican sandwiches on crusty rolls), tacos, and enchiladas. *Calle Cuauhtémoc 23, no phone. No reservations. Dress: casual. No credit cards. Inexpensive.*

**Puntarenas.** This plain place serves Mexican food and great breakfasts. It's a favorite with those in the know and there's often a line, but it's worth the wait. *Across the bridge at the end of Calle Juan N. Alvarez, no phone. No reservations. Dress: casual. No credit cards. Open only in high season. Inexpensive.*

**Lodging** Ixtapa/Zihuatanejo hotel rates vary widely, and after Easter they drop 30%-40% and sometimes more. Most of the budget accommodations are in Zihuatanejo. Rooms everywhere are clean and have private baths with showers.

| Category | Cost* |
|---|---|
| Very Expensive | over $160 |
| Expensive | $90–$160 |
| Moderate | $40–$90 |
| Inexpensive | under $40 |

*All prices are for a standard double room, excluding 10% sales (called IVA) tax.*

**Ixtapa** **Dorado Pacífico.** A high rise located on the beach in the center of Ixtapa, this hotel is noted for its spectacular atrium lobby, with fountains and panoramic elevators, and large pool. The rooms are spacious and very well kept. *Playa Palmar, 40880, tel. 753/3-2025. 305 rooms with bath. Facilities: 3 restaurants, bar, 2 lighted tennis courts, pool. AE, DC, MC, V. Expensive.*

★ **Krystal Ixtapa.** This attractive beachfront property is part of an excellent Mexican chain. Home to Christine's, Ixtapa's most popular disco, and Bogart's restaurant, the Krystal is one of the liveliest spots in town. *Playa Palmar, 40880, tel. 753/3-03-33. 260 rooms and suites with bath. Facilities: 2 restaurants, coffee shop, disco, 2 tennis courts, pool. AE, DC, MC, V. Expensive.*

**Posada Real.** Smaller and more intimate than most of the Ixtapa hotels, the colonial-style Posada Real sits on Palmar Beach, has lots of charm, and offers good value (Best Western hotel). *Playa Palmar, 40880, tel. 753/3-16-85 and 753/3-17-45. 108 rooms with bath. Facilities: 3 restaurants, 2 bars, disco, 2 pools, wading pool, tennis court. AE, DC, MC, V. Expensive.*

**Stouffer Presidente.** This is a beautifully landscaped resort that was among Ixtapa's first beachfront properties. The rooms are divided between colonial-style villas that line winding paths through the grounds and a tower with a glass elevator that provides a sensational view of Ixtapa. *Playa Palmar, 40880, tel.*

*753/3–00–18. 401 rooms with bath. Facilities: 3 restaurants, bar, 2 tennis courts, 2 pools, wading pool. AE, DC, MC, V. Expensive.*

★ **Westin Ixtapa.** Formerly known as the Camino Real, this is a pyramid-shaped hotel whose rooms (all with private balconies) seem to cascade down the hill to secluded Vista Hermosa beach. It is one of Ixtapa's largest hotels, and is noted for excellent service. *Playa Vista Hermosa, Box 91, 40880, tel. 753/3–21–21. 428 rooms with bath. Facilities: 3 restaurants, 2 bars, 4 tennis courts, 3 pools, wading pool. AE, DC, MC, V. Expensive.*

Zihuatanejo   The best hotels are on La Madera or La Ropa beaches or overlooking them; the least expensive ones are downtown.

**Puerto Mío.** This small hotel overlooking Zihuatanejo Bay is part of a marina and residential development. The suites, distributed among several Mediterranean-style villas, are tastefully furnished, and the decor makes wonderful use of the bright colors always associated with Mexico. *Playa del Almacen, Bahía de Zihuatanejo, 40880, tel. 753/4–37–45, fax 753/4–27–48. 26 suites. Facilities: pool, 2 tennis courts, restaurant, bar. AE, DC, MC, V. Very Expensive.*

★ **Villa del Sol.** A small hotel with a reputation as one of the best in Mexico, the Villa del Sol is set on the best beach in Zihuatanejo. Although the hotel has all the amenities of a large resort, guests are welcome to do nothing if they so desire. *Playa La Ropa, Box 84, 40880, tel. 753/4–22–39. 59 air-conditioned suites (1 and 2 bedrooms). Facilities: restaurant, pool, beach club, tennis court. Rate includes breakfast and dinner. Children under 14 not accepted in high season. AE, MC, V. Very Expensive.*

**Catalina-Sotovento.** Really two hotels in one, this oldie-but-goodie sits on a cliff overlooking the beach, to which you descend on stairs. The rooms are large and decorated in Mexican colonial style, with ceiling fans. *Playa La Ropa, Box 2, 40880, tel. 753/4–20–32 or 753/4–21–37. 124 rooms with bath. Facilities: 2 restaurants, 2 bars. Rate includes breakfast and lunch or dinner. AE, DC, MC, V. Expensive.*

**Avila.** Downtown and close to all the pier activity, the Avila has large clean rooms (some are air-conditioned), TVs, and ceiling fans. *Calle Juan N. Alvarez 8, 40880, tel. 753/4–20–10. 27 rooms with bath. AE, MC, V. Moderate.*

**Fiesta Mexicana.** The pretty Mediterranean-style rooms are surrounded by inviting palm-shaded gardens. Make reservations well in advance, especially for the winter season. *Playa la Ropa, Box 4, 40880, tel. 753/4–37–76. 63 rooms with bath. Facilities: restaurant, bar, pool. AE, DC, MC, V. Moderate.*

**Villas las Urracas.** Each of the units has a porch in a shaded garden, a kitchen, and a stove. Bungalows las Urracas is a great bargain—and lots of people know it, which places it in great demand. *Playa la Ropa, Box 141, 40880, tel. 753/4–20–49. 16 bungalows. No credit cards. Moderate.*

★ **Villas Miramar.** Overlooking La Madera beach, the pretty stucco rooms are nicely decorated and have tiled showers, air-conditioning, and ceiling fans. This all-suite hotel is an excellent value, but you need to book three months in advance and sometimes as much as two years ahead for Christmas and Easter. *Playa La Madera, Box 211, 40880, tel. 753/4–21–06. 18 suites. Facilities: restaurant, bar. AE, MC, V. Moderate.*

**Bungalows Pacíficos.** Each of these bungalows features two spacious, well-ventilated rooms (sleeping four between them), a kitchen, and a large terrace. *Playa la Madera, 40880, tel. 4–21–12. 6 bungalows. No credit cards. Inexpensive.*

**Irma.** Simple and clean, this hotel on a bluff overlooking Playa La Madera (and accessible by a stairway) gets lots of repeat visitors. Guests may use the beach club at the Fiesta Mexicana. *Playa la Madera, Box 4, 40880, tel. 753/4–37–76. 75 rooms with bath. Facilities: restaurant/bar, 2 pools, tennis. AE, DC, MC, V. Inexpensive.*

**The Arts and Nightlife**
A good way to spend an evening is at a happy hour in one of Ixtapa's hotels. Drinks are two for the price of one, and there is no cover charge to enjoy the live music. And don't miss the sunset. **The Bay Club,** on the road to Playa La Ropa, has a marvelous ocean view. **Mariano's** bar in Zihuatanejo is where the locals hang out. The decor is nothing special, but everyone goes, especially singles. **Benji-Pio Bar,** in the El Portal shopping center, and **Le Club,** at the Westin Ixtapa, are also popular. **Christine's** at the Krystal in Ixtapa is the town's liveliest disco. Two discos that attract a spirited young crowd are **Magic Circus** and **Visage.** Both are in the Galerías shopping mall across from the Ixtapa Palace hotel.

**Euforia** is a spectacular new disco across from the Posada Real hotel. Every night **Carlos 'n Charlies** has a dance party on a raised platform on the beach. On Friday night the **Sheraton Ixtapa** and the **Villa del Sol** hotel in Zihuatanejo stage lively Mexican Fiestas that are lots of fun.

There is a movie house with several screens, the **Multicinema Vicente Guerrero,** next to the Somex bank on Calle Vicente Guerrero. Tickets cost about $1.50. Movies in English generally have Spanish subtitles.

# 10 Oaxaca

Updated by Ron
Butler

Based in Tucson,
Arizona, freelance
writer Ron Butler
is the author of
The Best of the
Old West (Texas
Monthly Press)
and Fodor's Guide
to Santa Fe, Taos
and Albuquerque.
His work has
appeared in Travel
& Leisure, Travel
Holiday, and
Ladies Home
Journal.

The city of Oaxaca (Wah-HAH-kah), one of Mexico's colonial treasures, sits on the vast, fertile, mile-high plateau of the Oaxaca Valley, encircled by the majestic Sierra Madre del Sur mountain range. It is located in the geographic center of the state of Oaxaca, of which it is the capital.

The state, Mexico's fifth largest, is situated in the country's southernmost section, bordered by the states of Chiapas to the east, Veracruz and Puebla to the north, and Guerrero (whose touristic claims to fame are Acapulco and Ixtapa) to the west. The south of Oaxaca State spans 509 kilometers (316 miles) of lush tropical Pacific coastline with magnificent beaches. Until recently, las playas de Oaxaca (the beaches of Oaxaca) have been relatively unknown and unexploited, except for the long-established small fishing town and seaside hideaway of Puerto Escondido and the even smaller town of Puerto Angel. But now newly created Huatulco, 125 kilometers (75 miles) west of Puerto Escondido, is beginning to appear on maps and is scheduled to become a world-class resort that someday may rival Acapulco and Cancún (see The Oaxacan Coast, below).

Oaxaca is endowed with a vast geographic and ethnic diversity. Together with neighboring Chiapas, Oaxaca has the largest Indian population of any state in Mexico, which explains its richness and variety in handicraft, folklore, culture, and gastronomy. Most are descendants of the Mixtec or Zapotec Indians, whose villages dot the valleys, mountainsides, and coastal lowlands. Today two out of every three Oaxaqueños are Indians and come from one of 16 distinct groups within the Mixtecs and Zapotecs. They speak 52 dialects of eight distinct languages and for the most part can barely understand one another. If they speak Spanish, it is a second language to them.

The Zapotecs and Mixtecs flourished in the area thousands of years ago. The archaeological ruins of Monte Albán, Mitla, and Yagul are among the vivid reminders of their splendid legacies. Within a 40-kilometer (25-mile) radius of the city of Oaxaca, they all bear witness to highly religious, creative, advanced civilizations that were knowledgeable in astronomy and had a system of writing that may be the oldest in North America.

Their civilizations were conquered by the Aztecs, who in the 15th century gave Oaxaca its name: Huaxyaca. In the Náhuatl language it probably means "by the acacia grove," referring to the location of the Aztec military base. Then came the Spanish conquest in 1528. Cortés fell in love with the area and claimed much of it for himself, planning to build an estate there befitting his title, Marqués del Valle de Oaxaca. The estate was never built, although Cortés's descendants kept the property until Mexico's bloody 1910 Revolution.

Oaxaca's gift to Mexican politics was Presidents Benito Juárez and Porfirio Díaz, two of the country's most important leaders. Juárez, a Zapotec, was a sheepherder from San Pablo Gelatao, a settlement about 64 kilometers (40 miles) north of Oaxaca. As a child he spoke only his native Zapotec tongue. Often referred to as Mexico's Abraham Lincoln, Juárez was trained for the clergy but later studied law and entered politics. He was elected governor of the state (1847), chief justice of the Supreme Court of Mexico (1857), and then president (1859–1872), defeating efforts to convert the country into a monarchy under Maximilian. Porfirio Díaz, a Juárez general, seized the presi-

## Oaxaca and Huatulco

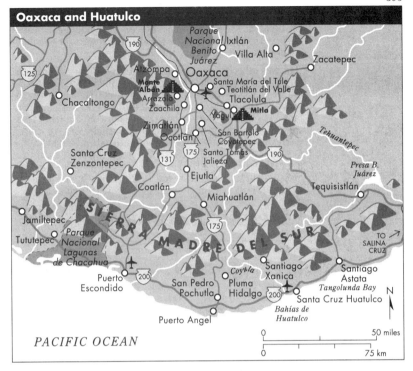

dency by coup in 1877 and held office until overthrown by the Mexican Revolution in 1911.

Today the capital is still the state's major attraction, with 2 million visitors a year. The city is traditionally Indian, but cosmopolitan touches are everywhere. Children sell woven bracelets and shoeshines around the city's many parks and squares, while painters and weavers display their wares on grassy lawns. Stark-white galleries exhibit the pottery, textiles, and fanciful wooden animals, called *animalitos*, that have drawn international attention to Oaxaca's artisans. Mariachis blare in the streets; salsa and jazz bands percolate in intimate clubs.

The large, lively, and very European-looking zócalo draws both visitors and locals to its shaded walks, commodious white park benches, and, in its center, an ornate bandstand. Closed to motor-vehicle traffic, the zócalo still bustles at all hours of the day—Indians on their way to the market early in the morning, schoolchildren hurrying to their lessons in midday, and tourists strolling to the sidewalk cafés surrounding the square for lunch or dinner.

Oaxaca celebrates Mexican holidays and its own state's fiestas with an intensity of color, tradition, and talent that attracts visitors in hordes. Hotels are usually booked solid around Christmas, but the tourist office (*see* Important Addresses and Numbers, *below*) can often help. On December 23, the *Noche de Rabanos* (Night of the Radishes), the zócalo is packed with growers and artists displaying their hybrid radishes carved and arranged in tableaux that depict everything from Nativity scenes to space travel. Prizes are awarded for the biggest and the best, and the competition is fierce. Other arrangements are made with *flores immortales* (small dried flowers) or *totomoxtl* (corn husks). Bring plenty of film.

Oaxaca's other major celebration is the *Guelaguetza* (Zapotec for offering or gift), held on the last two Mondays in July. Dancers from all the various mountain and coastal communities converge on the city bearing pineapples, baskets, weavings, and pottery. They perform elaborate dances in authentic costumes—everything from feathered headdresses to fluted white halos—from early morning until late at night at the Guelaguetza Auditorium, often shown on maps as *Lunes del Cerro* (Monday of the Hill). Contact the tourist office for information. Various hotels in town offer mini Guelaguetzas at night; the best is at the Stouffer Presidente on Fridays.

# Essential Information

## Important Addresses and Numbers

**Tourist Information** The English-speaking staff at the local tourist office can help plan your stay in the city as well as any excursions you might want to make to nearby ruins, such as Monte Albán, Mitla, and Yagul. *Cinco de Mayo 200 (corner of Morelos), tel. 951/6–48–28. Open daily 9–8.*

**U.S. Consulate** The U.S. consular representative has offices at Macedonio Alcalá 201, int. 204 (tel. 951/4–30–54). *Open weekdays 9–2.*

**Emergencies** Dial 06 locally for all emergencies, including police and hospital. The **police** direct line is 6–11–55 or 6–32–18; **hospital** (Red Cross) is 6–20–56.

## Arriving and Departing by Plane

**Airports and Airlines** There are no international flights to the city of Oaxaca, so travelers must fly into Mexico City and connect to either Aeroméxico or Mexicana, both of which fly nonstop to Oaxaca's **Zozocatlán Airport,** about 8 kilometers (5 miles) south of town. Their phone numbers in Oaxaca are: **Aeroméxico** (951/6–7101), **Mexicana** (951/6–7352). There is also service for triangle flight itineraries, including the Oaxacan coastal resorts of Huatulco or Puerto Escondido. Local domestic airlines serving Oaxaca are: **Aerocaribe** (tel. 951/6–2247) from Mérida, Cancún, and Villahermosa; **Aerovias Oaxaqueñas** (tel. 951/6–1600) from Puerto Escondido; **Aviacsa** (tel. 951/3–1809) from Tuxtla Gutiérrez, Villahermosa, and Palenque; **AeroVega** (tel. 951/6–27–77) from Puerto Escondido and Huatulco; and **Aeromorelos** (tel. 951/6–30–10) from Puerto Escondido and Huatulco. Taxis are plentiful, and microbuses are available from the airport to hotels in town.

## Arriving and Departing by Car and Bus

**By Car** From Mexico City, take Mexico 190 (Pan American Highway) south and east through Puebla and Izúcar de Matamoros to Oaxaca—a distance of 546 kilometers (338 miles).

**By Bus** There are direct bus trips from Mexico City to Oaxaca, with innumerable stops in between. The first-class bus terminal is at

Calzada Niños Héroes de Chapultepec, tel. 951/6–2270; the second-class bus station is on the Periferico at Las Casas, tel. 951/6–5776. Several bus lines serve the surrounding states and have desks at one or both terminals. Most routes are tortuous and grueling, going through narrow mountain roads.

### Guided Tours

Unless you're on a strict budget, take advantage of the many tour companies that offer guided trips to the archaeological sites, colonial churches and monasteries, the dozen or more outlying towns (some of which have weekly market days), and the folk-art centers. Several routes take in a sampling of each of the above, and each is different in character and color. The city tour runs $15 or so, and those to outlying areas cost $20 and more. There are licensed individual guides as well, available through the tourism office and the various agencies at $10–$20 per hour. **Turismo El Convento** (Calle Cinco de Mayo 300, in the main lobby of the Stouffer Presidente Hotel, tel. 951/6–0611), **Jade Tour Operators** (Porfirio Díaz 311, tel. 951/6–68–47), and **Agencia Marqués del Valle** (Portal de Clavería s/n, tel. 951/6–32–95) are among the most established agencies.

# Exploring Oaxaca City

*Numbers in the margin correspond to points of interest on the Oaxaca City map.*

The colonial heart of Oaxaca is laid out in a simple grid, with all major attractions within walking distance of one another. Most
❶ explorations of the town begin at the shady **zócalo**, the heart of the city and its pedestrian-only main square.

❷ On the zócalo's northwest corner is the **Catedral.** Begun in 1544, it was partially destroyed by earthquakes and not finished until 1733. The facade is Baroque, with a wood-cogged clock presented to the city by the king of Spain. *Av. Independencia 50, tel. 951/6–55–80. Open daily 8–8.*

Standing opposite the cathedral is the splendid 19th-century neoclassical **Palacio de Gobierno,** which serves as Oaxaca State House.

Walk north from the zócalo along the pedestrian mall, whose full name is Andador Turístico Macedonio Alcalá. Pastel, restored colonial mansions and some of Oaxaca's best galleries, shops, and restaurants line this street. It is also lively and well-lit at night, and there are frequent outdoor arts-and-crafts ex-
❸ hibits. After five short blocks you will come to the **Iglesia y Exconvento de Santo Domingo,** the church and ex-monastery of Santo Domingo. It is one of the most brilliantly decorated churches in Oaxaca, a city renowned for its many churches. The 16th-century monastery has an ornate carved facade between two high bell towers. The interior is a profusion of white and gold, typical of the energy with which Mexico seized on the Baroque style and made of it something unique. *Calle Macedonio Alcalá and Calle A. Gurrión, tel. 951/6–3720. Open Mon.–Sat. 7–1 and 4–8, Sun. 7–2.*

❹ The old convent alongside the church houses the **Museo Regional de Oaxaca,** or state museum, which is laid out in a series of galleries around the cloister. This ethnological collection

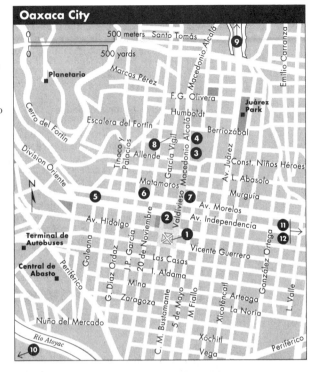

**Oaxaca City**

focuses on the various Indian groups (there were at least 52 dialects spoken in the state at last count) within Oaxaca. The centerpiece of the collection is the gold and jade treasures taken from the tombs at Monte Albán, the Mixtec and Zapotec ruin just outside Oaxaca. There is also a large collection of ceremonial masks and costumes from the different tribes of the valley; some of the Indian women who come into town for the market still wear traditional costumes, and with a bit of study here at the museum, you will be able to identify their home villages. *Tel. 951/6–2991. Small admission fee; free Sun. and national holidays. Open Tues.–Fri. 10–6, weekends 10–5.*

As you leave the church and enter the wide Santo Domingo Plaza, you are likely to be accosted by Indian boys selling rough sketches on bark (they make an easy-to-carry gift) and a variety of other crafts, or by smiling Indian girls with trays of fresh gardenias that they will want to put in your hair or pin to your clothes. From the front of the plaza, walk south, back down Macedonio Alcalá until, one block before the zócalo, you reach Avenida Independencia. Turn right and walk six blocks until you reach the Baroque **Basílica de la Soledad,** the Basilica of Our Lady of Solitude. This 1682 structure houses the statue of the Virgin, Oaxaca's patron saint. She stands in a gilded shrine and wears a magnificent robe of jewel-studded black velvet. She was found in the pack of a stray mule that had died. This event was construed by the faithful as a miracle, and the church was built to commemorate it. To the faithful the statue has supernatural healing powers and remains the object of fervent piety for the devout populace. *Av. Independencia 107 at Galeana, tel. 951/6–7566. Open daily 5:30 AM–9 PM.*

**6** Backtracking toward the zócalo, take the first street north to Morelos and head east on Morelos to the **Museo de Arte Prehispánico "Rufino Tamayo"** (Tamayo Museum of Pre-Hispanic Art). This old, carefully restored colonial mansion with interior courtyard has a small but excellent collection of pre-Hispanic pottery and sculpture. It was originally the private collection of the late painter-muralist Rufino Tamayo, who presented it to his hometown in 1979. There are exhibits from all over the country, arranged geographically and chronologically. Perhaps the most delightful item is the model of a ball court for sacred Indian games with figurines representing the participants and spectators. *Av. Morelos 25, tel. 951/6–4750. Small admission fee. Open Mon. and Wed.–Sat. 10–2 and 4–7, Sun. 10–3.*

**7** Oaxaca has almost as many small museums as it has churches. Of particular note is the **Museo de Oaxaca** (City Museum), housed in the Casa de Cortés (Cortés's House), a former colonial residence. Inside are exhibits featuring the crafts and artworks of local artists in a variety of media. *Calle Macedonio Alcalá 202–204, tel. 951/6–8499. Admission free. Open Tues.–Fri. 10–2 and 5–8, weekends 10–2.*

**8** Another colonial home is the **Museo Casa de Benito Juárez** (the Juárez House Museum). Memorabilia of the Mexican hero is displayed in this 19th-century house where he was a servant during his youth. *Calle García Vigil 609, tel. 951/6–1860. Small admission fee; free Sun. and holidays. Open Tues.–Sun. 9–7.*

**9** An impressive tribute to the natives of the region is the **Fuente de las Siete Regiónes** (the Fountain of the Seven Regions). It includes six statues of Indian women in regional garb and is topped by the figure of a male dancer from the Teotitlán del Valle wearing a plumed headdress.

**Time Out** **Choco-Chips,** at Macedonio Alcalá 200 in the middle of the pedestrian walkway, is a *fuente de sodas* (soda fountain) selling ice-cream cones, sundaes, sodas, and hot dogs and popcorn to nibble on as you stroll.

## Excursions from Oaxaca

**10** The onetime holy city of more than 40,000 Zapotecs, **Monte Albán** is among the most interesting and well-preserved archaeological ruins in the country. Monte Albán overlooks the Oaxaca Valley from a flattened mountaintop 8.8 kilometers (5.5 miles) southwest of Oaxaca. The Zapotecs leveled the area in about 600 BC. They arranged the buildings along a perfect north–south axis, with the exception of one structure thought to have been an observatory that is more closely aligned with the stars than with the earth's poles. The oldest of the four temples is the **Temple of the Dancers,** so named because of the remains of elaborately carved stone figures that once covered the building. The figures are nude and, because of their distorted positions, have since come to be thought of not as dancers but as patients in what might have been a hospital or school of medicine. Another major point of interest is the ball court,

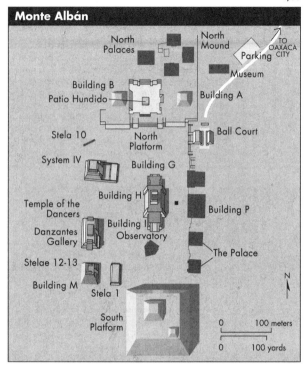

**Monte Albán**

North Palaces

North Mound

Parking

TO OAXACA CITY

Museum

Building B
Patio Hundido

Building A

Stela 10

North Platform

Ball Court

System IV

Building G

Building H

Building I

Temple of the Dancers

Danzantes Gallery

Observatory

Building P

Stelae 12–13

The Palace

Building M

Stela 1

N

South Platform

0          100 meters

0          100 yards

site of a complicated game—part basketball, part soccer. The players' objective was to navigate the ball into a lowered area in the opponents' court with only their hips and elbows. There is some speculation that the captain of the losing team was sacrificed, but this has never been confirmed. About 1,000 years ago, the Zapotecs were conquered by the Mixtecs. The Mixtecs never lived in Monte Albán but used it as a city of the dead, a massive cemetery of lavish tombs. More than 160 have been discovered, and in 1932 **Tomb 7** yielded a treasure unequaled in North America. Inside were more than 500 priceless Mixtec objects, including gold breastplates; jade, pearl, ivory, and gold jewelry; and fans, masks, and belt buckles of precious stones and metals. All are now on view at the Regional Museum of Oaxaca.

There are special tourist buses to Monte Albán from the Mesón del Ángel hotel running every hour on the half hour from 8:30 to 1:30, and one at 3:30; the last bus back is at 5:30. The fare is about $2 round-trip, or you can hire a taxi from your hotel or the zócalo. Most of the drive is straight up and tortuously slow but extremely scenic. *Follow 20 de Noviembre out of the city across the Atoyac River (Río Atoyac); at the end of the bridge, take the right fork to the site. Small admission fee; Sun. and holidays free. The ruins are open daily 8–6.*

⑪ Thirty-four kilometers (24 miles) southeast of Oaxaca is **Mitla,** another complex of ceremonial structures started by the Zapotecs but taken over and heavily influenced by the Mixtecs. The name, from the Aztec word *mictlan,* means "place of the dead." The architecture here is totally different from that of any of the other ruins in the area. The walls of stone and mud are inlaid with small stones cut into geometric patterns, forming a mosaic that is Grecian in appearance. Unlike other ancient buildings in North America, there are no human figures or mythological events represented—only abstract designs. Another unique feature of Mitla is the fact that it was still in use after the Spanish conquest of Mexico. A trip here can be nicely combined with a stop at the Tule Tree (*see* Off the Beaten Track, *below*), the colonial church of Mitla, built against the walls of other Mixtec ruins, and the large open-air crafts market by the ruins. *Small admission fee; Sun. and holidays free. Archaeological zone open daily 8:30–6.*

About 30 kilometers (19 miles) southeast of Oaxaca on the road to Mitla is **Yagul,** another group of ruins. Not as elaborate as Monte Albán, but set in a lovely spot on top of a hill, Yagul is certainly beautiful and interesting enough to make it worth the trip. This city is predominantly a fortress that is set slightly above a group of palaces and temples; it includes a ball court and more than 30 uncovered underground tombs. *Small admission fee; Sun. and holidays free. Archaeological zone open daily 8–6.*

## Off the Beaten Track

No trip to Oaxaca would be complete without visiting at least some of the dozen or more villages surrounding the city. Many are known for the skills of their artisans, who use both ancient and modern techniques to create indigenous folk-art pieces that sell for hundreds of dollars around the world. Few who purchase the treasures have the opportunity to see the tiny towns and humble homes where the artists live, often among generations of families who have their own special designs for pottery, woven rugs, and wood carvings. A trip to a few of these towns can be combined with a visit to at least one archaeological site, a colonial church or two, and a regional market.

A west-to-south counterclockwise route from the city takes in **Atzompa,** where the descendants of Teodora Blanca create fanciful *muñecas* (dolls) from clay and other potters make the region's traditional green-glazed plates, bowls, and cups, all in array on Tuesday market day. In **Arrazola,** artists carve *animalitos,* grand dragons, and snakes from copal wood, then paint them with surrealistic designs in vivid colors. On Thursdays, **Zaachila** has the most authentic livestock and food market in the area, while **Etla's** Wednesday market is famous for its cheeses, mole, and chocolate. The southern route includes **San Bartolo Coyotepec,** the center for glossy black pottery sold in people's yards and from a multistalled building on the side of the road. In **Santo Tomás Jalietza,** women work on small looms in the center of town, weaving elaborate belts and table runners from pastel cotton. Friday's market in **Ocotlan** is known for its handicrafts, especially woven baskets and cutlery.

An eastward route includes **Teotitlán del Valle,** where giant rug looms sit in front of many houses, and **Tlacolula,** where the Sunday market spreads for blocks around a Baroque 16th-century chapel. On Sundays it seems that all of Oaxaca take this route, starting at the Tule Tree (*see below*), moving to the ruins of Mitla, and then on to the crafts centers and market. The markets on other routes are held on special days throughout the week, and you can easily fill a week with tours and never see the same sight twice. If you have to budget your time, use tour guides for these trips so you don't miss out on the fascinating details.

(Prospective folk-art buyers should heed one major caveat, or risk being saddled with more than they expected. It is not too difficult to ship your purchases home from many of the city's shops and shipping services, provided you have a receipt showing that you paid the 10% sales tax on all items purchased. Since many of the artisans neither charge tax nor pay tax to the government, you may have a hard time finding someone to ship your wares for you, and when you do, it will be very expensive. Ask for receipts, and for referrals to shipping agents. Also, check out the displays at the shops in town and learn about quality and design before you start spending lots of pesos. The people of Oaxaca are deservedly proud of their arts and will help you make wise selections.)

Standing 6.5 kilometers (4 miles) east of Oaxaca in Santa María del Tule is the **Tule Tree** (located on Tehuantepec Highway en route to Mitla), a huge ahuehuete cypress that is estimated to be more than 2,000 years old. One of the biggest in the world, it is some 140 feet high with roots buried more than 60 feet in the earth; it takes 35 adults with their arms outstretched to embrace it. The tree is the traditional center of the town of Santa María and is larger than the church behind it.

# Shopping

Oaxaca City was and remains the focus of Indian life, mostly that of Zapotecs and Mixtecs who live in the valley and nearby mountains. They come to town to buy and sell, especially on Saturdays. Although the market is no longer as colorful as it was in D. H. Lawrence's day (see his *Mornings in Mexico*), it remains an authentic exotic spectacle. This is the largest Indian market in all of Mexico, and only Michoacán can rival Oaxaca in the variety and quality of crafts. Expect hectic activity and bright colors. (It might come as a surprise not to hear much Spanish spoken at the markets but rather the singsong Zapotec and Mixtec languages in which changes in the pitch of the voice change the meaning of the word.)

The Saturday market is held at the **Mercado Central de Abastos** (Central Supply Market) on the southern edge of town. Late Friday and Saturday, Indians stream to this site, spreading their wares over blocks and blocks of empty lots and through an enormous central warehouse. By noon on Saturday, the market is swarming with thousands of sellers and shoppers, and the experience can be quite overwhelming. Don't burden yourself with a lot of camera equipment or purses and bags; you'll have a hard enough time keeping track of companions in the jostling, bumping crowd. If you see something you really want, purchase it on the spot—you'll never find your way back. Check out the mounds of multicolored chilies and herbs, the piles of tropical fruit, the aisles of baskets, rugs, and jewelry. Some sections are filled with plastic household products, others with automotive and electronic gadgets. In the midst of it all are some great handicrafts: *huipiles* (embroidered blouses) that vary with the village of origin; *rebozos* (shawls) of cotton and silk; pottery shaped without a wheel; colorful woven baskets;

wooden and tin toys; machetes with leather sheaths. A long row of flower stands line the outside of the warehouse; buy some gladiolas or tuberoses for your room. Bargaining is expected in the market. Exercise sensible caution with what you eat, however; pineapple peeled and sprinkled with chile powder will quench your thirst just as well as drinks made with questionable water.

The several market areas in Oaxaca are active daily, though Saturday is the busiest day. **Mercado Juárez** (Juárez Market) and **Mercado 20 de Noviembre** are two blocks south of the zócalo between Calle las Cases and Calle Mine. This two-block area has some crafts, but most tempting are the food stalls, which serve simple meals for locals and budget travelers alike. Two blocks farther south is **Mercado de Artesanías** (Crafts Market), at the corner of Calles José P. García and Ignacio Zaragoza, which features mostly textiles. While they tend their stands, Trique Indian women and children weave wall hangings with simple backstrap looms.

Besides having a mother lode of markets, Oaxaca also has some spectacular shops and galleries, most near the zócalo. To get a good overview of the arts and crafts from throughout the region, start your serious shopping at **Aripo** (about nine blocks north of the zócalo on Av. García Vigil 809, tel. 951/6–9211), a large showcase for all the regions of Oaxaca. The **Fonart** store (García Vigil at Manuel M. Bravo 116, tel. 951/6–5764) also has a representative selection of arts and crafts. Several gallery-style shops have opened, featuring the works of the true masters of the folk arts. The prices can be astounding, but as your eye becomes adjusted to the differences in quality and technique, you can appreciate the talent involved. **Chimalli** (García Vigil 513–A, tel. 951/4–2101) has shelves and shelves of bright pink, orange, and purple carved copal cats, dogs, tigers, rabbits, and snakes with comical expressions. **La Mano Mágica** (Macedonio Alcalá 203, tel. 951/6–42–75) is an enormous gallery inside a hacienda, with rotating shows from Oaxaca's premier artists, working in pottery, textiles, wood, and paint. **Yalalag** (Macedonio Alcalá 104, tel. 951/6–2108) has delicately woven huipiles and a courtyard filled with pottery. Leading local artists exhibit and sell their paintings and sculptures at **Galería de Arte de Oaxaca** (Trujano 102, tel. 951/6–97–17).

Several shops specialize in gold and silver jewelry designed in the style of the jewels found at Monte Albán. Try **Palacio de las Gemas** (Morelos at Macedonio Alcalá, tel. 951/6–9596), **Artesanía Del Convento** (Macedonio Alcalá 503, tel. 951/6–4224), and **Oro de Monte Albán** (Adolfo C. Gurrión, tel. 951/6–4528). Most shops close from 2 to 4 in the afternoon; many are closed on Sunday.

# Dining

Though you can dine on overpriced Continental food, one of the highlights of visiting Oaxaca is the opportunity to enjoy its traditional cuisine, one of the finest and most elaborate in all Mexico. Oaxaca is known as "the land of seven moles" because of its seven distinct kinds of multispiced mole sauces. Only one of them is made with chocolate, rivaling that of Puebla (mole poblano) in thickness and flavor because of the outstanding quality of the local chocolate. Cheeses and tamales are another treat. The tamales are steamed corn dough stuffed with chicken or pork. The home- and factory-produced mezcal differs in flavor with its maker and can be as high as 80 proof, so be careful when you imbibe. One variety, slightly sweet, is flavored with oranges; others are sold in festive ceramic containers. The open-air cafés surrounding the zócalo are good for drinks, snacks, and people-watching, with the scene changing from peaceful serenity over early-morning coffee to pulsating frenzy in late evening. If you want to join the crowds at these restaurants, the *comida corrida* (set menu served at midday) makes an economical choice.

Highly recommended restaurants are indicated by a star ★.

| Category | Cost* |
|---|---|
| Expensive | $25–$35 |
| Moderate | $15–$25 |
| Inexpensive | under $15 |

*\*per person, excluding drinks and tip*

**Expensive** ★ **La Morsa.** The name means "walrus," the informal palapa setting is tastefully tropical amid gardens and fountains, and super-fresh seafood is the specialty. Try the *platón de mariscos* (shellfish platter) with oysters, shrimp, squid, and octopus; or fish fillet *a la veracruzana* (with tomato sauce), *a la mexicana* (with green chile sauce), or *amarillo* (with yellow *chile ancho* sauce). *Calzada Porfirio Díaz 240, Col. Reforma, tel. 951/5–2213. Reservations recommended. Dress: casual but neat. AE, DC, MC, V. Open weekdays 1–5. Closed Sun.*

**Il Refectorio.** The dining room at the Stouffer Presidente, a historic landmark hotel, does not disappoint. The best meal is the weekend brunch, served from 8 to noon. Fragrant strawberry soup simmers in huge green *ollas* (ceramic pots), and colonial wooden tables are laden with fresh papaya and pineapple, *pan dulce* (sweet rolls), egg dishes, and *chilaquiles* (corn tortillas simmering in chicken sauce). Choose a table overlooking the garden courtyard, and linger over breakfast in this 16th-century convent. *Stouffer Presidente, Cinco de Mayo 300, tel. 951/6–0611. AE, DC, MC, V.*

★ **El Tule.** On a hill to the west of town, the Victoria Hotel's prime location is enhanced by this veranda dining room that serves such Oaxacan specialties as tamales steamed in banana leaves and flavored with chocolate mole and *queso fundido*, a fonduelike bowl of melted Oaxaca cheese with slices of spicy Mexican sausage. The restaurant overlooks the hotel gardens and the countryside below. *Victoria Hotel, Km 545 of Rte. 190, tel. 951/5–2633. AE, DC, MC, V. Closed Sun.*

**Moderate** **El Asador Vasco.** Basque (*vasco*) cuisine is featured here along with an outstanding Oaxacan version of mole sauce—steamy, black, and marvelous on chicken and *cazuelas* (small casseroles of baked cheese, mushrooms, and garlic). The tables overlooking the zócalo are in great demand; dine before 8 and you'll have a chance at one if the dour waitresses approve of you. There's live music every night at 9 PM. Live serenading by the *tuna* student minstrels comes medieval Spanish style. *On the west side of the zócalo, upstairs, Portal de Flores 11, tel. 951/6–9719. AE, DC, MC, V.*

★ **Los Guajiros.** The inner courtyard of an old hacienda has been transformed into a tasteful restaurant/club where live salsa bands draw crowds after 10 PM. The waiters are pleasantly attentive, and the decor fascinating, with its pottery fountain, eclectic display of art and artifacts, and posters of jazz greats. *Macedonio Alcalá 303, tel. 951/6–5038. AE, MC, V. Open 6 PM–1 AM. Closed Sun.*

**Mi Casita.** Many in the know consider this the best place to enjoy the cuisine of Oaxaca. The actual dishes are displayed in the case by the door, so you can see what your food will look like before you order. This eatery is especially famous for *chapulines* (grasshoppers), but there are also more conventional dishes, such as enchiladas with chicken and spicy mole sauce. Try to get a table by the window (it's on the second floor), so you can watch the activity in the zócalo while you dine. *South side of the zócalo at Av. Hidalgo 616 altos, tel. 951/6–9256. AE, MC, V. Lunch only. Closed Thurs.*

★ **Ñuu-Luu.** The name in Mixtec, "picturesque place," couldn't be more appropriate. Located in a quaint colonial suburb in the northern part of town (just 8 minutes from the zócalo), this delightful veranda restaurant overlooks a large country garden lush with exotic fruit trees. Renowned chef-owner Guadalupe Salinas prepares gourmet Oaxacan specialties, including all seven kinds of mole, as well as pre-Hispanic delicacies. Also enticing is her fillet of grouper in green sauce wrapped in banana leaves. Delicate desserts follow. *Iturbide 100, San Felipe del Agua, tel. 951/5–3187. Reservations recommended, especially on weekends. (Private transportation is provided from and to your hotel.) Dress: casual. AE, MC, V. Open daily; breakfast from 8 AM, lunch until 6 PM.*

**Inexpensive** **Catedral.** This local favorite is nicknamed the House of Fillets. It offers no fewer than 11 tenderloin cuts, as well as regional dishes, hamburgers, sandwiches, and a variety of soups. Paintings by Guadalajara artist Miguel Angel Expanas fill the two pleasant dining rooms. *1 block from the zócalo, at the corner of Calle García Vigil and Av. Morelos, tel. 951/6–3285. MC, V.*

**El Mesón.** The spanking-clean dining room and open-air kitchen in this restaurant right off the zócalo make it a favorite for locals and visitors, who stop by for a snack or full meal from the long paper menu, where you check off your items of choice. Try the *cebollitas* (grilled whole green onions) as a side dish with your *enchiladas cecina* (grilled strips of pork covered with chile powder) and fresh corn tortillas made at the torilleria at the entrance. For an intense sugar fix, have a cup of rich Oaxacan chocolate and a slice of nut pie. *Av. Hidalgo 805, at Cinco de Mayo, tel. 951/6–2729. MC, V.*

# Lodging

Oaxaca has no high-rise hotels or luxury resorts, but it does have some magnificently restored properties and dozens of smaller, moderately priced accommodations, most in downtown locations.

Highly recommended lodgings are indicated by a star ★.

| Category | Cost* |
|----------|-------|
| Expensive | $90–$160 |
| Moderate | $40–$90 |
| Inexpensive | under $40 |

*All prices are for a standard double room, excluding 10% tax.*

**Expensive**
★ **Stouffer Presidente.** A monastic air lingers in the breezy patios and small enclosed gardens of this beautifully restored former convent (1576). One of the hotel's three courtyards, the one with the large stone basin in the center, is still called *La Lavenderia* (the laundry); it is where the nuns of the convent used to wash their clothes. Stouffer's rooms, of course, are far from austere; all have deluxe conveniences. Stop in for a drink and look around even if you don't stay here. On Friday nights, the restaurant offers a variety of traditional Oaxacan dishes, and there is an excellent performance of regional dances. *Cinco de Mayo 300, tel. 951/6–0611 or 800/468–3571, fax 951/6–0732. 91 rooms. Facilities: restaurant, bar, pool. AE, DC, MC, V.*

★ **Victoria.** Surrounded by terraced grounds and well-kept gardens, this sprawling salmon-colored complex is perched on a hill overlooking the city. Draw back your curtains at dawn and catch your breath at the view: Oaxaca awakening under the Sierra Madre. The two-story hotel has a very good restaurant, tennis courts, heated pool, and disco, and the property is strewn with picture-perfect bougainvillea vines. Rooms, bungalows, and suites are available; be sure to request one with a view. *Km 545 of Mexico 190, tel. 951/5–2633, fax 951/5–2411. 177 rooms, suites, and bungalows. Facilities: restaurant, disco, heated pool, tennis courts. AE, DC, MC, V.*

**Moderate**
**Fortin Plaza.** This modern six-story hotel, with beautifully landscaped gardens overlooking town and the surrounding mountains, is just downhill from the Victoria. Its rather modest exterior is offset by an exquisitely designed interior that makes lavish use of marble, wood, glass, and stone. Ancient Indian motifs show up in all of the rooms' marble and tiled decorations. Front balconied rooms offer the best views, but if you're looking for a good night's sleep, choose the quieter rear rooms (the hotel's nightclub is popular with local lovebirds). The hotel has a pool, but it's small and is sandwiched between the highway and the building. *Av. Venus 118, tel. 951/5–777, fax 951/5–1328. Facilities: restaurant, bar, pool. AE, DC, MC, V.*

**Misión de los Angeles.** Though this resort-style hotel is 10 blocks from the zócalo (a long, dark walk at night), its peaceful gardens, relaxed ambience, and colonial-style rooms make it a good choice. The hotel is near Plaza Juárez, a central park and plaza frequented more by locals than by tourists, and the commodious dining room is popular with tour groups. *Calzada Porfirio Díaz 102; tel. 951/5–1500, fax 951/5–1680. 155 rooms. Facilities: bar, disco, game room, heated pool, gardens, tennis court, and jogging path. AE, DC, MC, V.*

**Inexpensive**
**Marqués del Valle.** Right on the plaza and in the middle of things, the property's restaurant serves a good breakfast, from bananas and cream to hotcakes. The cavernous marble hallways act like echo chambers for the cathedral bells from next door, which ring with appalling frequency. *Portal de Clavería 1, tel. 951/6–3295, fax 951/6–9961. 95 rooms. Facilities: TV, restaurant. AE, DC, MC, V.*

**Mesón de Angel.** This huge, plain hotel near the markets is a favorite with Mexican families and traveling salesmen. There is a big pool with a playground nearby, but few decorative touches. Still, the rooms are clean, the mattresses firm, the water hot, and the rates low. Tourist buses to Monte Albán and Puerto Escondido leave from here, and the travel agency is one of the best in town. *Francisco J. Mina 518, tel. 951/6–6666. 50 rooms. Facilities: restaurant, pool, private parking. MC, V.*

**Principal.** This popular budget hotel fills up quickly, but the owners can refer you to other hotels in the area as well as provide insider touring tips. Rooms in this colonial hacienda face a central courtyard abloom with red geraniums. Each room has small folk-art touches, and the whole place has a friendly, homey feeling. *Cinco de Mayo 208, tel. 951/6–2535. 23 rooms. Facilities: small courtyard restaurant. No credit cards.*

**Señorial.** Beside El Jardín café on the zócalo, the Señorial caters quite comfortably to those who like being in the center of the action. Choose a room overlooking the zócalo if you like watching people rushing to work down freshly hosed-down streets, and enjoy the nightly reverie of mariachis and mingling. The rooms are large and casually comfortable, with little in the way of distinguishable touches. *Portal de Flores 6, off the zócalo, tel. 951/6–3933. 91 rooms. Facilities: bar, roof garden, pool. No credit cards.*

# The Oaxacan Coast

### Introduction

Oaxaca's 520-kilometer (322-mile) coastline is mainland Mexico's last Pacific frontier. Huatulco, 291 kilometers (180 miles) from the capital, is the newest project of Fonatur, the Mexican government's tourism developers. Already the tiny settlement has the state's only international airport, composed of a cluster of humble buildings with palm-frond roofs. So far, fewer than a dozen hotels are in operation. The Bahías de Huatulco, as the area is being called, covers 51,900 acres of mountain lowlands and coastal stretches, the vast majority of which have never been developed.

Today Huatulco's beauty can best be seen from a boat (*see* Guided Tours, in Essential Information, *below*), since most of the bays are inaccessible by road. Tangolunda Bay is the site of the first three major hotels, and more hotels, condos, and timeshare projects are under way. The towns of Santa Cruz de Huatulco and La Crucecita are being developed as well. Santa Cruz has the waterfront pier and sightseeing boats, a sprawling artisans' market, and the major banks; Crucecita has a lavishly landscaped town square and the best restaurants outside the hotels. The town of Santa María Huatulco, for which the tourism destination is named, is 18 kilometers (11 miles) from the bays and is largely ignored by developers.

Puerto Escondido, 111 kilometers (69 miles) northwest of Huatulco, has long been prime territory for international surfers seeking the thrills of the Mexican Pipeline. For much of the year the waves here are rated right up there with the surf in Hawaii and Australia by those who can handle the murderous undertow. International surfing champions congregate here for tournaments in August and November. And when the crowds of surfers are gone in June and July, the town turns into a peaceful village where those seeking solitude stay at shaded, bougainvillea-covered haciendas and cabanas and alternate between their hammocks and crystalline blue pools. Puerto Escondido has the coast's first airport (not international) and is in many ways better developed for travelers than Huatulco. Puerto Angel, midway between the two airports, is the budget traveler's destination, with a ragtag selection of hotels and bungalows spread into the hills overlooking the bay with, incongruously, a military installation smack in its center.

## Essential Information

**Arriving and Departing by Plane**
**Puerto Escondido** has a national airport with daily service from Oaxaca on **Aerovias Oaxaqueñas** (Av. Gasga, tel. 958/2–0132) and on tiny Cessnas run by **AeroVega** (tel. 958/2–0151). **Mexicana** (at the airport, tel. 958/2–0300) flies to Puerto Escondido daily from Mexico City and U.S. gateway cities.

**Aeropuerto Bahías de Huatulco,** the state's only international airport, is about 68 kilometers (42 miles) north of the Bahías de Huatulco. **Mexicana** (at the airport, tel. 958/4–0077) flies to Huatulco from Mexico City, Guadalajara, and several U.S. gateways. Regional carriers and private charters connect Huatulco with Oaxaca City, Mérida, and Cancún. Make reservations at the airport or through travel agencies, and be sure to confirm them 24 hours before your flight.

**Arriving and Departing by Bus and Car**
Don't attempt to take the bus from Oaxaca to Puerto Escondido or Huatulco unless you have an iron-clad stomach and lots of time. The twisting, jarring ride through the mountains takes about 10 hours. The 370-kilometer (230-mile) trip from Acapulco is less strenuous, and buses run hourly. The bus station in Puerto Escondido is on the main highway and Avenida Oaxaca (tel. 958/2–0427). Huatulco's bus station is in La Crucecita, on Avenue Gardenias (no phone; *see* Getting Around By Bus, *below*).

The drive from Oaxaca to the coast on Highways 175 and 190 is rough, and although the scenery through the mountains is superb, all your attention will be focused on the twisting, roughly paved road. Do not attempt this drive at night. Plan on taking 10 hours or so, and leave early enough to be at your destination before dark. *Note:* We received one report of a violent abduction of two tourists on Highway 200 between Salina Cruz and Puerto Angel at noon, so be careful even in daylight.

**Getting Around By Bus**
As yet there are no direct buses stringing together Puerto Escondido, Puerto Angel, and Huatulco. Instead you must change buses at Pochutla, just off the highway near Puerto Angel, where buses converge in a large dirt lot. Drivers yell out their destinations and refuse to leave unless the bus has a sufficient number of passengers. If you are going to Huatulco do not take the bus marked Huatulco, since it will leave you in the town of Santa María Huatulco, some 18 kilometers (11 miles) from the bays. Instead take a bus marked Santa Cruz or Salina Cruz, both of which stop in La Crucecita.

**By Car**
The drive on Highway 200 from Puerto Escondido to Huatulco should be relatively hassle-free (*see* Note, *above*), and having a car allows you to turn off the main road onto unmarked dirt roads leading to secluded beaches. But rental cars are extreme-

ly expensive (about $100 per day, including insurance and un-limited mileage), and there is an additional drop-off fee if you don't return the car where you picked it up. **Budget** has franchises in Huatulco (tel. 958/4–0078) and Puerto Escondido (tel. 958/2–0312), and **Hertz** is present in Puerto Escondido (tel. 958/2–0035); nonaffiliated local firms often quote lower rates, but their vehicles may be in questionable condition.

**Tourist Information** Information is scanty at best in this area. The **Puerto Escondido tourism office** (tel. 958/2–0358) is in the old part of town by the market, at the corner of Av. Hidalgo and Av. Oaxaca, on top of the Super Estrella grocery store. The office is open Monday–Friday 9–2 and 5–8, and Saturday 10–1. In Huatulco the **Fonatur** office (tel. 958/1–0094) is across from the Sheraton Hotel in Tangolunda Bay. Hours are erratic, information scarce, and there is no state tourism office yet. You're better off using the travel agents in the hotels.

**Guided Tours** In **Puerto Escondido** the most exciting tours are run by ornithologist Michael Malone, who offers dawn and sunset tours into the Manialtepec Lagoon, a prime bird-watching area. Tours are $30 per person and can be arranged through your hotel, through **Turismo Rodimar** (Av. Gasga, tel. 958/2–0734), or through the **Agencía García Rendon** (Av. Gasga, tel. 958/2–0114). This last agency is the most comprehensive in town for all sorts of information and is open daily 7 AM–9 PM.

The safest swimming and snorkeling beaches in Puerto Escondido are **Puerto Angelito** and **Carrizalillo,** a 10-minute boat ride from the town beach. Transportation is available from the Agencía García Rendon (*see above*) or from the many fishermen who park their *pangas* (small boats) on the sand near town. The ride should cost $5–$10.

In **Huatulco** you can't possibly grasp the beauty of the bays without touring them by boat. The venture takes four to six hours, with stops at Bahía San Augustín or El Maguey (where fishermen grill their catch over open fires) and at one of several secluded beaches for swimming and snorkeling. Bay cruises cost about $35 per person and are available at the boat dock in Santa Cruz.

**Turismo Tangolunda,** with offices in the Royal Maeva hotel (tel. 958/1–0000) and in Santa Cruz (Av. Oaxaca and Calle Zoquiapan, tel. 958/1–0024; in the U.S., 800/468–5639) is the most comprehensive travel agency in Huatulco and has bay and bus tours to Puerto Angel and Puerto Escondido (about $60 per person) and plane tours to Oaxaca ($220 per person). The **Sheraton** (Blvd. Benito Juárez, tel. 958/1–0055) and **Club Med** (Tangolunda Bay, tel. 958/1–0161) also have travel agencies.

## Exploring the Oaxacan Coast

**Puerto Escondido** is the first coastal town in Oaxaca south of Acapulco on Highway 200. The airport is on the northern edge of town, as are the hotels favored by charter groups. **Playa Bacocho,** just south of the airport, is being developed as a new housing-and-hotel development, and some inviting bars and restaurants have opened in this area. Be sure to catch the sunset at least once from the gardens of the **Posada Real hotel,** and walk down the cliff to Coco's Beach Club, a lavish restaurant (with erratic quality and service) and a pool right on the beach.

The main intersection in Puerto Escondido is at Highway 200 and Avenida Alfonso Perez Gasga, which travels south into the tourist zone. On the north side of the highway this street is called Avenida Oaxaca, which leads to the dirt streets and markets of the town. The bus station is on this corner. Traveling down a steep hill, Avenue Gasga passes many of the tourist hotels; at the bottom, traffic is prohibited and the street becomes a four-block-long pedestrian mall lined with shops, restaurants, and lodgings that spread to the sands of the main beach. The panga fleet is at the north end of this beach, where the water is calm albeit polluted. **Laguna Agua Dulce** is at the south end of the tourist strip, followed by **Marinero Beach,** then a sharp outcropping of rocks, and, finally, the most famous beach of all, **Zicatela.**

One of the top 10 surfing beaches in the world, Zicatela is a long stretch of cream-color sand battered by the **Mexican Pipeline,** as this stretch of mighty surf is called. In August and November international surfing championships are held here, and the town fills with sun-bleached blonds of both sexes intent on serious surfing and hard partying. Do not swim in these waters unless you can withstand deadly undertows and rip currents. Instead watch the surfers at sunset from the palapa restaurant at the **Hotel Santa Fe,** surely the prettiest hotel in town.

**Puerto Angel,** about 81 kilometers (50 miles) south of Puerto Escondido, is a small village on a beautiful bay that, sadly, shows signs of pollution these days. The central town beach has been taken over by the navy, and the most popular swimming-and-sunning territory is at **Playa Panteón,** just past the ocean-front cemetery. The biggest attraction in Puerto Angel is **Playa Zipolite,** a bay 6 kilometers (3.7 miles) west of town. Known for its nude sunbathing, Zipolite is a favorite with surfers and travelers who are content with a hammock on the beach and little else in the way of creature comforts. The undertow is dangerous here, and the local officials occasionally ban nudity.

**Bahías de Huatulco,** the Fonatur development, is suffering growing pangs, with some bizarre results. Modern streets and lightposts are in place, but telephones are scarce except in the first-class hotels. There are branches of Mexico's main banks, but pesos are sometimes hard to come by. Although rental cars are available, maps are nonexistent, and the vast majority of Huatulco's tourists rarely leave their hotels. The Huatulco of the future is most evident at **Tangolunda Bay,** where three major hotels are in full swing, and parasailers glide over fleets of sightseeing boats. A small shopping/restaurant center is located by the entrance to the Sheraton, but most of the shopping and dining take place in the towns of Santa Cruz and La Crucecita, each about 10 minutes from the hotels by taxi. **Santa Cruz** is located on the bay of the same name, where glass-bottom boats and sightseeing tours are available. The waterfront is lined with bright-blue, pink, and orange shacks offering a disappointing selection of crafts and souvenirs for sale. A central zócalo with a wrought-iron gazebo has been built nearby, and tourists and locals alike mingle in the grassy plaza.

**La Crucecita,** just off Highway 200, is more developed, with a few condominium complexes and a central park. Modern buildings with arches and balconies are going up along the streets by the park, and this is becoming the place for hanging out at sidewalk cafés and shopping in trendy boutiques. The bus station and long-distance telephone office are here, along with a smattering of budget rooms.

## Dining

Seafood is the coast's best dining bet; everything else is mediocre. Unfortunately, Oaxacan cuisine—the cheeses, mole sauces, and meats that make dining in the capital memorable—is in short supply here. The best choices for restaurants continue to be in the hotels or on the beach. Puerto Escondido now has three vegetarian restaurants; Puerto Angel has meager offerings; and Huatulco's restaurants are gradually struggling to their feet. Dress is casual at all restaurants except where noted, and reservations are not necessary.

Highly recommended restaurants are indicated with a ★.

| Category | Cost* |
|---|---|
| Very Expensive | over $35 |
| Expensive | $25–$35 |
| Moderate | $15–$25 |
| Inexpensive | under $15 |

*per person, excluding drinks and tip*

**Huatulco** **Cardinale.** Your only choice for glamorous dining thus far is in the Sheraton Hotel. The menu emphasizes northern Italian dishes—any of the pastas are a good choice—and the ambience is decidedly upscale, with heavy polished tables and chairs, stained-glass doors, and elaborate floral arrangements. Try the hotel's Mexican restaurant as well. *Sheraton Hotel, Blvd. Benito Juárez, Tangolunda Bay, tel. 958/1–0055. AE, MC, V. Closed lunch. Expensive.*

**1/2 Carlos 'n Charlie's.** The odd name refers to the size of this closetlike addition to the Carlos 'n Charlie's chain, with all the trappings of the famous franchise packed in meager space. 1/2 has dependable food—barbecued ribs, tortilla soup, burgers, fries, and platters of fresh oysters—and fun for those who like downing shots of tequila and beer. *Ave. Flamboyan, Crucecita, tel. 958/7–0005. Closed lunch. MC, V. Expensive.*

**Restaurante María Sabina.** This is a great place for sitting at a sidewalk table and watching the locals and tourists mingle in Crucecita's pretty plaza. No mystery exists here about how your food is prepared, since the grill is on the sidewalk, and the cook will chat with you as he chars your steak or fish. *West side of plaza, Crucecita, no phone. No credit cards. Moderate.*

**Puerto Angel** **El Capi.** There's nothing to distinguish this small hotel and restaurant from all the rest, except the gargantuan portions of fresh fish and Mexican dishes served by the friendly, talkative owners. In fact, this is one of the best spots in town to get the lowdown on what's happening. *Blvd. Virgilio Uribe, near cemetery, no phone. No credit cards. Moderate.*

**Posada Cañon Devata.** The communal health-food dinner at this small hotel is a local institution, and most travelers stop by at least once to compare notes with others. The menu changes daily, so you're never sure what the meal will be, but it's always healthy, filling, and unusual. *Posada Cañon Devata Hotel, past*

and Mexican families as well as lone travelers. The emphasis is on fun, fun, fun, and if you're not a fan of loud music, stay in a room that's away from the pool area. The ever-present, ever-upbeat recreation leaders here are fanatically in love with Huatulco and will do all they can to make sure you feel the same. The beach is colorfully littered with sunbathers sipping piña coladas while watching the tow boats depart for the more secluded bays; and the rooms are spacious, colorful, and adorned with heavy blue-and-peach fabric and light-wood furniture. The meals, included in your tab, are uninspired but generous; breakfast is by far the best. There are plenty of activities, from talent shows to sports demonstrations. *Tangolunda Bay, Blvd. Benito Juárez 227, Bahías de Huatulco, tel. 958/1–0000, fax 958/1–0220. Reservations in U.S., tel. 800/431–2822. 300 rooms. Facilities: 3 restaurants, 3 bars, pool, beach, tennis, water sports, fitness center. AE, MC, V. Very Expensive.*

**Sheraton.** The only hotel on Tangolunda Bay that's not all-inclusive, the Sheraton is also the most user-friendly, with boutiques, a travel agency, a selection of restaurants, and a triangular pool. The rooms are done in soft peaches and pinks, with blessedly powerful air-conditioning, heavy drapes to block the sun, and bathtubs—a real luxury in these parts. *Tangolunda Bay, Blvd. Benito Juárez, tel. 958/1–0055, fax 958/1–0113. Reservations in U.S., tel. 800/325–3535. 346 rooms. Facilities: 4 restaurants, 3 bars, pool, tennis courts, beach, fitness center, water sports. AE, MC, V. Very Expensive.*

**Hotel Castillo Huatulco.** The closest accommodations to the plaza and Santa Cruz Bay are the brand-new rooms at the Castillo, which overlooks the Santa Cruz Marina. This hotel resembles a motel from the front but looks like a quasi-resort inside. New in 1991, the Castillo is a good choice if you want to be near rental boats, close to the luxury hotels, and away from the business bustle of Crucecita. *Blvd. Bahía Santa Cruz, tel. 958/ 7–0051, fax 958/7–0131. 110 rooms. Facilities: restaurant, bar, pool, tennis court. MC, V. Moderate.*

**Posada Binniguenda.** The first hotel in Santa Cruz, the Binniguenda is not on the beach but stands close to the marina. As development continues the hotel will be in the center of the town's hotel/restaurant/shopping scene. The dusty-pink adobe, red-tile-roof building forms a "U" around the courtyard and pool. The rooms have heavy colonial furnishings, commodious showers, and wood-and-glass French doors leading to small wrought-iron balconies. The pool bar is an ideal retreat from the midday sun—try the fresh lemonade for a quick reviver. *Blvd. Benito Juárez 5, Box 44, Santa Cruz, tel. 958/7–0077, fax 958/7–0028. Reservations in U.S., tel. 800/262–2656. 75 rooms. Facilities: restaurant, pool. MC, V. Moderate.*

**Hotel Griffer.** Crucecita's only hotel is the least expensive place to stay in Huatulco and thus fills up quickly. Located on a busy in-town corner, the hotel feels like a business traveler's quarters, with a no-nonsense desk clerk, simple serviceable rooms, and no frills. The restaurant is operated separately from the hotel and is a good spot for down-home breakfasts and lunch with the locals. *Av. Guamuchil at Carrizal, Crucecita, tel. 958/7–0048. 18 rooms. Facilities: restaurant. MC, V. Inexpensive.*

**Puerto Angel**    **Angel del Mar.** The road to Puerto Angel's most expensive hotel is a steep, twisting affair you wouldn't want to attempt on foot except in the coolest hours of the morning. The view from the top takes in the panorama of town and coast, and sunsets are spectacular. The rooms, however, are only adequate, and the restaurant is expensive. Because all supplies must be carted up the hill, the hotel sometimes runs out of water, among other essentials. The telephone number is now simply 2; the hotel can be reached only through operator assistance since dial phones have yet to arrive in Puerto Angel. *Dirt road past Playa Panteón, in Puerto Angel, tel. 2. 45 rooms. Facilities: restaurant, pool. MC, V. Moderate.*

**Posada Cañon Devata.** The buildings look like colonial-style tree houses nestled in a shady, forested canyon. Rocking chairs carved from logs sit outside the rooms, which are small, clean, and cool. The beach is a three-minute walk away and is visible from the rooftop restaurant shaded by a giant palapa. The bungalows here have kitchenettes. *Off Blvd. Virgilio Uribe at end of road, Box 74, Pochutla, no phone. 10 rooms, 3 bungalows. Facilities: restaurant. No credit cards. Closed May–June. Moderate.*

**La Cabaña de Puerto Angel.** Just across from Playa Panteón, this is the best located hotel in town. The accommodating proprietors keep a big pot of coffee at the front desk for early risers, along with a library of paperback novels and maps of Mexico. The rooms have small balconies, louvered windows with screens, ceiling fans, and cheery yellow-stripe spreads on the thin mattresses. Some rooms don't have curtains. *Across from Playa Panteón. 23 rooms. MC, V. Inexpensive.*

**Puerto Escondido**    **Fiesta Mexicana.** Among the newest of the new, this hotel is a celebration of Mexico's Pacific Coast decor, with bold, sunny colors, thatch, and nautical designs. It has a warm ambience and a helpful staff. Rooms are large and simply furnished. *Blvd. Benito Juárez, tel. 958/2–0150, fax 958/1–6219. 90 rooms. Facilities: restaurant, bar, pool, tennis. AE, MC, V. Expensive.*

★   **Hotel Santa Fe.** Your room here will have colonial furnishings, a tiled bath, drapes and spreads of heavy woven Mexican cloth in soothing lavenders and blues, a telephone, air-conditioning and a ceiling fan, a television if you request one, and maybe a balcony overlooking the pool. All the fine details come from Mexico's crafts centers—the multicolor tiles lining the steps are from Puebla, the cowhide chairs from Guadalajara. No wonder more than half the hotel's guests come back year after year, and stay put for weeks at a time. The owners of the Santa Fe also operate a small country inn about two hours from Puerto Escondido, in the pine forests of the Oaxaca mountains, amid coffee plantations and crystal-clear rivers. *Calle del Morro by Zicatela beach, Box 95, tel. 958/2–0170, fax 958/2–0260. 39 rooms. Facilities: restaurant, pool, tours. AE, MC, V. Expensive.*

**Paraíso Escondido.** Puerto Escondido's only funky, colonial-style hotel climbs the hillside overlooking Avenue Gasga and has a down-home, friendly aura that encourages mingling around the pool. No two rooms are alike, and all are furnished with a mishmash of wood dressers, tin mirrors, and bright blue drapes and spreads. Take time to examine the stone statues spread about the property. *Calle Union 10, tel. 958/2–0444. Reservations: Box 20–187, Mexico 20, Mexico City D.F. 24 rooms. Facilities: restaurant, bar, pool. MC, V. Expensive.*

**Villas Los Delfines.** An enterprising couple from the capital have created this solitary paradise atop a hill overlooking the coast, with eight first-class cabanas spread along the hillside. The cabanas have full kitchens, separate bedrooms, and hammocks hanging outside. The husband is an architect with a fine eye for classical Mexican design, and blooming bougainvillea climbs all over the grounds. The cool blue pool sits in the middle of the compound, beside a palapa restaurant. Staying here is like visiting gracious friends who happen to have a few extra homes for guests. There's a long path down the hill to Zicatela Beach, and there is a market nearby. *Cerro de la Iguana, Carretera Costera del Pacifico Km. 71, Box 150, tel. 958/2–0467. 8 cabanas. Facilities: restaurant, bar, pool, satellite TV. MC, V. Expensive.*

**Casas de Playa Acali.** You can choose from four sizes and styles of accommodations at this cluster of cabanas by the main beach. The least expensive rooms are in small bungalows without air-conditioning or patios; prices rise with the size of the cabanas, number of beds, and the extent of kitchen facilities. This is a good choice for groups of four or six surfers who want to share expenses and prepare their own meals. *Calle del Morro, tel. 958/2–0754. 10 cabanas. Facilities: kitchens. MC, V. Moderate.*

★ **Jardín Escondido.** Of the dozens of bungalow/cabana hotels near the beach, this place stands out for its cleanliness and its long lap pool. The cabanas have hammocks hanging out front, mosquito nets over the beds, tile baths and showers, and freshly painted white brick walls. There's a small restaurant by the pool, and bottles of purified water to take to the beach are available at the front desk. Weekly and monthly rates are available. *Calle del Morro 300, Box 97, tel. 958/2–0348. 8 bungalows. Facilities: restaurant, pool. MC, V. Moderate.*

**Casa de Huespedes Pakololo.** Surfers congregate in the patios of this small guest house, keeping an eye on the waves while listening to the latest rock tunes on their boom boxes. The two bungalows have full kitchens; the eight simple rooms have refrigerators, ceiling fans, louvered windows, and mosquito netting over the beds. The rates are just about the lowest on the beach, and the clientele is young and ready to party. *Calle Morro, Zicatela Beach, tel. 958/2–0759. 2 bungalows, 8 rooms. No credit cards. Inexpensive.*

**Castillo del Reyes.** Proprietor Don Fernando runs an amiable show in his small, immaculately clean establishment. With no pool or restaurant, the clients tend to congregate around the front desk, drinking their own sodas and beer. The simple rooms have clean white walls and powerful showers with plenty of hot water. Some have air-conditioning. *Av. Gasga, tel. 958/2–0442. 17 rooms. No credit cards. Inexpensive.*

**Hotel Arco Iris.** This three-story colonial-style hotel is on Zicatela Beach, south of the Santa Fe, and is a good choice for those who want privacy and security but cannot afford the Santa Fe. Most rooms overlook the beach and have ceiling fans, fairly firm double beds, and private balconies with hammocks. Eight of the rooms have kitchenettes. The third-floor restaurant is a great spot for sunset-watching. *Calle del Morro, Zicatela Beach, Box 105, tel. 958/2–0432. 18 rooms. Facilities: restaurant, pool, surfboard rental. MC, V. Inexpensive.*

# 11 Chiapas and Tabasco

*By Erica Meltzer*

*Updated by*
*Barbara Franco*

Newcomers to Mexico might want to save Chiapas and Tabasco for a later visit. Although uniquely interesting, they are not an easy region to see and appreciate. For those truly looking for an outstanding travel experience, however, a well-planned trip to this area can be very satisfying, particularly if you arrange for your visit to coincide with a local festival. Though the two states have several American-style deluxe hotels, it is the smaller, locally run properties, with their foibles as well as their charms, that are more representative of the area's accommodations. Unlike beach resorts such as Cancún and Acapulco, this area is not one that visitors can jet to in a few hours from major U.S. gateways. Substantial ground transportation, either by bus or car, is absolutely necessary. People working in the tourist industry often don't speak English and are not as practiced in dealing with tourists as they are elsewhere in Mexico. Tourist information can be more difficult to obtain, and locals may be a bit more reserved.

On the other hand, the less touristic nature of these states has its own appeal. In Chiapas, at least, the locals are less self-conscious, less sophisticated, and they seem less out to make a quick buck. And though gringos are hardly a novelty, it can be refreshing to be noticed as an outsider rather than ignored as one more anonymous face in an ongoing "invasion."

The Indians' wariness of strangers has a historic basis. A bloody past of exploitation by and fierce confrontation with outsiders remains vividly present, as already impoverished indigenous communities in Chiapas are continually forced to compete for their lands with wave after wave of new settlers. Most of eastern Chiapas borders on Guatemala, and during the past 20 years it has been overrun, first by the landless poor relocated from other parts of Mexico, and then by tens of thousands of Guatemalan refugees. Because of its isolation, Chiapas has been at the margin of the nation's development. It is one of the poorest states in Mexico, with appallingly high rates of alcoholism, violence, illiteracy, and death due to unhygienic conditions. Land distribution, too, is skewed: 1% of the landowners hold 45% of the territory, keeping the colonial system nearly intact, and repression is rampant. Not surprisingly, tensions are high among the various Indian groups themselves; between the Indians and the mestizos (those of both Spanish and Indian descent); and between the Indians and PEMEX, the state oil monopoly, which has built a highway along the Guatemalan border, destroying lands and wildlife in the process.

Although it was nominally made rich half a century ago with the discovery of oil in the gulf, Tabasco maintains a rebellious tradition. During the 1920s and 1930s, Tomás Garrido Canabal, a vehemently anticlerical dictator, outlawed priests and had all the churches either torn down or converted to other uses. Riots, deportations, and property confiscations were common. When British writer Graham Greene visited Tabasco in 1938, he called it "the Godless state." No wonder he found people voicing "the rather wild dream . . . of a rising which will separate Chiapas, Tabasco, Yucatán, and Quintana Roo from the rest of Mexico and of an alliance with Catholic Guatemala"! These somber facts are not likely to intrude on the visitor's consciousness, although they should be borne in mind. The rest of Mexico, too, has a turbulent past. But if Tabasco's past is barely evident today, a wholly different spirit prevails in Chiapas.

Chiapas will not be off the tourist track for long. In the planning stage is an American-sponsored "Mayan Route," which will carve highways of tourism into the hinterland in the name of preservation and development. And the Lacondon jungle is already disappearing, its Indian inhabitants being driven to adopt poor imitations of Western lifestyle. Massive erosion and deforestation are taking their toll as the new settlers burn the forest and exhaust the soil by planting corn and raising cattle.

For the present, however, travelers threading their way along tortuous mountain roads—full of dramatic hairpin turns along the edges of desolate ravines—will come upon remote clusters of huts and cornfields planted on near-vertical hillsides. They will pass Indian women wrapped in deep blue shawls and coarsely woven wool skirts, and Indian children selling fruit and flowers by the roadside. Chiapas has 14 separate Indian groups, primarily the highland-dwelling Maya Tzeltals and Tzotzils, many of whom do not speak Spanish. As they have for centuries, the Indians travel seasonally between their homes in the highlands and the plantations in the lowlands, which still need subsistence-wage workers, and between Mexico and Guatemala.

Tabasco is of interest primarily to hardy adventure-seekers, lured by its minor ruins and the wild rivers surging through the jungle. Less adventurous travelers will find Villahermosa's CICOM museum of pre-Columbian archaeology and the collection of Olmec heads at Parque La Venta a good introduction to the Indian heritage so evident in Chiapas. (And no, Tabasco sauce does not come from here or from anywhere else in Mexico; it originated in Louisiana.)

The highlight of Chiapas and Tabasco is the town of San Cristóbal de las Casas. It can be reached by car or bus from either Tuxtla (**Tus**-tla) Gutiérrez, a convenient point of departure because of its airport and access to San Cristóbal, or Villahermosa, which also has a major airport. A sample itinerary might begin in Tuxtla, then head east to San Cristóbal for a few nights. From here move on to Toniná, Agua Azul, and Palenque, and finally on to Villahermosa. From Palenque you can arrange an excursion to the Mayan ruins of Bonampak and Yaxchilán (Yas-chee-**lan**). A popular day trip from San Cristóbal is to the Lagunas de Montebello (Lakes of Montebello).

# San Cristóbal de las Casas

San Cristóbal, the chief city of the Chiapas highlands, is a pretty town of about 150,000 situated in a valley of pine forests and orchards. Common sights are Indian women, who stand combing and braiding their hair, and hippies, because the place is inexpensive and relatively unfettered by tourism. More Europeans than Americans visit San Cristóbal, and it is the preferred stopping point before venturing on to Palenque and Guatemala.

San Cristóbal is also among the finest colonial towns in Mexico: It has churches, red-tile roofs, elegant Spanish mansions, and cobblestone streets. The cold, haunting atmosphere of the place is intensified by the remarkable quality of the early morning and late-afternoon light. Small enough to be seen on foot in the course of a day, San Cristóbal is also captivating enough to invite a stay of three days, a week, or even a month.

In addition to viewing the monuments from the colonial era, visitors usually plan an early morning visit to see the Indians gather at the *mercado* (market), browse for local handicrafts, or explore one of the indigenous villages in the vicinity. Just soaking up the ambience in one of San Cristóbal's little cafés or unpretentious restaurants is a pleasure. But more than anything else, San Cristóbal is safe and comfortable, and can serve as an unintimidating prelude to Guatemala.

In 1524, the Spaniards under Diego de Mazariegos decisively defeated the Chiapan Indians at a battle outside town. Mazariegos founded the city, which was called Villareal de Chiapa de los Españoles, in 1528. For most of the viceroyalty, or colonial era, Chiapas, with its capital at San Cristóbal, was a province of Guatemala. It was of greater strategic than economic importance to the Spaniards, lacking the gold and silver of the north. Instead, the state's agricultural resources became entrenched in the *encomienda* system, tantamount to slavery. "In this life all men suffer," lamented a Spanish friar in 1691, "but the Indians suffer most of all."

The situation improved only slightly through the efforts of Bartolomé de las Casas, the eponymous bishop of San Cristóbal who in the mid-1500s protested the colonials' torture and massacre of the Indians. The Indians protested in another way, murdering priests and other *ladinos* (whites) in infamous uprisings. (Chiapans still refer to whites as either ladinos or *Españoles*—Spaniards—whether they are "pure-blooded" or mestizo.)

Mexico, Guatemala, and the rest of New Spain declared independence in 1821. For a brief two years, Chiapas was independent of both Spain and Mexico, electing by plebescite to join the latter on September 14, 1824, the *día de la mexicanidad* of Chiapas (the day is still celebrated in San Cristóbal). In 1892, because of San Cristóbal's allegiance to the Royalists during the War of Independence, the capital was moved to Tuxtla Gutiérrez; with it went all hope that the town would keep pace with the rest of Mexico. It was not until the 1950s that the roads into town were paved and the first automobiles arrived. Modern times came late to San Cristóbal, for which most visitors are thankful.

## Arriving and Departing

**By Plane**
*Airports and Airlines*
The closest major airport is in Tuxtla Gutiérrez, 85 kilometers (52.8 miles) west. There are four daily flights from Mexico City on **Mexicana** (airport, tel. 961/3–49–21; in Tuxtla, 961/2–00–20 or 961/2–54–02, fax 961/2–16–92). **Aviación de Chiapas** (Aviacsa, tel. 961/2–80–81 or 961/2–68–80, fax 961/3–78–12; Mexico City, tel. 563–44–00, fax 590–25–64) also has daily flights between Tuxtla and Mexico City. For charter flights to the ruins of Bonampak and Yaxchilán, contact a travel agency or Na-Bolom. The San Cristóbal airport south of the city is no longer in operation.

*Between the Airport and Center City*
The easiest way to get from Tuxtla to San Cristóbal is by taxi. The two-hour ride costs about $65. Many travel agencies in both cities provide private taxi service. By car, follow Route

190. First-class bus service on **Cristóbal Colon** costs under $15; from the Tuxtla airport, you must first catch the *colectivo* (shared taxi service in a van or minibus) into town (about $8).

**By Car** From Tuxtla, Route 190 goes east through Chiapa de Corzo to San Cristóbal. Route 190 continues southeast to Comitán and the Guatemalan border. Route 199 is the preferred route from San Cristóbal to Villahermosa via Toniná, Agua Azul, and Palenque. Route 195 is a more circuitous route between San Cristóbal and Villahermosa. Though very expensive, car rentals are available at the Tuxtla and Villahermosa airports as well as in San Cristóbal.

**By Bus** The **Cristóbal Colon** terminal is at Avenida Insurgentes and Pan American Highway, Route 190. Second-class service to Tuxtla and Guatemala departs from the terminal at Allende and Pan American Highway. **Transportes Tuxtla** (Panamerican Highway at Allende) runs second-class buses northeast along the road to Ocosingo.

## Getting Around

The most enjoyable and thorough way to explore San Cristóbal, as with many other colonial Mexican towns, is on foot. Trying to maneuver a car on its narrow, cobblestone streets filled with pedestrians is a needless test of patience. If you do come to town with a car, leave it in the hotel garage except for excursions outside San Cristóbal. **Budget Rent-a-Car** has offices at Calle Diego de Mazariegos 36 in San Cristóbal (tel. 967/8–18–71). Taxis can be found at the *sitio* (taxi stand) next to the cathedral (tel. 967/8–03–96), and there is colectivo service to outlying villages, departing from and returning to the market. For maps and information, inquire at the tourist office.

## Important Addresses and Numbers

**Tourist Information** The **San Cristóbal tourist office** (tel. 967/8–07–15 and 967/8–06–60, fax 967/8–08–65) is on the ground floor of the Palacio Municipal, right on the *zócalo* (main square). Check the bulletin board here upon arrival for information on tours and side trips. *Open Mon.–Sat. 9–8, Sun. 9–2.*

**Emergencies** **Municipal police** (tel. 967/8–05–54). The **Hospital Regional** is located at Insurgentes 26 (tel. 967/8–07–70). The **Social Security Clinic** is outside of town on Calle Tabasco and Diagonal Centenario (tel. 967/8–03–50). You might also contact **Dr. Elisa Jimenez Pascasio** (tel. 967/8–18–31).

**English-language Bookstores** Good selections of English-language books can be found at **Cafetería El Mural** (Av. Crescencio Rosas 4), the **Casa de las Imagenes** (Av. B. Domínguez 9, tel. 967/8–03–70), and **Soluna** (Calle Real de Guadalupe 24-D).

**Travel Agencies** The best travel agencies are **A.T.C.** (Av. 5 de Febrero 15; tel. 967/8–25–50, 967/8–25–57, and 967/8–11–53; fax 967/8–31–45) and **Lacantún** (Calle Madero 19-2, tel. 967/8–25–87 or 967/8–25–88).

## Guided Tours

Most tour operators transport passengers in minibuses and can arrange hotel pickup.

**Orientation Tours**  A pleasurable way to explore this entire region is with a VTP (*Viajes Todo Pagado*) on **Mexicana** (tel. 800/531–7921) airlines. These all-inclusive packages are available in several combinations to fit your personal needs and budget. The A.T.C. travel agency (Av. 5 de Febrero 15, tel. 967/8–25–50 and 967/8–11–53, fax 967/8–31–45) runs full-day city tours that also cover Na-Bolom, San Juan Chamula, and the San Cristóbal Caves. Five-hour horseback tours to outlying villages can also be arranged.

**Regional Tours**  **A.T.C.** and **Lacantún** travel agencies organize tours to Bonampak, Yaxchilán, Palenque, Agua Azul, Lagunas de Montebello, Amatenango, Belize, Chincultik, Comitán, Guatemala, Sumidero Canyon, Tuxtla Gutiérrez, and Yucatán. Special-interest tours and treks—Lacandon Indians, bird-watching, flora and fauna, river trips, rain-forest excursions—are also available.

**Personal Guides**  The tourist office can put you in touch with Mercedes Hernández Gómez, a licensed English-speaking guide who leads tours to San Juan Chamula, Zinacantán, and the area ruins.

## Exploring

*Numbers in the margin correspond to points of interest on the San Cristóbal de las Casas map.*

San Cristóbal is laid out in a grid pattern and centered around the zócalo, with street names changing on either side of the square. For example, Francisco Madero to the east of the square becomes Calle Diego de Mazariegos to the west (rather like New York City's East and West 50th streets, divided by 5th Avenue).

The heart of San Cristóbal is small and can be seen on foot in
❶ two hours or less. Begin at the **zócalo,** around which the Spaniards built all their colonial cities. In its center stands the gazebo, which is used by musicians on festive occasions. Surrounding the square are a number of 16th-century buildings, many former mansions of the conquistadores. Tile roofs and wood-beamed ceilings adorn corridors flanking central patios, which are surrounded by arched columns and filled with huge potted plants. (Don't be afraid to go into buildings whose doors are open.) Perhaps the most famous mansion is the so-
❷ called **Casa de Diego de Mazariegos,** opposite the square on the southeast corner of Calle Diego de Mazariegos. One of the most exquisite specimens of colonial architecture in Mexico, the Casa is now the Hotel Santa Clara. The stone mermaid and lions outside it are typical of the period's Plateresque style, as ornate and busy as the work of a silversmith.

Continue in a northwesterly direction around the zócalo to the
❸ **Palacio Municipal,** which was the state capitol building until 1892, when San Cristóbal lost that honor to Tuxtla Gutiérrez. Stop at San Cristóbal's tourist office, on the ground floor, for maps and information.

Perpendicular to the Palacio Municipal, on the north side of the
❹ zócalo, is **La Catedral,** built in 1528, then demolished and rebuilt in 1693, with subsequent additions during the 18th and 19th centuries. Noteworthy attractions in the cathedral include the painting of Our Lady of Sorrows, to the left of the altar; the gold-plated *retablo de los Reyes* (altarpiece); the

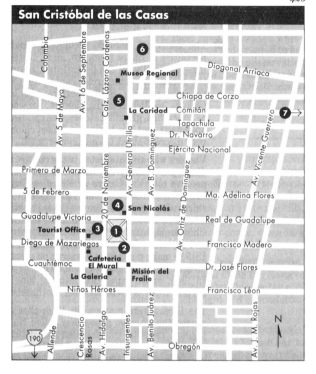

Casa de Diego de Mazariegos, **2**

Centro de Estudios Científicos Na-Bolom, **7**

La Catedral, **4**

Mercado, **6**

Palacio Municipal, **3**

Templo de Santo Domingo, **5**

Zócalo, **1**

### San Cristóbal de las Casas

Chapel of Guadalupe; and the gold-encrusted pulpit. *Open daily 7–2 and 4–8.*

**Time Out**  **Cafetería El Mural** (Crescencio Rosas 4 at the corner of Calle Diego de Mazariegos) is a pleasant café serving standard Mexican snacks. The café also has a bookshop.

**⑤** Head north about four blocks on Avenida General Utrilla toward the **Templo de Santo Domingo,** a three-block-long complex housing the church, former convent, regional history museum, and Templo de la Caridad. The church dates from 1547–1569, and the two-headed eagle—emblem of the Hapsburg dynasty that once ruled Spain and its American dominions—broods over its pediment. The pink stone facade, carved in an intensely ornamental style known as Baroque Solomonic, was clearly influenced by the church of Antigua, Guatemala: Saints' figures, angels, and grooved columns overlaid with vegetation motifs abound. The interior is dominated by lavish altarpieces; an exquisitely fashioned pulpit; a sculpture of the Holy Trinity; and wall panels of carved cedar, one of the precious woods of Chiapas that centuries later lured the woodsmen of Tabasco to the obscure highlands surrounding San Cristóbal. At the southeast corner of the church park lies the tiny **Templo de la Caridad,** built in 1711 to venerate the Immaculate Conception. Its highlight is the finely carved altarpiece. The **Ex-convento de Santo Domingo,** immediately adjacent to the church, now houses Sna Jolobil, an Indian cooperative selling rather expensive local weavings and a good selection of colorful postcards (open daily 9–2 and 4–6). The small regional history

## San Juan Chamula

The spiritual and administrative center of the Chamula Indians is justly celebrated, as much for its rich past as for its turbulent present. The Chamula are a Tzotzil-speaking Mayan group of about 16,000 individuals who live in hamlets scattered throughout the highlands; there are some 300 of them in San Juan Chamula. Virtually the only thing to see is the church and the rituals performed inside, which are central to the Chamula culture.

The village has been minutely studied for its economic and religious/political systems. The Chamulas grow subsistence crops on the region's badly eroded lands and trade actively with the outside world, despite their traditional distrust of strangers. They raise sheep for wool and manure, but their religion—a curious mélange of pagan and Christian rites and beliefs—forbids them to eat its flesh. As the land is depleted, Chamula men hire themselves out as laborers on the Soconusco coffee plantations in the south of Chiapas. Soil erosion is so severe that many Chamula have emigrated permanently, particularly to the selva lacandona.

The horrendous working conditions of the coffee pickers and woodcutters in the early part of this century have been tellingly described by B. Traven in such novels as *The Rebellion of the Hanged*. More recently, Ricardo Pozas drew a portrait that is nearly as abysmal in his classic monograph, *Juan the Chamula*.

Chamula society is organized around revolving *cargos*, or public posts. The chosen men must leave their homes and serve the community for a year in San Juan Chamula, frequently as policemen or religious leaders. The position carries with it much prestige, and although it is a burden for their families, it is willingly undertaken.

The Chamula are fiercely religious, a trait that has played an important role in their history. The Chamula uprising of 1869 started when some tribesmen were imprisoned for crucifying a boy in the belief that they should have their own Christ. Some 13,000 Chamula then rose up to demand their leaders' release and massacred scores of ladino villagers in the process.

As recently as 1968, the Chamula responded to an attempt to build a Catholic chapel in a neighboring hamlet with armed resistance and a warning to the priest. The priest later tried to stop indigenous ceremonies from being performed in the church and was evicted; he now returns only for mass and baptisms. Incursions by American evangelical groups have also met with resistance. Very recently, 10,000 Chamula were expelled from the region for rejecting ancient beliefs.

**Getting Around**  San Juan Chamula is 12 kilometers (7.5 miles) northwest of San
**By Car**  Cristóbal. Head west on Guadalupe Victoria, which forks to the right onto Ramón Larrainzar. Continue 4 kilometers (2.5 miles) until you reach the entrance to the village. Most of these roads are paved and they are far more interesting than the alternate route, which is to take the main road to Tuxtla 8 kilometers (4.9 miles) and then turn right when you see signs. You can catch one of the colectivos that run regularly from the market in San Cristóbal, or you can hire a taxi or ride horseback (*see* Sports, in San Cristóbal de las Casas, *above*). To get per-

mission to enter the church and to pay a small fee, go first to the office of the Presidente Municipal (Municipal President) in the main square.

**Exploring**   Physically and spiritually, life in San Juan Chamula revolves around the church, a white stucco building with red, blue, and yellow trim. Extreme care must be exercised in entering the church. A policeman will either accompany you in or meet you inside, and he is likely to tell you that taking photographs is absolutely prohibited.

There are no pews in the church, the floor of which is strewn with fragrant pine needles. Indian families sit chanting on low stone platforms, facing colorfully attired saints' statues that are so highly polished they resemble porcelain dolls. For the most part, worshipers appear oblivious to intruders, continuing with their sacraments: They burn candles of various colors, drink Coca-Cola, kill chickens, and break eggs over themselves to plead for help with crops, illness, and disaster.

Outside the church there is no taboo against photography. Visitors may be accosted by barefoot children speaking broken Spanish at best who want payment for being photographed. The children are eager for any handouts, but coins, *chicle* (chewing gum), and pens are favorites. If you are lucky, they will take you to their homes—mud-thatched huts—where a female relative will try to sell you locally woven goods. Village elders may question you as you leave the vicinity of the church. The best time to visit San Juan Chamula is on Sundays, when the market is in full swing and more formal religious rites are performed.

### Zinacantán

The village of Zinacantán (place of the bats) is even smaller than San Juan Chamula and is reached by taking a paved road west just before San Juan Chamula. Here photography is totally forbidden, even outside the churches. It is the scenery en route to Zinacantán—terraced hillsides with cornfields and orchards—that draws visitors. There isn't much to see in the village itself except on Sundays, when people gather from the surrounding parishes, or during religious festivals. The men wear bright pink *serapes* (ponchos); the women cover themselves with deep blue *rebozos* (shawls). Watch for the plethora of crosses around the springs and mountains on the way to Zinacantán: They are not Christian symbols, but instead mark the abodes of Mayan gods, honored and propitiated through gifts of food, drink, and candles. Zinacantán is 4 kilometers (2.5 miles) west of Chamula. From Chamula, follow signs along a paved road. From San Cristóbal, take the Tuxtla road about 8 kilometers (4.9 miles) and look for the turnoff on your right. Colectivos depart for the village from the San Cristóbal market.

# Villahermosa and Tabasco

*Numbers in the margin correspond to points of interest on the Chiapas and Tabasco map.*

Graham Greene's succinct summation of Tabasco as a "tropical state of river and swamp and banana grove" captures its essence. Though the state played an important role in the early history of Mexico, its past is rarely on view; instead, it is Tabasco's modern-day status as a supplier of oil that overwhelms the visitor. Set on a humid coastal plain and crisscrossed by abundant rivers, low hills, and unexplored jungles, the landscape is marred by shantytowns and refineries reeking

❶ of sulfur. The capital city of **Villahermosa** epitomizes the mercurial development of Tabasco (the airplane was here before the automobile). Though ugly and modern, Villahermosa is the home of a fine archaeology museum. It is also the place to see the giant stone heads carved by Tabasco's ancient inhabitants, the Olmecs.

This is not to say that the rest of Tabasco has nothing to offer the visitor. There are beaches, but the tourist infrastructure is minimal, and in some places strollers might come away with tar on their feet due to the oil industry. The fired-brick Mayan ruins of Comalcalco attest to the influence of Palenque. Probably the most interesting region is the rivers and canyons to the south and east of Villahermosa, which are home to jaguars, deer, and alligators; this was where the English pirate Sir Francis Drake hid from the Spaniards.

Tabasco—specifically the mouth of the River Grijalva—lay along the route of the Spanish explorations of Mexico in 1518–19. At that time, the state's rivers and waterways, along which the Olmecs and their descendants lived, served as a trade route between the peoples of the north and those of the south. When the Spaniards came to Tabasco, they had to bridge 50 rivers and contend with swarms of mosquitoes, beetles, ants, and almost unbearable heat, but the region was so lush that one early chronicler termed it a Garden of Eden.

The Spanish conquest was facilitated by the state of almost constant tribal warfare between the Tabascans and their Mayan and Aztec overlords, and by the fact that the Indians, who had never seen horses, perceived both horse and rider to be one supernatural being. Among the 20 slave women turned over to the victors was a Chiapan named Malintzín, who was singled out by the Spaniards for her beauty and her ability to speak both the Mayan and the Nahuatl languages. Called Marina by the Spaniards, she became not only Cortés's mistress and the mother of his illegitimate son but also the willing interpreter of Indian customs. Marina's cooperation helped the conquistador trounce both Moctezuma and Cuauhtémoc, the last Aztec emperors.

Until the early 20th century Tabasco slumbered; it did not become a state until 1824. After the American Civil War, traders from the southern United States began operating in the region and on its rivers, hauling the precious mahogany trees upstream from Chiapas and shipping them north from the small Tabascan port of Frontera. This was Tabasco's most prosperous era until the discovery of oil 50 years ago.

## Arriving and Departing

**By Plane** **Aeroméxico** has daily nonstop service from Mexico City. The Aeroméxico ticket office is at Periférico Carlos Pellicer, Camara No. 511. (airport, tel. 93/14–16–75 or 93/12–09–04; in town, tel. 93/12–69–91, 93/12–15–28 or 93/12–95–54). **Mexicana** has four daily nonstop flights from Mexico City, and both airlines

# Chiapas and Tabasco

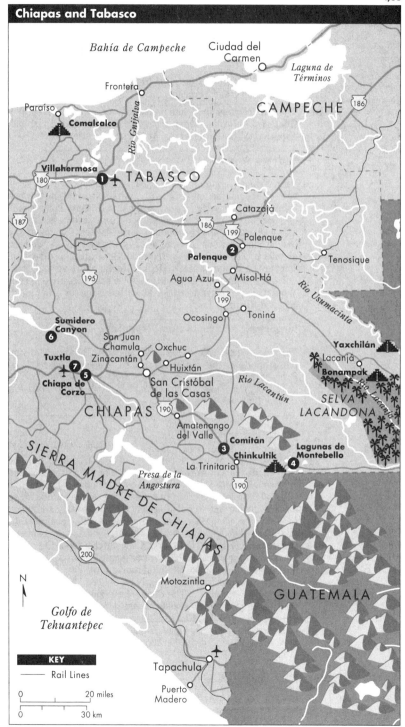

Bahía de Campeche

Ciudad del Carmen

Laguna de Términos

Paraíso

Frontera

Comalcalco

CAMPECHE

186

Río Grijalva

Villahermosa

180

TABASCO

187

Catazajá

186 199

Palenque

195

Palenque 2

Tenosique

Agua Azul

Misol-Há

199

Ocosingo

Toniná

Río Usumacinta

Sumidero Canyon 6

San Juan Chamula

Oxchuc

Zinacantán

Tuxtla 7

Huixtán

5

Chiapa de Corzo

San Cristóbal de las Casas

CHIAPAS

190

Río Lacantún

Yaxchilán

Lacanjá

Bonampak

SELVA LACANDONA

Río Lacanjá

Amatenango del Valle

Comitán 3

Chinkultik

Lagunas de Montebello 4

La Trinitaria

190

Presa de la Angostura

SIERRA MADRE DE CHIAPAS

200

GUATEMALA

N

Golfo de Tehuantepec

Motozintla

**KEY**

— Rail Lines

0        20 miles

0        30 km

Tapachula

Puerto Madero

offer connecting flights to other Mexican cities. Mexicana has a ticket office in the Tabasco 2000 complex, Ave. de los Rios 105 (tel. 93/16–31–32/33/34; airport, tel. 93/12–11–64). Travel agencies book charter flights to Palenque and Bonampak.

**By Car** Take Route 186 from Palenque and points east (Campeche, Chetumal, Mérida), Route 195 from Tuxtla, or Route 180 from Coatzacoalcos and Veracruz.

**By Bus** There is frequent first- and second-class service to Campeche, Chetumal, Mérida, Mexico City, Palenque, San Cristóbal, Tapachula, Tuxtla Gutiérrez, Veracruz, and elsewhere.

## Getting Around

Villahermosa—population 500,000—is surrounded by three rivers but oriented toward the River Grijalva to the east, which is bordered by the *malecón* (boardwalk). The city is huge, and driving can be tricky. The main road through town is almost a highway; exit ramps are about 1 kilometer (.62 mile) apart, and tourist destinations are not clearly marked. Nevertheless, driving is the best way to get around. Several major car-rental companies, including Avis, Dollar, Hertz, and National, have offices in Villahermosa. Most taxi service is collective and runs along fixed routes; information about buses, on the other hand, can be difficult to find.

## Important Addresses and Numbers

The main tourist office is located in the huge Tabasco 2000 complex, opposite the municipal palace. *Paseo Tabasco 1504, Tabasco 2000 complex, tel. 93/16–36–33, 93/16–28–89, or 93/16–28–91. Open weekdays 9–3 and 6–8. An auxiliary office at Parque La Venta is open daily 8–4.*

## Exploring

Downtown Villahermosa contains a pedestrian shopping mall, a museum of popular culture, and a folk-art shop, but the **CICOM Museum of Anthropology** should be seen first. Located on the right bank of the Grijalva, the museum is part of a huge cultural complex dedicated to research on the Olmec and Maya (which is what the Spanish acronym CICOM stands for) and provides one of the last tranquil vistas of Villahermosa as it might have looked 50 years ago. Although most of the explanations are in Spanish, that should not detract from the visual pleasure of the displays. The entire ground floor is devoted to Tabasco and the Olmec, or "inhabitants of the land of rubber," who flourished in Tabasco as early as 1800 BC and disappeared about 1,600 years later. The Olmecs have long been honored as the mother culture of Mesoamerica and as inventors of the numerical and calendrical systems that spread throughout the region, though recent research suggests that the Olmecs might actually have been influenced by the Maya, rather than the other way around.

Some of the most interesting artifacts of the Olmec, other than the giant stone heads on view at Parque La Venta (*see below*), are the remnants of their jaguar cult, which are displayed in the museum. The jaguar symbolized the earth fertilized by rain, and many Olmec sculptures portray werejaguars (half-human, half-jaguar, similar to a werewolf) or jaguar babies. Other sculptures portray jaguars swallowing human heads, bat gods, bird-headed humans, female fertility figurines, and the mysterious smiling faces of Veracruz. The collection of recently discovered burial urns, found in the Tapijulapa caves west of Palenque, is outstanding. All of Mexico's ancient cultures are represented on the upper two floors, from the red-clay dogs of Colima and the nose rings of Nayarit to the huge burial urns of the Chontal Maya, who built Comalcalco. Don't miss the vivid reproductions of the Mayan murals from Bonampak. CICOM also houses a handicrafts shop, restaurant, library, and theater. *Carlos Pellicer 511, an extension of the malecón, tel. 93/ 12–32–00. Admission: about $3.50. Open daily 9–8.*

**Time Out**   Stop off for a beer and a plate of fresh shrimp at the **Capitán Beulo,** a small riverboat restaurant that also runs 90-minute cruises along the Grijalva. *Paseo Malecón Madrazo and Zaragoza, no phone and no reservations necessary. No admission charge for the cruise, but passengers must order food (no minimum). Departures at 1:30, 3:30, and 9 PM. Closed Mon.*

The giant stone heads carved by the Olmec and salvaged from the oil fields of La Venta, on the western edge of Tabasco near the state of Veracruz, are on display in **Parque La Venta,** situated west of CICOM in a tropical garden on the Lago de las Ilusiones (Lake of Illusions). These six-foot-tall, baby-faced Negroid heads, weighing upwards of 20 tons, have sparked endless scholarly debate. It has been theorized that they depict ancient Phoenician slaves who wound up on the coasts of Mexico, that they were meant to represent space invaders, and that because of the obesity and short limbs of the figures, they are proof of endocrine deficiencies among the ancient Olmec. More likely, they simply celebrate the earth's fecundity. La Venta contains 30 sculptures, not all of them heads. There are also werejaguars, priests, monsters, stelae, and stone altars oddly reminiscent of ancient Mesopotamian art. *Blvd. Ruiz Cortines near Paseo Tabasco, tel. 93/15–22–28. Admission: about $3.50. Open daily 8–4.*

## Dining

For price categories, *see* Dining for San Cristóbal, *above*. Highly recommended restaurants are indicated by a star ★.

**Moderate**   **El Mesón del Duende.** This restaurant, which translates as the House of the Elf, serves Spanish cuisine similar to the food at El Mesón de Castilla, including a savory Galician broth, veal, goat, paella, and seafood. The modest decor is in keeping with the family-style atmosphere. *Gregorio Méndez 1703, tel. 93/16–13–24. MC, V.*

★   **Los Tulipanes.** Next door to the CICOM Museum, the spacious Los Tulipanes specializes in steaks and seafood and has a tranquil view of the river. Try the stuffed crab or shrimp. *Carlos Pellicer 511, tel. 93/12–92–09 or 93/12–92–17. AE, MC, V.*

**Restaurante Reyna.** Formerly the Mesón de Castilla, this newly renovated restaurant is still known for its paella as well as for its varied international menu; fresh seafood is always available. The decor suggests a medieval atmosphere, and the 24 tables are arranged around an inner garden. Music can be heard here daily. *Pagés Llergo 125, 93/12–56–21. AE, DC, MC, V.*

**Inexpensive** **Leo.** This is a very popular spot for tasty beef and pork tacos that has recently expanded its menu and enlarged its dining area. *Paseo Tabasco 429, tel. 93/12–44–63. MC, V. Open daily till 1 AM.*

## Lodging

Villahermosa hotels are relatively expensive, especially when compared with those in San Cristóbal. Generally speaking, the newer, American-style hotels are outside of town, near Tabasco 2000 and Parque La Venta, and the older and more modest hotels are downtown. For price categories, *see* Lodging for San Cristóbal, *above.*

Highly recommended lodgings are indicated by a star ★.

**Very Expensive**
★ **Exelaris Hyatt.** Built in 1983, this nine-story Hyatt has 211 air-conditioned rooms, all with color TVs, phones, and minibars. *Juárez 106, 86050; tel. 93/13–44–44, 93/15–12–34, or 800/228–9000; fax 93/15–12–35 or 93/15–58–08. Facilities: 2 restaurants, 3 bars, heated pool, 2 tennis courts, business center, disco. AE, DC, MC, V.*

**Holiday Inn.** Situated across from La Choca Park in Tabasco 2000, this nine-story resort property has 144 climate-controlled rooms, all with color TVs, minibars, and room service. There's live entertainment in the Jaguar Lounge. *Paseo Tabasco 1407, 86030, tel. 93/16–44–00 or 800/HOLIDAY, fax 93/16–45–69. Facilities: lounge, restaurant, pool, business center, gym. AE, DC, MC, V.*

**Expensive** **Calinda Viva Villahermosa.** This business traveler's hotel has 241 rooms, all with air-conditioning, FM stereos, color TVs, and phones; many have balconies. *Paseo Tabasco 1201, 86050, tel. 93/15–00–00, fax 93/15–30–73. Facilities: restaurant, 2 bars, coffee shop, disco, pool, gift shop. AE, DC, MC, V.*

**Cencali.** This colonial-style hotel in the new hotel zone is situated in parklike grounds and surrounded by lakes and lush greenery. All 116 rooms and 3 suites are air-conditioned. *Juárez and Paseo Tabasco, 86040, tel. 93/15–19–94 through 93/15–19–99, fax 93/15–66–00. Facilities: restaurant, lobby bar, pool. AE, DC, MC, V.*

**Maya Tabasco.** The recently renovated Maya Tabasco has 156 rooms, all with air-conditioning, TVs, and phones. *Ruiz Cortines 907, 86000, tel. 93/12–11–11 or 93/14–44–66, fax 93/12–10–97. AE, DC, MC, V.*

**Moderate** **Don Carlos.** Formerly the Manzur, this downtown hotel has always been popular for its unpretentious atmosphere and good service. TVs and phones are available in every room. *Ave. Madero 422, 86000, tel. 93/12–24–99, fax 93/12–46–22. Facilities: restaurant, bar, lounge. AE, MC, V.*

## Excursions from Villahermosa

The most important Mayan site in Tabasco is **Comalcalco,** about 60 kilometers (37.3 miles) northwest of Villahermosa off Route 187. The abundant cocoa plants in the region provided food and livelihood for a booming population during the late classic period (AD 600–900), when Comalcalco was built; the site marks the westernmost reach of the Maya. Descendants of the Chontal Maya, who constructed Comalcalco, still live in the vicinity. This site is unique among Mayan cities for its use of fired brick, as the Tabasco swamplands lacked the stone for building that was found elsewhere in the Mayan empire. The bricks were apparently inscribed and painted with enigmatic "anonymous messages" before being covered with stucco. The major pyramid, on the Great Eastern Acropolis, is decorated with large stucco masks and carvings, and the museum houses many of the artifacts that were uncovered there. *Admission: about $3.50. Open daily 9–4:30.*

If not seeing the Gulf of Mexico will leave you feeling deprived, continue 19 kilometers (11.8 miles) to **Paraíso.** Bear in mind, however, that Tabasco is not known for its beaches: For the most part, they are dirty and almost totally lacking in tourist infrastructure. There is one hotel on the beach and others in the town of Paraíso, a few kilometers inland.

# Palenque

② The ruins of **Palenque** are to many people the most beautiful in all Mexico. Chichén Itzá may be more expansive, and Teotihuacán more monumental, but Palenque possesses a mesmerizing quality, perhaps because of its intimacy. It is, after all, just a cluster of ocher buildings intermingled with grassy mounds and tall palm groves set in a rain forest. But in the early morning or late afternoon, sunlight illuminates the structures in a hazy, iridescent glow; there are the eerie shrill calls of birds, and the local Indians, descendants of the Maya, wander about collecting banana leaves, oranges, and avocados. Whether or not visitors are archaeology fans, they cannot fail to be moved by the sanctity of Palenque.

A Spanish priest first stumbled on the site in the 16th century; it was rediscovered in 1750, and in 1785 a royal Spanish expedition made its way to the site. In about 1833 an eccentric Austrian count set up house with his mistress for three years in a building known as the **Templo del Conde** (Temple of the Count). American explorers John Lloyd Stephens and Frederick Catherwood lived briefly in the palace during their 1840 expedition. In 1923 serious excavations began under the direction of Franz Blom, cofounder of Na-Bolom in San Cristóbal. Work continued intermittently until 1952, when Alberto Ruz Lhuillier, a Mexican archaeologist, uncovered the tomb of the 7th-century King Pacal beneath the Temple of the Inscriptions. Seeing Palenque, one can understand why archaeologist Sylvanus Morley honored the Maya as the "Greeks of the New World." The site dates from the mid- to late-classic period (6th–9th centuries), although it was inhabited as early as 1500 BC. Palenque marks the architectural apogee of the western Mayan empire, and it has been called "second only to the Acropolis in terms of unadulterated beauty." (Even Graham Greene, grumpier than usual because of illness, was impressed by the "gnarled relics.")

Ground-breaking work has been done on the Maya in the past 12 years by archaeologists, linguists, and astronomers. The deciphering of 98% of Palenque's hieroglyphics in 1988 has revolutionized scholars' understanding of both the Maya and the bloody history of Palenque. For example, the glyphs have revealed the complex history of the Palenque dynasties and shown how prevalent self-mutilation was. It is now hypothesized that Palenque reached its peak during a period of transition for Mayan civilization, when the rulers—Pacal in particular—were bent on expanding the city-state's power over rival polities. The site was abandoned around AD 800 for reasons still hotly disputed, making it one of the earliest Mayan sites to be deserted in a west-to-east extinction pattern. In its heyday, Palenque encompassed nearly 25 square miles; the excavated portions of the ruins cover only a half mile.

## Arriving and Departing

**By Plane** Chartered flights are available through travel agencies in San Cristóbal and Villahermosa; many of them continue on to the ruins of Bonampak and Yaxchilán.

**By Car** The 90-minute, 143-kilometer (89-mile) trip from Villahermosa on Route 186 to Catazajá, then on Route 199 to Palenque, is easy, as for most of the way the roads are straight and paved (if full of potholes). It takes about seven hours to drive from Palenque to San Cristóbal on scenic Routes 199 and 190. For the first 30 kilometers (18.6 miles) out of Palenque, the roads are flat and newly paved. The worst stretches of unpaved roadway are on the curvy 116 kilometers (72 miles) between Palenque and Ocosingo, with numerous hillocks, lush green riverbeds, and savannas. After Ocosingo the road becomes more mountainous and paved. It is also extremely beautiful, with dense vegetation, hillsides planted with maize, and occasional thatched huts of the indigenous villages. You may see *campesinos* (peasants), machetes in hand. Exercise caution during the rainy season (June through October), when the roads are slick.

**By Train** Daily trains from Mexico City take at least 24 hours. First-class service from Mérida takes 11 hours; second-class service makes more stops and takes 16 hours. The train station is 10 kilometers (6.2 miles) from town.

**By Bus** First- and second-class service is available from Villahermosa (2.5 hours), San Cristóbal (6 hours), and Mexico City (14 hours); there is second-class only from Mérida (8 hours), Campeche (6 hours), and Tuxtla Gutiérrez (9 hours).

## Getting Around

The town of Palenque, some 8 kilometers (5 miles) east of the ruins, is dusty, unsightly, and commercial, providing only the most basic dining and lodging facilities. Shops on the main street have an adequate selection of regional crafts, though there are much better offerings in San Cristóbal. The tourist office, on the second floor of the Palacio Municipal, on the zócalo, is open Monday through Friday 8–1 and 4–7 (tel. 934/5–01–14 or 934/5–01–53).

Visitors with a car will have the easiest time reaching both Palenque and its surrounding attractions, but colectivo service is available from the town center to the ruins and the neighboring waterfalls.

## Exploring

The ruins are open daily 8–5, and there is an admission charge of about $5. Since no formal guides are available, we suggest that you buy a guidebook in town.

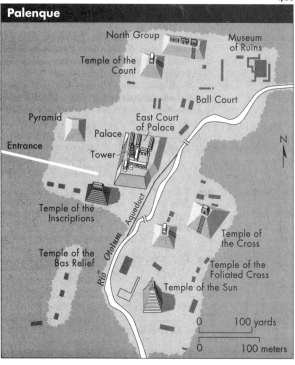

**Palenque**

North Group

Museum of Ruins

Temple of the Count

Ball Court

Pyramid

East Court of Palace

Palace

Entrance

Tower

N

Temple of the Inscriptions

Río Otolum

Aqueduct

Temple of the Cross

Temple of the Bas Relief

Temple of the Foliated Cross

Temple of the Sun

0          100 yards

0          100 meters

**Temple of the Inscriptions**  On your right as you enter the site is a 75-foot pyramid. Reaching the tomb inside involves a relatively easy, if slow, climb. The pyramid is dedicated to Pacal, the "Mesoamerican Charlemagne," who took Palenque to its most glorious heights during his 70-year reign, which ended circa AD 692.

Once at the summit, take a good, long look around you, particularly at the imposing palace to your right, which fills the field of vision. This is the best view of Palenque, and it provides an excellent orientation to the other buildings. Atop this temple and the smaller surrounding temples are vestiges of roof combs, one of the most distinctive architectural features of the southern Mayans. (Roof combs are delicate vertical extensions that resemble ornamental combs worn by Spanish women on the crown of their heads.) Then descend 80 feet down a steep, damp flight of stairs into the tomb, one of the only crypts ever found inside a Mexican pyramid. Pacal's diadem and majestic jade, shell, and obsidian mask were stolen from Mexico City's Museum of Anthropology in the early 1980s and recovered in 1989. The intricately carved sarcophagus lid, weighing some 5 tons and measuring 10 by 7 feet, however, remains. A "psychoduct," or hollow stone tube through which his soul was thought to have passed to the netherworld, leads up to the temple.

It can be difficult to make out the carvings on the slab, but they depict Pacal, prostrate beneath a sacred ceiba tree. The lords of the nine underworlds are carved into stucco reliefs on the walls around him; his more earthly companions were several youths, whose remains were uncovered alongside the sepulcher. *The tomb is open daily 10:30–4.*

**Palace** Built at different times, the palace is a complex of patios, galleries, and other buildings set on a 30-foot-high platform. Stucco work adorns the pillars of the galleries and the inner courtyards. There are numerous friezes and masks inside, most of them depicting Pacal and his dynasty. Remarkably well preserved, their style is sinuous and linear, stylized but restrained. Steam baths in the Southwestern Patio suggest that priests once dwelled in the adjoining cellars and that the galleries were probably used for religious ceremonies.

**Group of the Cross** To the right of the palace you'll cross the tiny Otulum River, which in ancient times was roofed over to form a nine-foot-high vaulted causeway, or aqueduct. Tombs were discovered beneath the largest, the Temple of the Cross, and the most exquisite roof combs are found on these buildings.

**Northern Group** To reach this cluster, walk north along the river (little more than a creek), passing the palace and then the unexcavated ball court on your left. This group includes five buildings in varying states of disrepair, of which the largest and best preserved is the Temple of the Count.

**Museum** The small but worthwhile museum includes fine stelae, hieroglyphs, and, especially noteworthy, the stucco fragments of handsome Mayan faces. There are also maps of the Mayan zone and of Palenque itself. The museum northeast of the ball court is open daily from late morning to late afternoon.

## Off the Beaten Track

Just 18 kilometers (11.2 miles) from Palenque is the waterfall of **Misol-Ha,** 2 kilometers (1.2 miles) to the right off Route 199; swimming is permitted in the pool formed by the 100-foot cascade. The falls of **Agua Azul** are another 22 kilometers (13.7 miles) toward Ocosingo (4 more kilometers—2.5 miles—off the highway). The falls are much larger and faster than Misol-Ha, and swimming is permitted. These cataracts are surrounded by giant palm fronds and tropical flowers; monkeys and toucans frolic in the vicinity. There are restaurants, camping facilities, and rest rooms.

Between San Cristóbal and Palenque, on a dirt road running along the Jatate River in the midst of the steamy jungle, is the archaeological site of **Toniná.** Currently under exploration, this site is closely linked to Palenque: Recent excavations indicate that the vanquished rulers of Palenque and Yaxchilán were brought here as prisoners for execution. To date, several ball courts and the main pyramid platform, taller than those of Tikal and Teotihuacán, have been uncovered. As one of the last major ceremonial centers to flourish before the Mayan decline in this area, the monumental architecture and noteworthy sculptures found here are rapidly adding to our knowledge of Mayan civilization. Toniná can be reached by following the dirt road from Ocosingo, off Route 199.

## Dining

Generally speaking, the food served in Palenque town is modest in both quality and price. On the other hand, most of the restaurants are open-air, which is where you want to be in this part of Mexico (except when it rains, and then the thatched roofs are welcome). Try **El Paraíso,** 2 kilometers (1.2 miles) from the ruins; **La Selva,** next door to the Hotel La Cañada, Merle Green 14; or the **Nututún Viva,** at the hotel of the same name. Don't expect to use credit cards.

## Lodging

For prices, *see* Lodging for San Cristóbal, *above*. Highly recommended lodgings are indicated by a star ★.

**Very Expensive** **Misión Palenque.** This new motel-style resort is the town's only luxury hotel. Located on the north side of town off Route 199, it has a free shuttle bus to the ruins. All rooms are air-conditioned and have a terrace, minibar, and phone. *Rancho San Martín de Porres, tel. 934/5–02–41 or 934/5–04–44, fax 934/5–03–00. 144 rooms. Facilities: restaurant/bar, pool, tennis court. AE, DC, MC, V.*

**Expensive** **Chan Kah.** Four kilometers (2.5 miles) from the ruins in a para-
★ disiacal jungle setting, this property has a stone-lined pool, a resident spider monkey, aromatic jasmine bushes, and a stream flowing around the back. The restaurant is overpriced, and meals are accompanied by Muzak and movie soundtracks, but the 14 bungalows feature mahogany furnishings and have ceiling fans (surprisingly adequate, despite the humidity); bungalows 6 through 10 offer views of both the pool and the stream. *Km. 3 Carr. Ruinas 29960, tel. 934/5–11–00, fax 934/5–08–20. 38 units. Facilities: restaurant/bar, lagoon-style pool. MC, V.*

**Moderate** **Nututún Viva Palenque.** This property has 60 air-conditioned rooms, restaurant/bar, disco, natural pool, and trailer park. *Apdo. 74, Carretera Ocosingo Km. 3.5, 29960, tel. 934/5–01–00 or 934/5–01–61, fax 934/5–06–20. AE, DC, MC, V.*

## Excursions from Palenque

Because access is difficult, only the most devoted Mayan fans will attempt the trip to the ruins of **Bonampak** and **Yaxchilán** (Yas-che-**lan**), 183 and 133 kilometers (113.7 and 82.6 miles), respectively, southeast of Palenque. Bonampak is renowned for its vivid murals of ancient Mayan life, though they are sadly deteriorated. (The reproductions at the archaeological museums in Mexico City and Villahermosa are better.) Recent excavations at Yaxchilán, on the other hand, have uncovered captivating temples and carvings in a superb jungle setting.

Bonampak, a satellite of Yaxchilán, was built on the banks of the Lacanjá River during the 7th and 8th centuries and remained undiscovered until 1946. Explorer Jacques Soustelle called it "a pictorial encyclopedia of a Mayan city." Indeed, the scenes portrayed in the three rooms of the Templo de las Pinturas graphically recall subjects such as life at court and the prelude and aftermath of battle with unusual realism.

Yaxchilán, which means "place of green stones," is a contemporary of Bonampak. It is dominated by two acropolises containing a palace, temples with finely carved lintels, and great staircases leading to the banks of the Usumacinta (Guatemala is on the other side). Until very recently, the Lacandon, who live in the vicinity, made pilgrimages to this site in the heart of the jungle, leaving behind "god pots" (incense-filled ceramic bowls) in honor of ancient deities. They were particularly awed by the headless sculpture of Xachtun (Wa-sha-**tun**) at the entrance to the temple (called structure 33) and believe that the world will end when its head is replaced on its torso.

Yaxchilán was situated on the trade route between Palenque and Tikal; the site was recently threatened with destruction by plans for a huge dam to be built by Mexico and Guatemala. The plans have been put on hold due to lack of funds, though they may yet come to fruition. Meanwhile, ambitious highways under construction in the region are already changing the ecosystem and lifestyle. Yaxchilán in its present state is probably doomed, so you should see it now.

**Arriving and Departing** Both sites can be reached by making arrangements for a small chartered plane in Palenque or San Cristóbal. In San Cristóbal, contact **A.T.C.** (5 de Febrero 15, tel. 967/82–5–50 or 967/8–11–53). The six-hour, round-trip tour costs about $300 (possibly less, with a minimum of four people) and includes lunch. The same agency has a branch in Palenque (Allende, Esq. Av. Juárez, Local 6, tel. 934/5–02–10 or 934/5–03–56). The trip takes five hours and costs the same as the trip from San Cristóbal. Some trips add the Lacandon village of Lacanjá. (For other tours to the ruins, *see* San Cristóbal, *above*). A road is being built that will connect Yaxchilán with Bonampak. In any case, wear sturdy shoes, carry insect repellent, and protect yourself from mosquitoes, ticks, sandflies, and undergrowth.

# Lagunas de Montebello

East of San Cristóbal lies one of the least explored and most exotic regions of Chiapas: the selva lacandona. In this largely uninhabited area, a major drama is being played out that rarely makes the news in North America. Incursions of developers, land-hungry settlers, and refugees from neighboring Guatemala are transforming Mexico's last frontier, which for centuries has been the homeland of the Lacandones, a small tribe descended from the ancient Maya. This trip can be done in a day, as the lakes themselves are 155 kilometers (96.3 miles) or about 2½ hours by car from San Cristóbal. If you are driving during the rainy season, however, the trip may take longer. For extended exploration of the lakes, we suggest an overnight stay in Comitán. The itinerary can be covered by car, bus, or tour, but a car is highly preferable because of the freedom it allows for exploration on one's own.

Head south 35 kilometers (21.7 miles) on Route 190 to **Amatenango del Valle,** a small village known for its handsome, primitive pottery. By the side of the road, women sell ocher, black, and brown clay flowerpots and animal figurines that have been fired on open kilns. The rugged foothills and pine groves surrounding San Cristóbal subside into a low plain along the next stretch of the road; the mountains appear to have been sliced in two, revealing their rust-red innards, sad artifacts of the devastating erosion caused by the clearing of the forests. **Comitán** is at the halfway point to the lakes, and though the city has few attractions, it is one of the few places on the way to Guatemala that offer lodgings and restaurants. From the zócalo there are fine views of the hills. Comitán's tourist office, located on the ground floor of the Municipal Palace, facing the zócalo, is open Monday–Saturday 9–8:30, Sunday 9–2, tel. 963/2–23–03 through 963/2–23–07, ext. 138 or 139.

Many of the Mexicans who work at the few remaining Guatemalan refugee camps in Chiapas live in Comitán. Beginning in 1981, some 46,000 Guatemalan peasants fled a wave of political repression by crossing the border into ramshackle camps only to be hunted down by the Guatemalan army. Mexico eventually moved more than half of the refugees to safer, more distant camps, but many Guatemalans preferred to remain in Chiapas, and there are still camps near Comitán at Las Margaritas and La Trinitaria. Comitán, whose original Mayan name was Balún-Canán, or "Nine Stars," flourished early on as a major center linking the lowland temperate plains to the edge of the Mayan empire on the Pacific. Even today, it serves as the principal trading point for the Tzeltal Indians and such Guatemalan goods as sugarcane liquor and orchids. The present city was built by the Spaniards, but few traces of the colonial era remain. Notable exceptions are two churches, Santo Domingo de Guzmán and San Sebastián, in which part of Chiapas's struggle for independence from Spain took place.

The **Casa-Museo Dr. Belisario Domínguez,** former home of a martyr of the revolution, opened as a museum in 1985 and re-creates that turbulent era with an array of documents and photographs. *Av. Dr. Belisario Domínguez Sur 17. Admission: about 35¢. Open Tues.–Sat. 10–6:45, Sun. 9–12:45.*

The small, late-classic Mayan site of **Chincultik** will interest only hard-core archaeology buffs, although it has a lovely forest location, a view of the Montebello Lakes, and a large *cenote* (sacred well). From Comitán, continue south 15 kilometers (9.3 miles) on Route 190 until you see a very small turnoff for the lakes (marked only by a green-and-white sign depicting a tree) outside of La Trinitaria. After 39 kilometers (24.2 miles), there is a dirt road on the left that leads to the ruins, which are another 5 kilometers (3.1 miles) off the highway; a 10-minute hike is then required. The ruins, which are only partially restored, include a ball court, pyramid, cenote, and stelae. *Admission: about $2.75. Open daily 8–4.*

**Time Out**  At Km. 22 is the **Parador Museo** (no phone), a modest lodging with seven rooms and a restaurant. These are adequate, inexpensive accommodations.

❹ Ample signs and guardposts mark the entrance to the **Lagunas de Montebello** (Montebello Lakes), 9 kilometers (5.6 miles) away. Together, the 60-odd lakes and surrounding selva compose a 2,437-acre national park. A different color permeates each lake, whose waters glow with vivid emerald, turquoise, amethyst, azure, and steel-gray tints, caused by various oxides. Practically the only denizens of the more accessible part of the forest are the clamorous goldfinch, mockingbirds, and the rare quetzal bird. To the east, wild animals roam: pumas and jaguars, deer and bears. The serenity and majesty of the place, with its clusters of oak, pine, and sweet gum, recall the Alps or the lakes of Minnesota.

At the park entrance, the road forks. The left leads to the Lagunas Coloradas (Colored Lakes). At **Laguna Bosque Azul,** the last lake along that road, there are picnic tables, rest rooms, and, at the end of the road, a shabby but serviceable café. At Laguna Bosque Azul you may encounter José Alvarez, who runs 10-day walking tours into the jungle, including a visit to the Lacandon village of Lacanjá (near the ruins of Bonampak). José is a bit of a charlatan, but he knows the region well; if he is not there, other quasi-"native" guides are sure to have taken his place. The right fork at the park entrance continues along dirt roads for 14 kilometers (8.7 miles) before dwindling into a footpath. If you walk down the right fork, you will see some of the more beautiful lakes. The largest, **Tziscao,** is on the Guatemalan border and is the site of the Tziscao Lodge and the Hospedaje La Orquidia hostelries, both of which are dirt-cheap and very basic (no hot water), but there are food service, horses, and boats, and the fishing is excellent. Buses leave infrequently from Comitán (2 Av. Poniente Sur #4, tel. 963/2–10–44) to Laguna Bosque Azul and Tziscao. There is also colectivo service.

From Comitán, head north on Route 190 to San Cristóbal and continue west to Tuxtla Gutiérrez, the capital. The 85-kilometer (52.8-mile) drive from San Cristóbal to Tuxtla winds through densely wooded peaks and valleys. Indians by the roadside sell food, crafts, flowers, and fruits. You'll gradually descend onto vast plains punctuated by hills. At the bottom—Tuxtla is only 1,739 feet above sea level—the change to a temperate climate is striking. Just a few kilometers before Tuxtla is Chiapa de Corzo.

"All pink wash and palms and tropical fruit and old wounded churches and dusty desolation," Graham Greene remarked in a **⑤** rather romantic vein. **Chiapa de Corzo** was founded in 1528 by Diego de Mazariegos, who one month later fled the mosquitoes and transported all the settlers to San Cristóbal (then called Chiapa de los Españoles, to distinguish it from Chiapa de los Indios, as Chiapa de Corzo was originally known).

Chiapa is still pink, still dusty, and perhaps because of its climate, the people smile more than they do in the colder highlands. Life in this small town on the banks of the Grijalva revolves, inevitably, around the zócalo, lorded over by a bizarre 16th-century Mozarabic fountain modeled after Isabella's crown. The interior is decorated with stories of the Indians.

Chiapa's lacquerware museum, facing the plaza, contains a modest collection of delicately carved and painted *jícaras* (gourds). ("The sky is no more than an immense blue jícara, the beloved firmament in the form of a cosmic jícara," explains the *Popul Vuh*, a 16th-century chronicle of the Quiché Maya.) The lacquerware on display is both local and imported, coming from Michoacán, Guerrero, Chiapas, and Asia. The museum is open Tuesday–Saturday 9–2 and 4–6, Sunday 9–1. A workshop behind the museum is open during the week and generally keeps the same hours as the museum.

**Time Out** Stop for lunch or refreshments at the **Jardines de Chiapa** (Portal Oriente s/n) on the opposite side of the square from the museum. Occupying a lovely patio setting, this restaurant serves an excellent and inexpensive variety of regional cuisines, including *chipilín con bolita* (a soup made with balls of ground corn paste cooked in a creamy herbal sauce and topped with Chiapas's famous cheese), *tasajo* (sun-dried beef served with squash-seed sauce), and *butifarra* (minced pork and beef sausage).

Several handicraft shops line the square, selling huaraches, ceramics, lacquerware, masks, and regional costumes. Just outside of town, behind the Nestlé plant, are some nearly unnoticeable Maya-Olmec ruins dating from 1450 BC.

**❻** The next stop—18 kilometers (11.2 miles) north of Tuxtla—is the **Sumidero Canyon**, whose gaping, almost vertical walls descend 4,000 feet for some 15 kilometers (9.3 miles). North Americans may compare it with the Grand Canyon; it was formed about 12 million years ago, and the Grijalva River slices through it, erupting in waterfalls and coursing through caves. Ducks, pelicans, herons, raccoons, iguanas, and butterflies live at the base, which can be viewed either from five lookout points off the highway or by boat (a two- to three-hour trip). As you visit the canyon, think about the fate of the Chiapa Indians, who jumped into it rather than face slavery at the hands of the Spaniards. Boat trips (about $5 for colectivo service) depart daily between 7 AM and 4 PM from the tiny island of Cahuaré and the dock at Chiapa de Corzo, also stopping at the hydroelectric dam in Chicoasen. You can rent your own boat for about $50.

# Tuxtla Gutiérrez

Tuxtla Gutiérrez is the thriving capital city of the state of Chiapas. In 1939 Graham Greene characterized it as "not a place for foreigners—the new ugly capital of Chiapas, without attractions . . . It is like an unnecessary postscript to Chiapas, which should be all wild mountain and old churches and swallowed ruins and the Indians plodding by." That bleak description is even truer today. Nonetheless, Tuxtla Gutiérrez is a city through which most visitors to Chiapas will pass, and it is of vital economic and political importance. It is the state's transportation hub, and it does have what is probably the most exciting zoo in Latin America, along with a comprehensive archaeology museum. It is also convenient for its proximity to Chiapa de Corzo and the Sumidero Canyon, which have little in the way of accommodations.

The state capital since 1892, Tuxtla's first name derives from the Nahuatl word *tochtlan*, meaning "abundance of rabbits." Its second name, Gutiérrez, honors Joaquín Miguel Gutiérrez, who fought for the state's independence and incorporation into Mexico.

## Arriving and Departing

**By Plane** **Mexicana** flies nonstop to Mexico City from the Tuxtla airport, which is in the town of Ocozocoautla, 22 kilometers (13.7 miles) west. Mexicana's ticket office is located at Av. Central Ote 1520, tel. 961/2–00–21 or 961/2–54–02, fax 961/2–16–92. **Aviacsa** also operates daily flights to Mexico City (Tuxtla, tel. 961/2–80–81 or 961/2–68–80, fax 961/3–78–12; Mexico City, tel. 5/559–1955).

**By Car** Route 190 goes from San Cristóbal to Tuxtla and west into Oaxaca. If you are skipping Palenque, an alternative road to or from Villahermosa is via Pichucalco, on Route 195. It's in excellent condition and the scenery en route is gorgeous.

**By Bus** Regular first- and second-class bus service runs between Tuxtla and Oaxaca, Villahermosa, Tapachula, and Mérida. For Palenque, you must transfer in Villahermosa or San Cristóbal.

## Exploring

**❼** The highway into town is endless and honky-tonk. **Tuxtla** (population 525,000) does not have many conveniences for tourists, and it can be difficult to get your bearings. If you stay on the main drag you will run smack into the zócalo, known locally as the *parque central*, which is fronted by huge government buildings. Marimba music is played here. The Tuxtla tourist office is on the mezzanine of Edificio Plaza de las Instituciones (Blvd. Dr. Belisario Domínguez 950, tel. 961/2–55–09 or 961/2–45–35). It is open weekdays 8 AM–9 PM.

Only the most obstinate animal-hater would fail to be captivated by the free-roaming inmates of the **Tuxtla Zoomat,** all native Chiapans. The 100-plus species on display include black widows, jaguars, marsupials, iguanas, quetzal birds, boa constrictors, tapirs, eagles, and monkeys. *Southeast of town off Libramiento Sur. Admission free but a donation is appreciated. Open Tues.–Sun. 8–6.*

Amateur archaeologists and botanists should head for **Parque Madero,** which includes the Regional Museum of Chiapas, (open Tues.–Sun. 9–4), the Botanical Garden (open Tues.–Sun. 8–6), and the orchid house (open Tues.–Sun. 10–1). One of the largest collections of Mayan artifacts worldwide is on the ground floor of the museum, an innovative structure of glass, brick, and marble. On the upper floor are displays of colonial pieces and regional handicrafts and costumes. *Northeast of downtown, between 5a Av. Norte and 11a Calle Oriente. Admission: approx. $3.50.*

A good selection of regional handicrafts is on sale in the **Casa de las Artesenias,** a government-run shop on the ground floor of the state tourism office (Blvd. Dr. Belisario Domínguez 950). Amber from Chiapas and gold filigree jewelry, lacquerware, and leather are among the local specialties.

## Dining

For price categories, *see* Dining for San Cristóbal, *above.* Highly recommended restaurants are indicated by a star ★.

**Moderate** **La Selva.** Specialties from Chiapas top a menu that satisfies multiple tastes with a broad sampling of international dishes. A tropical atmosphere sizzles with marimba music. *Belisario Dominguez 1360, tel. 961/5–02–03.*

**Inexpensive** **Cafeteria San Marcos.** For the youthful crowd, this is a popular place on weekends for light meals and mingling. *Plaza Crystal 2-D, tel. 961/3–52–02.*

★ **Las Pichanchas.** This restaurant features an outstanding variety of regional dishes, as well as live marimba music and weekly folkloric dances. *Central Oriente 837, tel. 961/2–53–51. AE, MC, V.*

## Lodging

Lodgings are plentiful in Tuxtla. For prices, *see* Lodging for San Cristóbal, *above*. Highly recommended lodgings are indicated by a star ★.

**Very Expensive**
★

**Hotel Flamboyant.** If you want something splashy and American style, try one of the 118 guest rooms in this luxury hotel. All rooms are air-conditioned and have TVs. Capacious is the byword: the pool is huge, and so are the public areas. The only disadvantage is the location—a 10-minute drive west of town. *Blvd. Dr. Belisario Domínguez Km. 1081, 29000; tel. 961/5-08-88 or 961/5-09-99, fax 961/5-00-87. Facilities: restaurant, bar, disco, gardens, travel agency, car rental, parking. AE, MC, V.*

**Expensive**

**Bonampak.** A fine hotel that has just been completely and tastefully redone, Bonampak has spacious rooms and an enormous pool set in lush gardens. The cafeteria and restaurant have a well-deserved reputation for good regional cooking, steaks, and soups. *Blvd. Dr. Belisario Domínguez 180, 29030, tel. 961/3-20-50, fax 961/2-77-37. 70 rooms. Facilities: restaurant, cafeteria, bar, gardens, tennis, pool, cable TV, travel agency, car rental, beauty shop. AE, MC, V.*

**Moderate**

**Gran Hotel Humberto.** Much closer to the main square is the Gran Hotel Humberto, which has 112 air-conditioned rooms, all with TVs. *Central Poniente 180; tel. 961/2-20-80 or 961/2-20-44, fax 961/2-97-71. Facilities: restaurant, cabaret, parking. AE, MC, V.*

# 12 Huasteca Country

By Jim Budd

Mexico City
bureau chief for
the Reed Travel
Group, Jim Budd
is the former
editor of The News
of Mexico City and
the Spanish-
language business
magazine
Expansion. He has
concentrated on
travel writing for
nearly 20 years.

Updated by
Eleanor S. Morris

Huasteca Country is not Mexico at its best. The Gulf Coast from the Rio Grande down to Veracruz and inland to the eastern Sierra Madre is not the Mexico touted in glossy color brochures and full-page magazine ads. Each of the three border towns—Nuevo Laredo, Reynosa, and Matamoros—seems more industrial and commercial than the next. However, with the new four-lane toll road from Nuevo Laredo and Reynosa to Monterrey completed, as well as stretches of other highways, the country is on its way to bringing major highways up to U.S. standards. The number of customs and immigration inspections has lessened, and most roadblocks have been discontinued.

The flip side of the Huasteca story is appreciated by day-trippers from Texas, who pop across the border to pick up excellent handicrafts in Nuevo Laredo and Matamoros, sample authentic Mexican dishes, and perhaps take in a bullfight—all at a bargain. Those seeking an urban respite make the three-hour drive from the border to Monterrey, an attractive cosmopolitan city founded on steel and beer. Sportsmen are lured by magnificent hunting and fishing at Lake Vicente Guerrero, not far from Ciudad Victoria. And the archaeologically curious visit the spectacular pyramid and stone carvings of El Tajín, one of Mexico's most fascinating and least-visited ruins.

The Huastecs, linguistically related to the Maya, have inhabited the region for the past 3,000 years. They developed a fairly advanced pre-Hispanic civilization, though they were scorned by the Aztecs for their immoral ways. It seems the Huastecs were more interested in worshiping the goddess of fertility and carnal pleasures than in building monuments. The lack of Huastecan ruins is more than compensated for by El Tajín, in the state of Veracruz, one of the premier archaeological zones in Mexico. It was built by the Totonacs, vassals of the Aztecs, and contains the 60-foot Pyramid of the Niches, several ball courts, and carvings of human sacrifice. El Tajín was apparently abandoned around the year AD 1100, but the Totonacs remained a tribe to be reckoned with: They were the people who greeted Cortés when he landed in Veracruz.

Many Texans weekend in Monterrey, Mexico's third-largest city and the area's cultural highlight. They come for the Alfa Cultural Center, museums of history and art, the Mexican Baseball Hall of Fame, the five-star hotels, restaurants, and shopping required of a major commercial center. Huasteca Country has its share of natural attractions, such as the dramatic Barranca de Huasteca (Huasteca Canyon) and Grutas García, caves with an underground lake and a stalactite and stalagmite forest both of which lie west of Monterrey. Cola de Caballo (Horsetail Falls), south of the city, sits amid wooded parkland right off Mexico 85.

A growing number of vacationers head to Huasteca Country, especially on coach tours down the coast, to visit only Tampico, but they occasionally travel as far as Veracruz. With unleaded gasoline becoming easier to find in Mexico, more motorists are venturing into Huasteca Country, the appeal being that they're able to go where and when they want and stay for as long as they choose.

# Essential Information

## Important Addresses and Numbers

**Tourist Information**  Ironically, the best information about Mexico is found in Texas border towns, especially at places that sell Mexican automobile insurance, which is mandatory in Mexico. This list will give you a head start in searching out such sources: **Sanborn's Viva Tours,** 2015 S. 10th St., McAllen, tel. 210/682–9872 or 800/395–8482; **Sanborn's Mexican Insurance,** 2009 S. 10th St., McAllen, tel. 210/686–0711; **Bravo Insurance,** 2212 Santa Ursula, Laredo, tel. 210/722–0931; **Sanborn's International Travel** (tourist information and insurance), 2235 Boca Chica Blvd., Brownsville, tel. 210/542–7222.

*Border Towns*  The Tamaulipas State Tourist Authority maintains information offices at Mexican customs and immigration posts in **Nuevo Laredo** (tel. 871/2–0104), in **Reynosa** (tel. 892/2–1189), and in **Matamoros** (tel. 891/2–3630). All are open weekdays, usually 9–3. The Matamoros telephone operates 24 hours a day.

*Monterrey*  The main information center (Infotur) of the Nuevo Leon State Tourism Office is at Zaragoza and Matamoros on the Gran Plaza (tel. 83/45–08–70, 83/45–09–02, or 800/235–2438). It is open daily 10–5 (closed Jan. 1, May 1, Sept. 16, Nov. 20, and Dec. 25). Recorded information in English and Spanish can be heard by dialing 83/42–21–66. For toll-free information, call 800/235–2430.

*Tampico*  The local tourism office is well hidden one flight up over Banco Mercantile del Norte at Olmos Altos and Carranza (tel. 12/12–26–68 and 12/12–00–07), but it has so little information that the walk up is rarely worth the effort. It is closed Monday and Friday and open 8–8 the rest of the week.

*Veracruz*  The **Direccion de Turismo** is located on Bajos Palacio Municipal on the east side of the zócalo (tel. 29/32–19–99 or 29/32–31–31, ext. 1500).

The federal government also maintains tourism offices in **Tamaulipas** (for Nuevo Laredo, Reynosa, Matamoros, and Tampico): Oaxaca 360 Altos, Col. Rodriguez, Reynosa, tel. 892/2–46–60 or 892/2–24–49; **Nuevo Leon:** Av. Loma Grande and San Francisco, Monterrey, tel. 83/44–43–43, 40–10–80, or 44–11–69; and **Veracruz:** Esq. (corner) Zaragoza and Prima Verdad, tel. 29/7–3030 or 7–3796.

**U.S. Consulates**  **Matamoros** (Primera at Azalias, tel. 891/6–7270); **Nuevo Laredo** (Allende 3330, tel. 871/4–0512); **Monterrey** (Constitución 411 Poniente, tel. 83/43–06–50 and 83/45–21–20); and **Veracruz** (Juárez 110, tel. 29/31–01–42).

**Emergencies**  **Matamoros: Police:** González and Calle Venteuno, tel. 891/2–
*Border Towns*  0732 and 891/2–03–22; **Cruz Roja (Red Cross) Hospital:** Garcia and L. Caballero, tel. 891/2–00–44 and 891/6–65–62. **Nuevo Laredo: Police:** Maclovio Herréa and Ocampo, tel. 871/2–2146; **San José Hospital:** Comonfort and Independencia, tel. 871/4–9506. **Reynosa: Police:** Morales between Veracruz and Nayarit, tel. 891/2–0008; **Cruz Roja (Red Cross) Hospital:** Morelos and Argentina, tel. 83/2–13–14 or 83/2–62–50.

*Monterrey* **Police:** Gonzalitos and Lincoln, tel. 83/43–25–76; **Cruz Roja (Red Cross) Hospital:** Universidad and Camelo, tel. 83/75–12–12.

*Tampico* **Police:** Mendez and Sor Juana Inés de la Cruz, tel. 12/12–11–57; **Cruz Roja (Red Cross) Hospital:** Tamaulipas and Gochicoa, tel. 12/12–13–33.

*Veracruz* **Police:** Playa Linda 222, tel. 29/38–06–64 or 29/38–06–93. **Hospital Regional de Veracruz:** 20th Nov. s/n, tel. 29/32–27–05 or 29/32–36–90, and **Cruz Roja (Red Cross),** tel. 29/37–55–00.

## Arriving and Departing by Plane

**Airports and Airlines** All major cities in Huasteca Country are served either by **Aeroméxico** (tel. 800/AEROMEX), **Mexicana** (tel. 800/531–7921), **Aeromonterrey** (reservations handled in the U.S. by Mexicana, tel. 800/531–7921; in Monterrey, tel. 83/40–55–11), and **Aerolitoral** (reservations handled in the U.S. by Aeroméxico, tel. 800/AEROMEX; in Monterrey 83/33–76–06, 83/33–74–17, or 83/33–74–56; elsewhere in Mexico 91/800–36–202).

*Border Towns* From Mexico City, Aeroméxico has service to Matamoros and Reynosa; Mexicana has service to Nuevo Laredo.

*Monterrey* **Mexicana** has flights from New York, San Antonio, and San Francisco. **Aeroméxico** has service from Houston, New Orleans, Miami, New York, San Diego, and Los Angeles. **Continental** (tel. 800/525–0280) has nonstop flights from Houston, and **American** (tel. 800/433–7300) flies to Monterrey from Dallas. **Aerolitoral** has service from McAllen and San Antonio, Texas.

*Tampico* **Mexicana** has flights from San Antonio, San Francisco, Los Angeles, and San Jose. **Aerolitoral** has flights from San Antonio and McAllen, Texas.

*Veracruz* **Mexicana** operates flights from San Antonio, San Francisco, Los Angeles, San Jose, and New York. **Aerolitoral** flies to Veracruz from McAllen and San Antonio, Texas.

## Arriving and Departing by Car, Train, and Bus

**By Car** With unleaded gasoline now more widely available, an increasing number of American motorists are exploring Mexican highways. A car trip is not without its red tape, however. Upon arriving at the 25-mile checkpoint, drivers must prove automobile ownership by presenting their vehicle registration and proof of both U.S. and Mexican insurance, as well as leave a credit-card imprint (canceled upon return) or post a bond. If there is a lien on the vehicle, written permission to take the car into Mexico must be provided. The vehicle must be registered in the driver's name. Car-rental agencies rarely permit their vehicles to be taken into Mexico. Although Mexico is busy building improved highways, driving at night should be avoided as many of the two-lane roads do not have shoulders; Mexico is also still an open-range country where animals meander back and forth across the roads. The old Pan-American Highway, Mexico 85 (now under construction as a four-lane toll road), leads from Laredo to Monterrey and on to Mexico City via Ciudad Victoria and Pachuca. From Monterrey, Mexico 57 is the preferred way to reach Mexico City, but it does not pass through what is called the Huasteca Country. From Matamoros (across from Brownsville), Mexico 180 runs down the Gulf Coast to Tampico, Veracruz, and beyond. A turnoff on Mexico 101 leads to the hunting and fishing camps at Lake Vicente Guerrero. Mexico 97 leads from Reynosa (McAllen) into Mexico 101.

Distances are deceiving in this part of Mexico because of the Sierra Madre Oriente. It generally takes 3 hours to drive from the border to Monterrey; from Monterrey to Cuidad Victoria is another 4 hours; from Cuidad Victoria to Pachuca (a mountainous route with hairpin turns) takes approximately 6 hours; and from Pachuca to Mexico City is about 2 hours.

*Border Towns*   Downtown Nuevo Laredo is reached by International Bridge 1, the point of entry required for vehicles heading to the interior. The New Bridge is the best route from downtown Brownsville to downtown Matamoros. U.S. 281 leads down to Hidalgo, Texas, and the bridge crossing into Reynosa.

*Monterrey*   Mexico's third-largest city is about 242 kilometers (150 miles) south of Nuevo Laredo on Mexico 85; it can also be reached from Matamoros and Reynosa on Mexico 40.

*Tampico*   The port is roughly a seven-hour drive from Matamoros on Mexico 180, or eight hours from Monterrey via Mexico 84.

*Veracruz*   The city can be reached within about eight hours by traveling south from Tampico via Mexico 180, or within six hours from Mexico City via Mexico 150.

## By Train

For trains between Matamoros and Reynosa, Monterrey, and Mexico City, contact Mr. Juan Alberto Peña Garcia (Calle Hidalgo between 9 and 10 s/n, Col. Centro, Matamoros, Tamps., tel. 891/667–06). For other train service to Huasteca Country, contact Mexico by Rail (800/228–3225). At present there is service from Nuevo Laredo to Monterrey daily and from Monterrey to Mexico City, with a daily train from Mexico City to Veracruz. For more information about travel from Mexico City, contact the Commercial Passenger Department at National Railways of Mexico (Buenavista Grand Central Station, 06358 Mexico D.F., tel. 52/547–86–55).

## By Bus

Huasteca Country is well connected by buses, and fares are low. Information on Mexican bus service is available from terminals in Laredo (tel. 210/723–4324), McAllen (Valley Transit, tel. 210/686–5479), and Brownsville (tel. 210/546–7171). There is first-class bus service between Nuevo Laredo and Monterrey, to connect with *El Tamaulipeco* to Mexico City (tel. 800/228–3225 in Texas; tel. 905/546–7171 in Mexico City). **Sanborn's Viva Tours** (2015 S. 10th St., McAllen, Texas, tel. 800/395–VIVA or 512/682–9872) runs daily tours to Monterrey and one weekly tour through Tampico to Veracruz.

## Guided Tours

Several U.S. tour operators, including **Sanborn's Viva Tours** (tel. 210/682–9872 and 800/395–VIVA), run shopping and sightseeing tours to the border towns and coach excursions into the interior of Huasteca Country. **Viva** has also inaugurated a four-day tour to El Tajín. **Viajes Pozo** (tel. 12/13–58–71 or 12/12–01–50) in Tampico, **Viajes Turismo** (tel. 29/31–01–98 or 29/31–01–99) in Veracruz, and **Servicios Turísticos** (tel. 83/76–21–41, 83/52–13–55, or 83/52–13–56) in Monterrey provide sightseeing excursions in their respective areas.

# Exploring

*Numbers in the margin correspond to points of interest on the Huasteca Country map.*

**❶** Two bridges connect **Nuevo Laredo** with Laredo, Texas. However, tourists must use International Bridge 1, the only one with facilities for clearing people and vehicles for travel to the interior of Mexico. The newer Juárez Lincoln Bridge leading into I–35 is obligatory for the trip back across the border. For brief excursions across the border, consider leaving your car in Laredo and walking over. This eliminates the hassle of purchasing Mexican auto insurance as well as the long wait—often a half hour or more—to bring a car back into the United States.

Nuevo Laredo is the major port of entry for trucks and trains heading into Mexico and also a manufacturing center for U.S. firms that take advantage of cheap Mexican labor. It in no way resembles a beautiful city and has no historical sights. Some of the shops, however, are quite attractive, and there are a few good restaurants in town. It's the shopping and dining that bring Americans to Nuevo Laredo. Avenida Guerrero, which runs from the border and eventually becomes Reforma, is the main shopping street. The Nuevo Laredo racetrack closed in 1988, and while there are promises of a reopening soon, don't bet on it. Occasionally there are bullfights on Sundays.

**❷** **Reynosa,** some 242 kilometers (150 miles) southeast of Laredo, is an oil-refining and gas-processing center of little charm. There are a few curio shops and a couple of bars and restaurants clustered around the **Zona Rosa** (Pink Zone) tourist district. Beyond lies a very typical Mexican town complete with cathedral and central square, the **Plaza Principal.**

The cathedral on the square is of some interest, too: The original colonial church has been joined like a Siamese twin to an ultramodern arched and stained-glass windowed, newer addition. There are also an inordinate number of dentists in this area (Texans save money by having their teeth fixed south of the Rio Grande). The main part of the city, around Plaza Principal, is nearly 20 blocks from the International Bridge. Hidalgo Street itself, leading from the plaza, is a colorful pedestrian mall of shops and street vendors.

**❸** While **Matamoros**—across from Brownsville, Texas (the southernmost point in the continental United States)—has much more to offer than Reynosa, it scarcely glitters. Some 20 years ago, Avenida Alvaro Obregón, which leads from the main bridge, was spruced up to "dignify" the Mexican side of the border, but the area has not been maintained and is decidedly shabby. Nonetheless, this is where you'll find some of the best shops, restaurants, accommodations, and the local museum. In fact, the **Casa Mata Museum** in the remains of old Fort Mata, whose stone walls, turrets, and cannon are a legacy from the

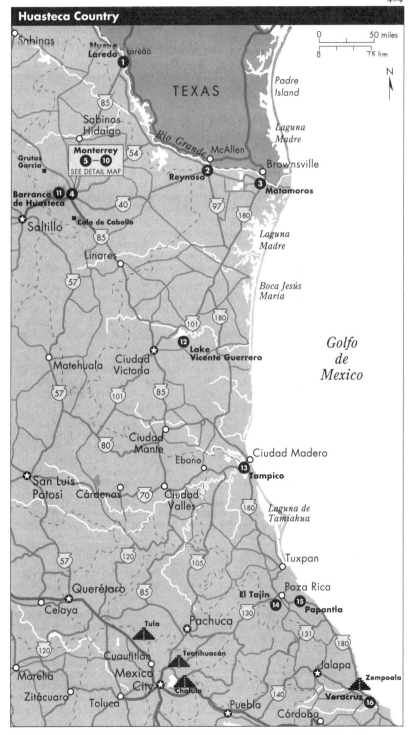

# Huasteca Country

TEXAS

Padre Island

*Laguna Madre*

*Rio Grande*

Sabinas

Nuevo Laredo / Laredo ❶

⑧⑤ Sabinas Hidalgo

McAllen

Brownsville

Monterrey
⑤ — ⑩
SEE DETAIL MAP

❷ Reynosa

❸ Matamoros

Grutas García

❶❶ ❹ Barranca de Huasteca

Cola de Caballo

Saltillo ✪

*Laguna Madre*

Linares

*Boca Jesús Maria*

*Golfo de Mexico*

Matehuala

Ciudad Victoria ✪

❶❷ Lake Vicente Guerrero

Ciudad Mante

Ebano

Ciudad Madero

❶❸ Tampico

San Luis Potosí ✪

Cárdenas

Ciudad Valles

*Laguna de Tamiahua*

Querétaro ✪

Tuxpan

Poza Rica

El Tajín ❶❹ ❶❺ Papantla

Celaya

Tula 🔺

Pachuca ✪

Cuautitlán

Teotihuacán 🔺

Jalapa ✪

Morelia

Mexico City ✪

Cholula 🔺

Zempoala 🔺

Veracruz ❶❻

Zitácuaro

Toluca

Puebla

Córdoba

0 — 50 miles
0 — 75 km

N

city's turbulent past, will hold special interest for local history buffs. *Calle Cuba and Lauro Villar. No phone. Admission free. Open Wed.–Mon. 9:30–5:30.*

Matamoros, the most historic of the border towns, dates from the 18th century. It is named H. Matamoros, or Heroic Matamoros, for one of the many rebellious priests who was executed by the Spaniards during the War of Independence (1810–1821). The first major battle of the Mexican-American War was fought here when guns in Matamoros began shelling Fort Brown on the north side of the river. Shortly afterward, troops of Zachary Taylor occupied Matamoros and began their march south. During the U.S. Civil War, nearby Bagdad became a major port for Confederate blockade runners. A wild and wicked place, Bagdad was destroyed by a hurricane a century ago; treasure hunters often discover bits and pieces of it among the dunes on the beach. Today Matamoros is the commercial center of a rich agricultural area and a manufacturing center for Mexico's in-bond industry.

❹ Mexico's third-largest city, **Monterrey** is home to some 3 million people who claim to be the hardest-working in Mexico. The capital of Nuevo León state, this is an industrial center, a brewer of beer and forger of steel, with nothing in the way of a laid-back lifestyle. Still, it is a favorite with weekenders and "winter Texans" from the Rio Grande Valley who find Monterrey so near—a three-hour drive from the border or a short flight from Dallas, Houston, or San Antonio—and yet so foreign. The top hotels are clustered close together downtown, and several streets, including Avenida Morelos—the main drag—are now pedestrian malls.

*Numbers in the margin correspond to points of interest on the Monterrey map.*

❺ The impressive **Gran Plaza,** which covers 100 acres and was completed in 1985 as part of an urban renewal scheme, is within walking distance of downtown hotels. The plaza extends from
❻ the new and modernistic **Palacio Municipal** (City Hall) several blocks past the cathedral, the old City Hall, and the Legislative
❼ Palace to the neoclassical **Palacio de Gobierno** (State Palace). Towering above it is a concrete slab topped by the Light of Commerce, a laser beam that flashes from 8 to 11 PM nightly. Handsome Saddle Mountain and the craggy Sierra Madre provide a majestic backdrop.

Gran Plaza now has the brand-new **Museum of Contemporary Art** to brag about as well. Its purpose is to promote the visual arts of Mexico and Latin America. *Gran Plaza, corner of Zuazua and Ocampo, tel. 83/42–4820 or 83/42–4830. Admission: about $3.35, free on Wed. Open Tues., Thurs., Fri., Sat. 11–7; Wed., Sun. 11–9; closed Mon.*

Monterrey dates from 1596, although for the first couple of centuries it was little more than an outpost. Construction of the cathedral—on the Gran Plaza a block or so from Palacio Municipal—began in 1600 but took some 250 years to finish. The
❽ **Obispado** (Bishop's House) is the only landmark to be completed in the colonial era (1788). About a mile from the city center, along Avenida Padre Mier and built on a hilltop as a home for retired prelates, the Obispado was used as a fort during the Mexican-American War (1847), the French Intervention (1862), and again during the Mexican Revolution (1915). Today

456

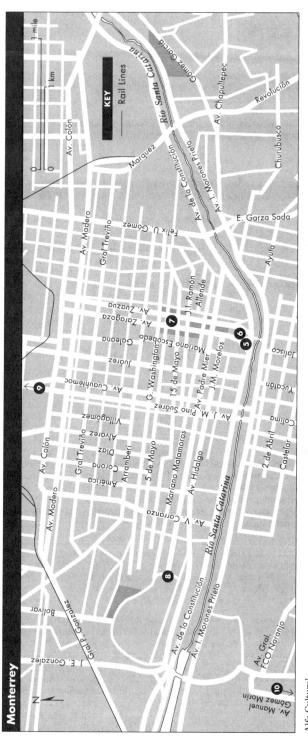

**Monterrey**

KEY
— Rail Lines

Alfa Cultural
Center, **10**
Gran Plaza, **5**
Mexican Baseball Hall
of Fame, **9**
Obispado, **8**
Palacio de Gobierno, **7**
Palacio Municipal, **6**

it is the **Regional Museum of Nuevo León,** its exhibits focusing on the history of the area, but the major appeal is the splendid view it provides of Monterrey. *Small admission fee. Open Tues.–Fri. 10–1 and 3–6; Sat., Sun. 10–5.*

In recent years, Mexican beer has taken the world by storm. Monterrey is where all this started when the Cuauhtémoc Brewery opened a century ago. Today the brewery complex includes the **Mexican Baseball Hall of Fame,** a sports museum, an art gallery, and a beer garden with free beer. *Av. Universidad 2202, tel. 83/72–48–94. Admission free. Open Tues.–Sun. 9:30–9. Brewery tours Mon.–Fri. 9–1 and 3–6, but call (tel. 83/75–22–00) to confirm.*

The brewery spawned a glass factory for bottles, a steel mill for caps, a carton factory, and eventually several industrial conglomerates, one of which, Alfa, gave Monterrey the **Alfa Cultural Center,** probably the best museum of science and technology in the country. The museum has many hands-on exhibits and an IMAX theater. Free buses to the museum run from downtown Alameda every half hour, returning on the hour from the museum. *Av. Gómez Morín at Roberto Garza Sada, tel. 83/78–35–10. Admission: about $3.50. Open Tues.–Fri. 3–9; Sat. 2–9; Sun. 12–9; closed Mon.*

*Numbers in the margin correspond to points of interest on the Huasteca Country map.*

Mexico 40 leads to scenic **Barranca de Huasteca** (Huasteca Canyon) in the western suburb of Santa Caterina. The canyon is about 2 miles down a paved road to the south of the village. Although the road is rocky and unpaved, the drive through the 1,000-foot-deep canyon is spectacular. **The Grutas García** (Garcia Caves) are farther west on 40, about 40 kilometers (25 miles) from downtown Monterrey. A swaying funicular leads to the caves, where guides lead the way through a mile of underground grottoes. This site is far less commercialized than are similar attractions north of the border. *Funicular cost is approximately $1; admission to caves approximately $6.25 adults, $4 children. Open daily 9–5.*

From Monterrey the Pan-American Highway, Mexico 85, runs south through Huasteca Country to Ciudad Victoria, capital of Tamaulipas state. This is the route to the man-made **Lake Vicente Guerrero,** a favorite with American bass fishermen year-round and, during the winter months, an excellent place to hunt duck and white-wing dove. Several camps in the area, such as El Tejon and El Sargento lodges, cater to American sportsmen. For information, contact Sunbelt Hunting and Fishing (Box 3009, Brownsville, TX 78520, tel. 210/546–9101 or 800/876–4868, fax 210/544–4731).

About 35 kilometers (20 miles) south of Monterrey on Mexico 85 is **Cola de Caballo** (Horsetail Falls), a magnificent waterfall park 4 miles off the highway at the small town of El Cercado.

Highway 40 continues toward the coast and to **Tampico,** a picturesque if raffish port adjoining Ciudad Madero, an oil-refining center. Because of its relative proximity to the border, Tampico gets a smattering of tourists and is a fascinating place in which to wander around for a spell. Plaza Libertad, near the harbor, is shaggy and unkempt—very much the tropical waterfront. A block away is the regal Plaza de Armas, with its majestic City Hall guarded by towering palms. The cathedral here, started in 1823, was completed with funds donated by Edward L. Doheny, an oil magnate implicated in the Teapot Dome scandal of the 1920s. Oil made Tampico what it is today. Shortly after the conquest, the Franciscans established a mission in the area near a Huastec fishing village, but the settlement was constantly battered by hurricanes and pirate attacks. In 1828 the Spaniards attempted to reconquer then-independent Mexico by landing troops at Tampico, but they were soundly defeated. With later invasions by the Americans and then the French, the port languished until oil was discovered in the region at the turn of the 20th century. The British and Americans developed the industry until a strike in 1938 led to its nationalization. Petroleum helped Tampico prosper but ruined the area for tourism. Río Pánuco is so polluted that it no longer attracts tarpon fishermen, although the big ocean freighters are a sight to see. Except for Mexicana flights from Texas and California, Tampico airport now handles only regional flights, and the hotel chains have returned their properties to local owners.

**14** The pyramids and temples at **El Tajín** compose the only major archaeological site in Huasteca Country. The center was built by the Totonacs, the people who met Cortés when he landed at Veracruz. El Tajín, being remote, is perhaps the least visited of the major archaeological sites in Mexico, but it is very much worth seeing even if you have to be your own guide. Much of the site remains unexcavated; the largest and most famous structure at El Tajín is the Pyramid of the Niches. Consisting of six levels into which 365 altars are carved, the pyramid towers some 60 feet. It is generally believed that the niches contained small altars, but this has not been confirmed. For the past year, 300 workers have been busy excavating the site and constructing a tourist center.

By some accounts, El Tajín was the most influential center in Mexico 1,000 years ago. It was a source of cacao beans, which were used as money in pre-Hispanic times. And the sacred ball game, similar to soccer, that was played throughout Mesoamerica is said to have originated here. In this game, players used a hard rubber ball that could not be touched with the hands. Two ball courts at El Tajín that have been fairly well restored show carvings of players suited up in knee pads and body protectors. They also indicate that games ended with human sacrifice. *El Tajín is 13 km (8 mi) west of Papantla. Small admission and parking fees. Open Tues.–Sun. 9–6.*

**15** The city that is closest to the ruins at El Tajín is **Papantla,** the center of a vanilla-producing region and home of the Flying Indians, who perform their ancient ritual all over Mexico. The ceremony, which in preconquest times had religious significance, consists of five men, called *voladores* (flyers), who climb to a tiny platform atop a 100-foot pole. There four of the five tie to their ankles ropes that have been wound around the pole maypole style. While the untied performer plays a flute and beats a drum, the others hurl themselves from their perches and whirl gradually toward the ground as the ropes unwind. At the last moment they flip neatly to their feet on the ground. The gods surely are impressed.

**16** **Veracruz** is about an eight-hour drive south from Tampico. This was the first European city to be established on the American mainland, although the spot where Cortés supposedly landed is about 50 kilometers (30 miles) north. What is professed to be his home, a rustic compound now in a state of decay, is located on the northern edge of the city and is worth seeing if only for its crumbling, roofless masonry, taken over by clinging vines and massive tree roots. During the viceregal era, Veracruz was the only east-coast port permitted to operate in New Spain. As a result, it was frequently attacked by pirates. The great fort of San Juan de Ulúa, built shortly after the conquest, is a monument to that swashbuckling era. The fort was the last territory in Mexico to be held by the Spanish Royalists. After independence, it was used in unsuccessful attempts to fight off first the invading French, the Americans, then the French again and, in 1914, the Americans. It also served as a prison, but today it is a museum. *Reached via causeway from downtown Veracruz. Small admission fee. Open Tues.–Sun. 10–6.*

Also of interest is **Baluarte de Santiago,** a fortress and museum. It's all that's left of old city walls and was also built (in 1636) as a defense against pirates. *Rayon and Gomez Farias. Open Wed.–Mon. 10 AM–7 PM.*

Until a few decades ago, Veracruz was Mexico's premier seaside resort and the port of entry for most foreign visitors; travelers arrived by ship, then boarded a train to Mexico City, often looking wistfully back. Today relatively few foreigners find their way to Veracruz's beaches, and domestic vacationers are lured into the area by prices that are far lower than those found in Acapulco, Puerto Vallarta, or Cancún. The beaches begin on the southern edge of town and extend to Mocambo, about 7 kilometers (4 miles) farther. Beyond Mocambo is the fishing village of Boca del Río, where a little Atoyac river meets the sea and every other house seems to be a restaurant. The seafood is some of the best in Mexico. Most of these cafés feature live musical entertainment, but customers are expected to pay for the songs they order.

Veracruz itself is famed as a musical city, hometown of La Bamba and its own special brand of song played by lively trios outfitted all in white and slapping away at tiny guitars and portable harps. In the evening, mariachis entertain outside the sidewalk cafés around the main plaza. The port is a fun-loving but not particularly sophisticated town, enjoyed by those who care little about spending hours baking on the beach. The best time of all, for many, is *Carnaval,* Mexico's version of Mardi Gras. It takes place during the week before Ash Wednesday and is wild, merry, and far less self-conscious than the better-known celebrations in Rio or New Orleans. The biggest problem at such times is finding a room, but the local tourist office can usually come up with acceptable accommodations. The same is true during Christmas and Easter week, when all of Mexico goes on vacation and heads for the beach.

# Shopping

**Matamoros** The most appealing shops are on Calle Obregón, the street that leads from the border bridge to the center of town. **Barbara** (Obregón 37, tel. 891/6–54–56) has an attractive assortment of quality handicrafts, carved wood, home furnishings, and even good costume jewelry and imported cosmetics. **Garcia's** (Obregón 82, tel. 891/2–39–29, 891/3–18–33, or 891/3–44–04), across from the Hotel Residencial, and **The Drive Inn** (tel. 891/2–

0022), also near the hotel, are both restaurants with gift shops as big as their dining room and a nice selection of craft items.

**Matamoros Market,** downtown, is the place to haggle for bargains; you get what you pay for.

**Nuevo Laredo** International Bridge 1 leads into Avenida Guerrero and the more prestigious stores. Few have street numbers, but their signs are big. **Marti's** (tel. 871/8–37–56) has perhaps the best selection of quality crafts, with prices to match. **Galva's** (tel. 871/2–8348), a few blocks farther, has a wider variety when it comes to prices, and **Rafael de Mexico** (tel. 871/4–25–88), where Guerrero widens into Avenida Reforma, is the biggest and finest shop in town. In between there are countless garish outlets selling plaster matadors, giant sombreros, sunsets painted on black velvet, and the like. Most shops remain open until 8 PM.

**Reynosa** **Trevino's** (Calle Los Virreys, tel. 871/22–14–44) has a good selection of Mexican arts and crafts, sculpture, papier mâché, perfumes, liquors, and clothing, with a cocktail lounge in the rear.

**Monterrey** Top-quality shops center on Plaza Hidalgo, near the major hotels, with leather and cowboy boots the local specialties. **Sanborns,** just off Plaza Hidalgo, has an excellent selection of silver, onyx, and other Mexican craft items, as does **Casa de las Artisanias de Nuevo Leon** on the corner of Allende and Dr. Coss. The **Mercado Indio,** at Bolivar Norte 1150, is another favorite with souvenir hunters. Superb lead crystal is made in Monterrey by **Krystaluxus** at José María Vigil 400 (take a taxi from your hotel), although there are showrooms (and higher prices) in town. There are guided tours of the factory Monday–Saturday at 10:30.

**Veracruz** There are many seashells and dried and varnished frogs, iguanas, and armadillos heaped in stacks at the stands lining the waterfront, and at the Mercado on Insurgentes you'll find all sorts of assorted goods, including leather and jewelry. Independencia, the main shopping street, has little to interest tourists.

# Sports

**Reynosa** **Bullfights** are becoming increasingly rare, although tickets and transportation are available from Sanborn's Viva Tours (2015 S. 10th, McAllen, TX, tel. 210/682–9872 or 800/395–8482).

**Monterrey** **Bullfights** alternate among three different locations on Saturdays and Sundays at 4:30; call the tourism office (tel. 83/45–09–02 or 83/45–08–70) or check a local newspaper for information and admission fees. Hotel travel desks can provide tickets and transportation, as well as arrange visits to **charreadas** (Mexican rodeos), held most Sunday mornings. Hotels can arrange temporary memberships in one of the area's three **golf courses** but only on weekdays.

**Tampico** **Golf** can be played at the local country club on weekdays; local hotels can arrange temporary memberships. **Tarpon and snapper fishing** is popular at Chairel Lagoon, with boats and equipment available for rent. Lake Vicente Guerrero, near Ciudad Victoria, has some of the best **bass fishing** and **duck hunting** in the country, while some very good fishing can be found at La

Pesca on the Tamaulipas coast between Matamoros and Tampico east of Ciudad Victoria and Soto La Marina.

# Beaches

**Matamoros** About 30 kilometers (18 miles) from downtown Matamoros is **Playa Lauro Villar,** sometimes referred to by its old name, Playa Washington. Facilities are limited, though there are some good seafood shanties.

**Tampico** **Playa Miramar,** about 5 kilometers (3 miles) from town, is a favorite with locals. Facilities are limited, but many people enjoy its unspoiled charm. Public transportation is available from Tampico.

**Veracruz** The beach begins on the southern edge of the city at **Villa del Mar** but is at its best down toward **Mocambo,** about 7 kilometers (4 miles) from downtown Veracruz. Buses run out this way. Umbrellas and chairs are available for rent, and wandering vendors peddle beer and seafood snacks.

# Dining

One of the most attractive features of Huasteca Country is the extensive variety and the low cost, compared with other regions of Mexico. *Cabrito* (roast kid) and *huachinango* (red snapper) are found on many menus. With the exception of Monterrey's Residence, where a jacket and tie are necessary, restaurants are generally casual. Highly recommended restaurants are indicated by a star ★.

| Category | Cost* |
| --- | --- |
| Expensive | over $25 |
| Moderate | $15–$25 |
| Inexpensive | under $15 |

*per person, excluding drinks, service, and tax*

**Border Towns** **The Drive Inn.** In spite of the name, it's a formal restaurant
*Expensive* with crystal chandeliers, linen tablecloths, orchestra, and dance floor. Expect a romantic evening, and stick with steak and seafood specialties. *Avenida Hidalgo at Calle 6a, Matamoros, tel. 891/2–00–22. Jacket advised. No reservations. MC, V.*

★ **Winery** (La Vinteria). This Mexican version of a Continental wine bar serves such regional specialties as *tampiqueña* steak and *queso fundido* (melted cheese), often served in a bowl with *chorizo* (spicy sausage) to be spread on tortillas. It has the best selection of Mexican wines in town. *Calle Victoria 2926, Nuevo Laredo, tel. 871/2–0895. Dress: casual. No reservations. AE, DC, MC, V.*

*Moderate* **Cadillac.** Dating from the Prohibition era, this spot is a favorite with the Texas crowd—a hangout better known for its atmosphere than for its cuisine. *Ocampo at Belden, Nuevo Laredo, tel. 871/2–0015. Dress: informal. No reservations. AE, DC, MC, V.*

★ **Garcia's.** Recently relocated across from the Hotel Residencial, this is a romantic place for dancing and dining on lobster or

steak. *Calle Alvaro Obregón, Matamoros, tel. 891/2–3939, 891/ 3–1833, or 891/3–4404. Reservations advised. AE, DC, MC, V.*
**Mexico Tipico.** This establishment offers both indoor and outdoor patio dining, with mariachis coming in off the street to entertain diners. The patio has both open and covered dining and a waterfall. Specialties are *carne asada* (grilled meat) and *cabrito* (baby goat). True to its name, Mexico Tipico serves the typical Mexican plate of beef, chicken, or cheese enchiladas with rice and refried beans. *Guerrero 934, Nuevo Laredo, tel. 871/2–1525. Dress: casual. No reservations. MC, V.*
**Sam's.** Wild game and seafood are the specialties here. Sam's is frequented by Americans from the Rio Grande Valley in the winter and snowbirds from Minnesota. *Allende 990, Reynosa, tel. 892/2–0034 or 892/2–3434. Dress: informal. No reservations. MC, V.*

*Inexpensive* **Tupinamba.** Cabrito, a northern Mexican specialty, is served at this restaurant beside the plaza. There is also a piano bar. *Zaragoza 660 Ote., Reynosa, tel. 89/22–42–98. Dress: casual. No reservations. No credit cards.*

**Monterrey** **Luisiana.** Perhaps the most elegant dining room downtown,
*Expensive* this is a taste of how New Orleans is imagined in Mexico. There
★ are no Cajun specialties on the menu, but rattlesnake is occasionally served. The usual menu consists of steak and seafood dishes. *Plaza Hidalgo, tel. 83/43–15–61, 83/40–21–85, or 83/ 40–37–53. Jackets appreciated but not required. Reservations advised. AE, DC, MC, V.*
★ **Residence.** A clubby meeting place for the industrialists and executives who make Monterrey what it is, the menu here features both Mexican specialties and Continental dishes. *Degollado and Matamoros, tel. 83/45–54–18, 83/45–50–40, or 83/45–54–78. Jacket and tie appreciated. Lunch reservations advised. AE, DC, MC, V.*

*Moderate* **El Pastor.** Roast kid is the regional specialty in northeastern Mexico, and this is where Monterrey folk go to enjoy it. *Madero Poniente 1067, tel. 83/46–89–54. Dress: informal. No reservations. MC, V.*
**Sanborns.** Part of a national chain that is a Mexican institution, this is the place for hamburgers and malts as well as tacos and enchiladas. *Just off Plaza Hidalgo, tel. 83/43–18–34. Dress: informal. No reservations. AE, MC, V.*

**Tampico** **Deligencias.** Stuffed crabs are the specialty at this plain water-
*Moderate* front café that ranks as one of the most famous seafood restaurants in Mexico. *Ayuntamiento 2702, Ribera Ote. 415, tel. 12/ 14–12–79. Dress: casual. No reservations. MC, V.*

*Inexpensive* **Cafe y Neveriá Elite** is a popular gathering spot for breakfast, coffee, and ice-cream treats as well as other short-order meals. Don't be put off by the noise and the rather worn Formica tables; it's all part of the local color. *Av. Diaz Miron 211 Ote., tel. 83/12–03–64. No credit cards.*

**Veracruz** **La Bamba.** On the waterfront with a lovely view, the menu at
*Expensive* this eatery includes steak and chicken as well as seafood. *Malecon at Avila Camacho, tel. 29/32–53–55. Dress: casual. No reservations. AE, DC, MC, V.*

*Moderate* **Pardiños,** in Boca del Rio about 10 kilometers (6.2 miles) south
★ of downtown, is a star in a village of seafood restaurants. Plain tables in a storefront setting belie the elegant preparation of

such dishes as crabs Salpicon, grilled sea bass, and huachinango à la Veracruzana, served with *plantanos fritos* (fried plantains). *Boca del Rio (take a bus or taxi). Dress: casual. MC, V.*

*Inexpensive* **La Paroquia.** Possibly the most famous sidewalk café in Mexico,
★ this is the place to breakfast on sweet rolls and *café con leche* (bang your glass for a refill) and sip a beer while munching shrimp as marimbas play around sunset. *Independencia 106 (adjacent to the cathedral), no phone. No credit cards.*

# Lodging

There are good hotels in a few Mexican border towns, and staying overnight in a foreign country can be fun. The interior Huasteca Country cities offer a wide choice of accommodations. Highly recommended lodgings are indicated by a star ★.

| Category | Cost* |
|---|---|
| Very Expensive | over $100 |
| Expensive | $85–$100 |
| Moderate | $50–$85 |
| Inexpensive | under $50 |

*All prices are for a standard double room; excluding taxes.*

**Border Towns** **Residencial.** A pleasant low rise built along Spanish Colonial
*Expensive* lines with a large pool in the patio, this is the center of activity for much of Matamoros. Rooms are plain but comfortable. *Alvaro Obregón at Amapolas (6 blocks from border bridge), Matamoros, tel. 891/3–9440. 122 rooms. Facilities: restaurant, bar, pool, satellite TV. AE, MC, V.*

*Moderate* **Astromundo.** Downtown and handy to the bullring, the market, and the few good local restaurants, this popular hotel gets a lot of traffic from weekending winter Texans. *Juárez at Guerrero, Reynosa, tel. 892/2–5625. 106 rooms. Facilities: restaurant, bar, pool. MC, V.*
**El Rio.** A modern white structure spread out on large landscaped grounds, this motel has a spacious lobby and large guest rooms decorated in white and burgundy with dark Spanish Colonial furniture. All units include shower and telephone. *5 km (3 mi) south on Hwy 85, tel. 871/4–3666. 152 rooms. Facilities: dining room, bar, 2 swimming pools, parking on grounds. AE, MC, V.*
**Hotel Reforma.** An older hotel just a few blocks south of Plaza Hidalgo, Reforma has a restaurant opening both off the lobby and the street, and secure parking a block away. Rooms in the older section, although somewhat small and rather nondescript, are comfortable; junior suites in the new section are spacious and modern. All units come with shower, TV, and telephone. *Guerrero 822, Nuevo Laredo, tel. 871/2–6250. 38 rooms. Facilities: restaurant, bar, parking. MC, V.*

**Monterrey** **Ambassador.** A downtown landmark recently restored as a
*Very Expensive* Westin/Camino Real with spacious, comfortable rooms, a piano
★ bar in the lobby, and a health club; this is the best hotel in Huasteca Country. *Hidalgo at Emilio Carranza, tel. 83/40–63–90 or 83/42–20–40, fax 83/45–19–84. 241 rooms and suites. Facilities: satellite TV, shops, travel desk. AE, DC, MC, V.*

★ **Gran Hotel Ancira Radisson Plaza.** A grand old lady, built in 1912 but kept like new, the property is reminiscent of the grand hotels of Europe. It features good dining, a popular bar, and large, comfortable rooms. *Hidalgo at Escobedo, tel. 83/45–75–75 or 800/333–3333, fax 83/44–52–26. 240 rooms and suites. Facilities: gymnasium, pool, meeting rooms, satellite TV, shops. AE, MC, DC, V.*

*Expensive* **Chipinque.** This hilltop resort property overlooking the city is
★ wonderful if you have a car. The view from the restaurant is extraordinary, especially at night. *Meseta de Chipinque, tel. 83/78–11–00. 43 rooms. Facilities: restaurant/bar, pool, tennis court. AE, MC, V.*

**Río.** A large commercial establishment, the Río is centrally located but somewhat noisy. *Padre Mier and Garibaldi, tel. 83/44–90–40 or 83/43–20–90, fax 83/45–14–56. 408 rooms. Facilities: restaurant, lobby bar, pool. MC, V.*

*Moderate* **Royalty.** Good location and low prices are the main attractions here. *Hidalgo Oriente 402, tel. 83/40–28–00, fax 83/40–58–12. 66 rooms. Facilities: restaurant, bar. MC, V.*

**Tampico** **Camino Real.** Attractively decorated, this low-rise property
*Expensive* near the city center comes close to being a resort. *Hidalgo 200, tel. 12/13–88–11 or 91/800–57–000, fax 12/13–92–26. 132 rooms. Facilities: pool, bar, restaurant, tour desk, evening entertainment. AE, MC, V.*

*Moderate* **Inglaterra.** The convenient location of this property may be a plus for business travelers, while others may find it too commercial and noisy. *Díaz Mirón 116 Oriente, tel. 12/12–56–78. Facilities: restaurant, bar, evening entertainment. AE, MC, V.*

**Veracruz** **Emporio.** This big commercial hotel, recently renovated, is fun
*Expensive* and well situated—right on the malecón. Ask for a room with a sea view. *Paseo de Malecon s/n, tel. 29/32–00–20 or 29/32–22–22, fax 29/31–22–61. 202 rooms. Facilities: indoor and outdoor pools, satellite TV, restaurant, lobby bar, disco. AE, MC, V.*

**Mocambo.** One of the first beach resorts in Mexico, this landmark is showing its age, and, thankfully, an ambitious renovation is under way. But in the meantime, it's still a must-see with its sprawling grounds and fine dark-wood fixtures. *Playa Mocambo, tel. 29/37–15–00 or 29/37–17–10. Facilities: beach, indoor and outdoor pools, restaurant, bar, evening entertainment. AE, MC, V.*

*Moderate* **Colonial.** A comfortable but unimpressive establishment, the Colonial is two blocks from the harbor. *Miguel Lerdo 105, tel. 29/32–01–93, fax 29/32–93–63. 180 rooms. Facilities: indoor pool, sidewalk café and bar. MC, V.*

*Inexpensive* **Gran Hotel Diligencias.** Centrally located, on the *zócalo* (main square), this hotel is quite clean and the rooms have an imaginative decor, such as frescoes around the door frames. *Independencia 1115, tel. 29/31–21–16 or 29/32–29–67, fax 29/31–31–57. 118 rooms. Facilities: restaurant/bar. MC, V.*

# Nightlife

**Border Towns** In Nuevo Laredo, **O'Henry's** is a noisy favorite, with **The Winery** and **Cadillac** somewhat more sedate; **The Lion's Den** is the local disco. **Garcia's, Blanca White's,** and the **Hotel Residencial**

are where the action is in Matamoros. The **Hosteria del Bohemio,** in downtown Reynosa, has traditional mariachi music. The **Zona Rosa** has several discos, and **Trevino's** has a piano bar.

**Monterrey** Fashionable folk, residents and visitors alike, flock to the downtown hotels for after-dark action. The **Crowne Plaza Lobby Bar** is loud enough to dismay guests who turn in early, but it delights the young-at-heart crowd. At the **Ambassador** the pianist is more reserved. **El Cid,** at the Hotel Monterrey, features cheek-to-cheek dance music, and **Bar 1900** (Gran Ancira Radisson Plaza), a classic but upscale Mexican cantina, has flamenco dancers every Friday night. **Baccarat** (Rio Grijalva and Mississippi) is a top new disco, best reached by taxi.

**Tampico** The **Camino Real, Inglaterra** and **Posada de Tampico** hotels usually have lively entertainment; **Plaza Casino** (Universidad 36) is Tampico's top disco, but don't expect the staff to understand English.

**Veracruz** Head to the hotels for the best nightlife, especially **Tilingo Charlie's,** at the Emporio, and the bars at the **Torremar** and **Mocambo,** with the **Puerto Bello** offering a cozy piano bar. Leading dance clubs seem to change almost yearly: The latest are **Ocean,** on Calle Ruiz, and **Jaque** on Calle Diaz Miron. Most typically Veracruz, though, are the street musicians entertaining happy crowds on the zócalo every evening.

white, porous limestone sand and clear blue waters here, and the sun shines an average of 240 days a year, reputedly more than at almost any other Caribbean spot. Temperatures linger appealingly at about 80° F. You can sample Yucatecan foods and watch folkloric dance demonstrations as well as knock back tequila slammers at the myriad night spots.

But there can be more to the resort than plopping down under a *palapa* (pre-Hispanic thatched roof). For divers and snorkelers, the surrounding reefs and other islands—Isla Mujeres and Cozumel—are among the best in the world. Cancún also provides a relaxing home base for visiting the stupendous ruins of Chichén Itzá, Tulum, and Cobá on the mainland—remnants of the area's rich Mayan heritage—as well as the Yucatán coast and its lagoons.

Cancún has gone through the life cycle typical of any tourist destination. At its inception, the resort drew the jet set; lately, it has attracted increasing numbers of less affluent tourists, primarily package-tour takers and college students, particularly during spring break when hordes of flawless, tanned young bodies people the beaches and restaurants.

As for the island's history, not much was written about it before its birth as a resort almost 20 years ago. The island does not appear on the early navigators' maps and little is known about the Mayans who lived here; apparently Cancún's marshy terrain discouraged development. It is recorded that Mayans settled the area during the preclassical era, in about AD 200, and remained until about the 14th or 15th century. In the mid-19th century minor Mayan ruins were sighted; however, they were not studied by archaeologists until the 1950s and mid-1970s. In 1970 then-President Luis Echeverría first visited the site that had been chosen to retrieve the state of Quintana Roo from obscurity and abject poverty.

## Important Addresses and Numbers

**Tourist Information** The **state tourist office** (Av. Tulum 29, S.M. 5, tel. 98/848073), located next to Multibanco Comermex, is open daily 9–9. At this office, at the airport, and at many hotels, you can pick up a copy of *Cancún Tips,* a free pocket-size guide to hotels, restaurants, shopping, and recreation that usually contains a discount card for use at various establishments. The staff also runs a number of information centers around town, including one at Plaza Caracol (tel. 98/832745) that is open daily 10–10.

The Mexican Ministry of Tourism recently established a 24-hour English-language help line for tourists; it's toll free, 800/90392.

**Consulates** **U.S. Consulate** (Av. Nader 40, S.M. 2A, Edificio Marruecos 31, tel. 98/842411 or 98/846399) is open daily 9–2 and 3–6.

**Canadian Consulate** (Plaza México Local 312, upper floor, tel. 98/843716) is open daily 11 AM–1 PM. For emergencies outside office hours, call the Canadian Embassy in Mexico City (tel. 5/254–3288).

**Emergencies** **Police** (tel. 98/841913); **Red Cross** (Av. Xcaret and Labná, S.M. 21, tel. 98/841616); **Highway Patrol** (tel. 98/840710).

**Late-night Pharmacies** **Farmacia Turística** (Plaza Caracol, tel. 98/831894) and **Farmacia Extra** (Plaza Caracol, tel. 98/832827) deliver to hotels

9 AM–10 PM. **Farmacia Paris** (Av. Yaxchilán, in the Marrufo Bldg., tel. 98/840164) also fills prescriptions.

**English-language Bookstores** **Fama** (Av. Tulum, tel. 98/846586) **La Surtidora** (Av. Tulum 17, tel. 98/841103).

## Arriving and Departing by Plane

**Airport and Airlines** **Cancún International Airport** is 16 kilometers (9 miles) southwest of the heart of Cancún City, 10 kilometers (6 miles) from the southernmost point of the hotel zone. **Aeroméxico** (tel. 800/237–6639, tel. 98/860079 in Cancún) flies nonstop from Houston and New York. **American** (tel. 800/433–7300, tel. 98/860055 in Cancún) has nonstop service from its hub in Dallas and from Miami. **Continental** (tel. 800/231–0856, tel. 98/860040 in Cancún) offers daily direct service from Houston and Newark, NJ. **Mexicana** (tel. 800/531–7921, tel. 98/860120 in Cancún) nonstops depart from Chicago, Los Angeles, Miami, and New York. **Northwest** (tel. 800/225–2525, tel. 98/860046 in Cancún) flies direct from Tampa. From mid-December through April, **United** (tel. 800/538–2929, tel. 98/860025 in Cancún) flies from Chicago via Washington, D.C. In Cancún, Mexicana subsidiaries **Aerocaribe** (tel. 98/842000 [downtown], 98/860083 [airport]) and **Aerocozumel** (tel. 98/842000 [downtown], 98/860162 [airport]) offer flights to Cozumel, the ruins at Chichén Itzá, Mérida, and other Mexican destinations.

*Between the Airport and Hotels* A counter at the airport exit sells tickets for buses (called *colectivos*) and for taxis; prices for the latter range from $15 to $20, depending on the exact destination. Buses, which cost about $6, are air-conditioned and vend soft drinks and beer on board, but may be slow if they're carrying a lot of passengers and need to stop at many hotels.

## Arriving and Departing by Car or Bus

**By Car** Cancún is at the end of Route 180, which goes from Matamoros on the Texas border to Campeche, Mérida, and Valladolid. The road trip from Texas to Cancún can take up to three days. Cancún can also be reached from the south via Route 307, which passes through Chetumal and Belize. Gas stations on these roads are few in number, so try to keep your tank filled.

**By Bus** The bus terminal (Av. Tulum and Av. Uxmal, tel. 98/841378 or 98/843948) downtown serves first-class buses making the trip from Mexico City and first- and second-class buses arriving in Cancún from Puerto Morelos, Playa del Carmen, Tulum, Chetumal, Cobá, Valladolid, Chichén Itzá, and Mérida. Public buses (Route 8) make the trip out to Puerto Juárez and Punta Sam for the ferries to Isla Mujeres.

## Getting Around

Motorized transport of some sort is necessary, since the island is somewhat spread out. Public bus service is good and taxis are relatively inexpensive.

When you first visit Cancún City (downtown), you may be confused by the layout. There are four principal avenues: Tulum and Yaxchilán, which run north-south; and Uxmal and Cobá, running east-west. Streets bounded by those avenues and running perpendicular to them are actually horseshoe-shaped, so you will find two parallel streets named *Tulipanes*, for instance. However, street numbers or even street names are not of much use in Cancún; the proximity to landmarks, such as specific hotels, is the preferred way of giving directions.

**By Bus**  Public buses run between the hotel zone and downtown from 6 AM to midnight; the cost is NP$2. There are designated bus stops, but drivers can also be flagged down along Paseo Kukulcán. The service is a bit erratic, but buses run frequently and can save you considerable money on taxis, especially if you're staying at the southern end of the hotel zone.

**By Car and Moped**  Renting a car for your stay in Cancún is probably an unnecessary expense, entailing tips for valet parking, as well as gasoline and rather costly rental rates. What's more, driving here can be harrowing when you don't know your way around. However, if you plan to do some exploring, using Cancún as a base, the roads are excellent within a 100-kilometer (62-mile) radius.

*Car Rentals*  Rental cars are available at the airport or from any of a dozen agencies in town. Try **Avis** (tel. 98/860222 at the airport, 98/830800 at Hotel Calinda Viva, or 98/830803 at Galería Mayfair); **Budget** (tel. 98/840730 or 98/840204 [reservations], with offices at the airport, downtown, and at the Galería Mayfair); **Econo-Rent** (tel. 98/842147 at the airport, 98/841826 or 98/841435 at Calle Tulipanes 16); **National** (tel. 98/864492 or 98/860152 on Av. Uxmal 12); or **Hertz** (9 locations, tel. 98/841326 or 98/876604 at Reno 35). The **Car Rental Association** (tel. 98/842039) can help you arrange a rental as well.

*Moped Rentals*  Mopeds and scooters are also available throughout the island. While fun, they are risky, and there is no insurance available for the driver or the vehicle. The accident rate is high, especially downtown, which is considered too congested for novice moped users.

**By Taxi**  Taxis to the ferries at Punta Sam or Puerto Juárez cost $5–$16 or more; between the hotel zone and downtown, $6 and up; and within the hotel zone, $2–$4. All prices depend on the distance, your negotiating skills, and whether you pick up the taxi in front of the hotel or go onto the avenue to hail a green city taxi (the latter will be cheaper). Since taxi rates fluctuate according to gasoline taxes and the drivers' whims, check with your hotel. Most list rates at the door; confirm the price with your driver before you set out. If you lose something in a taxi or have a complaint, call the **Sindicato de Taxistas** (tel. 98/886992 or 98/886990).

**By Ship**  Boats leave Puerto Juárez and Punta Sam (both north of Cancún City) for Isla Mujeres every half hour or so; *see* section on Isla Mujeres, *below*, for details.

## Guided Tours

There are few guided tours of Cancún per se, because other than several tiny Mayan ruins, there is virtually no sightseeing on the island. **Tranviás Turísticos** (tel. 98/844055), which has booths at Ki Huic Market, downtown, and Nautilus Shopping Center and Gypsy's restaurant in the hotel zone, runs sightseeing trolleys around the island. More popular are tours to the surrounding islands, the beaches along the Cancún-Tulum corridor (Akumal is the best known), or the Mayan ruins on the mainland—Chichén Itzá, Cobá, and Tulum (these trips usually include a stop at the lagoons at Xel-Ha (pronounced *shell-HA*) or Xcaret (pronounced *SHAR-et*).

**Cruises** A lobster-dinner cruise on board the 62-foot vessel ***Columbus*** (tel. 98/831488 or 98/831021) includes a full lobster or steak dinner, open bar, and dancing for $54; the boat departs the Royal Mayan Yacht Club Monday–Saturday, and sails from 4 to 7. The "Sun Tour" run by **Turismo Aviomar** (tel. 98/848944) to Isla Mujeres departs the Playa Linda dock daily at 10 AM and returns at 6 PM; the $48 price (half that for kids) includes a Continental breakfast, buffet lunch on a private beach, open bar, and live music. **Nautibus** (tel. 98/831004 or 98/832119), or the "floating submarine," has a 1½-hour Caribbean-reef cruise that departs the Playa Linda marina four times daily; during high season, boats sail at 10, 12, 2, and 4. The $28 price ($15 for children) includes music and drinks.

**Air Tours** A 15-minute, $50-per-person seaplane ride over the lagoons and Caribbean reefs departs from **Pelican Pier** (Paseo Kukulcán, Km 5.5, tel. 98/830315 or 98/831935), across from the Casa Maya; a 35-minute ride, covering the whole island, costs $90.

**Special-Interest** **Intermar Caribe** (tel. 98/844266) leads daily jeep tours through the jungle to unexcavated ruins. The $50 price includes lunch.

## Exploring

Cancún is comprised of two zones: the hotel zone, which is shaped roughly like the numeral 7, and Cancún City or downtown Cancún, known as *el centro*, 4 kilometers (2½ miles) west of the hotel zone on the mainland.

Paseo Kukulcán is the main drag in the hotel zone, and because most of the 7 is less than a kilometer wide, both the Caribbean and the lagoons can be seen from either side of it. Regularly placed kilometer markers on the roadside help indicate where you are; they go from Km 1 on the mainland, near downtown, to Km 20 at Punta Nizuc. The hotel zone consists entirely of hotels, restaurants and shopping complexes, marinas, and timeshare condominiums; there are no residential areas as such. It's not the sort of place you can get to know by walking. Paseo Kukulcán is punctuated by driveways with steep inclines turning into the hotels, most of which are set at least 100 yards from the road. The lagoon side of the boulevard consists of scrubby stretches of land, many of them covered with construction cranes, alternating with marinas, shopping centers, and restaurants. What is most scenic about Cancún is the dramatic contrast between the vivid turquoise-and-violet sea and the blinding alabaster-white sands.

*Numbers in the margin correspond to points of interest on the Cancún map.*

Cancún's scenery consists mostly of its beautiful beaches and crystal-clear waters. There are also a few intriguing sites tucked away among the modern hotels. Heading north from Punta Nizuc and keeping your eye on the seaside, as many as eight hotels are situated within the space of 1 kilometer, one right after the next, with barely any distance between them.

❶ The small **Ruinas del Rey** are located on the lagoon side at Km 17, roughly opposite Days Inn and Playa de Oro. Large signs

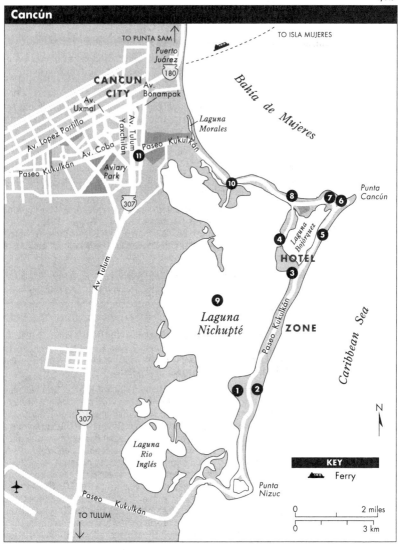

Cancún

TO PUNTA SAM

Puerto Juárez

TO ISLA MUJERES

CANCÚN CITY

Av. Bonampak

Av. Uxmal

Av. López Portilla

Av. Tulum Yaxchilán

Av. Coba

Paseo Kukulkán

Aviary Park

Paseo Kukulkán

Laguna Morales

Bahía de Mujeres

Punta Cancún

HOTEL

Laguna Bojórquez

Av. Tulum

Laguna Nichupté

ZONE

Paseo Kukulkán

Caribbean Sea

Laguna Río Inglés

Punta Nizuc

N

Paseo Kukulkán

TO TULUM

**KEY**

Ferry

0 ——— 2 miles
0 ——— 3 km

Bullring, **11**
Cancún Convention Center, **6**
Laguna Nichupté, **9**
Playa Chac Mool, **5**
Playa Linda, **10**
Playa Tortugas, **8**
Pok-Ta-Pok, **4**

Ruinas del Rey, **1**
San Miguelito, **2**
Shopping malls, **7**
Yamil Lu'um, **3**

point out the site, which is being incorporated into a complex that will include a hotel, golf course, shops, and residential units. At this writing, because of the construction, the ruins are closed to public access, and no one seems to know when they will open again. First mentioned in a 16th-century travelogue and then, in 1842 when they were sighted by American explorer John Lloyd Stephens and his draftsman, Frederick Catherwood, the ruins were finally explored by archaeologists in 1910, though excavations did not begin until 1954. In 1975 archaeologists, along with the Mexican government, began the restoration of El Rey and San Miguelto (*see below*).

Although El Rey is not particularly impressive, it is worth a look. The ruin is notable for its unusual architecture: two main plazas bounded by two streets. Most of the other Mayan cities, which were not in any sense planned but had developed over centuries, contained one plaza with a number of ceremonial satellites and few streets. The pyramid here is topped by a platform, and inside its vault are stucco paintings. Skeletons found buried both at the apex and at the base indicate that the site may have been a royal burial ground. Originally named Kin Ich Ahau Bonil, Maya for "King of the Solar Countenance," the 2nd–3rd-century BC site was linked to astronomical practices in the ancient Mayan culture.

About half a kilometer away from El Rey—between Km 16 and 17—but on the east side of Kukulcán, is another Mayan site: **❷ San Miguelito,** a very small stone building (about the size of a shack) with a number of columns about 4 feet high. There is no signage, so if you take a taxi, make sure the driver knows how to reach the site.

**❸** Another ruin, **Yamil Lu'um** (meaning "hilly land"), stands on the highest point of Cancún and is situated at Km 12, to the left of the Sheraton. A small sign at the hotel will direct you to the dirt path leading to the site. Although it's composed of two structures—one probably a temple, the other probably a lighthouse—this is the smallest of Cancún's ruins. Discovered in 1842 by John Lloyd Stephens, the remains date from the late 13th or early 14th century.

Just after Km 12, near the Melia Turquesa, Sheraton, and Radisson hotels, you'll come in sight of Laguna Bojórquez on your left; buildings span nearly the entire length of the spit of land that encloses the lagoon. On the far side of that spit, along the road that forks to the left (between Km 6 and Km 7), is **❹ Pok-Ta-Pok** golf course, whose Mayan name means "ball game." Situated on the 12th hole is yet another Mayan ruin, consisting of two platforms and vestiges of other buildings.

Approaching the northern tip of the vertical leg of the 7— **❺** Punta Cancún—you'll pass **Playa Chac Mool** at Km 10, one of the few beaches not associated with hotels on Cancún, with restaurants and changing areas. Leaving the beach, you'll round the corner to the bay side (Bahía de Mujeres). Calmer waters prevail here, as opposed to the sea side, where you can also swim, and which has the more beautiful beaches. On the sea side of the tip of Punta Cancún, look for the fourth Mayan ruin, a tiny shrine that is fairly insignificant except that it's been cleverly incorporated into the architecture of the **Hotel Camino Real.**

After the beach, you'll come upon a traffic circle at Km 9, where
**❻** the **Cancún Convention Center,** a large venue for cultural
events, is located. At press time (May 1993) the convention
center, damaged by Hurricane Gilbert, was still in the process
of being rebuilt.

Between the convention center and the Stouffer Presidente is a
**❼** ½-mile-long string of **shopping malls,** including Plaza Caracol,
La Mansión–Costa Blanca, Plaza Lagunas, Plaza Terramar,
and Galería Mayfair.

**❽** Right beyond the Stouffer Presidente, at Km 7, is **Playa Tortugas,** the other beach where those staying at the beachless
downtown hotels are welcome. To the south, on your left, you'll
**❾** reach **Laguna Nichupté,** the center for most of the watersports
activities. Also in the lagoon are swampy areas that host mangrove trees and more than 200 species of birds. Ask your hotel
to arrange for a boat and guide.

Continue along Paseo Kukulcán past the numerous hotels. Just
before you cross the causeway onto the mainland, at the Hotel
**❿** Calinda, you'll come to **Playa Linda,** from which ferries depart
for Isla Mujeres. The less expensive public ferries leave for the
island from Puerto Juárez, about 9 kilometers (6 miles) farther
north.

As you enter downtown Cancún, Paseo Kukulcán turns into
Avenida Cobá at the spot where it meets **Avenida Tulum,** the
main thoroughfare and the location of many restaurants and
shops. Life-size reproductions of ancient Mexican art, including the Aztec calendar stone, giant Olmec head, the Atlantids
of Tula, and the Mayan Chac Mool (reclining rain god), line the
grassy strip dividing Tulum's northbound and southbound
lanes. Visitors looking for shopping bargains, however, generally find better prices if they stick to the parallel Avenida
Yaxchilán.

**⓫** The Cancún **bullring,** a block south of the PEMEX station,
hosts year-round bullfights. *Paseo Kukulcán at Av.
Bonampak, tel. 98/845465 or 98/848248. Admission: $33, Wed.
3:30 PM.*

## Shopping

Resort wear and handicrafts are the most popular purchases in
Cancún, but the prices are high and the selection standard; if
you're traveling elsewhere in Mexico, it's best to postpone your
shopping spree until you reach another town. Still, you can find
a respectable variety of Mexican handicrafts ranging from
blown glass and hand-woven textiles to leather to jewelry made
from local coral and tortoiseshell. (Don't be tempted by the tortoiseshell products: The turtles they come from are endangered species, and it is illegal to bring tortoiseshell into the
United States and several other countries.)

*Caveat emptor* applies as much to Cancún as it does to the "bargain" electronics stores on Fifth Avenue in New York City or in
Hong Kong. Throughout Mexico you will often get better
prices by paying with cash (pesos or dollars) or traveler's
checks. This is because Mexican merchants are averse to the
commissions charged by credit-card companies, and frequently
tack that commission—6% or more—onto your bill. If you can

do without the plastic, you may even get the 10% sales tax lopped off.

Bargaining is expected in Cancún, but mostly in the market. Suggest half the asking price and slowly come up, but do not pay more than 70% of the quoted price. Shopping around is a good idea, too, because the crafts market is very competitive. But closely examine the merchandise you are purchasing: Some "authentic" items—particularly jewelry—may actually be shoddy imitations.

In Cancún, shopping hours are generally weekdays 10–1 and 4–7, although more and more stores are staying open throughout the day rather than closing for siesta between 1 and 4 PM. Many shops keep Saturday morning hours, and some are now open on Sunday until 1 PM. Shops in the malls tend to be open weekdays from 9–10 AM to 8–10 PM.

**Downtown** The wide variety of shops downtown along Avenida Tulum (between Avenidas Cobá and Uxmal) and Avenida Cobá (between Avenidas Bonampak and Tulum) includes the **Plaza México** (Av. Tulum 200, tel. 98/843506), a cluster of 50 handicrafts shops. Next door, visit **Pama** (Av. Tulum and Calle Lluvia, tel. 98/841839), a department store offering clothing, beachwear, sports gear, toiletries, liquor, and *latería* (crafts made of tin). Also on Tulum is the oldest and largest of the crafts markets, **Ki Huic** (Av. Tulum, between Bancomer and Banco Atlantico, no phone), which is open daily from 9 AM to 10 PM and houses about 100 vendors. Nearby is **Margarita's** (Av. Tulum 10, tel. 98/842359), one of the better silver shops.

**Hotel Zone** Fully air-conditioned malls (known as *centros comerciales*) are as streamlined and well kept as any in the United States or Canada. **Flamingo Plaza** (Paseo Kukulcán, Km 11, across from the Hotel Flamingo, tel. 98/832855), the latest addition, includes a full-service gym, exchange booth, some designer emporiums and duty-free stores, several sportswear shops, two boutiques selling Guatemalan imports, and a new Planet Hollywood boutique. At the food court, in addition to the usual McDonald's and fried chicken concessions, you'll find **Chicádole,** offering what might be the only fast-food molé enchiladas around.

Just across from the convention center site at Km 8.5 is **Plaza Caracol** (tel. 98/830905 or 98/831038), the largest and most contemporary mall in Cancún, with about 200 shops and boutiques, including two pharmacies, art galleries, and folk art and jewelry shops, as well as cafés and restaurants. Fashion boutiques include Benetton, Bally, Gucci, and Ralph Lauren; in all these stores, prices are less than those in their U.S. counterparts. One drawback: Aside from formal restaurants, there are no places here for shoppers to rest their feet.

To the back of—and virtually connected to—Plaza Caracol are two outdoor shopping complexes: the pink stucco **La Mansíon-Costa Blanca** (tel. 98/844261), which specializes in designer clothing and has several restaurants, a bank, and a liquor store; and **Plaza Lagunas** (tel. 98/831266), dedicated primarily to sportswear shops, such as Ellesse and Ocean Pacific. Also nearby, **Plaza Terramar** (tel. 98/831588, opposite the Hotel Fiesta Americana) sells beachwear, souvenirs, and folk art, and has a restaurant and a pharmacy.

Plaza Nautilus (Km 3.5, lagoon side, tel. 98/831903), the mall closest to downtown and a favorite of American shoppers, has a bookstore, liquor store, art gallery, perfumery, folk art shop, and Super Deli, as well as about 65 other shops.

## Sports and Fitness

Golf   The main course is at Pok-Ta-Pok (Paseo Kukulcán between Km 6 and Km 7, tel. 98/830871), a club with fine views of both sea and lagoon, whose 18 holes were designed by Robert Trent Jones, Sr. The club also has a practice green, swimming pool, tennis courts, and restaurant. The greens fees are $50; electric cart, $30; clubs, $15; caddies, $15; and golf clinics, $25 per hour. Playing hours are 6 AM–6 PM (last tee-off is at 4:30). There are also 18- and 5-hole golf courses at the Hotel Melia Cancún (Paseo Kukulcan, Km 12, tel. 98/851160) and a 9-hole course at the Oasis Hotel (Paseo Kukulcán Km 20, tel. 98/850867).

Health Clubs   Most of the deluxe hotels have their own health clubs, although few of them are very large. There are, however, two gyms in Cancún: Gold's Gym (Plaza Flamingo, tel. 98/832933 or 98/832966) and Michel's Gym (Av. Sayil 66, S.M. 4, tel. 98/842394 or 98/842550).

Jogging   Although to some people the idea of jogging in the intense heat of Cancún sounds like a form of masochism, fanatics should know that there is a 14-kilometer (9-mile) track extending along half the island, running parallel to Paseo Kukulcán from the Punta Cancún area into Cancún City.

Water Sports   Water sports—particularly snorkeling, scuba diving, and deep-sea fishing—are popular pastimes in Cancún, because some 500 species of tropical fish, including sailfish, bluefin, marlin, barracuda, and red snapper, live in the adjacent waters. Snorkeling gear can be rented for $10 per day. Sailboards are available for about $50 an hour; classes go for about $35 an hour. Parasailing costs $35 for eight minutes; waterskiing, $60–$65 per hour; jetskiing, $50–$55 per hour.

*Fishing*   Deep-sea fishing boats and other gear may be chartered from outfitters for about $320 for four hours, $420 for six hours, and $520 for eight hours. Charters generally include a captain, a first mate, gear, bait, and beverages. Tiki Island (tel. 98/833481) and Marina Aqua Ray (tel. 98/853007) are just a couple of the companies that operate large fishing fleets.

*Sailboarding*   Although some people sailboard on the ocean side in the summer, activity is limited primarily to the bay between Cancún and Isla Mujeres. If you visit the island in July, don't miss the National Windsurfing Tournament (tel. 98/843212), in which athletes test their mettle. The International Windsurfer Sailing School (tel. 98/842023), located at Playa Tortugas, rents equipment and gives lessons.

*Snorkeling and Scuba Diving*   Snorkeling is best at Punta Nizuc, Punta Cancún, and Playa Tortugas, although you should be especially careful of the strong currents at the latter. Some charter-fishing companies offer a two-tank scuba dive for about $100. As the name implies, Scuba Cancún (tel. 98/831011) specializes in diving trips and offers NAUI, CMAS, and PADI instruction. Aqua Tours Dive Center and Marina (tel. 98/830400 or 98/830227) offers scuba tours and a resort course, as well as snorkeling trips. If you've brought your own snorkeling gear and want to save money, just take a city bus down to Club Med and walk along the resort's beach for about a mile until you get to Punta Nizuc.

## Dining

*By Judith Glynn*

At last count, there were more than 1,200 restaurants in Cancún, but—according to one profiting restaurateur—only about 100 are worth their salt, so to speak. Finding the right restaurant in Cancún is not easy. The downtown restaurants that line the noisy Avenida Tulum often have tables spilling onto pedestrian-laden sidewalks; however, gas fumes and gawking tourists tend to detract from the romantic outdoor-café ambience. Many of the hotel-zone restaurants, on the other hand, cater to what they assume is a tourist preference for bland, not-too-foreign-tasting food.

One key to good dining in Cancún is to find the haunts—mostly located in the downtown area—where locals go for Yucatán-style food prepared by the experts. Many menus are highlighted by seafood made with fresh lime juice and other authentic Mexican specialties, but it takes more to make a Cancún dining experience: Look for a place where the waiters artistically prepare meals at tableside or where cocktails are served flaming. Fish caught from the waters around the island, then grilled and seasoned with lime juice, is a sure bet. Grilled pork and chicken prepared with spices used in Mayan cooking, such as *achiote*, are other local specialties.

When reviewing Cancún's restaurants, we looked for places where your money will best be spent and your meal most enjoyed. It's important to note that although hotels make strong efforts to keep guests on the premises, you'll be paying high prices for what may well be an average meal. Therefore, only the truly exceptional hotel restaurants are listed, allowing for more comprehensive coverage of independently operated cafés. Unless otherwise stated, restaurants serve lunch and dinner daily.

Highly recommended restaurants are indicated by a star ★.

| Category | Cost* |
| --- | --- |
| Very Expensive | over $35 |
| Expensive | $25–$35 |
| Moderate | $15–$25 |
| Inexpensive | under $15 |

*per person, excluding drinks and service*

## Hotel Zone

*Hotel Zone restaurants are located on the Cancún Hotel Zone Dining and Lodging map.*

**Very Expensive** **Bogart's.** Whether you consider it amusingly elaborate or merely pretentious, it's hard to be neutral about Bogart's, probably the most expensive and talked-about restaurant in town. Taking off from the film *Casablanca*, the place is decorated with Persian rugs, fans, velvet-cushioned banquettes, and fountains; waiters wear fezzes and white suits. A menu as

**Dining**

Bogart's, **11**
Captain's Cove, **2, 18**
Carlos 'n Charlie's, **5**
Casa Rolandi, **9**
El Mexicano, **8**
Grimond's Mansion, **4**
Gypsy's, **14**
Hacienda El
Mortero, **11**
Lorenzillos, **15**

**Lodging**

Albergue CREA, **1**
Calinda Viva
Cancún, **7**
Camino Real, **12**
Cancún Playa, **19**
Conrad Cancún, **20**
Fiesta Americana
Condesa, **17**
Fiesta Americana
Coral Beach
Cancún, **10**
Hyatt Regency
Cancún, **13**
Krystal Cancún, **11**
Meliá Cancún, **16**
Stouffer Presidente, **6**
Villas Tacul, **3**

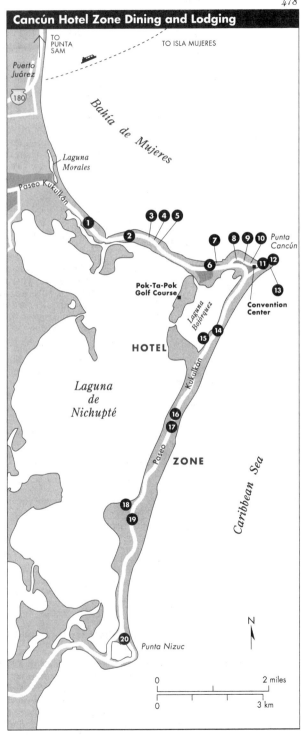

eclectic as the patrons of Rick's Cafe features many seafood and Mediterranean dishes. The food is good, but don't expect large portions; servings are nouvelle style. *Paseo Kukulcán, Hotel Krystal, tel. 98/831133. Reservations required; seatings at 7 and 9:30. Dress: casual but neat. AE, MC, V. No lunch.*

**Grimond's Mansion.** Although the management has changed—this restaurant was formerly called Maxime's—the French chef and 19th-century French-country decor, with its ornate furnishings, remain. The outside terrace, with lush greenery and a fountain, is a relaxing spot for lunch; in the evening, you'll dine to the strains of a piano and classical guitar. An upstairs bar features a billiard table. Although there are many standard French dishes, the menu bears a decided Mexican influence; specialties include a fillet of beef served with *cuitlacoche*, an Aztec sauce made with corn and mushrooms. *Calle Pez Volador 8, tel. 98/830438. Reservations suggested during high season. Dress: casual but neat. AE, MC, V.*

**Expensive** **El Mexicano.** One of Cancún's largest restaurants seats 320 for a folkloric dinner show in a room resembling the patio of a hacienda. Details such as elaborately hand-carved chairs created by Indians from central Mexico and numerous regional Mexican dishes convey a feeling of authenticity. Be forewarned, however: Though indisputably popular, this is a touristy spot, and the dancing-girl show is not a window into Yucatecan culture. Granted that, try the *empanxonostle* (steamed lobster, shrimp, fish, and herbs); it promises to be as extravagant as El Mexicano's surroundings. When the final show ends, you're invited to dance until midnight. *La Mansión-Costa Blanca Shopping Center, tel. 98/832220 (restaurant), 98/844261 (reservations). Reservations required; show begins at 7:30. Dress: casual but neat. AE, MC, V.*

**Hacienda El Mortero.** Pampering waiters, strolling mariachi, lush hanging plants, fig trees, and candlelight make this reproduction plantation home a very popular spot to dine. The menu offers a selection of country cooking, and the steaks and ribs are first class. *Paseo Kukulcán, Hotel Krystal, tel. 98/831133. Reservations required for 7 and 9:30 seatings. Dress: casual but neat. AE, MC, V. No lunch.*

**Moderate** **Captain's Cove.** Both waterfront locations feature popular breakfast buffets served under palapa roofs. The decor is decidedly nautical, with rigging draped on the walls and chandeliers in the shape of ships' steering wheels. The restaurant near the Casa Maya Hotel overlooks the Caribbean Sea toward Isla Mujeres; the other is situated beside the Nichupté Lagoon. Both present lunch and dinner menus filled with seafood dishes and charbroiled steak and chicken. Parents appreciate the lower-priced children's menu, an unusual feature in Cancún. *Lagoonside, across from the Royal Mayan Hotel, tel. 98/850016; beachside, next to Casa Maya Hotel, tel. 98/830669. No reservations. Dress: casual. MC, V.*

★ **Carlos 'n Charlie's.** A lively atmosphere, a terrific view overlooking the lagoon, and good food make this restaurant—part of the popular Anderson chain—Cancún's best-known hot spot. You'll never run out of bric-a-brac to look at: The walls are catchalls, with tons of photos; sombreros, bird cages, and wooden birds and animals hang from the ceilings. For dinner you may be tempted by the barbecued ribs sizzling on the open grill, or one of the steak or seafood specials. After your meal, dance off the calories under the stars at the Pier Dance Club.

*Paseo Kukulcán, Km 5.5, tel. 98/830846. No reservations. Dress: casual. AE, MC, V.*

**Casa Rolandi.** Authentic northern Italian and Swiss dishes are skillfully prepared by the Italian owner-chef, who grew up near the Swiss border. Homemade lasagna, baked in the large stucco oven, and an ample salad bar make for a satisfying dinner. Many fish and beef dishes are also on the menu. The decor is appropriately Mediterranean—white walls, lots of plants, and copper plates decorating the tables—and the back room offers a view of the beach. *Plaza Caracol, tel. 98/831817. Reservations suggested during high season. Dress: casual. AE, MC, V.*

★ **Gypsy's.** This all-time favorite restaurant sits upon stilts and overlooks an illuminated lagoon where crocodiles and fish can be seen. The decor hints at Spain, and the two dinner shows (7:30 and 9:30) with flamenco dancers convey the message loud and clear. Don't pass up the paella prepared by a Spanish chef from León. *Paseo Kukulcán, Km 10.5, tel. 98/832015. Reservations suggested. Dress: casual. AE, MC, V. Buffet brunch served 7:30 AM–noon.*

**Lorenzillos.** Perched on its own peninsula in the lagoon, this nautical spot provides a pleasant spot to watch the sunset, sip a drink on the outdoor patio, or sample excellent seafood. Specialties include grilled or broiled lobster (you can pick your own) and whole fish Veracruz-style. The seafaring theme extends to the names of both the dishes (like Jean Lafitte beef) and the restaurant itself (Lorenzillo was a 17th-century pirate). *Paseo Kukulkán Km 10.5, tel. 98/831254. Reservations advised. Dress: casual. AE, MC, V.*

---

### Downtown

*Downtown restaurants are located on the Downtown Cancún Dining and Lodging map.*

**Expensive** **du Mexique.** The combination of an upstairs art gallery and a restaurant that serves Mexican fare with a nouvelle twist presents a creative alternative for diners who are looking for something new. The decor features dark-wood floors, a vaulted white stucco ceiling, and sleek contemporary design. *Av. Cobá 44, tel. 98/841077. Reservations suggested. Dress: casual but neat. AE, MC, V. No lunch.*

**Moderate** **Bucanero.** Quiet dining in a candlelit marine atmosphere is the drawing card for this seafood restaurant, and the seafood—especially lobster specialties—is tops. For starters, try the lobster bisque or black bean soup, and round the meal out with the seafood combination, which includes lobster in garlic sauce, shrimp and squid brochette, and a fish fillet. Piano music played throughout the evening and waiters dressed as pirates add character to the place. *Av. Nader, tel. 98/842280. Reservations accepted. Dress: casual but neat. MC, V. No lunch.*

★ **El Pescador.** It's first-come, first-served, with long lines, especially during high season. But people still flood into this rustic Mexican-style restaurant with nautical touches; the open-air patio is particularly popular. Heavy hitters on the menu include red snapper broiled with garlic and freshly caught lobster specials. For dessert consider sharing the cake filled with ice cream and covered with peaches and strawberry marmalade. *Tulipanes 28, tel. 98/842673. No reservations. Dress: casual. MC, V.*

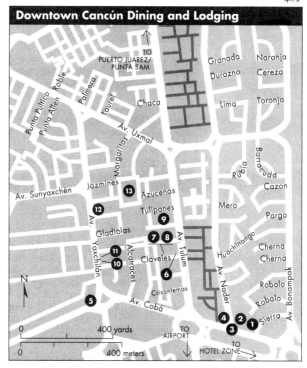

**Dining**
Bucanero, **2**
du Mexique, **3**
El Pescador, **9**
El Tacolote, **5**
La Fonda Del Angel, **1**
La Habichuela, **13**
La Parrilla, **10**
Rosa Mexicano, **7**

**Lodging**
Antillano, **6**
Holiday Inn Centro
Cancún, **4**
María del Lourdes, **11**
Plaza Carrillo's, **8**
Plaza del Sol, **12**

**La Fonda Del Angel.** This unpretentious restaurant in a Mexican colonial-style setting has walls that are painted pink, lemon, and aqua; wood beams and wrought-iron details add a bit more pizzazz. The menu, which includes a variety of Mexican dishes, features the special Fillet Angel (beef covered with melted cheese and mushroom sauce). During high season, the outside patio offers a quiet alternative. Live music is played nightly. *Av. Cobá 32, tel. 98/843393. Reservations suggested. Dress: casual. AE, MC, V.*

★ **La Habichuela.** This charmer—once an elegant home—is perfect for hand-holding romantics or anyone looking for a relaxed, private atmosphere. The candlelit garden, with white, wrought-iron chairs, pebbled ground, and thick, tropical greenery, exudes peacefulness, while a statue of Pakal, the Mayan god of astronomy and culture, surveys all. Try the *cobichuela*—lobster and shrimp in a light Indian sauce served on a bed of rice inside a coconut—a specialty of the house. *Margaritas 25, tel. 98/843158. Reservations suggested. Dress: casual but neat. MC, V.*

★ **La Parrilla.** If you're looking for the place where local Mexicans—young and old—hang out, you've found it in this popular downtown spot, an old classic by Cancún standards (it opened in 1975). Everything from the food to the bougainvillea and palapa roof is authentic. Popular dishes include the grilled beef with garlic sauce and the *tacos al pastor* (tacos with pork, pineapple, coriander, onion, and salsa). *Av. Yaxchilán 51, tel. 98/845398. No reservations. Dress: casual. AE, MC, V. No lunch; closed Christmas.*

★ **Rosa Mexicano.** One of Cancún's prettiest Mexican colonial-style restaurants presents waiters dressed as *charros* (Mexican cowboys), pottery and embroidered wall hangings, floor tiles with floral designs, and a cozy, softly lighted atmosphere. For extra romance, make a reservation for the candlelit patio. Savory appetizers include *nopalitos* (a tamale-type treat with cactus, corn, cilantro, and cheese). Specialties are *filete Rosa* (beef and onions in a tequila-orange sauce) and *camarones al ajillo* (shrimp sautéed in olive oil and garlic, with chili peppers). *Calle Claveles 4, tel. 98/846313. Reservations advised. Dress: casual. MC, V. No lunch.*

**Inexpensive** **El Tacolote.** Only tacos are served here, and the standard order includes three. Mix-and-match fillings, but don't overlook the filet mignon taco. Bowls of sliced limes and salsa come with your order, in keeping with the very casual tone of this brightly tiled and comfortable place. *Av. Cobá, tel. 98/844453. No reservations. Dress: casual. MC, V.*

## Lodging

The most important buildings in Cancún are its hotels, which presently number more than 100 (the number of new hotels is increasing by 5–10 per year). Choosing from this variety can be bewildering, because most hotel brochures sound—and look—alike. Many properties were built in the mid-1970s by international hotel chains known for their streamlined, standardized versions of hospitality, and some were substantially renovated following the damage wrought by Hurricane Gilbert in 1988. Hotels here tend to favor "neo-Mayan" architecture (palapa roofs, massive pyramidal stone structures, and stucco walls interspersed with red tile roofs and quasi-Mediterranean Moorish arches), bland contemporary-style furniture, and pastel hues.

All hotels have air-conditioning and private bathrooms unless otherwise noted. In addition, all properties in the Very Expensive and Expensive categories have water-sports facilities and parking unless otherwise noted. All Cancún hotels are within the 77500 postal code. Rates quoted refer to the peak winter season, mid-November–March. For more information, but *not* for reservations, contact the **Cancún Hotel Association** (Box 1339, Cancún, QR 77500, tel. 98/842853 or 98/845895, fax 98/847115).

Highly recommended hotels are indicated by a star ★.

| Category | Cost* |
| --- | --- |
| Very Expensive | over $160 |
| Expensive | $90–$160 |
| Moderate | $40–$90 |
| Inexpensive | under $40 |

*All prices are for a standard double room, excluding the 10% tax.*

## Hotel Zone

*Hotel Zone properties are located on the Cancún Hotel Zone Dining and Lodging map.*

**Very Expensive** **Camino Real.** This Westin resort, situated at the tip of Punta
★ Cancún, was selected as one of the Leading Hotels of the World because of its luxury accommodations and excellent management, staff, housekeeping, and maintenance. The hotel comprises two very different structures—a four-story building incorporating a small Mayan ruin and a newer high rise—that are strikingly coordinated in design. Rooms in both units are unusually attractive. In the tower, the 85 Royal Beach Club accommodations, with pink and turquoise color schemes and well-wrought rattan furniture, capture the spirit of Cancún; a number have Jacuzzis, and each has its own balcony. Rooms in the older building were recently redone in a similar style. In the evening, guests can dance to live salsa at the hotel's popular Azucar disco (*see* Nightlife, *below*). *Punta Cancún (Box 14), tel. 98/830100 or 800/228–3000, fax 98/831730. 381 rooms. Facilities: 5 restaurants, 4 bars, 3 lighted tennis courts, disco, pool, 2 beaches, water sports, shopping arcade. AE, DC, MC, V.*

**Fiesta Americana Condesa.** This sprawling, friendly hotel has the same casual elegance and luxurious amenities of its older sister, the Fiesta Americana Cancún. Situated toward the southern end of the hotel zone, the Condesa has a Mediterranean-style facade featuring balconies, rounded arches, and alternating ocher, salmon, and sand-colored walls. But it's the huge palapa fronting the structure that makes it hard to miss. An attractive and spacious lobby bar has Tiffany-style stained-glass awnings, tall palms, and ceiling fans. Three seven-story towers overlook a tranquil inner courtyard with hanging plants and falling water. The rooms, highlighted by dusty-pink stucco walls and gray-blue carpets, offer the same tranquility. Balconies are shared by three standard rooms; costlier rooms have their own balconies. Suites are available. *Paseo Kukulcán (Box 5478), tel. 98/851000 or 800/FIESTA–1, fax 98/851800. 502 rooms. Facilities: 4 restaurants, 2 bars, health club, 3 indoor tennis courts, 15 meeting rooms, beauty parlor, boutiques, in-room safes. AE, DC, MC, V.*

**Fiesta Americana Coral Beach Cancún.** Opened in late 1990, this all-suite hotel lies just in front of the convention center and shopping malls at the rotary opposite the Hyatt Regency. The large salmon-colored structure—built in Mediterranean style with blue wrought-iron balconies—houses a lobby with marble-tiled floors, potted palms, and a stained-glass skylight. All rooms are ample in size, with oceanfront balconies, marble floors, rounded doorways, and stained-glass windows; slate-blue, lavender, and beige tones create a soothing, pleasant mood. As for outdoor activities, choose between the 1,000-foot beach and the 660-foot pool. This is Cancún's largest convention hotel; expect the clientele to match. *Paseo Kukulcán, Lote 6 (Box 14), tel. 98/832900 or 800/FIESTA–1, fax 98/832502. 602 suites. Facilities: 3 restaurants, 3 bars, pool, health club, 3 indoor tennis courts, shopping arcade. AE, MC, V.*

**Hyatt Regency Cancún.** A cylindrical 14-story tower with the Hyatt trademark—a striking central atrium filled with tropical greenery and topped by a skylit dome—affords a 360° view of the sea and the lagoon. Plants spill over the inner core of the cylinder, at the base of which is a bar. Pink and purple tones prevail in the rooms, which also feature glossy gray-marble floors and warm hardwood furniture. This hotel, much larger and livelier than its sister property, boasts an enormous two-level pool with a waterfall. The Punta Cancún location is convenient to the convention center and several shopping malls. Suites are available. *Paseo Kukulcán (Box 1201), tel. 98/ 830966, 98/831566, or 800/228–9000, fax 98/831349. 300 rooms; rooms for disabled people available. Facilities: 2 restaurants, 4 bars, shops, car rental, travel agency, game room, pool, fitness center. AE, DC, MC, V.*

**Krystal Cancún.** Its rooms, done in nondescript contemporary style, are nothing to write home about, and its lobby can be rather hectic; but the location of this hotel, part of a Mexican chain, can't be beat. At the tip of Punta Cancún, within walking distance of three major shopping malls and across the street from the convention center, the Krystal affords spectacular views of the entire ocean coast of the island, the lagoon, and parts of downtown. The property also hosts Bogart's and Hacienda El Mortero, two of the best-known restaurants in town (*see* Dining, *above*), as well as the popular Christine disco (*see* Nightlife, *below*). *Paseo Kukulcán, Lote 9, tel. 98/831133 or 800/231–9860. 330 rooms. Facilities: 5 restaurants, 3 bars, pool, tennis and racquetball courts, weight room, Jacuzzi, sauna, shops. AE, DC, MC, V.*

★ **Meliá Cancún.** The stunning new Meliá Cancún is a boldly modern version of a Mayan temple, fronted by a sheer black marble wall and a sleek waterfall. The spacious, airy atrium, filled with lush tropical flora, is dappled with sunlight flooding in from corner windows and from the steel-and-glass pyramid skylight overhead. Public spaces, displaying loving attention to detail, exude elegance; the boutiques could not be more chic. Ivory, dusty-pink, and light-blue hues softly brighten rooms (all with private balconies); white-lacquered furniture and wall-to-wall carpeting create a luxurious ambience. The long two-level pool is deliciously unobstructed; service is unusually courteous and fast. Suites are available. *Paseo Kukulcán, Km 16, tel. 98/851160 or 800/336–3542, fax 98/851263. 450 rooms. Facilities: 5 restaurants, 4 bars, 2 pools, in-room safes, shopping arcade, beauty salon, car rental, travel agency, 18-hole-golf course, health center, 3 tennis courts. AE, DC, MC, V.*

**Stouffer Presidente.** Located five minutes from Plaza Caracol, this hotel has a striking Mexican-pink facade. One of the first to open in Cancún, but extensively remodeled in 1988, it boasts a quiet beach and a waterfall in the shape of a Mayan pyramid by the pool. Well-appointed, larger-than-average-size rooms offer either one king-size or two queen-size beds, and are decorated in blue, cream, and pink pastels with light wood furnishings and tile floors. The property prides itself on its superior service. *Paseo Kukulcán, Km 7.5, tel. 98/830200, or 800/HOTELS–1, fax 98/832602 or 98/832515. 294 rooms; rooms for disabled people and no-smoking rooms available. Facilities: 4 restaurants, bar, in-room safes, fitness center, 2 pools, 5 Jacuzzis, lighted tennis court, travel agency, car rental, beauty parlor, shops. AE, DC, MC, V.*

**Villas Tacul.** The accommodations in this large complex, set on its own stretch of beach en route to downtown, are appointed with red-tile floors and authentic Mexican colonial–style furniture, wagon-wheel chandeliers, and tin-work mirrors. Each villa has a kitchen and from two to five bedrooms, making this a good place for families and couples traveling together. An individual housekeeper keeps each unit spotless and serves private breakfasts for an extra charge. The grounds are beautifully landscaped, with well-trimmed lawns and palm trees surrounding the pool. *Paseo Kukulcán, Km 5.5, tel. 98/830000, 98/ 830080, or 800/842–0193, fax 98/830349. 23 villas. Facilities: restaurant, bar, pool, 2 tennis courts. AE, DC, MC, V.*

**Expensive**   **Cancún Playa.** This hotel's airy lobby, with plenty of marble
★   and cozy sunken sofas, is a popular gathering spot: You can get a quick breakfast of good coffee and pastries here in the morning; make arrangements for car rentals and tours during the day; and enjoy a drink to the strains of a piano player in the evening. Smartly modern, the property has white facades and royal blue canvas-topped lean-tos at the pool area, which is nicely divided by lawns. The rooms are equally spiffy, with lovely pine furniture, and corner suites are equipped with private hot tubs and large terraces. *Paseo Kukulcán, Km 19.5, tel. 98/ 851111, 98/851115, or 800/44–OASIS, fax 98/851151 or 713/622– 5955 (Houston). 388 rooms. Facilities: 3 restaurants, 3 bars, 3 pools, car rental, travel agency. AE, MC, V.*

**Conrad Cancún.** Opened in 1991, this luxury property stands at the southern end of the island, on Punta Nizuc. It is one of the few hotels with direct access to both a 1,600-foot beach and Laguna Nichupté, which it shares with Club Med. The hotel comprises four nondescript low-rise concrete blocks, and the reception area is post-modern almost to the point of austerity, with scattered pieces of art posed against large, empty areas. In contrast, the restaurant set dramatically below the lobby floor is cheerfully decorated and has stunning beach views. Understated beige guest rooms are enhanced by handsome rustic furnishings. Concierge towers and suites are available. *Paseo Kukulcán, Km 20 (Box 1808), tel. 98/850086, 98/850537, or 800/ 445–8667, fax 98/850074. 391 rooms. Facilities: 2 restaurants, 3 bars, 5 pools, fitness center, 2 lighted tennis courts, 7 whirlpools, in-room safes, hair dryers. AE, DC, MC, V.*

**Moderate**   **Calinda Viva Cancún.** This white stucco 10-story building— part of a Mexican chain—is not one of the most attractive in town, but it makes a reliable standby and is in a good location, on the north beach near many malls. The rooms have marble floors; some have private balconies, ocean views, and kitchenettes. The property also features a small garden, a beach, and Mexican-theme restaurants. *Paseo Kukulcán, Km 8.5 (Box 673), tel. 98/830800. 216 rooms. Facilities: 2 restaurants, bar, pool, 2 lighted tennis courts, boutique. AE, DC, MC, V.*

**Inexpensive**   **Albergue CREA.** This modern, government-run youth hostel on the beach has glass walls, cable TV, a pool, and dormitory beds (separate rooms for men and women). A cafeteria and lounge on the ground floor lend themselves to the sort of congenial mingling one expects of a youth hostel. *Paseo Kukulcán, Km 3, tel. 98/831337. 33 rooms (350 beds) with shared baths. Facilities: cafeteria, basketball, volleyball, Ping-Pong. No credit cards.*

## Downtown

*Downtown properties are located on the Downtown Cancún Dining and Lodging map.*

**Expensive**   **Holiday Inn Centro Cancún.** The place to stay if you want to be downtown and have all the amenities, this is the newest (built

1990) and most upscale hotel in the area. It's less expensive than similar properties in the hotel zone and provides free transportation to the beach of the Holiday Inn Crowne Plaza. The attractive pink four-story structure, with a Spanish tile roof, affords easy access to restaurants and shops. Although rooms are somewhat generic motel modern, with mauve and blue color schemes, they have appealing Mexican touches. *Av. Nader 1, S.M. 2, tel. 98/87455, fax 98/847954. 190 rooms. Facilities: restaurant, 2 bars, nightclub, pool, shops, beauty salon, travel agency, car rental agency, conference rooms. AE, DC, MC, V.*

**Moderate** **Antillano.** This old but prettily appointed property features
★ wood furnishings, a cozy little lobby bar, and a tiny pool. Extras such as tiled bathroom sinks and air-conditioning in the halls and rooms make this hotel stand out a bit from the others in its league. Suites with kitchenettes are available. *Av. Tulum at Calle Claveles, tel. 98/841532 or 98/841132, fax 98/ 841878. 48 rooms. Facilities: pool, bar, travel agency, shop. AE, DC, MC, V.*

★ **Plaza del Sol.** Popular with students, Europeans, and Canadians, this three-story Spanish colonial-style hotel is situated on one of the less-trafficked main streets downtown. Inside the large lobby is a pleasant bar. Rooms feature above-average (for this price category) carved furnishings but tend to be somewhat dark; bathrooms are large. *Av. Yaxchilán 31, tel. 98/ 843888. 86 rooms. Facilities: 2 bars, restaurant, pool, laundry service, car rental, free shuttle to beach, travel agency, parking. AE, DC, MC, V.*

**Inexpensive** **María del Lourdes.** The María del Lourdes has some nice touches throughout, such as the colonial-style restaurant with rust-and-white stucco walls and the garden surrounding a small pool in the back. The rooms are bright, with sparse, functional decor. *Av. Yaxchilán 80, tel. 98/844744, fax 98/841242. 51 rooms. Facilities: restaurant, pool. AE, MC, V.*

★ **Plaza Carrillo's.** One of the first hotels to be built in Cancún City, this one is conveniently located in the heart of the downtown area next to the Plaza Carrillo shopping arcade and Carillo's restaurant (*see* Dining, *above*), which are under the same ownership. The rooms are simply furnished but clean and well maintained and are equipped with small refrigerators. *Calle Claveles 35, tel. 98/841227 or 98/844833. 43 rooms. Facilities: restaurant, pool. AE, MC, V.*

## The Arts and Nightlife

**Film** Local movie theaters showing American and Mexican films include **Espectáculos del Caribe** (Av. Tulum 44, tel. 98/840449) and **Cines Cancún 1 and 2** (Av. Cobá 112, tel. 98/841646).

**Performances** The **ballet folklórico** dinner show consists of stylized performances of regional Mexican dances including the hat dance and *la bamba*. Admission includes the buffet—a sampling of regional Mexican cooking—the show, and one drink. *Hotel Continental Villas Plaza, Paseo Kukulkán, Km 11, tel. 98/821583. Admission: about $40. Performances Tues.–Sun.; dinner 7 PM, show 8:30 PM.*

Cancún's **Jazz Festival** (tel. 800/542–8953) premiered in May of 1991 and featured Wynton Marsalis and Gato Barbieri. Sponsored by the Cancún Office of Special Events, part of the Hotel

Association, the jazz fest is scheduled to continue as an annual event and is being included in tour packages from the U.S. At press time, the 1994 schedule was not yet available.

**Discos** Cancún wouldn't be Cancún without its glittering discos and hotel-lobby bars. Generally discos start jumping about 10:30. **Dady'O** (Paseo Kukulcán, Km 9.5, tel. 98/833184 or 98/833333) is presently a very "in" place. **Christine** (Krystal Cancún hotel, tel. 98/831133) is among the most spectacular and popular joints in town. **La Boom** (Paseo Kukulcán, Km 3.5, tel. 98/831458; closed Sun.) includes a video bar with a light show and is not always crowded, although it can squeeze in 1,200 people. Visit the **Hard Rock Café** (Plaza Lagunas, Paseo Kukulcán, tel. 98/832024) for nostalgic rock music. The new **Azucar** disco in the Camino Real hotel (tel. 98/830100, ext. 8037) sizzles to a salsa beat from 8 PM to 4 AM daily.

**Music** **Cat's Reggae Bar** (Av. Yaxchilán 12, tel. 98/840407) plays island music starting at 9 PM. You can also hear live reggae at **Jalapeños** (Paseo Kukulkan, Km 7, tel. 98/8328960) and **Tequila Boom** (Paseo Kukulcán, Km 3.5, tel. 98/831458 or 98/831641) nightly from 8. **Batacha** (Hotel Miramar Misión, tel. 98/831755) is a piano bar with a small dance floor. **La Palapa** (Club Lagoon Hotel, tel. 98/831111), offering dancing on a pier over the lagoon, inspires romance. **Reflejos** (Hyatt Regency, tel. 98/830966) has a chic lounge with a small dance floor. Other popular places include **Jarro Café** (Plaza Laguna, tel. 98/832024) and **Pat O'Brien's** (Flamingo Plaza, tel. 98/83–0832).

# Isla Mujeres

*Updated by Edie Jarolim*

A tiny fish-shaped island just five miles off Cancún, Isla Mujeres (*IS-lah moo-HAIR-es*) is a tranquil alternative to its bustling western neighbor. Only about five miles long by a half-mile wide, Isla has flat sandy beaches on its northern end and steep rocky bluffs to the south. Because of its proximity to Cancún, it has turned into a small-scale tourist destination, but it is still a peaceful island retreat with a rich history and culture centered on the sea.

Part of that history is blessed by the presence of Isla's first known inhabitants, the ancient Mayas. Their legacy lies in the names, features, and language of their descendants here, but not, unfortunately, in the observatory they built on the southern tip (Hurricane Gilbert obliterated the well-preserved ruin in '88; restoration efforts are ongoing). The Spanish conquistadores followed: After setting sail from Cuba in 1517, Hernández de Córdoba's ship blew here accidentally in a storm. Credited with "discovering" the island, he and his crew dubbed their find "Isle of Women." One explanation of the name's origins is that Córdoba and company came upon wooden idols of Mayan goddesses. Another theory claims the Spaniards found only women when they arrived—the men were out fishing.

For the next several centuries, Isla, like many Caribbean islands, became a haven for pirates and smugglers, then settled into life as a quiet fishing village. In this century, it started out as a vacation destination for Mexicans; the '60s witnessed a hippie influx; since the late '70s, day-trippers from Cancún increasingly disembark here, and Isla's hotel, restaurant, and shop owners are seeing more activity than ever.

## Important Addresses and Numbers

**Tourist Information** The tourist office (Calle Hidalgo 6, behind the basketball court, tel. 987/70316), located on the main square, two blocks from the ferry, is open weekdays 9–2 and 6–8.

**Emergencies** Medical Service (tel. 987/70195); Health Center (tel. 987/70117); Police (tel. 987/70082).

**Late-night Pharmacies** Farmacia Isla Mujeres (Av. Juárez, next to the Caribbean Tropic Boutique, no phone) and Farmacia Lily (Avs. Madero and Hidalgo, no phone) and open Monday–Saturday 9 AM–9 PM.

---

## Arriving and Departing by Boat

**Arriving** Passenger ferries leave from Puerto Juárez, on the mainland, for the main ferry dock in Isla Mujeres at approximately 6, 8:30, 9:30, 10, 10:30, and 11:30 AM, and at 12:30, 1:30, 2:30, 3:30, 4:30, 5:30, 6:30, 7:30, and 8:30 PM; the schedule varies depending on the season, so check the times posted at the dock. The one-way fare is only about $1.50 and the trip takes 45 minutes, but delays and crowding are frequent. Preferable is the private *lancha*, or motorboat, which makes the crossing from Punta Sam, 5 kilometers (3 miles) north of Punta Juárez, in about 15 minutes. The fare is usually about $4 per person but varies: Water taxis charge a flat fee, about $20, divided by the number of passengers; a full load keeps the price low. Another convenient, more expensive service, the Shuttle (tel. 98/846433, in Cancún), runs directly from the Playa Linda dock in Cancún's hotel zone and costs $12 round-trip. Cars are unnecessary on Isla (*see* Getting Around, *below*), but municipal ferries that accommodate passengers and vehicles leave from Punta Sam and take about 45 minutes. Check departure times posted at the pier, but you can count on the schedule running from about 7 AM to 9 PM, and until 11 PM in the summer. The fare is under $1.50 per person.

**Departing** The passenger ferry departs from the main dock at Isla Mujeres to Puerto Juárez at approximately 5, 6:30, 7:30, 8:15, 8:45, 9:30, 10:30, and 11:30 AM, and at 12:30, 1:30, 2:30, 3:30, 4:30, 5, 5:30, and 6:30 PM. The first car ferry from Isla Mujeres to Punta Sam leaves at about 6 AM and the last departs at about 7:15 PM. The 91-foot *Caribbean Queen* (tel. 987/70254 or 987/70088, fax 987/70253), an air-conditioned ship with a bar, makes one or two 30-minute crossings daily; the fare is under $3 per person. Again, schedules vary, so you should call ahead or check the boat schedule posted at the pier.

---

## Getting Around

**By Car** There is little reason for tourists to bring cars to Isla Mujeres, because there are plenty of other forms of transportation that cost far less than renting and transporting your own private vehicle. Moreover, though the main road is paved, speed bumps abound and some areas are poorly lighted.

**By Taxi** If your time is limited you can hire a taxi (Av. Rueda Medina, tel. 987/70066) for a private island tour at about $8 an hour. Fares run $1–$2 from the ferry or downtown to the hotels on the north end, at Playa Cocoteros. Taxis line up right by the ferry dock between 5 AM and well past midnight.

**By Moped** The island is full of moped rental shops. Among them are: **Motorent Kankin** (Calle Abasolo 15, tel. 987/70071), **Pepe's Motorenta** (Calle Hidalgo 19, tel. 987/70019), and **Ciro's Motorent** (Calle Guerrero N 11 at Calle Matamoros, tel. 987/70351). Rentals cost about $5 per hour, $25 per day.

**By Bicycle** Bicycles are available for hardy cyclists, but don't underestimate the hot sun and the tricky road conditions. **Rent Me Sport Bike** (Calles Juárez and Morelos, 1 block from the main pier, no phone), offers five-speed cycles starting at less than $2 for an hour; a full day costs about $5. You can leave your driver's license in lieu of a deposit, and it's open daily 8–6.

Moped and bicycle riders should watch for the many speed bumps, which can give you an unexpected jolt. Avoid riding at night; some roads have no street lights.

## Guided Tours

**Tour Operators** Local agencies include **Club de Yates de Isla Mujeres** (Av. Rueda Medina, tel. 987/70211 or 987/70086), open daily 9–noon; and **La Isleña** (Calles Morelos and Juárez, tel. 987/70578), half a block from the pier, open daily 7–6.

**Boat Tours** **Cooperativa Lanchera** (waterfront, near the dock, no phone) offers four-hour launch trips to the Virgin, the lighthouse, the turtles at Playa Lancheros, the coral reefs at Los Manchones, and El Garrafón, for $35. **Cooperativa Isla Mujeres** (Av. Rueda Medina, tel. 987/70274), next to Mexico Divers, rents out boats at $120 for a maximum of four hours and six people, and $15 per person for an island tour with lunch (minimum six people). A trip to **Isla Contoy** (45 minutes to the north), with a minimum of 10 people, costs $30 per person and includes a light breakfast, snorkeling, lunch, and drinks; it departs at 8 AM and returns at 4 or 5.

## Exploring

*Numbers in the margin correspond to points of interest on the Isla Mujeres map.*

We start our itinerary in the island's only town, known simply as *el pueblo*, which extends the full width of Isla's northern "tail." The village is sandwiched between sand and sea to the north, south, and east; no high rises block the view. Activity
**❶** centers around the waterfront **piers** and on the coastal main drag, Avenida Rueda Medina. Two blocks inland you'll find the
**❷** other spot where everyone gathers—the **main square,** *la placita* or *el parque*, bounded by Calle Morelos, Avenida Bravo, and Calles Guerrero and Hidalgo. This is an ideal place to take in the life of the town.

**❸** Follow any of the north–south streets out to **Playa Cocoteros,** one of the finest beaches on the island, where you can wade far out in the placid waters. Along the way sit congenial palapa bars for drinks and snacks, and stands where you can rent snorkel gear, jet-skis, floats, sailboards, and sometimes parasails. At the northernmost end of Cocos, you'll find Punta Norte and come upon a hotel on its own private islet. A wood-planked bridge leads to the property, which has changed hands several times and is supposed to open by 1994 as an all-inclusive resort

# Isla Mujeres

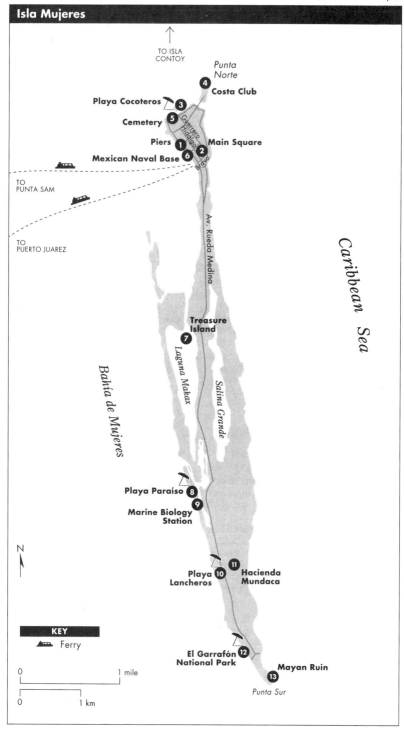

TO ISLA
CONTOY

*Punta Norte*

**④ Costa Club**

**Playa Cocoteros ③**

**Cemetery ⑤**

Herrería

Hidalgo

**Piers ①** **② Main Square**

**Mexican Naval Base ⑥**

Bravo

TO
PUNTA SAM

*Av. Rueda Medina*

TO
PUERTO JUAREZ

*Caribbean Sea*

**Treasure Island ⑦**

*Laguna Makax*

*Salina Grande*

*Bahía de Mujeres*

**Playa Paraíso ⑧**

**⑨**
**Marine Biology Station**

N

**⑪**
**Playa Lancheros ⑩** **Hacienda Mundaca**

**KEY**

⚓ Ferry

0 _____ 1 mile

0 _____ 1 km

**El Garrafón ⑫**
**National Park** **Mayan Ruin**
**⑬**

*Punta Sur*

**4** called **Costa Club.** (The other building you'll see jutting out on a rocky point is a private home.)

On the road parallel to Playa Cocos (Lopez Mateos), you'll find
**5** Isla's **cemetery,** with its hundred-year-old gravestones. Among the lovingly decorated tombs, many in memory of children, is that of Fermín Mundaca (*see* Hacienda Mundaca, *below*). A notorious 19th-century slave trader (often billed more glamorously as a pirate), Mundaca is said to have carved his own tombstone with a skull and crossbones. On one side of the tomb an inscription reads in Spanish: "As You Are, I Once Was"; the other side warns, "As I Am, So Shall You Be." Mundaca's grave is empty, however; no one knows exactly where his remains lie. The monument is not easy to find—ask a local to point out the unidentified marker.

To explore the rest of the island, you'll need to take a moped or taxi south along the Avenida Rueda Medina, which leads out of town. The first landmark you'll pass after the piers is the
**6** **Mexican naval base,** which is closed to the public. From the road, however, you can see (but don't photograph) the modest flag-raising and -lowering ceremonies at sunrise and sunset. Continuing southward, the *salinas* (salt marshes) will be on your left, and on your right you'll see the **Laguna Makax,** where pirates are said to have anchored their ships as they lay in wait for the hapless vessels plying Spanish Main (the geographical area in which Spanish treasure ships trafficked).

Follow the road until you come to an unmarked turnoff that
**7** leads to a bridge across the lagoon and out to **Treasure Island,** where there's **Pirates Cove,** a small theme park visited mostly by Cancún day-trippers. Though few overnighters take an interest in this attraction, families who stop in enjoy the model shipwreck, open-air theater, shops, restaurant, and some caged birds and animals.

Head back to the main road and travel south for about 4 kilome-
**8** ters (2½ miles); take the right turnoff at the sign to **Playa Paraíso.** The lovely beach is fronted by Hacienda Gomar, a good restaurant featuring a buffet lunch and marimba music. If you'd rather not put your shoes back on, try the barbecued grouper, snapper, or barracuda at Blacky's open grill on the beach. Also in the area you'll find boutiques and a beach bar with small palapas.

Walk about ½ kilometer south, either along the beach or on the soon-to-be-paved dirt road, until you come to the sign that says "Pesca." This signals the entrance to the government-run
**9** **marine biology station,** which is devoted primarily to the study and preservation of the sea turtle, the lobster, and coral reefs. Technically the station is not open to the public, but during working hours visitors can examine various species and talk to the biologists about their work.

**10** Just south of Paraíso lies **Playa Lancheros,** where you can eat lunch in the modest restaurant or shop for handicrafts, souvenirs, and T-shirts at the small stands. Also housed here, in a sea pen, are some pet sea turtles and harmless *tiburón gato* (nurse sharks). On the ocean side live the carnivorous *tintorera* (female sharks), which have seven rows of teeth and weigh as much as 500 kilograms (1,100 pounds). There is a small entrance fee to the beach, and you can buy refreshments and souvenirs. Live music is played on certain afternoons.

Off the main road, across from the entrance to Playa Lancheros, a tiny footpath cut through the brush leads to the remains of the **Hacienda Mundaca,** built by Fermín Mundaca de Marechaja, the 19th-century slave-trader-cum-pirate mentioned above. When the British navy began cracking down on slavers, he settled on the island and built an ambitious estate with resplendent tropical gardens. The story goes that he constructed it to woo a certain island woman who, in the end, chose another man.

What little remained of the hacienda has mysteriously vanished, except for a sorry excuse of a guardhouse, an arch, a pediment, and a well. If you push your way through the jungle— the mosquitoes are fierce—you'll eventually come to the ruined stone archway and triangular pediment, carved with the following inscription: *Huerta de la Hacienda de Vista Alegre MDCCCLXXVI* (Orchard of the Happy View Hacienda, 1876).

The next major site along the main road is **El Garrafón National Park,** the much-hyped, overvisited snorkeling mecca for thousands of day-trippers from Cancún. Although still beautiful, Garrafón—which lies at the bottom of a bluff—was once almost magical in its beauty. Now, as a result of the hands and fins of eager divers, Hurricane Gilbert, and anchors cast from the fleets of tourist boats continually arriving from Cancún, the coral reef here is virtually dead. Still, visitors will be impressed by the scenery—parrotfish, angelfish, and the rich blue-greens of the water. Arriving early is essential if you wish to avoid the hordes that begin arriving around 10 AM. There are food stands and souvenir shops galore, as well as palapas, lockers, equipment rental, and a small aquarium. *No phone. Admission: $5. Open daily 9–5.*

Continuing around the southern tip of Isla Mujeres, about 1 kilometer (⅗ mile) from Garrafón, you'll come to the sad vestiges of a **Mayan ruin,** formerly a temple dedicated to Ixchel, the goddess of fertility. Though Hurricane Gilbert whalloped the ruin and succeeded in blowing most of it away, restoration efforts are underway. The adjacent **lighthouse** still stands, and the keeper sometimes allows visitors to go up. Just past that point, on the windward side, is one of the island's most scenic patches of coastline, from which you can also make out the skyline (and lights, if it's dark) of Cancún. From here, follow the road into town; it's about an hour's walk. Flag a cab on the road if you wish.

---

### Shopping

Shopping on Isla Mujeres used to be limited to basic resort wear, suntan lotions, and groceries. Now, more Mexican crafts shops offering good deals on silver, fabric bags, and handcrafted objects are opening here. Even the smaller shops often accept credit cards. Shopping hours are generally daily 10–1 and 4–7, although many stores now stay open through siesta and after 7.

**La Loma** (Calle Guerrero 6, 2nd floor, on the east side of the main square, tel. 987/70446) has a selection of exquisite crafts from all over Mexico and Guatemala, including amber, silver, black jade, leather jewelry, and masks, pottery, and textile bags. Although the shop is not inexpensive, La Loma offers the biggest and best collection on the island. **Tienda Paulita** (Calles

Morelos and Hidalgo, tel. 987/70014) features a standard selection of folk art and handmade clothing in a fairly large space. **Rachat & Rome** (Av. Rueda Medina, tel. 987/70250), housed in the pink building by the dock, sells gold, silver, and gemstones. **Casa del Arte Mexica** (Calle Hidalgo 6, no phone) has a good choice of clay reproductions, silver jewelry, batiks, rubbings, wood carvings, leather, and hammocks.

## Sports and Fitness

**Fishing** Billfish are a popular catch in spring and early summer; the rest of the year, you can fish for barracuda and tuna, as well as for shad, sailfish, grouper, and red snapper.

**Bahía Dive Shop** (Av. Rueda Medina, across from the pier, tel. and fax 987/70340) charges $250 for a day of deep-sea fishing, $200 a day for cast fishing (tarpon, snook, and bonefish), and $20 an hour for offshore fishing (barracuda, snapper, and smaller fish).

**Snorkeling and** **Bahía Dive Shop** (Av. Rueda Medina 166, across from the pier, **Scuba Diving** tel. and fax 987/70340) rents snorkeling and scuba equipment and runs three-hour boat and dive trips to the reefs and the Cave of the Sleeping Sharks. Snorkel gear goes for $4 a day; tanks, $40–$55, depending on the length of the dive. **Mexico Divers** (Av. Rueda Medina and Av. Medero, 1 block from the ferry, tel. 987/70131 or 987/70274), also called **Buzos de México,** runs three-hour snorkeling tours for $15; trips for certified divers start at $40 per tank. Dive master Carlos Gutiérrez also gives a resort course for $80 and open-water PADI certification for $350.

## Dining

Dining on Isla Mujeres offers what you would expect on a small island: plenty of fresh-grilled seafood—lobster, shrimp, conch, and fish. You can also try Mexican and Yucatecan specialties like *carne asada* (broiled beef), *pollo píbil* (chicken baked in banana leaves in a tangy sour orange sauce), and *poc chuc* (pork marinated in sour orange sauce with pickled onions). Those who crave more familiar fare can opt for pizza, steak, or shish-kebob. Highly recommended restaurants are indicated by a star ★.

| Category | Cost* |
| --- | --- |
| Very Expensive | over $20 |
| Expensive | $15–$20 |
| Moderate | $8–$15 |
| Inexpensive | under $8 |

*per person, excluding drinks and service*

**Expensive** **Chez Magaly.** A very elegant establishment on the grounds of ★ the Nautibeach Condo-hotel, this mostly French restaurant is tastefully furnished with wood floors, plants, leather chairs, Chinese blinds, and handsome place settings. Seafood grills, lobster quiche, jambalaya (Caribbean paella), and tequila-flambéed mangos are among the specialties. To complement the meal, choose from an extensive wine list. *Av. Rueda Medi-*

*na, Playa Norte, tel. 987/70259. Reservations advised. MC, V.
Closed 2 weeks in June.*

**Maria's Kan Kin.** Near El Garaffón, at the southern end of the
island, this beach restaurant features gourmet seafood. Choose
a live lobster or try one of the specialties, which tend to be prepared with a French twist, like lobster bisque and chocolate
mousse. It's the perfect spot for a long lunch that extends to
sunset. *On the main road to Garaffón, tel. 987/70015. MC, V.*

**Moderate**   **El Limbo.** This restaurant—housed in the Hotel Roca Mar,
which has been carved into the side of a cliff—offers a sensational view of the sea, which laps up to the lower level windows.
The decor remains typical for the island: Nets, seashells, and
tortoiseshells adorn the walls, while rustic wood furniture fills
the dining area. Included on the menu are pollo píbil, pork
chops, and steak, as well as many seafood specials. You have the
choice of fish or shellfish broiled, breaded, fried, or in garlic, all
served with rice or french fries and salad. *Av. Bravo and Calle
Guerrero, at Hotel Roca Mar, tel. 987/70101. No reservations.
MC, V.*

★ **Pizza Rolandi.** Red tables, yellow director's chairs, green walls
and window trim, and dark wood beams set the cozy tone at this
very "in" chain restaurant. Select from a broad variety of Italian food: lobster pizzas, calzones, and pastas. Grilled fresh fish
and shrimp are highly recommended, and salads are excellent.
Or just stop in for a drink at one of the outside tables; the
margaritas are the best in town. *Calle Hidalgo (between Calles
Madero and Abasolo), tel. 987/70430. No reservations. MC, V.*

**Inexpensive**   **Lonchería Poc Chuc.** This tiny restaurant is named for the famous Yucatán dish of pork marinated in sour orange, which is a
house specialty. The no-frills Mexican eatery has a decent
breakfast, too. *Calle Juárez (between Calles Madero and Morelos), no phone. No reservations. No credit cards.*

**Mirtita's, Tropicana,** and **Villa del Mar.** Next to each other on
Av. Rueda Medina across from the ferry dock, these are favorite local hangouts. All serve fresh seafood and Yucatecan specialties. *Av. Rueda Medina. No phone. No credit cards.*

### Lodging

The approximately 25 hotels (about 600 rooms) on Isla Mujeres
generally fall into one of two categories: The older, more modest places are situated right in town, and the newer, more expensive properties tend to have beachfront locations. Most
hotels have ceiling fans and air-conditioning. All share the
77400 postal code. Highly recommended hotels are indicated by
a star ★.

| Category | Cost* |
|---|---|
| Very Expensive | over $90 |
| Expensive | $60–$90 |
| Moderate | $25–$60 |
| Inexpensive | under $25 |

*\*All prices are for a standard double room, excluding service
and the 10% tax.*

**Expensive** **Na-Balam.** This intimate, informal hostelry set on Playa Cocos
★ will fulfill all your tropical-paradise fantasies. Three corner
suites with balconies affording outstanding views of sea and
sand are well worth $75. The simple, attractive rooms have tur-
quoise-tiled floors, carved wood furniture, dining areas, and
patios facing the beach; photos of Mexico in its bygone days and
Mexican carvings grace the walls. Breakfast at the hotel's restaurant is a delightful way to kick off the day. *Calle Zazil Ha
118, tel. 987/70279, fax 987/70446. 12 suites. Facilities: air-conditioning, restaurant, bar, beach. AE, MC, V.*

**Moderate** **Belmar.** Right in the heart of town, above Pizza Rolandi, this
small hotel shares a charming plant-filled inner courtyard with
the restaurant, which means it can be noisy here until 11 PM.
Standard rooms are pretty, with tiled baths and light-wood furniture. One enormous suite features a private Jacuzzi on a patio, a
tiled kitchenette, and a sitting area. All rooms have cable TV and
air-conditioning. *Calle Hidalgo 110 (between Calles Madero
and Abasolo), tel. 987/70430. 11 rooms. AE, DC, MC, V.*

★ **Cabañas María del Mar.** A rather mind-boggling assortment of
rooms is available in this unusual beachfront hotel, but all have
a great deal of character, and the place as a whole has a unique
Mexican atmosphere. There are hand-carved wood furnishings
by local artisans in a combination of Spanish and Mayan styles,
folk art, tiled baths, hand-painted sinks, and, for Yucatecan
visitors who don't like beds, some rooms even have hammock
rings. The hotel has a prime location on Playa Cocos, next to
Na-Balam, and its reasonable room rates include Continental
breakfast. *Av. Carlos Lazos 1, tel. 987/70213, 987/70179, or
800/826–6842, fax 305/531–7616 or 987/70173. 51 rooms, including 12 cabanas. Facilities: air-conditioning, pool, moped
rental, restaurant/bar, travel agency, car and boat service.
MC, V.*

**Posada del Mar.** This hotel's assets include its prime location
between town and Playa Cocos and its reasonable prices.
Rooms have balconies overlooking a main road and beyond to
the waterfront. The simple wood furnishings appear somewhat
worse for wear, although baths are clean, with cheerful sea
green tiles. Inexpensive private bungalows are also available.
A new bar, in the process of construction, promises to be as
popular as the current palapa-roofed local hangout. *Av. Rueda
Medina 15, tel. 987/70300, 987/70044, fax 987/70266. 42 rooms.
Facilities: 2 restaurants, bar, pool. AE, MC, V.*

**Inexpensive** **Poc-Na.** The island's youth hostel, located at the eastern end of
town, rents bunks or hammocks (which cost less), but it re-
quires a deposit that's almost twice the cost of the accommodations. One bonus is its proximity to the beach. *Calle
Matamoros 15, tel. 987/70090 or 987/70059. Facilities: dining
room, lockers, showers. No credit cards.*

## The Arts and Nightlife

**The Arts** Festivals and cultural events occur on many weekends, with
live entertainment on the outdoor stage in the main square.
The whole island celebrates events like the spring regattas and
the Caribbean music festivals. **Casa de la Cultura,** near the
youth hostel, offers folkloric dance and aerobics classes year-
round. The center also operates a small public library and book
exchange. *Av. Guerrero, tel. 987/70307. Open Mon.–Sat. 9–1,*

*4–8*. For English-language films visit **Cine Blanquita** (Calle Morelos, between Calles Guerrero and Hidalgo, no phone).

**Nightlife** Most restaurant bars feature a happy hour from 5 to 7; the palapa bars at Playa Cocos are an excellent place to watch the sunset. The bar at the **Posada del Mar** (Av. Rueda Medina 15, tel. 987/70300) can be subdued or hopping, depending on what's going on in town. **Buho's,** the bar/restaurant at Cabañas María del Mar (Calle Carlos Lazo 1, tel. 987/70213), serves food and is another good choice for a relaxing drink at sunset or later at night. **Restaurante La Peña** (Calle Guerrero 5, tel. 987/70321) has music and dancing on its open-air terrace overlooking the sea. Locals swear by the down-home ambience at **Calypso** (Av. Rueda Medina, near the lighthouse and Playa Cocos, no phone). Go watch music videos or sports events at **Tequila** (Calle Hidalgo 19, tel. 987/70019), which also hosts a disco in high season. Hours vary, but you will find it open weekend nights. Head for the main square if you're in the mood for Caribbean, salsa, or other live music.

# Cozumel

*Updated by Edie Jarolim* Cozumel provides a balance between Cancún and Isla Mujeres: Though attuned to North American tourism, the island has managed to keep development to a minimum. Its expansive beaches, superb coral reefs, and copious wildlife—in the sea, on the land, and in the air—attract an active, athletic crowd. Rated one of the top destinations in the world among underwater enthusiasts, Cozumel is encircled by a garland of reefs entrancing divers and snorkelers alike. Despite the inevitable effects of docking cruise ships (shops and restaurants actively recruit customers on an increasingly populous main drag), the island's earthy charm and tranquility remain intact. The relaxing atmosphere here is typically Mexican—friendly and unpretentious. Cozumel's rich Mayan heritage is reflected in the faces of 60,000 or so isleños; you'll see people who look like ancient statues come to life, and occasionally hear Mayan spoken.

A 490-square-kilometer (189-square-mile) island 19 kilometers (12 miles) to the east of Yucatán, Cozumel is mostly flat, its interior covered by parched scrub, dense jungle, and marshy lagoons. White sandy beaches with calm waters line the island's leeward (western) side, which is fringed by a spectacular reef system, while the powerful surf and rocky strands on the windward (eastern) side, facing the Caribbean, are broken up here and there by calm bays and hidden coves. Most of Cozumel is undeveloped, with a good deal of the land and the shores set aside as national parks; a few Mayan ruins provide what limited sightseeing there is aside from the island's glorious natural attractions. San Miguel is the only established town.

## Important Addresses and Numbers

**Tourist Information** The **state tourism office** (tel. 987/20218 or tel. and fax 987/23318) is located upstairs in the Plaza del Sol mall, at the east end of the main square, or *la plaza*, and is open weekdays 8:30–3. A good source of information on lodgings (as well as of general information) is the **Cozumel Island Hotel Association** (Calle 2 N at 15a, tel. 987/23132, fax 987/22809), open weekdays 8–2 and 4–7.

**Emergencies** **Police** (Anexo del Palacio Municipal, tel. 987/20092); **Red Cross** (Av. Rosada Salas at Av. 20a S, tel. 987/21058); **Air Ambulance** (tel. 987/20912); **Port Captain** (tel. 987/20169); **Recompression Chamber** (Calle 5 S 21-B, between Av. Rafael Melgar and Av. 5a S, tel. 987/22387).

**Late-night** **Farmacia Joaquín** (plaza, tel. 987/20125) is open Monday–Sat-
**Pharmacies** urday 8 AM–10 PM and Sunday 9–1 and 5–9.

## Arriving and Departing by Plane, Ferry, and Jetfoil

**By Plane** **The Cozumel Airport** is 3 kilometers (2 miles) north of town. **Continental** (tel. 800/231–0856, tel. 987/20847 in Cozumel) provides nonstop service from Houston. **Mexicana** (tel. 800/531–7921, 987/22945 in Cozumel) flies nonstop from Dallas/Fort Worth, Miami, and San Francisco; **Aerocaribe** and **Aerocozumel** (tel. 987/20877 or 987/20928), both Mexicana subsidiaries, fly to Cancún (12 round-trip flights daily) and other destinations in Mexico, including Chichén Itzá, Chetumal, Mérida, and Playa del Carmen.

*Between the Airport* Because of an agreement between the taxi drivers' and the bus
*and Hotels* drivers' unions, there is no taxi service from the airport; taxi service is available to the airport, however. Arriving passengers reach their hotels via the *colectivo*, a van with a maximum capacity of eight. Buy a ticket at the airport exit: the charge is $5 per passenger to the hotel zones, a little under $3 into town. If you want to get to your hotel without waiting for the van to fill and for other passengers to be dropped off, you can hire an "especial"—an individual van costing a little under $20 to the hotel zones, about $8 to the city. Taxis to the airport cost about $8 from the hotel zones and approximately $5 from downtown.

**By Ferry** Passenger-only ferries depart from the **Playa del Carmen dock** (no phone) for the 40-minute trip to the main pier in Cozumel. They leave approximately every hour between 5:30 AM and 9 PM and cost about $7. Return service to Playa operates from roughly 4 AM to 10 PM. Verify the regularly changing schedule. A new 320-passenger boat, *La Vikinga,* now provides fast service between Cozumel, Cancún, and Isla Mujeres; departures for Cancún from Cozumel are at 10:45 AM and 6:30 PM, and the cost is $27 one way. Call 987/20477 or 987/21588 for more information. The older car ferry from **Puerto Morelos** (tel. 987/21722) is not recommended unless you *must* bring your car. The three- to four-hour trip costs about $30 depending on the size of the car or $4.50 per passenger. Again, schedules change frequently, so we advise you to call ahead. Tickets can be bought up to a day in advance.

**By Jetfoil** Two waterjet catamarans make the trip between Cozumel (downtown pier, at the zócalo) and Playa del Carmen. This service, operated by **Aviomar** (tel. 987/20588 or 987/20477), costs the same as the ferry and takes as much time, but the vessel is considerably more comfortable and offers on-board videos and refreshments. The boats make at least eight crossings a day, leaving Playa del Carmen approximately every two hours between 7:30 AM and 9:30 PM and returning from Cozumel between 6:30 AM and 8 PM. Tickets are sold at the piers in both ports one hour before departure, but call to confirm the schedule.

## Getting Around

**By Bus** Because of a union agreement with taxi drivers, no public buses operate in the north and south hotel zones; local bus service runs mainly within the town of San Miguel, although there is a route from town to the airport. Service is irregular but inexpensive (under NP$1).

**By Car** Open-air Jeeps and other rental cars, especially those with four-wheel drive, are a good way of getting down dirt roads leading to secluded beaches and small Mayan ruins (although the rental insurance policy may not always cover these jaunts). The only gas station on Cozumel, at the corner of Avenida Juárez and Avenida 30a, is open daily 7 AM–midnight.

*Car Rentals* Try **Avis** (Calle 20 between Calle Rosada Salas and Calle 3 S, tel. 987/21923; at Hotel Stouffer Presidente, tel. 987/20322), **Budget** (Av. 5a, between Calle 2 N and Calle 4 N, tel. 987/20903; at the cruise-ship terminal, tel. 987/21732; and at the airport, tel. 987/21742), **Fiesta Cozumel** (Hotel Mesón San Miguel, tel. 987/21389), or **Hertz** (Av. Juárez and Calle 10, tel. 987/22136). Car rates start at $50 a day.

**By Moped and Motorcycle** Mopeds and motorcycles are very popular here, but also extremely dangerous. Mexican law now requires all passengers to wear helmets. For mopeds, go to **Fiesta Cozumel, Rentadora Caribe** (Calle Rosada Salas 3, tel. 987/20955), or **Rentadora Cozumel** (Calle Rosada Salas 3 B, tel. 987/21429, and Av. 10a S at Calle 1, tel. 987/21120). Mopeds rent for $25 per day.

**By Taxi** **Taxi service** is available 24 hours a day, with a 25% surcharge between midnight and 6 AM, at the main location (2 Calle N, tel. 987/20041 or 987/20236) or at the *malecón*, as the oceanside walkway is called, at the main pier in town. You can also hail taxis on the street, and there are taxis waiting at all the major hotels. Fixed rates of about $3 are charged to go between town and either hotel zone, about $8 from most hotels to the airport.

## Guided Tours

**Orientation** Island tours are offered for about $30 by at least two of Cozumel's leading travel agencies. The **Intermar Caribe** (tel. 987/21535) version includes swimming at a beach on the windward side, a visit to a "coral factory" in town, and snorkeling and lunch at Chankanaab. **Turismo Aviomar** (tel. 987/20588) sells the same tour and a variation: the Mayan ruins at San Gervasio, swimming, beach games, and jetskiing at Playa del Sol (near Palancar Beach, on the leeward side).

**Specialty Tours** **Snorkeling tours** go for anywhere from $18 to $35, depending on the length, and take in the shallow reefs off Palancar or the Colombia lagoon. Lunch on a beach and equipment are usually included. **Diving tour** rates begin at about $56 per day; snorkelers wishing to accompany dive boats may do so for about $25.

Strictly for professional divers is the all-inclusive scuba trip to **Banco Chinchorro,** a ship graveyard 16 kilometers (10 miles) off the coast of southern Quintana Roo, almost due east of Chetumal. **Barbachano Tours** (1570 Madruga Ave., Ph. #1, Coral Gables, FL 33146, tel. 305/662–5971) sponsors the trip.

Glass-bottom-boat trips provided by **Turismo Aviomar** (tel. 87/20588) appeal to people who don't want to get wet but do want to see the brilliant underwater life around the island. Four times a week, the air-conditioned semisubmarine *Mermaid* glides over a number of reefs that host a dazzling array of fish; the tour, which costs $30, lasts 1 hour and 45 minutes and includes soft drinks and beer.

**Off-island tours** to Tulum and Xel-Há, run by **Intermar Caribe** and **Turismo Aviomar,** cost about $54 and include the 30-minute ferry trip to Playa del Carmen, the 45-minute ride to Tulum, 1½–2 hours at the ruins, entrance fees, guides, lunch, and sometimes a stop for snorkeling at Xel-Há lagoon.

The Cozumel Museum offers evening **turtle-watching tours** during which visitors aid in the preservation of the endangered turtle species. The tours run between May and September, when the babies hatch. *Av. Rafael Melgar, between Calles 4 and 6 N, tel. 987/21545. Suggested donation: $10. May–Sept., check museum for weekly tour schedules.*

## Exploring

Cozumel is about 53 kilometers (33 miles) long and 15 kilometers (9 miles) wide, but only a small percentage of its roads—primarily those in the southern half—are paved. Dirt roads can be explored, with care, in a four-wheel-drive vehicle. Aside from the 3% of the island that has been developed, Cozumel is made up of vast expanses of sandy or rocky beaches, quiet little coves, palm groves, scrubby jungles, lagoons and swamps, and a few low hills (the maximum elevation is 45 feet).

*Numbers in the margin correspond to points of interest on the Cozumel map.*

❶ Cozumel's principal town, **San Miguel,** serves as the hub of the island; its Avenida Rafael Melgar, along the waterfront, is the main strip of shops and restaurants. The **Plaza del Sol** is the main square, most often simply called *la plaza* or *el parque.* Directly across from the docks, it's hard to miss. The square is the heart of the town, where everyone congregates in the evenings. Heading inland (east) from the malecón (the walkway along the ocean) takes you away from the touristy zone and toward the residential sections.

The **Museo de la Isla de Cozumel** is a good place to begin orienting yourself. Housed on two floors of what was once the island's first luxury hotel are four permanent exhibit halls of dioramas, sculptures, charts, and explanations of the island's history and ecosystem. The museum also presents temporary exhibits, guided tours, and workshops. *Av. Rafael Melgar between Calles 4 and 6 N, tel. 987/21545 or 987/21475. Admission: $3. Open Sun.–Fri. 10–6; closed Sat.*

**Time Out**  On the terrace off the second floor of the museum, the **Restaurante del Museo** (Av. Rafael Melgar, between Calle 4 and 6 N, tel. 987/20838) offers breakfast, drinks, or a full meal of *fajitas* or grilled red snapper; all enhanced by a great waterfront view.

Heading south of town, divers and snorkelers may want to take ❷ a plunge off the pier at **La Ceiba:** About 100 yards offshore lie the remains of a small airplane that was placed there in 1977 during the making of a Mexican movie. An underwater trail

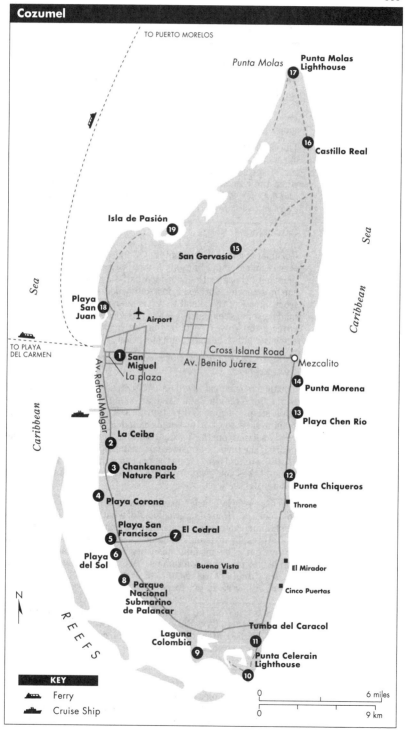

# Cozumel

TO PUERTO MORELOS

*Punta Molas*

**Punta Molas Lighthouse**

**17**

**16** **Castillo Real**

*Sea*

*Caribbean*

**Isla de Pasión**

**19**

**15**

**San Gervasio**

*Sea*

**Playa San Juan** **18**

Airport

TO PLAYA DEL CARMEN

Cross Island Road

**1** **San Miguel**

La plaza

*Av.* *Rafael Melgar*

Av. Benito Juárez

Mezcalito

**14** **Punta Morena**

**13** **Playa Chen Río**

**La Ceiba**

**2**

*Caribbean*

**3** **Chankanaab Nature Park**

**12** **Punta Chiqueros**

■ **Throne**

**4** **Playa Corona**

**Playa San Francisco**

**5** **El Cedral** **7**

**Playa del Sol** **6**

■ **El Mirador**

**Buena Vista** ■

**8** **Parque Nacional Submarino de Palancar**

■ **Cinco Puertas**

N

**Tumba del Caracol**

R E E F S

**Laguna Colombia**

**11**

**Punta Celerain Lighthouse**

**9**

**10**

**KEY**

Ferry

Cruise Ship

0 ——— 6 miles

0 ——— 9 km

marks various types of sea life, including sponges and enormous coral formations; visibility is excellent to about 30 meters (about 98 feet).

About a 10-minute drive south of San Miguel you will find **Chankanaab Nature Park** (the name means "small sea"), a lovely saltwater lagoon that the government has made into a wildlife sanctuary and botanical garden. Underwater caves, offshore reefs, a protected bay, and a sunken ship attract droves of snorkelers and scuba divers. Some 60-odd species of marine life, including fish, coral, turtles, and various crustaceans, reside in the lagoon. Sadly, swimming through the underwater tunnels from the lagoon to the bay is now forbidden, but visitors may walk through the shallow lagoon. Be warned, however, that the bottom is rocky, so wear shoes with rubber soles. Four dive shops, a restaurant, four gift shops, a snack stand, and a dressing room with lockers and showers are on the premises. *Carretera Sur, Km 9, no phone. Admission: $4. Open daily 9–5.*

Just south of Chankanaab, **Playa Corona** offers the same brilliant marine life as the park by sharing access to the Yucab reef. Snorkeling equipment is available for rent, and the restaurant here serves conch and shrimp ceviche, fajitas, and more. The crowds that visit Chankanaab haven't yet discovered this tranquil neighbor.

More southerly still lies **Playa San Francisco,** an inviting 5-kilometer (3-mile) stretch of sandy beach that's considered one of the longest and finest on Cozumel. Environmental concerns have halted plans to build five new luxury hotels here, but there are two outdoor restaurants, a bar, dressing rooms, gift shops, volleyball nets, beach chairs, and snorkeling equipment. Just past San Francisco is **Playa del Sol.** Now open to the public, this beach was once privately owned by the tour operator Aviomar; it has complete facilities, including a restaurant-bar, shops, and snorkeling and jetskiing equipment; you can also rent horses and trot down the beach.

A turnoff at Km 17.5 leads about 3 kilometers (2 miles) inland to the village and ruins of **El Cedral,** once the largest Mayan site on Cozumel and the temple sighted by the original Spanish explorers in 1518. The first Mass in Mexico was reportedly celebrated at this temple, most of which was torn down by the conquistadores. All that remains is a small structure capped by a Mayan arch and covered by faint traces of paint and stucco. A defiant tree grows from its roof.

More interesting than the ruin is the small green contemporary church housing 92 crosses shrouded in embroidered lace mantles. The crosses, which were thought to have oracular qualities, testify to the cult of the "Speaking Cross," which inspired the rebellious Mayas during the War of the Castes in the mid-1800s.

Backtrack to the coast and continue south, and you'll come to **Parque Nacíonal Submarino de Palancar,** whose beach, with a gently sloping shore enlivened by palm trees, is far more deserted than San Francisco. Offshore lies the famous **Palancar Reef,** which is practically Cozumel's raison d'être.

At the island's southern tip and most commonly reached by boat (although there is a trail) is the **Laguna Colombia,** a prime site for jungle aficionados. Fish migrate here to lay their eggs, and barracuda, baby fish, and birds show up in great numbers in season.

If you continue east on the paved road, you'll reach the Caribbean coast. Make a right turn off the paved road onto a dirt road and follow it for 4 kilometers (3 miles) south to get to the

⑩ **Punta Celerain Lighthouse,** surrounded by sand dunes at the narrowest point of land. The lighthouse affords a misty, mesmerizing view of pounding waves, swamps, and scraggly jungle. On Sunday at noon, the point comes to life when Primo the lighthouse keeper serves fried fish and beer, and locals and tourists gather to chat.

After visiting the lighthouse, backtrack on the dirt road north.

⑪ You will first pass the **Tumba del Caracol,** another Mayan ruin that may have served as a lighthouse. The east coast of Cozumel, at which you have now arrived, presents a splendid succession of mostly deserted rocky coves and narrow, powdery beaches—sadly garbage-strewn in spots—posed dramatically against astoundingly turquoise water. Swimming can be treacherous here, but there is nothing (except perhaps the lack of changing facilities, since most of the beaches can be seen from the road) to prevent solitary sunbathing on any of the several beaches.

⑫ **Punta Chiqueros,** a moon-shaped cove sheltered from the sea by an offshore reef, is the next attraction en route; you'll be back on the paved road by the time you get to this point. Part of a longer stretch of beach that most locals call **Playa Bonita,** it has fine sand, clear water, and moderate waves. You can swim and camp here, watch the sun set and the moon rise, and dine at the Playa Bonita restaurant. A little less than 5 kilometers (3

⑬ miles) away, is **Playa Chen Río,** another good spot for camping or exploring, where the waters are clear and the surf is not too strong.

Nearly 1 kilometer (½ mile) north of Chen Río along the main

⑭ road is **Punta Morena,** where waves crash on the rocky beach and, on June nights when the moon is full, turtles come to lay their eggs.

The cross-island road meets the east coast at **Mezcalito Café;** here you can turn back to town or continue north. If you choose the latter, you'll have to travel along a dead-end dirt road; eventually you'll have to turn around.

At this point you may decide to detour inland to the jungle, and

⑮ view the ruins of **San Gervasio,** the largest extant Mayan site on Cozumel. San Gervasio was once the island's capital and probably its ceremonial center, dedicated to the fertility goddess Ix-Chel. The classical- and postclassical-style site was continuously occupied from AD 300 to AD 1500. What remains today are several small mounds scattered around a plaza and several broken columns and lintels that were once part of the main building or observatory. *Admission: $1 for access to the road, $3.50 for access to the ruins; $1 for use of a video camera. Open daily 8–5.*

The road to the ruins is a good one, but a nearly unmaneuverable dirt road leads northeast of San Gervasio back to the unpaved coast road. At the junction is a marvelously deserted beach where you can camp. At the northern end of the

⑯ beach you'll find **Castillo Real,** another Mayan site comprising a lookout tower, the base of a pyramid, and a temple with two chambers capped by a false arch.

A number of other minor ruins are spread across the northern
⑰ tip of Cozumel, which terminates at the **Punta Molas Lighthouse,** an excellent spot for sunbathing, birding, and camping. This entire area is accessible only by four-wheel-drive vehicles (or by boat), but the jagged shoreline and the open sea offer magnificent views, making it well worth the trip.

Back on the leeward side of the island, north of town, is a long
⑱ expanse of sandy beach known as **Playa San Juan,** which culminates in Punta Norte. The island's northern cluster of hotels occupies the sea side of the highway here; across the way are several restaurants. Just beyond Punta Norte, smack in the
⑲ middle of Abrigo Bay, you'll find **Isla de Pasión.** The secluded beaches of this tiny island are now part of a state reserve, and fishing is permitted. Backtrack along the coast road to return to San Miguel.

### Shopping

Cozumel has three main shopping areas: **downtown** along the waterfront, on Avenida Rafael Melgar, and on some of the side streets around the plaza (there are more than 150 shops in this area alone); at the **crafts market** (Calle 1 S, behind the plaza) in town, which sells a respectable assortment of Mexican wares; and at the cruise-ship **passenger terminal** south of town, near the Casa Del Mar, La Ceiba, and Sol Caribe hotels. There are also small clusters of shops at **Plaza del Sol** (on the east side of the main plaza), **Plaza de las Garzas** (Av. Rafael Melgar at Calle 8), and **Plaza Maya 2000** (across from the Sol Caribe). As a general rule, the newer, trendier shops line the waterfront, while the area around Avenida 5a houses the better crafts shops. The **town market** (Calle Rosada Salas, between Avs. 20a and 25a) sells fresh produce and other essentials.

**Department Stores** **Orbi** (Av. Rafael Melgar S 27, tel. 987/20685) sells everything from liquor and perfume to snorkeling gear and luggage; **Pama** (Av. Rafael Melgar S 9, tel. 987/20090), near the pier, features imported food, luggage, snorkeling gear, jewelry, and crystal; and **Prococo** (Av. Rafael Melgar N 99, tel. 987/28113) offers a good selection of liquor, jewelry, and gift items.

**Specialty Stores**
*Clothing* Several trendy sportswear stores line Avenida Rafael Melgar (between Calles 2 and 6), including **Aca Joe, Bye-Bye Cozumel,** and **Explora. La Fiesta Cotton Country** (Av. Rafael Melgar N 164-B, tel. 987/22032) sells a variety of T-shirts as well as souvenirs.

*Jewelry* Jewelry on Cozumel is pricey, but it tends to be of higher quality than the jewelry you'll find in many of the other Yucatán towns. **Van Cleef** (Av. Rafael Melgar N 54, tel. 987/21143) offers a good collection of silver jewelry and gemstone rings. Down the block from Van Cleef, is **Casablanca** (Av. Rafael Melgar N 33, tel. 987/21177), which specializes in gold, silver, and gemstones, as well as expensive crafts. **La Fiesta Silver Country** (Av. Rafael Melgar N 164-A, tel. 987/22143 or 987/22054) offers silver, much of it of the cheap, junky variety, but with some nice-looking pieces. Nothing but fine silver, gold, and coral jewelry is sold at **Joyería Palancar** (Av. Rafael Melgar N 15, tel. 987/21468).

*Mexican Crafts*  **La Concha** (at the corner of Rafael Melgar and Calle 2a N, tel. 987/20571) offers a selection of good, if somewhat pricey, Mexican and Guatemalan folk art, jewelry, and clothing. **Na Balam** (Av. 5a N 14, no phone) sells high-quality Mayan reproductions, batik clothing, and jewelry. **Xaman-Ek: The Bird Sanctuary** (Av. Rafael Melgar, tel. 987/20940), specializes, as its name implies, in all manner of artificial birds.

Your best bet for one-stop shopping, the nearly block-long **Los Cinco Soles** (Av. Rafael Melgar N 27, tel. 987/20132), features an excellent variety of well-priced, well-displayed items, including blue-rim glassware, brass and tin animals from Jalisco, tablecloths and place mats, cotton gauze and embroidered clothing, onyx, T-shirts, papier-mâché fruit, reproduction Mayan art, Mexican fashions, silver jewelry, soapstone earrings and beads, and other Mexican wares.

## Sports and Fitness

Most people come to Cozumel to take advantage of the island's water-related sports—particularly scuba diving, snorkeling, and fishing (*see below*), but jetskiing, sailboarding, water-skiing, and sailing remain popular as well. You will find services and rentals throughout the island, especially through major hotels and water-sports centers such as **Del Mar Aquatic** (Carretera a Chankanaab, Km 4, tel. 987/21665 or 987/21833) and **Agua Safari** (Av. Rafael Melgar 39A, tel. 987/20101 or 987/20892).

*Fishing*  The waters off Cozumel swarm with more than 230 species of fish, the numbers upholding the island's reputation as one of the world's best locations for trolling, deep-sea fishing, and bottom fishing. Beaky jawed billfish—including swordfish, blue marlin, white marlin, and sailfish—are plentiful here in late April through June, their migration season. World records for catches are frequently set on the island in these months.

High-speed fishing boats can be chartered for $350 for a half-day or $400 for a full day, for a maximum of six people, from the **Club Naútico de Cozumel** (Puerto de Abrigo, Av. Rafael Melgar, Box 341, tel. 987/20118 or 800/253–9701), the island's headquarters for game fishing. Daily charters are easily arranged from the dock or at your hotel, but you might also try **Aquarius Fishing and Tours** (Calle 3 S, tel. 987/21092) for a 4½-hour fishing trip ($125; maximum 3 people) or **Yucab Reef Diving & Fishing** (Av. Rosado Salas between Rafael Melgar and 5a, tel. 987/24110 or tel. and fax 987/21842).

*Scuba Diving*  With more than 30 charted reefs whose average depths range from 15 to 24 meters (50 to 80 feet) and a water temperature that hits about 75–80°F during peak diving season (June–August, when hotel rates are coincidentally at their lowest), Cozumel is far and away Mexico's number-one diving destination. The diversity of options includes deep dives, drift dives, shore dives, wall dives, and night dives, as well as theme dives focusing on ecology, archaeology, sunken ships, and photography. With all the shops to choose from, divers should look for high safety standards and documented credentials. Members of CADO, the **Cozumel Association of Dive Operators** (at Yucab

Reef Fishing and Diving, Av. Rafael Salas between Av. Rafael Melgar and Av. 5 S, Box 450, Cozumel, 77600, tel. 987/24110, tel. and fax 987/21842), are required to meet a number of safety standards. Make sure your instructor has PADI certification (or FMAS, the Mexican equivalent) and is one of the 25 or so shops affiliated with the **SSS recompression chamber** (Calle 5 S 21B, between Av. Rafael Melgar and Av. 5a S, next to Discover Cozumel, tel. 987/22387) or the new recompression chamber recently set up at the **Hospital Civil** (Av. 11 S, between calles 10 and 15, tel. 987/20140 or 987/20525).

*Dive Shops and Tour Operators*   Most dive shops can provide you with all the incidentals you'll need, as well as with guides and transportation. You can choose from a variety of two-tank boat trips and specialty dives ranging from $46 to $56; three-hour resort courses cost about $60, and 1½-hour night dives, $35. Certification courses are available from $300 to $350, while dive-master courses cost as much as $700. Equipment rental is relatively inexpensive, ranging from $6 for tanks or a lamp to about $8 for a regulator or jacket; underwater cameras can cost as much as $35, and videos of your own dive, about $75.

Because dive shops tend to be competitive, it is well worth your while to shop around when choosing a dive operator. In addition to the dive shops in town, many hotels have their own operations and offer dive and hotel packages starting at about $350 for three nights, double occupancy, and two days of diving. Before choosing a shop, check credentials, look over the boats and equipment, and consult experienced divers who are familiar with the operators here. Here's a list to get you started on your search: **Aqua Safari** (Av. Rafael Melgar 39a, tel. 987/20101), **Blue Angel** (next to Hotel Villablanca, tel. 987/21631), **Blue Bubble** (Av. 5a S at Calle 3 S, tel. 987/21865), **Dive House** (Av. 1a, no. 6, tel. 987/21953, fax 987/23068), **Dive Paradise** (Av. Rafael Melgar 601 at Calle 3 S, tel. 987/21007, fax 987/21061), **Fantasia Divers** (Av. 25, enter at Adolfo Rosado Salas and Av. 35, tel. 987/22840, fax 987/21210), **Marine Sports** (Hotel Fiesta Inn, tel. 987/22900), **Pro Dive** (Av. Rosado Salas at 5a, downtown and at the Holiday Inn Cozumel Reef, tel. 987/20816 or 987/20700), **Scuba Shack** (next to Hotel Sol Caribe, tel. 987/20145, or 800/445–4716), **Yucab Reef** (Av. Rosado Salas 11, between Rafael Melgar and 5a, tel. 987/24110, tel. and fax 987/21842).

**Snorkeling**   There is good snorkeling in the morning off the piers at the Stouffer Presidente and La Ceiba, where fish are fed. The shallow reefs in Chankanaab Bay, Playa San Francisco, and the northern beach at the Club Cozumel Caribe also provide clear views of brilliantly colored fish and sea creatures. Tour operators that specialize in snorkeling include **Fiesta Cozumel** (tel. 987/22935 or 987/20974) and **Turismo Aviomar** (tel. 987/20477 or 987/20588). As its name suggests, **Snorkozumel** (Calle 5 S 11A, between Av. Rafael Melgar and Av. 5, tel. 987/24166) is devoted to running snorkeling excursions. Directly off the beach, excellent snorkeling is to be had near the Stouffer Presidente and the Holiday Inn Cozumel Reef, as well as at Chankanaab and Playa Corona; snorkeling equipment is available for less than $10 a day at these locations.

**Dining**

Dining options on Cozumel reflect the nature of the place as a whole, with some harmless pretension at times but mainly the insouciant, natural style of the tropical island. More than 80 restaurants in the downtown area alone offer a broad choice, from air-conditioned, Americanized places serving Continental fare and seafood in semiformal "nautical" settings to sensible, simple outdoor eateries that specialize in fish. Highly recommended restaurants are indicated by a star ★.

| Category | Cost* |
|----------|-------|
| Expensive | $25–$35 |
| Moderate | $15–$25 |
| Inexpensive | under $15 |

*per person, excluding drinks and service*

**Expensive**
★ **Arrecife.** A well-trained staff and impeccably prepared seafood and Continental fare put this hotel restaurant in a class by itself. Tall windows and excellent views of the sea complement the stylish decor—potted palms, white wicker furniture, pink walls—while jazz quartets, which play regularly, further enhance the romantic mood. *Hotel Stouffer Presidente, tel. 987/20322. AE, DC, MC, V. Closed Sept.–Nov. 15*

**Donatello's.** Pale pink walls, pink marble floors, and dim lighting lend a certain elegance to this place. Although not yet world-class, Donatello's ranks as one of the most sophisticated restaurant in town; it offers less formal dining in the back garden. Italian accents enhance the menu, which includes such specialties as scampi, lobster, veal, and pasta. *Av. Rafael Melgar S 131, tel. 987/20090 or 987/22586. AE, MC, V. No lunch.*

★ **La Cabaña del Pescador.** To get to this rustic palapa-covered hut, you've got to cross a gangplank, but it'll be worth it if you're looking for well-prepared fresh lobster. The tails are sold by weight, and the rest—including a delicious eggnog-type drink served at the end of the meal—is on the house. Seashells and nets hang from the walls of this small, dimly lit room and geese stroll outside. *Across the street from Playa Azul Hotel, north of town, no phone. No credit cards. No lunch.*

**Moderate**
★ **El Capi Navegante.** Locals say you'll find the best seafood in town here: The captain's motto is: "The fish we serve today slept in the sea last night." Specialties like whole red snapper and stuffed squid are skillfully prepared and sometimes flambéed at your table. Highly recommended dishes include conch ceviche and deep-fried whole snapper. Nautical blue-and-white decor adds personality to this place. *Av. 10a S 312 at Calle 3, tel. 987/21730. AE, MC, V.*

★ **La Choza.** Home-cooked Mexican food is the order of the day at this family-run establishment. Doña Elisa Espinosa's specialties include chicken mole, red snapper in mustard sauce, and grilled lobster; meals come with soup and fresh tortillas. The informal palapa-covered patio is furnished with simple wood tables and chairs, oilcloth table coverings, and hand-painted pottery dishes. *Calle Rosada Salas 198 at Av. 10a S, tel. 987/20958. AE, MC, V.*

★ **Rincón Maya.** Spicy Yucatecan specialties are the order of the day in this festive, friendly eatery. Miguel Mena Mendosa serves up fresh seafood, beef, pork, and chicken prepared with *achiote* and other traditional herbs used in Mayan cooking. Lamps decorated in the colors of the Mexican flag, hats, and masks line the walls. *Av. 5a S between Calles 3 and 5, no phone. No credit cards. No lunch.*

**Inexpensive**  **El Foco.** A *taqueria* serving pork, *chorizo* (spicy Mexican sausage), and cheese-soft tacos, this eatery also does ribs and steak. Graffitied walls and plain wood tables make it a casual, fun spot to grab a bite and a *cerveza. Av. 5 S and Calle 13, no phone. MC, V.*

★  **El Moro.** This family-run restaurant on the eastern edge of town specializes in low-priced local cuisine—seafood, chicken, and meat. Inside, the decor follows the regional theme, beginning with Yucatecan baskets hanging on the walls. Divers flock to this place, so you know portions are hearty and the food is delicious. Take a taxi; it's too far to walk. *Calle 70, no phone. No credit cards. Closed Thurs.*

**Sports Page Video Bar and Restaurant.** Signed team T-shirts and pennants line the walls and ceilings of this popular restaurant and watering hole. The main attraction is the sports coverage—large TVs simultaneously broadcast at least four athletic events—but the food's good too. Cheeseburgers are juicy and served with generous portions of crispy fries; Mexican specialties as well as seafood and steak dinners are offered. The place is open from 9 AM for breakfast, so you can have your eggs with ESPN. *Corner Av. 5a N and Calle 2 N, tel. 987/21199. MC, V.*

## Lodging

Most of Cozumel's hotels are located on the island's western, or leeward, side. Because of the proximity of the reefs, divers and snorkelers tend to congregate at the southern properties. Sailors and anglers, on the other hand, prefer the hotels to the north, where the beaches are better. Most budget hotels—with various architectural styles—are located in town. All hotels have air-conditioning unless otherwise noted, and all hotels share the 77600 postal code. Highly recommended hotels are indicated by a star ★.

| Category | Cost* |
|---|---|
| Very Expensive | over $160 |
| Expensive | $90–$160 |
| Moderate | $40–$90 |
| Inexpensive | under $40 |

*All prices are for a standard double room, excluding service and the 10% tax.*

**Very Expensive**  **Stouffer Presidente.** This hotel, dramatically refurbished since
★  the 1988 hurricane, exudes luxury, from the courteous, prompt, and efficient service to the tastefully decorated interior. The Stouffer is famed not only for possessing one of the best restaurants on the island, Arrecife (*see* Dining, *above*), but also for its respectable and professional water-sports center. Located on its own beach near the end of the southern hotel zone,

the property ranks among the best on the island for snorkeling. All rooms are done in bright colors with pine furnishings; deluxe rooms, with private terraces fronting the pool or beach, are huge. *Carretera a Chankanaab, Km 6.5, tel. 987/20322, 987/21520, or 800/HOTELS-1, fax 987/21360. 253 rooms. Facilities: 2 restaurants, coffee shop, 3 bars, pool, Jacuzzi, 2 lighted tennis courts, dive shop, water sports, boutiques, car and motorcycle rental, travel agency. AE, DC, MC, V.*

**Expensive** **Fiesta Americana Sol Caribe.** The largest hotel in Cozumel, the Sol Caribe is south of town, just across the street from its own small beach. The lobby in the 10-story main building is dramatically designed, with a high, wood-beamed palapa roof and waterfall. Rooms in the newer (1990) tower are slightly more expensive, but those in the main building are the same size and furnished in a lighter, more cheerful fashion. Nicely landscaped grounds and a large pool with a swim-up bar are among the hotel's pluses. *Box 259, Playa Paraíso, Km 3.5, tel. 987/20700 or 800/FIESTA-1, fax 987/21301. 321 rooms. Facilities: 3 restaurants, 4 bars, satellite TV, minibars, pool, dock, 3 tennis courts, water sports, travel agency, motorcycle and car rental, dive shop, boutiques, beauty salon. AE, DC, MC, V.*

**Fiesta Inn.** This three-story Spanish-roofed structure, south of town and across the street from the beach, has all the trademarks of the Fiesta name: a comfortable lobby with a fountain and garden, brightly decorated modern rooms with archways, a large pool, and an international dining facility. Carpeted rooms are painted light blue, with cream-color wicker furniture and private balconies. This property is less expensive than its larger sister property (*see above*). *Carretera a Chankanaab, Km 1.7, tel. 987/22811, 987/22900, or 800/FIESTA-1, fax 987/22154. 180 rooms. Facilities: restaurant, 2 bars, beach club, water sports, pool, Jacuzzi, tennis court. AE, DC, MC, V.*

★ **Holiday Inn Cozumel Reef.** Opened in 1991, this property is ideally situated for snorkeling and scuba diving. Located on the less developed southern end of the island, near the Stouffer Presidente and Chankanaab, the hotel's beach offers easy access to spectacular underwater scenery. Standard rooms are large, with sea-green headboards and well-made light-wood furnishings; all have balconies looking out on the ocean as well as hair dryers and direct-dial phones. *Carretera a Chankanaab, Km 7.5, tel. 987/22622 or 800/HOLIDAY, fax 987/22666. 162 rooms. Facilities: 3 restaurants, 3 bars, 2 lighted tennis courts, gym, 2 pools, dive shop, water sports. AE, MC, V.*

**Meliá Mayan Cozumel.** Lush tropical foliage and spectacular sunsets over the beach combine with modern architecture and amenities to make this hotel north of town a memorable place to stay. Large windows in the light, cheerful lobby look out onto a pool and swim-up palapa snack bar. Standard rooms, some with small patios opening out onto the lawn, are attractively decorated with colorful tropical print bedspreads and light-wood furniture; larger superior rooms, somewhat more austere in decor, have balconies overlooking the water. *Box 9, Carretera a Sta. Pilar 6, tel. 987/20523, 987/20411, or 800/336-3542, fax 987/21599. 200 rooms. Facilities: 2 restaurants, 2 bars, beach, 2 pools, water-sports center, 2 tennis courts, minibars, travel agency, shop. AE, MC, V.*

**Moderate** **Bahía.** The lobby here is small but the hallways are pleasant enough, with white walls and red tile floors. The large rooms, decorated with the standard stucco, wood, and tile, come with sofabeds and kitchenettes. Ask for a room with a sea view; the balconies overlook the malecón and go for the same price as those facing town. *Av. Rafael Melgar and Calle 3 S, tel. 987/ 21387, fax 987/20209. 27 rooms. AE, MC, V.*

★ **Casa del Mar.** Located south of town near several boutiques, sports shops, and restaurants, this three-story hotel is frequented by divers. An unpretentious but tasteful lobby, which has natural wood banisters and overlooks a small garden, exemplifies the overall simplicity of the place. Cheerful rooms feature yellow-tiled headboards, nightstands, and sinks; Mexican artwork; and small balconies with views of the pool or the sea. The bi-level suites sleep three or four. *Box 129, Carretera a Chankanaab, Km 4, tel. 987/21900 or 800/777–5873, fax 987/ 21855. 96 rooms, 8 cabanas. Facilities: 2 restaurants, 2 bars, pool, Jacuzzi, dive shop, car rental. AE, MC, V.*

★ **Villas Las Anclas.** Conveniently located parallel to the malecón and rated as a three-star hotel, these villas are actually furnished apartments for rent by the day, week, or month. The duplexes include a downstairs sitting room, dining area, and kitchenette, which is fully stocked with dishes, refrigerator, and hot plate; a spiral staircase leads up to a small bedroom with a large desk (but no phone) and inset shelves over the double bed. Rooms are extremely attractive, with tastefully bright patterns set off against white walls. You can buy fresh-ground coffee at the front desk, or head over to the nearby Café Caribe for a breakfast of cappuccino and croissants. *Box 25, Av. 5a S 325 between Calles 3 and 5 S, tel. 987/21955, tel. and fax 987/ 21403. 7 units. Facilities: kitchenettes, garden in back. No credit cards.*

**Inexpensive** **Bazar Colonial.** This attractive modern three-story hotel, located over a small cluster of shops, has pretty red tile floors and bougainvillea, which add splashes of color. Natural wood furniture, kitchenettes, bookshelves, sofa beds, and an elevator make up for the lack of other amenities, such as a restaurant and a pool. *Av. 5a S 9, tel. 987/20506, fax 987/30309 or 987/ 21387. 28 rooms. Facilities: shops, kitchenettes. AE, MC, V.*

★ **Mesón San Miguel.** Situated right on the square, this hotel sees a lot of action because of the accessibility of its large public bar and outdoor café, which are often filled with locals. The architecturally eclectic San Miguel, with four stories and an elevator, has a black-and-white–tiled lobby floor and a contemporary-style game room with a pool table. The remodeled rooms are clean and functional, with balconies overlooking the plaza—a good bet for your money. Sip a drink in the evenings at Cafe Alladino, the hotel's bar on the square. *Av. Juárez 2 bis, tel. 987/20323 or 987/20233, fax 987/21820. 100 rooms. Facilities: bar, café, small pool, game room. AE, MC, V.*

**The Arts and Nightlife**

Although Cozumel doesn't have much in the way of highbrow performing arts per se, it does offer the visitor an opportunity to attend performances that reflect the island's heritage, including Maya Night on Monday and Fiesta Mexicana on Thursday, both at 7 PM at the **Meliá Mayan Cozumel** (tel. 987/20411); Viva México, Wednesday (and Saturday during high season) at

6 PM at the **Fiesta Americana sol Caribe** (tel. 987/20700); or Caribbean Night on Sunday at the **Stouffer Presidente** (tel. 987/20322).

Cozumel offers enough daytime activities to make you want to retire early, but the young set keeps the island hopping late into the night. For a quiet drink and good people-watching, try **Alladino** at the Mesón San Miguel, at the northern end of the plaza. Serious bar-hoppers like **Carlos 'n Charlie's** (Av. Rafael Melgar, between Calles 2 and 4 N; tel. 987/20191) and **Chilly's** (Av. Rafael Melgar at Calle 2N, tel. 987/21832), both on the waterfront north of the plaza. You and your friends provide the live entertainment at the new **Laser-Karaoke Bar** (Fiesta Inn, tel. 987/22811); the more inhibited can play video games or check the latest football scores at the **Sports Page Video Bar and Restaurant** (corner Av. 5 N and Calle 2 N, tel. 987/21199).

# Mexico's Caribbean Coast

*Updated by Maribeth Mellin*

Above all else, beaches are what define the eastern coast of the Yucatán peninsula. White, sandy strands with offshore coral reefs, oversize tropical foliage and jungle, Mayan ruins, and abundant wildlife make the coastline a marvelous destination for lovers of the outdoors. The scrubby limestone terrain is mostly flat and dry, punctuated only by sinkholes, while the shores are broken up by freshwater lagoons, underwater caves, and cliffs.

The coast consists of several destinations, each catering to different preferences. The lazy fishing village of Puerto Morelos so far has been only slightly altered to accommodate foreign tourists. Rustic fishing and scuba diving lodges on the even more secluded Boca Paila and Xcalak peninsulas are gaining a well-deserved reputation for fly-fishing and superb diving on virgin reefs. The beaches, from Punta Bete to Sian Ka'an, south of Tulum—beloved of scuba divers, snorkelers, birders, and beachcombers—offer accommodations to suit every budget, from campsites and bungalows to condos and luxury hotels. Ecotourism is on the rise, with special programs designed to involve visitors in preserving the threatened sea-turtle population. Then, too, there are the Mayan ruins at Tulum, superbly situated on a bluff overlooking the Caribbean, and Cobá—a short distance inland—whose towering pyramids evoke the magnificence of Tikal in Guatemala. At the Belizean border is Chetumal—a modern port and the capital of Quintana Roo—which, with its dilapidated clapboard houses and sultry sea air, is more Central American than Mexican. The waters up and down the coast, littered with shipwrecks and relics from the heyday of piracy, are dotted with mangrove swamps and minuscule islands where only the birds hold sway.

## Important Addresses and Numbers

**Tourist Information** *Chetumal*

The **main tourist office** (Palacio del Gobierno, 2nd floor, tel. 983/20266, fax 983/20855) is open weekdays 9–2:30 and 6:30–9:30.

*Playa del Carmen*

The unreliable tourist information booth is located one block from the beach on Avenida 5 (no phone). It is supposed to be open Monday–Saturday 7–2 and 3–9 and Sunday 7–2, but it is often closed during these times.

| | |
|---|---|
| **Emergencies**<br>*Chetumal* | **Police** (Av. Insurgentes and Av. Belice, tel. 983/21500); **Red Cross** (Av. Efraín Aguilar at Av. Madero, tel. 983/20571). |
| *Playa del Carmen* | **Police** (Av. Juárez between Av. 15a and Av. 20a, next to the post office, no phone). |
| **Pharmacies**<br>*Chetumal* | **Farmacia Social Mechaca** (Av. Independencia 134C, tel. 983/20044). |
| **Car Rental**<br>*Playa del Carmen* | **Rent-a-Car** (Av. Juárez between Avs. 10a and 15a, no phone) and **APSA** (Av. 5 between Av. Juárez and Playacar, 987/30033). |

## Arriving and Departing by Plane, Ferry, Car, and Bus

**By Plane**
*Chetumal*

The Chetumal airport is located on the southwestern edge of town, along Avenida Alvaro Obregón where it turns into Route 186. **Aerocaribe** (tel. 983/26675) has flights three times a week to Mérida, Cozumel, Mexico City, Guatemala City, and Flores, Guatemala (near the ruins at Tikal).

**By Ferry**

Ferries and jetfoils—which can be picked up at the dock—run between Playa del Carmen and Cozumel about every two hours and take about 40 minutes on the old ferry, and 30 minutes on the two enclosed hydrofoils. The fee varies depending on which boat you choose, but the one-way trip costs approximately between $2 and $5.

**By Car**

The entire coast, from Punta Sam to the main border crossing to Belize at Chetumal, is traversable on Route 307. This straight road is entirely paved and is gradually being widened to four lanes from Cancún south. Gas stations are becoming more prevalent, but it's still a good idea to fill the tank whenever you can.

**By Bus**
*Playa del Carmen*

There is first-class service on the **ADO** line (Av. Juárez, 4 blocks from the beach, tel. 987/30141) between Playa and Cancún, Valladolid, Chichén Itzá, Chetumal, Tulum, Xel-Há, Mexico City, and Mérida daily. **Autotransportes del Caribe** (Av. Juárez, no phone) has second-class service to the above destinations, and express service to Chetumal. **Autotransportes Oriente** (Av. Juárez, no phone) has express service to Mérida twice daily, and three buses daily to Cobá. **Playa Express** (Av. Juárez at Av. 5, no phone) has express minibus service to Cancún every half hour 6 AM–9 PM, and to Tulum four times daily; the buses do not have space for luggage.

*Chetumal*

The bus station (Av. Héroes at Av. Insurgentes) is served by ADO (tel. 983/20629) and other lines. Buses run regularly to Cancún, Villahermosa, Mexico City, Mérida, Campeche, and Veracruz.

## Exploring

*Numbers in the margin correspond to points of interest on the Mexico's Caribbean Coast map.*

Our north-south exploration of the Caribbean coast takes you from Puerto Morelos to Chetumal, with brief detours inland to
**❶** the ruins of Cobá and Kohunlich. **Puerto Morelos,** a small coastal town about 36 kilometers (22 miles) south of Cancún, is home to the car ferry that travels to Cozumel. The town has been left remarkably free of the large-scale development so common far-

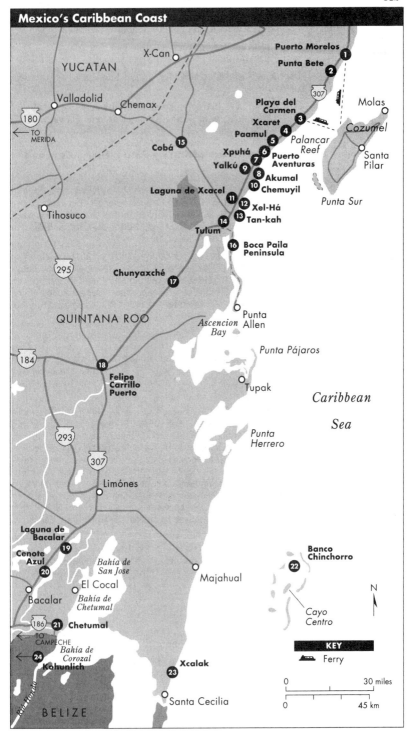

512

Mexico's Caribbean Coast

Puerto Morelos 1
Punta Bete 2
YUCATAN
X-Can
Valladolid
Chemax
180
TO MERIDA
Cobá 15
Molas
Cozumel
Playa del Carmen 3
Xcaret 4
Paamul 5
Palancar Reef
Santa Pilar
Xpuhá 6
Puerto Aventuras 7
Yalkú 9
Akumal 8
Chemuyil 10
Punta Sur
Laguna de Xcacel
11
Xel-Há 12
Tan-kah 13
Tulum 14
Boca Paila Peninsula 16
Tihosuco
Chunyaxché 17
QUINTANA ROO
Ascencion Bay
Punta Allen
Punta Pájaros
295
Tupak
Caribbean
Sea
184
Felipe Carrillo Puerto 18
Punta Herrero
293
307
Limónes
Laguna de Bacalar 19
Banco Chinchorro
Cenote Azul 20
Bahía de San Jose
22
Bacalar
El Cocal
Majahual
Bahía de Chetumal
Cayo Centro
N
186
Chetumal 21
TO CAMPECHE
Bahía de Corozal
Kohunlich 24
Xcalak 23
KEY
Ferry
0    30 miles
0    45 km
Santa Cecilia
BELIZE

ther south, though each year more and more tourists stop here
to take in its easygoing pace, cheap accommodations, and convenient oceanside location near a superb offshore coral reef.
For obvious reasons, this place is particularly attractive to divers, snorkelers, and anglers. The reef at Morelos—about 550
meters (1,800 feet) offshore—has claimed many ships over the
centuries, and nowadays divers visit the sunken wrecks. Snorkeling gear, fishing tackle, and boats can be rented from the
**Ojo de Agua Dive Shop** (no phone) at the Ojo de Agua hotel,
north of town.

**②** About 32 kilometers (20 miles) south of Puerto Morelos is
**Punta Bete,** a 6½-kilometer (4-mile) white sand beach between
rocky lagoons. This point is the setting for several bungalow-
style hotels that have almost become cult places for travelers
who love being in or on the water. All the properties are set off
from Route 307 at the end of a 2³⁄₁₀-kilometer (1⅝-mile) rutted
road.

**③** A 10-minute drive farther south will take you to **Playa del Carmen,** a once-deserted beach where only a few decades ago Indian families raised coconut palms to produce copra. Nowadays
its alabaster-white beach and small offshore reefs lend themselves to excellent swimming, snorkeling, and turtle-watching,
and the town has recently become the preferred destination of
hip young Europeans who want to skip Cancún and go on to see
the archaeological sights of Yucatán.

The busiest parts of Playa are down by the **ferry pier** and at the
**zócalo.** Take a stroll north from the pier along the beach and
you'll see the essence of the town: simple restaurants roofed
with palm fronds, where people sit around drinking beer for
hours; two campgrounds; and lots of hammocks. Now head all
the way south, along Avenida 5a (the first street in from the
beach), a street lined with *tienditas* (little shops) selling crafts
and groceries; the crafts stands are concentrated especially at
the south end, where the street meets the ferry ramp. On the
south side of the pier is **Playacar,** a first-class, lavish hotel that
has brought a sense of luxury and style to Playa del Carmen.
Playacar, which opened in 1991, has become a stunning success, particularly with European tour groups. A second hotel,
the all-inclusive **Diamond Resort** has opened farther south
along the beach. If you walk away from the beach, you'll come
upon the affluent section: several condominium projects and
well-tended gardens and lawns that can be seen from the
street. From here, only the sandy streets, the small vestiges of
Mayan structures, and the stunning turquoise sea on the horizon suggest you're in the tropics. The streets at both ends of
town peter out into the jungle.

**④** Six kilometers (4 miles) south of Playa is a paved road leading
to **Xcaret,** which has been transformed from a tranquil cove into
a waterside amusement park. A mind-boggling combination of
construction and destruction has changed an idyllic hidden
cove with a few small ruins into an expanse of winding jungle
trails leading to man-made *caletas,* or inlets, with white sand
beaches and waters that are still a bit clouded from the distur-
bances of bulldozers and trucks. The main feature at the new
Xcaret park is an underground river ride, included in the admission price. Swimmers don life jackets (snorkels, masks, and
fins come in handy as well) and float with the cool waters' currents through a series of caves. Lockers, showers, and chang-

ing rooms are available. *No phone. Admission: $17. Open daily 9–6.*

**⑤** Beachcombers and snorkelers are fond of **Paamul** (10 kilometers/6 miles south of Xcaret), a crescent-shaped lagoon with clear, placid waters sheltered by the coral reef at the lagoon's mouth. Shells, sand dollars, and even glass beads—some from the sunken pirate ships at Akumal—wash onto the sandy parts of the beach. Trailer camps, cabañas, and tent camps are scattered along the beach; a restaurant sells cold beer and fresh fish.

**⑥** **Puerto Aventuras** is a 900-acre self-contained resort, which will eventually include condominiums, a 250-slip marina, a tennis club, a beach club, a dive center, an 18-hole golf course, a shopping mall, a movie theater, and five deluxe hotels with a total of 2,000 rooms. At press time, facilities in operation included several restaurants and shops, nine holes of the golf course, an excellent dive shop, the marina, and the **CEDAM underwater archaeology museum** (open daily 9–6), where old ships, coins, and nautical devices are exhibited. Accommodations including two hotels and several condo and time-share units were also open.

**⑦** Nine kilometers (5½ miles) south of Paamul along a narrow path is a little fishing community called **Xpuhá,** where residents weave hammocks and harvest coconuts. Some small, overgrown pre-Hispanic ruins in the area still bear traces of paint on the inside walls.

**⑧** **Akumal** lies about 35 kilometers (22 miles) south of Playa del Carmen and consists of three distinct areas. Half Moon Bay to the north is lined with private homes and condominiums and has some of the prettiest beaches and best snorkeling in the area. Akumal proper consists of a large resort and small Mayan community with a market, laundry facilities, and pharmacy. More condos and homes and an all-inclusive resort are located at Akumal Aventuras to the south. People come here to dive or simply to walk on the deliciously long beaches filled with shells, crabs, and migrant birds. The long curved bay and beach are rarely empty now; but although Akumal can be crowded—especially at lunchtime, when tour buses stop here en route from Tulum—it is also expansive and generally much less developed than Cancún.

First and foremost, however, Akumal is famous for its diving. Area dive shops sponsor resort courses and certification courses, and luxury hotels and condominiums offer year-round packages comprising airfare, accommodations, and diving. Deep-sea fishing for giant marlin, bonito, and sailfish is also popular.

**⑨** Devoted snorkelers may want to walk to **Yalkú,** a practically unvisited lagoon just north of Akumal along an unmarked dirt road. Wending its way out to the sea, Yalkú hosts throngs of parrot fish in superbly clear water with visibility to 160 feet, but it has no facilities.

**⑩** In stark contrast to the man-made finery of Akumal is the beautiful little cove at **Chemuyil,** about 5 kilometers (3 miles) south, where you can stop for lunch and a swim. The crescent-shaped beach is small and secluded, but has been discovered by tour groups and is far less tranquil than it was in the past.

Continue south for a couple of kilometers along Route 307 to the **Laguna de Xcacel,** which sits on a sandy ridge overlooking yet another long white beach. The calm waters provide excellent swimming, snorkeling, diving, and fishing; birders and beachcombers like to stroll in the early morning. Camping is permitted, and a restaurant (closed on Sunday) is on the site. Tour buses full of cruise-ship passengers stop here for lunch, and the showers and dressing rooms get crowded at dusk.

A natural aquarium cut out of the limestone shoreline 6 kilometers (4 miles) south of Akumal, **Xel-Há** (pronounced *shel-HA*) national park consists of several interconnected lagoons where countless species of tropical fish breed; the rocky coastline curves into bays and coves in which enormous parrotfish cluster around an underwater Mayan shrine. Several low wooden bridges over the lagoons have benches at regular points, so you can take in the sights at leisure. Lockers and dressing rooms are available, and you can rent snorkel gear ($10) and underwater cameras (the $18 fee includes a roll of film). Those who choose not to snorkel can rent chaise longues ($3) for sunbathing. The park holds other attractions as well. A shrine stands at the entrance, and there are other small Mayan ruins throughout, including one named Na Balaam (Mayan for "tiger") for a yellow jaguar painted on one of its walls. There is also a huge but overpriced souvenir shop, food stands, and a small museum. The enormous parking lot attests to the number of visitors who come here; you should plan to arrive in the early morning, before all the tour-bus traffic hits. For a pleasant breakfast or lunch, you may want to try the restaurant, which serves reasonably good ceviche, fresh fish, and drinks. *Admission: $5. Open daily 8–5.*

About 9½ kilometers (6 miles) south of Xel-Há, in the depths of the jungle, stands a small grouping of pre-Hispanic structures that cover 10 square kilometers (4 square miles) and once served as a satellite city of Tulum. **Tan-kah,** as the place is known, has still not been fully explored, and while the buildings themselves may not warrant much attention, a curious bit of more recent history does. In the 1930s an airstrip was built here; Charles Lindbergh, who was making an aerial survey of the coast, was one of the first to land on it.

A couple of kilometers farther south lies one of the Caribbean coast's biggest attractions: **Tulum.** The most visited Mayan ruin, it is the only Mayan city built on the coast, and the spectacle of those amber-gray stones etched against the fiercely blue-green Caribbean waters is nothing less than riveting. Almost Grecian in its stark, low grayness, and vaguely medieval in the forbidding aspect of its walls, this site surpasses all others for the sheer majesty of its setting. Unfortunately, access to many of the most impressive structures is now limited; visitors can no longer climb or enter the buildings.

Resting about 130 kilometers (80 miles) south of Cancún, Tulum is comprised of 60-odd structures, most of which date from the 12th to the 15th centuries. Only about three structures merit visiting, so you can see the site in two hours, but you may wish to allow extra time for a swim or a stroll on the beach. A path leads from the cliff down to the sea, where it's likely that the ancient Maya beached their canoes.

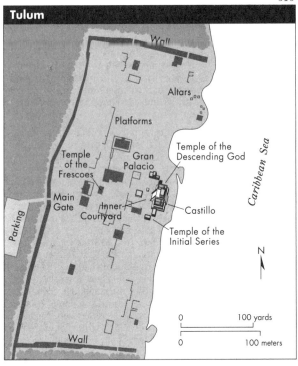

**Tulum**

Tulum—which means "City of the New Dawn," and which the ancient Maya called Zama ("sunrise")—is the only Mayan city known to have been inhabited when the conquistadores arrived. Its largest building, the **Temple of the Descending God**—so called for the carving of a winged god plummeting to earth over the doorway—has skillfully rendered stucco masks in the corners. *Admission: $4; free Sun. and holidays. Open daily 8–5.*

Tourist services are clustered at the crossroads (El Crucero) between the highway and the turnoff to the ruins, marked by a bulky shopping center, which was under construction at press time. At the parking lot by the ruins, souvenirs, handicrafts, and snacks are sold from a semicircular row of stands, but prices tend to be excessive. You will also encounter unofficial guides who profess various degrees of expertise on Mayan archaeology. Using their services will help the local economy, but you should take their stories with a grain of salt. Tour buses arrive at the ruins by midmorning, so it is wise to get there early. There is also a present-day village of Tulum, just off Route 307 and about 4 kilometers (2½ miles) south of the ruins. This small community is undergoing changes as prosperity rises. Markets, taco stands, and other businesses line the highway close to town.

**⓯** Beautiful but barely explored, **Cobá** is a 35-minute drive northwest of Tulum down a well-marked and well-paved road that leads straight through the jungle. Two tiny pueblos, Macario Gómez and Balché, with their clusters of thatched-roof white huts, are the only signs of habitation en route. Once one of the most important city-states in the entire Mayan domain, Cobá now stands in solitude; the spell this remoteness casts is intensified by the silence at the ruins, broken occasionally by the shriek of a spider monkey or the call of a bird. Processions of huge hunter ants cross the footpaths, and the sun penetrates the tall hardwood trees, ferns, and giant palms with fierce shafts of light.

Archaeologists estimate the presence of some 6,500 structures in the area, but only 5% have been uncovered, and it will take decades before the work is completed. Discovered by Teobert Maler in 1891, Cobá was subsequently explored in 1926 by the Carnegie Institute but not excavated until 1972, when the road from Tulum was built. At present there is no restoration work underway.

The city flourished from AD 400 to 1100, probably boasting a population of as many as 40,000 inhabitants. Situated on five lakes between coastal watchtowers and inland cities, its temple-pyramids towered over a vast jungle plain (one of them is 138 feet tall, the largest and highest in northern Yucatán). Cobá (meaning "ruffled waters") exercised economic control over the region through a network of at least 16 sacbeob, one of which, at 100 kilometers (62 miles), is the longest in the Mayan world. In the elegance of its massive, soaring structures and in its sheer size—the city once covered 210 square kilometers (81 square miles)—Cobá strongly resembles Tikal in northern Guatemala, to which it apparently had close cultural and commercial ties.

The main groupings are separated by several miles of intense tropical vegetation, so the only way to get a sense of the immensity of the city is to scale one of the pyramids. Maps and books about the ruins are sold at the makeshift restaurants and shops that line the parking lot. None of the maps are particularly accurate, and unmarked side trails lead temptingly into the jungle. Stay on the main, marked paths unless you have a guide; several men with guide licenses congregate by the entrance and offer their services. When you go, bring plenty of bug repellent, and if you plan to spend some time here, bring a canteen of water (you can also buy sodas and snacks at the entrance).

Cobá can be comfortably visited in a half-day, but if you want to spend the night, opt for the Villa Arqueólogica Cobá (*see* Lodging, *below*), operated by Club Med and only a three-minute walk from the site along the shores of Lake Cobá. Spending the night is highly advised—the nighttime jungle sounds will lull you to sleep, and you'll be able to visit the ruins in solitude when they open at 8 AM. Even on a day trip, consider taking time out for lunch and a swim at the Villa—an oasis of French civilization—after the intense heat and mosquito-ridden humidity of the ruins. *Buses depart Cobá for Playa del Carmen and Valladolid twice daily. Check with your hotel and the clerk at the ruins for the times, which may not be exact. Admission: $4; free on Sun. Open daily 8–5.*

Return to the coastal road heading south to Tulum and continue to the Boca Paila turnoff from Route 307. Several kilometers south, past a few bungalows and campsites, the paved road ends, and a rope over the sand marks the entrance to the **Sian Ka'an Biosphere Reserve.** The reserve includes the 1.3-million-

❻ acre **Boca Paila peninsula,** a secluded 35-kilometer (22-mile) strip of land established by the Mexican government in 1986 as one of UNESCO's internationally protected areas and named a World Heritage Site by UNESCO in 1987.

Sian Ka'an, meaning "where the sky is born," was first settled by the Xiu tribe from Central America in the 5th century. The area once flourished with countless species of wildlife, many of which have fallen into the endangered category, but the waters here still teem with banana fish, bonefish, mojarra, snapper, shad, permit, sea bass, and alligator. Flat fishing and fly-fishing are especially popular, and the peninsula's few lodges run deep-sea fishing trips as far away as **Ascensión Bay,** two hours south of the lodges by boat. Birders take launches out to **Cajo Colibrí** (Hummingbird Cay) or to **Isla de Pájaros** to view the pelicans, frigate birds, woodpeckers, sparrow hawks, and some 350 other species of birds that roost on the mangrove roots or circle overhead. The beaches are wide and white. The more adventuresome travelers can explore the caves with which the waterways are riddled or trek out to the tiny ruins of Chunyaxché (*see below*).

The narrow, rough dirt road down the Boca Paila (meaning "mouth of the river") peninsula is dotted with campgrounds, fishing lodges, and deserted palapas and copra farms. It ends at **Punta Allen,** a fishing village whose main catch is the spiny lobster, and the site of a small guest house. In 1990 some muggings involving tourists took place on the Boca Paila road, but they seem to have been isolated events. In any case, you should travel by car or private plane, or charter a flight from Playa del Carmen or Cozumel.

Continue along the main route to the extensive archaeological
❼ site of **Chunyaxché**—known in ancient times as Muyil—which is currently under excavation by Tulane University and the Mexican government, with the help of local Maya and the latest laser and satellite technology. Dating from the Late Preclassical era (300 BC–AD 200), it was connected by road to the sea and served as a port between Cobá and the Mayan centers in Belize and Guatemala. Today, all that stands are the remains of a 56-foot **temple-pyramid.** From its summit you can see the Caribbean, 15 kilometers (9 miles) in the distance. Chunyaxché sits on the edge of a deep blue lagoon and is surrounded by a nearly impenetrable jungle. You can swim or fish in the lagoon, and there is a small restaurant on the highway next to the dirt road leading to the ruins. *Admission: $4. Open Tues.–Sun. 9–6.*

Twenty-four kilometers (15 miles) to the south, at Km 73 on
❽ Route 307, is **Felipe Carrillo Puerto,** named for a local hero who preached rebellion. In 1920 Carrillo Puerto eventually became governor of Yucatán and instituted a series of reforms that led to his assassination. This town, formerly known as Chan Santa Cruz, also played a central role in the 19th-century War of the Castes. It was here that the Talking Cross first appeared— carved into a cedar tree near a cenote. The Indian priest Manuel Nahuat, translating from behind a curtain, interpreted the cross as a sign for the Indians to attack the *dzulob* (white Christians) under the protection of the cross. Although Mexican soldiers cut down the tree and destroyed the cross, the Indians made other crosses from the trunk and placed them in neighboring villages, including Tulum. The last messages were given in 1904; by then half the local population had been annihilated

in the war. Several humble hotels, some good restaurants, and a gas station may be incentives for stopping here on your south-bound trek.

Route 307, a dreary and monotonous road to Belize, continues south for another 112 unremarkable kilometers (69 miles), until the sudden appearance of the spectacularly vast and beautiful **Laguna de Bacalar.** Also known as the Lake of the Seven Colors, this is the second largest lake in Mexico (56 kilometers/35 miles long) and is frequented by scuba divers and other lovers of water sports. Seawater and fresh water mix in the lake, intensifying the aquamarine hues, and the water contrasts starkly with the dark jungle growth. If you drive along the lake's southern shores, you'll enter the affluent section of the town of Bacalar, with elegant turn-of-the-century waterfront homes. Also in the vicinity are a few simple hotels and campgrounds.

Just beyond Bacalar exists the largest sinkhole in the world, the **Cenote Azul,** 607 feet in diameter, with clear blue waters that afford unusual visibility even at 200 feet below the surface. Surrounded by lush vegetation and underwater caves, the cenote attracts divers who specialize in this somewhat tricky type of dive.

**Chetumal**—38 kilometers (24 miles) farther along Route 307—is the last Mexican town on the southern Caribbean. It was founded in 1898 as Payo Obispo in a concerted and only partially successful effort to gain control of the lucrative traffic in the region's precious hardwoods, arms, and ammunition, and also to put down the rebellious Indians. The city, which overlooks the Bay of Chetumal at the mouth of the Río Hondo, was devastated by a hurricane in 1955 and rebuilt as a modern state capital and major port. Because of its status as a free port (in the past it was a haven for smugglers), Mexican merchants come to buy imported goods not found elsewhere in the country. In ancient times it was one of the major Mayan ports.

Overall, Chetumal feels more Central American than Mexican; this is not surprising, given its proximity to Belize, with which there is both commercial and tourist traffic. Chetumal's streets are also vaguely reminiscent of some parts of the American South, with monotonous rows of run-down (but often charming) clapboard houses interspersed with low-lying ramshackle commercial establishments. The mixed population includes many black Caribbeans and Middle Easterners, and the arts reflect this eclectic combination—the music includes reggae, salsa, calypso, and Belizean bruckdown; there is not much mariachi. The cuisine represents an exotic blend of Yucatecan, Mexican, and Lebanese.

The town's most attractive thoroughfare, the wide **Boulevard Bahía,** runs along the waterfront and is a popular gathering spot at night (though on the weekend Chetumal practically shuts down). The main plaza sits between the boulevard and Avenidas Alvaro Obregón and Héroes; unremarkable modern government buildings and some especially bland patriotic statues and monuments to local heroes wall in the plaza on two sides. Brackish bay waters lapping at the dock create a melancholy rhythm, but if you sit at one of the sidewalk cafés by the square, you will have an appealing view of this huge, placid bay.

Downtown Chetumal contains a small zoo, a few discos, and a cultural institute; the reasonably priced hotels, which seem to cater mostly to the modest needs of traveling salesmen, are generally clean. For shopping, you can stroll along Avenida Héroes, where most of the stores are located, but the merchandise tends to be a humdrum, functional miscellany.

Surrounding attractions offer alternatives to downtown Chetumal. **Banco Chinchorro,** a 42-kilometer (26-mile) coral atoll and national park (fishing prohibited), is situated two hours offshore and littered with shipwrecks. The reef, which is popular with divers, is accessible by boat from the fishing village of **Xcalak,** near the tip of the Xcalak peninsula, which divides the bay from the ocean. The peninsula is accessible from Highway 307 by way of the Majahual exit, north of Laguna Bacalar. The road is paved to Majahual on the coast, then turns to dirt, sand, and ruts running south to Xcalak—about a one-hour drive.

Sixty-eight kilometers (42 miles) west of Chetumal, off Route 186, lies **Kohunlich,** renowned for the giant stucco masks on its principal pyramid, for one of the oldest ball courts in Quintana Roo, and for the remains of a great hydraulic system at the Stelae Plaza. *Admission: $4. Open daily 8–5.*

## Shopping

There aren't many high-quality crafts available along the Caribbean coast, although stands on the road leading to the ferry in Playa del Carmen and in the parking lot at the Tulum ruins do their best to unload a mediocre and overpriced selection of embroidered clothing, schlock reproductions of ancient carvings and statues, knickknacks made from shells, and hammocks. Several roadside artisans' markets have sprung up along Route 307; most feature a repetitive display of cotton rugs. If you drive, stock up on groceries, pharmacy items, hardware, and auto parts in Puerto Morelos, Playa del Carmen, Felipe Carrillo Puerto, or Chetumal. As for Chetumal, while Mexicans go there to buy imported and black-market appliances, North Americans will find the merchandise inferior and the prices no bargain. Save your shopping dollars for Mérida or Cozumel.

## Sports and Fitness

**Water Sports** Diving, snorkeling, and fishing are among the most popular activities along the coast. The following is a brief list of outfitters. For details about where to dive, *see* Exploring, *above.*

*Akumal* **Kapaalua Dive Shop** (tel. 800/351–1622), **Akumal Dive Shop** (tel. 987/22453, 987/41259, or 800/777–8294), and **Cedam Dive Centers** (tel. 987/22211) rents diving equipment.

*Chetumal* **Casa Lucy** (Av. Héroes No. 52, between Plutarco Elias and Ignacio Zaragoza) rents diving gear.

*Puerto Aventuras* **Mike Madden's CEDAM Dive Centers** (in the Club de Playa hotel, tel. 987/22233, fax 987/41339) is a full-service dive shop with certification courses; cave and cenote diving is a specialty.

*Puerto Morelos* Scuba gear is available from the **Ojo de Agua Dive shop** (no phone) and at the dive stand on the beach by the plaza.

Punta Bete **La Posada del Capitan Lafitte** and **Shangri La Caribe** (tel. 800/
538–6802 for both), located on Carretera 307 just north of
Playa del Carmen, run deep-sea fishing trips and have full-
service dive shops on the premises.

Xcalak The **Costa de Cocos Hotel** (Box 316, Bloomingdale, IL 60108,
tel. 800/443–1123) runs deep-sea fishing and diving trips.

## Dining and Lodging

Dining Most of the restaurants along the Mexican Caribbean coast are
simple beachside affairs with outdoor tables and palapa roofs.
The few luxury hotels in the area have fancy establishments offering Continental cuisine, elegant service, and of course high
prices. Many of the restaurants have limited hours or close
down in summer and during the hurricane season (September–
November). Generally, all restaurants maintain a casual dress
code and do not accept reservations. Highly recommended restaurants are indicated by a star ★.

| Category | Cost* |
|---|---|
| Very Expensive | over $20 |
| Expensive | $15–$20 |
| Moderate | $8–$15 |
| Inexpensive | under $8 |

*per person, excluding drinks and service*

Lodging Accommodations on the Caribbean coast run the gamut from
campsites to simple palapas and bungalows to middle-range
functional establishments to luxury hotels and condominiums.
Many of these hotels include two or three meals in their prices.
The fanciest accommodations are in Playa del Carmen,
Akumal, and Puerto Aventuras, while the coastline (including
the Tulum area) is sprinkled with small campgrounds and hotels on solitary beaches. Note that hotel rates drop as much as
25% in the low season (June–October). Highly recommended
hotels are indicated by a star ★.

| Category | Cost* |
|---|---|
| Very Expensive | over $90 |
| Expensive | $60–$90 |
| Moderate | $25–$60 |
| Inexpensive | under $25 |

*All prices are for a standard double room in the high season
(Nov.–June), excluding service and the 10% tax.*

Akumal **Luna Chueca.** "The Broken Moon" is the official name of this
Dining tiny restaurant, but locals call it Katie's Place. Owner Katie
Robinhawk has taken a one-bedroom condo at Half Moon Bay
and turned it into a cult café, where locals and enterprising
tourists congregate at the three indoor tables and tiled bar, or
on the patio by the sea, and savor Katie's creative cuisine. Maya
cooks prepare authentic tortillas, licuados, panuchos and flan,
vegetarian chili rellenos, fried onion rings, thick French toast,

and whatever else strikes Katie's fancy, especially at dinner. You'll need a car, a cab, or strong legs to reach Katie's, but it's worth it. *Go through the entranceway at Club Akumal Caribe, then turn left at the dirt road heading north to Half Moon Bay to the Hacienda de la Tortuga, tel. 987/22421 (condo office). No credit cards. Open Mon.–Sat. 7–10, 5:30–8. Moderate.*

*Dining and Lodging* **Club Aventuras Akumal.** An all-inclusive luxury hotel managed by the Spanish hotel group Oasis, this sprawling property started as the private preserve of millionaire Pablo Bush Romero, a friend of Jacques Cousteau. Today the beautiful beach—protected by an offshore reef—and the pier are used as the starting point for canoeing, snorkeling, diving, fishing, and windsurfing jaunts. The U-shaped building, with nautical decor, features handsome mahogany furniture and sunken blue-tile showers between Moorish arches (no doors!). All rooms have balconies (you can choose a sea view or a garden view) and air-conditioning or ceiling fans (same price). *For reservations: Adventure Tours, 111 Avenue Rd., 5th floor, Toronto M5R 3J8, tel. 416/967–1112 or, in Akumal, 987/22887. 44 rooms plus 49 condominium units and penthouses. Facilities: restaurant, indoor and outdoor bar, beach, 2 pools, game room, dive shop, tennis court, boutiques, travel agency, car rental. AE, MC, V. Very Expensive.*

**Club Akumal Caribe & Villas Maya.** Accommodations at this resort, situated on the edge of a cove overlooking a small harbor, range from rustic but comfortable bungalows with red tile roofs and garden views (Villas Maya) to beachfront rooms in a modern three-story hotel building. All have air-conditioning, ceiling fans, and refrigerators. Also available are the more secluded one-, two-, and three-bedroom condominiums called the Villas Flamingo, on Half Moon Bay and a half-mile from the beach. The bungalows and hotel rooms are cheerfully furnished in rattan and dark wood, with attractive tile floors; the high-domed condominium units, Mediterranean in architecture and room decor, have kitchens and balconies or terraces overlooking the pool and beach. The best of the three restaurants is Lol Ha: Breakfasts come with a basket of fresh sweet breads, and the grilled steak and seafood dinner entrées are bountiful. An optional meal plan includes breakfast and dinner. *Km 104, Carretera Cancún-Tulum, no phone. For reservations: Akutrame, Box 13326, El Paso, TX 79913, tel. 915/584–3552 or 800/351–1622. 40 bungalows, 21 rooms, 4 villas, 3 condos. Facilities: 3 restaurants (Moderate–Expensive), snack bar, ice cream parlor, pizza parlor, bar, pool, beach, 2 dive shops, boutique, grocery. AE, DC, MC, V. Expensive.*

*Bacalar* **Rancho Encantado.** On the shores of Laguna Bacalar, five min-
*Lodging* utes north of Chetumal, the Rancho comprises six private *casitas* (cottages), each with its own patio and hammocks, kitchenette, sitting area, and bathroom. The casitas and public areas feature hand-carved hardwood furnishings, woven Oaxacan rugs, and sculptures of Maya gods; lush green lawns border the water, where a gaggle of snow-white geese honk at passersby. Both breakfast and dinner are included in the room rate, and guests applaud the homemade breads and ice creams, curries, gumbo, lasagna, and other exotic fare (no red meat is served). You can swim and snorkel off the private dock leading into the lagoon. When traveling by car on Route 307, watch for the road sign on your left. *For reservations: Turquoise Reef Group, Box 2664, Evergreen, CO 80439, tel. 303/674–9615 in*

*CO or 800/538–6802 outside CO, fax 303/674–8735. 6 units. Facilities: restaurant, bar, lagoon excursions. No credit cards. Expensive.*

**Boca Paila** **Caphé-Ha.** Originally built as a private home by an American
*Lodging* architect, this small guest house—located between a lagoon
★ and the ocean—is a perfect place to stay if you're interested in
bonefishing and birding. A private two-bedroom house, with a
kitchen, private bath, and living room, and a two-unit bungalow (with shared baths) are your choices; though neither has
fans or electricity, all the windows have screens and catch the
ocean breeze. The room rates include breakfast and dinner; advance reservations must be accompanied by a 50% deposit, and
a three-day or longer stay is required during high season.
Caphé-Ha is located 30 kilometers (19 miles) south of Tulum, on
the road to Sian Ka'an, 5 kilometers (3 miles) past the bridge at
Boca Paila and around the next rocky point. *For reservations:
tel. 99/213404 in Mérida or 212/219–2198 in NY. 1 villa, 1 bungalow. Facilities: fishing packages. No credit cards. Very Expensive.*

★ **Sol Pez Maya.** An idyllic fishing resort smack in the middle of
the Boca Paila peninsula and the Sian Ka'an Biosphere Reserve, this property consists of only seven cabañas and a small
restaurant. The simply furnished bungalows, with small patios, are set back slightly from the expanse of white beach, palm
trees, and sea pines. Table fans are provided for morning and
evening use, but the generator shuts down in the daytime and
after 11 PM, when you must rely on the screen door to let in the
sea breeze and keep out the fierce mosquitoes. Manager Nestor
Erazo can arrange boat trips for bonefishing, fly-fishing, deep-
sea fishing, birding, or exploring the savannah and the mangrove
swamps and even an obscure Mayan ruin, Chunyaxché. Turtles
come to the beach to lay their eggs between May and July. Sol Pez
Maya is well worth the price, since fabulous fresh meals, daily
fishing, and transfers to and from Cancún or Playa del Carmen
are included. Follow the dirt road south of the Tulum ruins for
about 24 kilometers (15 miles); the hotel is another kilometer (%10
mile) beyond a small wooden bridge that cuts the peninsula in
two. This road is very difficult to maneuver, and the trip takes
about one hour. Call the reservations number for road conditions.
*For reservations: Box 9, Cozumel, Quintana Roo 77600, tel.
987/20072 or 800/336–3542, fax 987/21599. 7 bungalows. Facilities: restaurant, beach, fishing boats. No credit cards. Very
Expensive.*

**Chemuyil** **Chemuyil.** This gorgeous little cove and coconut grove sur-
*Dining and Lodging* rounding a very quiet beach has its own campground and restaurant. Facilities include hammock rentals (for sleeping under
palm trees) and tiny open-air palapas with mosquito netting
and hammocks. At Marco Polo, the restaurant, you can sit at
the bar or at a small table, or you can lounge on a hammock under the palapa as you sip a delicious freshly squeezed limonada.
The seafood- and chicken-based cuisine is much the same as
you'd find at any of a number of palapa eateries in the area. *Km
110, Carretera Cancún–Chetumal, no phone. 6 rooms. Facilities: restaurant (Moderate). Inexpensive.*

**Chetumal** **Casablanca.** This informal, air-conditioned restaurant is one of
*Dining* the favorite local hangouts. Overall, the food—mostly Mexican
dishes—is good and the wine list is better. *Av. Madero 293, tel.
983/22355. AE, MC, V. Moderate.*

**Mandinga.** The best place in town for the freshest seafood, Mandinga is best known for its octopus and conch seafood soup, a spicy blend of the daily catch. *Av. Belice 214, tel. 983/21824. No credit cards. Moderate.*

**Sergio's.** This popular pizza parlor is situated in a small, simply decorated frame house. Locals rave about the grilled steaks. *Av. Alvaro Obregón 182 at Av. 5 de Mayo, tel. 983/22355. AE, MC, V. Moderate.*

*Lodging* **Príncipe.** The best three-star hotel in Chetumal is located between the bus station and downtown. The rooms are air-conditioned, clean, and modern, with satellite TV. There is also a restaurant-bar on the premises. *Av. Héroes 326, 77000, tel. 983/24799 or 983/25167. 52 rooms. Facilities: restaurant-bar, color TV, parking. AE, MC, V. Moderate.*

**Cobá** **Villa Arqueólogica Cobá.** This Club Med property, a three-minute walk from the entrance to the Cobá ruins, overlooks one of the region's vast lakes, where turtles swim to the hotel's dock for a breakfast of bread and rolls. Tastefully done in white stucco and red paint, with bougainvillea hanging from the walls and museum pieces throughout the property, the hotel has a clean, airy feel; corridors in the square, two-story building face a small pool and bar. Although the air-conditioned rooms are small, they feel cozy. Dining choices near the isolated Cobá ruins are quite limited, so the restaurant here is an attractive option. For regional fare, try the grouper, ceviche, shrimp, chicken píbil, or enchiladas. On the more international side are pâtés, salad nicoise, marinated artichokes, and a superb chocolate mousse. *For reservations: tel. 800/CLUB–MED. 40 rooms. Facilities: restaurant (Expensive), bar, pool, tennis court, gift shop. AE, MC, V. Moderate.*
*Dining and Lodging*
★

**El Bocadito.** Though nowhere near as lavish as the Villa, El Bocadito is a friendly, satisfactory budget alternative and only a five-minute walk from the ruins. There is no hot water, and only fans to combat the heat, but the camaraderie of the clientele and staff make up for the discomforts. The restaurant is decent, clean, and popular with tour groups. *On the road to the ruins, APDO 56, Valladolid, Yucatán, Mexico 97780, no phone. 8 rooms. No credit cards. Inexpensive.*

**Felipe Carrillo Puerto** **El Faisán y El Venado.** Given the paucity of hotels in Felipe Carrillo Puerto, this one is your best bet. It's bare-bones, but you can choose between air-conditioned rooms or rooms with ceiling fans. The rooms also come with color or black-and-white TV and refrigerators. The pleasant restaurant does brisk business with locals at lunchtime because it is so centrally located. Yucatecan specialties such as poc chuc, *bistec a la yucateca* (Yucatecan-style steak), and pollo píbil are served in a simple but rustically decorated setting. *Av. Juárez 781, 77200, tel. 983/40043. 21 rooms. Facilities: restaurant. No credit cards. Inexpensive.*
*Dining and Lodging*

**Playa del Carmen** **Albatros.** This beachfront palapa restaurant-bar is owned by Americans, and it rates high with compatriots who come to hang out as well as to sample the food. Suggestions for lunch include fish or sandwiches; breakfasts are also very good. *6 blocks north of ferry pier, tel. 987/30001. MC, V. Moderate.*
*Dining*

★ **Limones.** Probably the most romantic place in town, this restaurant offers dining by candlelight, either alfresco in a courtyard or under the shelter of a palapa indoors. House favorites include copious entrées such as fettuccine, lasagna, and lemon-sautéed beef scaloppini. *Av. 10a at Calle 2, 3 blocks north of the pier, no phone. AE, V. Moderate.*

★ **Máscaras.** The wood-burning brick oven here produces exceptionally good thin-crusted pizzas and homemade pastas and breads. Fresh-squeezed, sweetened lime juice, margaritas, wine, and beer help wash down the rich Italian fare. *Av. Juárez (on the plaza), tel. 987/21300. MC, V. Moderate.*

**Tacos al Pastor.** Fans of the wickedly delicious little pork tacos frequent this stand opposite the Posada Sian Ka'an. *Av. 5a at Calle 2, no phone. No credit cards. Inexpensive.*

*Lodging* **Albatros.** Owned and managed by Americans, the Albatros is a
★ set of 18 homey thatched cabanas situated on the beach and complete with hammocks hanging on the patios. The one-, two-, and three-bedroom cabanas are gaily painted in pastel colors and have hot water and ceiling fans. Purified water is available from large demijohns, and extra care is taken to keep the premises free of insects. *6 blocks north of ferry pier. Box 31, Playa del Carmen, Quintana Roo, 77710, tel. 987/30001 or 800/527–0022. 18 cabanas. Facilities: restaurant, bar. MC, V. Moderate.*

**Alejari.** The nicest hotel on Playa's north beach is this new two-story complex set amid lush gardens. Some rooms have kitchenettes and fans, others provide air-conditioning. A small market and a long-distance phone booth sit on the premises. *Calle 6N; for reservations: Box 166, Playa del Carmen, Quintana Roo, 77710, tel. 987/22754, fax 987/20155. 15 rooms. Facilities: store, kitchenettes. MC, V. Inexpensive.*

**Posada Sian Ka'an.** Located in town, three blocks north of the pier, the Posada features clean rooms with pine furnishings, plus kitchenettes, ceiling fans, and hot water, in a pleasant garden setting where you can hang up your own hammock by a natural cenote. *For reservations: Box 135, Quintana Roo, 77710, tel. in Mérida, 992/97422. 11 rooms. No facilities. No credit cards. Inexpensive.*

*Dining and Lodging* **Continental Plaza Playacar.** Playa del Carmen became a first-class tourism destination when the Playacar hotel opened in October 1991. The centerpiece of an 880-acre master-planned resort, Playacar faces the sea on the south side of the ferry pier. A pastel, blush-colored palace, it possesses all the amenities of its competitors at the larger resort towns. The tropical-style rooms have ocean views and balconies or patios, marble baths, blonde wood furnishings, satellite TV, and in-room safes. The beach is one of the nicest in Playa del Carmen, and far less crowded than those to the north. Mexican and international dishes are served at a restaurant in the main building and a palapa by the pool; the breakfast buffet is excellent. *Fraccionamiento Playacar, tel. 987/21583 or 800/882–6684. 188 rooms, 16 suites. Facilities: 2 restaurants, bar, pool, dive shop, boutique, travel agency. AE, MC, V. Expensive.*

**Diamond Resort.** Opened in 1992 as part of the Playacar development, Diamond is an all-inclusive resort that sprawls down a sloping hill to the sea. The 296 rooms are spread out in small thatch-roofed villas along winding paths; the dining room, bar, lobby, and entertainment areas are housed in a gigantic multi-peaked, two-story palapa. Unlike many all-inclusives, Diamond's design allows peace and privacy. Buffet-style meals are plentiful and imaginatively prepared. Playa del Carmen is a 20-minute walk or $5 cab ride north. *In the Playacar development, tel. 987/30340 or 800/858–2258, fax 987/30345. 296 rooms. Fa-*

*cilities: dining room, bar, 2 pools, dive shop, 4 tennis courts, gift shop, car rental, sports equipment. Expensive.*

★ **Las Palapas.** Las Palapas is an ideal get-away-from-it-all destination resort where many guests stay for 10 days or more. White cabanas with blue trim lend a rustic feel, and duplexes feature balconies or porches, palapas, and hammocks. The thatch roofs and hexagonal shape of the buildings enhance the ocean breezes, making air-conditioning unnecessary. The beach and pool are complemented by a shuffleboard area, clubhouse, beach bar, palapa bar, and attractive palapa restaurant, where Chef Roberto Kappes prepares spectacular Mexican buffets and German specialties as well as hamburgers, tacos, and other snacks. German tour groups keep the hotel's occupancy up to 80 percent year-round; make reservations early. Room rates include breakfast and dinner. *Km 292 on Rte. 307 (Box 116), Playa del Carmen, Quintana Roo, 77710, tel. 987/ 22977, fax 5/379–8041 in Mexico City. 50 cabanas. Facilities: restaurant, 2 bars, pool, beach, in-room safes, 3-night minimum stay. AE, MC, V. Expensive.*

**Puerto Aventuras**

*Dining* **Papaya Republic.** The owners of this small gourmet restaurant refused to sell out to the developers of Puerto Aventuras, and continue doing business at the end of a dirt road to the south of the resort. Fresh ceviche, gazpacho, and local fish in almond sauce are among the offerings, which change with the availability of ingredients. *Off the main road into Puerto Aventuras, down a dirt road to the right marked by a sign, no phone. No credit cards. Moderate.*

*Lodging* **Club de Playa.** A small 30-room hotel with stunning views of the Caribbean. The swimming pool seems to flow right into the sea, and guests have use of a health spa. The spacious rooms are decorated in pinks and greens, with first-class amenities. The Swiss-trained chef prepares international cuisine at the small dining room. *Near the marina, tel. 987/35100 or 800/44OASIS, fax 404/240–4513 in the U.S. 30 rooms. Facilities: restaurant, pool, marina, spa, water sports. AE, MC, V. Very Expensive.*
**Oasis.** A larger hotel at the other end of the marina (opened in 1992), the Oasis bustles with activity as European tour groups on great package deals fill the hotel. The rooms include kitchenettes with microwaves; some have whirlpool baths. The resort's excellent dive shop is on the premises, along with a great gift shop featuring folk art from throughout Mexico. A shuttle bus runs to both hotels, the golf course, commercial center, and marina. *On the beach at the north end of the complex, tel. 987/ 35051 or 800/44OASIS, fax 404/240–4513 in the U.S. 70 rooms. Facilities: 2 pools, 3 restaurants, dive shop, gift shop, tour desk. AE, MC, V. Very Expensive.*

**Puerto Morelos**

*Dining* **Los Pelícanos y las Palmeras.** If you're looking for good fresh fish—fried, grilled, or steamed—stop by these two small thatched huts on the beach. *Puerto Morelos, no phone. No credit cards. Inexpensive.*

*Lodging* **Los Arrecifes and Casa Miguel.** Located on an isolated (and sometimes windy) beach, Los Arrecifes is an older hotel that's been remodeled and redecorated by Vicki Sharp, who is also creating a bed-and-breakfast inn called Casa Miguel across the street from the beach. Arrecifes has eight one-bedroom apartments with kitchenettes, large living rooms and balconies, in an ideal setting. Casa Miguel has four private bedrooms with private baths and a central kitchen and dining area; the house is available for use by families and groups or individuals. Sharp also has information on condo and house rentals in Puerto Morelos. *Arrecifes is 8 blocks north of town on the street closest to the beach; Casa Miguel is 6 blocks north of town on the same street. For reservations: Box 986, Cancún, Quintana Roo, 77500, tel. 98/871011, fax 98/832244. Facilities: kitchens. No credit cards. Moderate.*

*Dining and Lodging* **Caribbean Reef Club at Villa Marina.** This gorgeous white condo complex is one of the nicest hideaways along the coast, especially because of its location on an isolated beach south of town. The colonial-style suites have marble floors, air-conditioning, ceiling fans, blue-tiled kitchenettes, floral pastel linens, and arched windows. Sliding glass doors lead to balconies outside, where you can slip in an afternoon nap on your own private hammock. The adjacent restaurant is easily the most picturesque in town, with a balcony overlooking the sea, handpainted tile tables, and candlelight at night. The menu has a Texan flair, offering chicken-fried steak, BBQ ribs, fajitas, and key lime pie. *South of the ferry dock. For reservations: Box 1526, Cancún, Quintana Roo, 77500, tel. 98/832636, fax 98/832244 or 800/3–CANCUN. 21 suites. Facilities: restaurant, bar, pool water sports. AE, MC, V. Expensive.*

**Punta Bete** **Posada del Capitán Lafitte.** Set on an invitingly long stretch of
*Dining and Lodging* beach just 10 kilometers (6 miles) north of Playa del Carmen at
★ Punta Bete, this lodging is known for its genuinely chummy, unpretentious atmosphere. This is no luxury resort, but a simple cluster of two-unit cabanas, each with its own private bath and ceiling fan. Breakfast, dinner, tax, and tips are included in the room rate, so you rarely need to carry money. In the evening the European and American clientele congregates around a small but pretty pool/bar decorated with red tiles and coral-pink stucco. A small hotel was under construction at press time. *On a dirt road (follow the signs), 2⁸⁄₁₀ km (1⅝ mi) off Rte. 307. For reservations: Turquoise Reef Group, Box 2664, Evergreen, CO 80439, tel. 303/674–9615 in CO or 800/538–6802 outside CO, fax 303/674–8735. 39 rooms, 2-bedroom duplex cabin. Facilities: restaurant (Moderate), bar, beach, pool, dive shop, car rental. All reservations (minimum 3 nights) must be prepaid. No credit cards. Closed around Sept. 1–Nov. 1. Expensive.*

**Tulum** **Casa Cenote.** Don't miss this outstanding restaurant beside a
*Dining* large cenote—this one's a mini-pool of fresh and salt water full
★ of tropical fish. The beef, chicken, and cheese are imported from the United States, and the burgers, chicken fajitas, and nachos are superb. On Sunday afternoon the expats living along the coast gather at Casa Cenote for a lavish barbecue featuring ribs, chicken, beef brisket, or lobster kebabs. The restaurant operates without electricity or a generator (perishables are packed in ice coolers) and closes at dark. *On a dirt road off Rte. 307, between Xel-Há and Tulum, 987/41368. No reservations. No credit cards. Moderate.*

*Dining and Lodging* **Osho Oasis.** On the site of the long-standing Cabañas Chac Mool
★ along the dirt road south of the ruins now emerges a holistic, New-Age–style resort. Only four of the 22 cabanas have private baths, but all have hammock-like mattresses suspended from the ceiling, rock floors, and mosquito nets (the windows have no screens). Communal showers are equipped with hot water, and a generator provides electricity at night. The res-

taurant (Expensive) serves superb vegetarian meals, plus fish and lobster, and is worth visiting even if you aren't staying here. It's best to write or fax ahead for reservations. *For reservations: Box 99, Tulum, Quintana Roo, 77780, tel. 987/42772, fax 987/30230, reservations in the U.S. 415/381–9861 (Sun.-Thurs. 5–7 PM). No credit cards. Moderate.*

**Xcalak Lodging ★**  **Costa de Cocos.** For the ultimate in privacy and scenery you can't beat the southern tip of the Xcalak peninsula, where divers and explorers congregate for trips to the famed Chinchorro Banks. Costa de Cocos is one of the precious few resorts in this area, and is easily the most hospitable and comfortable. Eight cleverly crafted cabanas have exquisite handcrafted mahogany furnishings, screened windows, tiled baths, and bookshelves stocked with an eclectic selection of paperbacks. Small pangas (launches) transport divers to the nearby reefs, and day trips by boat to Belize's Ambergris Caye and the town of San Pedro can be arranged. While guests must rely on the two or three restaurants in town for full meals, coffee, homemade muffins, and fresh fruit are served under the resort's central palapa for breakfast, and cold drinks are available throughout the day. *Xcalak Peninsula, 56 kilometers (35 miles) south of Majahual. For reservations: Box 316, Bloomingdale, IL 60108, tel. 800/443–1123, fax 983/21676. 8 cabanas. Facilities: dive shop, airstrip. No credit cards. Moderate.*

**Xcaret Dining**  **Restaurant Xcaret.** This small palapa restaurant, with walls lined with photos from diving expeditions, serves conch ceviche, lobster, poc chuc, and french fries. *Off Rte. 307, Xcaret, no phone. No credit cards. Inexpensive.*

## Nightlife

There isn't much in the way of nightlife along the coast, unless you happen upon some entertainment in a luxury hotel bar. If you're staying in Akumal, try **Discoteca Akumal** at the Hotel Akumal Cancún; if you're in Playa del Carmen, try **Ziggy's** or **Bambu.** At Puerto Aventuras **Carlos 'n Charlie's** is the most happening place at night.

# Campeche City

*Updated by Maribeth Mellin*  The city of Campeche has a run-down but lovely feel to it: No self-conscious, ultramodern tourist glitz here, just an isolated, friendly city (population 250,000) content to rest on its staid old laurels. That good-humored, lackadaisical attitude is enshrined in the Spanish adjective *campechano*, meaning easygoing, hearty, genial, cheerful. The city gets only about 20,000 tourists a year, its strongest attraction being its sense of history. You can easily imagine pirates attacking the formidable stone walls that surround the downtown, and several Mayan ruins and undisturbed Mayan towns are within driving distance. The city's coastline is cluttered with commercial fishing operations, and there are a few popular public beaches. It is possible to see much of Campeche City in a day or two, but you will probably want to stay longer to absorb the traditional lifestyle, whiling away the hours at a café near the plaza.

## Important Addresses and Numbers

Tourist Information — The **main tourist office** is located at Plaza Moch Cohuo (Av. Ruíz Cortines, tel. 981/66068 or 981/66767), near the Baluarte San Carlos, and is open weekdays 9–3 and 4–9; volunteers sometimes staff the office on Saturday morning. There are also **information modules** at the bus station (Av. Gobernadores 289 at Calle 45, tel. 981/60663 or 981/60419) and the airport (same phone). Modules are open Monday–Saturday 8–noon and 4–8.

Emergencies — **Red Cross** (Av. Resurgimiento s/n, tel. 981/60666 or 981/65202). **Police** (Calle 12 between Calles 57 and 59, tel. 981/62111, 981/62329, or, in town, 06).

Late-night Pharmacies — **Farmacia Ah-Kin-Pech** (Calle Pedro Sainz de Baranda 100, Centro Comercial Ah-Kin-Pech Local 113, tel. 981/68602) is open 24 hours and delivers to hotels.

## Arriving and Departing by Plane, Car, Train, and Bus

By Plane — **Aeroméxico** (tel. 981/66656 in Campeche or 800/237–6639) has one flight daily from Mexico City.

By Car — Campeche can be reached from Mérida in about 1½ hours along the 160-kilometer (99-mile) *via corta* (short way, Rte. 180). The alternative route, the 250-kilometer (155-mile) *via larga* (long way, Rte. 261), takes at least three hours but crosses the major Mayan ruins of Uxmal, Kabah, and Sayil. From Chetumal, take Rte. 186 west to Francisco Escárcega, where you pick up Rte. 261 north; the drive takes about seven hours.

By Train — The **Mexican National Railroad** (Av. Héroes del Nacozari, s/n, tel. 981/62009 or 981/61433) has routes to Campeche from Mérida and Mexico City, but the lines are not among those that have been recently upgraded. It may be difficult to book a sleeper on the Mexico City line (the trip is 24 hours long), so this journey is recommended only for the most stoic traveler. Two trains depart daily from Campeche, at 8 AM and 11 PM, for the 10-hour trip to Palenque.

By Bus — **ADO** (Av. Gobernadores 289 at Calle 45, along Rte. 261 to Mérida, tel. 981/60002), a first-class bus line, runs service to Campeche from Coatzacoalcos, Ciudad del Carmen, and Mérida every half hour, and from Mexico City, Puebla, Tampico, Veracruz, and Villahermosa regularly, but less frequently. There is second-class service on **Autobuses del Sur** (tel. 981/63445) from Chetumal, Ciudad del Carmen, Escárcega, Mérida, Palenque, Tuxtla Gutiérrez, Villahermosa, and intermediate points throughout the Yucatán Peninsula.

## Getting Around

By Bus — The municipal bus system covers the entire city, but you can easily visit the major sights on foot. Public buses run along Avenida Ruíz Cortines and cost under $1.

By Car — Rental agencies include **Hertz** (Hotel Baluartes, Av. Ruíz Cortines s/n, tel. 981/63911 or 981/68848) and **AutoRent** (Ramada Inn, Calle 57 No. 1, tel. 981/62714 or 981/62233).

By Taxi — Taxis can be hailed on the street, or—more reliably—commissioned from the **taxi stand** (Calle 8 between Calles 55 and 53, tel. 981/62366 or 981/65230) or at stands by the bus stations and market.

## Guided Tours

There are no organized tours of Campeche. Ask at the tourist office for a guide, who will set his or her price. You should be able to take a three-hour walking tour for about $10.

## Exploring

Because it has been walled since 1686, most of historic Campeche is neatly contained in an area measuring just five blocks by nine blocks. Today, for the most part, streets running north–south are even-numbered, and those running east–west are odd-numbered. The city is easily navigable (on foot, at least); the historical monuments and evocative name plaques above street numbers serve as handy guideposts.

*Numbers in the margin correspond to points of interest on the Campeche City map.*

Our Campeche itinerary highlights attractions in Campeche City then takes you into the countryside. While it may sound dauntingly ambitious to accomplish the city tour in one day, many of the sights described here can be seen in just a few minutes; the more leisure-minded visitor, however, should schedule two days.

**❶** The **Centra de Información de Turistica** (between Av. 16 de Septiembre and Av. Ruíz Cortines, tel. 981/66068 or 981/66767) is housed in a modern red and white building on the Plaza Moch Cohuo. Here you can pick up maps of the city and its environs.

Across the way, what appears to be a flying saucer is actually **❷** the **Congreso del Estado,** the State Congress building, where government activities take place. Across Calle 8, notice the rather handsome neoclassical Municipal Palace, built in 1892.

Continue southeast on Avenida 16 de Septiembre; on your left, where the avenue curves around and becomes Circuito **❸** Baluartes, you'll arrive at the first bastion, the **Baluarte San Carlos.** Because this one contains only scale models of the original defense system, you may prefer to save your energy for some of the more elaborate installations.

One block east, occupying the full city block between Calles 10 **❹** and 12 and Calles 63 and 65, stands the **Ex-Templo de San José.** The Jesuits built this fine Baroque church in 1756, and today its facade stands as an exception to the rather plodding architectural style of most of the city's churches. Its immense portal is completely covered with blue Talavera tiles and crowned by seven narrow, stone finials that resemble the roofcombs on many Mayan temples.

Now head north on Calle 12 for two blocks, then turn right onto **❺** Calle 59, where you will pass the tiny **Iglesia de San Francisquito,** whose architecture and ambience do justice to the historic street's old-fashioned beauty. Behind the genteel lace curtains of some of the homes, you can glimpse equally genteel scenes of Campeche life, with faded lithographs on the dun-colored walls and plenty of antique furniture and clutter. Along Calle 59 once stood some of Campeche's finest homes,

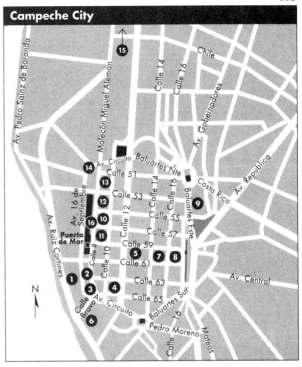

Campeche City

many of them two stories high, with the ground floors serving as warehouses and the upper floors as a residence.

**6** Take Calle 10 south to Calle Bravo, home of the **Iglesia de San Román.** Though it went up in the 16th century, the church became central to the lives of the Indians only when an ebony image of Christ, the "Black Christ," was brought in about 1565. The legend goes that a ship that refused to carry the tradesman and his precious statue was wrecked, while the ship that did take him on board reached Campeche in record time. To this day, the Feast of San Román—when the icon is carried through the streets as part of a colorful and somber procession—is the biggest such celebration in Campeche. People still come to see the black wood Christ mounted on a silver filigree cross. *Calle 10 s/n, no phone. Open Mon.–Sat. 7–noon and 4–8:30; Sat. Mass at 7:30 PM, Sun. Mass at 10 AM and 7:30 PM.*

**7** One block beyond San Francisquito, at the corner of Calle 59 and Calle 14, is the **Museo Regional,** for which you should allow at least two hours. The museum occupies the former Casa del Teniente del Rey, or House of the King's Governor, who lived here between 1804 and 1811. *Admission: $4.50. Open Tues.– Sat. 8–8, Sun. 8–1.*

**8** Old Campeche ends one block east of the museum at the **Puerta de Tierra,** the only one of the four city gates that still stands with its basic structure intact. A light-and-sound show here highlights the city's history on Friday at 8 PM. *Admission: $3.*

To take in the heart of a true Mexican inner city, walk north on Calle 16 for three blocks, then turn east (right) onto Calle 53,

**❾** which leads to the **Mercado Municipal,** where locals congregate en masse to shop for seafood, produce, and housewares.

After browsing through the market, walk four blocks west on Calle 55 to an exquisite mansion highlighted by Moorish arcades. In 1865 Empress Carlotta, wife of the doomed Maximilian, stayed here briefly.

**❿** Just opposite the mansion stands the **Parque Principal,** the southern side of which—Calle 57—is lined with several agreeable cafés and hotels; the park is the focal point for the town's activities. Concerts are held on Sunday evening, when it seems all the city's residents come out for a stroll.

**⓫** Situated across from the Parque Principal on Calle 57 is the **Campeche hotel** (*see* Lodging, *below*), a dilapidated but likable inn with colorful tile floors, an iron balustrade, and what must once have been a striking courtyard.

**⓬** Across the street from the north side of the park—on Calle 55 between Calles 8 and 10—is another exception to the generally somber architecture rule of colonial Campeche. The **Catedral** took two centuries (from 1650 to 1850) to build and incorporates Neoclassical and Renaissance elements.

**⓭** Walk one block north of the cathedral to the corner of Calles 10 and 53, where you'll find the eclectic **Mansión Carvajal.** Built in the early 20th century by one of the wealthiest plantation owners in Yucatán, this structure did time as the Hotel Señorial before arriving at its present role as a government office center and headquarters for the state governor's wife and her staff. *Calle 10 s/n, between Calles 53 and 55, no phone. Admission free. Open Mon.–Sat. 8–2:30 and 5–8:30. Closed Sun.*

**⓮** Just a short block north on Calle 8 (which becomes Malecón Miguel Alemán) is the **Baluarte Santiago,** the last of the bastions to be built (1704). It has been transformed into a botanical garden. The original bastion was demolished at the turn of the century, but it was rebuilt in the 1950s. *Calle 8 at Calle 49, tel. 981/66829. Admission free. Open Tues.–Sat. 9–1 and 4:30–8, Sun. 9–1.*

**⓯** At this point, devotees of religious history may wish to venture three long blocks north, away from the city center and into a residential neighborhood, to the ruins of the **Iglesia de San Francisco** (1546), the oldest church site in Campeche. Possibly more significant is that it marks the spot where—in 1517—the first Mass on the North American continent was said.

**⓰** Campeche has one other bastion museum that warrants visiting: the **Baluarte de la Soledad,** otherwise known as the **Museo de los Estelas.** The largest of the bastions, this one has comparatively complete parapets and embrasures that offer a sweeping view of the cathedral, the municipal buildings, and the Gulf of Mexico. *Calle 8 at Calle 57, no phone. Admission: 50¢; free on Sun. Open Tues.–Sat. 8–8, Sun. 8–1.*

## Shopping

Folk art in Campeche is typical of the rest of Yucatán's handicrafts: basketry, gold and silver filigree, leather goods, embroidered cloth, clay trinkets, and tortoiseshell (which is illegal to import into the U.S., because the animals from which the shells come are an endangered species).

Visit the **municipal market** (Circuito Baluartes at Calle 53), at the eastern end of the city, for crafts and food.

Also try **Artesanía Típica Naval** (Calle 8 No. 259, tel. 981/65708), **México Lindo** (Calle 57 No. 30, tel. 981/67206), and **Baluarte San Pedro** (Calle 51 at Calle 18, no phone).

## Sports

Hunting, fishing, and birding are popular throughout the State of Campeche. Contact the **Hotel Castelmar** (Calle 61 No. 2, tel. 981/65186) for information regarding the regulations and the best areas for each sport.

## Dining

There is nothing fancy about Campeche's restaurants, but its regional cuisine is renowned throughout Mexico—particularly the fish and shellfish stews, shrimp cocktails, squid and octopus, crabs' legs, *panuchos* (tortillas stuffed with beans and diced fish), and Yucatecan specialties. Because regional produce is plentiful, most restaurants—including those listed below—fall into the inexpensive (under $15 for a three-course meal excluding drinks and tips) category. Restaurants throughout Campeche have casual dress codes (no shorts) and do not require reservations. Highly recommended restaurants are indicated by a star ★.

**Barbillas.** The relaxed atmosphere, accented by creamy white walls and tropical touches, makes this mostly seafood restaurant a good spot for a lunch break. Specializing in fish (pompano and snapper) and shellfish (shrimp, oysters, conch, and crabs' legs), this restaurant offers a real taste of Yucatecan fare. Located on the edge of town, Barbillas is somewhat out of the way, but the excellent service and extensive menu are worth the trip. *Av. Lázaro Cárdenas Fracc. 2000 at Av. López Portillo, no phone. AE, MC, V. Closed for dinner.*

**Miramar.** These two restaurants—one across from Hotel Castelmar and one near the town hall building—attract locals and foreign visitors with their fabulous *huevos motuleños* (fried eggs served on corn tortillas and topped with ham, beans, peas, and cheese), red snapper, shellfish, soups, and meat dishes. The wooden tables and chairs and the paintings of the coat-of-arms of the Mexican Republic give Miramar a colonial feel. *Calle 20 No. 8, tel. 981/20923 and Calle 8 No. 73, tel. 981/62883. MC, V.*

**Video Taco.** The young folk of Campeche hang out at this small café, where inexpensive tacos are served to the beat of music videos. *Av. Madero s/n. No phone. No credit cards.*

## Lodging

Most of Campeche City's hotels are old (and several are in disrepair), reflecting the city's lackadaisical attitude toward tourism. Hotels tend to be either luxury accommodations along the waterfront, with air-conditioning, restaurants, and other standard amenities, or basic downtown accommodations offering only ceiling fans and a no-credit-card policy. Those in the latter category tend to be either seedy and undesirable or oddly charming, with some architectural and regional detail unique to each. Highly recommended hotels are indicated by a star ★.

| Category | Cost* |
|---|---|
| Moderate | $40–$90 |
| Inexpensive | Under $40 |

*All prices are for a standard double room, excluding service and the 10% tax.*

**Moderate** **Alhambra.** A great choice away from the bustle of the city, the Alhambra is a modern hotel facing the waterfront near the university. A wide-screen TV plays softly in the lobby; TVs in the rooms get U.S. stations, sometimes including CNN. Rooms are carpeted and clean, with king- and double-size beds. Bathtubs are a welcome addition, rare in these parts. *Av. Resurgimiento 85 between Av. Universidad and Av. August Melgar, tel. 981/66800, fax 981/66132. 98 rooms. Facilities: restaurant, bar, pool. MC, V.*

★ **Ramada Inn.** A whitewashed, four-story modern hotel right on the seafront, the luxurious Ramada offers a relaxing pool area with greenery and a bar. Fairly large rooms, with all the necessary amenities, are decorated in blues with rattan furnishings; balconies overlook the pool or the bay. The lobby restaurant, El Poquito, is extremely popular with locals at breakfast and at night before the disco Atlantis opens. *Av. Ruíz Cortines 51, tel. 981/62233 or 800/228–9898, fax 981/11618. 119 rooms. Facilities: restaurant, coffee shop, pool bar, gift shop, disco, travel agency. AE, MC, V.*

**Inexpensive** **Colonial.** This building—the former home of a high-ranking army lieutenant—dates from 1850 but was made over as a hotel in the 1940s, when its wonderful tiles were added. Pastel-colored rooms with ceiling fans (only some of the units are air-conditioned) are clean and functional, but the hotel's public areas have become extremely run-down. *Calle 14 No. 122, tel. 981/62222 or 981/62630. 30 rooms. No facilities. No credit cards.*

**Lopez.** Pink, yellow, and white walls reflect the airy ambience found in this small, pleasant, two-story accommodation. Standard rooms include colonial-style desks and armoires, luggage stands, and easy chairs. Although the restaurant serves basic Continental fare, it's a convenient enough stop for breakfast, lunch, or dinner. *Calle 12 No. 189, tel. 981/63344. 39 rooms. Facilities: restaurant (closed Sun.). AE, MC, V.*

### Nightlife

For entertainment, check out the sound-and-light show at the **Puerta de Tierra** (Calle 59 at Calle 18 and Circuíto Baluartes, no phone) every Friday evening at 8:30 ($2). If you're in the mood to dance, try Campeche's one disco, **Atlantis,** in the Ramada Inn.

# Mérida and the State of Yucatán

*Updated by Maribeth Mellin*

There is a marvelous eccentricity about Mérida. Fully urban, with maddeningly slow-moving traffic, it has a self-sufficient, self-contented air that would suggest a small town more than a state capital of some 600,000 inhabitants (locals say there are

850,000). Gaily pretentious turn-of-the-century buildings have an Iberian-Moorish flair for the ornate, but most of the architecture is low-lying and although the city sprawls, it is not imposing. Grandiose colonial facades adorned with iron grillwork, carved wooden doors, and archways conceal marble tiles and lush gardens; horse-drawn carriages hark back to the city's heyday as the wealthiest capital in Mexico.

Mérida is a city of subtle contrasts, from its opulent yet faded facades to its residents, very Spanish yet very Mayan. The Indian presence is unmistakable: People are short and dark-skinned, with sculpted bones and almond eyes; women pad about in *huipiles* (hand-embroidered, sacklike white dresses), and craftsmen and vendors from the outlying villages come to town in their huaraches. So many centuries after the conquest, Yucatán remains one of the last great strongholds of Mexico's indigenous population. To this day, in fact, many Maya do not even speak Spanish, primarily because of the peninsula's geographic and, hence, cultural isolation from the rest of the country. Additionally, the Maya—long portrayed as docile and peace-loving—for centuries provided the Spaniards and the mainland Mexicans with one of their greatest challenges. As late as the 1920s and 1930s, rebellious pockets of Mayan communities held out against the outsiders, or *dzulobs*. Yucatecos speak of themselves as *peninsulares* first, Mexicans second.

Physically, Yucatán, too, differs from the rest of the country. Its geography and wildlife have more in common with Florida and Cuba—with which it was probably once connected—than with the central Mexican plateau and mountains. A mostly flat limestone slab possessing almost no bodies of water, it is riddled with underground cenotes, caves with stalactites, small hills, and intense jungle.

But it is, of course, the celebrated Mayan ruins, Chichén Itzá and Uxmal especially, that bring most tourists to Mérida. The roads rank among the best in the country, and the local travel agencies are adept at running tours. High season generally corresponds to high season in the rest of Mexico: Thanksgiving week, the Christmas period, Easter week, and the month of August. Rains fall heaviest between May and November, bringing with them an uncomfortable humidity. Levels of service differ drastically between the high and low seasons, so you should be prepared for a trade-off.

## Important Addresses and Numbers

**Tourist Information**
The main **Tourist Information Center** (Teatro Peón Contreras, corner of Calles 60 and 57, tel. 99/249290 or 99/249389) is open daily 8–8. Kiosks, open 8–8, can be found at the airport (tel. 99/246764), the ADO bus terminal (no phone), and next to the Palacio Municipal on Calle 62 (no phone).

**Emergencies**
**Police** (tel. 99/233456); **Red Cross** (Calle 68 No. 583, at Calle 65, tel. 99/212445); **Fire** (tel. 99/214122).

**Late-night Pharmacies**
**Farmacia Yza Aviación** (Calle 71 at Av. Aviación, tel. 99/238116); **Farmacia Yza Tanlum** (Glorieta Tanlum, tel. 99/251646); and **Farmacia Canto** (Calle 60 No. 513, at Calle 63, tel. 99/210106).

If you love Mexican crafts, you may want to trek several blocks
⓰ east of the plaza, along Calle 59, to the **Museo de Arte Popular,**
which is housed in a fine old mansion. The ground floor, devoted to Yucatecan arts and crafts, displays weaving, straw
baskets, filigree jewelry, carved wood, beautifully carved
conch shells, exhibits on huipil manufacture, and the like. The
second floor focuses on the popular arts of the rest of Mexico.
*Calle 59 between Calles 50 and 48, no phone. Admission free.
Open Tues.–Sat. 8–8.*

## To Chichén Itzá and Valladolid

*Numbers in the margin correspond to numbers on the State of
Yucatán map.*

Chichén Itzá attracts a large number of visitors who come for
the famous ruins. For those traveling by car, the trip can be enhanced by stopping at several villages on the way. Route 80
passes through **Tixkokob,** a Mayan community famous for its
hammock weavers. By cutting south at Tekanto and east again
at Citilcúm (the road has no number, and there are few road
⓱ signs), you'll reach **Izamal,** nicknamed Ciudad Amarillo (Yellow City) for the painted earth-tone-yellow buildings. In the
center of town stands an enormous 16th-century **Franciscan
monastery** perched on—and built from—the remains of a pre-
Columbian pyramid.

⓲ Probably the best-known Mayan ruin, **Chichén Itzá,** the Maya-
Toltec center, was the most important city in Yucatán from the
11th to the 13th century. The architectural mélange encapsu-
lates Mexican history, showing foreign domination and the
intermingling of cultures. Chichén was altered by each succes-
sive wave of inhabitants, and archaeologists are able to date the
arrival of new inhabitants by the changes in the architecture;
however, they have yet to explain the long gaps of time when
the buildings seem to have been uninhabited. The site is believed to have been first settled in AD 432, abandoned for an unknown period of time, then rediscovered in 964 by the Maya-
speaking Itzás from the Tabasco region, who gave the site its
name; *Chichén Itzá* means "the mouth of the well of the Itzás."
The Itzás also abandoned the site, and in 1185 it was rediscovered by the central-Mexican Toltecs, who abandoned it forever
in 1224. Francisco de Montejo established a short-lived colony
here in the course of his conquest of Yucatán in the mid-1500s.
At the beginning of this century, U.S. Consul General Edward
Thompson carried out some of the earliest excavations at the
site, basing himself at a hacienda (now the Hacienda Chichén)
and carting most of the treasure away to the Peabody Museum
at Harvard University.

The majesty and enormity of this site are unforgettable. An architectural hybrid, it incarnates much of the fascinating and
bloody history of the Maya, from the steep temple stairways
down which sacrificial victims were hurled, to the relentlessly
ornate beauty of the smaller structures. Its audacity and vitality are almost palpable. Chichén Itzá encompasses approximately 6 square kilometers (2 square miles), though only 20 to
30 buildings of the several hundred at the site have been fully
explored. These buildings include the often-photographed
Mayan pyramid, a sprawling colonnade evoking imperial
Rome, the largest ball-playing court in Mesoamerica, a sacrifi-

# State of Yucatán

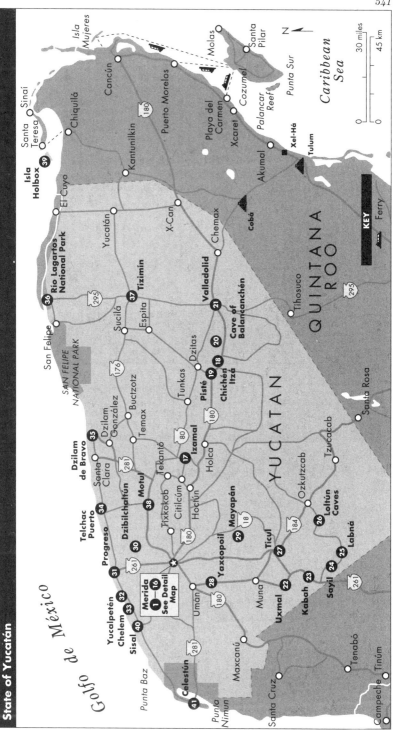

Golfo de México

Caribbean Sea

QUINTANA ROO

YUCATAN

SAN FELIPE NATIONAL PARK

Río Lagartos National Park

KEY

Ferry

30 miles

45 km

N

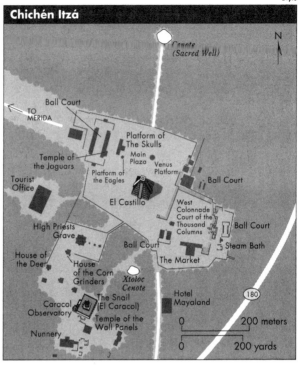

cial well once filled with precious offerings, and one of the only round buildings in the Mayan lands. Stone sculptures of the feathered serpent god, reclining *Chac Mools* (rain gods, associated with human sacrifice), steam baths for ritual purification, ruined murals, astronomical symbols, and broad *sacbeob* (white roads usually used for ceremonial purposes or as trade arteries) leading to other ancient centers endow the site with nearly all the celebrated visual elements of the Mayan civilization.

Chichén Itzá is divided into two parts—Old and New—though architectural motifs from the classical period are found in both sections. A more convenient distinction is topographical, since there are two major complexes of buildings separated by a dirt path. The martial, imperial architecture of the Toltecs and the more cerebral architectural genius and astronomical expertise of the Maya are married in the 98-foot-tall pyramid called **El Castillo** (The Castle), which dominates the site and rises above all the other buildings.

Atop the castle is a temple dedicated to Kukulcán (known as Quetzalcóatl in central Mexico), the legendary leader-turned-deity who was incarnated by the plumed serpent.

The sound-and-light show in the evening is not as well done as the one at Uxmal, but the engineering is astounding and the colored lights that enhance the wall carvings of El Castillo provide after-dark entertainment. *Sound-and-light show in Spanish, $1, 7PM; in English, $2, 9PM.*

In 1937, archaeologists discovered a more ancient temple inside the Castillo. A humid, slippery stairway leads upward to an altar that once held two statues: a Chac Mool and a bejeweled red tiger. The tiger wears a mosaic disc of jade and turquoise and is now housed in the Anthropology Museum in Mexico City. The inner temple is open to the public for only a few hours in the morning and again in the afternoon.

The temple rests on a massive trapezoidal square, on the west side of which is Chichén Itzá's largest **ball court,** one of seven on the site. Its two parallel walls are each 272 feet long, with two stone rings on each side, and 99 feet apart. The game was something like soccer (no hands were used), but it had religious as well as recreational significance. Bas-relief carvings at the court depict a player being decapitated, the blood spurting from his severed neck fertilizing the earth. Acoustics are so good that someone standing at one end of the court can hear the whispers of another person clearly at the other end. Sadly, the western wall of the court has been blackened by acid rain blown eastward from the oil fields on the Gulf of Mexico.

Between the ball court and El Castillo stands a **Tzompantli,** or stone platform, carved with rows of human skulls. In ancient times it was actually covered with stakes on which the heads of enemies were impaled.

The predilection for sacrifice was once believed to have come from the Toltecs, but recent research suggests that the pre-Toltec Maya had already been indulging in their own forms of the ritual. The **Sacred Well,** a cenote 65 yards in diameter that sits half a mile north of El Castillo at the end of a 900-foot-long *sacbe* (a white stone causeway usually used for ceremonial purposes or as a trade artery), was used only for sacrifices; another cenote at the site supplied drinking water. Skeletons of men, women, and children were found in the first well; they were thrown in to placate the rain gods and water spirits. The slippery walls were impossible to scale, and most of the victims could not swim well enough to survive until noon, when those who did hang on were fished out to recount what they had learned. Thousands of gold, jade, and other artifacts, most of them not of local provenance, have been recovered from the brackish depths of the cenote. Trees and shrubs have washed into the well over the centuries, and their remains have prevented divers from getting to the bottom; because the cenote is fed by a network of underground rivers, it cannot be drained. More treasure undoubtedly remains.

Returning to the causeway, on your left is the **Group of the Thousand Columns** with the famous **Temple of the Warriors,** a masterful example of the Toltec influence at Chichén Itzá. This temple so resembles Pyramid B at Tula—the Toltecs' homeland, north of Mexico City—that scholars believe the architectural plans must have been carried 1,280 kilometers (800 miles) overland.

To get to the less visited cluster of structures at Chichén Itzá—often confused with Old Chichén Itzá—take the main road south from the Temple of the Jaguar past El Castillo and turn right onto a small path opposite the ball court on your left. You'll pass several thatched huts (as well as young children and turkeys) en route. The ancient edifices here, overgrown with flowering vines, are as intriguing as the more visited ones, but the astronomical observatory dubbed **El Caracol** is the most impressive. The name, meaning "snail," refers to the spiral staircase at the building's core. Built in several stages, El Caracol is possibly the sole round building constructed by the Maya. Although definitely used for observing the heavens (judging by the tiny windows oriented toward the four cardinal points, and the alignment with the planet Venus), it also appears to have served a religious function.

After leaving El Caracol, continue south several hundred yards to the beautiful **Casa de las Monjas** (Nunnery) and its annex, which have long panels carved with flowers and animals, latticework, hieroglyph-covered lintels, and Chac masks (as does the nunnery at Uxmal). It was the Spaniards who gave the structure this sobriquet; no one knows how the Maya used it.

At Old Chichén Itzá, south of the remains of Thompson's hacienda, "pure Mayan" style—a combination of Puuc and Chenes styles, with playful latticework, Chac masks, and gargoyle-like serpents on the cornices—dominates. Mayan guides will lead you down the path by an old narrow-gauge railroad track to even more ruins, barely unearthed, if you ask. A fairly good restaurant and great ice-cream stand are located in the entrance building, and there are refreshment stands by the cenote and on the pathway near El Caracol. *Admission to site and museum: $6, free on Sunday and holidays. Parking: $1. Use of video camera $8. Open daily 8–5.*

⑲ The town of **Pisté**, about 1 kilometer (⅗ mile) west of the ruins on Route 180, serves mainly as a base camp for travelers to Chichén Itzá. Hotels, campgrounds, restaurants, and handicrafts shops tend to be cheaper here than south of the ruins. At the west end of town are a PEMEX station and a bank.

From Chichén Itzá, drive east along Route 180 for about 4 kilometers (2½ miles), then turn left at the first dirt road you come to and continue for about ½ kilometer (³⁄₁₀ mile) to the ⑳ **Cave of Balancanchén.** This shrine, whose Mayan name translates as "hidden throne," remained virtually undisturbed from the time of the conquest until its discovery in 1959. Within the shrine is the largest collection of artifacts yet found in Yucatán—mostly vases, jars, and incense burners once filled with offerings. In order to explore the shrine you must take one of the guided tours, which depart almost hourly, but you must be in fairly good shape, because some crawling is required; claustrophobes should skip it, and those who go should wear comfortable shoes. Also offered at the site is a sound-and-light show that fancifully recounts Mayan history.

Following Route 180 east for another 40 kilometers (25 miles) will take you to the second-largest city in the State of Yucatán, ㉑ **Valladolid.** This picturesque, pleasant, and provincial town (population 50,000) is enjoying growing popularity among travelers en route to or from Río Lagartos (*see below*) who are harried by more touristy towns. Montejo founded Valladolid in 1543 on the site of the Mayan town of Zací. The city suffered during the Caste War, when it was besieged by the rebellious Maya (who killed all the Europeans they could find), and again during the Mexican Revolution.

Today, however, placidity reigns in this agricultural market town. The center is mostly colonial, although it has many 19th-century structures. The main sights are the **colonial churches,** principally the large **cathedral** on the central square and the 16th-century **San Bernardino church and convent of Sisal,** three blocks southwest. The latter were pillaged during the insurrection.

## To Uxmal and the Puuc Route

If you opt for the southward journey from Mérida, follow Route 180 south and turn onto Route 261 at Umán; 80 kilometers (50 miles) farther south you'll reach **Uxmal.** If Chichén Itzá is the most impressive Mayan ruin in Yucatán, Uxmal is arguably the most beautiful. Where the former has a Toltec grandeur, the latter seems more understated and elegant—pure Maya. The architecture reflects the late classical renaissance of the 7th–9th centuries and is contemporary with that of Palenque and Tikal, among other great Mayan metropolises of the southern highlands.

It is considered the finest and largest example of Puuc architecture, which embraces such details as ornate stone mosaics and friezes on the upper walls, intricate cornices with hooked noses, rows of columns, and soaring vaulted arches. Lines are clean and uncluttered, with the horizontal—especially the parallelogram—preferred to the vertical. Many of the flat, low, elongated buildings were built on artificial platforms and laid out in quadrangles.

While most of Uxmal remains unrestored, three buildings in particular merit attention. The most prominent, the **Pyramid of the Magician,** is, at 92 feet high, the tallest structure at the site. Unlike most Mayan pyramids, which are stepped and angular, it has a strangely elliptical design. Built five times, each time over the previous structure, the pyramid has a stairway on its western side that leads through a monster-shaped doorway to two temples at the summit.

West of the pyramid lies the **Nunnery,** or Quadrangle of the Nuns. You may enter the four buildings; each comprises a series of low, gracefully repetitive chambers that look onto a central patio. Elaborate decoration—in the form of stone latticework, masks, geometric patterns, representations of the classic Mayan thatched hut (*na*), coiling snakes, and phallic figures—blankets the upper facades.

Continue walking south; you'll pass the ball court before reaching the **Palace of the Governor,** which archaeologist Victor von Hagen considered the most magnificent building ever erected in the Americas. Interestingly, the palace faces east while the rest of Uxmal faces west. Archaeologists believe this is because the palace was used to sight the planet Venus. Covering five acres and rising over an immense acropolis, the palace lies at the heart of what must have been Uxmal's administrative center.

First excavated in 1929 by the Danish explorer Frans Blom, the site served in 1841 as home to John Lloyd Stephens. Today a sound-and-light show recounts Mayan legends, including the kidnapping of an Uxmal princess by a king of Chichén Itzá, and focuses on the people's dependence on rain. The artificial light brings out details of carvings and mosaics that are easy to miss when the sun is shining. The show is performed nightly in Spanish and English and is one of the better such productions.

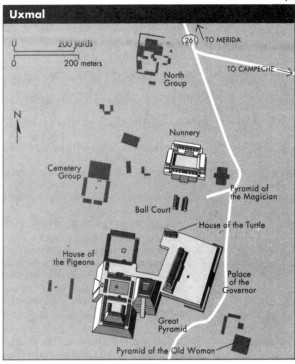

**Uxmal**

200 yards
200 meters

TO MERIDA
261

TO CAMPECHE

North Group

N

Nunnery

Cemetery Group

Pyramid of the Magician

Ball Court

House of the Turtle

House of the Pigeons

Palace of the Governor

Great Pyramid

Pyramid of the Old Woman

*Admission to site and museum: $6, free on Sunday and holidays. Parking: $1. Use of video camera $8. Open daily 8–5. Sound-and-light show in Spanish, $2, 7 PM; in English, $2.50, 9 PM.*

Four smaller Puuc sites near Uxmal are also worth visiting, **㉓** and en route you pass through beautiful hilly jungles. **Kabah,** 23 kilometers (14 miles) south of Uxmal on Route 261, lies almost entirely in ruins; its mounded landscape has a soft, almost Grecian beauty. Linked to Uxmal by a *sacbe*, at the end of which looms a great independent arch, is the 151-foot-long **Palace of the Masks,** so called because of the huge number of Chac masks with their hooked noses. Another 270 can be seen at the Codz-Poop temple, located on the east side of the road.

Five kilometers (3 miles) to the south you'll see the turnoff to **㉔** **Sayil,** the oldest site of the group, renowned primarily for its majestic three-story **palace** with 100 rooms. The structure recalls Palenque in its use of multiple planes, its columned porticos and sober cornices, and in the play of its long, solid horizontal masses, heightened by colonnades. *Admission: $4, free on Sunday and holidays. Open daily 8–5.*

Another 9 kilometers (6 miles) beyond Sayil, on Route 261, **㉕** rests the monumental arch at **Labná.** While most Mayan arches linked inner passageways at door height, this one is more characteristic of the great imperial arches of classical antiquity except for the corbels. *Admission: $4, free on Sunday. Open daily 8–5.*

Continue along the road from Labná for another 18 kilometers
**㉖** (11 miles) to the **Loltún Caves,** a 500-meter (⅗₀-mile) series of
caverns containing Mayan and neolithic remains and stalactites
and stalagmites. *Admission: $4. Open Tues.–Sun. 9–5; guided
tours at 9:30, 11, 12:30, 2, and 3.*

From Loltún, drive 10 kilometers (6 miles) northeast to
**Oxkutzcab,** where, to the left, you can pick up Route 184. An
**㉗** additional 17 kilometers (10½ miles) will bring you into **Ticul,**
where most of the Yucatecan pottery is produced, along with
huipiles and shoes. Many descendants of the Xiu dynasty,
which ruled Uxmal before the conquest, still live here. One of
the larger towns in Yucatán, Ticul boasts a handsome 17th-cen-
tury church.

**Time Out** If you save your appetite for **Los Almendros Restaurant,** in
Ticul, you'll be rewarded by what is considered the best regional restaurant in Yucatán.

From this point you can either head back to Mérida or continue
on to Mayapán, about 49 kilometers (30 miles) to the east (*see
below*).

If you wish to get back to Mérida, turn right off Route 184 at
Muna onto Route 261 and follow Route 261 back to Route 180.
Along Route 261, about 62 kilometers (38 miles) north of
**㉘** Uxmal, you may want to stop at **Yaxcopoil,** a restored 17th-cen-
tury hacienda that offers a nice change of pace from the ruins.
The building, with its distinctive Moorish double arch out
front, has been used as a film set and is the best-known henequen plantation in the region.

Those who are really enamored of Yucatán and the ancient
Maya can detour at Ticul on Route 18 to the ruined city of
**㉙** **Mayapán,** the last of the great city-states on the peninsula.
There have been few excavations here, however, so archaeolog-
ical evidence of past glory is limited to a few fallen statues of
Kukulcán, and today the site is mainly of historical interest.

## To Progreso and the North Coast

If you have decided to take the easterly course toward Progreso and the north coast, follow the Paseo de Montejo north out of
Mérida, where it becomes Route 261. After 14 kilometers (9
**㉚** miles) you'll come to the ruins of **Dzibilchaltún** ("the place
where there is writing on flat stones"), which is thought to have
been the capital of the Mayan states at one time. The site occupies more than 65 square kilometers (25 square miles) of land
cluttered with thousands of mounds, low platforms, piles of
rubble, plazas, and stelae. It was established around 2000 BC
and is now surrounded by a national preserve.

Dzibilchaltún's significance lies in the stucco sculpture and ceramics, from all periods of Mayan civilization, that have been
unearthed here. The **Temple of the Seven Dolls** (circa AD 500),
the only structure excavated on the site to date, is the only
Mayan temple known to have windows. Low and trapezoidal,
the temple exemplifies the late preclassical style, which pre-
dates such Puuc sites as Uxmal. The remains of stucco masks
adorn each side, and there are vestiges of sculptures of coiled
serpents. The **Xlacah cenote**—at 144 feet one of the deepest in

Yucatán—apparently supplied ceremonial as well as drinking water.

A small **museum** at the entrance to the site displays the seven vulcanized-rubber deformed male "dolls"—thought to be used against sickness—that were found deep inside the temple. The dolls, dating to the 13th and 14th centuries, are unusual because rubber is virtually unknown in the region, though the Lacandón Indians in Chiapas (descendants of the ancient Maya) make similar ones. There is a small refreshment stand. *Admission: $4, free on Sunday and holidays. Open daily 8–8.*

About 16 kilometers (10 miles) farther north on Route 261 is **Progreso,** the waterfront town closest to Mérida. Progreso, which is not particularly historical, is noisy with traffic and not at all picturesque, but on summer weekends it becomes a popular vacation destination for families from Mérida. It has fine sand and shallow waters that extend quite far out, making for nice walks, although its beaches are inferior to those of Quintana Roo.

The approach requires crossing some very foul-smelling swamps, and these remind you of Progreso's main raison d'être: It has been the chief port of entry for the peninsula since its founding in 1872, when the shallow port at Sisal, to the southwest, proved inadequate for handling the large ships that were carrying henequen cargo.

The town's attractions include its **malecón,** Calle 19, which is lined with seafood restaurants. Fishermen sell their catch on the beach east of the city between 7 and 8 AM, so it's a good place to come for fresh fish. Some 120 kilometers (75 miles) offshore are the **Alacranes Reef,** where divers can explore sunken ships, and **Pérez Island,** which supports a sizeable population of sea turtles and seabirds. Sportfishing, for such catch as grouper, red snapper, dogfish, sea bass, and pompano, is popular at the **marina** in nearby Yucalpetén (*see below*). For more information on the town and on guides who provide service to the reef, visit the **tourist office,** where representatives are friendly and helpful. *Calle 80 No. 176, at Calle 37, tel. 993/50104. Open Mon.–Sat. 9–1 and 3–7.*

Three kilometers (2 miles) west of Progreso, at the end of the narrow, marshy promontory, is **Yucalpetén.** The harbor here dates only from 1968, when it was built to provide shelter for small fishing boats during the hurricane season. Little goes on here other than some activity at the yacht marina and the fancy Fiesta Inn, though more hotels are planned for the future. Just beyond Yucalpetén is the even tinier village of **Chelem,** which has a few beachfront bungalow hotels.

A short drive (43 kilometers/27 miles) to the east of Progreso along the same road and past time-shares in progress, palm groves, henequen fields, and tiny villages, sits **Telchac Puerto,** now known as Nuevo Yucatán—the state government's latest venture in tourism development. One reason for this location is its proximity to **Laguna Rosada,** where the flamingos come to nest; another is its lovely, empty (at least that's how they were at this writing) beaches.

If you continue east on the coastal road, eventually you'll get to **Dzilam de Bravo,** where a better road—Route 281—heads back toward Mérida and points south. The pirate Jean Laffite supposedly lies buried just outside this village; at least there's a grave so marked, and two locals claim to be his descendants. Stop here for a swim in the gentle waters.

If you're a flamingo fan (flamingo season runs from April to May), take Route 281 13 kilometers (8 miles) to Dzilam Gonzá-
36  lez, then follow the unpaved road to Buetzotz, where you'll pick up Route 176 to Route 295 to Río Lagartos and **Río Lagartos National Park.** Actually a long estuary, not a river, the park was built with ecotourism in mind, though the alligators for which it and the village were named have long since been hunted into extinction. In addition to flamingos, birders can spot egrets, herons, ibis, cormorants, pelicans, and even pere-
grine falcons flying over these murky waters; fishing is good, too, and hawksbill and green turtles lay their eggs on the beach at night.

If you wish to extend this tour rather than return to Mérida, continue 104 kilometers (64 miles) south of Río Lagartos on Route 295 to Valladolid and then westward to Chichén Itzá (*see above*).

To return to Mérida, you'll have to backtrack, but you may want to make a brief stop in two villages to break up the monot-
37  ony of the drive. **Tizimín,** renowned as the seat of an indigenous messianic movement during the 1840s Caste War, is situated at the junction of Highways 176 and 295. The town boasts a 17th-
century church dedicated to the Three Kings.

38  Farther along Route 176 is **Motul,** for which *huevos motuleños* are named. This is the birthplace of the Indian rebel leader Felipe Carrillo Puerto, whose former house is now a museum containing displays on the life and times of the Socialist governor of Yucatán. *Open daily 8–noon and 4–6.*

39  Even farther afield is **Isla Holbox,** a tiny island (25 kilometers/
16 miles long) at the eastern end of the Río Lagartos estuary and just across the Quintana Roo state line. A fishing fan's heaven because of the pompano, bass, barracuda, and shark thronging its waters, the island also pleases seekers of tranquillity who don't mind rudimentary accommodations (two ho-
tels, plus rooms and hammocks for rent) and simple palapa restaurants.

### Sisal and Celestún

Traveling westward from Mérida, take an hour-long drive on
40  Route 25 to the town of **Sisal,** which gave its name to the hene-
quen that was shipped from the port in great quantity during the mid-19th century. With the rise of Progreso, Sisal dwindled into little more than a fisherman's wharf. Today the attrac-
tions are few: a **colonial customs house** and the private 1906 **lighthouse.** Sisal livens up a bit in July and August when Méridanos come to swim and dine.

41  To reach the fishing town of **Celestún,** take Route 180 southwest to Umán, then Route 281 west for 92 kilometers (57 miles). The town sits at the end of a spit of land separating the Celestún estuary from the gulf on the western side of Yucatán. It is the only point of entry to the **Parque Natural del Flamenco Mexica-
no,** a 147,500-acre wildlife reserve with one of the largest colo-
nies of flamingos in North America. From September through April clouds of pink wings soar over the pale blue backdrop of

the estuary, which also features rocks, islets, cenotes, and mangroves, and make for stunning scenery; cormorants, ducks, and herons also fly overhead. There is good fishing in both the river and the gulf; and you can see deer and armadillo roaming the surrounding land.

## Shopping

For the most part Mérida is the best place in Yucatán to buy local handicrafts at reasonable prices. The main products include *hamacas* (hammocks), *guayaberas* (short, loose shirts), huaraches, huipiles, *ternos* (hand-embroidered dresses), baskets, *jipis* or Panama hats, leather goods, gold and silver filigree jewelry, masks, painted gourds, vanilla, and piñatas.

On the second floor of the **central municipal market** (between Calles 65 and 56 and Calles 54 and 59) you'll find crafts, food, flowers, and live birds, among other items. On Sunday in Mérida, you will find an array of wares at three bazaars: the **Handicraft Bazaar,** in front of the Municipal Palace across from the main square, starting at 9; the **Popular Art Bazaar,** a flea market in Parque Santa Lucía, at the corner of Calles 60 and 55, also at 9; and the **Book Bazaar,** in the Callejón del Congreso, Calle 60, starting at 10.

*Crafts* The best places for hammocks are **La Poblana** (Calle 65 No. 492) and **El Aguacate** (Calle 58 No. 492); for guayaberas, **Camisería Canul** (Calle 59 No. 496); and for jipis, **La Casa de los Jipis** (Calle 56 No. 526). **Mayakat** (Paseo de Montejo 498, tel. 99/236385) specializes in handpainted tiles.

*Jewelry* Probably the largest and finest selection of crafts—particularly silver jewelry—is at **Sonrisa del Sol** (Calle 62 No. 500 Altos, between Calles 61 and 59, almost on the main square, tel. 99/281255). Good selections of earrings and onyx beads can be found at **El Paso** (Calle 59 No. 501).

## Sports and Fitness

*Fishing* Those interested in sportfishing for such catch as grouper, red snapper, and sea bass, among others, will be sated in **Yucalpetén,** west of Progreso. **Río Lagartos** also offers good fishing in its murky waters. In the Parque Natural del Flamenco Mexicano in **Celestún,** you have your choice of river or gulf fishing.

*Golf* There is an 18-hole championship golf course (and restaurant, bar, and clubhouse) at **Club Campestre de Mérida** (Calle 30 No. 500, tel. 99/71100 or 99/71700), 16 kilometers (10 miles) north of Mérida on the road to Progreso.

*Tennis* The **Holiday Inn** (Av. Colón 498 at Calle 60, tel. 99/256877) has tennis courts, as do the **Club Campestre de Mérida** (*see* Golf, *above*), the **Centro Deportivo Bancario** (Carr. a Motul s/n, Frac. del Arco, tel. 99/60500 or 99/77819), and the **Deportivo Libanés Mexicano** (Calle 1-G No. 101, tel. 99/70669).

*Bullfights* Bullfights are most often performed from November to January, or during other holiday periods at the **bullring** (Paseo de la Reforma), near Avenida Colón.

## Dining and Lodging

**Dining** Dining out is a pleasure in Mérida. The city's 50-odd restaurants offer a superb variety of cuisine—primarily Yucatecan, of course, but also Lebanese, Italian, French, Chinese, and Mexican—at very reasonable prices.

Pisté, the village nearest to Chichén Itzá, is not a gourmand's town: The food in most of its restaurants is simple, overpriced, and only fair. For the most part, the hotel restaurants are even worse. Try one of the palapa-covered cafés along the main road. The small markets and produce stands can provide the makings for a modest picnic.

The restaurants near the ruins in Uxmal are nothing to write home about either. The exception is Los Almendros, in Ticul, which is well worth the 15-minute drive.

Highly recommended restaurants are indicated by a star ★.

| Category | Cost* |
| --- | --- |
| Very Expensive | over $20 |
| Expensive | $15–$20 |
| Moderate | $8–$15 |
| Inexpensive | under $8 |

*per person, excluding drinks and service*

**Lodging** Outside of Mérida you'll find that accommodations fit the low-key, simple pace of the region. Internationally affiliated properties are the exception rather than the rule; instead, charmingly idiosyncratic old mansions offer visitors a base from which to explore the countryside and Mérida itself—which merits at least a two-day stay. Properties in Mérida have a 97000 postal code. Highly recommended hotels are indicated by a star ★.

| Category | Cost* |
| --- | --- |
| Very Expensive | over $90 |
| Expensive | $60–$90 |
| Moderate | $25–$60 |
| Inexpensive | under $25 |

*All prices are for a standard double room, excluding service and the 10% tax.*

**Chichén Itzá** **Mayaland.** The hotel closest to the ruins, this charming 1920s
*Dining and Lodging* property belongs to the Barbachano family, whose name is
★ practically synonymous with tourism in Yucatán. Accommodations include a wing and several bungalows set in a large garden on a 100-acre site. The observatory is visible from the alcoves on the road side of the hotel. Colonial-style rooms in the main building feature decorative tiles, ceiling fans, air-conditioning, television, and mosquito netting; bungalows do not have television or air-conditioning. The hot water often runs cold. Tour buses fill the road in front of the hotel, so choose a room at the back. Light meals served poolside and at tables overlooking the

garden are a far better choice than the fixed-price meals served in the dining room. *Carretera Mérida–Cancún, Km 120, tel. in Chichén Itzá 985/62777; in Mérida, Mayaland Tours, Av. Colón 502, tel. 99/252122, 99/252133, or 800/235–4079, fax 99/257022. 65 rooms. Facilities: restaurant (Expensive), bar, pool. AE, MC, V. Expensive.*

**Dolores Alba.** The best low-budget choice near the ruins is this family-run hotel, a long-time favorite in the country south of Pisté. The rooms are simple, clean, and comfortable; some have air-conditioning. Hammocks hang by the small pool, and breakfast and dinner are served family-style in the main building. Free transportation to the ruins is provided. *Carretera Pisté-Cancún, 1½ mi. south of Chichén Itzá, reservations in Mérida Calle 63 No. 464, tel. 99/285650, fax 99/283163. 28 rooms. Facilities: dining room, pool. MC, V. Inexpensive.*

**Mérida**
**Dining**
★

**Alberto's Continental Patio.** You can probably find this restaurant praised in just about every guidebook and it merits the kudos: The setting is romantic and the food is excellent. The building, which dates from around 1727, is adorned with such fine details as mosaic floors from Cuba. If you order Lebanese food, your plate will be heaped with servings of shish kebab, fried kibi, cabbage rolls, hummus, eggplant, and tabbouleh, accompanied by pita bread, almond pie, and Turkish coffee. Black bean soup, enchiladas, fried bananas, and caramel custard make up the Mexican dinner; there are also a Yucatecan dinner, an Italian dinner, and à la carte appetizers and entrées. *Calle 64 No. 482, at Calle 57, tel. 99/285367. AE, MC, V. Open daily 11–11. Very Expensive.*

★ **La Bella Epoca.** For a truly special dinner, nothing matches the elegance and style of this second-story dining room, the former ballroom of an old mansion that has been restored well beyond its original grandeur. Crystal chandeliers sparkle over tiny balcony tables overlooking Parque Cepeda Peraza. An ambitious menu includes French, Mexican, Middle Eastern, Yucatecan, vegetarian, and unusual Maya dishes—try the *sikil-pak*, a dip with ground pumpkin seeds; the charcoal-broiled tomatoes and onions; or the succulent *pollo píbil* (chicken baked in banana leaves). Arrive for dinner before 8 PM to claim one of the small balcony tables overlooking the street. *Calle 60 between Calles 57 and 59, tel. 99/281928. AE, MC, V. Open daily 12 PM–1 AM. Expensive.*

**Express.** Young and middle-aged Méridano men in guayaberas spend hours in this plain café-style restaurant that reeks of Madrid café ambience (and of cigar smoke as well). That ambience is reinforced by the paintings of old Spain (and old Mérida) on the walls, the ceiling fans, and the old-fashioned globe lights. On the menu are broiled garlic chicken, sandwiches, shrimp, and red snapper. Service can be slow, but then Express is a place for lingering. *Calle 60 No. 502, at Calle 59, tel. 99/281691. No credit cards. Moderate.*

**Los Almendros.** Another Mérida classic, this chain restaurant credits itself with the invention of poc chuc, and though perhaps overrated, it does know how to cater to the tourists and businesspeople who frequently fill its chairs and tables to the limit. The two dining rooms have both ceiling fans and air-conditioning. The food tends to be on the greasy, oily side, and sometimes the taste of the food itself is all but drowned in wonderful local spices. Nonetheless, the restaurant provides a more than passable introduction to the variety of Yucatecan cuisine, including cochinita píbil, panuchos, pork sausage, papadzules, and *pollo ticuleño* (boneless, breaded chicken in tomato sauce, accompanied by fried beans, peas, red peppers, fried bananas, and ham and cheese). The sangria—with or without alcohol—washes it all down. *Calle 50-A No. 493, between Calles 57 and 59, tel. 99/212851. AE. Moderate.*

★ **Santa Lucía.** Locals crowd this small dining room, a few steps below the sidewalk, at lunch time, when the bountiful *comida corrida* is served. The bargain three-course lunch usually includes such Yucatecan specialties as *sopa de lima* (lime soup) and *pollo píbil*. Before you order, browse through the book of guests' comments to get tips on favorite meals—the pepper steak constantly wins rave reviews. Soft tropical music plays in the background, and the service is friendly and efficient. *Calle 60 No. 481, next to Parque Santa Lucía, tel. 99/285957. MC, V. Closed for breakfast. Moderate.*

**Ananda Maya Ginza.** One of a handful of vegetarian restaurants in town, this one is light on the decor, which includes wood tables, white walls, and stone floors, and heavy on the health drinks, made mostly with local vegetables, fruit, and herbs. Regular coffee and Yucatecan beers are also served, and the salads are made with fresh local vegies washed with purified water. The terrace of this old historic home provides a quiet dining atmosphere beneath a big tree. *Calle 59 No. 507, between Calles 60 and 62, tel. 99/282451. No credit cards. Open Mon.–Sat. 9–10; closed Sun. Inexpensive.*

★ **Cafetería Pop.** A favorite with the student crowd (the university is across the street), this place—with some 12 white-linoleum-covered tables—resembles a crowded American diner. The busiest time is 8 AM–noon, but for late risers the breakfast menu can be ordered à la carte all day, and the noteworthy coffee is freshly brewed round the clock. In addition, sandwiches, hamburgers, spaghetti, chicken, fish, beef, and tacos are featured. Beer, sangria, and wine are served only with food orders. *Calle 57 No. 501, at Calle 62, tel. 99/216844. MC, V. Inexpensive.*

*Lodging* **Casa del Balam.** This very pleasant hotel on well-heeled Calle
★ 60 (opposite the Opera House) was built 60 years ago as the home of the Barbachano family, pioneers of Yucatán tourism. Today the hotel—owned and managed by Carmen Barbachano—has a lovely courtyard ornamented with a fountain, arcades, ironwork, and a black-and-white tile floor; rocking chairs in the hallways impart a colonial feeling, as do the mahogany trimmings and cedar doorways. The rooms are capacious and well maintained, featuring painted sinks, wrought-iron accessories, and minibars. The suites are especially agreeable, with large bathrooms, tiny balconies, arched doorways, and mahogany bureaus. *Calle 60 No. 488, Box 988, tel. 99/248844, 99/248044, or 800/437–9607, fax 99/245011. 54 rooms. Facilities: restaurant, 2 bars, minibars, pool, sun deck, travel agency, car rental, gift shop. AE, MC, V. Very Expensive.*

**Mérida Misión.** Part of the city's landscape for decades (in its earlier incarnation it was the Hotel Mérida), the Misíon has two major assets: an excellent location in the heart of downtown and a genuine colonial ambience, with chandeliers, wood beams, archways, patios, fountains, and a pool. Handsome public areas make it a pleasure to spend time here; it is not just a place to retire for the night. *Calle 60 No. 491, tel. 99/237665 or 800/221–6509, fax 99/239500. 145 rooms. Facilities: restaurant, night-*

club, snack bar, pool, travel agency, gift shop. *AE, DC, MC, V. Expensive.*

**Casa Mexilio.** One would never guess that behind the drab exterior of this guest house sits an exquisitely decorated bed-and-breakfast. Two partners—one Mexican, one American—have brought the best of their respective architectural and decorating traditions to bear on this small house with seven guest rooms (one on each floor), which is being restored to something beyond its original splendor. From the dark entrance you approach a tiny pool adjacent to a charming kitchen, painted as extravagantly as the kitchen that belonged to Frida Kahlo, the celebrated Mexican painter. At the top of the narrow stairs is a sun deck laden with cacti; one entire wall of the house is covered with vines. Middle Eastern wall hangings, French tapestries, colorful tile floors, black pottery, tile sinks, rustic furniture, loft beds, and white walls make up the eclectic decor. The price includes breakfast. *Calle 68 No. 495, tel. 99/282505; for reservations tel. 303/674-9615 or 800/538-6802, fax 303/674-8735. 7 rooms. Facilities: restaurant, pool. AE, MC, V. Moderate.*

**Caribe.** The Caribe has all the makings of an authentic colonial hotel, including tile floors, dark wood furniture, and a large inner courtyard with arcades. It is located on Parque Hidalgo, but most of its rooms overlook the inner courtyard and restaurant, as do the open balconies, which are lined with comfortable chairs. The rooftop sun deck and swimming pool have a great view of the plaza and downtown. The hotel's café, El Meson, is one of the better restaurants in Parque Hidalgo. *Calle 60 No. 500, tel. 99/249022 or 800/826-6842, fax 99/248733. 56 rooms. Facilities: restaurant, outdoor cafeteria, pool, travel agency, parking. AE, DC, MC, V. Moderate.*

★ **Gran Hotel.** Cozily situated on Parque Hidalgo, this 1901 hotel is the oldest in the city, and it still lives up to its name. The five-story neoclassical building, with an Art Nouveau courtyard complete with wrought-iron bannister, variegated tile floors, Greek columns, and a myriad of potted plants, exudes charm. High ceilings in rooms drenched in cedar provide a sense of spaciousness. All units have balconies and some have air-conditioning. Ask for a room overlooking the park. Porfirio Díaz, Fidel Castro, and Sandino stayed in sumptuous Room 17, and Room 12½ has an enormous sitting room. TVs are available upon request. *Calle 60 No. 496, tel. 99/236963 or 99/247633, fax 99/247622. 34 rooms. Facilities: restaurant, sun roof. MC, V. Moderate.*

**Galería Trinidad.** Eccentricity holds sway at this impossibly original, slightly ramshackle, bizarre little hotel, nearly unidentifiable unless you are looking specifically for it. In its previous lives it has been a hacienda, an auto rental shop, and a furniture store, but in the late 1980s owner Manolo Rivero made it into a hotel. The large, chaotic lobby is filled with plants, a fountain, and yellow wicker furniture; making your way through the maze that is the rest of the hotel, you'll encounter painted wooden angels, curved columns, and even a green satin shoe mounted on a pedestal. The rooms are small and equally odd. *Calle 60 at Calle 51, tel. 99/232463. 30 rooms. Facilities: pool, gallery. AE, MC, V. Inexpensive.*

**Progreso**
**Dining**
**Capitán Marisco.** This large and pretty restaurant-bar on the malecón features a nautical motif, with a ship's rudder in the center of the main dining room and a fountain adorned with sea-

shells. The house specialty is *filete a la hoja de plátano* (fish fillet—usually grouper, sea bass, or pompano—cooked in a banana leaf), but the entire menu is dependable. For a superb view of the sea, visit the outdoor terrace on the second floor. *Malecón between Calles 10 and 12, tel. 993/50639. AE, MC, V. Expensive.*

**Soberanis.** This branch of a respected Mexican chain of seafood houses is a dependable choice for fish dishes and traditional Mexican meals. *Calle 30 No. 138, between Calles 27 and 29, tel. 993/50582. AE, MC, V. Moderate.*

*Lodging* **Sian Ka'an.** These four whitewashed, thatched-roof, two-story villas, right on the beach in Chelem (just west of Yucalpetén and near Progreso) all come with kitchenettes, ceiling fans, and terraces that overlook the water. Decorated in rustic Mexican-Mediterranean style, the suites feature handwoven bedspreads, *equipales* (leather chairs from Jalisco), and hand-blown glassware. Prices include breakfast. Ask about off-season discounts. *Calle 17, s/n, tel. in Mérida, 99/282582, fax 99/244919; in Chelem, tel. 993/54017. 8 suites. Facilities: restaurant, beach, pool. AE, DC, MC, V. Expensive.*

**Progreso.** This clean, modest-but-tasteful three-star hotel in the heart of Progreso opened in 1990. The rooms, some with balconies, are furnished in pine, with arched window frames and tiled baths. *Calle 29 at Calle 28, tel. 993/50038. 9 rooms. Facilities: restaurant. MC, V. Inexpensive.*

**Uxmal** **Los Almendros.** Located in Ticul, a small town 28 kilometers (17
*Dining* miles) east of Uxmal (turn left at Santa Elena), this restaurant
★ offers fresher and juicier foods than do the other members of the Los Almendros chain; poc chuc and cochinita píbil are good choices. This is one place, however, where you can expect to wait in line for a table, especially during high season. *Calle 23 No. 196, tel. 99/20021. MC, V. Moderate.*

**Las Palapas.** A great alternative to the hotel dining rooms at Uxmal, this family-run restaurant specializes in Yucatecan dishes served with homemade tortillas. When tour groups request it in advance, the owners prepare a traditional feast, roasting the chicken or pork píbil style in a pit in the ground. If you see a tour bus in the parking lot stop in—you may chance upon a memorable fiesta. *Hwy. 261, 5 kilometers (3 miles) north of the ruins, no phone. No credit cards. Inexpensive.*

*Lodging* **Hacienda Uxmal.** The oldest hotel at the site, built in 1955 and still owned and operated by the Barbachano family, this pleasant colonial-style building has lovely floor tiles, ceramics, and iron grillwork. The rooms—all with ceiling fans and air-conditioning—are tiled and decorated with worn but comfortable furniture. Inside the large courtyard are a garden and pool. Across the road and about 100 yards south you'll find the ruins. Ask about packages that include free or low-cost car rentals for the nights you spend at Uxmal and at the Mayaland hotel in Chichén Itzá. *Tel. in Uxmal, 99/247142; in Mérida, Mayaland Tours. Av. Colón 502, tel. 99/252122, 99/252133, or 800/235–4079; fax 99/252397. 80 rooms. Facilities: restaurant, bar, pool, gift shop. AE, DC, MC, V. Expensive.*

**Villa Arqueológica Uxmal.** The hotel closest to the ruins is this two-story Club Med property built around a large Mediterranean-style pool. The functional rooms have cozy niches for the beds, tiled bathrooms, and powerful air conditioners. Mayan women in traditional dress serve well-prepared French cuisine in the restaurant, and large cages located around the hotel contain tropical birds and monkeys. *Within walking distance of the ruins, tel. 99/247053; in the U.S., tel. 800/CLUB-MED. 44 rooms. Facilities: restaurant, bar, pool, tennis court, gift shop. AE, MC, V. Expensive.*

**Valladolid**
**Dining and Lodging**

**El Mesón del Marqués.** This building, on the north side of the main square, is a well-preserved, very old hacienda built around a lovely courtyard. Rooms in the modern addition at the back of the hotel have air-conditioning and are attractively furnished with rustic and colonial touches; rooms in the older section have ceiling fans. Unusually large bathrooms boast bathtubs—a rarity in Mexican hotels. As an added draw, El Mesón features a pool, a crafts shop, and a restaurant that serves local specialties. *Calle 39 No. 203, tel. 985/62073, fax 985/62073. 25 rooms, plus 9 suites. Facilities: restaurant (Moderate), bar, gift shop, pool. MC, V. Moderate.*

**María del Luz.** Another choice by the main plaza, this hotel is built around a small swimming pool and courtyard. The rooms have been recently renovated with new floors, fresh paint, and tiled bathrooms. Air-conditioning and televisions are being added to all the rooms. The street-side restaurant is attractively furnished with high-backed rattan chairs and linen cloths; Mexican dishes are predictable and inexpensive. *Calle 2 No. 195, tel. 985/62071, fax 985/62098. 30 rooms. Facilities: restaurant (Inexpensive), bar, pool. MC, V. Inexpensive.*

## The Arts and Nightlife

**The Arts**
**Mérida**

Mérida enjoys an unusually active and diverse cultural life, including free government-sponsored music and dance performances nightly in local parks. For information on these and other performances, consult the tourist office, the local newspapers, or the billboards and posters at the Teatro Peón Contreras (Calle 60 at Calle 57) or Café Pop (Calle 57 between Calles 60 and 62). Among a variety of performances presented at the **Teatro Peón Contreras** is "The Roots of Today's Yucatán," a combination of music, dance, and theater presented by the Folkloric Ballet of the University of Yucatán. *Admission: $4. Tues. 9 PM.* Another theater that regularly hosts cultural events is the **Teatro Daniel Ayala** (Calle 60 between Calles 59 and 61).

**Nightlife**
**Mérida**

The **Hotel Calinda Panamericana** (Calle 59 No. 455, tel. 99/239111 or 99/239444) stages folkloric dances most nights by the pool. **Tulipanes** (Calle 46 No. 462-A, tel. 99/270967), a restaurant and nightclub built over a cenote, stages a folkloric ballet and "Mayan ritual" performance nightly at 8.

A number of restaurants feature live music and dancing, including **El Tucho** (Calle 60 No. 482, between Calles 55 and 57, tel. 99/242323), **La Prosperidad** (Calle 53 at Calle 56, tel. 99/240764), and **Pancho's** (Calle 59 between Calles 60 and 62, tel. 99/230942).

**State of Yucatán**

Both Chichén Itzá and Uxmal offer elaborate nighttime sound-and-light shows accompanied by narrations of Mayan legends (*see* Exploring, *above*).

# Spanish Vocabulary

**Note:** *Mexican Spanish differs from Castilian Spanish.*

## Words and Phrases

| | *English* | *Spanish* | *Pronunciation* |
|---|---|---|---|
| **Basics** | Yes/no | Sí/no | see/no |
| | Please | Por favor | pore fah-**vore** |
| | May I? | ¿Me permite? | may pair-**mee**-tay |
| | Thank you (very much) | (Muchas) gracias | (**moo**-chas) **grah**-see-as |
| | You're welcome | De nada | day **nah**-dah |
| | Excuse me | Con permiso | con pair-**mee**-so |
| | Pardon me/what did you say? | ¿Como?/Mánde? | ko-mo/mahn-dey |
| | Could you tell me? | ¿Podría decirme? | po-**dree**-ah deh-**seer**-meh |
| | I'm sorry | Lo siento | lo see-**en**-toe |
| | Good morning! | ¡Buenos días! | **bway**-nohs **dee**-ahs |
| | Good afternoon! | ¡Buenas tardes! | **bway**-nahs **tar**-dess |
| | Good evening! | ¡Buenas noches! | **bway**-nahs **no**-chess |
| | Goodbye! | ¡Adiós!/¡Hasta luego! | ah-dee-**ohss/ah**-stah-**lwe**-go |
| | Mr./Mrs. | Señor/Señora | sen-**yor**/sen-**yore**-ah |
| | Miss | Señorita | sen-yo-**ree**-tah |
| | Pleased to meet you | Mucho gusto | **moo**-cho **goose**-to |
| | How are you? | ¿Cómo está usted? | **ko**-mo es-**tah** oo-**sted** |
| | Very well, thank you. | Muy bien, gracias. | **moo**-ee bee-**en**, grah-see-as |
| | And you? | ¿Y usted? | ee oos-**ted**? |
| | Hello (on the telephone) | Bueno | **bwen**-oh |
| **Numbers** | 1 | un, uno | oon, **oo**-no |
| | 2 | dos | dos |
| | 3 | tres | trace |
| | 4 | cuatro | **kwah**-tro |
| | 5 | cinco | **sink**-oh |
| | 6 | seis | sace |
| | 7 | siete | see-**et**-ey |
| | 8 | ocho | **o**-cho |
| | 9 | nueve | new-**ev**-ay |
| | 10 | diez | dee-**es** |
| | 11 | once | **own**-sey |
| | 12 | doce | **doe**-sey |
| | 13 | trece | **tray**-sey |
| | 14 | catorce | kah-**tor**-sey |
| | 15 | quince | **keen**-sey |
| | 16 | dieciséis | dee-es-ee-**sace** |
| | 17 | diecisiete | dee-**es**-ee-see-**et**-ay |
| | 18 | dieciocho | dee-**es**-ee-**o**-cho |
| | 19 | diecinueve | **dee-es**-ee-new-**ev**-ay |
| | 20 | veinte | **vain**-tay |
| | 21 | veinte y uno/veintiuno | **vain**-te-oo-no |

| | | |
|---|---|---|
| 30 | treinta | **train**-tah |
| 32 | treinta y dos | train-tay-**dose** |
| 40 | cuarenta | kwah-**ren**-tah |
| 43 | cuarenta y tres | kwah-**ren**-tay-**trace** |
| 50 | cincuenta | seen-**kwen**-tah |
| 54 | cincuenta y cuatro | seen-**kwen**-tay **kwah**-tro |
| 60 | sesenta | sess-**en**-tah |
| 65 | sesenta y cinco | sess-**en**-tay **seen**-ko |
| 70 | setenta | set-**en**-tah |
| 76 | setenta y seis | set-**en**-tay **sace** |
| 80 | ochenta | oh-**chen**-tah |
| 87 | ochenta y siete | oh-**chen**-tay see-**yet**-ay |
| 90 | noventa | no-**ven**-tah |
| 98 | noventa y ocho | no-**ven**-tah **o**-cho |
| 100 | cien | see-**en** |
| 101 | ciento uno | see-en-toe **oo**-no |
| 200 | doscientos | doe-see-**en**-tohss |
| 500 | quinientos | keen-**yen**-tohss |
| 700 | setecientos | set-eh-see-**en**-tohss |
| 900 | novecientos | no-veh-see-**en**-tohss |
| 1,000 | mil | meel |
| 2,000 | dos mil | dose meel |
| 1,000,000 | un millón | oon meel-**yohn** |

| | | | |
|---|---|---|---|
| **Colors** | black | negro | **neh**-grow |
| | blue | azul | ah-**sool** |
| | brown | café | kah-**feh** |
| | green | verde | **vair**-day |
| | pink | rosa | **ro**-sah |
| | purple | morado | mo-**rah**-doe |
| | orange | naranja | na-**rahn**-hah |
| | red | rojo | **roe**-hoe |
| | white | blanco | **blahn**-koh |
| | yellow | amarillo | ah-mah-**ree**-yoh |

| | | | |
|---|---|---|---|
| **Days of the Week** | Sunday | domingo | doe-**meen**-goh |
| | Monday | lunes | **loo**-ness |
| | Tuesday | martes | **mahr**-tess |
| | Wednesday | miércoles | me-**air**-koh-less |
| | Thursday | jueves | who-**ev**-ess |
| | Friday | viernes | vee-**air**-ness |
| | Saturday | sábado | **sah**-bah-doe |

| | | | |
|---|---|---|---|
| **Months** | January | enero | eh-**neh**-ro |
| | February | febrero | feh-**brair**-oh |
| | March | marzo | **mahr**-so |
| | April | abril | ah-**breel** |
| | May | mayo | **my**-oh |
| | June | junio | **hoo**-nee-oh |
| | July | julio | **who**-lee-yoh |
| | August | agosto | ah-**ghost**-toe |
| | September | septiembre | sep-tee-**em**-breh |
| | October | octubre | oak-**too**-breh |
| | November | noviembre | no-vee-**em**-breh |
| | December | diciembre | dee-see-**em**-breh |

| | | | |
|---|---|---|---|
| **Useful phrases** | Do you speak English? | ¿Habla usted inglés? | **ah**-blah oos-**ted** in-**glehs**? |

| | | |
|---|---|---|
| I don't speak Spanish | No hablo español | no **ah**-blow es-pahn-**yol** |
| I don't understand (you) | No entiendo | no en-tee-**en**-doe |
| I understand (you) | Entiendo | en-tee-**en**-doe |
| I don't know | No sé | no **say** |
| I am American/ British | Soy americano(a)/ inglés(a) | soy ah-meh-ree-**kah**-no(ah)/ in-**glace**(ah) |
| What's your name? My name is . . . | ¿Cómo se llama usted? Me llamo . . . | **koh**-mo say **yah**-mah oos-**ted** may **yah**-moh |
| What time is it? | ¿Qué hora es? | keh **o**-rah es? |
| It is one, two, three . . . o'clock. | Es la una; son las dos, tres | es la **oo**-nah/sone lahs dose, trace |
| Yes, please/No, thank you | Sí, por favor/No, gracias | **see** pore fah-**vor**/no **grah**-see-us |
| How? | ¿Cómo? | **koh**-mo? |
| When? | ¿Cuándo? | **kwahn**-doe? |
| This/Next week | Esta semana/ la semana que entra | **es**-tah seh-**mah**-nah/lah say-**mah**-nah keh **en**-trah |
| This/Next month | Este mes/el próximo mes | **es**-tay mehs/el **proke**-see-mo mehs |
| This/Next year | Este año/el año que viene | **es**-tay **ahn**-yo/el **ahn**-yo keh vee-**yen**-ay |
| Yesterday/today/ tomorrow | Ayer/hoy/mañana | ah-**yair**/oy/mahn-**yah**-nah |
| This morning/ afternoon | Esta mañana/tarde | **es**-tah mahn-**yah**-nah/**tar**-day |
| Tonight | Esta noche | **es**-tah **no**-cheh |
| What? | ¿Qué? | keh? |
| What is it? | ¿Qué es esto? | keh es **es**-toe |
| Why? | ¿Por qué? | pore **keh** |
| Who? | ¿Quién? | kee-**yen** |
| Where is . . . ? the train station? the subway station? the bus stop? the post office? the bank? the . . . hotel? the store? | ¿Dónde está . . . ? la estación del tren? la estación del Metro? la parada del autobús? la oficina de correos? el banco? el hotel . . . ? la tienda . . . ? | **dohn**-day es-**tah** la es-tah-see-**on** del **train** la es-ta-see-**on** del **meh**-tro la pah-**rah**-dah del oh-toe-**boos** la oh-fee-**see**-nah day koh-**reh**-os el **bahn**-koh el oh-**tel** la tee-**en**-dah |

| | | |
|---|---|---|
| Pancho or blanket | Serape | seh-**ra**-peh |

## Dining Out

| | | |
|---|---|---|
| A bottle of . . . | Una botella de . . . | **oo**-nah bo-**tay**-yah deh |
| A cup of . . . | Una taza de . . . | **oo**-nah **tah**-sah deh |
| A glass of . . . | Un vaso de . . . | oon **vah**-so deh |
| Ashtray | Un cenicero | oon sen-ee-**seh**-roh |
| Bill/check | La cuenta | lah **kwen**-tah |
| Bread | El pan | el pahn |
| Breakfast | El desayuno | el day-sigh-**oon**-oh |
| Butter | La mantequilla | lah mahn-tay-**key**-yah |
| Cheers! | ¡Salud! | sah-**lood** |
| Cocktail | Un aperitivo | oon ah-pair-ee-**tee**-voh |
| Dinner | La cena | lah **seh**-nah |
| Dish | Un plato | oon **plah**-toe |
| Dish of the day | El platillo de hoy | el plah-**tee**-yo day oy |
| Enjoy! | ¡Buen provecho! | bwen pro-**veh**-cho |
| Fixed-price menu | La comida corrida | lah koh-**me**-dah co-**ree**-dah |
| Fork | El tenedor | el ten-eh-**door** |
| Is the tip included? | ¿Está incluida la propina? | es-**tah** in-clue-**ee**-dah lah pro-**pea**-nah |
| Knife | El cuchillo | el koo-**chee**-yo |
| Lunch | La comida | lah koh-**me**-dah |
| Menu | La carta | lah **cart**-ah |
| Napkin | La servilleta | lah sair-vee-**yet**-uh |
| Pepper | La pimienta | lah pea-me-**en**-tah |
| Please give me | Por favor déme | pore fah-**vor** **day**-may |
| Salt | La sal | lah sahl |
| Spoon | Una cuchara | **oo**-nah koo-**chah**-rah |
| Sugar | El azúcar | el ah-**sue**-car |
| Waiter!/Waitress! | ¡Por favor Señor/Señorita! | pore fah-**vor** sen-**yor**/sen-yor-**ee**-tah |

# Index

# Personal Itinerary

| | | |
|---|---|---|
| **Departure** | *Date* | |
| | *Time* | |
| **Transportation** | | |
| | | |
| | | |
| | | |
| | | |

| | | |
|---|---|---|
| **Arrival** | *Date* | *Time* |
| **Departure** | *Date* | *Time* |
| **Transportation** | | |
| | | |
| | | |
| **Accommodations** | | |
| | | |
| | | |

| | | |
|---|---|---|
| **Arrival** | *Date* | *Time* |
| **Departure** | *Date* | *Time* |
| **Transportation** | | |
| | | |
| | | |
| **Accommodations** | | |
| | | |
| | | |

| | | |
|---|---|---|
| **Arrival** | *Date* | *Time* |
| **Departure** | *Date* | *Time* |
| **Transportation** | | |
| | | |
| | | |
| **Accommodations** | | |
| | | |

*Personal Itinerary*

**Arrival** *Date*      *Time*

**Departure** *Date*      *Time*

**Transportation**

**Accommodations**

**Arrival** *Date*      *Time*

**Departure** *Date*      *Time*

**Transportation**

**Accommodations**

**Arrival** *Date*      *Time*

**Departure** *Date*      *Time*

**Transportation**

**Accommodations**

**Arrival** *Date*      *Time*

**Departure** *Date*      *Time*

**Transportation**

**Accommodations**

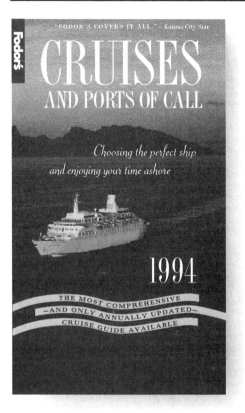
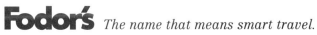

*Personal Itinerary*

**Arrival** *Date*        *Time*

**Departure** *Date*        *Time*

**Transportation**

**Accommodations**

**Arrival** *Date*        *Time*

**Departure** *Date*        *Time*

**Transportation**

**Accommodations**

**Arrival** *Date*        *Time*

**Departure** *Date*        *Time*

**Transportation**

**Accommodations**

**Arrival** *Date*        *Time*

**Departure** *Date*        *Time*

**Transportation**

**Accommodations**

# Announcing the only guide to explore
# a Disney World you've never seen before:

# The one for grown-ups.

This terrific new guide is the only one written specifically for the millions of adults who visit Walt Disney World each year <u>without</u> kids. Upscale, sophisticated, packed full of facts and maps, *Walt Disney World for Adults* provides up-to-date information on hotels, restaurants, sports facilities, and health clubs, as well as unique itineraries for adults, including: a Sporting Life Vacation, Day-and-Night Romantic Fantasy, Singles Safari, and Gardens and Natural Wonders Tour. Get essential tips and everything you need to know about reservations, packages, annual events, banking service, rest stops, and much more. With *Walt Disney World for Adults* in hand, you'll get the most out of one of the world's most fascinating, most complex playgrounds.

At bookstores everywhere, or call 1-800-533-6478

*Addresses*

| *Name* | *Name* |
| *Address* | *Address* |
| | |
| *Telephone* | *Telephone* |
| *Name* | *Name* |
| *Address* | *Address* |
| | |
| *Telephone* | *Telephone* |
| *Name* | *Name* |
| *Address* | *Address* |
| | |
| *Telephone* | *Telephone* |
| *Name* | *Name* |
| *Address* | *Address* |
| | |
| *Telephone* | *Telephone* |
| *Name* | *Name* |
| *Address* | *Address* |
| | |
| *Telephone* | *Telephone* |
| *Name* | *Name* |
| *Address* | *Address* |
| | |
| *Telephone* | *Telephone* |
| *Name* | *Name* |
| *Address* | *Address* |
| | |
| *Telephone* | *Telephone* |
| *Name* | *Name* |
| *Address* | *Address* |
| | |
| *Telephone* | *Telephone* |

*Escape to ancient cities and exotic*

*islands*  *with CNN Travel Guide, a*

*wealth of valuable advice. Host Valerie Voss will take you*

*to all of your favorite destinations,*

*including those off the beaten path.*

*Tune into your passport to the world.*

# CNN TRAVEL GUIDE
SATURDAY 10:00 PMᴘᴛ   SUNDAY 8:30 AMᴇᴛ

# Fodor's Travel Guides

*Available at bookstores everywhere, or call 1–800–533–6478, 24 hours a day.*

## U.S. Guides

Alaska

Arizona

Boston

California

Cape Cod, Martha's Vineyard, Nantucket

The Carolinas & the Georgia Coast

Chicago

Colorado

Florida

Hawaii

Las Vegas, Reno, Tahoe

Los Angeles

Maine, Vermont, New Hampshire

Maui

Miami & the Keys

New England

New Orleans

New York City

Pacific North Coast

Philadelphia & the Pennsylvania Dutch Country

The Rockies

San Diego

San Francisco

Santa Fe, Taos, Albuquerque

Seattle & Vancouver

The South

The U.S. & British Virgin Islands

The Upper Great Lakes Region

USA

Vacations in New York State

Vacations on the Jersey Shore

Virginia & Maryland

Waikiki

Walt Disney World and the Orlando Area

Washington, D.C.

## Foreign Guides

Acapulco, Ixtapa, Zihuatanejo

Australia & New Zealand

Austria

The Bahamas

Baja & Mexico's Pacific Coast Resorts

Barbados

Berlin

Bermuda

Brazil

Brittany & Normandy

Budapest

Canada

Cancun, Cozumel, Yucatan Peninsula

Caribbean

China

Costa Rica, Belize, Guatemala

The Czech Republic & Slovakia

Eastern Europe

Egypt

Euro Disney

Europe

Europe's Great Cities

Florence & Tuscany

France

Germany

Great Britain

Greece

The Himalayan Countries

Hong Kong

India

Ireland

Israel

Italy

Japan

Kenya & Tanzania

Korea

London

Madrid & Barcelona

Mexico

Montreal & Quebec City

Morocco

Moscow & St. Petersburg

The Netherlands, Belgium & Luxembourg

New Zealand

Norway

Nova Scotia, Prince Edward Island & New Brunswick

Paris

Portugal

Provence & the Riviera

Rome

Russia & the Baltic Countries

Scandinavia

Scotland

Singapore

South America

Southeast Asia

Spain

Sweden

Switzerland

Thailand

Tokyo

Toronto

Turkey

Vienna & the Danube Valley

Yugoslavia

# Fodor's Travel Guides

*Available at bookstores everywhere, or call 1–800–533–6478, 24 hours a day.*

## Special Series

**Fodor's Affordables**

Caribbean

Europe

Florida

France

Germany

Great Britain

London

Italy

Paris

**Fodor's Bed & Breakfast and Country Inns Guides**

Canada's Great Country Inns

California

Cottages, B&Bs and Country Inns of England and Wales

Mid-Atlantic Region

New England

The Pacific Northwest

The South

The Southwest

The Upper Great Lakes Region

The West Coast

**The Berkeley Guides**

California

Central America

Eastern Europe

France

Germany

Great Britain & Ireland

Mexico

Pacific Northwest & Alaska

San Francisco

**Fodor's Exploring Guides**

Australia

Britain

California

The Caribbean

Florida

France

Germany

Ireland

Italy

London

New York City

Paris

Rome

Singapore & Malaysia

Spain

Thailand

**Fodor's Flashmaps**

New York

Washington, D.C.

**Fodor's Pocket Guides**

Bahamas

Barbados

Jamaica

London

New York City

Paris

Puerto Rico

San Francisco

Washington, D.C.

**Fodor's Sports**

Cycling

Hiking

Running

Sailing

The Insider's Guide to the Best Canadian Skiing

Skiing in the USA & Canada

**Fodor's Three-In-Ones (guidebook, language cassette, and phrase book)**

France

Germany

Italy

Mexico

Spain

**Fodor's Special-Interest Guides**

Accessible USA

Cruises and Ports of Call

Euro Disney

Halliday's New England Food Explorer

Healthy Escapes

London Companion

Shadow Traffic's New York Shortcuts and Traffic Tips

Sunday in New York

Walt Disney World and the Orlando Area

Walt Disney World for Adults

**Fodor's Touring Guides**

Touring Europe

Touring USA: Eastern Edition

**Fodor's Vacation Planners**

Great American Vacations

National Parks of the East

National Parks of the West

**The Wall Street Journal Guides to Business Travel**

Europe

International Cities

Pacific Rim

USA & Canada

# WHEREVER YOU TRAVEL, $\mathcal{H}$ELP IS NEVER FAR AWAY.

From planning your trip to replacing
lost Cards, American Express® Travel Service
Offices* are always there to help.

## MEXICO

**ACAPULCO**
*Costera Miguel Aleman 709-1*
*74-845550*

**CANCUN**
*Av. Tulum and Brisas, Suite A*
*98-841999*

**COZUMEL**
*Fiesta Cozumel*
*Ave. Rafael Melgar, # 27*
*98-720925*

**GUADALAJARA**
*Plaza Los Arcos*
*Vallarta 2440*
*36-158910*

**MANZANILLO**
*Agencia de Viajes*
*Bahias Gemelas*
*33-332100*

**MAZATLAN**
*Plaza Balboa*
*Cameron Sabalo S/N*
*69-830466*

**MERIDA**
*Paseo de Montejo #494*
*Por La 43 Y 45*
*99-284222*

**MEXICO CITY**
*Paseo de Reforma #234*
*55-330380*

**MONTERREY**
*Padre Mier 1424. Esq. Bravo*
*83-430910*

**OAXACA**
*Viajes Mexico Itso Y Caribe*
*Dr. Aurelio Valdiviesco, No. 2*
*95-166522*

**SAN JOSE DEL CABO**
*Tourcabos*
*Plaza de los Cabos Local B*
*68-420982*

# INTRODUCING

At last, your own personalized list of what's going on in the cities you're visiting.

Keyed to the days when you're there, customized for your interests, and sent to you before you leave home.

Exclusive for purchasers of Fodor's Guides...

# Introducing a revolutionary way to get customized, time-sensitive travel information just before your trip.

Now you can obtain detailed information about what's going on in each city you'll be visiting <u>before</u> you leave home—up-to-the-minute, objective information about the events and activities that interest you most.

This is a special offer for purchasers of Fodor's guides – a customized Travel Update to fit your specific interests and your itinerary.

Travel Updates contain the kind of time-sensitive insider information you can get only from local contacts – or from city magazines and newspapers once you arrive. But now you can have the same information before you leave for your trip.

The choice is yours: current art exhibits, theater, music festivals and special concerts, sporting events, antiques and flower shows, shopping, fitness, and more.

The information comes from hundreds of correspondents and thousands of sources worldwide. Updated continuously, it's like having your own personal concierge or friend in the city.

You specify the cities and when you'll be there. We'll do the rest — personalizing the information for you the way no guidebook can.

It's the perfect extension to your Fodor's guide and the best way to make the most of your valuable travel time.

Reg
The
in th
domain
tion as
worthwhil
the perform
Tickets are u
venue. Alter
mances are canc
given. For more i
Open-Air Theatre, I
NW1 4NP Open Air
Tel: 935-5756. Ends: 9-

**International Air Tattoo**
Held biennially, the world
military air display
demostra-
tions, mili-
band

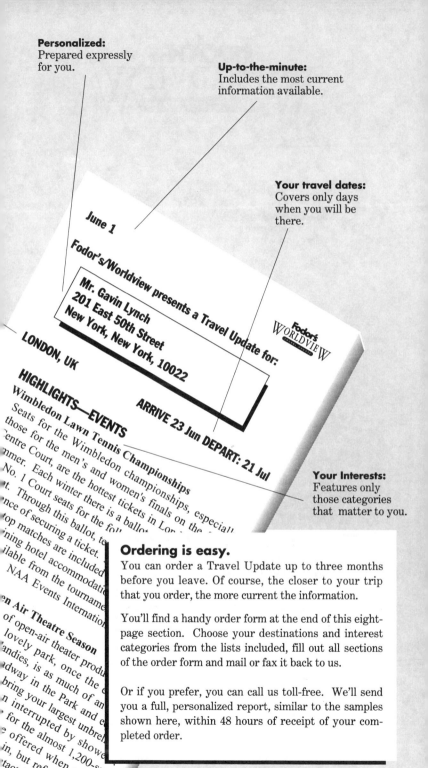

**Personalized:**
Prepared expressly for you.

**Up-to-the-minute:**
Includes the most current information available.

**Your travel dates:**
Covers only days when you will be there.

June 1

Fodor's/Worldview presents a Travel Update for:

Mr. Gavin Lynch
201 East 50th Street
New York, New York, 10022

Fodor's
WORLDVIEW

LONDON, UK

ARRIVE 23 Jun DEPART: 21 Jul

**HIGHLIGHTS—EVENTS**

**Wimbledon Lawn Tennis Championships**
Seats for the Wimbledon championships, especiall
those for the men's and women's finals on the
entre Court, are the hottest tickets in Lon
mmer. Each winter there is a ballo
No. 1 Court seats for the fo
t. Through this ballot, te
nce of securing a ticket.
op matches are included
ning hotel accommodati
ilable from the tourna
NAA Events Internatio

**n Air Theatre Season**
of open-air theater produ
lovely park, once the
andies, is as much of an
dway in the Park and e
bring your largest unbre
n interrupted by showe
for the almost 1,200-seat
offered when perfor
in, but refunds are not
tact Sheila Benja
ent's Park

**Your Interests:**
Features only those categories that matter to you.

### Ordering is easy.

You can order a Travel Update up to three months before you leave. Of course, the closer to your trip that you order, the more current the information.

You'll find a handy order form at the end of this eight-page section. Choose your destinations and interest categories from the lists included, fill out all sections of the order form and mail or fax it back to us.

Or if you prefer, you can call us toll-free. We'll send you a full, personalized report, similar to the samples shown here, within 48 hours of receipt of your completed order.

**Special concerts—
who's performing
what and where**

**One-of-a-kind,
one-time-only events**

**Special interest,
in-depth listings**

## Children — Events
### Angel Canal Festival
The festivities include a children's funfa[ir]
entertainers, a boat rally and displays on th[e]
water. Regent's Canal. Islington. N1. Tub[e:]
Angel. Tel: 267 9100. 11:30am-5:30pm. 7/04[.]
### Blackheath Summer Kite Festival
Stunt kite displays with parachuting tedd[y]
bears and trade stands. Free admission. SE3[.]
BR: Blackheath. 10am. 6/27.
### Megabugs
Children will delight in this infestation o[f]
giant robotic insects, including a praying
mantic 60 times life size. Mon-Sat 10am-
6pm; Sun 11am-6pm. Admission 4.50
pounds. Natural History Museum, Cromwel[l]
Road. SW7. Tube: South Kensington. Tel:
938 9123. Ends 10/01.
### Childminders
This establishment employs only women,
providing nurses and qualified nannies to

## Music — Jazz & Blues
### Tito Puente's Golden Men of Latin Jazz
The father of mambo and Cuban rumba king
comes to town. Royal Festival Hall. South Bank.
SE1. Tube: Waterloo. Tel: 928 8800. 8pm. 7/15.
### Georgie Fame and The New York Band
Riding a popular tide with his latest album, the
smoky-voiced Fame and his keyboard are on a
tour yet again. The Grand. Clapham Junction.
SW11. BR: Clapham Junction. Tel: 738 9000.
7:30pm. 7/07.
### Jacques Loussier Play Bach Trio
The French jazz classicist and colleagues.
Kenwood Lakeside. Hampstead Lane.
Kenwood. NW3. Tube: Golders Green, then bus
210. Tel: 413 1443. 7pm. 7/10.
### Tony Bennett and Ronnie Scott
Royal Festival Hall. South Bank. SE1. Tube:
Waterloo. Tel: 928 8800. 8pm. 7/11.
### Santana
Royal Festival Hall. South Bank. SE1. Tube:
Waterloo. Tel: 928 8800. 8pm. 7/12.
### Count Basie Orchestra and Nancy Wilson Trio
Royal Festival Hall. South Bank. SE1. Tube:
Waterloo. Tel: 928 8800. 8pm. 7/14.
### King Pleasure and the Biscuit Boys
Royal Festival Hall. South Bank. SE1. Tube:
Waterloo. Tel: 928 8800. 6:30 and 9pm. 7/16.
### Al Green and the London Community Gospel Choir
Royal Festival Hall. South Bank. SE1. Tube:
Waterloo. Tel: 928 8800. 8pm. 7/13.
### BB King and Linda Hopkins
Mother of the blues and successor to Bessi[e]
Smith, Hopkins meets up with "Blues Boy[."]
[Royal F]estival Hall. South Bank. SE[1]

## Music — Classical
### Marylebone Sinfonia
Kenneth Gowen conducts music by Pu[rcell]
and Rossini. Queen Elizabeth Hall. S[outh]
Bank. SE1. Tube: Waterloo. Tel: 928
7:45pm. 7/16.
### London Philharmonic
Franz Welser-Moest and George Ben[jamin]
conduct selections by Alexander G[oehr,]
Messiaen, and some of Benjamin's ow[n com-]
positions. Queen Elizabeth Hall. South
SE1. Tube: Waterloo. Tel: 928 8800. 8[pm.]
### London Pro Arte Orchestra and Forest [Choir]
Murray Stewart conducts selectio[ns by]
Rossini, Haydn and Jonathan Willcock[s.]
Queen Elizabeth Hall. South Bank[.]
Tube: Waterloo. Tel: 928 8800. 7:45p[m.]
### Kensington Symphony Orchestra
Russell Keable conducts Dvorak's

# Here's what you get . . .

## Detailed information about what's going on — precisely when you'll be there.

**Show openings during your visit**

**Reviews by local critics**

### Exhibitions & Shows—Antique & Flower
**Westminster Antiques Fair**
Over 50 stands with pre-1830 furniture and other Victorian and earlier items. Thu-Fri 11am-8pm; Sat-Sun 11am-6pm. Admission 4 pounds, children free. Old Royal Horticultural Hall. Vincent Square. SW1. Tel: 0444/48 25 14. 6-24 thru 6/27.

**Royal Horticultural Society Flower Show**
The show includes displays of carnations, summer fruit and vegetables. Tue 11am-7pm; Wed 10am-5pm. Admission Tue 4 pounds, Wed 2 pounds. Royal Horticultural Halls. Greycoat Street and Vincent Square. SW1. Tube: Victoria. 7/20 thru 7/21.

**...mpton Court Palace International Flower Show**
Major international garden and flower show ...king place in conjunction with the British

### ...eater — Musical
**Sunset Boulevard**
In June, the four Andrew Lloyd Webber musicals which dominated London's stages in the 1980s (Cats, Starlight Express, Phantom of the Opera and Aspects of Love) are joined by the composer's latest work, a show rumored to have his best music to date. The 1950 Billy Wilder film about a helpless young writer who is drawn into the world of a possessive, aging silent screen star offers rich opportunities for Webber's evolving style. Soaring, aching melodies, lush technical effects and psychological thrills are all expected. Patti Lupone stars. Mon-Sat at 8pm; matinee Thu-Sat at 3pm. In-person sales only at the box office; credit card bookings, Tel: 344 0055. Admission 15-32.50 pounds. Adelphi Theatre. The Strand. WC2. Tube: Charing Cross. Tel: 836 7611. Starts: 6/21

**Leonardo A Portrait of Love**
A new musical about the great Renaissance arti... and inventor comes in for a London premie... tested by a brief run at Oxford's Old Fire Stati... ...utumn. The work explores the relation... ...Vinci and the woman '...

Alberquerque • Atlanta • Atlantic City • N... Baltimore • Boston • Chicago • Cincinnati Cleveland • Dallas/Ft.Worth • Denver • De... • Houston • Kansas City • Las Vegas • Los Angeles • Memphis • Miami • Milwaukee • New Orleans • New York City • Orlando • ... Springs • Philadelphia • Phoenix • Pittsburg... Portland • Salt Lake • San Antonio • San Di... • San Franc... • Se... • ...ouis • Tamp... Oslo • Wash... • ...lu • Island ... Hawaii • Kauai • Maui • Abacos • Bimini Ber... • ...a Countryside • Hamilton • ...lar... Antigua & B... • ...v... • Angui...

### Spectator Sports — Other Sports
**Greyhound Racing: Wembley Stadium**
This dog track offers good views of greyhound racing held on Mon, Wed and Fri. No credit cards. Stadium Way. Wembley. HA9. Tube: Wembley Park. Tel: 902 8833.

**Benson & Hedges Cricket Cup Final**
Lord's Cricket Ground. St. John's Wood Road. NW8. Tube: St. John's Wood Tel: 289 1611. 11am. 7/10.

### ...siness-Fax & Overnight Mail
**Post Office, Trafalgar Square Branch**
Offers a network of fax services, the Intelpost system, throughout the country and abroad. Mon-Sat 8am-8pm, Sun 9am-5pm. William IV Street. WC2. Tube: Cha...
Cross T...

## Fodor's WORLDVIEW
### TRAVEL UPDATE

...Gorda • Barbados • Dominica • Gren... ...cia • St. Vincent • Trinidad &Tobago ...ymans • Puerto Plata • Santo Doming... ...Aruba • Bonaire • Curacao • St. Ma... ...ec City • Montreal • Ottawa • Toro... ...Vancouver • Guadeloupe • Martiniqu... ...helemy • St. Martin • Kingston • Ixta... ...o Bay • Negril • Ocho Rios • Ponce ...n • Grand Turk • Providenciales • S... St. John • St. Thomas • Acapulco • ...& Isla Mujeres • Cozumel • Guadal... ... • Los Cabos • Manzinillo • Mazatl... ...City • Monterrey • Oaxaca • Puerto ...do • Puerto Vallarta • Veracruz • Ix... ...dam • Athens • B...

# Interest Categories

For your personalized Travel Update, choose the categories you're most interested in from this list. Every Travel Update automatically provides you with *Event Highlights* – the best of what's happening during the dates of your trip.

| | | |
|---|---|---|
| **1.** | **Business Services** | Fax & Overnight Mail, Computer Rentals, Photocopying, Secretarial , Messenger, Translation Services |

**Dining**

| | | |
|---|---|---|
| **2.** | **All Day Dining** | Breakfast & Brunch, Cafes & Tea Rooms, Late-Night Dining |
| **3.** | **Local Cuisine** | In  Every Price Range—from Budget Restaurants to the Special Splurge |
| **4.** | **European Cuisine** | Continental, French, Italian |
| **5.** | **Asian Cuisine** | Chinese, Far Eastern, Japanese, Indian |
| **6.** | **Americas Cuisine** | American, Mexican & Latin |
| **7.** | **Nightlife** | Bars, Dance Clubs, Comedy Clubs, Pubs & Beer Halls |
| **8.** | **Entertainment** | Theater—Drama, Musicals, Dance, Ticket Agencies |
| **9.** | **Music** | Classical, Traditional & Ethnic, Jazz & Blues, Pop, Rock |
| **10.** | **Children's Activities** | Events, Attractions |
| **11.** | **Tours** | Local Tours, Day Trips, Overnight Excursions, Cruises |
| **12.** | **Exhibitions, Festivals & Shows** | Antiques & Flower, History & Cultural, Art Exhibitions, Fairs & Craft Shows, Music & Art Festivals |
| **13.** | **Shopping** | Districts & Malls, Markets, Regional Specialities |
| **14.** | **Fitness** | Bicycling, Health Clubs, Hiking, Jogging |
| **15.** | **Recreational Sports** | Boating/Sailing, Fishing, Ice Skating, Skiing, Snorkeling/Scuba, Swimming |
| **16.** | **Spectator Sports** | Auto Racing, Baseball, Basketball, Football, Horse Racing, Ice Hockey, Soccer |

Please note that interest category content will vary by season, destination, and length of stay.